W9-AGT-703

PEARSON

Popping Culture

Seventh Edition

Edited by
Murray Pomerance
John Sakeris

Pearson Learning Solutions, 501 Boylston Street, Suite 900, Boston, MA 02116
A Pearson Education Company
www.pearsoned.com

Printed in Canada

1 2 3 4 5 6 7 8 9 10 V0ZN 17 16 15 14 13 12

000200010271656756

BK/TP

ISBN 10: 1-256-84016-5
ISBN 13: 978-1-256-84016-9

Contents

Race for the Screen

Screened Ideologies

Cultural Moments

They get what they are looking for, but they get it wrapped up in the illusions which their future employers think suitable for them.

—George Orwell (1939)

Acknowledgments

Many who read anthologies are unaware of the inordinate amount of work required of a great many people to bring them to reality. In the case of a book that deals with motion pictures, television programs, popular literature and music, and mass culture, everything—as the saying goes—is in the details, and the details can be overwhelming. We wish to express gratitude to our many colleagues whose words are contained in these pages, who acted with extraordinary grace and speed to help us make the volume. Our students, who have been generous with feedback over the years, have been especially helpful—by expressing their taste, by openly wondering, and by telling us without reserve how critical essays have touched their thoughts.

Particular credit goes to Gilaine Waterbury, our many friends and collaborators at Pearson, especially Bradley Keist, Jamie Wilson, Eric Tamlin, Christine Judge, and Ben Wright. These are cultural workers whose labor is very intensive and at the same time quite invisible. Thanks to them, as much as to the authors here, books like this can help all of us examine, re-examine, and hopefully understand popular culture.

Murray Pomerance
John Sakeris

Toronto, June 2012

Introduction

John Sakeris and Murray Pomerance

Welcome to the seventh revised and expanded edition of *Popping Culture*. Here you will find five new challenging and interesting articles that expand on our central themes with exciting and current examples. There are some revised and updated articles as well, and all of these deal with important issues in popular culture today. Since the first edition of this book, much has changed in the world: the widening arena of war, the continuing economic crisis, the upsurge in religiosity, racism, and homophobia are issues that challenge us all, as do the global spread of electronic imaging and new technologies such as the iPad and 3-D projection. We are hopeful that these thoughtful and challenging articles will help contribute to a wider understanding of these issues and ultimately a wider understanding of our complex social and economic world.

The landscape of popular culture shifts daily, to such a degree that it is often difficult to make any coherent sense of it. The authors included in this book have all attempted to do so, each in different ways and each within his or her own specific areas of interest and using a particular critical language. That the languages, areas, and materials included here are so different, yet so perceptive, is, we hope, one of the delights to be found in these pages. The articles you are about to read concern a wide and varied examination of films, television news and entertainment shows, and images. From Quentin Tarantino to Michael Jackson, *Star Wars* to *Avatar,* Paul Verhoeven to Gus Van Sant, from *The Hunger Games* to *Harry Potter,* from Juvenile to the NBA, from *Clueless* to *"Modern Family,"* from "American Idol" to "Glee," and much more, our authors cover popular culture with a multidisciplinary approach and an eye for important structures and events. Pop cultural product is flattened by our culture industries to a vast screen of globally accessible imagery in the service of illusion, reorientation, indoctrination, and cultivated "understanding." Our authors are concerned with issues such as filmic point of view, propaganda and the state, war, sexuality, camerawork, editing, media framing, racism, and the depiction of social class.

This book, which is organized according to the most central themes and issues in popular culture today, expands our new section, <u>Cultural Moments</u>, with essays about a number of phenomena and concerns that have very recently sprung onto the pop cultural scene. We have new articles on apocalyptic films, the serial killer genre, Harry Potter and fantasy films, the persistence of the vampire genre, and "Glee." With all of the diversity of content here, the overriding perspective that all the authors and articles share is a critical one; modern mass culture is dissected and probed here with an eye to its consequences for us and for all members of society. With this critical eye comes an unspoken assumption that we can improve our society. Resistance is not futile and change is possible. But before we can change things, we must come to understand them. We live in a system of advanced capitalism that is proceeding to gobble up resources and people on a global scale unheard of in human history. Multinationals or trans-nationals straddle the boundaries of the nation state while the state and its institutions are increasingly under attack. The ideology of neoliberalism is still dominant and anything that is seen as interfering with the so-called free market is denigrated. Social programs, environmental safeguards, and labor protections are under attack internationally as "austerity" takes the front seat, and under the onslaught of liberal free-trade rules governments are becoming less and less masters of their own houses. The current situation in Greece is a case in point.

Multinational media corporations are of course part of the process of globalization and the last few years have seen the rise of huge international media conglomerates that cover all aspects of information dissemination: from the Internet to blockbuster films, television, and the music industry. Many of our authors must deal implicitly with the fact of increasing conglomeration since modern popular culture cannot be analyzed without some consideration of the incredible concentration of ownership in the media business. Giant American, European, Australian, and Canadian firms dominate the production of material that is available internationally as news, entertainment, and music, and a smaller and smaller number of owners seem to be wielding more and more influence over that product.

In a way that has not been as blatant since the days of William Randolph Hearst, many of these media magnates are using their vast holdings to put forward viewpoints that they see as suitable to their own interests. Fox News has surpassed CNN as one of the most watched newsgathering institutions in the world and the views of its notoriously conservative owner, Rupert Murdoch, are evident in all aspects of his empire, even as he increasingly comes under attack. Murdoch and others like him hold great control over information that we read, see, and hear, in ways that vary from direct interference with content to setting an atmosphere in the newsroom that reporters dare not violate. The constant attacks on "liberalism," environmentalism, and in the USA on the Democratic Party and Barack Obama in particular, are examples of this enormous power.

It is no surprise that during the invasion of Iraq, the media seemed overwhelmingly on the side of President George W. Bush. American television news media in particular, a primary source of information for the majority of North Americans, seemed to be no more than a cheering section for the military with endless demonstrations of patriotism and "support for the troops," as William Hoynes makes clear in these pages. Barack Obama's continuation of the use of US military power internationally seems to be met with similar enthusiasm from the major news media. No analysis of current war coverage is complete without considering the power of the media conglomerate today.

But not all information is news and many of our authors note how the entertainment media also contain messages that support the status quo. For example, race continues to be a central lens through which people interpret the world and ultimately experience it. While it has long been discredited as a useful scientific concept, it persists in our day-to-day lives as if it were real. Racism is still a major issue in the world today and it dominates our lives everyday. Even though there is a black American president. Racism persists not only in the US presidential race, but in the continued incarceration of people of color in percentages far beyond their proportion of the population. And significantly, racism provides a major justification for wars of conquest and for both privilege and discrimination in the society at large.

Gender also persists as a defining theme in popular entertainment; in fact all of our experience of popular entertainment is gendered in both its presentation and its experience. The articles that we have included consider romance films, homoeroticism, and sexual orientation as but a few of the areas of gender that are significant in our society. Our world continues to be divided by both race and gender and it is important to consider why this division persists, even after generations of struggle to eradicate sexism and racism. Some authors argue that these ways of seeing continue to exist because they benefit certain vested interests. Others make no such claim, but assume nevertheless that the eradication of these ideologies is an important goal.

"Buying into Social Class" examines one aspect of popular culture that persists in remaining largely unanalyzed today, omnipresent though it is in popular cultural narratives and depictions. Here we look at inequality from the aspect of consumerism. Class is certainly influential on all our lives even though it is often effectively invisible as a social form. While inequality surrounds us and its consequences are there for all to see, we continue to insist that our position in the class structure is earned and that that position is a sign of our moral superiority or inferiority. Popular culture seems to revel in this idea, so much so that Social Darwinism, largely dormant since the early 1900s, has seen a resurgence in popular forms of thought such as reality television, game shows, and even many news arenas. Does our society in fact broadly and generally offer a promise of social mobility, as these shows implicitly claim? And since we all live in the real world, what is our reaction to such promises when our own experiences contradict them? The recent upsurge in demonstrations with the theme "We are the 99%" are perhaps one consequence of living in the real world.

The amazing popularity of so-called reality television has an economic explanation, certainly; these shows are extremely cheap to produce by comparison with high-budget sitcoms or drama shows involving actors, locations, scripts, and complex production styles. Reality TV is a source of human drama and an opportunity for the fifteen minutes of fame our celebrity-obsessed culture so cherishes (and that Andy Warhol promised us all). But for something to be popular, it has to touch some kind of nerve in us with meaning. We are hardly passive consumers of mass culture: television and movie theatres are vast graveyards of failed attempts to capture our attention and imagination. People actively interpret what they are shown and evaluate things through their own experience.

The questions that persist are: What makes something popular? Why do we revel in someone else's triumph or humiliation? (The popularity of shows like "TMZ," "The Soup," and "Chelsea Lately" and other forms of tabloid entertainment illustrate this desire.) How is it that we identify with the characters that populate the dramas we love, and why must the characters be drawn in very particular ways for us to relate to them? How, indeed, do media images work to affect our ways of thinking about the world, considering reality and illusion, and forming belief? What does popular culture tell us is "natural," what is "obvious," what is "universal," what is "authentic," what is "successful," what is "true"? One thing is certain: we cannot always be told what to think, but we can be directed to what should be thought about. It is in this interesting area that critics of popular culture find themselves. Does big business control our lives or are we more active participants than some would have us believe?

If media operate on the battlefield where our interests clash with those of big business, we can certainly not consider this clash without considering the concept of ideology. Ideology is a fundamental concept in the study of popular culture, one that is worthy of more explanation and analysis than we can possibly give here. But we do make the attempt to connect ideology to social class and the results are provocative. Consider that we live in a society where the ideology of consumption is the driving engine of the economy, that in order for consumption to take place on a large (and profitable) scale we have to be convinced that consuming is central to our own lives. Historically, this was not an easy task, but modern mass advertising has been very effective in its central mission. So it is that much popular culture, linked to consumerist logic, puts forward the dramatic importance of "need"—emotional, chemical, informational, economic—as though our lives are perpetually insufficient and shopping—for friends, for pleasures, for knowledge, for success—is a panacea for all problems. As members of society we must consider the consequences of such an ethos on our environment, social relations, and self-image, but we are rarely given the opportunity to see the negative implications of mass consumption in our mass-mediated world. We search for "authenticity" as a form of resistance to this ideological prescription, but even as we do that, the advertising industry has devised ways to co-opt our taste, our desire, our memory, our anticipation, and our passion in the service of its own interests.

Within this ambitious framework, our authors have endeavored to illuminate some fascinating aspects of our world and have done so with a view to "popping" the pop culture of our times. Since much of what is written about in these essays is very current and critiques currently available media materials, the reader is encouraged to see the films and shows before, and while, reading about them here, and also to become introduced to the fascinating and ever-growing volume of critical material about visual culture, much of which has been written by the authors represented here. If, in the end, these views are limited, even as they engage us to ponder, they will serve the important function of making us look twice at images we have long taken for granted. But it is also possible that in popping pop culture a new and heightened pleasure will be available for readers, that of seeing the cultural and social world with new critical insight, new questions, and new urgency to understand ourselves, our relationships, and our future.

Toronto, June 2012

Section 1

Buying into Social Class

*T*he reality of social class and inequality is woven through all aspects of our social world and throughout this book. And of course, inequality is intimately connected to our ability to consume, an activity that is central to the very economic structure of advanced capitalist societies. Current social movements against increasing inequality around the world are important indicators of social change and they will have an impact on all parts of our social life. Consumption, production, and politics are intricately intertwined and it is from these areas that our first group of authors approach the reality of inequality.

Timothy Shary looks at important depictions of youth and social class in films such as *Clueless, Kids,* and *Superbad,* showing how sex and sexuality in those films are connected to class identification and class awareness. Thomas Wartenberg considers the film *Good Will Hunting* and its apparently positive depiction of the working class. But his close examination reveals that the film itself is in fact very supportive of the current class structure and ends up justifying the "American Dream." Stuart Ewen gives a fascinating historical depiction of the uses of the photographic image in propaganda designed to protect the status quo. Curtis Maloley establishes a connection between "American Idol" and democracy and comes up with some surprising conclusions. Douglas Kellner shows us how consumer societies originated and examines the important role of advertising in their continuation. Both of them consider the rapid growth of enormous multinationals on our day to day life and on inequality and social class.

Chapter 1

"The only place to go is inside"

Confusions about Sexuality and
Class from *Kids* to *Superbad*

Timothy Shary

*I*n 1995 two distinctly different films about teenagers
were released to distinctly different audiences: Larry
Clark's *Kids* was a low-budget *vérité*-style examination
of a group of teens in Manhattan which contained such
frank discussion of sexuality, particularly sexuality
among minors, that it was initially given an NC-17 rating by the Motion Picture Association of America and
was eventually released unrated only in limited distribution; Amy Heckerling's *Clueless*, with a larger budget
and a star teen performer whose tale of high school
struggle centered around social acceptance based on
class and attitude as well as sex, became, with its PG-13
rating and wide release, the highest-grossing teen film
in recent years. At first glance one may find the differences and similarities between these two films to be
purely academic, but the release of *Kids* and *Clueless*
represents a crucial movement in the way cinema
addresses teens on screen and in the audience, that

population David Considine has labeled "screenagers."[1] The ways in which *Clueless* and *Kids* examine sex and class for their young characters indicate the precise reasons why these films are such important teen texts.

Ultimately, what is radical about *Kids* is obvious: its graphic confrontation with the dangerous and detached lifestyles of a group of urban teens whose engagement in sex and drugs is killing them. The radical aspect of *Clueless* seems less apparent, if only because the film presents itself as a vapid exposé that treats teen issues casually if not condescendingly; we are tuned in to the idiosyncrasies of current youth in such a way that young people's confrontations with serious youth issues appear relatively unthreatening. However, these two films are significant especially because they enforced lasting perspectives on the American cinema's presentation of teenage sex and class, topics that were problematized, if not minimized, after the release of *Pump Up the Volume* in 1990. During the '90s, teen screen sexuality was suppressed under the dark cloud of AIDS, and class divisions among youth were dismissed after the divisive Reagan era, at least for white youth. Still, in recent years, with the exception of a few unexpected tales of losing virginity at the turn of the century—such as *American Pie* (1999), *Cruel Intentions* (1999), and *The Virgin Suicides* (2000)—sexual and class conflicts among screen teens have remained generally dubious issues, as recent popular films will illustrate.

In the early '80s such films as *Porky's* (1981), *Fast Times at Ridgemont High* (1982) and *Risky Business* (1983) inaugurated the modern teen sex comedy, a genre that was closely linked with the traditional teen drama in which young people struggled to come of age. Throughout the later '80s the popular teen film refined its take on sex as the era of AIDS took hold: previously carefree sexual adventures were gradually replaced by either melodramatic visions of "troubled" youth (e.g. *River's Edge* [1986], *Less Than Zero* [1987], *Heathers* [1989]) or sanitized fables that largely averted sex (e.g. *Can't Buy Me Love* [1987], *Some Kind of Wonderful* [1987], *Dead Poets Society* [1989]). By the release of *Pump Up the Volume*, a film that points to a multiplicity of complex youth problems while enjoying the entertainment value of teen angst, Hollywood seemed to have reached a limit in addressing young adults, as the number of teen films declined considerably between 1991 and 1994. The critical exception was the African American crime drama.

When *Boyz N the Hood* and *Straight Out of Brooklyn* premiered in 1991, their gritty realism and street-smart style granted the films an instant credibility. These films were far removed from the adolescent adventures of the '80s, revealing a population of young people confronted on a daily basis by murder, drugs, and poverty. Like their '80s predecessors, they still explored issues about sex and love, family problems, and the difficult quest for adulthood, but here that difficulty was more daunting—and the consequences more threatening—than in the vast majority of teen films made in the past 20 years. With the release of *Juice* (1992) and *Menace II Society* (1993), Hollywood took on the dramatic (and financial) potential of the black urban youth crisis, leaving television to address the white suburban milieu in shows like "Beverly Hills, 90210," "Blossom," and "Saved by the Bell."

By the mid-'90s the brief wave of African American youth films had nonetheless subsided, leaving open many meaningful questions about the representation of current screenagers. Was the prevailing male perspective going to be maintained? (Of the many African American youth films in the early '90s, only one, *Just Another Girl on the I.R.T.* [1993], focused on the female experience.) Were attitudes about poorer youth shifting toward class awareness and away from ambivalence? Were serious problems like crime, drugs, and sexual disease going to be confronted as well; and if so, how authentically? Indeed, if Hollywood was going to present the youth experience at all, would it welcome a heightened realism or resort to a safer naivité? With *Kids* and *Clueless*, Hollywood did both.

The five years before *Clueless* and *Kids* may well have been a hibernation period during which the minimizing of teens on screen reflected a Hollywood predisposition against dealing with youth. 1991 could have been a watershed year for teen films with the publication of Douglas Coupland's eponymous book *Generation X* and the release of Richard Linklater's equally eponymous film *Slacker*, but these texts shifted attention to the post-teen twentysomething population, as the wave of corresponding movies over the next few years (e.g. *Singles* [1992], *Reality Bites* [1994], *Threesome* [1994]) attested. With the emergence of the "Generation X" genre in the early '90s, Hollywood could have avoided addressing teens even longer, and may have, had the new genre been more successful. By 1995 the time was ripe for Hollywood to reconsider not only the teen box office potential but more so the conditions of teen life that had been renegotiated in the past five years, especially in the wake of the African American youth films. What remained to be seen was the form that new teen films would take.

The teens and pre-teens that populate *Kids* not only exist in a world removed from structures such as high school and family (we are led to believe that the story takes place during summer vacation and only one parent is featured), but seem to be removed from any livelihood other than the conquest for sex, drugs, and alcohol. In films like *Clueless* and earlier teen dramas like those of the John Hughes variety (e.g. *Sixteen Candles* [1984], *The Breakfast Club* [1985], *Ferris Bueller's Day Off* [1986]), high school and family provide the system against which teens rebel and through which they develop their social roles. *Kids* posits that its characters' roles have been firmly developed outside of school—to be sure, even though there are dozens of teen characters in the film who associate with each other, not once is a reference to school friends or activities made by any of them. Unlike the vaguely similar *Where the Day Takes You* (1992), in which the out-of-school teen characters are homeless runaways dealing with troubled pasts and seeking more promising futures, *Kids* presents its characters as familiar with, and at home in, their territory and otherwise content to just make it to the next party. Thus, they have little discernable identity other than hedonistic ignorance. In praising the film, Amy Taubin deduced that *Kids* "suggests that adolescent socialization is less determined by culture than biology."[2] These teens obviously didn't need school or parents to develop their streetwise instinct for sexual and chemical gratification.

The lack of institutionalized social structure allows for moral conditions in which youths are forced to make decisions usually reserved for adults, and this is especially problematic since these children lack the wisdom needed to comprehend the consequences of their actions. The minimal adult presence in *Kids* calls attention to the guile of a culture that necessarily but unrealistically excludes all but the young (as if these characters function in the same artificial environment of the *Peanuts* comics, only with excessive decadence) and further blurs the distinction between youthful innocence and adult accountability. In terms of sexuality, these teens' actions can be a matter of life (pregnancy) or death (disease), and yet *Kids* allows the gravity of its characters' circumstances to be spoken in an aloof visual and verbal irony. This tactic may be effective in appealing to the young viewers who were supposedly prevented from seeing the film, but it evacuates the kids in *Kids* of much literal understanding about the dangers (or certainly the joys) of sexuality. In comparing the directors of *Clueless* and *Kids*, Tom Doherty proposed that "if Heckerling is an indulgent mother having fun with her kids, Clark is the absent father, looking on detachedly, counting on the spectator to invest the narrative with moral meaning."[3] *Kids* is thereby oddly reactionary: we are ultimately shown that sex can be bad despite how much people claim to enjoy it, and the moral and philosophical complexities of this position are left largely unexplored.

Perhaps much of the conquest for pleasure that permeates *Kids* is based on its distinctly masculinist perspective; or, as bell hooks claimed in more aggressive terms, "What is being exploited [in *Kids*] is precisely and solely a spectacle of teenage sexuality that has been shaped and informed by patriarchal attitudes."[4] The film revolves around two teen boys, Telly (Leo Fitzpatrick) and Casper (Justin Pierce), the first of whom begins the film's day-in-the-life by deflowering an apparently pubescent girl while the other is drinking a 40-ounce beer and reading *Hate* comics. The few girls who are presented in the film are less developed characters but, as an early scene shows, they are just as sexually excitable as the boys who pursue them. The one conspicuous exception is Jennie (Chloe Sevigny), who reveals that she only ever had sex one time, with Telly, and soon afterward discovers that he has infected her with HIV. The film's narrative thus becomes something of a picaresque journey for Jennie as she tries to find Telly before he infects another girl by the end of the day.

Despite Jennie's presence in the story and the one dialogue scene offered between girls, Harmony Korine's script never offers a balance or reprieve from its objectified positioning of young women. Perhaps Korine was making a statement on the difficulty girls face in dealing with urban boys today, for he appears himself as a friendly nerd who meets Jennie at a rave and, with empty consolations, forces her to take a drug that he insists will make her feel better. By the end of the film Jennie is so stoned that she cannot even protest when Casper rapes her, in a scene made all the more brutal by the fact that immediately before it she finds Telly but is too late to stop him from having sex with yet another virgin, and by Clark's sustained filming of it for two and a half minutes. Thus the film cheaply offers a false empowerment for its female characters, who initially appear confident in their knowledge and appropriation of sex, but who are ultimately victimized by it. The film is not merely sexist or patriarchal, it endorses an understanding of youthful sexuality that is degrading for both genders.

Clueless offers a more complex hypothesis on the nature of sexuality among teens, as its virginal main character, ironically named Cher (Alicia Silverstone), negotiates a wider range of social roles that are not all related to sexuality *per se*. Cher narrates her story in a voiceover that recalls and accentuates the style of the film's inspiration, Jane Austen's *Emma*. In describing her perspective on boys, Cher notes that high school boys are unacceptably immature for her tastes (making the extra-textual reference, "Searching for a boy in high school is as useless as searching for meaning in a Pauly Shore movie"), and for the first half of the film she remains uninterested in pursuing romantic or sexual involvements. Instead, she devotes her time first to the "project" of matchmaking two of her teachers, clearly for the purpose of improving her grades, and then to transforming a new student named Tai (Brittany Murphy) from a frumpy outcast to a costumed cutie so that she can become part of the small but popular crowd that in which Cher travels. Only after she has achieved these romantic and sexual changes in others does she turn to herself.

Meanwhile, a dramatic tension is set up through a rather candid conversation between Cher, Tai, and Dionne (Stacey Dash) about Cher's virginity. After Tai expresses her preference that men have straight (as opposed to crooked) penises, Dionne points out that Cher is "hymenally challenged," to which Cher rejoins, "You see how picky I am about my shoes, and they only go on my feet." Cher's implication that she has been careful and patient, not to say discriminating, in waiting to have sex (at the age of 15) is thus equated to a fashion statement and, as Amanda Lipman points out, Cher's "strong sense of morality is purely pragmatic."[5] Sex for Cher must be rationalized and purposeful. Tai makes no such concessions to virginity and Dionne, who initially resists losing her virginity with her boyfriend, later gives in after the "emotional" experience of surviving a drive on the L.A. Freeway. This leaves Cher with the tension of being inculcated into sexual practice for the rest of the film.

What happens in the second half of the film in terms of Cher's sexual development is most unusual considering the traditions of young romance. First she develops a crush on a new guy at school (Justin Walker), who is sophisticated and cool and who clearly shows an interest in her. Despite Cher's best efforts at attracting him, which include sending herself presents, she later discovers that he is gay (an over-informed friend tells her he is "a disco-dancing, Oscar Wilde-reading, Streisand-ticket-holding friend of Dorothy"). This revelation prevents Cher from further pursuing her awkward crush (at least her gay friend becomes a great shopping companion), but as if her romantic/sexual momentum can't be stopped, she next finds herself in the conflict of being attracted to her college-age stepbrother, Josh (Paul Rudd). Heckerling sets up this relationship with scenes that do not alleviate its incestual implications: Josh gazes longingly at Cher when she dresses up for a party and then tells her father (his stepfather) that he's going to the party to look after her; two scenes later, Cher encourages Josh to stay around for spring break, reminding him that he's not really her brother. Then, in what turns out to be a serendipitous soul-searching shopping trip, Cher realizes that she's in love with Josh, and next finds herself trying to hide her tense feelings for him. Josh and Cher eventually break this tension when, after a session of mutual compliments, they share a passionate kiss. While such an attraction between stepsiblings may be understandable, the potential problems that could arise from acting on it are diminished for the sake of preserving the romantic trajectory of the film. When Heckerling ends *Clueless* with Cher and Josh kissing at the wedding of her teachers, after Cher has fought hard to catch the bouquet, we are left to infer that the world of sexuality has become so difficult for teens to navigate that Cher's choice of her stepbrother for a boyfriend is completely rational despite its dilemmas. Literally "staying close to home" may ironically be the smartest sexual choice of all.

Kids does not make sexuality for youths appear effortless either, however, the film's one-dimensional perspective, i.e. that boys are dogs and girls are no better, denies the psychological intricacy of the issue. The main, if only, consequence of sexuality in *Kids* is the potential spread of HIV, a serious issue to be sure; but Telly's habitual practice of deflowering virgins is left on the moral surface. When Telly's friend Casper tells him, "How you gonna fuck two virgins in one day? It's gotta be against the law," Telly takes further pride in his pursuit. Unlike the morality lessons learned in other movies about youth, the dangerous lesson of *Kids*—that sex and drugs can be deadly—is never realized onscreen. The film concludes with Telly visibly infecting another girl with HIV and reciting in a voiceover, "When you're young, not much matters . . . Sometimes when you're young, the only place to go is inside. That's just it—fucking is what I love. Take that away from me and I really got nothing." This ending may be meant as further ironic commentary on the fact that Telly is likely to die from his fucking practices, but he is never forced to confront them while we watch. As Owen Gliberman said in his review of the film, "We never get to see if the little son of a bitch has a soul after all."[6] I am not proposing that *Clueless* necessarily offers a more "realistic" perspective on teen sexuality, only that the perspective offered by *Kids* is incomplete and misogynistic when compared to *Clueless*, and that such a perspective, when presented in the "graphic" style that Clark works in, is dubious and deceptive.

Sexuality and gender have been issues central to many films about young adults, but there is another potentially radical address that *Kids* and *Clueless* pose, which is their ways of handling class. Some youth movies in the '80s highlighted the economic status of their characters for the sake of considering intragenerational differences of privilege (e.g. *Valley Girl* [1983], *The Breakfast Club, Say Anything* [1989]). These films usually highlighted the struggles of couples as they recognized their class differences or the class disparities within a group, and in every case the point was made that friendship or love could transcend financial status. That transcendence is not a goal of the narratives of *Kids* and *Clueless*, for these are films that indifferently acknowledge the class of their characters and then proceed to reinforce the false "privilege" that their status represents: in the case of *Kids*, the characters' lack of wealth can be seen to justify their lifestyles of crime and hedonism, while in *Clueless* the characters' excess of wealth rationalizes their consumption and their nonchalance.

Some mention should also be made of the differing commercial practices connected to the productions of *Kids* and *Clueless*. Clark's film is adamantly independent and low-budget (although it was distributed by Disney-owned Miramax), shot on location with high-speed film in predominantly natural light, and thus it preserves on a technical level the meager moral conditions inhabited by its characters that are metaphorically manifested in their surroundings. Heckerling had the backing of a substantial budget from Paramount (allowing for an extensive wardrobe, expensive cars, and spectacular sets), and several companies' products are clearly displayed and used throughout the film, commenting further on the literal and figurative consumption that is intrinsic to the characters' lives and Hollywood filmmaking practice. In one particularly telling scene, we see from Cher's point of view as she walks through a room looking at teachers. Suddenly she is seized by the sight of a candy bar, naming it aloud as if its material presence and personality in the room cannot be avoided. Both films are thus produced within the class conditions that are depicted in their narratives.

Kids portrays a rather ambiguous group of youths in terms of their living situations—some only mention having parents while others seem to have no family at all. We become aware that Steven (Jon Abrahams), whose parents own the rather swank high-rise apartment where the kids have their climactic party, is at least upper-middle-class, while it remains unclear if most of the characters in the film are really from the poor backgrounds that they appear to be from. Telly's class status is the one most clearly articulated, and it becomes an index for his peers. When he briefly returns home in the afternoon, his family's modest apartment speaks of their working-class position: Telly's father is away at his job while his mother is home breast-feeding, and the apartment is decorated with a sparse mixture of family snapshots and newspaper photos or posters. Telly lies to his mother that he and Casper have been unsuccessfully looking for jobs and thus he needs money; when his mother refuses, Telly goes into her room and steals some cash, which he soon afterward uses to buy drugs. Clark films this sequence in the same casual, familiar manner as the rest of the film, demonstrating that the stealing and lying these youths engage in is routine and systematic. For Telly, Casper, and the rest of the group, jobs and money are indeed irrelevant, as their lives revolve around the ongoing acquisition of drugs and alcohol, which they steal or share, and sex, which is only slightly more negotiated.

This condition of excessive consumption is nonetheless figured very differently from that which is engendered by conspicuous wealth. In *Kids*, consumption has become a means of celebrating squalor and aimlessness while preserving communal bonding. These young characters not only lack jobs, they don't have any discernable skills other than the ability to maintain consumption. In another revealing scene, after Telly and Casper buy marijuana with their stolen money, a friend demonstrates how to hollow out a blunt cigar to smoke the dope. Clark films this sequence in a how-to manner, as the character takes us through the process ("break it, scrape it, lick it, dump it, smoke it"), instructing us on a technique which demonstrates the humble sophistication of dope smoking. This yields an attitude which is again indicative of the film's ambivalence toward class: you don't need a lot of money to be a hip youngster, but you do need to know how to engage in the common customs relative to your peer group.

A striking parallel is found in *Clueless*, although this film necessarily presents a considerably different class perspective since the main character comes from apparently unlimited wealth and is well-versed in the practices of conspicuous consumption. Richard Corliss succinctly claimed, indeed, that the film is entirely about conspicuous consumption: "wanting, having and wearing in style. And in L.A."[7] Because that consumption is so conspicuous it is easy to perceive as being harmless, too: the shopping trips and fashion concerns of Cher and her friends are not as dangerous, we may think, as the more private sexual and drug experiences of the youths in *Kids*. Nonetheless, the characters in *Clueless* are still having sex and, in lesser quantities, indulging in drugs– potential crises which are alleviated by the more visible practices of buying clothes, driving in fancy cars, and hanging out at cafés. If money seems to have the effect of diversifying teen hedonism, it really only serves as a distraction from potential problems common to all young people.

Cher, like the characters in *Kids*, is certainly not interested in employment, but this is because her father apparently provides all the money she asks for. What becomes the more crucial class question in *Clueless* is how the fortunate use their financial power to influence— or stifle—change, as Cher attempts to become altruistic in her efforts to help people around her, gaining popularity (and a boyfriend) for herself and molding Tai into an acceptable member of her clique. There is a distinct sense of irony behind Cher's attempts to "improve" the world through her good fortunes: she struggles to help others in a way that is not self-serving, and finds this most difficult. When she joins a cause like the Pismo Beach disaster relief, Heckerling further parodies Cher's ability to actually help people by having her donate such impractical items as caviar and skis. There seems to be no escape from the vapid consumption that ensures her upper-class status, and even though it makes her more popular and visible at school, her wealth is nonetheless a liability in her understanding of the world around her.

The level of teen acceptance that is sought by characters in *Kids* via sex and drugs is thus figured very differently in *Clueless*, which incorporates upper-class materialism as a means of de-emphasizing sex and drug problems and thereby shifts the notion of acceptance to a more idealized vision of self-improvement and social change. Perhaps in this sense *Kids* speaks more of the truth about the disempowerment and *ennui* of most youth, who do not enjoy upper-class lifestyles; yet where *Clueless* demonstrates Cher's strained efforts to understand and utilize her privilege, *Kids* encourages its characters to wallow in their under-privileged conditions. Again bell hooks' critique is to the point: "There is no resistance to domination in [*Kids*], merely a primitive embrace of ruling paradigms."[8] [The characters in *Kids* never speak of an interest in future life goals because the film is too busy celebrating the pleasure-filled present. Even Jennie, who fears she is going to die, never has an opportunity to consider the tragedy of her life. In the end, both films demonstrate class conditions for their young characters, but both are unable to offer any meaningful alternatives to the problems class conditions pose: the rich and the poor are locked in different prisons of nescience.

Despite the wide appeal of a film like *Clueless* and the art-house interests of a film like *Kids*, both films indicate that the traditional representations of youth that were seen in American cinema since the early '80s were changing considerably by 1995. The graphic aspects of *Kids* would be enough evidence of this, but I argue that there could be a deeper change, in that *Clueless* and *Kids* became new paradigms for addressing youth issues today. On one hand, we have a seemingly innocuous comedy which highlights issues important to teens without exploring how paramount those issues actually are to teens themselves; on the other we see teens engaged in a level of serious behavior that is so extreme in its representation that the protagonists' lives are reduced to vulgar debauchery. *Clueless* presents the supposed "Hollywood" version of '90s youth, paying lip service to social change while remaining steadfastly concerned with self-fulfillment; *Kids* presents youth strictly in adult terms, inflaming adult viewers with its nihilistic vision of the kind of teen crisis they most fear. There is thus a split, even schizophrenic, image of youth propagated by these films, as sexuality remains an inherently confusing prospect to youth and class becomes a deceptively apolitical characteristic of youth.

Even at the end of the '90s, when more sexualized roles reappeared in mainstream teen films—*American Pie, Cruel Intentions, Coming Soon* (all 1999)—their otherwise prominent class issues were averted by the overwhelming emphasis these films placed on the gravity of sexual experience. *Cruel Intentions* and *Coming Soon* revealed this most visibly, as their wealthy teens trafficked in luxury goods at elite schools with nary a thought about their financial status; rather, status for these teens remained tied up in their sexual conquests and pleasures. As in *Clueless, Cruel Intentions* also featured a romantic tension between teenage stepsiblings, although in the latter film the sexual force between them has risen to a graphic and moral level worthy of Larry Clark: the stepsister promises her stepbrother he can "put it anywhere" if she loses a bet about his seductive proficiency. Meanwhile, Clark himself has sustained a notorious output of increasingly vilifying films about teenagers, as with *Bully* (2001) and *Ken Park* (2003), both of which managed to be even more ethically bankrupt than *Kids* and more pornographic in their sex and violence, while neither film had the capacity to present troubled teens as anything other than psychopathic predators and cannibals.

The confusions of sex and class in teen films of recent years remains prominent, as exhibited by the two highest-grossing examples from 2004: *Mean Girls* and *Napoleon Dynamite*. The first film is indebted to *Heathers* with its tale of a girl negotiating her space among an elite clique at a new school, and the latter hearkens back to the "slacker" films of the early '90s in its tale of a distraught teenager who seems to have no ambition beyond hoarding tater tots. Both films are humorous and satirical, yet *Mean Girls* has an explicit agenda to interrogate and expose the oppressive attitudes of acceptance within the high school caste system, and *Napoleon Dynamite* takes on an implicit challenge to middle-American racism when a Latino asks his white friend to help him run for his high school class presidency. Despite these potentially political aspects, however, both films manage to jettison the core power issues that fuel their conflicts: in *Mean Girls*, the sexual practice of its heroine, and in *Napoleon Dynamite*, the class limitations of its two male heroes.

More recently, the celebrated *Superbad* (2008) further illustrated the subtle intrusion of class and the direct disruption of sex so common in contemporary teen films. The story focuses on three male friends who together pursue liberation from their uncomfortable status as awkward high schoolers: one is nerdy, another overweight, and another shy. They share the common goals of acquiring alcohol and bedding girls, although the traditional hierarchy of acceptance typical of high school is broken down in their pursuits. Rather than exhibiting wealth, good looks, or athletic ability, the boys paradoxically achieve their triumph through a progressive acceptance of their own inadequacies. The film thereby validates young male diffidence in the process of rewarding its heroes—they overcome great trouble in bringing a bounty of drinks to the climactic party, achieving social recognition and approval—yet they are thwarted in their sexual ambitions. Even though each guy pairs off with a girl, the only one to even start coitus is interrupted by cops—an intervention of law that is no less symbolic than the ultimate confession of the other two boys that they love each other. The homosocial ending of the film, with these boys looking longingly at each other as they walk away to go shopping with their new girlfriends, provides another example of sexual confusion for screen teens, and its displacement onto a less satisfying consumer exercise.

Given the appeal of these films, and the continuing common themes of most teen movies, we may well wonder if the impact of social class has become all but invisible for youth, while sexual experiences continue to trump all other interests, even if the young characters are never provided with the consummating pleasure they seek.

Notes

[1] David Considine, *The Cinema of Adolescence* (Jefferson, North Carolina: McFarland, 1985), 14.

[2] Amy Taubin, "Chilling and Very Hot," *Sight and Sound* (Nov. 1995), 17.

[3] Tom Doherty, "Clueless Kids," *Cineaste* 21: 4 (1995), 16.

[4] bell hooks, "White Light," *Sight and Sound* (May 1996), 10.

[5] Amanda Lipman, "Clueless" review, *Sight and Sound* (Oct. 1995), 46.

[6] Owen Gliberman, "Bold Before Their Time," *Entertainment Weekly* (July 21,1995), 47.

[7] Richard Corliss, "To Live and Buy in L.A.," *Time* (July 31, 1995), 65.

[8] hooks, 11.

Chapter 2

"What's a smart boy like you doing in a class like this?"

Intelligence and Class in *Good Will Hunting*

Thomas E. Wartenberg

A great deal of the interest of Gus Van Sant's 1997 popular and successful film, *Good Will Hunting*,[1] results from its focus upon intelligence as an issue for men. Three of the central characters in the film have superior intelligence and the film presents this as a significant concern in their lives. This is particularly true of Will Hunting (Matt Damon), the film's hero, a young mathematical genius who is faced with the question of how and whether to square his intellect with his working-class identity. But both Sean Maguire (Robin Williams), the therapist who eventually helps Will find a balm for his psychic wounds, and Gerald Lambeau (Stellan Skarsgård), the MIT mathematics professor who "discovers" Will, also have had to figure out how to cope with their intelligence and its impact on their lives.

But *Good Will Hunting* is not just a film about intelligence and men; it also foregrounds issues of class for, as I have said, Will belongs to the working class. The question that the film presents is whether Will's superior intelligence is at odds with his membership in the working class.

To many viewers, it may seem as if I am belaboring the obvious. After all, the film presents Will as showing up the pretensions and elitism of a pseudo-intellectual Harvard graduate student as well as his erstwhile mentor, while coming to a deeper understanding of his own psychic compulsions. What else could the film's view of class be, viewers might be inclined to think, but that working-class men are more authentic, less pretentious and snobby than upper-class men? On such an interpretation of the film, *Good Will Hunting* would fit the model of the populist romances of the 1930s with their affirmation of populist values over elitist ones.

A more nuanced interpretation of the film will show, however, that *Good Will Hunting* is more ambivalent in its depiction of the working class than this interpretation allows. Using an ascent narrative, the film presents the behavior of most working-class men as justifying, if not the disrespect that others show them, then at least their inferior social position. Only the exceptional Will Hunting is seen as deserving to escape from the vicious environment that the film depicts working-class men as creating as well as inhabiting. Rather than offering a sympathetic portrait of the difficulties faced by working-class men, *Good Will Hunting* endorses class hierarchy, provided that those exceptional individuals with superior talent wind up in the privileged social positions they deserve. Using intelligence as a marker of class, *Good Will Hunting* treats membership in the working class as a form of disability from which "brains" provide one of the few avenues of escape.

Ascent Narratives

My interpretation of *Good Will Hunting* places it in the context of films that I have called "unlikely couple films."[2] The narratives of unlikely couple films focus upon the development of romantic couplings that are transgressive in some socially significant way. One important sub-category of the unlikely couple film includes films that depict cross-class romances. There are many films that fit this category, from Frank Capra's 1934 comedy *It Happened One Night* to Erick Zonca's tragic 1988 film, *The Dreamlife of Angels* (*La Vie rêvée des anges*). These films often feature *ascent narratives*, that is, plots depicting a romance in which one of the partners is elevated to the other's privileged social position.

The mere presence of an ascent narrative does not determine the political perspective of a film, however. Although many theorists of Hollywood cinema have contended that popular narrative films of this type—from *It Happened One Night* to *Pretty Woman*—are particularly designed to deny the significance of the social difference that the successful couple transcends, such a broad generalization is not valid. The story of a character's successful social ascent could be used, as it is in the first half of Anthony Asquith's 1938 film version of *Pygmalion*, to attack the validity of a social hierarchy such as the class structure by demonstrating that there is no legitimate reason why members of the lower class are relegated to inferior social positions.[3] On the other hand, as Gary Marshall's 1990 film *Pretty Woman* clearly demonstrates, a character's social ascent can be used to validate class hierarchy by showing that justice demands that an exceptional member of the working class ascend to her rightful social location.[4] As we shall see, I believe *Good Will Hunting* falls into the latter camp, i.e., it uses an ascent narrative to justify a class hierarchy based on intelligence.

Intelligence Trumps Class

It is against this background of unlikely couple films employing ascent narratives that I want to look more closely at *Good Will Hunting*. Let's begin by considering a scene that might be taken to establish the film's validation of the working class. That the working class might stand in need of validation by a film is itself an interesting notion, one that points toward the question of what role the film sees for itself in regard to the class hierarchy. As we shall see, the film presents a simplified set of options for men's class positions: being in the working class, having ascended out of the working class, or being in the upper class. Upper-class men are presented as having condescending attitudes toward the working-class men, as this scene illustrates, so the need for a response seems natural, called for by the pompous attitudes of the upper class itself. Will and his friends have gone to the Bow and Arrow Pub, a crowded Harvard bar. Will's best friend, Chuckie (Ben Affleck), tries to pick up Skylar (Minnie Driver), a Harvard undergrad, by pretending to recognize her from a class. At this point, a pretentious male graduate student, Clark (Scott Winters), tries to publicly humiliate Chuckie by showing that he has no idea what the course in question was about and thus establish that the working-class Chuckie is not the sort of person who could possibly have taken a course at Harvard:

> CLARK: What class did you say that was?
> CHUCKIE: History.
> CLARK: How'd you like that course?
> CHUCKIE: Good, it was all right.
> CLARK: History? Just "history"? It must have been a survey course then. Pretty broad. History of the world? . . .
> CHUCKIE: To tell you the truth, I wasn't there much. The class was rather elementary.
> CLARK: Elementary? Oh, I don't doubt that it was. I remember the class—it was just between recess and lunch.
> CHUCKIE: All right, are we gonna have a problem?
> CLARK: There's no problem. I was just hoping that you could give me some insight into the evolution of the market economy in the early colonies. My contention is that prior to the Revolutionary War, the economic modalities, especially of the southern colonies, could most aptly be characterized as agrarian precapitalist and . . .
> (24–25)

Clark attempts not only to catch Chuckie in his lie, but to use the knowledge he, Clark, gained in that class to put Chuckie down, to demonstrate his, Clark's, class superiority by humiliating Chuckie.

Things will not turn out the way Clark intends, however, for Will steps in to rescue Chuckie and shows that the ideas Clark has been spouting are all derivative and do not demonstrate that Clark possesses superior intelligence.

WILL: Of course that's your contention. You're a first-year grad student. You just finished reading some Marxian historian, Pete Garrison prob'ly, and so naturally that's what you believe until next month when you get to James Lemon and get convinced that Virginia and Pennsylvania were strongly entrepreneurial and capitalist back in seventeen forty. That'll last until sometime in your second year, then you'll be in here regurgitating Gordon Wood about the prerevolutionary utopia and the capital-forming effects of military mobilization.
CLARK: Well, as a matter of fact, I won't, because Wood drastically underestimates the impact of—
WILL: —Wood drastically underestimates the impact of social distinctions predicated upon wealth, especially inherited wealth. . . . You got that from Vickers's *Work in Essex County*, was it pages ninety-eight to one-oh-two, what? Do you have any thought of your own on the subject or were you just gonna plagiarize the whole book for me?

To finish things off, Will hands Clark this judgment of him:

WILL: The sad thing is, in about fifty years you might start doin' some thinkin' on your own and by then you'll realize that there are only two certainties in life. . . . One, don't do that. Two, you dropped a hundred and fifty grand on an education you coulda picked up for a dollar fifty in late charges at the public library. (25–27)

By the end of the exchange, Clark limps away, tail between his legs, having been shown up by the working-class genius whose victory in this intellectual contest has perked Skylar's interest, too.

Throughout the scene, while our attention is riveted by the conversation between the three men, the camera rarely focuses upon them alone. Most of the shots, even the close-ups, also include other characters as well: Clark's fellow Harvard students, eagerly anticipating Clark's humiliation of Chuckie; Skylar, the undergraduate who occasions the exchange in the first place; Will, watching Clark carefully as he sizes up the situation. The exchange between these three young men takes place in a highly public space of contestation. The film thus makes us aware that the men are all acting before their various audiences, but it also calls attention to the role we play, bystanding as the film's actual audience, in the creation of this drama.

What does this scene actually establish? First, it shows that Clark is a poseur who does not really possess superior intelligence to Chuckie. This is established by Will's ability to walk circles around him intellectually and to show that all Clark really possesses is some second-hand knowledge he has acquired in his courses at Harvard. Such knowledge, however well it might serve him in graduate school—and the film is unremitting in its negative portrayal of graduate students, especially Lambeau's and these in the bar—does not reflect his possession of superior intelligence. But this means, secondly, that Clark's position of social privilege in relation to Chuckie is not justified by his possession of superior intelligence. While Clark believes it is, his inability to contend with Will invalidates that belief. The superficial knowledge that he does possess is simply the result of his privileged access to Harvard and can't be used to justify that privilege. Only Will, lacking as he does Clark's privileges, has the sort of intelligence that, in the film's eyes, justifies a superior social position, for Will not only possesses a great deal of information garnered from his wide reading but knows how to assess it and deploy it in an argument.

Since this scene demonstrates that Clark's arrogant pretense is nothing but that, the question remains open as to whether superior intelligence such as Will's justifies a privileged social position. As we shall see, the film winds up endorsing this idea and, in so doing, naturalizes the class structure as based upon genuine differences of intelligence, itself something the film sees as genetic.

I characterize this scene as pseudo-populist. Such scenes can be found in a variety of recent films. *Pretty Woman*, once again, will function as my paradigm. There, Vivian Ward (Julia Roberts), a prostitute who has been snubbed by a saleswoman in a Rodeo Drive boutique, returns to the scene of the crime laden with bags full of her many expensive purchases from other stores and intones, "You work on commission, don't you? Mistake. Big, big, mistake," as she turns around while displaying the goods she has bought that cost a small fortune. By putting down the saleswoman, Vivian makes up for the rejection she suffered at the saleswoman's hands, although her doing so, ironically, makes her guilty of the very same crime, something the film seeks to keep us from noticing. Snobbery suffers an inversion as the saleswoman recognizes that Vivian deserved to be treated with respect, her hot pants and go-go boots notwithstanding. The populist moment of a snob receiving her comeuppance is mitigated by the film's assertion that Vivian—because of her great beauty—really belongs among the privileged and should be treated as such. It is interesting to note that both films attempt to *naturalize* class position, but do so in different ways. *Pretty Woman* focuses upon a woman and treats her exceptional beauty as requiring her social elevation. *Good Will Hunting*, dealing as it does with men, uses not beauty but intelligence as the supposedly natural marker that ought to be reflected in the class hierarchy. Although both films exceptionalize their hero in order to justify a heroic ascent, the terms they use reflect differences in how we think of men and women in relation to class position.

Returning to *Good Will Hunting*, we can see that the bar scene is equally remote from fully endorsing the populist idea that all human beings deserve equal respect. Its populist feel comes from Will's ability to defeat Clark's attempt to show that he is superior to Chuckie. The pretension of a false elite to deserve its social privilege because of superior intelligence is thus shown to be ungrounded. This is accomplished, however, only by subtly positing a true elite, one to which Will belongs because of his genius. Indeed, the film even grants Will "the girl," for Skylar approaches him at the end of the scene, thus reinforcing our sense of him as the "victor" in this battle for recognition.[5]

This scene, then, suggests that an individual's actual class position may not reflect his or her intelligence. Education is a privilege granted to those in the upper class, and that they can use to demean members of the working class. But Will's upbraiding of the Harvard snot shows that differences in intelligence do not coincide with class distinctions. Despite its exceptionalizing of Will, the film still seems headed on a trajectory that will expose the illegitimacy of justifying class hierarchy on supposed differences in intelligence. However, as we shall see, this appearance is deceptive.

Pathologizing Class

Central to *Good Will Hunting*'s narrative is Will's ascent out of the working class. An important question to ask is why this ascent is necessary. Even though Will is shown to be a mathematical genius, it is not clear why that requires him to leave his working-class environment and friends, as he does when he decides to follow Skylar to San Francisco where she has gone to pursue her medical education.

The answer to this question, unfortunately, is that *Good Will Hunting* pathologizes Will's class position. Despite the fact that Will was born into the working class, the film treats his position in that class—and other peoples' position there as well—as a disability that requires a cure.

That this is the case emerges in two stages. In the first stage we see Will engaging in self-destructive behavior with his working-class pals, behavior that winds him up in jail. Because Lambeau has discovered Will's mathematical talents, he bails Will out under the proviso that he undergo counseling. As a last resort, Lambeau turns to his old college buddy, Sean Maguire, a therapist whose career has been sidetracked by the illness and subsequent death of his wife. During Maguire's therapy sessions with Will, the second stage of the film's pathologizing of Will and the working class emerges: it turns out that Will suffers from self-doubts and insecurities as the result of the vicious abuse he suffered at the hands of his step-father.

What exactly is Will's psychological problem? In the pop psychological terms furnished by Maguire during Will's analysis, Will believes he deserves the mistreatment he suffered as a child. This phenomenon is actually quite common: a young child internalizes his own mistreatment, seeing it as a result of some defect on his part, rather than a flaw in his or her caretaker. As a result, Will repeatedly relives the scene of his own victimization, seeking out confirmation that he is a "bad boy" from whatever authorities he can find. Hence, his misdeeds and his trouble with the police. He puts himself in jail, as it were, to confirm his negative self-image.

Will's position in the working class is thus, from the point of view of the film, an injustice on two scores. First, his inferior social position belies his superior intelligence which should place him among the privileged members of society. But Will's remaining in the working class also reflects his perduring lack of self-esteem as a result of the mistreatment he suffered as a child. His ascent out of the working class will therefore simultaneously right both wrongs: it will put him in the class that is appropriate for his intelligence while at the same time recuperating his sense of self and allowing him to escape the prison of his own childhood.

To achieve this psychological "ascent," however, Will has to learn a lesson from Maguire, for it won't be enough if Will simply decides to respect his intellect and go to work for one of the firms that Lambeau has selected. He needs to discover that, despite his intelligence, human relationships should be the primary focus of his life.

This lesson comes across most clearly in a story that Maguire tells Will about how he met his future wife. He had slept out on the street to get tickets for game six of the World Series in 1975, the game in which Carlton Fisk hit a home run in the bottom of the twelfth inning to give the Red Sox the Series. Maguire was sitting in a bar with his friends, waiting for the game to start, when a woman walked into the bar. Maguire explains: "I just slid my ticket across the table and said, 'Sorry fellas, I gotta go see about a girl.'" Will is astounded and asks how Maguire's friends could let him give up that ticket for "a girl." Maguire explains again:

> If I had gone to see that game I'd be in here talkin' about a girl I saw at a bar twenty years ago. And how I always regretted not goin' over there and talkin' to her. I don't regret the eighteen years we were married. I don't regret givin' up counseling for six years when she got sick. I don't regret being by her side for the last two years when things got real bad. And I sure as hell don't regret missing that damn game.
> (86)

Maguire is telling Will a number of things here. First, he is suggesting that moving from a focus on male bonding to an intimate relationship with a woman is a mark of socio-psychological development. Secondly, and more importantly from the point of view of my argument here, he is explaining that achievement does not bring happiness, for that can only come from intimate human relationships no matter what their "cost." These lessons conflict deeply with Lambeau's urgent desire that Will simply accept his gift and dedicate himself to pushing back the frontiers of knowledge.

The contrast between Maguire and Lambeau is instructive here. (The film script even refers to Maguire, but not Lambeau, by his first name, establishing our intimacy with him and our distaste for Lambeau.) Although both men seek to mentor Will, Lambeau's interest in Will is portrayed as highly suspect. It is as if Lambeau's career as a mathematician will finally be validated by his discovery of this young genius. His interest in Will is based on attention to not Will himself but only his amazing facility with math. Although Maguire clearly benefits from his relation with Will—he is freed from his own depression over the death of his wife through his interaction with Will and makes his own decision to leave town at the film's end—he is motivated by a genuine desire to help Will overcome his destructive impulses and discover the nature of his real desires.

While I find this aspect of the film's narrative less problematic than its class politics, let me point out that the film here plays on anti-intellectual attitudes that are very common, it seems, in contemporary society. Maguire's decision to use his intellect to help people cope rather than to advance knowledge is presented as simply the correct thing to do. Indeed, the film explicitly claims that Einstein—one of Lambeau's models for intellectual achievement—was an unhappy human being who made a wreck of his intimate relationships. Clearly, this is a naive and simplistic view of how intelligence can be used to benefit life on the planet.

So let us now consider the film's representation of the working class. I believe that the film's use of an ascent narrative undermines its earlier support and affirmation—if only partial—of the working class in the face of intellectual snobbery. If Will's being in the working class is the result of his pathology, his lacking an adequate self-image, what does this say about his friends and other members of the working class? How are we to understand *their* being in the working class?

As we will see, the film treats their membership in the working class as inevitable, something from which they have no means or hope of escape, for it is only Will, with his exceptional intelligence, who has the option of ascending out of the stultifying environment the film characterizes as that of working-class males. *Good Will Hunting* simply uses the working-class men who are Will's friends as foils for his ascent, treating the self-destructive and demeaning lives it depicts *them* living as simply their natural lot. Instead of actually valorizing the working class, *Good Will Hunting* ultimately presents working-class men as deserving their inferior social position because of their pathologies.

The scene that exposes this aspect of the film's class politics takes place between Will and his best buddy, Chuckie. They are drinking beer after work, standing in front of the construction site where they labor.[6] The two seem to be catching up, for Will tells Chuckie that Skylar has left some time ago to go to medical school. As the two continue to talk, it becomes clear that Will and Chuckie have different ideas about Will's future.

CHUCKIE: So, when are you done with those meetin's [with Maguire]?
WILL: Week after I'm twenty-one.

CHUCKIE: Are they hookin' you up with a job?

WILL: Yeah, sit in a room and do long division for the next fifty years.

CHUCKIE: Yah, but it's better than this shit. At least you'd make some nice bank.

WILL: Yeah, be a fuckin' lab rat.

CHUCKIE: It's a way outta here.

WILL: What do I want a way outta here for? I want to live here for the rest of my life . . .

CHUCKIE: Look, you're my best friend, so don't take this the wrong way, but in twenty years, if you're livin' next door to me, comin' over, watching the fuckin' Patriots' game and still workin' construction, I'll fuckin' kill you. And that's not a threat; that's a fact, I'll fuckin' kill you.

WILL: Chuckie, what are you talkin' . . .

CHUCKIE: Listen, you got somethin' that none of us have.

WILL: Why is it always this? I owe it to myself? What if I don't want to?

CHUCKIE: Fuck you. You owe it to me. Tomorrow I'm gonna wake up and I'll be fifty and I'll still be doin' this. And that's all right 'cause I'm gonna make a run at it. But you, you're sitting on a winning lottery ticket and you're too much of a pussy to cash it in. And that's bullshit 'cause I'd do anything to have what you got! And so would any of these guys. It'd be a fuckin' insult to us if you're still here in twenty years.

(133–34)

The logic of this discussion is somewhat elusive. It begins with the assumption that Will's exceptional talent gives him a ticket out of the working class. Chuckie concludes that Will has an obligation to ascend to a position of social privilege because all working-class men desire such ascent, but only Will has the exceptional capabilities that are necessary for it. Why the others' desire for an ascent that they cannot, but Will can, make should place him under the obligation to make it, remains unclear, though Chuckie clearly believes this to be true. Therefore, Will's not making the ascent that is available only to him would, according to Chuckie's logic, degrade him as well as the others.

Chuckie's reasoning here seems a clear case of projection. Since *he* cannot ascend out of his working-class environment, and since Will can, Chuckie projects an obligation for Will to do so. It is as if Chuckie thinks that Will's doing so will satisfy his, Chuckie's, desire to ascend. But whatever psychological pleasure Will's ascent will give Chuckie, it certainly won't change the basic terms of his existence.

Nonetheless, the very same logic that the film uses to place a burden on Will—he must flee from the working class in order to validate the pain that characterizes Chuckie's daily existence—condemns Chuckie and all of his non-exceptional working-class mates to a life that Chuckie himself claims to be only slightly short of hell. And this problematic life is made to seem somehow right and proper if only Will saves himself by escaping from it. But if Will is portrayed as engaging in self-destructive behavior characteristic of his milieu because of psychological scarring from his abusive childhood, the other working-class men are simply behaving in accord with their "natures." No redemption for them—psychological or social; simply lives lived out in not so quiet desperation. *Their* condition is represented as something that is not ameliorable, as if what in Will is the result of destructive parenting in them is simply the result of their natures as working-class men.

The film's emphasis on Will's exceptionality as the grounds for his elevation out of the working-class into a position of social privilege thus has its mirror in its representation of working-class men as deserving their social subordination and disempowerment. Will's childhood wound and his outstanding intellect both mark him as different, render him capable of ascent. *Good Will Hunting*, despite its sympathy for its main character and the circumstances of his life, paints a negative portrait of the lives of working-class men. Compared to Will, they are stupid, and they lack the sophistication provided by social privilege as well as that special wound that might entitle them to it. If their only hope for validation is Will's escape from the life they are destined for, that is less a problem with their lives than with this film's own elitism. A film that allows its main character to best an upper-class student for attempting to demean a working-class rival ultimately enacts a similar humiliation of that rival. While Will can save Chuckie from unfairly being shown up, he can't keep *Good Will Hunting* from enacting its own deeper humiliation of Chuckie and working-class men in general.

Notes

[1] All subsequent quotations from the film are taken from the published screenplay: Matt Damon and Ben Affleck, *Good Will Hunting* (New York: Hyperion, 1997).

[2] This term is explained in Thomas E. Wartenberg, *Unlikely Couples: Movie Romance as Social Criticism* (Boulder, CO: Westview Press, 1999).

[3] For an extended discussion of this claim, see my *Unlikely Couples*, chapter 2.

[4] I defend this interpretation in *Unlikely Couples*, chapter 4.

[5] Skylar's class position is interesting: She is a trust-fund baby, but she announces that she only has the money because her father is dead and she would gladly give it all back to see him again. Although this fact is intended to distance Skylar from those who accept their privileged position as their just desert, she has not actually renounced the privilege that she has and that allows her to attend Harvard and then medical school in California. But the film wants to protect her from the same critique of elite pseudo-intellectuals that it is in the process of assembling.

[6] Incidentally, Will now talks as if he has chosen construction as his life-long career goal. But earlier in the film he had been employed as a custodian at MIT. His profession seems to switch to satisfy the momentary needs of the narrative. Earlier, Will's mathematical genius turned out to also result in his reading difficult historical studies of the prerevolutionary economy in the United States. These inconsistencies point to the film's lack of care in articulating a coherent narrative.

Chapter 3

Fashion, Advertising, and the Consumer Society

Douglas Kellner

*F*or decades, billions of dollars has been spent on advertising in contemporary capitalist societies, often more than on education. When one considers that an equal amount of money is spent on design, packaging, marketing, and product display one sees how much money is squandered on advertising and marketing. For example, only eight cents of the cosmetics sales dollar goes to pay for ingredients; the rest goes to packaging, promotion, and marketing. Consequently, a tremendous amount of resources, talent, and money is invested in advertising.

The expansion of marketing and advertising was a necessary consequence of the system of mass production developed in modern capitalist societies. By the early years of the twentieth century, industrial capitalism had already perfected techniques of mass production. The assembly line, scientific management of the labor process, and the emergence of the modern corporation revolutionized production and made possible the creation of new mass-consumer goods. New modes of advertising, marketing, packaging, and design helped produce mass consumption and consumers who would purchase and utilize the new world of commodities. The result is the now familiar consumer society within which most of us were born and in which we work, consume, amuse ourselves, and suffer.

Advertising and fashion are two of the dominant mechanisms in the production and reproduction of the consumer society. Advertising attempts to produce consumer needs for commodities which will allegedly solve a wide range of our personal problems and which will supposedly provide a large number of gratifications. Advertising tells us that new commodities will make us happier, more popular, and more successful. Fashion in turn provides the constant cycle of new products, styles, and images which keep consumer demand at a high level. Advertising tells us that to be "with it" and up to date we must be fashionable, and buy and exhibit all the latest products and fashions. Both advertising and fashion therefore work together to manage consumer demand and thus to reproduce the consumer society.

Yet ads and fashion not only play a crucial role in consumer demand management, they promote a view of the world complete with an ethics, politics, gender-role models, and sense of appropriate and inappropriate daily social behavior. Advertising and fashion thus have crucial economic *and* socializing functions in shaping behavior and inducing people to participate in the consumer society.

Advertising: Information or Persuasion?

The mainstream media and much academic social science essentially defends the institutions, life-styles, and values of consumer capitalism. Throughout the past century, members of the advertising industry claimed that they were merely providing consumers with information that would enable them to make intelligent, informed, and rational choices. The fashion industry, too, claimed that it was promoting innovation, style, and novelty that provided for a richer, more diverse life. Apologists for the advertising industry interpret it as a form of information which provides consumers with up-to-date news concerning commodities and which provides the impetus necessary to maintain a high level of production and affluence.[1] Advertisers defended their wares in terms of the democratic effects of promoting "freedom of choice" through the information provided citizens which expanded their range of options. Likewise, defenders of the fashion industry claim that they too are merely providing a constant turnover of new products and styles that meet consumer needs for novelty, change, and desire for trendiness. Its apologists claim that fashion opens up and "with all its new developments, new horizons, enriches and diversifies life and makes it more attractive; it also acts as a powerful stimulus to the economy."[2]

In most standard textbooks and theories, fashion and advertising are therefore presented as beneficial aspects of an innovative and dynamic consumer society that provides individuals with the goods and styles they themselves desire. According to standard conventional wisdom, advertising that is primarily informative appeals to "rational" motivations while persuasive advertising appeals to more irrational motivations; it is thus conceded that there are two basic forms of advertising and that at least persuasive advertising appeals to some "irrational" aspect of the consumer's self. In the words of one mainstream theorist, while informative advertising aims to appeal to reason and provides "reasons-why" individuals should purchase products, by contrast, "advertising that addresses itself chiefly to the emotions, rather than to reason or intellect, is called human interest copy. This kind of advertising is based on appeals to . . . emotions to which the average person reacts."[3]

Yet how much advertising is really "informative"? Scrutiny of the various types and media of advertising discloses a continuum from purely informative ads, such as one can find in the classified section of newspapers, to television ads that provide no information whatsoever about their products but simply associate the product with luxury, or success, or happiness, or other obviously desired conditions. Close scrutiny of most magazine and television ads reveals that advertising in the U.S. is overwhelmingly persuasive, relying on emotional appeals, dramatic or comic images, and manipulation of basic fears and desires.

For example, Marlboro cigarette ads have been aimed primarily at male smokers and have attempted to associate smoking with virile masculinity, while Virginia Slims ads have traditionally associated smoking with hip femininity to try to convince women that it is cool to smoke and that the product being advertised is perfect for the "modern" woman. Images of health abounded in these ads, despite the fact that cigarettes are a well-documented source of cancer—a fact that the government finally forced cigarette makers to acknowledge on their packaging. The images of nature and a "natural" look cover over the fact that the cigarettes contain a variety of synthetic chemicals, preservatives, and flavoring devices, while the tobacco itself has been drenched in dangerous pesticides. In any case, no information is presented (beyond the mandatory government warnings) in these ads which—like most ads—rely primarily on emotional, non-conscious appeal conveyed through carefully constructed images.

Thus, it is fair to conclude that advertising is primarily "persuasive," serving to manipulate consumers into purchasing products by channeling, steering, and directing behavior into certain gender and role models and by offering commodities as magical solutions to every conceivable problem and as vehicles to life's most intense joys. In any case, it is clear that advertising, fashion, and consumerism are of crucial social importance in producing the needs, values, and behavior that dominate our lives in the contemporary United States and Canada. Advertising and fashion are thus crucial aspects of the system of manipulation and domination within consumer capitalism. Consumerism is not just a form of pleasure and fun, but is an all-important instrument of social control and a means by which individuals are integrated into society. Today in North America, and increasingly globally, individuals are manipulated and indoctrinated by advertising and consumerism into social conformity and accepting the consumerist way of life as the only way to live. And it is fashion that spins out ever more numerous and ever more rapid cycles of "the new" to keep the consumer machine in motion.

To support this argument, let us look at some historical studies of advertising and consumer culture by Stuart and Elizabeth Ewen, whose books *Captains of Consciousness* and *Channels of Desire* interpret both advertising and fashion as modes of social control that manipulate our desires and fantasies into consumption and always for market commodities.

Advertising and Fashion as Channels of Desire

Today we are constantly bombarded by the messages and images of the consumer society. We wake up and turn on the radio, television, or a record player, MP3 player, Blackberry, iPad, or other electronic device. We go to school or work and observe the styles of clothes worn by those around us, talk about and perhaps admire people's possessions, enjoy household gadgets and products, and are assailed on all sides with advertising messages to buy, consume, and possess the wonders of the commodity society.

Yet we rarely raise such questions as: When, where, and how did the consumer society arise and why did it become such a central force in our lives? Does consumption makes us happier, freer, and better off than people were in a less consumer-oriented environment? How are our attitudes, behaviors, and values shaped by advertising, fashion, and all the institutions of the consumer society? What roles do advertising, fashion, and consumerism play in legitimating the current socio-economic system, and in making us compliant players in the capitalist game of competition, success, and material consumption? And how can we become more rational consumers and free ourselves from media manipulation and advertising indoctrination?

Probably few of us raise these questions. Most of us have grown up in a society populated by magazines, television, and radio with their ubiquitous ads. Most of us go to shopping malls or stores and are confronted with slickly packaged goods and a wealth of services—all for the right price, of course. We are used to everything from medical to sexual services having a price tag and are told that there is no free lunch: everything in the society is a commodity and we are led to believe that consumer capitalism is the best socio-economic system in the world. Is this so? And how did the consumer society come to play such an important role in our lives?

In *Captains of Consciousness,* Stuart Ewen tells of how corporations, advertising agencies, and market research organizations began planning ways to produce consumers and to promote consumption as a way of life in the United States during the 1920s.[4] Individual resistance to new products had to be broken down and individuals had to be convinced that it was "good" to consume, to spend money, to gratify their desires. Previously, a work ethic and puritan savings ethic prevailed which held that getting what you wanted, when you wanted it, and enjoying the process were immoral; advertising had to convince individuals on the contrary that consumption was a new route to happiness and satisfaction. Advertising also attempted to create fears that unless individuals bought products to combat bad breath, body odor, and oily or tangly hair, they would not be socially acceptable. Thus, advertising attempted to create problems and fears to which commodities and desires for new products were offered as solutions. In this way, a commodity culture self emerged in which different products allowed individuals to develop or present different aspects of "their" personality. The personality could be produced or shaped by using the right products and producing the right image.

To keep a high level of consumer demand in place, individuals also needed to be constantly persuaded that they continually needed new products to be fashionable and up to date. The advertising and fashion industries thus had to persuade consumers to throw away old products and continually buy new ones. The fashion industry began to accelerate the turnover of models, trends, styles, and products. While formerly individuals purchased products for durability, now style and fashion began to dictate consumer choices. Previously, automobiles, for instance, followed more or less the same design and style and one presumably bought an automobile for life. In the consumer boom after World War II, however, new automobile styles, new fashion styles, and constant refashioning of products and designs promoted a frenzied orgy of consumption in which individuals bought, borrowed, and stole to constantly purchase the latest models and fashions which the fashion and consumer industries set out to promote.

Advertising and fashion combine individuality and conformity in curious ways. Individuals consume and pursue fashion to individuate themselves yet do so in order to be socially accepted, to fit in, to be popular. Moreover, and ironically, it is mass-produced goods and fashion that are used to produce individuality. Such a commodified self and presentation of "individuality" in terms of fashion and mass goods could emerge only in a society controlled by "image." How did such a social order emerge, and what role did mass images play in the production of the consumer society and commodity self?

As Elizabeth and Stuart Ewen tell us in their important history of consumer culture, consumerism and Americanism were promoted by mass images beginning in the 19th century when newspapers began selling advertising and when corporations attempted to impress their brand name and their product's image on the consumer.[5] The Ewens tell the story of how a young Czech girl, Anna Kuthan, was fascinated by the labels on bales of cotton and the products she handled as a servant girl in Vienna; these "channels of desire" promised a new world of commodity paradise, of happiness through consumption. She eventually immigrated to the United States where the down-to-earth reality of the "American dream" was a life of hard work and suffering compensated by a few brand name products that she had always dreamed of. Was she, in fact, better off leaving her home and traditions to toil in a New York ghetto? Was the possibility of enabling her children to own a house in the suburbs worth her own life of toil? Is consumption the way to happiness?

The consumer society evolved into the dominant form of American society after World War II. It had its origins in the big department stories (Macy's, Gimbel's, Marshall Field's) and the mail order houses (Sears, Ward's) that began in the nineteenth century.[6] It was promoted by the advertising agencies and corporate campaigns of the 1920s but was postponed first by the Great Depression of the 1930s, which dramatized the failures of capitalism to provide a rational society without state intervention,[7] and then by World War II, which dramatized the darker side of twentieth-century drives for power and profits. After World War II, returning servicemen came home with large amounts of back pay and the corporations tooled up to make the consumer society a reality. New goods, services, shopping centers, and marketing techniques appeared, and the move toward the suburbs and the rise of television helped promote the consumer society.[8]

The era from the 1950s to the present might be seen in retrospect as the Age of Consumption. But how do advertising, fashion, and consumption socialize us into being compliant participants in the dream world of consumer culture? On one level, advertising and fashion function to manage consumer demand, to get us to buy products, but on a deeper level what is significant about advertising and fashion is not the fact that they sell us this or that toothpaste, shampoo, or car, but that they sell us *consumerism as a way of life* and promote the belief that happiness is to be found through consumption. Advertising implies that a solution to every problem can be found through the purchased commodity, and thus offers commodity solutions to all the problems of life. Fashion tells us that products, styles, and trends are constantly changing and that one must keep up with fashion and all the new products to be with it, to be popular, to make it. You're not getting enough dates? Buy the proper mouthwash, deodorant, perfume, or after-shave lotion and all will be well. You're not successful sexually? Buy a new car, better clothes, more up-scale alcohol and toys, and you'll score. This sounds crude but it is the clear message of most fashion ads, and a large percentage of magazine ads that use sexual desires and insecurity to sell their products.

Advertising also promises commodity solutions to health problems. You're not feeling well? Just take Geritol for tired blood; XY and Z for headaches; A or B for heartburn or indigestion; or eat Wheaties, the breakfast of champions, or Total or K or whatever, and you'll supposedly be bursting with vim, vigor, and vitality. Sexually dysfunctional? Gobble Viagra or Cialis, but watch out for side-effects . . .

Advertising also plays on fears that one is either not attractive enough or not properly playing one's role in life. Do you want to be a good housewife and mother? Buy M soap to eliminate ring-around-the-collar; brand P frozen pizza to bring your family to quasi-orgasmic ecstasies; and Q bathroom deodorant and sweetener to give your toilet more appetizing smells and colors. Want to have a happy family life?: go to McDonald's, pig out on Big Macs, and enjoy the pleasures promised to all good Americans (and be sure to have plenty of stomach remedies at home to deal with the aftermaths of junk food orgies).

Do you want to have fun, enjoy community, and social acceptance? Join the Pepsi generation, or be a Pepper, or drink Coke; or swill the uncola, 7-Up (and be sure to have a good dentist for when your teeth start rotting). And girls, do you want to be a TOTAL WOMAN? Easy, just buy a twenty-four-hour perfume so you can work your ass off at the office or school, then come home and fix dinner and clean up house, and still be sexy and sweet-smelling for hubby or boyfriend. And do you want to be really respected and desired, boys? Merely get a new luxury car, read *Playboy* or *Hustler* to see what you need for your pad, and sit back and wait for the bunnies to come running over.

The point that I am trying to make is that ads offer commodity solutions to all problems, and present consumption as the route to happiness. Therefore, advertising not only sells products but also tries to sell consumerism as a way of life, the capitalist way of life. It provides role models showing us how to be a proper man or woman, and sells specific values such as romance and sexuality as crucial, of fundamental importance. In turn, it uses desires for sex and romance to sell specific products.

Advertising also sells institutions like the family, and capitalist values like individuality, gratification through consumption, and the joys of ownership. As Robert Goldman has argued, certain ads promote an idealized version of history and the institutions and values of corporate capitalism as they try to huckster their products.[9] For instance, McDonald's ads frequently contain charming images of small-town America, family life, middle-class affluence, and integrated Americana that surround the images of the Big Macs and McMuffins that they are trying to sell.

Other ads promote consumerist ideology by equating consumerism with "Freedom of Choice" (i.e. between their light or their regular beer) or tell you to be an "individual" by buying this or that product, or dousing yourself in this or that perfume or after-shave. And note that "individualism" here is defined in terms of possession, consumption, and style—as opposed to thought, action, dissent, rational behavior, and autonomy, which were previous definitions of individualism in earlier stages of modern societies.

What Is to Be Done?

In conclusion, one might ask: what's wrong with all of this and what can be done about it? First of all, the rise of the consumer society has meant the homogenization of contemporary capitalist societies and has contributed to the incredible power enjoyed by corporations that have come to control all facets of life in consumer societies. Marty Jezer points out in his history of life in the U.S. after World War II that there were once literally hundreds of brands of beer and soft drinks, locally produced by small businesses. But with the development of corporate capitalism these smaller companies were driven out of business and a handful of brands of beer produced by monopoly corporations came to dominate the market.[10] The result was the homogenization of mass consumer societies. Indeed, corporate control of the economy has made the United States and Canada look virtually the same all over: drive down Anystreet and you will see generic North America in the form of filling stations selling the same brands of gas everywhere, fast-food chains selling the same junk food, video stores renting the same (quite small) selection of (almost always very recent blockbuster) films, and chains of other products everywhere selling the same goods. How has this come about and what have we lost?

Through advertising, price-fixing, mergers, and other corporate developments, giant corporations have come to dominate the economy and society in the West and in most other capitalist societies. Thus, commodity production and distribution has become standardized, homogenized, and centrally controlled—all of the standard accusations against socialism! There are thus fewer products produced locally, less craft and artisan production, and less variety and diversity of goods. Moreover, the consumer must pay for the entire corporate infrastructure and advertising, marketing, packaging, etc. Any corporation advertising products on television or in other media passes down costs to the consumer. All packaging and marketing expenses are part of what we pay for brand-name goods. Thus in effect we are subsidizing entire industries and agencies that are working to manipulate, indoctrinate, and exploit us.

What can we do to avoid manipulation by the advertising and fashion industries? First, we should become rational consumers and see that anything advertised on television is probably overpriced since astronomical advertising expenses have been factored into the price. Generally, generic products can be had of the same or better quality and at a lower price. Moreover, when it comes to nutrition, corporate food has been sprayed with pesticides, preserved with chemicals, and treated with synthetics that are often harmful to one's health. Of course, the very term "junk food" suggests edibles that are lacking in nutrition. Many other products are over-priced and are shoddily constructed. "Planned obsolescence," for example, has been one of the scandals of the American automobile industry and one of the reasons why this industry is no longer competitive on the world market: as early as the 1950s, Vance Packard argued that American automobiles were produced to self-destruct after a short time to force consumers to buy new models,[11] and Toyota's recent problems with new models requiring recall reminds us that automobiles are still unsafe.

Secondly, we must learn to resist the machinations of fashion, choosing our clothes and products because they fulfill our own wants and please us, rather than merely because they fit into the latest cycle of fashion. I do not want, however, to polemicize here against consumption and commodities per se. Consumption can be a legitimate pleasure and commodities can be of use and value to us. One does not have to buy junk food, worthless nostrums, overpriced cars, silly fashions, or shoddy goods. If one looks, one can always find alternatives. But I am suggesting that one should be very careful in buying any products produced by giant corporations which are likely to be overpriced, injurious to health, shoddily constructed, likely to self-destruct, and so on. Moreover, you may be buying something simply because you were manipulated by advertising to do so. To avoid such manipulation and exploitation: Buy generic; buy from small businesses or local producers, or craftspeople; or buy used products from friends or someone you trust. Most important: seek out alternative institutions like food coops, or more healthy products like fruit juices instead of soft drinks, the desire for which is no doubt the product of behavioral conditioning and bad habits.

Thirdly, we must learn to read and decipher advertising, learning to see through the hype and puffery so as to be able to analyze and criticize its manipulative techniques. One should learn to protect oneself against domination by advertising through becoming aware of how ads are constructed; of what techniques are being used; of what devices are used to manipulate us; and of what general social messages one is receiving. Finally, despite propaganda from corporations and advertising agencies to the contrary, one should see advertising itself as a parasitical industry dedicated to manipulation, and not providing information as advertisers claim—at least this is true of most TV and magazine advertising. Advertising is a tremendous social drain that a rational society would either eliminate or radically restructure from an instrument of manipulation into solely an instrument of socially necessary and beneficial information. Arguably, advertising is a disgraceful waste of resources, talent, and time, and anyone who tells you differently is deceived or is prostituting himself. A rational society would ban advertising completely or would simply use it for informational purposes.

However, in capitalist societies, advertising is a prime manipulator of consumer demand and a source of political socialization and propaganda for the system, though it is not usually perceived as such. Moreover, advertising has come to dominate broadcasting and our media system. While it appears that television is "free," one actually pays higher prices for goods and services because costs of producing advertisements and purchasing advertising time are passed down to consumers. Thus it is not only the case that one literally pays for the indignity of having one's television programs interrupted but advertising-dominated programming ensures that the television networks will keep providing mediocre programming that manages not to offend significant segments of the mass audience in order that a huge audience may be offered to advertisers at a high rate.

Eventually, citizens of advanced capitalist societies are going to have to seriously question the priorities, values, and institutions of consumer capitalism. Each individual and society as a whole needs to consider the social effects of advertising and fashion and whether the consumer society provides the most rational and beneficial social order, or whether we can produce better alternatives. The many-sided failures of neo-liberalism in the 2000s provide the incentive for critical scrutiny of our current social organization and require that we find better forms of everyday life and social organization if we wish to preserve the democracy, freedom, and individuality to which we pay lip service.

Notes

[1] Ronald Berman, *Advertising and Social Change* (New York: Sage, 1981).

[2] Rene Konig, *A la mode* (New York: Seabury Press, 1973), 29.

[3] Abraham Switkin, *Ads: Design & Make Your Own* (New York: Van Nostrand Reinhold, 1981), 66.

[4] Stuart Ewen, *Captains of Consciousness* (New York: McGraw-Hill, 1976).

[5] Stuart Ewen and Elizabeth Ewen, *Channels of Desire* (New York: McGraw-Hill, 1982).

[6] *Ibid.*

[7] Ewen, *Captains.*

[8] Marty Jezer, *The Dark Ages* (Boston: South End Press, 1982).

[9] Robert Goldman, "We Make Weekends: Leisure and the Commodity Form," *Social Text* 8 (1984), 84–103.

[10] Jezer, *Dark Ages.*

[11] Vance Packard, *The Waste Makers* (Baltimore and London: Penguin, 1960).

Chapter 4

The Public Mind and the Pictures in Our Heads

A Riff

Stuart Ewen

I want to explore some of the ways that intelligence and stupidity are portrayed in television, film and popular culture from a somewhat different vantage point. Rather than talking about representations of intelligence and stupidity in the media, I want to talk a little about the ways that ideas about human intelligence, or its absence, have worked behind the scenes, shaping the broad texture of the media culture that surrounds us.

I will be speaking, particularly, about important 20th century developments, and the ways that certain assumptions about public intelligence often invisible on the surface of media representations have exerted a weighty influence on them and have, in the process, affected the character of public discourse. Because of this influence, it is a question of moment, something that reflects on the quality and possibility of democracy itself. I want to open with a writer whom I first encountered when I was an undergraduate at the University of Wisconsin, and then re-visited as I was commencing

© 2003 by Stuart Ewen

research for a book I wrote on the history of public relations. His name was Gustave Le Bon. Le Bon was a French sociologist, who, in 1895, published a book entitled *The Crowd: A Study of the Popular Mind.* This book took this relatively obscure French academic and transformed him into an internationally acclaimed intellectual. Within a year of its publication in France, *The Crowd* was translated into 19 languages and was being read by middle class readers throughout the Western World. Within twenty years of its publication Le Bon's ideas influenced the thinking of a modern, emerging profession of persuasion specialists who were interested in reaching and shaping public perception and behavior.

Let me say a little bit about Le Bon, not because I am interested in trundling out an old academic, but because I think that, although he is largely unknown today, during his lifetime he was clearly a much more influential figure in sociology than, say, Max Weber was. I am not talking about the relative merits of their work. I am talking about the acclaim, the eminence they enjoyed. Although Le Bon is not well known today, the indelible marks of his thinking remain all around us. *The Crowd* was the fearful tirade of a middle class academic, alarmed by the rise of working class militancy, and you have to remember that he was from France and was terrified by the modern deterioration of hierarchy and deference that had, for centuries, been the glue that had held many aristocratic European societies together. These traditions seemed to be crumbling around him, and I should add that an event that had taken place in the early 1870s, when the workers of Paris seized control of the city—the Paris Commune—had shaken the foundations of bourgeois life, and intensified the kinds of fears that run through Le Bon's book, *The Crowd.* Le Bon's work was not simply a theoretical concern, it was based on recent experiences of upheaval.

Le Bon, like many social scientists of his generation, yearned for order, and his book was an attempt to lay out a strategy for establishing it. A knowledge of the psychology of crowds, he warned, was the last resource of the statesman and *The Crowd* was nothing less than Le Bon's urgent attempt to scientifically analyze the workings of "the popular mind," as he termed it, for the purposes of knowing how to better control it.

Le Bon rejected a basic principle that had affected liberal political thought since the 18th Century, the idea that people are inherently rational and that if one offers people a coherent, well-substantiated argument, public reason will be capable of evaluating that argument and on the basis of this, arriving at sound judgments. This is an idea that stands behind the principle of democracy, the notion that an informed public is capable of rationally determining its own destiny. Le Bon rejected this assumption. While he still believed that educated, middle-class people, such as himself, were capable of reason and reflection, he diagnosed the crowd, the urban masses, as being a lower life form, a kind of protoplasm driven by dark, irrational forces, by "its spinal cord."

Le Bon and those who followed his lead were the founders of the modern science of social psychology, a field worth noting, in part, because it continues to expand as the 21st Century commences. It is one of the most prevalent features of our society, of the political dynamics of our society, and of our media environment. According to the outlook of social psychology, and other social sciences, the capacity to scientifically monitor, analyze and appeal to the irrational within people was the key to social stability in the modern era. If you look at political scientists and political theorists at the turn of the century—for example, people like Graham Wallace, an English academic who came to teach at Harvard and was the political theory professor of someone whose ideas will come into play a little bit later in this talk, Walter Lippmann—Le Bon's ideas provided a foundation.

In 1908, Graham Wallace published a book called *Human Nature in Politics* in which he argued that much of the political theory that had existed up until then was garbage and had to be tossed. The idea of politics as a rational process unfolding, of social checks and balances, was out of touch with political realities. "The empirical art of politics," he wrote, "consists largely in the creation of public opinion by the deliberate exploitation of subconscious, non rational inferences." With Wallace, and others like him, political science was moving into the realm of cabalistic behavior, the idea that in a democracy, where popular support is essential, it was necessary to appeal to people's unconscious psyches in order to achieve one's political goals.

In the United States, where working class militancy and a middle class reform movement were troubling the sleep of business and political elites at the threshold of the 20th Century, Le Bonian ideas found a receptive audience. Theodore Roosevelt, it is said, kept a copy of *The Crowd* next to his bed, and from World War I onward, social psychology became the intellectual foundation for an emerging American persuasion industry, and continues to be. That is where polling comes from; this is what focus groups are about. The ubiquitous apparatus for continually taking the temperature of the public is rooted in the rise of social psychology, and it is not insignificant that these tools are used, primarily, to examine public feelings above thought.

This was the moment when survey research emerged as a fixture of life—endless studies of popular emotion, studies done to inform strategies for creating emotional bonds between a presumably mindless crowd and its would-be leaders.

At the end of the 19th Century, Le Bon paved the way for these practices. "To know the art of impressing the imagination of crowds," he wrote, "is to know at the same time the art of governing them. Crowds have always undergone the influence of illusions. Whoever can supply them with illusions is easily their master."

One of the central ideas that emerged in Le Bon, something that is particularly pertinent to contemporary culture, is an insight which related to the pivotal role of images within thinking about the crowd's mental life. "When studying the imagination of crowds," he wrote, "we say that their imagination is particularly open to the impressions produced by images. A crowd thinks in images and the image, itself, immediately calls up a series of other images that have no logical connection with the first." Given this penchant for what Le Bon termed "collective hallucination," specialists interested in managing public opinion or public feeling believed they could not rely on rational argument.

This is a rather curious argument that Le Bon is making, because all of this stuff about playing to the gut, and to the irrational is, in fact, being articulated at a moment when working-class people, in France and elsewhere, are becoming increasingly literate. So, if anything, one could say this is a culture in which the possibility of factual and literary argument is becoming more possible. Yet what Le Bon is arguing is that you can't use rational approaches to communication, and you can't employ literary means. You need to speak visually, and simplistically, in order to influence the crowd.

"Ideas," he wrote, "must assume a very absolute and simple shape." They must be presented "in the guise of images."

Crowds, being only capable of thinking in images, are only to be impressed by images. For this reason theatrical representations, in which the images are shown in their most clearly visible shape, always have an enormous influence on crowds. It is not . . . the facts in themselves that strike the popular imagination, but the ways in which they take place and are brought under notice. It is necessary that by their condensation, if I must thus express myself, they should produce a startling image, which fills and besets the mind.

What is interesting is that Le Bon is arguing that "collective hallucination," which is so rampant among the urban working classes, is a particular factor of crowd life. Le Bon still holds to the idea that middle-class individuals—as I said before, people like himself—were perfectly capable of reason and reflection and that, in fact, this was their greatest strength. This stood behind their ability to benefit from the methods of social psychology.

What is fascinating is that by the 1920s the analysis of public emotions was predicated on the idea that the degraded mental capacity of the masses was not just an aspect of crowd life but, in fact, a characteristic of all people, except those people who were scientifically trained to apply reason in order to examine public mental life. All others, regardless of class, were motivated, for the most part, by unconscious, instinctual baggage. In 1922 Sigmund Freud wrote a book called *Group Psychology and the Analysis of the Ego*, which was basically a response to Le Bon. He wrote that Le Bon's book was very insightful, accurate in its description of the mental life of the crowd. The blind spot in Le Bon, Freud contended, was that he assumed that middle-class individuals were capable of reason. No, says Freud. Except for those who are scientifically trained to use reason as a tool for social or psychological analysis, all people tend to react from the gut. Visual suggestibility was for Freud, "an irreducible primitive phenomenon of fundamental fact in the mental life of man" overall.

By the 1920s the analysis of public emotion was becoming a basic drill of compliance professionals and persuasion experts, and an eloquence of images was being employed as the favored instrument of public address. The strategic wisdom of the day was that in order to sell products to consumers, or link public loyalties to big business, or to lead populations into war, the capture of the eye was essential.

I mentioned Walter Lippmann before. I would argue that Lippmann was among the most influential American intellectuals of the 20th Century. From around 1910 onward, he had the ears of politicians, businessmen, military leaders, and the public at large. He was America's senior newspaper columnist into the 1970s. Lippmann transplanted Le Bon into American soil in 1922, in a book called *Public Opinion*, in which he laid out, for those interested in shaping political agendas for society, what needs to be known about the public and its mental processes, in order to package messages for general consumption.

One of the basic arguments that Lippmann made was that the public is incapable of comprehending its political environment. Ordinary people, he maintained, are driven primarily by "pictures in their heads." Because of this, and because people take those pictures to be reality, it is critical for people in leadership positions to know how to create the pictures that will occupy the public mind, to establish palpable "pseudo environments" that will guide public perception. These were his instructions, written in *The Phantom Public* (1927), a sequel to *Public Opinion*.

The making of one general will out of a multitude of general wishes consists essentially in the use of symbols which assemble emotions after they have been detached from their ideas. Because feelings are much less specific than ideas and yet more poignant, the leader is able to make a homogeneous world out of a heterogeneous mass of desires. The process, therefore, by which general opinions are brought into cooperation consists of *an intensification of feeling and a degradation of significance* (emphasis added).

Simply put, the calculated use of images will enable leaders to harness the psychological energy of the masses, provoking their passions, while at the same time marginalizing the meaning of what is actually being said. You don't want people focussing on what you are actually saying. What you want to do is touch them deeply.

I should add that I am not going into it at great length now, but it is certainly pertinent that Lippmann, particularly in *Public Opinion*, wrote of the ways that Hollywood films—how they gathered the emotions of an audience—provided a useful template for persuasion engineers. He wrote, for example, of the ways that movies create handles for identification, so you very quickly know who is the hero, who is the villain. You know, you have only an hour and a half to tell the story. You can't, in fact, let character development get in the way, so you have only signals: black hat, white hat, so to speak. You need to develop a routine, formulaic semiotic language that will allow the audience to know who is good, who is evil.

Lippmann also wrote of the ways that Hollywood films were "public fictions" that stimulated a sense of "private urgency" in their audiences. Political leaders, too, he counseled, must learn to stage public events in a way that can arouse a sense of personal urgency for constituents.

Now, of course, a question remains, and it is a question that is lurking behind this whole spiel I am giving you and that is: first of all, are they right? Is it true that images are mechanisms for dumbing people down, for bypassing critical thinking? I would argue we have no way of knowing, because we live in a world where that is the way that images are routinely used, but this doesn't necessarily mean this approach to images exhausts the vast possibility of how visual eloquence might be used differently.

I should say that a very big part of my life, and of my creative work, has been devoted to exploring how imagery can function as a language which doesn't necessarily detonate stupidity, but encourages people to see more clearly, to understand their world more completely. The other thing is that, for the most part, our education doesn't encourage us to be literate in relation to visual media.

"Media literacy" too often means inoculating people against the "virus" of the media, which I am not sure is the best way of approaching the media or the tools of communication. A serious approach to visual literacy is not a part of our education. We are all taught how to look at the structure of written language, about paragraph structure and adjectives, and the way that written arguments get made. We may not have learned that stuff, but that is what grammar is about.

But the grammar of the visual is something that is largely absent from our educational system, and I would say that even the great minds of our world have no idea what is going on. We haven't reached a point where we know really how to talk about this, so I don't think we are in a position to judge whether the anti-image critics are right—and I tend to think that they are probably wrong—about the power of images to neutralize critical thought.

We need to ask another question as well. What was it about images that made people like Le Bon and Lippmann see them as powerful tools for shaping the public mind? During these people's lifetimes powerful new media technologies and new aesthetic outlooks were transforming the physics of perception, the relationship between the physical world and the ways that people see and understand it. Photography and motion pictures, in particular, I would say, signaled changes in how both objective truth and subjective experience were popularly understood and communicated. If you look at some of the initial impacts of photography and cinema, one can easily see why men like Lippmann and Le Bon looked to the visual realm as a very powerful arena of persuasion.

Now I'm sure that this is old hat for most of you, but it is worth saying again. Photography, as a technology, emerged in the 1830s and 40s, and it was a medium that took off very dramatically and very quickly. And photography was a kind of magic. It represented a "sea change" in the ability to replicate, or at least apparently replicate, facts observable to the human eye, observable truths. If a conventional artist could only mimic the countenance of reality, there was a sense that photography was a truthful record of events. We all know, intellectually, that this isn't true about photography, but I don't think photography's power is something that can simply be dismissed intellectually. There was a powerful sense that photography was able to capture and preserve "the real" in a way never before possible.

If you listen to the idiom surrounding photography, people still talk about "taking pictures," not making them. It is as if the act of photographing, even if you know it is an art form, is not about something you make; rather, you are taking something that is already out there. You are skinning the surface off the visible world, so to speak.

Lippmann was very interesting about photographic media, which he examined extensively in *Public Opinion*. He wrote that "photographs exert a kind of authority over the imagination which the printed word had yesterday or the spoken word before that." Photographs, he wrote, seemed utterly real. "They come, we imagine, directly at us without human meddling and (I like this language) they are the most effortless food for the mind conceivable."

He talks about the movies in particular. He says that "on the screen the whole process of observing, describing, recording and then imagining has been accomplished for you." The film doesn't just create objective pictures of reality, but movies, because of editing, lens work, and other techniques, are able to guide the imagination process in ways that were previously not so easy to achieve. Without any more trouble needed to stay awake, he wrote, "the result which your imagination is always aiming at, is reeled off on the screen."

I raise this, in part, because Lippmann was very aware of this sort of double-edged nature of photography and film. On the one hand, these media could create a credible likeness of observable truth. They seemed real, they convincingly mimicked what the eye would see. The hand of the artist was invisible. Photographs looked real.

It is amazing to me that even now, at the beginning of the 21st Century, one of the major things that people who study photography go on and on about, is that photographs aren't real, that photographs are framed, that photographs are not what they appear to be. The fact that people are still making that argument, in a certain way, is testimony to the enduring power of photographs to be accepted as imprints of reality.

What Lippmann was also talking about, however, was the way that, alongside of photographs and film having a kind of "phantom objectivity" to them, they also have an uncanny ability to connect to the inner imagination, the subconscious psychological lives of people; the visceral level of imagination; the mimicry of dreams and the unconscious.

Let me say a little bit about this. You have all seen *Citizen Kane*, I imagine. At the beginning of the picture, you'll remember, Charles Foster Kane dies. He was a very rich and powerful man who ran a media empire and, unaccountably, the final word to pass through his lips was, "Rosebud." The whole film is an attempt on the part of a reporter to go around and talk to people who knew Charles Foster Kane: his ex-girlfriend, people he had worked with, others, to find out what the enigmatic term *rosebud* might have meant.

One of the people the reporter goes to visit is an old guy named Bernstein. When Kane took over his first newspaper—I think it was called *The Inquirer*—Bernstein had been his business manager. So the reporter goes to see Bernstein, who is now an old man, and he asks him what he thinks *rosebud* was. Bernstein says, "Well, I don't know. Could have been something he lost." Then he starts to ruminate a bit, this old guy Bernstein, on the texture of human memory, and he recalls an incident from his own youth, and here is what he says:

> A fellow will remember a lot of things that you wouldn't think he would remember. You take me. One day back in 1896 I was crossing over to New Jersey on the ferry and as we pulled out there was another ferry pulling in. On it there was girl waiting to get off, a white dress she had on and she was carrying a white parasol. I saw her only for one second. She didn't see me at all, but I will bet a month hasn't gone by since that I haven't thought of that girl.

That's his story, that's his explanation. This haunting tale, a very moving moment in the film, evokes, to some extent, the psycho-dynamics of the mind and the power of the incidental, the momentary, the things that inscribe themselves very deeply upon a life: the ability for apparently minor incidents to assume a suggestive significance which far outweighs the objective magnitude at the moment from which they were drawn.

From early on this was an uncanny capacity of photography. Part of what photographs do, part of what we like about them, is that they are able to entrap and crystallize evanescent moments. They defy the passage of time itself, and they engrave the past upon the future. They are able to grab transient gestures to enshrine the commonplace, the incidental, and hold onto things that previously, before photography emerged, survived only as faint yet seductive glimmers of memory, like the story that Bernstein tells.

Freud, of course, wrote extensively of the powers that such ephemeral impressions exerted within people's dreams and in the unconscious workings of the psyche. Incidental moments, he argued, stand at the heart of people's character development and within each of us as fragmentary mementos, asserting their influence and awaiting rediscovery. This is the premise of psychoanalysis, the idea that there are these deeply buried incidents and that psychoanalysis is a process by which they can be discovered, and that people will come face to face with themselves in a way that they haven't before.

Photographs provided a visual paradigm which was totally in sync with this perspective. Part of what was amazing about photography, part of what made it seem effective and powerful to a first generation of persuasion specialists, was that photographs could preserve "the girl in the white dress," they could mimic the impassioned eyes of the young man on the ferry boat and could stroke the depths of longing.

Movies, with their ability to emulate subliminal processes of mental association for montage and cross-cutting and close-ups which tell us what is important, were even more adept at speaking the inner language of the mind. Minute details could be magnified in the close-up. These are things that previously had been less possible, the ability to link visual communication to the matrix of people's inner lives.

So, to some extent, what photography and film suggested to that first generation of social psychologists, that first generation of modern persuasion specialists, was that because of the image's ability to mimic truth, and at the same time touch people in ways that they are not even conscious of, the image was a peculiarly useful tool of public address to be exploited, and the "intelligence" of the social analyst, or the psychological analyst, was to be used, in order to plumb the ostensible "stupidity" of a public that was, it was supposed, incapable of thought and was, primarily, an organism driven by feeling.

To some extent that assumption is a theme that has served as an assumed ground-work for the compliance professions from the 1920s onward, and still does today—the idea that images and inner life are connected in ways that suggest the possibility of increasingly psychological strategies of visual communication.

In 1925, the first course in New York City to deal with "Influencing Human Behavior" was offered at the New School for Social Research by a man named Harry Overstreet. Overstreet taught his students that the key to influencing human behavior is what he called "selective picturizing." Assume the objectivity of the picture, the way pictures seem real to people, and then select that part of the picture that will guide them to see that reality in a particular kind of way.

What he is really talking about is embedding the power of suggestion within the communication process itself. "The secret of all true persuasion," he told his students, "is to induce the person to persuade himself. The chief task of the persuader, therefore, is to induce an experience. The rest will take care of itself. The secret of it all is that a person is led to do what he overwhelmingly feels. Practice in getting people to feel themselves in situations is therefore the surest road to persuasiveness."

I have raised these issues in part because Overstreet's kind of thinking, about inducing feelings within the public, is a strategy that surrounds us at every turn—specifically, the assumption that the most effective way to speak to the public is to use calculated intelligence in order to bypass whatever critical thought processes the public may have, and to speak to them on a more gut level.

Of course, the price of this, and the danger of this, are its implications for the possibility of a democratic society, because democracy is not about people doing whatever they feel like doing. A democracy is about people's ability to understand their world, and to make judgments on the basis of that understanding, which are presumably in their own best interests. As long as public communications are continually aimed at bypassing public thought and discussion, then the possibility of democracy has become fugitive. This, unfortunately, is an embedded condition of contemporary culture, and I assume it is an issue we are going to be grappling with in the future.

Chapter 5

"American Idol"atry

The Practice of Democracy in the Age of Reality Television

Curtis Maloley

After performing Kara DioGuardi's song "Terrified" during Hollywood Week of "American Idol" (Season 9, Episode 9), twenty-three-year-old contestant Didi Benami stared eagerly at the often ornery Simon Cowell as he judged her potential for the competition: "I like the idea of somebody like you, a waitress, coming on a show like this, doing well. That's what it's all about." Cowell's uncommon blessing set Benami on her way to a coveted spot in the Top Ten, one small step closer to becoming America's next Idol. It also spoke candidly to the branding of the enormously successful "Idol" franchise: this is a show about the fulfillment of the American dream; it is about the discovery of anonymous everyday people who are sitting in the audience right now, and who have the undiscovered talent that makes them deserving of a shot at musical stardom. Billing itself as a reality television series that "empowers contestants and viewers to share their voice in deciding who will be America's next singing superstar,"[1] "American Idol" is positioned as a vehicle for participation and involvement within the music industry, a kind of benevolent facilitator of public tastes and desires, where the public gets to write the ending.[2] Implicit in the show's format is the promise of participatory democracy. The contestants are chosen from the audience, and the audience chooses "who will be the next American Idol." Casting a text ballot is framed as an active form of industry citizenship that appears to provide viewers with "voice" or agency within the system of popular music production.

Conceived by former Spice Girls manager Simon Fuller in collaboration with FremantleMedia, the format of the "Idol" franchise was established in the United Kingdom in 2001 on a show called "Pop Idol," which was an immediate ratings success and led to the development of "American Idol" in 2002. Fuller's company, 19 Management, controls the franchising rights that the Fox Network reportedly paid one million dollars per episode to acquire.[3] Since then, the "Idol" format has spawned 137 series in over forty-three countries, including in Canada where "Canadian Idol" became one of the highest rated shows in Canadian television history during its first season in 2003.[4] In the United States, "American Idol" continues to be a number one series, gaining audiences of more than thirty-seven million, and breaking new records in 2009, with over 100 million votes cast in the season finale and 624 million votes cast over the season as a whole.[5]

The enduring popularity and success of "American Idol" provides sociologists and popular culture scholars with fertile ground for examining how the political economy of the entertainment industry is related to the democratic practices of North American society. In the past two decades a series of structural changes in the entertainment industry, in both the production and consumption of popular music and television, has led to the increasing vertical integration of cultural production.[6] These changes have led to a new entertainment landscape in which viewers are encouraged to become active participants in the media industry. "American Idol" is a prime example, as its very premise is based on empowering contestants and viewers alike. This growing inclusion of "democratic participation" in the media industry speaks to the ways in which popular notions of citizenship and participation have become increasingly entwined with consumer capitalist hegemony. That so many young people are more interested in casting votes for reality-television idols than for the people who actually govern them, is a fact that has disconcerted many cultural critics who lament what they see as the decline of civic participation in the daily life of our communities.[7] Even in the historic election of Barack Obama in 2008, only 57.1% of the eligible electorate actually cast votes for President of the United States.[8] In the same year, voter turnout reached an all-time low in the history of Canadian Confederation as only 59.1% of eligible voters turned out to vote in the Federal Election.[9] Perhaps more significant, however, is not *what* we desire to vote for, but *how* the very meaning of "voting" and democratic participation more generally is configured within the "Idol" format. Democracy in this case is superficially associated with a menu of potential choices to be consumed, rather than with any real civic concern for the actual methods by which, or structures within which, these choices are made possible.

This chapter will apply a political-economic framework in order to examine the production context and inner workings of the media conglomerates and companies behind the "Idols" brand, as well as the parameters for expression that they provide for both contestants and viewers to express their "voice" within the larger systems of music industry production and consumption. It will then move to draw parallels between the consumerist discourse of participatory democracy encouraged by "American Idol" and the declining interest in civic participation that seems to pervade the governing relations of 21st-century liberalism.

Technology, Economy, and Entertainment Industry Synergy

The rapid proliferation of new digital communications technologies completely transformed the landscape of the entertainment industry over the last two decades, especially with regard to the structure of the music business. Forced to adapt to a generation of music consumers increasingly more likely to download their favorite songs, often illegally, rather than pay for physical CDs, the recording industry has faced significant challenges to its traditional revenue model. The growing popularity and accessibility of technologies such as laptops, MP3 players, cellphones, smartphones and iPhones, along with the increasing speed with which media can be shared using these technologies, has forced record companies to embrace "cross-media 'synergies'" in order to address deteriorating profits.[10] Increasingly, "[k]ey aspects of the music industry, such as talent development and the distribution of recorded music, are being undertaken by the broadcast industry, retailers, and electronics manufacturers."[11] In short, to ensure its continued success, the record industry has had to reach out to other industries that can facilitate the profitable distribution of its products. The "Idol" phenomenon has been at the forefront of these industry changes.

Having undergone its own technological revolution in the 1990s with the shift from analog to digital technology, the television industry established models for profiting from changes in the creation and delivery of content in the digital universe. Digital technology led to a rapid increase in the number of cable channels, decreasing the market share of the traditional networks (CBS, NBC, ABC, Fox, etc.). The networks responded by embracing reality television programs that could be produced at roughly a third of the cost of traditionally scripted dramas and sitcoms, due in large part to the use of amateur performers willing to appear on television voluntarily.[12] Shows like CBS's "Survivor," which was launched in 2000, had proven that not only were these programs cheap to produce, they could also become top ratings successes; the finale of the first "Survivor" season garnered the second highest ratings of all programs that year behind only the Super Bowl.[13] The overall increase in cable channels and the popularity of reality shows also served to give advertisers more clout within the broadcast industry, as networks had to work harder to keep advertisers from jumping to other stations or programs. Consequently, networks opened themselves up to the increased commercialization of programming, particularly within the content of the newly popular reality genre.[14] Amidst the usual fare of product placements, contestants on reality shows like "Survivor" began to compete for prizes from corporate sponsors.[15] These shows became virtual infomercials for advertisers, with the contestants acting as unpaid spokespeople for the products on display. This process of what Robert McChesney has called "media hyper-commercialism" gained increasing momentum over the next decade and is nowhere more evident than in the "American Idol" format. In 2008, the show featured a total of 4,636 total product placements,[16] and incorporated its sponsors into the very format and delivery of the show, most notably through the use of SMS text message voting, which it helped AT&T Mobility to launch in 2003. More recently, Apple iTunes signed on as a sponsor (Season 7), and in addition to product placement and promotion within the show, "American Idol" now uses Apple's iTunes platform on its website to allow viewers to download performances.[17]

It is within this synergistic media environment that partnerships between companies like the Fox Network, FremantleMedia, and Fuller's 19 Entertainment have allowed music conglomerates like Sony Music Entertainment to find a profitable new framework for the recording industry. Traditionally, the process of finding, cultivating, and promoting new musical talent was both laborious and expensive, but the "Idol" format has helped to turn this process into what Charles Fairchild calls a "profitable promotional spectacle and marketing juggernaut":[18]

> The "Idol" phenomenon shows us how the music industry can incorporate existing pieces of the media environment to establish and maintain connections with audiences through almost every type of media and the varied formats and inventive ways in which we consume them.[19]

The broadcast and telecommunications industries have facilitated a transition that has seen the expensive and unpredictable "back stage" workings of the record industry turned into a profitable "front stage" enterprise for all of the media groups involved. As Richard Sutherland and Will Straw argue, "Popular success is achieved prior to recordings, which now become almost secondary, responsible for only one portion of overall revenues."[20] By the time a season of "Idol" is over, the show has not only served as a vast platform for advertising revenues, it has also created a whole slate of "authentic" new pop stars with devoted fan followings. These fans have been "participants" in the creation of their favorite idol's success and they are encouraged to remain responsible for it after the conclusion of the season by attending concerts, buying albums, and purchasing "Idol"-endorsed products. When a winning "Idol" contestant finally puts out a traditional studio album, successful sales are virtually guaranteed for RCA (a label under the umbrella of Sony Music Entertainment, and the company responsible for all of the "Idol" recordings).[21] To date, the top ten most successful American Idols have sold in excess of 40 million albums.[22] FremantleMedia and 19 Entertainment control all aspects of merchandizing and any events associated with "American Idol" and its worldwide franchises. Fuller's 19 Entertainment also controls the management of all "Idol" finalists who enter into the recording business, including "advertising, endorsements, sponsorships, and merchandise associated with the contestants on the show."[23]

What this political economy reveals is a very different motivation behind the "Idol" franchise than is presented to viewers. Although continually promoted as both a chance for contestants to decide their own fate through their performances and a chance for audiences to respond to those performances with their votes, the "Idol" brand is meticulously controlled by a very powerful and staggeringly profitable media company.

Becoming an Idol: Identity, Image, and the Labor of Idolatry

Viewer identification with the "Idol" contestants is carefully crafted throughout each season of "American Idol." Using dramatic stories of each contestant's ascent from "Idol" auditions to the Top Ten, the show follows the contestant's "transformations" as they seek to become "America's next singing superstar." The show's narrative presents these stories within a meritocratic framework that appears to unfold naturally. The judges, along with a series of "mentor" guest stars, such as recording artist Usher (under contract to Sony Music subsidiary Arista Records), help coax out the best of each contestant's natural talents and "identity" in time for the elimination rounds, at which point the audience begins to cast their votes. What these narratives of ascent conveniently hide, however, is the actual lack of agency that "Idol" contestants have from the moment they sign a release form to audition for the contest. In agreeing to appear on the show, potential idols sign away "control of their voices, images and likenesses" and agree that "other parties . . . may reveal and/or relate information about [them] of a personal, private, intimate, surprising, defamatory, disparaging, embarrassing or unfavorable nature, that may be factual and/or fiction."[24] In short, the idol contestant is turned into a "product with market value" whose image, actions, and personal history are now available to be exploited by the "Idol" brand in whatever way the show's producers see fit.[25]

Over the course of a single season, the "image" of each idol is shaped into a product to be consumed and attached to the myriad sponsors and advertisers of the show. The idols themselves have no say as to which products they promote or how they promote them, and their labor is unpaid because it is voluntary, thus falling outside performance union contracts and industry labor practices.[26] It is assumed that this is "all part of the process" of becoming an idol in the contest, but it is precisely because "Idol" contestants have willingly volunteered themselves as amateur hopefuls within the competition that they are stripped of the democratic rights and entitlements that usually go along with being a "real" recording artist; namely, the ability to use their voice in order to create music that reflects their own vision, and to align themselves with whatever causes they see fit. In "American Idol," the self is turned into an idol of consumption and the "Idol" loses control over the self.

Perhaps no one is more familiar with this contractual entrapment than the first "American Idol" winner, Kelly Clarkson. In 2007, it was widely reported that Clarkson and her manager Clive Davis (Chief Creative Officer of Sony Music Entertainment) were feuding over the direction of her new album. Reportedly, Davis had failed to identify a "guaranteed radio hit" and thought the album lacked commercial appeal; he was pushing Clarkson to take her album in another direction.[27] Despite Clarkson's repeated criticisms of Davis in the public media,[28] the album "My December" was finally released, but seemingly without all of the major promotional support normally provided by the record company. Clarkson's tour for the album ended up being cancelled due to poor ticket sales, and eventually she was forced to publicly apologize to Davis and "set the record straight" about the feud. Her subsequent albums have been fully backed by the record label but have also, generally speaking, produced the same formulaic pop music as her first album. This is the price one pays for becoming "America's Idol."

Consuming Citizenship: Democratic Participation in the Age of "American Idol"

Much of the political economy of "Idol" may not come as a surprise to a new generation of media-savvy television viewers who recognize that reality TV is highly crafted, not really "real," and designed to sell products and maximize revenues. The agency of the audience within the show is often less critically considered by "media literate" consumers, however it is this audience's votes that are presumably responsible for crowning the eventual "American Idol." Each week of the elimination round, "Idol" host Ryan Seacrest prefaces the voting results with the declaration that "America has spoken!" By definition, the process is transparently democratic! Of course, *when* and *how* America gets to speak and *what* they get to speak about has long since been decided and packaged by the producers of "Idol," who have worked to shape audience perceptions of the contestants. By the time audience voting begins, the menu of potential choices has already been narrowed by producers and each contestant has become a brand that is already potentially worthy of being called an "Idol." As Doris Baltruschat observes, "Media participation and interactivity therefore take place within pre-established frameworks determined by producers and website developers, which delimit the degree of audience engagement to a pre-determined spectrum of choices."[29] Voting or participating within the show via text message, blog, or contest is prescribed entirely by the network of corporate sponsors that shape the content of the show and is more akin to processes of consumption than it is to any process of democratic citizenship. Viewers do not actively participate in the creation of America's next idol, they merely engage actively in consuming the industry idols on display.

By incorporating popular notions of citizenship and democracy into the framework of its brand, the "Idol" phenomenon provides a rich example for considering how the popular meanings of political participation have been altered by the contemporary media environment. The democratic pretense of the show offers a useful analogy for the current state of political discourse in North America. In their examination of the way that television news programs engage the public sphere, for example, Justin Lewis, Sana Inthorn, and Karin Wahl-Jorgenson argue that "we have seen the concept of the citizen replaced by the more limited idea of the consumer. Citizens are actively engaged in the shaping of society and the making of history; consumers simply choose between the products on display."[30] This critique aptly applies to the "American Idol" format and speaks to the way that media narratives have increasingly framed consumption as an act of democratic participation. It is precisely within this association of consumption and citizenship that the waning interest in civic and political participation should be understood.

Recent studies of declining voter turnouts and potential first-time voters indicate that the public has become disenfranchised from civic participation because of what voters perceive as a lack of "real choices" when it comes to voting in elections. This problem is particularly acute in countries like Canada that have "first past the post" electoral systems that do not reward citizens for voting for smaller parties or more progressive viewpoints.[31] Only the largest and wealthiest political parties have the necessary resources to carry out widespread public relations and advertising campaigns, and thus they come to be portrayed to Canadians as the only "real" choices. It is this emphasis on "choices," however, that is perhaps the real problem with the political discourse of our time. Just as "American Idol" has adopted the language and discourse of political participation, our political establishments have increasingly adopted the language and practices of public relations firms, branding experts, and image consultants. It is attention to the conditions under which candidates in the political system come to be potential choices that is required for informed citizenship. By establishing voting as the primary exercise of democracy, and presenting "image" as reality, the framework of shows like "Idol" serves ultimately to convince us that meaningful public and democratic dialogue can be replaced by a single "text or toll-free" vote.

Notes

[1] About the Show: American Idol. http://www.americanidol.com/about/

[2] Charles Fairchild, "Building the Authentic Celebrity: The 'Idol' Phenomenon in the Attention Economy," *Popular Music and Society* 30: 3 (2007), 360.

[3] Gabrielle Dann, "*American Idol:* From the Selling of a Dream to the Selling of a Nation," *Mediations* 1: 1 (2004), 17.

[4] Doris Baltrushat, "Reality TV Formats: The Case of Canadian Idol," *Canadian Journal of Communications* 34 (2009), 47–48.

[5] Associated Press, "American Idol Crowns New Winner," *msnbc.com* (May 21, 2009). Available online at: http://www.msnbc.msn.com/id/30855119/

[6] Fairchild, "Building," 355.

[7] Justin Lewis, Sanna Inthorn and Karin Wahl-Jorgenson, *Citizens or Consumers? What the Media Tell Us About Political Participation* (Maidenhead, UK: Open University Press, 2005).

[8] U.S. Census Bureau, "Resident Population of Voting Age and Percent Casting Votes—States: 2000 to 2008," Available online at: http://www.census.gov/compendia/statab/2010/tables/10s0409.pdf

[9] Canadian Broadcasting Corporation, "Voter Turnout drops to record low," *cbcnews.ca* (Oct. 15, 2008). Available online at: http://www.cbc.ca/canada/story/2008/10/15/voter-turnout.html

[10] Fairchild, "Building," 356.

[11] Richard Sutherland and Will Straw, "The Canadian Music Industry at a Crossroads" in David Taras, Frits Pannekoek, and Maria Bakardjieva, eds., *How Canadians Communicate II: Media, Globalization and Identity* (Calgary: University of Calgary Press, 2007), 142.

[12] Evan Pattak, "Cable Nets Get Real and Love It," *Multichannel News* (May 4, 1998).

[13] Justin Dini, "Survivor Finale Posts Second-Highest Ratings of the Season," *The Street* (August 24, 2000). Available online at: http://www.thestreet.com/brknews/media/1053408.html

[14] Robert W. McChesney, *Rich Media, Poor Democracy: Communication Politics in Dubious Times* (New York: The New Press, 1999), 42.

[15] The Associated Press, "Burnett: Survivor is Life," *cbsnews.com* (June 5, 2001). Available online at: http://www.cbsnews.com/stories/2001/06/05/survivor/main294978.shtml

[16] The Nielson Company, "Product Placements Decline by 15% in First Half, Nielsen Reports," News Release (Sept. 15, 2008). Available online at: http://en-us.nielsen.com/etc/medialib/nielsen_dotcom/en_us/documents/pdf/press_releases/2008/september.Par.41713.File.dat/pr_080915_download.pdf

[17] Season 8 Downloads: American Idol. http://www.americanidol.com/itunes

[18] Fairchild, "Building," 356.

[19] Fairchild, "Building," 359.

[20] Sutherland and Straw, "Canadian Music," 161.

[21] Dann, "American Idol," 19.

[22] Access Hollywood, "Top 10 best-selling 'American Idols,'" *msnbc.com* (April 5, 2010). Available online at: http://www.msnbc.msn.com/id/36126063/ns/entertainment-access_hollywood/

[23] Dann, "American Idol," 17.

[24] Alison Hearn, "'John, a 20-year-old Boston native with a great sense of humor': on the spectacularization of the 'self' and the incorporation of identity in the age of reality television," *International Journal of Media and Cultural Politics* 2: 2 (2006), 138.

[25] Hearn, "John," 137–38.

[26] Baltruschat, "Reality TV," 54.

[27] Variations of these reports appeared in numerous celebrity oriented magazines, such as *People, Blender, US Weekly,* and on online entertainment blogs like *Perez Hilton.* Although the exact details of the feud differed slightly, they generally all reported a clashing between Davis and Clarkson over "creative differences."

[28] See the August 2007 edition of *Blender* magazine.

[29] Baltruschat, "Reality TV," 51.

[30] Lewis, Inthorn and Wahl-Jorgenson, "Citizens," 5.

[31] Lewis, Inthorn and Wahl-Jorgenson, "Citizens," 3.

The Genders of Popular Culture

*P*opular culture is infused with sex and gender and there is no escaping it; gender formulates our view of the world and the world's view of us. Nothing is more deeply ingrained in the human psyche than our sexual identity and yet our understanding of our basic human biology and its connections to our behavioral expectations is ultimately rooted in myth. And it is myth that fuels our behavior towards one another at home, in the workplace, and in our communities. The media are of course part of the process of mythmaking, both reflecting and creating our common set of cultural understandings. Sexism, heterosexism, and homophobia still mark our ideological framework and legitimate a whole set of institutional and systemic inequities.

Our authors wrestle with these ideologies in popular culture to present creative and challenging ideas in this section. John Sakeris and Michael DeAngelis look at the new representations of gays and lesbians on television and film. De Angelis examines the career of Keanu Reeves and looks at the ways actors and stars deal with their public personae in the wake of changing societal expectations. Both of these articles consider the "new gay images" prevalent in popular culture and examine the changing face of homophobia. Sakeris's revised and updated article includes a look at the current crop of "gay" films, including the controversial *Brüno* and television programs like "Modern Family." Kristen Hatch's article on the recent history of romantic films looks critically at the apparent erosion of feminist values in films such as *Sweet Home Alabama,* and finds a complexity that has been overlooked by many viewers. She gives a cogent analysis of the effects of women's current socioeconomic situation on the production and marketing of such films. Jennifer Brayton, in another substantially revised article, looks at the past and present depictions of virtual reality in commercial films and shows how old heterosexist and homophobic assumptions are still reinforced while cloaked in a futuristic technological framework. Also included is Tison Pugh's forceful and interesting analysis of Gus Van Sant's relationship to queer cinema, and his films' role in changing perceptions of homosexuality. And finally, Fred Turner takes a look at reality-based crime shows, uncovering the hidden psycho-sexual messages in their narrative and showing how they relate to social class.

Chapter 6

From "Ellen" to a "Modern Family"

The Love That Dared Not Speak Its Name Goes Big

John Sakeris

*T*he depictions of gays and lesbians in North American mass media have been described by many authors as negative and stereotypical. Gay men and women have been routinely portrayed as figures of fun and ridicule, or even as villains who meet a well-deserved fate of death or destruction.[1] Film and television have historically reinforced homophobia as have the state and many religious institutions. These negative media portrayals have been increasingly under attack, however, as have the considerable inequities that have been institutionalized in law over generations, and many gains have been made. Legalization of homosexuality is still to be achieved in many countries and persecution of gay men and lesbians continues resulting in incarceration and even death; the struggle for full equality under the law continues today even where homosexuality has been made legal (gay marriage has been made legal in eight countries and civil unions are recognized in about twenty, as well as in individual jurisdictions). These institutional gains have been made by committed activists around the world; attitudinal changes in the general population have been slow in coming but indicators say that tolerance is increasing. Many groups have targeted TV, radio, newspaper news, and fictional film and television for fairer representation. GLAAD (The Gay and Lesbian Alliance against Defamation) is but one group that is routinely approached by the big media outlets for their comments on film and television portrayals of Lesbians and Gay men. There have been different levels of success: the words "gay and lesbian" rather than "homosexual" are used normally in news reports now and the use of the term "hate crime" in describing attacks against gays has reached a broader acceptance both in the law and in the media; in news reports, gays are no longer routinely described deserving beating or killing. Positive portrayals of gays and lesbians are found increasingly in films and television shows and these portrayals are therefore finding a much wider audience.

Gay and Lesbian Visibility: Queers are Everywhere!

Gay- and lesbian-centered shows have exploded in the last few years in North American film and television. The first major show featuring a lesbian was the groundbreaking "Ellen" (1994–1998), with the much publicized "coming out" episode that made its star Ellen DeGeneres famous. "Ellen" was one of the first mainstream situation comedies to feature (albeit after several episodes) a lesbian character played by a lesbian actor. DeGeneres was the subject of many news and entertainment stories, both in Canada and in the U.S. Her subsequent, much publicized love affair with Anne Heche (followed by Heche's much publicized breakdown and marriage to a man) added another dimension to the whole presentation of same-sex themes in the media; actors were finally coming out, an action that had been considered as a source of career suicide just a year earlier. Nonetheless, at the time of the broadcast of the "coming out" episode of April 30, 1997, there was a concerted campaign against the show by religious groups, directed at advertisers who were wary of being associated with any controversy. Ironically, this campaign had an effect opposite to the one intended; the publicity created a substantial ratings success.

"Ellen" surprised advertisers and network executives alike and created an opportunity for more shows featuring lesbians and gays. When a subsequent ratings decline led to the show's cancellation, media pundits opined that gay material was simply not acceptable to mainstream American audiences. However, gay and lesbian lobby groups, and the star herself, openly speculated that it was because of the homophobia of the executives that the show was no longer being supported by the network and sponsors; others claimed that the show did not have wide enough appeal to carry a large audience, while still others saw entrenched homophobia in the TV audience as an explanation of its failure. A subsequent situation comedy with Ms. DeGeneres also failed after only one season even though it was a critical success; nevertheless, the actor-comedian returned to television in 2003 with a highly successful talk show that has come to rival even "Oprah" in ratings.

Gay and lesbian characters and themes suddenly grew up everywhere on both cable and network TV. Positive portrayals and themes are now to be found in situation comedies like "Modern Family" (2009), "Glee" (2009), "The New Adventures of the Old Christine" (2006), "30 Rock" (2006), "Ugly Betty" (2006), and "Will and Grace" (1998); but also in reality TV shows like "The Amazing Race" (2001), "Survivor" (2000), and "The Real World"

(1992); detective and crime shows like "Cold Case" (2003) and "Law & Order" (1990) or any of its many spin-offs; docu-dramas like "Prayers for Bobby" (2009) and "The Matthew Shepard Story" (2002); dramas like "Smash" (2012), "Revenge" (2011), "Brothers & Sisters" (2006), and "Desperate Housewives" (2004); fantasy and science fiction shows like "Torchwood" (2006) and the classic "Buffy the Vampire Slayer" (1997); and premium cable TV shows like "Nurse Jackie" (2009), "Sex and the City" (2008), "True Blood" (2008) (vampire stories have always had a homoerotic subtext), "The L Word" (2004), "Six Feet Under" (2001), and "The Sopranos" (1999). From a period of gay and lesbian invisibility just a few short years ago, the TV landscape has changed dramatically with a plethora of characters and gay themes (both positive and negative).

This new climate has allowed high-profile celebrities to come out, declaring that they are gay or bisexual: Rosie O'Donnell, Lindsay Lohan, Neil Patrick Harris, and Ricky Martin are but a few. Nevertheless, male sports stars and major male film stars are still hesitant to announce their sexuality, persisting in the thought that doing so would constitute career suicide.

Homophobia, Sexism, Capital, and the Struggle for Equality

Homophobia has long been a mainstay of North American popular culture. Since the rise of gay activism in the 1960s, there have been several strategies in the struggle for gay rights and the end of homophobia. Activists have focused their energies for change on both civil rights (most recently on same-sex marriage), legislative change, and representation in the mainstream media. The mass media have been the targets of highly publicized campaigns by gay lobby groups—such as GLAAD—against negative and stereotypical representations. These campaigns, coupled with a militant new gay spirit, were seen by activists as a step in ending discrimination and prejudice in the larger social system; the assumption was that changing people's attitudes would be part of the road to social change. However, the huge defeats in state legislatures and in state referenda for marriage equality in the U.S. seem to indicate that homophobia is hardly on the decline. (The Canadian case is different: the legislative route has been more successful partially because the neo-conservatives and the religious right are not as powerful or politically connected as they are in the United States.)

The reasons for the persistence of homophobia lie in the economic structure of our society and in the cultural ideas that legitimate it. Homophobia is a primary means of enforcing gender identity; the social disapprobation that greets nonconforming gender behavior is a powerful force that serves as a lesson to all members of society to conform or face the consequences. Sexism is an ideology that reinforces the idea of the natural biological superiority of males, and gender definitions and expectations reflect that ideology. (For example, men aren't supposed to cry and use violence as a defining characteristic while women are nurturing and emotional.) Our very economic and social organization is built on gender and racial discrimination and sexism and racism provide its legitimization. Gender, sexism, racism and discrimination are central to the economic order of capitalism, since they result in higher profits.

Sexism justifies a divided labor force that maintains an increased level of profit for corporations. The international labor force is primarily female, young, and low paid. With few unions and many repressive governments, the rate of return on overseas investment is staggering, and the global sweatshop is overwhelmingly female. In North America, working women are primarily concentrated into what has been termed the "pink collar ghetto," earning wages that are still approximately three quarters of what men earn for similar jobs. This divided labor force drives the cost of all labor down.

Sexism also justifies free labor in the home, still performed largely by women. This free labor benefits corporations' bottom line since companies require a clothed and fed workforce to run smoothly, and women, primarily, provide it free.

Sexism also plays a central role in the realization of profit through consumption. Buying products is central to capital and advertisers must delve deep into our consciousness to be successful. For example, the commodification of women's, and increasingly men's, bodies is central to creating a climate for consumption. Many shows and films ultimately serve to increase our insecurity so that we will buy products we do not need, but that producers and marketers need to sell to us.

Sexism enforces aggression, violence, and competition among males. A competitive male is central not only to a shrinking labor market (we must compete for the few jobs that are there) but also to a militarized and imperialist power; the warrior male is an essential component of wars of aggression and domination that ultimately benefit corporate interests.[2]

In short, capitalism benefits from sexism. But homophobia is also a central component of sexism. *Homophobia serves to reinforce sexist ideology by maintaining fairly rigid gender rules for behavior.* The murders and bashings of lesbian, gay, and transgendered people attest to the effectiveness of gender socialization; the penalties are severe for those who step out of their defined gender roles. Homophobia is then a major variable in maintaining the gender status quo, and the mass media, which are central to reproducing capitalist relations of production, have historically been prime vehicles for reinforcing it.

No doubt there are more and more challenges to homophobia (as with sexism and racism) that have met with some success, but this success has not really challenged the status quo. It is possible for capital to allow for a new attitude towards homosexuality without disturbing the primary gender definitions that already exist. The defeat of homophobia would of course not alter the structure of capital. But it would eliminate that convenient deviant "other" that is so useful to the powerful when economies are in trouble and social unrest is upon us.

TV, Film, and the Heterosexual Narrative: A Recent History

Among the many shows that saw their debut on NBC in 1998 was "Will and Grace," a half-hour sitcom produced and written by both gay and straight men and women that debuted with considerable anticipation and network concern. The show quickly became successful and continues to be a top earner in syndication. Initially controversial, it was scheduled on late-night prime time but network tolerance for gay subject matter having broadened, it is now often televised earlier, sometimes at dinner hour when there is a younger viewing audience. The main characters are a gay lawyer, Will (Eric McCormack), his longtime friend Grace, a designer (Debra Messing), Will's old friend Jack (Sean Hayes), an unsuccessful actor who is also gay, and Karen (Megan Mullaley), Grace's bored and wealthy assistant.

The series was a conventional sitcom but its plots often concerned gay issues (marriage, adoption, discrimination, homophobia, coming out). Like many other characters that populate the small screen, the central focuses here were young, attractive professionals rather than blue-collar workers. They formed a "family" in a non-traditional sense, but then most shows use a family of friends as a structural center. As for addressing traditional working class concerns, "Will and Grace" was no different than other shows: for the most part, it didn't.

There was rarely any display of physical affection or eroticism involving the gay characters in this ostensibly "gay" show. Any kissing between two men was either fleeting or played for laughs. The female characters, in particular Grace, were allowed a more all-encompassing sex life. One particular episode made reference to that double standard. Deciding to confront NBC about its apparent censorship of acts showing physical affection between two men, Jack and Will kissed each other in a mock-up of the "Today Show" crowd milling around Rockefeller Center. Even though that kiss was played for laughs, the episode was heavily marketed by the network, seemingly winking at its own policy. Generally, a traditional heterosexual narrative is reflected and reinforced by this show, but it is interestingly reconfigured to fit the gay characters and plot. (Indeed, a few of the writers and producers, some of whom are gay themselves, have spoken publicly about the apparent necessity to be "cautious" in their depiction of male-to-male eroticism.)

Often, there is an undercurrent of critical assessment of heterosexual dominance in the program, which is not surprising given its creators. This homo/hetero dichotomy can best be explained by the increased tolerance for gays and lesbians among younger people, who consistently accept gay marriage in greater numbers than their older counterparts. They also are more likely to accept critiques of the dominant culture of their elders. Younger people and particularly women are the target demographic for this show and it is clear that profitability sometimes takes precedence over the reinforcement of traditional mores.

"Queer as Folk" and "The L Word": The New Queer Sensibility

The British show "Queer as Folk," about the sex lives of gay twenty something Brits, was broadcast to a large audience in Britain in the 1990s and was a huge success. Its subsequent success on its broadcast in North America was a surprise to the producers, who expected a backlash for the graphic depiction of gay male sex. But a North American cable-television version was produced and shown in Canada on Showcase. In the U.S. it was also shown on cable but on Showtime, a premium pay-tv channel. The show has been successful enough to continue for many seasons and is one of the most profitable shows ever produced by Showtime. The newer series "The L Word" has also enjoyed a successful run on cable television and has attracted a broad cross section of the TV viewing public.

In the North American "Queer as Folk," a group of young gay men and women ranging in age from the teens to the thirties live in a large eastern American city (Toronto standing in for Pittsburgh). Brian Kinney (Gale Harold) and his friend Michael (Hal Sparks) are the two central characters; they are long-time friends who are opposite in their activities and attributes. Brian is a professional gay man in his thirties who has many sex partners but lives with Justin (Randy Harrison) in what is an open relationship. Michael seeks long-term relationships and was partnered with a man with HIV. Their friends Ted (Scott

Lowell), Emmett (Peter Paige), Melanie (Michelle Clunie) and Lindsay (Thea Gill) (a lesbian couple whose baby has been fathered by Brian), and Michael's mother Debbie (Sharon Gless), a waitress in a diner, and her brother and Justin's mother Jennifer, form the rest of the large ensemble cast.

The producers portray a cross section of urban gay life (albeit one that appears to lack visible minorities). The show itself is clearly aimed at the gay "market" as the situations that are portrayed in this hour-long drama series are deliberately current and relevant to gay men and women: the problems of gay parenting, ageism in the gay community, HIV, drug abuse, gay bashing, anonymous sex, jealousy, social class, police entrapment, workplace sexual harassment, pornography, parental rejection, marriage, religion, workplace discrimination, outing, human rights, and many other topics. While most of the cast members are heterosexual, some are prominently "out" in both the gay and mainstream media. The heterosexual cast members have even appeared on talk shows discussing the graphic sex scenes for which the show is famous. The gay actors, too, have been upfront about their own sexuality and its implications for the show and their careers outside "Queer as Folk." One has expressed fears about having difficulty landing straight roles if he were too identified as a gay actor, giving more evidence of the widespread homophobia in the industry.

The graphic nature of the sexual activity portrayed onscreen in both "Queer as Folk" and "The L Word" is noteworthy. It clearly could not be broadcast on network television. Nudity, both male and female, simulated sex of all sorts, anonymous sex, and sex between lovers are evident in most episodes. Before each shoot, the actors even have sessions about the sexual segment in which they participate. It seems that cable TV is the first frontier for portraying gay sex. If it is commonplace to see sex acts between heterosexual characters in the mainstream media, it is far less common to see acts between gay and lesbian characters. Even film has been slow to pick up on the trend, but with the increase in gay films marketed to the gay population, the so-called New Queer Cinema has seen this longstanding taboo broken as well. Cable television, because of the resultant fragmentation of the audience, has been able to step forward on this issue where network television has not. Premium pay cables are much less subject to pressure from organized groups than is network television.

Gay Cowboys, Political Martyrs, and Brüno

Mainstream commercial films have fallen behind in their inclusion of a wide variety of gay characters. The 2006 film *Brokeback Mountain*, based on the Annie Proulx short story of the same name, was a surprise success and captured much media attention with its central love story about two gay cowboys in Wyoming. The film, directed by the much admired Ang Lee, begins in the 1960s and spans over twenty years in the life of Ennis Del Mar (Heath Ledger) and Jack Twist (Jake Gyllenhaal) as they navigate the effects of their relationship. *Brokeback Mountain* has been both a commercial and critical success, garnering eight Academy Award nominations and winning three, one for Best Director; but losing for Best Picture and—tellingly—the major acting awards.

The film and short story are essentially about homophobia and its effects on both of the protagonists and the people with whom they come in contact. (Social class, too, is central to understanding the powerlessness of the main characters, particularly Ennis, the poorer of the two.) Yet the marketing and the critical reception of the film seemed to pointedly downplay the gay aspects of the film, choosing instead to focus on the so-called universal aspects of the story (i.e. "It's not *just* about gay men"). The posters for the film were different for different geographic areas of the United States: in predominately rural areas and strong "red" or Republican states the two lovers are photographed with their wives, while in the larger urban centers the two men face away from each other. The central homosexual theme of the film is almost minimized in all of the advertising campaigns (except, of course, the ones aiming at the gay audience).

Critics' responses to the film were in the same vein: most emphasized the "universality" of the love story, while at the same time calling the film a "breakthrough." It should be noted that other major films about homophobia have come out of Hollywood before, most notably *Philadelphia* (1993), in which Tom Hanks played a gay lawyer with AIDS fighting discrimination, or *V for Vendetta* (2006), about a futuristic British fascist state with echoes of Nazi Germany and George Bush's America, where three gay characters are killed by Josef Mengele-like doctors and police storm troopers because of their sexuality and their opposition to the regime. Most recently Colin Firth, in another Oscar-nominated performance, is a grieving gay man who has lost his lover in a car accident. *A Single Man* was a critical and commercial success for its depiction of closeted gay life in 1960s America. *Brokeback Mountain* continues a line of "serious" treatments of homosexuality and homophobia onscreen; what makes it different is that its two young leading men are shown engaging in scenes of sex and affection. The homosexual sex is limited, however, and far less graphic than the heterosexual sex scenes, or, for that matter, similar scenes on cable TV. Nevertheless, Ledger and Gyllenhaal were consistently asked what it was like to play these scenes while being hailed as "brave" for taking these roles; roles that the commentators emphasized would have in the past been shunned by male actors as sure paths to "career suicide."

Rarely are actors asked what it is like to play scenes of murder and mayhem or called "brave" when they do. Interestingly, this film about homophobia is surrounded by a homophobic popular culture industry. Audiences are no less immune. Young heterosexual males are less likely than females to attend this film with their male friends, or on their own, probably for fear of being labeled as gay. Older heterosexual males are similar. One columnist in a major U.S. daily wrote about how difficult it was for him to go to the film or convince his friend to do so. The mainstream news organizations have yet to comment on this very evident irony.

The U.S. political elite has been drawn into the discussions about the film as well. This group has not been particularly known for its acceptance of gay rights or even the positive depiction of gay lives. Top-ranking members of the former Bush administration (including Bush himself) and their Right-wing supporters were asked if they had seen the movie, and none of them had done so. Of course, it is this same political regime which promoted homophobia in order to gain support from the rest of the population for their class-based socioeconomic policies. Bush's fight against gay marriage, for example, diverted attention from his more significant agenda of tax cuts for the rich, the redistribution of wealth upwards, and support for the military industrial complex.

Brokeback Mountain has clearly been a cultural touchstone in North America and has created an opportunity for discussion on a broader scale of an issue that has unfortunately not been explored as fully as it might. Yet critics and commentators did not explore Ennis's internalized homophobia, Jack's death at the hands of gay bashers, and the characters' lack of power, aspects of the characters that have to be placed in the broader context of class, gender, and politics. Had the film engendered this broader discussion, rather than provoking questions about the feelings of the leading actors, it might truly have been a "breakthrough."

Milk (2008), directed by Gus van Sant and starring Sean Penn as the political activist and San Francisco city politician Harvey Milk, was one of the most political of the recent films about gays in America. This film was a critical and commercial success garnering an academy award for Penn's portrayal and for Dustin Lance Black's original screenplay. A straightforward biography of America's first elected openly gay politician, *Milk* opens with documentary shots of the arrests of men at a gay bar and their subsequent humiliation at the hands of the police and the press. Milk, a closeted somewhat conservative man who moved to the Castro Street district in the 1970s with his then lover Scott Smith (James Franco), became gradually politicized by the war in Vietnam and the violence directed towards gay men and lesbians by the police and sanctioned by the government. After four attempts to run for political office, Harvey is finally successful and becomes one of San Francisco's most popular politicians only to be assassinated, along with the Mayor, George Moscone, by Dan White (Josh Brolin), the only member of the Board of Supervisors to refuse to vote for a gay civil rights bill. White was subsequently released on what became to be known as the "Twinkie Defense" (he was supposedly subject to mood swings brought on by consuming too much sugar). His release was met with riots and massive demonstrations in the streets of the city. Years later he committed suicide.

Both Penn and Black used their Oscar acceptance speeches to advocate for equal rights for gays in all areas including marriage, to great applause from the audience. Van Sant, a prominent gay director, has made gay themed films before (*My Own Private Idaho* [1991] and *Elephant* [2003]) but this film, coming on the heels of the success of California's Proposition 8, banning gay marriage, was seen as an important vehicle in the fight for gay rights even though it was released after the referendum was voted on. While Van Sant's other films are more introspective and personal, this film falls easily into the category of "agit-prop." Despite its obvious political message, the actors were subject to questions about their (rather tame) love scenes (just as Ledger and Gyllenhaal were, earlier). David Letterman asked Franco what it was like to kiss Penn ("The Late Show", CBS Nov 21, 2008): "It had to be odd . . . Do you really want to be good at kissing a guy?"—blatant homophobia played for laughs as usual. While introducing Penn at the Oscars, Robert De Niro quipped, "How did he do it? How for so many years did Sean Penn get so many roles playing straight guys?" (ABC, Feb. 22, 2009). Despite the large number of homosexual workers and executives in the film industry, comments like these continue to go unchallenged and even unnoticed.

Many mainstream films about gay men and lesbians highlight homophobia. An interesting independent film called *Humpday* (2009) takes a somewhat different approach by examining the fear of gay intimacy between two straight friends, Ben (Mark Duplass) and Andrew (Joshua Leonard), who reconnect after some years. One evening at a party, drunk and stoned, they make a pact to produce a "porno" about two straight guys having gay sex for an amateur pornography festival called "Humpday." There is much discussion about the event beforehand: "It scares me more than anything else, and that is a reason to go through with it," says Ben, in one of the more telling moments. While they are ostensibly doing this to be "nonconventional" and "artistic," it becomes clear that the two friends have great affection for each other. The final scene where they get together is instructive. They agree not to kiss: "It's too intimate, I can't think about it, let's just let our bodies take over." Writer and director Lynn Shelton is clearly interested in something that appears easier for women—physical affection between members of the same sex. She noted that while she was in the audience for a screening of the film, most of the women audience members stayed while a large number of men left the theatre, thus adding another dimension to her exploration of male fear of intimacy and homophobia.

A more commercially successful approach to the buddy film is John Hamburg's *I Love You, Man* (2009). Peter Klaven (Paul Rudd) goes on a series of "man dates" since he has no male friends from whom to chose a best man for his wedding. Although it's about male intimacy, the film nevertheless resorts to familiar territory when one of Peter's "dates" turns out to be gay. The fear of homosexuality is part of the theme but not in a way that challenges conventional wisdom. (On the other hand, *Pineapple Express* [2008] manages to depict male friendship and love without resorting to homophobia.)

Sacha Baron Cohen's *Brüno* (2009), follows his highly successful *Borat* (2006) and uses much the same confrontatory formula as that film and his television show "Da Ali G Show" (2003), setting up unsuspecting people to respond to his outrageousness. The character of Brüno "wants to be the biggest gay movie star since Schwarzenegger" by leaving the Austrian fashion world (in which he has been unsuccessful) and going to America to become famous there. His clothes and style are "over the top" gay: sometimes yellow short shorts with suspenders and a matching yellow Austrian fedora, Zebra striped body shirts, army boots, a dried blond page boy flip haircut, and equally often nothing at all. His mannerisms are stereotypical, but different in effect from more traditional images of gay men as in *The Birdcage* (1996). Cohen is deliberately attempting to point out peoples' fear of homosexuals and the film is an exercise in confronting raw homophobia in the general population. Some of the scenes are surprising in their audacity: Paula Abdul and Brüno sitting on Mexicans placed as chairs while the two converse; a focus group where Brüno's penis speaks to them on television; an attempt to get Ron Paul, a Republican presidential candidate, to make a sex film; a scene in the Middle East where Brüno dresses up as a gay Hasidic Jew and gets chased down the street; a sex scene with his young lover who is strapped into a chair that Brüno pulls toward himself, for anal sex, with giant elastic bands; a bicycle with a dildo attached to the seat; a talk with a gay "converter" who tells him to do "straight" things to get rid of his homosexuality (join the National Guard, find Jesus, go hunting with some backwoods rednecks who chase him away when tries to enter their tent naked in the middle of the night . . .); and a staged cage fight in which he starts to make love to his partner in front of an enraged southern audience. No one is spared from Cohen's "in your face" theatrical style—neither the people in the film nor the audience watching it. Cohen is clearly a brave (or disturbed!) man to put himself in literally dangerous situations, and the film is not an easy one to watch.

Gay critics and audiences were divided on the effect of the film. Some thought that it exposed homophobia and others said that it increased it. In fact it probably did both. The most telling episode is the cage fight in the southern U.S. The audience is drunk and rowdy, wearing T shirts that say "straight pride" and "my asshole's for shitting." Brüno is in straight "drag," playing Straight Dave, a typical wrestling announcer who whips the crowd into a frenzy against gays by making outrageous anti-gay comments. His partner Lutz (Gustaf Hammarsten) challenges him from the audience and enters the ring to boos and catcalls. They start to fight while the audience cries for blood, then suddenly they start to make love on the floor of the cage. A near riot begins and men and women throw things (a folding chair) into the ring, try to scale the cage (surrounded by faux barbed wire) to get at them, and become more and more enraged. Cohen commented in the DVD that audience members were primed for violence and when they were met with expressions of love and affection, they were unable to handle it and resorted to violence themselves. Of course, gay people know that expressions of public affection can get them beaten or even killed; this film certainly brings that point home. The box office receipts were not as big as those of his earlier film but *Brüno* did reach a rather large audience nonetheless. As for the cultural effect of the film, one can certainly say that it was far less conventional than *Milk* in that it reached into areas of people's psyche where no one has dared (or thought) to go before. As for countering homophobia, time will tell.

Entertainment involving lesbians and gays does not call into question the dominant social structure as indeed it could. Instead these shows and films reinforce the idea of homosexuality as a separate category rather than as an integral part of all human sexuality. The fundamentals of gender socialization and their connection to our economic base could be called into question but they are not. Now, sexuality is conceived as something we can find in our genes rather than in our culture; and in this way our attention is diverted from any critical examination of the structure and culture of our society which clearly needs to be critiqued.[3] It is not hard to see how biological explanations of sexuality and behavior allow conventional explanations of the world to go unquestioned, unexamined, and unchallenged. Of course, the rise of neo-liberalism and Social Darwinism have cemented this mindset. Meanwhile, homophobia still remains, even though mainstream media are presenting more and more positive images of lesbian, gay, and transgendered individuals. The President of the United States has even publically supported gay marriage and some have argued that the representation of homosexual relationships in film and television has cultured more positive voter attitudes. Yet the deep divisions in the population remain. Gay and straight activists will continue to effect change in both the media and in human rights, yet the structural and cultural sources of homophobia and its functions in the larger social order stubbornly remain. Perhaps a broader perspective in this struggle needs to be considered—one that involves a social movement targeting homophobia, sexism and inequality together.

Notes

[1] See Vito Russo, *The Celluloid Closet*, Revised Edition (New York: Harper & Row, 1985).

[2] Sexism and homophobia have existed in most societies since the invention of agriculture. Feudal and semi-feudal societies today often exhibit extreme forms of sexism and homophobia. The end of state-sanctioned patriarchy and the growth of industrial wage labor have created the conditions for modern-day women's and gay liberation movements.

[3] Ruth Hubbard and Elijah Wald, *Exploding the Gene Myth* (Boston: Beacon Press, 1993).

Chapter 7

Girl Meets Boy

Romantic Comedies After Feminism

Kristen Hatch

In *Are Men Necessary: When Sexes Collide, New York Times* columnist Maureen Dowd despairs over the erosion of feminist values: "Maybe we should have known that the story of women's progress would be more of a zigzag than a superhighway, that the triumph of feminism would last a nanosecond while the backlash lasted 40 years."[1] Her central concerns are women's willingness to embrace domesticity rather than career success, and men's unwillingness to embrace successful women. Dowd points to several studies that appear to support her contention that men would rather marry their secretaries than their bosses. A University of Michigan study, for example, found that male undergraduates would prefer marrying subordinates to marrying their supervisors; "Men think that women with important jobs are more likely to cheat on them."[2] And a 2005 report by British researchers claims that men's marriage prospects increase by thirty-five percent for every sixteen-point rise in their I.Q., whereas women's prospects decrease by forty percent for every sixteen-point jump in theirs. Apparently, smart women don't get married.

Hollywood, argues Dowd, supports viewers' tendency to perceive successful women as poor marriage partners by offering romantic fantasies in which men marry the women who are hired to take care of them.

"In all those Tracy-Hepburn movies more than a half-century ago, it was the snap and crackle of a romance between equals that was so exciting. . . . Moviemakers these days are more interested in exploring what Steve Martin, in his novel *Shopgirl*, calls the 'calm cushion' of romances between unequals."[3] Dowd cites three films in which wealthy and successful men fall for subordinate and nurturing women. In James Brooks' *Spanglish* (2004), Adam Sandler plays a New York chef who is tempted to leave his neurotic, overachieving wife (Téa Leoni) for the Spanish-speaking maid (Paz Vega) who sees to the care and feeding of his family. In Richard Curtis's *Love, Actually* (2003), a British prime minister (Hugh Grant) is enamored of the woman who brings him his tea and scones every afternoon (Martine McCutcheon), a businessman (Alan Rickman) falls for his secretary (Heike Makatsch), and a novelist (Colin Firth) falls for his Portuguese-speaking maid (Lúcia Moniz). And in Wayne Wang's *Maid in Manhattan* (2002), a wealthy politician (Ralph Fiennes) marries a hotel maid (Jennifer Lopez).

While these thumbnail plot outlines do suggest that Hollywood has sounded a warning to career-oriented women that success in the boardroom leads to failure in the bedroom, a consideration of recent "career girl" comedies indicates no such thing. Indeed, the eponymous maid in *Maid in Manhattan* is hardly the nurturing domestic that Dowd's characterization implies. Lopez plays a single mother who aspires to be promoted to a management position, though her identity as a working-class Latina makes this goal seem almost impossible for her to achieve. It is an unusual Cinderella story, in which the heroine develops a successful career and then marries her prince. In *The Nanny Diaries* (2007), Annie (Scarlett Johansson) flees a corporate interview for a job as a nanny. In her new job, she witnesses the misery of a Manhattan housewife, Mrs. X (Laura Linney) who is married to a selfish and unsympathetic executive. Eventually, Annie learns that she can't spend her life looking after other people instead of herself, and she quits the job to attend graduate school. Likewise, in *27 Dresses* (2008), Jane (Katherine Heigl) is secretly in love with her boss. However, rather than winning her man by doting on him, she discovers that she must put her own needs and desires first if she's ever going to find happiness. She quits her job as an administrative assistant, determined to pursue a more fulfilling career, and finally becomes a bride when she falls in love with the man who insists she must learn to say "no" to people.

Contrary to Dowd's contention that Hollywood romantic comedies suggest that women will find happiness through domesticity rather than careers, Hollywood has turned increasingly to stories about young professional women who struggle to balance their career ambitions and their personal lives and, more often than not, earn more money than do their romantic partners. These being romantic comedies, it should come as no surprise that the films will offer love as the solution to the women's problems. However, the films do not necessarily suggest that career and marriage don't mix. Occasionally, as in *Kate and Leopold* (2001) and *13 Going on 30* (2004), the heroine will forego her professional aspirations once she recognizes her true love. In at least one instance, *Little Black Book* (2004), the heroine discovers she's not in love with the person she thought was the man of her dreams, and the realization helps her land her dream job. More often, however, the heroine discovers that she must make compromises in order to attain both love and professional success, as in *Sweet Home Alabama* (2002), *How to Lose a Guy in 10 Days* (2003), *Raising Helen* (2004), *The Devil Wears Prada* (2006), and *The Proposal* (2009).

Regardless of the outcome of their romantic plots, the generic conventions that shape these films reflect a preoccupation with concerns that have surprisingly little to do with the question of whether women belong in the home or the office. Instead, these films reflect disillusionment with corporate life that is akin to that expressed by men in the 1950s. These career-girl romantic comedies represent women negotiating the concerns that have arisen for middle-class women in the wake of second-wave feminism, and in doing so they suggest that these problems will be resolved through the marriage of the feminine characteristics of industry and ambition and the masculine ones of integrity and individuality.

Second-wave feminism is widely perceived to have been sparked by Betty Friedan's 1963 characterization of the suburban home as a "comfortable concentration camp."[4] In the 1950s and 1960s, although white, middle-class women were attending colleges in record numbers; they had little opportunity to put their educations towards anything other than marriage and childrearing. Women were informally discouraged from attending graduate school or pursuing professional careers, unless as a stop-gap before marriage, and employers had the legal right to reject women's job applications on the basis of their sex alone, regardless of their marital status. In the decades that followed Friedan's call to arms, feminists fought and won legal protections that would make it possible for women to achieve economic independence. No longer would a woman need permission from her husband or father to apply for a loan. No longer would she be barred from entering publicly funded graduate schools. No longer would want ads be segregated by sex, with men invited to apply to professional positions, women to clerical ones.

By the mid 1980s, women college graduates were expected to pursue careers in addition to marriage. Indeed, the disappearance of the "family wage"—the ideal that an entire family should be able to live comfortably, if modestly, on one person's salary—meant that most women had little choice but to work, regardless of their marital status. As this generation aged, middle-class women began to face the challenges that had long plagued working-class women, namely how to cook, clean, and care for children while holding down a full-time job outside the home. In July, 2002, *Time* magazine ran a cover story, "Babies vs. Career: Which Should Come First for the Women Who Want Both?" The sub-heading gave a hint at the answer: "The harsh facts about fertility."[5] The article is largely based on the argument made by Sylvia Ann Hewlett in her book, *Creating a Life: Professional Women and the Quest for Children* that professional women have pursued careers at the expense of bearing children, leading to an "epidemic of childlessness." "Time passes, work is relentless. The travel, the hours—relationships are hard to sustain. By the time a woman is married and settled enough in her career to think of starting a family, it is all too often too late."[6]

Hewlett's association of childlessness with disease in her characterization of childlessness as an "epidemic" should alert us to her position on the subject. In fact, she has been sounding the same alarm since 1986, when she published *A Lesser Life: The Myth of Women's Liberation in America*. And, as in 1986, her claims have been roundly proven to be erroneous. *Forbes* magazine, for example, found that among America's top female executives, 71% had children, hardly an epidemic of childlessness.[7] Nonetheless, Hewlett's book has captured national attention because it touches a nerve. Middle-class women, it would appear, are feeling the pressures of competition and overwork that have long plagued middle-class men.

Not surprisingly, the sentiment has been echoed in Hollywood. In the past decade, there has developed a cycle of romantic comedies that explore the concerns of women who struggle to balance their professional careers with their personal lives. Often in Hollywood's romantic comedies, the uniting of the lovers symbolically signals the reconciliation of opposing ideals. In the screwball comedies of the 1930s, for example, the concerns of Depression-era audiences were addressed in narratives in which men and women from divergent class backgrounds overcame their differences and fell in love. As Thomas Schatz argues, "their personal union serves to celebrate integration into the community at large, into a social environment where cultural conflicts and contradictions have been magically reconciled . . . within a classless utopian environment."[8] In *It Happened One Night* (1934), for example, a runaway heiress (Claudette Colbert) and an out-of-work journalist (Clark Gable) recognize their shared American values—individualism, self-reliance, integrity—despite the social distinctions that threaten to divide them. When the couple embraces, the economic differences that threatened to divide the nation are symbolically reconciled.

Similarly, twenty years later, comedies starring Doris Day and Rock Hudson address the concerns of a nation on the brink of a sexual revolution. In such films as *Pillow Talk* (1959) and *Lover Come Back* (1961), Day and Hudson are divided not by social class but by their attitudes toward sex and marriage. Hudson invariably plays men who approach sex as a game of seduction. Day plays self-reliant women who uphold their commitment to love and monogamy. In *Pillow Talk,* for example, Jan (Day) and Brad (Hudson) share a telephone line.[9] She needs to keep the line free so that she can take calls from her clients. He constantly has it in use, seducing women with charming lies. When Jan and Brad finally meet and fall in love, their different approaches to sexuality are resolved; she will ensure that theirs is a monogamous and productive union, while he will ensure that it is neither prudish nor stifling.

Contemporary romantic comedies, too, represent the resolution of competing ideals that have become apparent in the twenty-first century. In this case, the films are concerned with affirming hard work and individuality at a time when the workplace has become increasingly corporate. In the case of recent career-girl comedies, the woman invariably represents industriousness. She is driven to succeed in a competitive marketplace, though the values of her workplace are questioned. The man more often than not represents individuality, dictating the terms of his own existence, though in some instances he is not sufficiently aggressive. Once again, the marriage of the couple represents the integration of competing values and the resolution of seemingly irreconcilable divisions brought about by an alienating workplace, women's ambition harmonizing with men's independence and self-reliance. With surprising consistency, the women in these films work for the corporate media, which demand that they put aside their personal beliefs for the sake of "what sells." In *The Devil Wears Prada,* Andy (Anne Hathaway) briefly loses sight of loftier aspirations when she goes to work for a prominent fashion editor (Meryl Streep). In *How to Lose a Guy in 10 Days* (2003), Andie (Kate Hudson) is a columnist for a women's magazine who longs to write about more substantive things than how pick up a guy at a bar. In *Little Black Book,* Stacy (Brittany Murphy) gets a job as an Associate Producer for a reality television show. While the rest of the staff proposes episodes on the lurid topics we have come to expect from daytime reality shows ("My Grandmother's a Hooker") Stacy impulsively suggests one on literacy in inner-city schools, only to be greeted with laughter. And in *The Ugly Truth* (2009) Abby (Katherine Heigl) is forced to hire Mike (Gerard Butler) for her news show, though she finds his humor offensive.

With equal consistency, the men in these films work in professions that allow them to maintain their individuality and integrity. In *Sweet Home Alabama,* Jake (Josh Lucas) turns his fascination with the effects of lightning on sand into a business making glass. In *13 Going on 30,* Matt (Mark Ruffalo) is a photographer who may be short on cash but has kept his values intact, while *Raising Helen*'s romantic lead is Pastor Dan (John Corbett), a Lutheran minister. In *The Backup Plan* (2010), Zoe (Jennifer Lopez) falls for a man (Alex O'Loughlin) who makes artisanal cheese from the milk of goats he has raised on his farm in upstate New York. And Pete (Ed Burns), in *Life or Something Like It,* is a cameraman who left his job with the networks in New York to raise his daughter in Seattle. He insists on dictating the terms of his work rather than jumping to the station's every call and has deliberately cut back his working hours so that he can spend his afternoons browsing in bookstores rather than filming fluff pieces for the nightly news. The coupling of these characters, the driven corporate women and the independent men, represents a reconciliation of traits that are opposed in corporate life—ambition and individuality, industriousness and integrity.

The consequences of these unions go beyond the personal pursuit of happiness, however, and suggest a solution to the problems produced by a profit-driven mass culture. One of the damaging effects of mass culture, the films suggest, is the repositioning of sex not as an expression of personal identity confined to the private sphere of the monogamous home, but as a commodity that becomes a spectacle within these media. In *27 Dresses,* Jane is horrified when her status as a perennial bridesmaid becomes the subject of a widely read newspaper article. In *The Ugly Truth* Mike engages the husband-and-wife news team, Georgia (Cheryl Hines) and Larry (John Michael Higgins) in some live, on-air marriage counseling when he berates Georgia that Larry's impotence stems from the fact that she has "economically emasculated" him. In *Little Black Book,* Stacy's reality show runs episodes on topics— "Pregnant Strippers"—that mock what was once sacred. In the show's ultimate betrayal, it makes a spectacle of Stacy's own love life when she is tricked into appearing on live television with her boyfriend and three of his exes. Similarly, in *How to Lose a Guy in 10 Days,* Andie is assigned to write a column on the "don'ts" of dating. She picks up a man at a bar with the intention of driving him away within ten days. However, in order to get an important advertising account selling diamonds to women, he has made a bet that he can get a woman to fall in love with him in ten days. Thus, characters' private lives have become fodder for the mass media.

The antidote to the mass market's commodification of sex, these films suggest, is to contain sexuality within marriage. Romantic love is offered as a solution to life's problems not only because it promises to resolve the competing drives that complicate modern life, but because it is something divine and mystical, something beyond the market's ability to control or manipulate. In these films we know that love will be transcendent because fate has dictated that these couples meet and fall in love. Over and over again, we are told that the protagonists' love is something beyond the ordinary, something that is fated to be, whether it is fulfilled because of divine intervention or through the rediscovery of a childhood sweetheart.

Transcendent love is proposed as an alternative to the rabid consumerism that characterizes the marketplace, a marketplace that is gendered feminine. With surprising consistency, the women in these films are employed within the culture industry the mass audience for which is explicitly identified as feminine. *The Devil Wears Prada, How to Lose a Guy in 10 Days,* and *13 Going on 30* are set in the offices of women's magazines. Likewise, in *How to Lose a Guy,* Ben (Matthew McConaughey), an advertising executive, nearly loses an account because his boss thinks the campaign needs "a woman's touch." And in *Little Black Book,* the "Kippie Kann Do Show" reaches an audience that is ninety percent female. *The Proposal* directly attributes the decline of American culture to the feminization of the mass media. Margaret Tate (Sandra Bullock) is a powerful book editor who bullies a literary author into appearing on "Oprah." He clings to the romantic notion that a writer can remain aloof from the marketplace, but she insists that literary success—measured by book sales and a Pulitzer Prize—rests on his entering into the feminine sphere of the popular media by submitting to an interview by the *grand dame* of daytime television. Thus the problems of American corporate life are the product of a marketplace and culture industry that caters exploitatively to feminine tastes.

Suburbia, too, is a place dominated by commercialized, feminine tastes, and therefore offers little refuge to the heroines of these films. In *Raising Helen,* for example, Helen jokingly complains to her sister and brother-and-law that their home looks like a Pottery Barn catalog. If anything, the images of suburban home life in these films are dull and sexless, hardly a compelling alternative to the glamour and excitement of the cities in which these women live. Helen's sister, Jenny (Joan Cusack), may be the perfect mother, but her home is stuffed to bursting with chintz and potpourri. Worse, while she caters to everyone else's needs, no one seems to notice what lengths she has gone to in order to make them comfortable; even on Mother's Day, she cooks the celebratory dinner. By contrast, Helen uses her sister's kitchen to primp for a night out in Manhattan, looking at her reflection in the toaster as she fixes her hair and hikes up her skirt to the evident approval of her brothers-in-law. The suburbs, it appears, are a place where self-abnegating women cater to men who find other women far more exciting.

Rather than in the suburbs, these films suggest, salvation is to be found in escaping the feminizing effects of mass culture altogether. The most consistent moments of communal joy occur, tellingly, in sports arenas, at the basketball, hockey, and baseball games that the characters attend with surprising regularity. Though, of course, professional sports are every bit as commercialized as the magazines and television shows for which the women work, the games nonetheless represent a masculine ritual of communal bonding, an escape from the feminine world of mass culture that these films deride. Likewise, on the city streets, mixing with the working-class and immigrant populations that live, presumably, beyond the grasp of the culture industry, characters find a taste of the community and authenticity that are lacking in their work lives. On these bustling streets, the middle-class protagonists will briefly experience a sense of community with the gruff men who sell them their hotdogs or newspapers or the immigrant neighbors who ask after their personal lives.

Often, the modern city is a feminine space that threatens the masculinity and virility of its male inhabitants. In *The Proposal,* the antidote to matriarchal city life is to be found in the masculine realm of rural Alaska. In New York, Margaret terrorizes the people who work with her, particularly her assistant, Andrew Paxton (Ryan Reynolds). His morning begins with the humiliation of being doused with coffee in his rush to serve Margaret. The tables are turned, however, when Margaret and Andrew travel to his home in Alaska, where nearly every storefront is emblazoned with the name of his father. Here it is Margaret who is humiliated, doused with sea water and rescued from drowning by Andrew, who has recovered his masculinity. When they return to the city, Margaret may still have the higher salary, but Andrew has assumed the dominant role in their relationship. Similarly, in *The Backup Plan,* the city is the site of maternity gone awry. Zoe shares her Manhattan apartment with an inbred dog that scoots about on a wheelchair, having lost the use of its back legs due to bad breeding. By contrast, Stan's farm is inhabited by a healthy herd of goats that provide the milk necessary for his artisanal cheese. In this film, the plot complications center around the fact that Zoe has decided to have a child without the benefit of a male lover, having been artificially inseminated with the sperm of a stranger. The film suggests that such a pregnancy is far from ideal. Much is made of the fact that the unknown sperm donor has red hair and freckles and that the insemination has resulted in multiple births. The film suggests that there is something freakish about the red-headed twins to whom Zoe gives birth. Further, the unmarried mothers who populate the film are characterized as gross and atavistic. Zoe unwillingly attends the birth of a child whose lesbian mother brays like a sheep with every contraction and is surrounded by a bevy of women ritualistically thumping a tribal drum and chanting nonsense as she delivers the child in an inflatable bathtub in the living room of her apartment. The scene is characterized by chaos and scatological humor, in contrast to the orderly visits to Zoe's male obstetrician.

In *Sweet Home Alabama,* the Southern town—a perfect image of community and traditional values—offers a similar antidote to modern urban life, though this film acknowledges the difficulties women face in such an environment. While Melanie's (Reese Witherspoon) home town is hardly the film's answer to the question of what women want—her own mother is bitter that she spent her life raising children rather than pursuing her own desires and pushes Melanie to get out of town—it also offers an antidote to the superficiality of Manhattan. Melanie's first husband (Josh Lucas) assures her that, when she became pregnant in high school, though he was initially excited he eventually understood what early motherhood would have meant to her: "I thought that baby would be an adventure. And it took me a while to realize it would have been your only adventure." Nonetheless, the film suggests, the glamorous life of a successful Manhattanite is no answer, either, for Manhattan is ruled by Melanie's future mother-in-law, a domineering mayor (Candice Bergen), who is overly concerned with appearances. The film suggests that happiness lies in the marriage of North and South, of old and new. The South of *Sweet Home Alabama* is a place still living in the past. Melanie's father participates in reenactments of Civil War battles, and an eccentric neighbor recreates the war in the back yard of his own plantation home. It is a town that has rejected the cash economy symbolized by Manhattan. Years after leaving home, "Felony Melanie" is still remembered, and celebrated, for having blown up the bank as a child. If anything, though, the film is unclear about how these opposing ideals—of adventure and success vs. authenticity and community—should be resolved. In the end, Melanie returns to her childhood sweetheart rather than marry the mayor's son (Patrick Dempsey). As the closing titles run, we see what look like home movies of Melanie and her husband raising a daughter while Melanie continues to design clothes and he continues his glass-blowing business. With her drive and his individualism, they have found happiness by becoming entrepreneurs.

The modern city and feminine mass culture are no more roundly despised than in the cinematic fable *Kate and Leopold,* in which Leopold (Hugh Jackman), an impoverished duke living in nineteenth-century New York, is transported to modern-day Manhattan where he meets and falls in love with Kate (Meg Ryan), an executive at a market research firm. The film opens at a ceremony to celebrate the building of the Brooklyn Bridge in 1876. Like other achievements of the nineteenth century—electricity, movies, automobiles, and elevators—this is the product of human creativity and vision, a tribute to the industriousness and ingenuity that helped to produce modern life. The masculinity of such endeavors is emphasized in the speech at the dedication ceremony, in which the bridge's designer boasts,

"As the pyramids testify to the Egyptians, so my glorious erection shall represent our culture in perpetuity. Behold, rising before you the greatest erection on the continent. The greatest erection of the age! The greatest erection on the planet!" Only a visitor from the present finds this turn of phrase amusing.

If the nineteenth century that is so idealized in the film is characterized by the ingenuity of masculine scientific pursuits, modern-day Manhattan is demonized as a culture that caters to the banal tastes of a feminine mass market. When he arrives in the present, Leopold marvels at the nineteenth-century inventions that have come to fruition in the twenty-first century, but he bemoans the inauthenticity of this new world. Food is no longer one of life's pleasures to be savored, but a tasteless mass pulled from the freezer and popped into a microwave. Leopold is hired to be the spokesperson in a margarine advertisement because women find him handsome and sexy. Such tastes are demonstrated to be single-handedly responsible for the sorry state of American culture. Worse, Kate's work in market research has contributed to a loss of integrity and inventiveness in American business. The duped mass audience buys products that advertisers sell to them, rather than the products that meet their needs. When Leopold tastes the margarine that he has been hired to endorse, he walks out of the taping rather than promulgate a lie and claim it is delicious. And when Kate uses her market research to force a film director to re-edit his film, the director bitterly complains that "you people are sucking the life out of America."

In this film, the problem is resolved when Kate returns to nineteenth-century New York to join Leopold in his home epoch. The film suggests that a return to old-fashioned values, including sexual decorum and courtship, are needed. More importantly, however, it suggests a return to a golden and more innocent world in which the mass media—radio, television, magazines—that are designed to shape audiences' desires had not yet completely infiltrated American life.

In the end, these films suggest that the discontents felt by women won't be cured by feminism alone. Betty Friedan and the feminists of her generation showed us that domesticity would not bring meaning and pleasure to all women's lives. But these films show women today coming up equally empty when they pin their happiness to corporate careers. This is a discovery that professional men made half a century ago, when the image of "the man in the grey flannel suit" conjured thoughts of rigid conformity and rabid competition. At that time, women were widely held responsible for men's problems; women's competitive drive to "keep up with the Joneses" kept men tethered to emasculating jobs. The solution proposed by men like Hugh Hefner, whose *Playboy* magazine was created in answer to these problems, was to avoid marriage altogether.[10] Now, these films suggest, women are being held responsible for the effects of both consumerism and the profit-driven marketplace. And the solution proposed by romantic comedy is to contain women's drives by tethering them to men. These films address very real problems that plague a nation of men and women who must work increasing hours for decreasing compensation in an economy that has become overwhelmingly dominated by corporate business. However, rather than suggest that these problems might be solved by changes to the corporate economy, these films assure audiences that happiness is to be found in the pursuit of love.

Notes

[1] Maureen Dowd, "What's a Modern Girl to Do?" *New York Times Magazine* (October 20, 2005), 52.

[2] Dowd, 53.

[3] Dowd, 54.

[4] Betty Friedan, *The Feminine Mystique* (New York: Dell, 1964).

[5] *Time* (April 15, 2002).

[6] Nancy Gibbs, "Making Time for Baby," *Time* (April 15, 2002).

[7] Garance Franke-Ruta, "Creating a Lie: Sylvia Ann Hewlett and the Myth of the Baby Bust," *The American Prospect* (July 1, 2002), 30.

[8] Thomas Schatz, *Hollywood Genres: Formulas, Filmmaking, and the Studio System* (New York: McGraw-Hill, 1981), 155.

[9] From the earliest days of telephone service through the 1950s in some communities, telephone service was available on what was called a "party line," an arrangement where a number of subscribers would share a telephone number; party line etiquette became necessary, and the comedy of *Pillow Talk* is in part based on infractions of it.

[10] Barbara Ehrenreich, *The Hearts of Men: American Dreams and the Flight from Commitment* (New York: Anchor Books, 1983).

Chapter 8

This Is for Fighting, This Is for Fun

Camerawork and Gunplay in Reality-Based Crime Shows

Fred Turner

Several years ago, I interviewed a Vietnam veteran named Brian Winhover. He had survived three tours of combat duty, but when he tried to tell me how he felt when he was under fire, it took him a while to find the words. Eventually he said, "[you could] call me a piece of ice. . . . You couldn't impregnate me with anything."[1] At first I was taken aback—I hadn't expected a word like "impregnate" to crop up in a war story—but the more we talked, the clearer the psychology of his combat experience became. Winhover had lived out all the confusions embedded in the ubiquitous boot camp chant, "This is my rifle, this [penis] is my gun. One is for killing, one is for fun."[2] Killing could be sex, the chant implied, and sex of a very particular kind. For Winhover, as for generations of soldiers before and since, to be a man, to belong to the unit, was to penetrate; to fail at those tasks, to be an enemy to the unit, was to be penetrated like a woman or a homosexual "bottom." The battlefield was a site of sexualized conflict, one at which it was Winhover's duty to assert his difference from the enemy by proving it "feminine." This Winhover did with aplomb: by his own description, he became a mechanical, rifle-like creature in Vietnam, hard and numb. He dedicated his days in the field to killing, to trying to penetrate the bodies of enemy soldiers, to trying to "impregnate" the enemy with his weapon. In short, he became the perfect soldier.

Winhover came home in 1969, yet the psychosexual dynamics that characterized his combat experiences remain very much alive. In fact, they are a defining feature of the now ten-year-old American television genre of "reality-based" crime programs. In these highly popular and resilient shows, viewers encounter a world much like the one Winhover saw in Vietnam, a world in which heavily armed, uniformed men move among impoverished civilians, trying to sort guerrilla-like criminals from the population. They also encounter the psychosexual economy of that realm. In boot camp, Winhover's drill sergeants trained him to confuse his penis and his rifle and thus to take a physical pleasure in being a soldier. In the far less coercive world of television, and toward a similar end, reality-based crime programs urge viewers to confuse the guns of the police with the cameras through which they see events. Just as military training has long sought to break down the psychic barriers between killing and sex in the minds of its soldiers, so the visual styles of these programs work to intermingle the processes of seeing and shooting, of knowing and arresting, and of consuming goods and upholding the law. As the producers of reality-based crime programming acknowledge, these shows aim not to be watched, but to be experienced.[3] With the full support and cooperation of the police themselves, the cameramen of reality-based crime programs invite viewers—both male and female—to feel the highly sexualized, hyper-masculine power of the state within their sedentary bodies.[4]

They extend this invitation by carefully equating their own cameras with the guns of the policemen and bounty hunters the cameras depict. After watching ten episodes of each of four of the most popular reality-based crime shows in the United States—"Cops" (1989), "Bounty Hunters" (1996), "America's Most Wanted" (1988), and "LAPD: Life on the Beat" (1995)—I've noticed that guns most frequently appear onscreen in three contexts: as weapons aimed at suspects, as holstered emblems of police authority, and, in advertising trailers especially, as explicit echoes of the cinematic six-shooter. These three incarnations correspond to three televisual devices common to the real-life crime genre: hand-held camera work, computer graphics, and intertextuality. Like aimed pistols, hand-held video cameras grant the viewer a policeman's power to pursue and arrest the suspect, albeit visually. Like holstered weapons, computer graphics make visible an omnipresent power—in this case, the power of TV producers, cooperating state authorities, and the viewer to embed potentially disruptive criminal activity in a body of knowledge. Finally, as symbols manipulated by TV producers, guns link the local realm of the arrest scene to the mythology of the American frontier. In these ways, guns and cameras work together to transform real-life crime programs into a sort of visual boot camp for the TV audience, one in which viewers are subtly coerced into taking pleasure in the feminization and domination of the poor and of people of color by a well-armed, fun-craving masculinized state.

The link between cameras and guns naturally precedes the advent of real-life crime programming (consider the phrase "shooting a movie"), just as the link between weapons and penises preceded the Vietnam War. Yet, in the four programs I will focus on, producers put extraordinary effort into maintaining and naturalizing the gun-camera analogy.

This is true despite the fact that each show features its own unique aesthetics. "Cops" and "Bounty Hunters," for instance, offer seemingly raw (though in fact heavily edited) video-verité accounts of pursuit and capture. Each half-hour episode of "Cops" follows the exploits of police in a single American city, and includes between three and five sequences of police officers in action.[5] These are preceded by a video-montage title sequence which depicts some of the most dramatic moments from footage already gathered in that city, accompanied by the show's now-infamous reggae theme song ("Bad boys, bad boys— What'cha gonna do when they come for you?"). Each action sequence opens with a shot of the policeman centrally involved—a shot in which the officer frequently describes his motives for joining the force—and proceeds to show him responding to a radio call.[6] It then depicts the officer pursuing and usually capturing a suspect and concludes with that officer or one of his colleagues commenting laconically on the events that have just unfolded. "Bounty Hunters" follows a similar pattern. Each half-hour episode focuses on the work of one or two teams of bail enforcement agents and includes two to four sequences in which they discuss how to find and capture a particular bail jumper, pursue that person, arrest him, and bring him to jail.[7]

"LAPD" and "America's Most Wanted" feature a more varied menu of police activities and a correspondingly wider range of televisual devices. As its name suggests, "LAPD" attends exclusively to the activities of the Los Angeles Police Department. In addition to depicting pursuits and arrests, this half-hour show focuses considerable attention on the gathering of evidence. It also often has detectives recount the circumstances of unsolved crimes and ask the viewer for leads. At the end of many episodes, Los Angeles Mayor Richard Riordan appears on screen to encourage those with an interest in law enforcement to sign up for the force.

"America's Most Wanted" similarly encourages viewer participation. Hosted by John Walsh, an actor whose son Adam was murdered, the program's hour-long episodes tend to eschew capture sequences in order to introduce an average of three to five unsolved crimes or missing criminals, sometimes through re-enactments, and then ask viewers to assist in bringing the "bad guys" to justice. If they should spot one of these fugitives among their neighbors or can offer other leads, viewers are instructed to call "1-800-CRIMETV." Periodically, the program's producers present updates in which they show viewers how their calls have led to the arrest of fugitives from previous episodes.

With the exception of "America's Most Wanted," then, each of these programs regularly features several sequences in which law enforcement officials pursue and capture suspects. These pursuits normally culminate in an arrest vignette. In one common form, this vignette depicts a group of policemen or bounty hunters bursting into a house, guns drawn, tackling an often half-naked suspect, and throwing him to the ground. In another form, it consists of a group of officers pointing their pistols at a suspect some feet away, forcing him or her to lie on the ground, face down, and then creeping closer until they loom over the suspect's prone figure. In a third, the arrest vignette features officers fingering their weapons while forcing a suspect to bend forward over the hood of a police cruiser, legs spread in preparation for an imminent frisking (itself often depicted as well).

Monotonously styled and frequently repeated, these vignettes are the equivalents of the "money shot" or "cum shot" in a porn movie: they are moments at which the full masculine potency of the leading character is revealed. These moments differ slightly from their pornographic equivalents, though, in the forms of pleasure they offer. In the conventional, heterosexual cum shot, the camera closes in strategically on the hard body and erect penis of the male performer. It thus offers the viewer at least two possible pleasures: of watching a powerful male control a female and of imagining himself as that male. The cameras of reality-based crime shows, on the other hand, go several steps further in enforcing an identification between the viewer and the protagonist (in this case, a police officer). Repeatedly, cameramen seek out not just the point of view of the officers, but points of view suggested by their weapons. In police cars on the way to crime scenes, camera operators record the dashboard and radio from the waist-level vantage point of a gun belt. At the moment of capture, they point their lenses down at prone suspects like pistols. When those lenses zoom in on key parts of a suspect's body—a pocket, a scarred chest, and, especially often, the buttocks (a place where a weapon or drugs might be hidden and where the suspect might be penetrated sexually)—they draw the viewer toward the suspect along the trajectory of an imaginary bullet. Unlike their counterparts in heterosexual pornography, the cameramen of reality-based crime shows will not simply let their viewers watch. Rather, by conflating camera and pistol, they demand that the viewer personally experience the power of penetration embodied in the weapons of the officers of the state.[8]

This power is highly sexualized, but only in a limited sense. As in much heterosexual pornography, the twinned phallic weapons of camera and gun are used here in order to humiliate and subjugate rather than excite a feminized Other. The pleasure on offer is not a fantasy of congress, but a fantasy of control. And what needs to be controlled is the sexualized agency of the "enemy"—in this case, the poor and people of color. Sometimes, this agency is represented by a weapon, or at least the possibility of one. Virtually every arrest vignette features a police pat-down of a suspect for knives and guns, a search conducted as though the almost-always impoverished suspect could actually have the same access to weapons that the police themselves have. In this way, reality-based crime shows imply that the agency of the "enemy" may be masculine—that is, that it may be able to "penetrate" the bodies of the police on the screen (and by implication, of police and viewers in the off-screen world as well).

More often though (and sometimes simultaneously), these programs suggest that the agency of suspects and their friends and families is symbolically female. When police arrive at a crime scene, cameras quickly record any signs of difference between the police and the citizenry. They peer over the uniformed shoulders of the police and zoom in on unkempt hair, scars and bruises, and tattoos. Likewise, when cameramen follow officers into a home, they focus on disorder, on piles of dishes, unwashed children, unmade beds. In contrast to the officers—who stand erect and uniformed, their bodies often hard with muscles or body armor—the suspects are depicted as unruly, messy, corpulent and disorderly. They are "soft" where the officers are "hard." Often upset, they appear "hysterical" where the officers appear commanding and "rational." In these ways, producers imply that the poor are not only undisciplined individuals, but stereotypically feminine as well. Producers here do much the same psychological work as Army drill sergeants: faced with the symbolically masculine potential of those whom they've defined as antagonists to assault policemen and viewer alike, to "penetrate" them so to speak, they assist viewers in labelling these antagonists not as "men," but as "women" who must themselves be symbolically penetrated by the forces of the state. Like Army recruits, viewers are invited to join the masculine community of these forces and to take pleasure in the domination of a feminized enemy.

That feminized enemy, however, constantly threatens to devour its masculine counterpart. Even weaponless, the poor are dangerous: in episode after episode, the sexualized entropy of their lives threatens to overwhelm the orderly police. And while this is true for all such suspects, it is especially so for people of color. In keeping with centuries-old American stereotypes, both male and female African Americans are often depicted as having uncontrollable libidos. In an episode of "Cops" set in Kansas City, Kansas, for instance, several white officers pull up to a disturbance in the middle of the night. At the edges of the light cast by the camera team, we can see black figures running here and there, like escaped slaves in some 19th-century plantation owner's nightmare. Then, a large African American woman rushes to the center of the frame, wielding a pipe. She points out a young black man and accuses him of lifting up her teenage daughter's shirt in front of her. The policemen chase, tackle and arrest the young man, who is clearly intoxicated. Later, a policeman explains: "A lot of the people we deal with out here are on what we call 'water'—that's marijuana dipped in formaldehyde. That gentleman obviously was, trying to have sex with a young girl in front of the child's mother. Now it's time to do a lot of paperwork and move on to the next one."[9] The implied alignment of forces is clear: young black men run wild in the streets looking for sex; young white men work to preserve a chaste world of order and reason. White men work with their minds on "paperwork," whereas young black men are out of their minds on "water."

This episode of "Cops" presents a fairly extreme example, but the principles at work within it run throughout reality-based crime programming. By depicting the poor and people of color as symbolically female, producers of real-life crime programs remind viewers of the pleasures of aligning themselves with a dominant and symbolically male state. Nor are these pleasures merely intellectual: when producers force viewers to look down (and sometimes, seemingly, out of) the barrels of police guns, they invite viewers to feel those weapons as extensions of their own bodies.

Alongside this form of camerawork, however, these programs also feature an abundance of computer-generated graphics. At the outset of each arrest sequence on LAPD, for instance, an icon appears on the screen, looking much as it might in a Windows computer interface, giving the title of the segment. Subsequent icons introduce the officers involved, describe the type of crime under consideration, and even present a map of the area the officers routinely patrol. "America's Most Wanted" regularly features a graphic drawing of a target zone into which the images of criminals are drawn as if dragged and clicked by a mouse across a screen. It also presents surveillance photographs from stores and banks, photographs which producers manipulate on screen as if they were digitized images on a home computer. Even the comparatively low-tech "Cops" and "Bounty Hunters" present onscreen tags at the start of each segment identifying the time, city, crime at hand, and officer in pursuit.

On one hand, these graphics are the products of a larger change in television style. As television critic John Caldwell has noted, the 1980s saw a shift across the medium "from programs based on rhetorical discourse to ones structured around the concepts of pictorial and stylistic embellishment."[10] Having come into being at the end of the decade, the reality-based crime genre reflects this shift. On the other hand, however, I think we can read the uses of computer graphics as an extension of an already-established conflation of gun, camera and masculine agency. In much the way that holstered pistols signal an omnipresent power to contain a given situation, so too do computer graphics seem to surround and neutralize dangerous individuals without necessarily assaulting them directly. When the computer does assault a suspect, it acts as a pistol might: by tearing apart the body. With the click of an off-screen mouse, producers reduce people to mug shots; that is, they eliminate their bodies and surround the faces that remain with statistics and icons. They take all that is dangerous and original in the criminal and embed it in the seemingly safe, rational world of information. In other words, they dam the flow of "water" with "paperwork."[11]

Computer graphics thus extend the camera/gun analogy in two ways: first, by fragmenting the bodies of suspects, they recall the pistol's ability to violate the boundaries of a human body; secondly, by surrounding the suspect with information, they suggest the power of the police to surround and arrest any individual—a power assured on the scene by weapons. These same visual techniques also work to normalize police activities by linking them to other, seemingly unrelated practices. Drag-and-click graphics, for instance, suggest a link between the pursuit of criminals on television and the pursuit of information on home computers. The penetrating style of camerawork that offers viewers a chance to look through the eyes of a weapon echoes the point of view available in many video and computer games and in broadcast news accounts of contemporary military actions (most notably the Gulf War of 1991, in which Americans delighted in being able to see through the eyes of "smart" bombs).

Extensive use of statistics and of overhead helicopter shots even suggests a resemblance between the televised monitoring of crime and the televised monitoring of sports such as baseball. This is not to say that viewers confuse crime, war and baseball in any conscious sense, but rather to note that to the extent that real-life crime programs share a visual style with other activities, they may also be able to borrow the perceived legitimacy of those activities. That is, to the extent that the viewer watches war or crime on TV as he watches baseball—from high above, from the heights reserved for the owners of luxury boxes, or, in the case of war, from the aerial vantage points usually reserved for government authorities—he may well be inclined to feel that war and the pursuit of criminals are naturally right and rule-bound in the manner of a sport.

Nor are such linkages confined to the predominantly masculine domains of the battlefield, the baseball diamond, or the video game. Real-life crime programs are shown in a highly commercial context and for the purpose of selling ad time, and in many ways, the structure of pursuit and arrest—a structure controlled in the material field through the use of weapons and in the televisual field through the use of cameras and computer graphics—mirrors that of the pursuit and acquisition of consumer goods. With each new crime, the viewer joins the police or the bounty hunters in a process of revealing a need to make an acquisition (in this case, of a suspect), of identifying the target for acquisition, of capturing that target, and finally, of taking that target "home" to jail. In real-life crime programming, the sexualized landscape of crime and its containment soon overlaps the commercial landscape of desire and its satisfaction, and producers know this.

To take one particularly glaring example, the Sam Adams Brewing Company advertises its beer (in California, at least) on "Bounty Hunters." Their ad features a man drinking a beer who sees another man steal a woman's purse. The beer drinker flicks a bottle cap at the suspect's head and knocks him out cold, thus saving the day—and thus suggesting that the buying of beer and the capturing of suspects might each represent the exercise of a masculine agency.

That agency does not belong to the viewer alone, however, nor even to the law enforcement officials on the TV screen; it belongs to the American nation. In the same way that boot camp taught Brian Winhover not only to be a killer, but to be an American soldier, reality-based crime programs teach their viewers to feel not only the power of individual men within themselves, but the masculine power of the state itself. They do this by referring constantly to the Old West of American myth. The opening of "Bounty Hunters," for instance, features four men wearing black vests or long range coats with silver badges on their chests. Scruffy, macho, they carry pistols and a rifle. "When the West was won," explains the voiceover, "bounty hunters helped to create law and order. In 1873, federal law gave them the power to enter residences and cross state lines in pursuit of bail jumpers. Today, modern bounty hunters continue to use that power to return fugitives to justice. Their motto: You can run, but you can't hide."

With such references, the America of today, like the Vietnam of yesterday and the Wild West before it, becomes a landscape in which to act out a national drama of justice. In this landscape, the gun symbolizes the link between past and present, and with it the link between the righteousness of American laws and the masculinity of their enforcers. By means of its conflation with the camera, the gun offers viewers a chance to walk alongside the bounty hunters, to undertake a mission on behalf of the nation, a mission to penetrate the dank, dark regions of American society, to "see" the suspect there, to "know" his crimes and thereby to humiliate him. In the slums of the twentieth century, as on the prairies of the nineteenth, those whom the government has identified as wanton and uncivilized "can run, but they can't hide."

But why should Americans and Canadians want to "see" criminals in the first place? And how is it that enough Americans and Canadians want to watch these shows that they should appear, in first-run and serialized episodes, twice a day, every day of the week, in a number of major North American media markets?

In part, the answer is economic: reality-based crime programs typically cost between $150,000 and $250,000 per episode to produce, while a typical news magazine program might cost between $250,000 and $400,000.[12] Primetime dramas and action adventure programs usually run between $900,000 and $1 million per episode.[13] Thus, even before they take the often substantial revenues from syndication into account, producers know that they need not attract either huge audiences or high-budget advertisements to turn a profit. Moreover, because viewers often perceive these shows as resembling news, producers see them as effective programs with which to lead into and out of the local evening news or with which to counter-program against other genres, such as sitcoms.[14]

Yet, I think these shows remain popular for more historical reasons as well. The first reality-based crime programs, "America's Most Wanted" and "Cops," emerged in 1988 and 1989 respectively. These years fall toward the end of a nearly decade-long period in which first the Reagan administration and then the Bush administration sought to marginalize the poor and people of color. Under Reagan, this process took the form of cuts in aid to the poor, including $6.8 billion from the food stamp budget and $5.2 billion from child nutritional services between 1981 and 1987.[15] During the Bush administration, this process gained particular momentum as part of the "War on Drugs"—a war started under Reagan. In 1989, for instance, drug czar William Bennett implemented the National Drug Control Strategy. Even as it acknowledged that "the typical cocaine user is white, male, a high school graduate employed full time and living in a small metropolitan area or suburb," the Bennett plan devoted some 70% of its resources to law enforcement and focused most of its attention on the inner cities—areas inhabited predominantly by people of color and areas in which full-time employment outside the drug trade can often be hard to find.[16] As Michael Omi and Howard Winant have pointed out, these policies have been accompanied by "a regressive redistribution of income and a decline in real wages [across the country], a significant shift to the ideological right in terms of public discourse, and an increase in the use of coercion on the part of the state."[17] This broader process in turn, they argue, has resulted in the creation of an impoverished, disproportionately dark-skinned Third World inside the United States.

In that sense, then, reality-based crime shows represent the propaganda arm of a multi-tiered American state. Produced with the active assistance of local police departments (and at times national forces such as the F.B.I.), they serve as an ideological reservoir from which politicians and citizens alike can draw justifications of oppressive actions. This is particularly true of "LAPD: Life on the Beat," a program first aired in 1995, two years after the Los Angeles Riots. As historian Mike Davis has pointed out, the Los Angeles Police Department considered South Central Los Angeles an internal Vietnam throughout the late 1980s. It thought of African American housing projects as "strategic hamlets" and regularly launched "search-and-destroy" missions in the area.[18] The 1992 riots exposed this process on live television. It should be no surprise, then, that the Los Angeles Police Department was eager to join MGM Television in producing a new series about its activities. As Chief of Police Willie L. Williams told a reporter in 1994, "For some time, the Los Angeles Police Department has been searching for a forum that would allow the public to see firsthand the dedication and selfless efforts of the men and women of the L.A.P.D. as they go about serving our community. The reality-based television series L.A.P.D. is a window through which the viewer will be able to see the truth of department activities."[19]

Yet despite their obvious propaganda function, we must be careful not to read reality-based crime programs only in the light of the services they provide to the state or to the television industry. We need to acknowledge the ways in which these programs deliberately confuse and intermingle several struggles, including the struggle of the state to justify its policies, the struggle of men and women at times to affirm and at times to tear down systems of racial and sexual distinction, and the struggle of people throughout our society to manage their economic and social anxieties.

We should also continue to examine the ways in which visual technologies and styles translate these sometimes abstract struggles into felt experiences of the body. As Kevin Robins and Les Levidow have written, "War converts fear and anxiety into perceptions of external threat; it then mobilizes defenses against alien and thing-like enemies. In this process, new image and vision technologies can play a central role."[20] Over the last two decades, the American government has fought a low-intensity war on the poor. For generations, American society has been plagued by persistent conflicts over racial and gender boundaries. By equating guns and cameras and by sexualizing the work of each, reality-based crime shows not only define the poor and people of color as external threats to their viewers, but engage viewers in a process of defining the poor and people of color as alien and thing-like. As in the military, the "good guys" are "men like us," men who take pleasure in being well-equipped, so to speak, and "hard." The "bad guys" are (symbolically) women or perhaps homosexual males, creatures who deserve to be penetrated and who indeed must be penetrated if their threat to the heterosexual male social order is to be contained. In the world of reality-based crime programs, as formerly on the battlefields of Southeast Asia, to be a good American is to be impregnable.

* * *

March 15, 2006

I wish I could say that in the years since this essay first appeared, the phenomena it examines have faded from view. But they haven't. Two of the four shows the piece analyzes— "LAPD: Life on the Beat" and "Bounty Hunters"—ran for three seasons each before going off the air. But "Cops" and "America's Most Wanted" are still going strong. Both shows are still producing new material and in the case of "Cops", the actual episodes I analyzed can still be seen, cycling through reruns, on almost any weeknight. Over the last few years, a number of new reality-based crime programs have also appeared, largely drawing on the formulae established in the early 1990s. Fans of the old "Bounty Hunters," for example, can now check out "Dog: The Bounty Hunter" (2004-present), which tracks the exploits of a husband-and-wife-and-friends bounty hunting company, as well as numerous offerings from the Court TV network.

At the same time, thanks to the rise of digital media, both reality-based crime programs and the psychosexual economy they encode have migrated across media platforms and across social worlds. Today, for instance, you can not only watch "Cops"; you can visit the "Cops" website and play a computer game called "Air Pursuit" in which you control your own helicopter as it spotlights perps on the ground below (http://www.tvcops.com). You can practice fusing seeing and shooting in any number of first-person shooter computer games, as well as in an online recruiting game sponsored by the American military called "America's Army" (http://www.americasarmy.com/).

Perhaps most frightening, at least for citizens of the United States, the visual styles of reality-based crime shows have become staple resources for what George W. Bush calls "The War on Terror." As America launched its assault on Baghdad in the spring of 2003, television reporters and producers were embedded with American troops in much the way their counterparts at "Cops" had been embedded with local police forces. And like them, they offered viewers the chance to fuse the power to see with the power to control a feminized enemy. Rolling out with mechanized units, looking down from rooftops on scurrying Iraqi troops, American cameramen once again aligned their lenses with the guns of America's state security forces. Since the invasion of Iraq, camerawork and computer graphics have played a role in the "War on Terror" much like the one they used to play in the "War on Drugs." Once again, they have translated the powers of the state into the pleasures of the text and provided Americans with an affective ideological reservoir with which to justify enmity.

Notes

[1] Fred Turner, Echoes of Combat: The Vietnam War In American Memory (New York: Anchor Books, 1996), 76. Brian Winhover is a pseudonym for a veteran who requested anonymity.

[2] Ibid.

[3] As John Langley, co-creator of "Cops", puts it, "What we try to do is capture the experience of being a cop. We put the viewers as close to being a cop as possible, to let them experience what a cop experiences. My ideal segment would have no cuts. We have very few cuts as it is. We try to be as pure as possible and take viewers through the experience from beginning to end." (Quoted in Cynthia Littleton, "True Blue: John Langley helped set the tone for the reality genre with 'Cops'," Broadcasting & Cable [May 20, 1996], 26).

[4] Ratings have consistently shown that men and women watch reality-based crime programs in similar numbers. For example, a summary of the February, 1997 Nielsen ratings for *"LAPD: Life on the Beat"* broadcast on KUSI, San Diego, California, shows that in the Monday–Friday 5:30–6:00 pm time slot, an average of 9,000 females and 15,000 males between the ages of 25 and 54 watched the show. Another local station, KNSD, reports similar figures for February, 1996: an average of 7,000 females and 9,000 males watched the show when it was broadcast Monday through Friday from 3:00 to 3:30 pm (Source: Tapscan, Inc.). The broad appeal of these programs is widely recognized by both producers and advertisers. As Cynthia Littleton has noted, the "broad-based demographics" of these shows have made them very popular with merchants selling such staples as frozen foods (Cynthia Littleton, "Reality Television: Keeping the heat on," Broadcasting & Cable [May 20, 1996], 25). For a discussion of the economics of reality-based crime programs, see "Special Report: Reality's Widening Role in the Real World of TV," Broadcasting & Cable (April 12, 1993), 24–38.

[5] With one glaring exception: In 1989, "Cops" broadcast a one-hour special on Russian police.

[6] And it is almost always a "him"—female police officers appear rarely in these programs.

[7] Bail jumpers do include women of course, but on *"Bounty Hunters"*, males outnumber females approximately 2 to 1.

[8] We need to note that the stimulation on offer brings violence and power together in a highly structured way: the viewer is never allowed to see through the "enemy's" weapons and is never allowed to look back at the officers at work. Much as boot camp limits the range of relationships open to a new recruit, and thus makes it easier and more pleasurable for him to give himself over to membership in the platoon, so the camerawork in these shows limits the range of identifications open to the viewer and makes it easier for him to enjoy an imaginary allegiance with the police.

In this respect, the camera style of reality-based crime television differs from that used most often in television news reporting. While reality-based crime shows work hard to position the viewer within the onscreen action, television news accounts tend to present that action in ways that allow the viewer to retain a greater emotional distance from the events depicted. Even in the network reporting of the deeply disturbing shootings in Littleton, Colorado, Atlanta, Georgia, and Forth Worth, Texas, which filled television screens during the spring, summer, and autumn of 1999, news teams' camerawork rarely allowed viewers to approach the events from the point of view of an individual policeman. Cameras circled overhead in helicopters and moved in close among mourners, but in each case, the techniques of news reporting urged viewers to remain voyeurs. They brought viewers close to the action, but never structured the viewer's point of view in such a way as to demand that he or she see events through the eyes of a participant onscreen.

[9] "Cops", Kansas City, KS; Broadcast XETV, Ch.6, January 17, 1998.

[10] John Caldwell, Televisuality: Style, Crisis, And Authority in American Television (New Brunswick, NJ: Rutgers University Press, 1995), 233.

[11] I'm drawing here on concepts outlined by Klaus Theweleit in Male Fantasies, Volume 1: Women, Floods, Bodies, History (Minneapolis, MN: University of Minnesota Press, 1987). For the Freikorps soldiers Theweleit studied, as I believe for the policemen here,

the labeling of an enemy as feminine and the generation of masculinized response to that enemy occur simultaneously. One metaphor which participants have used to describe this process, Theweleit notes, is one of damming a flood.

12 Mike Freeman, "The economics of first-run reality," Broadcasting & Cable (April 12, 1993), 35.

13 Caldwell, Televisuality, 289.

14 According to Greg Meidel, president of syndication for Twentieth Television, "All our research says that viewers closely identify "Cops" content with that of similar sorts of law enforcement coverage on newscasts locally. That's why ["Cops"] has been so compatible as a lead-in or lead-out from local news programming. It looks, feels and tastes like a first-run news program." (Quoted in Mike Freeman, "Ratings are reality for off-net," Broadcasting & Cable [April 12, 1993], 32.) For a lengthy discussion of reality-based crime shows and programming tactics, see Cynthia Littleton, "Reality matures into 'utility' player," Broadcasting & Cable (May 20, 1996).

15 Michael Z. Letwin, "Report from the Front Line—The Bennett Plan: Street-Level Drug Enforcement in New York City and the Legalization Debate," Hofstra Law Review, Vol. 18, No. 4 (Spring), 810; cited in Robin Andersen, Consumer Culture and TV Programming (Boulder, CO: Westview Press, 1995), 184.

16 Office of National Drug Control Policy 1989, 4; Quoted in Andersen, Consumer Culture, 182.

17 Michael Omi and Howard Winant, "The L.A. Race Riot and U.S. Politics" in Robert Gooding-Williams, ed., Reading Rodney King/Reading Urban Uprising (New York and London: Routledge, 1993), 108.

18 Mike Davis, City of Quartz (New York: Vintage, 1990), 268 and 244; Quoted in Caldwell, Televisuality, 311.

19 Quoted in David Tobenkin, "MGM Television follows 'LAPD' into syndication," Broadcasting & Cable (August 19, 1994), 20.

20 Kevin Robins and Les Levidow, "Soldier, Cyborg, Citizen," in James Brook and Iain A. Boal, eds., Resisting The Virtual Life: The Culture and Politics of Information (San Francisco: City Lights Books, 1995), 106.

Chapter 9

The Completely Accessible Star Persona of Mr. Keanu Reeves

Michael DeAngelis

Keanu Reeves has had a devoted following of gay male fans throughout his career, and media speculations on the star's own sexual orientation began with his portrayal of a homosexual character in the play *Wolfboy* in Toronto in 1984, two years before he became a film actor.[1] His role of a male hustler, Scott, who fields the sexual desire of River Phoenix's Mike in the 1991 film *My Own Private Idaho* only fueled public inquiries into the "truth" of the star's sexuality. After 1994, with Keanu's rise to superstar status in *Speed*, speculations on his sexuality became more strategic as a result of simultaneous cultural and industrial developments. The widespread success of the film *Philadelphia*, also released in 1994, and of *In and Out* three years later, ushered in an era of increased visibility of gay representations and themes in mainstream cinema. These changes in the production of images are linked to a proliferation of new reception strategies: with statistics indicating that homosexuals have higher levels of discretionary income, gays now constitute a targetable market sector from the perspectives of the film and advertising industries. In the past several years, new diversities of sexual orientation have been constructed, documented, and classified by the popular press, culminating in a series of articles in mainstream magazines in the summer of 1995, confirming the presence of a "New Bisexuality" in contemporary culture—a phenomenon which, not incidentally, opens up a new field of possibilities in the realm of target marketing.[2]

If, as a result of these developments, there has been much greater interest in maintaining an image of the star persona that is accessible to multiple audience sectors across the lines of gender and sexuality, we can find a fascinating example of how such an image might be constructed by examining the case of Keanu Reeves. We can trace an interconnection of many of the media texts which Richard Dyer identifies as integral to the construction of the star image[3]—publicity materials, interviews, commentary and criticism, and character types and narrative—in order to see how the star image retains its heterosexual appeal while also becoming susceptible to queer readings. Facilitated in this process are gay male fantasy positions that depend upon the spectator's affective engagement. As I will demonstrate, this accessibility to both heterosexual and homosexual fans is enabled by the strategic use of discursive ambiguities which promote the stars' non-exclusivity and receptivity, and by the construction of a star image worthy of his audience's trust.

Fantasy operates as a structure that permits the spectator to introject him or herself as a participant in scenarios of desire. According to Elizabeth Cowie, pleasure in fantasy is derived not from the ultimate attainment of a desired object, but from the process itself of sustaining desire. As such, fantasy involves a "happening and continuing to happen," elicited through a series of stagings which enable the subject's continued participation.[4] Intersupportive yet ambiguous star texts can be seen as highly conducive to fantasy engagement: such texts afford pleasure not only by permitting spectators to fill in the gaps according to their desires, but also by promoting the work of staging and overcoming obstacles to fulfillment, which Cowie describes as "the making visible, present, of what isn't there, of what can never *directly* be seen" (emphasis hers).[5] Thus, in gay male fantasy relations between spectators and stars, the pleasure lies not in the prospect of a moment of closure when the star's sexual orientation will ultimately be known or verified, but in the negotiation of obstacles to the construction of a coherent and ideal fantasy figure.

Henry Jenkins stresses the importance of this notion of the obstacle in fantasy in his analysis of the Slash phenomenon.[6] Jenkins argues that the establishment of a "homosocial-homosexual continuum" poses the greatest challenge for Slash writers; at the same time, it offers the greatest pleasure because it dramatizes a crisis of a "traditional masculinity" in which intimacy between men is not socially tolerated.[7] In the star/spectator relations I examine here, the obstacle retains its potential for sustaining pleasure in fantasy only as long as the star earns and maintains the spectator's trust, and agrees not to disrupt the network of ambiguity that has been constructed within the star texts.

Although the publicity discourses surrounding the figure of Keanu Reeves have often overtly emphasized his sexual appeal to women, the star's heterosexuality or heterosexual appeal is not constructed as exclusive, and the star is promoted as universally accessible. Reeves's persona is especially wrought with ambiguities: a writer for *The Independent* describes Keanu's "hyper-modern unisex quality. Reeves is, well, evolved. In interview he talks with an open-spirited, complex positivity that could easily come from either gender."[8] Other articles promotes Reeves's passivity, and in attempting to explain his appeal, *Speed* director Jan de Bont remarks that "He's young, he has a vulnerable quality—open, romantic."[9]

Popular press constructions of the Keanu's universal sex appeal are often enhanced through locative ambiguities, in an effort to construct the "pan-accessibility" of the star. Keanu has no determinate place: he does not comfortably or conveniently "fit in" with mainstream culture on the basis of national, ethnic, racial, or indeed domestic ties and allegiances. Keanu has no place to call home: he crashes occasionally as his sister's, but for the most part he lives in hotels. Several articles emphasize his multi-ethnic heritage (Hawaiian, Chinese, and British) as well as his nomadic wanderings (born in Lebanon, raised in Canada and Australia). *The Independent* remarks that Keanu is "fashionably ethnic-looking (but not too ethnic-looking, his name means 'cool breeze over the mountains')."[10] The *Chicago Tribune* remarks upon "the angular face with its ethnic and sexual ambiguities," and comments that "The actor's enigmatic face suggests a computer-generated composite of every known race and gender. His affect is pansexual and so is his appeal. At the trill of his name—say key-AH-noo—fans female and male heave libidinal sighs."[11] Even Bernardo Bertolucci remarks that "[Reeves] has a beauty . . . that's not Eastern or Western."[12]

In these articles, star accessibility is often highlighted through discourses that construct the body as a site of receptivity and invitation. The body is firm and agile, muscular but not imposingly bulky; the hair is short; facial features resonate with an emotional, unthreatening quality. Receptivity at the site of the eye is mentioned in several of the articles about Keanu Reeves in *Speed*; a *USA Today* piece includes director Jan de Bont's observation that "[Keanu's] eyes are very open to the world"[13]; with more focus, de Bont comments that "You can read emotion in [his eyes]. There's nothing going on behind the eyes of most action heroes."[14] Some popular press articles include testimonials for Keanu's receptivity, such as the following comment from a 19-year-old woman: "I feel I could step into his soul, just slide in."[15] And discussions of Keanu's sexual appeal on the active alt.fan.keanu-reeves newsgroup often focus on the expressivity and impenetrable mystery of his face. In one heated debate over the range of Keanu's acting skills, a participant provides the following response, with indirect reference his performance in *Johnny Mnemonic*:

> "I don't know how to distinguish acting from performing, Keanu aside. I DO know that his eyes, his looks—this man does NOT need morphing software, he's got the morph deep inside his DNA. I think a.lot [sic] about how he looks. . . . Our Keanu's appearance is not an average face or look.[16]

Out magazine relates Keanu's ocular receptivity to the probing eyes of his gay male fans: "Reeves can seem all things to all people. Why he has caught the eye of gay men isn't such a mystery, given his tough-but-tender looks, his dude-acious bod, those eyes."[17]

Receptivity is also figured as a natural sexuality which derives its power from its lack of self-consciousness, as well as from the star's refusal to take the constructed image too seriously. For example, Keanu offers modest, objective and scientific reactions to the course taught on his films at the Art Center College of Design in Pasadena:

> My understanding of it is that [Professor Prima]'s using an artist as a jumping-off point or a sort of strobe light on popular culture. . . . and I'm flattered he used me as that jumping-off point.[18]

One *People* article highlights the fact that, at director de Bont's request, Keanu Reeves "pumped iron for two months at Gold's Gym in L.A. to add manly umpf to his formerly lanky frame"[19]; however, the association of image construction with active, goal-oriented labor serves to deflect any potential suspicions of the star's distancing obsession with his own sexual appeal. Keanu's own commentary on this subject confirms his disinterest in narcissism: "I like my body . . . and I know what it feels like when I'm in good shape—but I don't want to work at it all the time. Sometimes I do but if I'm not feeling as cool then I get into my whole other worlds and going to the gym is not at the top of my list."[20]

These constructed ambiguities are both reinforced and contextualized through elements of character and plot in the narrative of *Speed*. Certainly the character of Jack Traven demonstrates the strength, agility and resourcefulness which have come to be associated with the traditional action hero; however, these attributes are tempered by a physical and emotional vulnerability that adds resonance to the characterization, and which ultimately serves to expand the limits of acceptable masculine heroic behavior in the context of this genre. In conjunction with this vulnerability, the ravaged, strained body of the hero is frequently objectified sexually. Jack Traven's vulnerability is conveyed not only by frequent high angle and overhead shots which emphasize his helplessness, but also through plot devices which require that the hero's body undergo various gymnastic contortions. Toward the beginning of the film, Jack is suspended upside-down, then lowered and raised, by cable in an elevator shaft as he attempts to latch a hook to the top of a fallen car to rescue its terrified passengers. In several scenes, the hero is placed in a prone position to emphasize his passivity and vulnerability. Near the beginning of the film, an explosion propels him through the air and against a wall; groaning as rubble falls around his helpless body, he sinks to the floor in slow motion with his legs spread open. The scene in which he is transported by mechanic's dolly underneath the bus in an attempt to disassemble a bomb is marked by crosscutting between shots of Annie (Sandra Bullock) looking down at him from the driver's seat, and overhead shots of Jack from Annie's point-of-view. Once he is under the bus, the shot composition changes to a series of close-ups of the hero's body in severely cramped quarters. The dolly is propelled out of control and ground-level shots show Jack frantically groping for any part of the underside of the bus that might provide a supportive, steadying anchor. The mise-en-scene of one extreme close-up features Jack's left biceps flexing and straining in the foreground right, while in the background left his legs and feet dangle off the now wildly swerving dolly. After the dolly permanently veers away from his body a few shots later, another ground-level shot offers a more dramatic fragmentation of body parts, revealing only a clenched torso and pair of legs that strain anxiously to avoid scraping against the pavement.

The most emphatic revelations of vulnerability are conveyed by the intensity of Jack's reactions to his own helplessness as he confronts the forces of the villain, Howard Payne (Dennis Hopper). After Payne telephones Jack to inform him that his partner Harry (Jeff Daniels) has been killed, the hero emits a slow, agonized, low-pitched, groan; his head and back slumped over in despair, he suddenly erupts into a wild, convulsive state, gripping and shaking the handrail of the bus as the camera lingers on his straining arm muscles. After Annie manages to calm him down, he resignedly informs her, "We're gonna die." Interestingly, however, it is this very vulnerability that ultimately places Jack in a position of power both to defeat the villain and save his own life: in the closing moments of the final struggle between the two men on the roof of a speeding subway car, Howard manages to pin Jack underneath him, beating him senseless with a steel bomb trigger, and boasting that he has outsmarted and outmaneuvered him. But Jack's supine, submissive, and seemingly helpless position ironically becomes a position of safety; in a desperate effort, he succeeds in raising the head of his aggressor ever so slightly, just enough for it to be lopped off by a safety light mounted to the subway tunnel ceiling.

Vulnerability is also a function of locative ambiguities constructed through the publicity discourses, and reinforced within the film narrative: both establish the hero as alone and socially unconnected, suggesting an alienation resulting from an unidentified loss. In *Speed*, Jack Traven's alienation depends upon his lack of personal history. A man without a past, Jack harbors a despair defined by various absences. While the viewer may assume that Jack belongs to a family and has a home, the narrative reveals no such domestic space. Despite the social connections afforded to him as a police officer, he remains unconnected, unfixed. The day after receiving a medal for his rescue of the elevator passengers, when a local merchant comments that he must have celebrated his success the night before, Jack responds, "It can't have been too great—I woke up alone."

The narrative's corrective to this alienation emerges with the hero's role temporary and functional alliance with a community, an alliance which is also integral to the construction of the star as a universal fantasy figure. In *Speed*, human survival depends upon the organized efforts of the community to withstand threats imposed by the outside world. Community is confined within tight, containable public spaces—an elevator car, a bus, a subway car—vulnerable to the forces that attempt to disband it. And it is the action hero who comes to assume responsibility for establishing and maintaining the community as a cohesive space; he does so by encouraging cooperation, dispelling dissent, and establishing trust. Before Jack Traven arrives on the scene, community membership on the bus is distinguished only by common disadvantage: in a city plagued with traffic problems brought about to some extent by those who travel alone in cars, the group of bus passengers comprises those who can't afford private vehicles, those like Annie whose driving privileges have been revoked, and those like the tourist, Stephens (Alan Ruck), who cannot find their way. The common disadvantage uniting them in this public space of mass transit establishes a spirit of mutual tolerance more than unity of purpose, and while some passengers know each other by name, their interaction is fleeting and tentative, lasting only as long as it takes to reach their respective stops.

In an effort to establish its political correctness, *Speed* insistently emphasizes the diversity of the community by representing differences in age, race, ethnicity, gender, and domestic situation. Such differences appear to be tolerated until Jack makes the passengers aware of the bomb that threatens them. From this point forward, when the goal of the passengers is no longer to reach a specific destination, but to remain alive, differences between the community members become a source of conflict, and their cooperative effort is consistently in danger of being vitiated. Jack himself is initially greeted with suspicion and distrust, since he appears to them as a "madman" who disrupts their daily routine, and also because his identity as a police officer places him in a position of power and privilege. The disruption becomes life-threatening when one passenger suspects that Jack will arrest him; the passenger panics, inadvertently shoots the bus driver, consequently risking the other passengers' lives.

Jack's mission is to organize cooperative activity according to rules that Howard, the "real" madman, has established: the bus must not decrease its speed below fifty miles per hour; no passenger may be permitted to alight. His mission is complicated because he must (a) impose order without posing himself as a threat; but also (b) neutralize the stratification of the community by establishing his trustworthiness and inspiring people to trust one another. His first goal requires him to prove that under the present circumstances, his role of police officer is secondary to his role of fellow human being who is willing to risk his life for them. He accomplishes this as soon as he boards the bus: after Ray pulls out his gun when Jack displays the policy badge, Jack responds reflexively by pulling out his own gun, but then he makes a plea to the frightened passenger:

> I don't know you, man. I'm not here for you. Let's not do this. . . . Listen! I'm putting my gun away, okay? Okay? Now, listen. I don't care about your crime. Whatever you did, I'm sure that you're sorry. So it's cool now. I'm not a cop right now. See? We're just two cool guys hanging out.

To achieve the second goal he must serve as mediator of the conflicts that erupt as tension mounts within the enclosed space. When one passenger exclaims that he cannot die because he has a family to support, an unmarried passenger reacts vehemently that his own life is no more expendable because he is single; conflicts also arise between Ortiz (Carol Carrasco) and Stephens, the tourist who is in one sense an "outsider" since he uses mass transportation by choice rather than out of necessity. Jack gradually guides the community to celebrate mutual accomplishments, and to identify and resolve differences. They attribute this resolution not only to Jack's organizing presence, but to their own resourcefulness. Through the trust which the action hero figure establishes in this diverse community, spectators are invited to perceive the star persona's absences and ambiguities not as contradictions, but as evidence of character depth, complexity, and coherence.

While these qualities also support spectators' efforts to construct the star according to their own desires, his universal accessibility is not without its deterrents. Perhaps the strongest of these are the markings or hints of the hero's heterosexuality, as evidenced by his relationship with Annie. While these deterrents cannot be disavowed, heterosexuality remains a negotiable element within the narrative. Although *Speed* concludes with the promise of Jack and Annie's romantic involvement, it is a promise that blooms only after his partner Harry is killed. Up to this point, the film stresses an evolving homosocial intimacy between the male partners. This "couple" is constructed as two aspects of a unifiable whole: Harry possesses technical knowledge and psychological insight, while Jack demonstrates a complementary physical agility and fearlessness. Together they are able to confound Howard's scheme and save the passengers in the falling elevator. Savoring their accomplishment immediately afterwards at the elevator shaft, Jack inquires, "Was it good for you?" "It was great for me," responds Harry. When he shoots Harry in the leg in order to confuse Howard, he loses not only his partner, but also his own ability to perform his own duties effectively; rendered impotent, he can now communicate with Harry only by phone, yet this separation of the partners does not result in a weakening of the homosocial bond between them.

If the ambiguous narrative of *Speed* poses surmountable obstacles in the realm of gay male fantasy relations, the ultimate challenge to this tenuous contractual arrangement between spectator and star occurs when the actor is asked to disclose his views on the issue of his own sexual orientation, or that of his fans. Since disclosure can settle the mystery of a star's sexuality, the trust which spectators have invested in the star figure is most directly at risk of betrayal. Attempting to explain his reaction to a blatant homophobia of star figures once desired, a London *Gay Times* writer describes his emotional response to the news that male star figures whom he once desired have made homophobic remarks: "Yes, it does hurt: and you do what you did when you ended your first teenage love affair, when you tried madly to convince yourself the ex is ugly now, all attraction is gone."[21] But Keanu takes his appeal to gay audiences in stride. He remains entirely unmoved by the rumors of his secret marriage to David Geffen, and refuses to lend any definitive closure to the matter of his own sexual orientation; indeed, Keanu prefers not only to maintain the ambiguous, universal appeal of his image, but also to cultivate this ambiguity in the interests of a cool, progressive political correctness that echoes his community role in *Speed*. When asked whether or not he was gay in an article for *Interview* magazine in 1990, Keanu responded, "No, but ya never know."[22] In an interview for *Vanity Fair*, when Keanu is asked whether it might be better for him to outwardly deny rumors of his homosexuality, he replies: "Well, I mean, there's nothing wrong with being gay, so to deny it is to make a judgment. And why make a big deal of it? If someone doesn't want to hire me because they think I'm gay, well, then I have to deal with it, I guess. Or if people were picketing a theater. But otherwise, it's just gossip, isn't it?"[23]

In a 1995 cover article in the "straight" issue of *Out* magazine, the interviewer, aiming for a limiting and defining statement, boldly poses the hypothetical question, "What would be the best thing about being straight?" Keanu's response is appropriately opaque: "But wouldn't whatever that *thing* is be the best thing about being gay as well? There are no lines. I mean it's humans, man. I mean . . . what would I say? . . . We can go to different bathrooms in a restaurant!"[24] And it is the maintenance of such ambiguities which helps to perpetuate Keanu's accessibility to both gay and straight fans. Among the Internet pages of "KeanuNet" is one entitled, "Is Keanu Gay?" And the writer's response?: "If Keanu is a fantasy figure for you, imagine that he prefers YOU. The truth is really not so important, is it?"[25]

In the years since the release of *Speed*, the persona of the now demonstrably bankable Keanu has ventured into personal and narrative territories that at first glance seem to compromise once and for all the pan-accessibility sustained early in his career. The announcement of his expectant fatherhood with partner Jennifer Syme in 1999 might have signaled a star identity permanently secured in the realm of heterosexual desire. As it played out, however, the relationship itself was never highly publicized until its tragic dimension unfolded, when the female child was stillborn, and Keanu and Jennifer split soon afterwards. Ms. Syme's fatal California car crash in 2001 received some public attention primarily because of her connection with Reeves, but the couple had already ended their relationship shortly after the death of their child. Since this time, Keanu's personal life has continued to remain enigmatic and largely private, with the devoted care he has given to his ailing sister Kim receiving far more publicity than any of his sexual relationships.

Neither of the two most prominent "post-*Speed*" onscreen versions of Keanu Reeves that have emerged since the actor's mid-thirties situate the actor's sexuality as decidedly heterosexual. The first version comprises the lover/suitor to whom central female protagonists are attracted initially on the basis of his handsome looks, but ultimately much more because of his compassion, empathy, and trustworthiness. In *Sweet November* (2001), the short-lived relationship between Nelson Moss (Reeves) and Sara Deever (Charlize Theron) thrives less from sexual passion than from Nelson's never waning commitment and self-imposed responsibility to the enigmatic Sara, especially after it is revealed that she is dying of cancer. Dr. Julian Mercer (Reeves) represents a younger, more handsome, more stable, and undeniably saner choice of lover for Erica Jane Barry (Diane Keaton), who has been busying herself with attempting to deny her attraction for the wilder and less predictable Harry Sanborn (Jack Nicholson), her daughter's much older ex-lover in *Something's Gotta Give* (2003). Despite her better judgment, however, Erica predictably chooses Harry by the end of the film.

The second, much more prevalent version of an onscreen Keanu Reeves slowly approaching middle age is the spiritual figurehead popularized by the role of Mr. Anderson/"Neo" in the *Matrix* Trilogy (*The Matrix* [1999]; *The Matrix Reloaded* [2003]; and *The Matrix Revolutions* [2003]), and assuming a much darker version in his portrayal of detective/exorcist John Constantine in the critically reviled *Constantine* (2003). This persona is largely consonant with the role of dependable if predictable lover/suitor, since in both "versions" Keanu demonstrates loyalty, resourcefulness, and a perduring sincerity. The construction of the spiritualist role is also, however, an ingenious fusion of the vulnerable action hero figure that Reeves perfected as Jack Traven and his depiction of Prince Siddhartha in Bernardo Bertolucci's *Little Buddha* (1993), released only months before *Speed*. The juxtaposition of these two disparate parts startled critics when the films were released. John Simon, for instance, found Reeves more convincing as Jack Traven, yet he was also impressed by the actor's startling "transmigration" from emaciated Buddhist monk to beefed-up action hero figure, and others perceived Reeves's image/body/character transformation as a sign of the actor's untapped potential and suitability for roles that seemed entirely antithetical to his former image.[26]

The importance of *Little Buddha* both as a synthesis of prior Keanu roles and as a foundation for future emanations of the pan-accessible star persona was foreseen in a now famous mid-1990s web shrine entitled "The Society for Keanu Consciousness."[27] Here, Keanu takes residence in Keanumandu, a virtual temple in which the star's pronouncements through his character portrayals comprise world revelations which the moderator "Lama Jahvah" interprets for the enlightenment of devoted "acolytes." The figure of Buddha becomes her logical culmination of a star persona whose propensity to serve as "this century's premier symbol of enlightenment and peace" is revealed to have been evident from the start of his career, dating back to Ted's Socratic speculations in *Bill and Ted's Excellent Adventure* (1989), a propensity that forms the basis of a "Tao of No (or the No Way)." What critics had often described as the star's "airhead" image is transformed into the magical state of an emptiness that connotes purity and essence, suggested in the index page's epigram by Ted's pronouncement to Bill: "Ah, here it is, So-crates. . . 'The only true wisdom is in knowing that you know nothing.' That's us, dude." Reeves's role as a messenger who has disposed of his brain so that his head can serve as a polygigabyte data storage unit in *Johnny Mnemonic* (1995) inspired several critics to correlate the star's blank-slate acting style with the vacuousness of Johnny's character. In the realm of Keanumandu, however, the emptying of Johnny's head becomes the requisite condition for Buddhist spiritual harmony, offering acolytes a model of Keanu's teachings on meditation, described as "Mind Expansion Techniques."

These reworked oxymorons of plenitude and emptiness—of a figure who seems most present when he is also "elsewhere"—resonate with new "locative ambiguities" in Keanu's more recent spiritualist films. Through the characterization of Mr. Anderson in the first *Matrix* film, Keanu once again harbors a persona marked by dislocation and placelessness from the start. Mr. Anderson has no friends, and he doesn't socialize. His domestic environment comprises a cramped, cluttered, and windowless cell with no traces of personalized identity, and his sterile, brightly lit office cubicle appears just as alienating, if even less human in this world that is soon revealed to be nothing more than a simulated projection in which synthetically manufactured cyborgs play a game designed to resemble life. Yet the wisdom and capacity for enlightenment of the loner figure reveals itself from the start: even before the guru Morpheus (Laurence Fishburne) enlightens the Keanu (now known as "Neo") about the tragic developments of world history that led to the design of the matrix, Mr. Anderson has already begun to suspect that something is not quite right with this world, and he is sufficiently curious to want to find out what it is.

An emerging Prince Siddhartha with Jack Traven-like problems, Mr. Anderson/Neo lives in two worlds (one of which doesn't really exist). In a paradoxical turn characteristic of this enigmatic star, Mr. Anderson's spiritual transformation into the potential savior Neo correlates with a more literal human transformation of a man who is not real, whose emotions, feelings, and indeed history have been manufactured. The transformation itself requires a traumatic and wholly invasive violation of the spirit as well as the body, whose vulnerability is foregrounded in the film as scorpion-like electronic tracking devices are injected and extracted from his abdomen, and as his body is jolted, thrashed, and plugged in the purgative process of removing all traces of the electronically constructed artifice that he has known as home and reality.

The eponymous hero of *Constantine* is given (or plagued with, as the case may be) a similar sense of locative ambiguity that finds him struggling between identities in two worlds. The cynical detective is perhaps the most tortured loner figure to date for Keanu Reeves: not only does John Constantine have no close friends, but he seems intent upon alienating anyone who attempts to get close to him, and the chain-smoked cigarettes that have become his closest companions have left him with a case of terminal lung cancer. His cynicism stems from the fact that the detective already perceives himself as doomed to eternal Hell because of an attempt to commit suicide that left him literally "dead" and in the underworld for two excruciatingly long minutes. The dislocation of Constantine's identity originates from his psychic gift of being able to recognize "half-breeds"—dead human figures doomed to damnation but still wandering about the planet—whom he is commissioned to escort back to Hell. While the dichotomies of place in *The Matrix* are set forth as real vs. constructed versions of human experience, Constantine's journeys take him between the earth to which he has already said his goodbyes, and the Hell where Lucifer has reserved for him a special place.

Mimicking Jack Traven's plot trajectory in *Speed,* the unanchoredness and spatial dislocation of Neo and Constantine secure a range of possibilities for audience identification and desire, since in both cases the state of belonging nowhere tends to anticipate some form of reconnection that ultimately invites the audience's affective participation. *The Matrix* and *Constantine* are spiritually themed films demanding that their heroic figures enact a process of redemption that will help them to find a new place for themselves and others in the world. For Neo, this redemption involves an emergence of "true" identity, an anticipated verification of the question that his underground companions and indeed the narrative itself repeatedly ask: is he The One? The extensively withheld answer to this question determines the ability of Neo's "acolytes" to sustain the very human attributes of faith and hope, and to foresee realistically a change to the intolerable circumstances of living in what Morpheus describes as a "world that has been pulled over your eyes to blind you from the truth." For John Constantine, redemption is initially a much more personal matter, and the changing of what he perceives as his own fate—eternity in Hell because of his suicide attempt—can only be accomplished by repeatedly purging the world of damned half-breeds, a strategy by which he hopes to secure a place in Heaven. As circumstances unfold, however, much more is at stake for this world than the hero's reversing of religious doctrine, when it is revealed that the delicate balance between earth and the underworld threatens to be disrupted by the birth of Lucifer's child.

Spiritually gifted heroic figures are not automatically sexually appealing ones: as demonstrated by Reeves's role in *Little Buddha*, the ascetic and spiritually immersed hero sometimes seems entirely removed from the realm of human affect, aspiring as he does to something greater, higher, and ultimately less accessible to other humans. Both *The Matrix* and *Constantine* avert such distancing between spiritual hero and audience by rendering the spiritual journey in inter-human terms. The heroes feel pain: if Neo's vulnerability is demonstrated through poking, prodding, and injecting, Constantine endures the physical pain of chronic and (seemingly) terminal illness, coughing up blood and fortifying his compromised system by swigging bottles of cough medicine. Indeed, even the remarkable process of instantaneous "cure" to his lung cancer is played out as a test of physical endurance, as Lucifer (Peter Stormare) gropes through skin, muscle, and bones to dig out the sticky accumulations of tar on his lungs, so that he might live long enough to damn himself to Hell once again.

If, as action hero, Jack Traven's redemption required a connection to the world outside himself, the journeys of Neo and Constantine are presented as internalized paths of personal/spiritual reflection that also constitute a moving out into the world, and the narratives work to secure them as entirely human even in their extraordinary state of spiritual attainment. These heroes ultimately realize an obligation to their believers, and a sense that their actions most vitally *matter* to others—certainly to communities (and, indeed, the larger human race) that have grown to rely upon them, but also localized networks of believers. Neo comes to realize that the fulfillment of what increasingly appears to be his destiny is bound inextricably with Morpheus's own fate; Constantine finds in the suicide of Isabel (Rachel Weisz)—and in her twin sister Angela's determination to uncover the motive for this suicide—not only a reason to figure out what has gone wrong in his own life, but an obligation to help someone with whom he shares an affective, if self-destructive, affinity. At the same time, consonant with the path of most of Keanu's onscreen romantic encounters, the sexual investment in the promise of sustained "couple" relationships between Constantine/Angela and Neo/Trinity (Carrie-Anne Moss) is minimized, even though it is Trinity's prophecied belief in Neo that returns him to life at the end of the film.

The ultimate testament to Keanu Reeves' effectively sustained ambiguity in relation to audience desire in these films arises from the heroes' successful questioning of the hegemonically enforced status quo, of a set of prescribed laws that dictate what is right and wrong, normal and abnormal. If the ultimate narrative goal of *Constantine* lies in the successful containment of the problem of Lucifer's son's birth, the more remarkable accomplishment of the film is the hero's demonstrated ability to reverse, and even overturn, a systems of religious law that has dictated the hero's damnation for an act that he never considered to be criminal. And in *The Matrix*, the victory over the corporate, bureaucratic, ultimately fascist dominion of the clonelike Mr. Smiths (Hugo Weaving) of the world—along with the pristine and sterile version of virtual reality which they have enforced—is also a victory for the fate of the differentiated human spirit, described in Neo's final words of the film, with his promise of "A world without rules and controls, without borders or boundaries—a world where anything is possible. . . ."

The problems of attempting to "be oneself" in a world that relentlessly imposes arbitrary and senseless versions of normality are explored in *Thumbsucker* (2005), Keanu Reeves's fortieth film, made when he was forty-one. Here, rather than aspiring to redeem the world from the forces of evil or promising to emerge as a new and powerful spiritual entity, Keanu plays Perry Lyman, a very lonely and troubled orthodontist who has once more been put in the position of fixing the teeth of the thumb-sucking teenager Justin (Lou Pucci).

Although Keanu does not have a leading role in the film, the part is significant in the context of his greater career not only in its alignment with the spiritually enlightened persona he has been inhabiting recently, but also in his remarkable ability to reflect upon it—indeed, even make playful fun of it. Like Mr. Anderson and Jack Traven before him, Perry Lyman has no back story or historical past, except for what is revealed to us through brief references to past conversations with Justin. He is entirely without friends or companions. In the first half of the film he is curiously obsessed with sporting competition, but his athletic life is confined to activities which he can play by himself (running and biking). A man desperately in search of a philosophy, he tries out a number of spiritually enlightened positions that place him in the position of a healer, spouting psychoanalytic explanations of Justin's obsession, and convincing him to focus upon his "power animal" as he hypnotizes the teenager in his office, alerting him to the fact that his thumb will henceforth taste like Echinacea. After Justin once and for all rejects his therapeutic advances, the version of Perry that emerges at the end of the film might be called pathetic were it not for the fact that this orthodontist has also revealed himself to be capable of self-criticism. Apologizing to Justin for his past attempts at "curing" him, Perry has come to attain an enlightenment attuned to the narrative's strategy, in which the protagonists' perceptions of each other are challenged, modified, and ultimately renewed as though they were seeing each other—and themselves—with new eyes. Admitting the flaw of having prejudged Justin and his parents for their faulty child-rearing practices, by the end of the film Perry has learned to question himself, and indeed to forgive himself for not being the spiritually enlightened figure to which he has aspired.

"The trick is living without an answer—I think," Perry explains. While Neo would never have accepted such a tentative resolution, the vulnerability that Perry risks revealing in such a statement makes him mirror the Keanu that his audiences have grown to admire.

Notes

1. *Wolfboy*, by Brad Fraser and directed by John Palmer, was produced with Reeves as "Bernie" at the Main Space of Theatre Passe Muraille, Toronto, beginning February 10, 1984.

2. For accounts of this sexual phenomenon, see John Leland, "Bisexuality Emerges as a New Sexual Identity," *Newsweek* (17 July 1995) 44ff; Lynn Darling, "Bisexuality," *Harper's Bazaar* (June 1995), 136ff; Rachel Cohen, "A Bisexual Journey," *Harper's Bazaar* (June 1995), 138ff; Robert S. Boynton, "Going Both Ways," *Vogue* (June 1995), 132, 143; Anastasia Higginbotham, "Chicks goin' at it," *Ms.* (May/June 1995), 29–33; and Greta Christina, "Are we having sex yet?" *Ms.* (November/December 1995, 60–2.

3. Richard Dyer, *Stars* (London: BFI Publishing, 1979), 68–72.

4. Elizabeth Cowie, "Fantasia," m/f 9 (1984), 159.

5. Cowie, 154.

6 In *slash* fiction, fans rewrite old (and construct new) narratives around the presumably heterosexual relationships between television characters now cast as homosexual relationships. Slash fiction is often circulated among the members of fan communities. The slash refers to the mark between the names of the two characters whose "relationship" is being established. For example, Henry Jenkins documents "Kirk/Spock" slash written by "Star Trek" fans and "Blake/Avon" slash written by fans of the British cult science fiction series "Blake's 7."

7 Henry Jenkins, *Textual Poachers: Television Fans and Participatory Culture* (New York: Routledge, 1992), 204ff.

8 Angela Holden, "Blissed out, switched on perfect boy: what makes Keanu Reeves not just a movie star but a total babe?" *The Independent* (September 19, 1994), Living Page section, 22.

9 Mary Harron, "Picture that Majors on Motion," *The Independent* (October 9, 1994), Sunday Review section, 21.

10 Holden, 21.

11 Carrie Rickey, "The Importance of Being Keanu: the heartthrob hero of *Speed* talks about his transformation from airhead to man of action," *Chicago Tribune* (June 26, 1994), Arts section, 16.

12 Carrie Rickey, "Call it the cult of Keanu Reeves—Toronto actor is speeding away from adolescence at a record clip," *The Toronto Star* (June 13, 1994), F4.

13 Tom Green, "Built for *Speed*/Keanu Reeves, catching a bus to the big time/Former dude is a dynamo in demand," *USA Today* (June 9, 1994), Life section, 1-D.

14 Rickey, "Importance," 16.

15 Holden, "Blissed," 22.

16 Entry in alt.fan.keanu-reeves Internet newsgroup, signed, "a.fan" (February 20, 1996).

17 Tim Allis, "Keanu Sets the Record Straight," *Out* (July/August 1995), 65.

18 Kristine McKenna, "Keanu's Eccentric Adventure: from stoner dude to computer brain, 29-year-old Keanu Reeves has racked up 16 films during his eight hard-working years of acting, and emerged almost untarnished by the corrosive glitter of Hollywood," *Los Angeles Times* (June 5, 1994), Calendar Section, 3.

19 Natasha Stoynoff, et.al., "A Most Excellent Enigma," *People* (July 11, 1994), 49.

20 *Keanu Reeves: A Tear-Out Photo Book* (London: Oliver Books, 1994), 8.

21 Joseph Mills, "Can You Forgive Them?" *Gay Times* (March 1994), 40.

22 Dennis Cooper and Matthew Rolston, "Keanu Reeves," *Interview* 20 (September 1990), 132–137.

23 Michael Shnayerson, "Young and Restless," *Vanity Fair* (August 1995), 146.

24 Allis, "Record," 117.

25 "Is Keanu Gay?" Internet site, http://www.users.intrerport.net/!eperkins.gay.html

26 John Simon, "Polished Thriller, Polish Joke," *National Review* (July 11, 1994), 62.

27 "The Society for Keanu Consciousness," Internet site, http://www.empirenet.com/~rdaeley/ skc/index.html, accessed 16 February 1996. The site is currently offline but accessible by archive through the following site: http://web.archive.org/web/20010428233530/http:// homepage.mac.com/daeley/skc/. This discussion borrows heavily from a broader treatment of sprirituality in Keanu's films in Michael DeAngelis, *Gay Fandom and Crossover Stardom: James Dean, Mel Gibson, and Keanu Reeves* (Durham: Duke University Press, 2001), 197.

Chapter 10

Gus Van Sant's History of Homosexuality

Tison Pugh

*T*o view the films of Gus Van Sant is to witness shifts both in cultural perceptions of homosexuality over the roughly twenty-five years comprising his career and in his own portrayals of homosexuality. Cinema is implicated within its historical moment, and it thus provides a compelling locus to examine social transitions related to issues of sexuality as depicted on the silver screen and in the wider culture that films, to varying degrees, represent. And so when one watches Van Sant's films, one sees interlocking sexual histories: that of homosexuality in the United States, that of cinematic depictions of homosexuality, and that of one gay filmmaker's depictions of homosexuality.

At the same time, viewers need to examine Van Sant's films closely to locate the queerness—and the meaning of queerness—in his corpus: in some of his films the depictions of homosexuality are forthright, yet homosexuality is entirely absent in others. But, then, what is queer cinema? Is every film by a gay director somehow representative of a queer sensibility? Are films created by heterosexual directors and actors that depict homosexuality part of queer cinema? To be designated as queer cinema, must a film portray homosexuality in an uplifting manner and refrain from any negative portrayals? These questions are not answerable with pat definitions that circumscribe the amorphously protean body of work that constitutes queer cinema, but the very malleability of the term highlights that every director and his/her every film needs to be analyzed separately for its unique contributions, if any, to the genre.

Complicating Van Sant's relationship to queer cinema is his refusal to be labeled a gay filmmaker, his preference instead to see himself as an artist seeking to connect with as wide an audience as possible: "I don't think of myself as a gay filmmaker. I'm referred to as one, which is okay. But the political position of my films is not exclusively gay. If you put your sexual orientation into your job description, it makes it more specific, it suggests you make films for gays and not for anyone else."[1] With this ecumenical view of his audience, Van Sant delineates film as an inherently open and allegorical medium, one that invites audiences to occupy subject positions distinct from their own. Yet at the same time that Van Sant claims the inherent lability of cinema to address divergent perspectives in a single storyline, he also admits his tendency to bring gay stories to life, suggesting that they reflect the inter-section of his private and public lives: "The subjects of my films have sort of . . . they were about gay characters. They were what brought me out of the closet. . . . Yeah, the films brought me out. That's what my interest was. These gay characters and gay stories. And I was gay. My private life became my public life."[2] Several of Van Sant's films do not directly depict gay life, however, and so it appears that he sees homosexuality both as a sexual identity and as a metaphor for various conflicts—not necessarily sexual ones—between an individual and society. Due to the overlapping of sexuality as a representation of human desire and as a metaphor for non-erotic desires, conflicts within Van Sant's films often resonate with queer-ness even when homosexuality is absent. Along these lines, Van Sant proclaims, "I think you can be a normal rebel. Normal sometimes is being rebellious,"[3] and peering through the veneer of normality in his films exposes a hotbed of desires that could be labeled as queer, if not necessarily as homosexual.

In this regard, Van Sant's queer sensibility emerges from his overarching focus on alien-ation as a key component of the human condition, but it is a refracted and at times asexual or even heterosexual queerness. "Heterosexual queerness" may appear to be an oxymoronic term, but if one defines *queer* as representing sexual acts and identities deemed non-normative by ideological structures, it is apparent that ostensibly "straight" desires can upend normativity. As Janet Staiger argues, Van Sant thematically addresses a range of cultural issues through "references often expressed in ironic/sarcastic tones which occasionally deal with 'openly gay' issues but strikingly often raise instead class, gender, generational, and . . . race matters."[4] Building on the intersection of sexuality with other markers of per-sonal identity, Van Sant's sense of queer alienation concentrates on otherwise normative characters who are denied full franchise within our society.

Because Van Sant is gay, some viewers—in particular, some gay viewers—expect him to depict homosexuality in an exclusively positive light. Van Sant, however, expressed his frustration with viewers desiring to see a sanitized portrayal of gay life in his films. His first feature-length film, an independent venture entitled *Mala Noche* (*Bad Night* [1985]), depicts a somewhat unappealing lead in Walt (Tim Streeter), a gay Portland store clerk who falls in love (or merely lust) with a young Mexican immigrant named Johnny (Doug Cooeyate). Walt takes full advantage of his financial advantages and attempts to purchase Johnny's sexual attention: "I'll give you fifteen dollars if I can sleep with Johnny," he propositions one of

Johnny's friends, thus denigrating Johnny and his friend to the status of prostitute and pimp respectively. This blatant commercialization of amatory desire degrades both Walt and Johnny, but Van Sant defends his unsympathetic character: "He's an antihero . . . His cultural observations are somewhat red-necky and not politically correct. So, I've been presented with questions about that the whole time: 'What's the deal? You're gay, why aren't you making positive gay films? . . . Get to work!'"[5] Van Sant's exasperation with this viewpoint—that to advance acceptance of homosexuality within the wider culture, gay filmmakers should depict model gay citizens—illuminates his oeuvre as focused more on character-driven studies of alienation from American culture than on sentimental fantasies of idealized homosexuals. Walt's passion is both unique and universal, pointing to the shared human plight of finding love.

Following *Mala Noche,* Van Sant released *Drugstore Cowboy* (1989), a film concerning the sordid and often criminal lives of a group of drug addicts. If homosexuality is absent from the film, so too is any sense of heterosexuality beyond the clichéd coupling of the four lead characters, and this elision of heterosexual desire imprints the film with a latent queerness. Matt Dillon plays Bob, the leader of the group, who shows little sexual interest in his wife Dianne (Kelly Lynch); in a memorable line of angst and erotic frustration, she complains, "You won't fuck me, and I always have to drive." Dianne seeks romance with her partner, as evident when she shoplifts a copy of Erich Segal's *Love Story* (a novel made into a beloved film starring Ryan O'Neal and Ali McGraw in 1970, which serves as *Drugstore Cowboy*'s temporal setting). With their emotional handicaps in full view, the four friends dysfunctionally and parodically embody the American nuclear family. Bob and Dianne treat Rick (James LeGros) and Nadine (Heather Graham) as their children, as Bob explains: "Hell, it's like trying to raise a couple of kids when you take on a couple like that, trying to teach 'em to steal. . . . These kids, they're all TV babies." In this satiric recasting of the nuclear family, Bob's surrogate father is Tom the Priest (William S. Burroughs), an elderly junkie to whom Bob, attempting to wean himself from drugs, donates his stash. Bob's attempt to integrate himself into society abjectly fails when a rival addict kills him for the drugs he no longer possesses. Casting choices affect how viewers read a given film's queerness, and Van Sant's selection of Burroughs, the famed gay author of such works as *Junkie* (1953) and *Naked Lunch* (1962), to play Tom the Priest imbues this family of drug addicts with a queer grandfather figure, which complements Bob's apparent asexuality.

My Own Private Idaho (1991) tells the story of Mike (River Phoenix) and Scott (Keanu Reeves), two gay hustlers of the Pacific Northwest. The film is candid in its depiction of gay sexuality—one of the film's opening shots presents Mike receiving fellatio, and later Mike and Scott engage in a threesome with a German admirer—yet it is less certain in its depiction of homosexuality as a sexual identity. Scott denies any interest in homosexuality other than the financial rewards of prostitution: "It's when you start doing things for free that you start to grow wings. . . . You grow wings and become a fairy." When the two men embark on a quest to find Mike's lost mother, Mike confesses his feelings for Scott as they rest before a campfire:

> MIKE: I don't feel I can be close to you. . . .
> SCOTT: I only have sex with a guy for money.
> MIKE: Yeah, I know
> SCOTT: And two guys can't love each other.

MIKE: Yeah. Well, I—I don't know. I mean, I mean, for me, I could love someone even if I . . . you know, wasn't paid for it. I love you, and you don't pay me.

SCOTT: Mike . . .

MIKE: I really want to kiss you, man. Good night, man. I love you, though. You know that. I do love you.

Scott invites Mike to sleep by him, and his hand caresses his hair, but the scene fades off before viewers can ascertain whether they consummate their relationship. Soon after this emotionally fraught encounter, Scott rejects homosexuality: when he and Mike travel to Italy, he falls in love with Carmella (Chiara Caselli) and abruptly abandons his friend, telling him, "I'm going to take a little time off . . . maybe I'll run into you down the road." For Scott, homosexuality does not involve any emotional investment in sexual acts, and it threatens his access to the life of financial privilege that he stands to inherit from his rich and powerful father.

Van Sant incorporates numerous plot points and themes from Shakespeare's *Henry IV, Parts I* and *II* in *My Own Private Idaho,* most notably in Scott's rejection of his boisterous mentor Bob (William Richert) in a manner analogous to Prince Hal's renunciation of Falstaff. When Bob seeks Scott's favor after the young man inherits his father's fortune, Scott refuses to recognize him, speaking most of the following lines with his back turned to Bob: "I don't know you, old man. Please leave me alone. When I was young and you were my street tutor, an instigator of my bad behavior, I was planning a change. . . . And although I love you more dearly than my dead father, I have to turn away. Now that I have and until I change back, don't come near me."[6] Scott's words hint that his transformation into heterosexuality may be temporary ("until I change back"), and the closing shots of the film—as Mike and Scott attend funerals in the same cemetery, with Mike joyously celebrating Bob's memory while Scott stoically mourns his father's death—establish the sheer pleasure of life among a band of gay prostitutes and junkies in comparison to the banal uniformity of Scott's new life of wealth.

Even Cowgirls Get the Blues (1994), based on Tom Robbins's novel of the same name, presents a plethora of lesbian cowgirls, with protagonist Sissy (Uma Thurman), who boasts two abnormally long and notably phallic thumbs, challenging women's need for men to help them enjoy their sexuality. Beyond its celebration of lesbianism, the film subverts any sense of normativity when the Countess (John Hurt), the gay male owner of the beauty ranch that the cowgirls later commandeer, proclaims the universality of diversity: "All of us are freaks in one way or another. Try being born a male Russian countess into a white, middle-class Baptist family in Mississippi and you'll see what I mean." In response, Sissy praises her non-normative identity and declares, "Well, I've always been proud of the way nature singled me out. It's the people who have been deformed by society I feel sorry for." The film's defense of queerness—it is better to be true to oneself than to allow a sense of social propriety to strip one of one's essence—invites viewers to identify with a parade of queer characters who seek nothing more than to live as themselves.

In *To Die For* (1995), Nicole Kidman plays Suzanne Stone, a woman plotting to kill her husband Larry (Matt Dillon) because she believes he is handicapping her inevitable rise to stardom. Throughout the film, Van Sant employs numerous camera shots to highlight the polymorphousness of sexual desire, such as when Larry is playing with his band and the camera rests respectively on three female fans obviously enamored by him, and then rests on a male fan in the same manner. Likewise, when Suzanne enters the town's high school, male and female faces are shown registering the multifaceted nature of erotic attraction. She enlists local teenagers to abet her in her murderous scheme, physically seducing Jimmy (Joaquin Phoenix) on numerous occasions while also playing on the more nebulously formed affections of his classmate Lydia (Alison Folland). After they become suspected of killing Larry, Suzanne blames Lydia for the crime and ascribes her latent lesbianism as its motivation: "You had this crazy fixation about me, and you were getting some kind of perverted kick out of it, like people with your sexual problems tend to do." She later accuses Lydia of "lesbian tendencies." In regard to sexuality and normativity, the film contrasts Suzanne with Lydia, tacitly positing that the heterosexual Suzanne disrupts social standards of moral decency more than the likely lesbian Lydia, who is seduced into crime through Suzanne's machinations.

Good Will Hunting (1997) does not depict homosexuality, but it addresses the ways in which homosocial relationships queerly build heterosexuality: to achieve heteronormativity, the film illustrates, one must first successfully navigate away from childhood pastimes into a form of adult masculinity modeled by an appropriate male mentor. Young genius Will Hunting (Matt Damon) is wasting his life, hanging out with friends and drinking beer, and numerous scenes mark these men's psychosexual maturation as stunted: Will is arrested for beating up the bully who tormented him in kindergarten, and his friend Morgan (Casey Affleck) masturbates to porn videos in one of their mother's bedrooms. For Will to achieve heteronormativity, he must surpass these puerile attachments, and during his counseling sessions with therapist Sean Maguire (Robin Williams), he overcomes the childhood traumas of abuse and neglect that crippled his emotional growth. The potential homoeroticism of the scene that marks Will as cured, in which the two men embrace each other to celebrate their mutual accomplishments, is squelched:

> WILL: Hey, does this violate the patient-doctor relationship?
> SEAN: Naw. Only if you grab my ass.

After this unnecessary moment of homophobia, the film ends as Will drives from Massachusetts to California to reunite with his girlfriend Skylar (Minnie Driver). This concluding gesture toward heterosexuality ironically highlights that Van Sant has focused predominantly on the relationships between men rather than those between men and women throughout his film. This paean to the homosocial foundations of heterosexuality ends with a dedication to two of the twentieth century's greatest gay writers—"In memory of Allen Ginsberg and William S. Burroughs"—which further inscribes the film's queer subtext.

In terms of its skeletal plot structure, Van Sant's *Finding Forrester* (2000) matches *Good Will Hunting* in numerous elements. Both films feature young geniuses whose talents are not widely recognized, yet who tap into their full potential through the intercession of an adult mentor. Also similar to Will Hunting, Jamal Wallace (Rob Brown), the young protagonist here, needs amatory advice from his mentor William Forrester (Sean Connery) if he is to succeed in his courtship of Claire (Anna Paquin). In this movie, too, heterosexual romance is made possible through homosocial fellowship. William's somewhat trite advice for Jamal—to give an unexpected gift at an unexpected time—succeeds, and Jamal and Claire are established as a couple for the audience. This intergenerational dyad enables each male to overcome his handicaps—Jamal's unnurtured genius, William's agoraphobia—through their shared love of writing. Van Sant's interest in homosociality again stresses the ways in which males create erotic possibilities for one another, even in films with no explicit interest in homosexuality.

In *Elephant* (2003), the lead characters Eric (Eric Deulen) and Alex (Alex Frost) attack their fellow high-school students in a Columbine-type massacre, but Van Sant provides scant motivation to assist viewers in understanding the horrific assault. True, the two teens watch documentaries on Nazism and play violent videogames, but Alex also shows a sensitive side, such as when he practices Beethoven's "Für Elise" on the piano. Eric and Alex might be gay. When preparing for their assault, Eric declares, "I guess this is it. We're gonna die today," to which Alex responds, "Yeah, I've never even kissed anybody. Have you?" They then embrace in the shower, but if their closeted homosexuality provides the ostensible motivation for their rampage, it seems unwarranted at their rather progressive high school, which features a Gay Straight Alliance. In this setting, numerous teens and supportive adults discuss issues of sexuality candidly and in a mutually supportive environment, yet they are not spared as targets of Eric and Alex's attack. Before Eric kills the school principal, he berates him for not stopping the students from harassing one another, but Van Sant refrains from depicting Eric and Alex being mistreated due to their presumed homosexuality or for any other reason. Rather, Michelle (Kristen Hicks), the somewhat dorky character who refuses to wear shorts in gym class and who hears her classmates refer to her as "that nerd girl who sits behind you in math class," is Eric and Alex's first victim. Much of the thematic power of *Elephant* resides in its refusal to address the roots of Eric and Alex's alienation with pat answers: sexuality might play a role in their violence, but in the end, such violence remains incomprehensibly terrifying, and sexuality—heterosexuality, homosexuality, bisexuality—cannot help viewers to understand its insidious roots.

Paranoid Park (2007) recounts the experiences of Alex (Gabe Nevins), a Portland teenager who accidentally kills a security guard during a late night of skateboarding. Similar to *Good Will Hunting* and *Finding Forrester*, the film does not directly address homosexuality, but homosocial desires nonetheless circulate queerly in Alex's motivations and confuse any clear understanding of his erotic attractions. Foremost, he does not appear sexually interested in his girlfriend Jennifer (Taylor Momsen), who is jealous of his male friends: "You like hanging out with him better than me, it seems, and it's kind of annoying," she pouts about one of them. Alex's assessment of their relationship reveals that he does not eagerly anticipate consummating their affections: "Jennifer was nice and everything, but she was a virgin, which meant she'd want to do it at some point. And then I knew things would get all serious." After they have sex, Jennifer purrs, "That was amazing." She believed intercourse would cement their affections, but he grows increasingly emotionally divested from her:

> JENNIFER: You sure act weird. You'd think, after what we did, you'd be a little happier to see me.
> ALEX: It was your idea.

After Alex breaks up with Jennifer, one of his male friends asks, "Why would you give up free sex? She was even hot." The idea expressed here—that a male should continue a relationship with a sexually willing female, no matter whether he feels any affection for her or not—presents heterosexuality among teens as an emotionally vacuous enterprise. Nonetheless, such enactments of heterosexuality shield one against aspersions based on possible homosexuality, and Van Sant hints at latent male-male desires in his camera shots, such as when Alex's friend Jared (Jake Miller) looks slowly at him while driving or when they join another male friend in a hot tub in the scene following Alex's sexual encounter with Jennifer. When Alex shows Jared his new skateboard, Jared expresses his contempt for homosexuality to dissipate any latent homoeroticism between the two: " 'Cause I gotta skate with you, and I can't have some fag board riding next to me." The blatant homophobia of this scene is jarring but underscores the toxicity of teen angst brewing under the veneer of normativity.

That Alex is mostly uninterested in heterosexuality need not imply he is gay, but it does raise a question: if he is uninterested in sex with women, in what is he interested? His passion is skateboarding, and this pastime allows him to participate in a homosocial setting mostly devoid of female companionship. While skating at Paranoid Park, Alex meets a somewhat older man, Scratch (Scott Green), who wants to borrow Alex's skateboard: "Tell you what. Let me ride the board. If I don't come back, you can have the little hottie right here." With his sexual identity so muted throughout the film, it is unclear whether Alex would prefer this female "little hottie" whom Scratch so casually offers as a suitable trade for Alex's skateboard, should Scratch ride off with it. After his ride, Scratch invites Alex to join him in additional recreations: "Wanna ride a train, man, wanna get some beer?" The film slows while Alex considers the offer, with the camera resting on Alex's face, panning across Scratch's friends, and then focusing on Scratch's face as it breaks into a winsome grin. The two jump on a freight train, but a security guard spots them; as he tries to arrest them, Alex hits him with his skateboard, knocking him into an oncoming train. From the outside, Alex appears to be a typical teenager, but his apparent normalcy cannot conceal the ways in which heterosexuality frustrates his sense of self, with dire repercussions for those around him.

Van Sant's final film to date, *Milk* (2008), is a biopic depicting the life and times of Harvey Milk (Sean Penn), the first openly gay man elected to public office in the United States. The film is virtually a hagiography in its treatment of its eponymous protagonist, and here Van Sant delivers to gay audiences a paean to its progressive roots. The film's opening shots feature raids on gay bars in Miami and Los Angeles in the 1960s, thus establishing the virulent homophobia of the era; its dramatic action begins in New York City in 1970, several months after the Stonewall Riots of June 28, 1969, when drag queens and gay bar patrons fought back against a police raid in an event that is now widely recognized as the foundational moment of the modern gay rights movement in the United States. Van Sant dramatizes Milk's numerous failed campaigns prior to his election to the San Francisco Board of Supervisors, and the film also addresses the controversy over Proposition 6, a ballot initiative requiring that all gay teachers in California schools be fired. In terms of the historical interplay of film and fact, the release of *Milk*—and the many accolades it was subsequently awarded—provides an ironic commentary on the passing of California's Proposition 8 in 2008, which prohibited gay marriage in the state. Given Van Sant's sometimes obfuscated and conflicted treatment of homosexuality in some of his films, *Milk* is refreshingly open in its depictions of gay eroticism and affection.

Regardless of their individual treatment of homosexuality or heterosexuality, queerness permeates Van Sant's films. His personal biography as a gay filmmaker, one who began independently of the Hollywood system yet who increasingly worked within this system, records a continually oscillating treatment of homosexuality, from its forthright depictions in *Mala Noche*, *My Own Private Idaho*, *Even Cowgirls Get the Blues*, and *Milk* to its more muted and allegorical deployment in *Drugstore Cowboy*, *To Die For*, *Good Will Hunting*,

Finding Forrester, Elephant, and *Paranoid Park.* Furthermore, it should be noted that Van Sant's body of work contains several other short and feature-length films not addressed in this essay, including *Psycho* (1998), his shot-by-shot remake of Alfred Hitchcock's classic; *Gerry* (2002), on which he re-teamed with *Good Will Hunting* stars Matt Damon and Casey Affleck; *Last Days* (2005), a fictionalized account of a singer's suicide that was modeled on the death of Nirvana vocalist Kurt Cobain; and *Thanksgiving Prayer* (1991) and *Ballad of the Skeletons* (1997), two very brief films in homage, respectively, of William S. Burroughs and Allen Ginsberg.

Van Sant's history of homosexuality is as yet incomplete, and he will undoubtedly continue to create films that may or may not address gay life but that will influence how subsequent viewers assess both his body of work and cinematic treatments of sexuality. To date, his corpus allows viewers to assess snapshots of gay and straight life from a variety of vantage points, all of which contribute to an understanding of queer cinema, its cultural work, and its unfolding history. It is an inherently conflicted body of work, often endorsing homosociality yet disparaging homosexuality while nonetheless celebrating male beauty. Indeed, many of Van Sant's camera shots of the teen male leads of *Elephant* and *Paradise Park* focus almost pederastically on their attractiveness, with the camera resting on them as time slows in the film's narrative action. In Van Sant's cinematic tensions between squeamishness and sensuality, between his obfuscatory and celebratory treatments of homosexuality, a queer sensibility emerges in his films, often to the lingering discomfort of some viewers.

Notes

[1] Steve Kokker, "Back at the Ranch with Gus Van Sant," *Visions* 9 (1993): 43–45, at p. 44.

[2] James Robert Parish, *Gus Van Sant: An Unauthorized Biography* (New York: Thunder's Mouth, 2001), p. 44.

[3] Gary Indiana, "Gus Van Sant," *Bomb* 45 (Fall 1993): 34–38, at p. 38.

[4] Janet Staiger, "Authorship Studies and Gus Van Sant," *Film Criticism* 29.1 (2004): 1–22, at p. 9.

[5] Interview with Gus van Sant, in *Fabulous! The Story of Queer Cinema,* prod. and dir. Lisa Ades and Lesli Klainberg, DVD (Orchard Films and Independent Film Channel, 2005), track 4.

[6] Compare Scott's lines with those of Prince Hal, newly ordained King Henry V, at the close of *Henry IV, Part II* at 5.5.47–71. For a study of the interplay between Shakespeare's play and Van Sant's film, see Hugh Davis, "'Shakespeare, he's in the alley': *My Own Private Idaho* and Shakespeare in the Streets," *Literature / Film Quarterly* 29.2 (2001): 116–21.

11

Virtually Getting It On

"Sex" in Film and Television Narratives, 1992–2012

Jennifer Brayton

Setting the Stage

In the first virtual reality premised film, *The Lawnmower Man* (1992), a housewife named Caroline (Colleen Coffey) and her scientist husband Dr. Lawrence Angelo (Pierce Brosnan) have a bitter fight over the nature of virtual reality as a new technology. Caroline angrily asks of this technology, "Falling, floating, flying—so what's next? Fucking?" To answer her question bluntly, yes, sex is what the future holds for virtual reality, or perhaps "sex," at least as far as cinematic and televised representations would have contemporary society believe.

First, second, and third generational cinematic and televised narratives utilizing virtual reality all reproduce the same encoded messages about sex and gender roles, sexuality and sexual identity, sexual orientation, and the dominance of traditional social groups with power. Specifically, virtual reality narratives present a virtual realm where able-bodied men, superior and in control, use women for sexual purposes. Women are nameless sexual objects for the consumption and pleasure of male participants. Female sexuality, desire, and pleasure are negated in favor of male sexuality. Monogamy and heterosexuality dominate as the appropriate forms of sexual relationship. Similarly, real world social inequalities regarding sex/gender roles are reproduced that privilege the perspectives and voices of heterosexual white men who act as the narrating point-of-view. The predominance and valuing of male intellect is further manifested through the use of heterosexual white men serving as the extraordinary innovators of technology—creators of new virtual worlds where social inequalities that benefit men are reinforced. Although these three waves of virtual-reality visual narratives share similar framings that reinforce contemporary norms surrounding social location and power, the three waves differ over time in their thematic focus.

In a sense, virtual reality has failed as a technology. Once hyped as the next technological wave that would revolutionize society, human relationships, and methods of communication, virtual reality never succeeded in establishing itself in the public sphere as a functioning technology. As a result, the mass audience's experiences and understandings of virtual reality typically stem not from direct personal encounters with this technology but from mass-mediated messages that define it. My own doctoral research suggested that films and television are the most common sources of information about virtual reality, shaping the way the public has come to conceptualize it as a new information and communication technology.

Virtual reality is the use of computer technology with peripheral tools to credibly and realistically recreate the sensory impression of 3-D reality within an artificially-generated graphical environment.[1] The ideal of virtual reality is to produce an environment that is fully interactive and that utilizes and manipulates all sensory impressions. Virtual reality would be indistinguishable from the real external world.[2] The participant would experience and control her virtual environment as if it were a real world physical space with smells, tastes, sights, sounds, and tactile sensations. Further, VR calls for the interaction within a shared virtual realm of multiple participants who are not limited to the use of their own physical bodies but can interact in real time using any available graphical imagery to represent their bodies. As many contemporary writers suggest, the appeal of ideal virtual reality lies in the belief that with this technology people will be able to shed their bodies and create new virtual characters or digitized symbols—called avatars—to signify their presence to others. The participant would be able to explore a variety of options and experiences from a diversity of social positions, including gender identity, sexual orientation, age, height, species and inanimate object identity. In particular, the utilization of virtual realms for the exploration of sexuality and sexual identity has become of primary interest.

The avatar is an iconic representation of the participant within the virtual realm.[3] In all three waves of visual narratives, there exist avatars that serve as stand-ins for the real world people, though the avatars themselves vary dramatically. Many of these avatars are 3-D visual representations of a fictionalized character that may or may not share the same personality, appearance, beliefs, and interests of the creator. Avatars are thus able to be personalized and customized, their appearance chosen, manipulated, and controlled by the player. Other avatars exist only within the virtual realms, created by the developers and designers of these virtual environments. As we shall see with third wave visual narratives, the avatar becomes even more complex, moving away from the visual representation of a character to actual physical bodies (artificial or biological) that are controlled by the self-aware player or operator.

In 1990, Howard Rheingold circulated to the Internet a short theoretical essay on the concept of "teledildonics" and the implications of virtual reality for sex. Rheingold used the term to describe a possible (and ideal) computer system combined with software, a telecommunications system, and an interactive tactile effector system. People would be able to put on a body suit, load in a program, and have sexual encounters with other people—real and/or fictitious—in a virtual realm. These encounters would be as realistic as sexual encounters experienced in the physical world. As Rheingold suggested, virtual reality would be able to push the boundaries of human sexual experience, and sexual encounters would be bounded only by the limits of imagination: "Through a marriage of virtual reality technology and telecommunications networks, you will be able to reach out and touch someone—or an entire population—in ways humans have never experienced."[4] Such erotic possibilities include sexual encounters occurring across long distances, sex with strangers, sex with celebrities, creating one's own fantasy sexual partner, and changing one's own personal sexual identity. However, this form of virtual reality for sexual exploration has never been accomplished as envisioned by Rheingold. Susan Bright takes the idea ever further: "Using VR there is no reason that you have to be you. You could look like anything and be any gender or combination of genders that you want. There's no reason for you to even to be a person. You could be the vibrator. You could be the bed or the TV at the end of the bed."[5]

But while claims are made that ideal virtual reality will be an open and liberating space for challenging dominant social norms of human sexuality, contemporary visual representations of VR contradict this message of technologically-fueled sexual liberation. While the ability to have fully interactive and realistic virtual sex with others is a theoretical concept at present, what is important is that cinematic and televised representations of virtual reality have already narrowly constructed this technology in terms of male heterosexuality, male dominance in sexual relations, and the privileging of masculine traits. Films such as *The Lawnmower Man, Strange Days* (1995), *Virtuosity* (1995), *eXistenZ* (1999), *The 13th Floor* (1999), *The Matrix* trilogy (1999, 2003), *Surrogates* (2009), *Gamer* (2009), *Avatar* (2009) and the short-lived "Battlestar Galactica" spin-off "Caprica" (2009-2010) have all used VR as a narrative plot device and have similarly represented this new technological realm as being a sexualized space where men take pleasure in having control and dominance over women. In these virtual environments, women are constructed and represented based on contemporary norms of idealized female beauty, with perfect skin, long flowing manes of groomed hair, predominantly large-breasted with small waists, and wearing sexualized clothing (if any clothes at all).

With the meteoric rise of virtual reality as a new technology, the film industry in North America in the early 1990s had a new plot device in which to drive the cinematic narrative: a futuristic technology that allowed participants to enter a computer-generated realm. The focus of these films was a technology by which participants could access the virtual realms and play with their identities and the surrounding environment. First wave VR films (1991-1995) were criticized for unrealistically portraying the present-day configurations of this new technology, being more focused on its idealized and theoretical future potentials. However, the films were successful in introducing virtual reality to a public with little personal access to it and the appearance and mass acceptance of the Internet displaced interest in VR.

The second wave of VR films (1999-2003) had a markedly different focus: technologies that reconfigure human perceptions and societal understandings of the nature of reality. The focus was upon the philosophical questions surrounding reality and artificiality, not the hardware and the virtual realm. And the nature of the worlds inside the virtual realm was clearly delineated from the representations in the earlier films; second-generation films presented a more complex world indistinguishable from the physical world. In fact, the major plot device for second-wave films was the surprise ending revelation that the physical world inhabited by human beings was yet another embedded virtual reality. In such nested worlds, players can inhabit one virtual realm, and use it to slide between other internalized virtual realms. Pomerance has labeled such narrative techniques "elevator cinema", clearly illuminating the transitory nature of motion within these narratives where one smoothly moves between layers of virtual realities.[6]

The third and most likely last wave of VR narratives (2009-2010), though similarly reinforcing sex/gender, sexuality, and social inequalities, focuses instead upon the mediated relationship between the human operator who controls a virtual avatar, or even real people, in virtual and real world spaces. No longer is the attention given to technology itself (as characterized by the first wave), or the blurring of layers of virtual reality (as characterized by the second wave.). Instead, self-aware operators or players of avatars are offered to the audience. People are always conscious of their status as humans or as avatars in the real and virtual realms. Like puppet masters directing the actions and movements of their puppets, avatars are fully controlled by their players/operators. In this wave, the very nature of what an avatar is has changed compared to early VR narratives.

First Wave Virtual Reality Narratives

The Lawnmower Man was the first commercial film to consciously, albeit unrealistically, utilize the technology of virtual reality for a plot device. Jobe (Jeff Fahey), a mentally-challenged adult, becomes a super-genius through a combination of drugs and the use of virtual reality to stimulate his brain activity. In one sequence, he enters the virtual environment with his girlfriend Marnie (Jennie Wright) for a sexual encounter, saying to her, "In here, we can be anything we want to be." They begin having virtual sex, and while they are kissing their avatars merge to form a butterfly. Though Jobe claims to Marnie, "Nothing can hurt us in here," he soon turns into a huge phallic shape that ejaculates red ooze all over the virtual avatar of Marnie. In the external physical world, Marnie goes into shock, trembling in terror, unable to speak, permanently brain damaged.

In the world of *The Lawnmower Man*, virtual sex is presented as being fantastic and fluid, but strictly for men. Men have orgasms and experience pleasure in virtual sex; women die. In this context, men's sexuality becomes paramount, the standard against which women's sexuality is judged lacking. Jobe controls the virtual experience, his sexuality ultimately acting as a violent and deadly force against Marnie. The message about virtual reality and sexuality is clear: men's sexuality is dominant and controlling, and exists at the expense and subordination of women's sexuality. While ideal virtual reality is strictly theoretical, the manner in which *The Lawnmower Man* deliberately constructs its virtual reality narrative around a sexual encounter between a woman and a man implies that virtual reality sex by and for men is an objective of virtual reality for the future.

In *Strange Days*, sexuality is still heterosexually constructed and based on male desire; virtual reality is depicted as the direct recording of a person's memory and experiences, called SQUID recordings. Memories can be replayed, packaged as disks, sold, and then experienced by others. The lead character, Lenny (Ralph Fiennes), is obsessed with replaying memories of sex with his ex-girlfriend Faith (Juliette Lewis), these scenes recorded from his subjective point of view. Memories of the sexual encounter from the female subjective perspective are presumably not memorable or worthy of recording for posterity in the same way. Lenny is a former detective who turns to selling illegal and underground SQUID recordings, specifically explicit sex-based content, for those who can afford his prices.

More disturbing in *Strange Days* are the graphic sequences of violent VR rape scenes. An unknown man kidnaps a young call girl and records himself violently raping her while wearing the VR technology. By setting up a system feedback loop, he forces her to simultaneously experience the rape from his point of view. Thus, the victim experiences the rape physically from her own perspective while simultaneously seeing and feeling it from the rapist's point of view—his sight of her, his pleasure, his orgasm. As Lenny explains to the police, "She feels what he feels while he's inside her, the thrill while he's killing her." The rape SQUID recording also shows the moment of choking the woman to death during climax. Faith is also raped and murdered in this manner, her dead body left for Lenny to find in a hotel room. Not only is sex seen from a male point of view but it is ultimately deadly for women to experience.

Second-Wave Virtual Reality Narratives

The second wave of virtual reality films began to appear in the late 1990s, once the hype over this technology had become an accepted part of contemporary culture. The Internet had by then supplanted public interest in virtual reality. In cinematic representations during this wave, virtual reality was no longer represented as an astounding new technology but instead assumed a common cultural understanding of VR and emphasized its philosophical implications for human perceptions of reality itself. These second-wave films are all what Pomerance calls elevator films, since they rely upon a shift between virtual realms as the accepted norm for VR technologies. Yet, for all the musings to be found in these films about the nature of reality and human consciousness, sex is an element that is always present.

In *eXistenZ*, virtual reality is plotted as the future of entertainment gaming. The users are beta-testing the multi-player virtual game system called eXistenZ, where numerous people can interact both with the virtual environment and with each other throughout the duration of game play. Players use an organically manufactured entertainment pod to access the virtual space of the game. Virtual reality is advanced and realistic to a sophisticated enough degree that for the players, the virtual realm is indistinguishable from the physical world. Inside the realm of eXistenZ, players are subsequently able to enter another nested virtual realm—a "virtual reality game" that one can utilize from within the eXistenZ realm. Players can thus interact with other players' avatars sharing the same virtual reality game realm, or with virtual avatars unique to the game environment. A pre-existing plot line drives the virtual reality game narrative, to which players have select freedom and limitations to their actions.

The film narrative starts with Allegra, the world's top game designer (Jennifer Jason Leigh), and Ted, a security guard (Jude Law), fleeing an attempt on Allegra's life that is made at the public beta test. The two enter the world of eXistenZ for safety, and from there also move their avatars into the nested internal virtual reality "game." However, the conclusion of the film inverts the nature of reality within the narrative. Allegra is not the actual game designer of eXistenZ, but a terrorist fighting with Ted's help against tranCendenZ, a new virtual reality game created by master game designer Yevgeny Nourish (Don McKellar). All of Allegra and Ted's experiences in the external world or inside eXistenZ are revealed to be virtual experiences within the game realm of tranCendenZ.

On first viewing, it would appear that the construction of virtual reality and virtual realms within *eXistenZ* is conceptually different from the dominant messages of other films that link virtual reality with male sexuality. Allegra actively possesses the technological expertise as the game designer and creator, whereas Ted is the passive VR virgin. In a sequence involving Ted's bio-port implantation procedure—to make him susceptible to input from the internal "game"—we find a highly codified sexual experience in which Allegra is the seducer. She lies on the hotel bed, softly touching his lower spine while suggestively cooing, "Once you're ported, there's no end to the games you can play." Both the game console and the bio-port are socially constructed as feminine – a framing of technology rarely presented in mass media. Allegra calls the game console "her" at times, and allocates emotions and feelings like pain and excitement to the organic pod. The bio-port is clearly encoded as a vagina that is penetrated by phallic objects such as the game console cord, or body parts like fingers and tongues. As Allegra says to Ted while inserting her wet finger into his bio-port, "It's not infected, it's excited. It wants action." Allegra is the experienced sexual aggressor, seducing Ted into accepting his bio-port against his fears, and penetrating him first with her finger and then with the console cord. Ted, meanwhile, has a hysterical fear of being penetrated by technology: "I have this phobia about having my body penetrated."

As with the other films discussed so far, *eXistenZ* contains a carefully structured sequence in which the principal characters engage in a sexual encounter within a virtual realm. Proceeding to insert Allegra's micropod plug, Ted begins licking her spine and sliding his tongue in and out of her bio-port in a highly sexualized manner. Surprised, and claiming it is his avatar that is acting out sexually, Ted is still the instigator of the first sexual contact between the two. They begin to make out passionately, touching each other and rubbing up against each other's bodies. Allegra murmurs to Ted, "Our characters are obviously supposed to be jumping each other." The virtual realm is a place in which to engage in heterosexual encounters, and Ted finally submits to one, turning Allegra to face the camera as he begins fondling her breasts. Allegra and Ted both take pleasure in the experience, though it is an encounter and pleasure outside of their personal choice and control, imposed upon their avatars by the parameters of the "game programming."

However, these cinematic messages supporting women's active sexual pleasure within virtual reality are overturned by the conclusion of the film where we see that all of Allegra and Ted's experiences in the external physical world or inside eXistenZ were in fact virtual experiences within a game called tranCendenZ. The sexualized insertion of Allegra's finger into Ted's bio-port in the hotel room, as well as their sexual encounter in the second virtual realm, all existed inside the game play world of tranCendenZ. As participants in that game, the two have been avatars unaware of their own status as players, and unaware of their ongoing insertion as avatars into the various virtual game levels. As a result, the sexualization of gaming, Ted's homophobic response to penetrative technology, and the sexual encounter in which the avatars Ted and Allegra cannot control themselves are all game creations and manifestations of a programmer's masculinist beliefs and values.

The Matrix was the first highly successful commercial film utilizing virtual reality as a driver of the plot. What is experienced by human beings in this film as reality is, in fact, a virtual realm created by artificial intelligence agents. This realm, called The Matrix, is realistic to a high enough degree that humans do not know they are actually living within an artificially generated computer world. Humans unknowingly exist as avatars. This virtual world is fully realistic, interactive, immersive, and impossible to detect for the majority of humanity. In the real world, humanity is physically prisoner to the artificial intelligence agents, who use human energy to power themselves and maintain their global domination. Virtual reality is used to train humans who have been freed from the virtual realm of The Matrix in how to fight against the artificial intelligence agents. And while those within the Matrix experience the world of 1999, humans are actually living in the year 2199.

As with the other VR films, The Matrix presents both the physical world and the virtual world of the Matrix as heterosexual spaces. Neo (Keanu Reeves) is the principal character, a highly intelligent computer hacker who develops the ultimate ability to control the Matrix. Though she is a superior computer hacker herself, Trinity (Carrie-Anne Moss) is instead constructed as his love interest, the intended partner for the chosen one (Neo), her technological prowess never seen by the audience. Heterosexual desire is so dominant and powerful that Trinity can bring Neo back from the dead with one kiss. As in The Lawn-mower Man, the virtual realm of the Matrix is a place for falling, floating, flying, and even fucking.

In the agent training virtual reality program, Neo's eye is captured by a flirtatious young blonde woman (Fiona Johnson) in a skin tight red dress that reveals her cleavage. Later, when the female freedom fighter Switch (Belinda McClory) makes a crack about digital pimping, Mouse (Matt Doran) says slyly to Neo, "The woman in the red dress? I designed her! She doesn't talk very much, but if you'd like to meet her, I can arrange a much more personalized meeting." Heterosexuality is the assumed norm inside the Matrix, and no images of other sexual orientations are ever presented.

The Matrix Reloaded (2003) further reinforces messages about the norms of male-dominated heterosexuality. Hot sweaty adult women and men passionately bump and grind as they simulate sex, with other characters clearly engaging in exclusively opposite-sex encounters. Neo and Trinity have candle-lit, missionary-style sex in their private room. Heterosexual expression is the true expression of life, freedom, and love. Even the avatars of the artificial intelligence agents of The Matrix are constructed as heterosexual, with The Architect (Helmut Bakaitis) and The Oracle (Gloria Foster) as the so-called "father" and "mother" of virtual domain.

Third Wave Virtual Reality Narratives

2009 was the year in which additional film and new television narratives about virtual reality technologies and realms re-appeared in mainstream popular culture. These narratives do not significantly differ from early VR narratives in their depiction of social identities, inequalities, social groups, gender traits, normative heterosexuality, white cultural normativity, and negative stereotyping of people with disabilities.

"Caprica," a prequel to the successful "Battlestar Galactica" series, was the first of the virtual reality narratives in this wave to appear for public consumption. This is also the last time in which virtual reality technology, as depicted in the first and second waves, still maintains the standard visual interface between the user and the virtual avatar and environment. Daniel Greystone (Eric Stoltz) is the CEO and founder of Greystone Industries, which creates virtual reality technologies in which to interact with legalized and licensed corporate virtual environments. As in all other virtual reality films, Greystone is depicted as an extraordinary technological innovator, a white man with a beautiful wife and an elite lifestyle filled with luxuries and a home-based research facility. He is the inventor of the Holoband, the virtual reality interface that a user puts over their eyes to become immersed in virtual realms. In this narrative universe, virtual reality and Holobands are highly profitable corporate business integrated into society. Most people use it through the "v-world."

In the opening episode, partially clad and naked young teen women gyrate, dance, and have sex accompanied to the heavy musical beats of a rave-like event. It may at first glance resemble the mass dance celebration in *The Matrix Reloaded* but this is V-club, a hacked virtual space communally designed by predominantly teenagers. It is outside the corporate licensed V-world sector, a social space where teenagers hang out and have random sex, including group sex and public sex. Same sex female intimacy is positioned for the pleasure of the young teen men who watch appreciatively as observers.

For the first time in virtual reality narratives, teenagers exist as a social group. However, teenagers are negatively stereotyped as being highly sexual but without emotional involvement, participating in socially unacceptable forms of sex. They are also shown engaging in risk-taking behaviors including taking virtual drugs, drinking alcohol, and hurting other people. They may be hanging out and socializing, but not in ways that are accepted by the adult world.[7] Teenagers are shown as uncaring and unfeeling, because everything that happens is virtual and not real. Everything is entertainment and there are no consequences to their actions in V-club. Masculine attributes are prioritized and made dominant, where young men are shown engaging in violent free-for-all fight clubs and participating in the killing room, where virtual participants can happily murder anyone else, with any type of weapon or choice of method. There are even suicide rooms where teens can experience killing themselves for fun. Sex, drugs, murder . . . anything is possible.

Although the film *Gamer* still relies upon a relationship between a player and an avatar mediated by technology, we now see a very different type of avatar and interface come into play. However, masculinity still dominates in the real and virtual worlds, where women continue to be sexual conquests for men, and violent masculinity is rewarded. In *Gamer*, two virtual games/worlds exist, both created by Ken Castle (Michael C.Hall), a global media conglomerate owner who first designed Society (similar to Second Life or The Sims) and then Slayer (a first-person style shooter game). He is the wealthiest man on the planet, white, heterosexual, and with superior intelligence.

What is most commonly depicted through Society is men choosing to be the controllers of female avatars, women who allow their avatars to be controlled in exchange for pay. Angie (Amber Valletta), desperate for money to make ends meet while her husband is in prison, regularly logs into Society to have players pay to manipulate her avatar and determine what she will do. For Angie, this is commonly a male player utilizing her avatar for sexual purposes, yet another form of virtual prostitution. She is always shown clothed in a strongly sexualized manner – as are all the female avatars depicted in-game. Plenty of female avatars are in bikinis or little clothing, and have handles such as "Bo Peep," "Bubble Yum," "Trouble," "Kama Sutra," and "Booty Shaker." Society is a bright vibrant world where the sun always shines, avatars are gaily dressed (or barely dressed), and entertainment of all types can presumably be had, though the images of the world within Society depict the sexualized forms of entertainment. As Castle said of his creation Society: "You can get paid to be controlled, or you can pay to control."

What is illuminating is that in this narrative men are allowed to have a diversity of body types, though the large obese bodies of male players are negatively depicted in an unattractive manner, sweating and oily and eating junk food. Regardless, they still wield power. By contrast, Society only presents images of idealized male bodies that are slender, hairless and perfect. These virtual bodies are predominantly white, though racialized identities are existent but only in the background. Their chosen avatar names also reinforce power and authority of men, and their sexual prowess: "Big Guns," "Hardman," "Myballshurt," and "Vagina Blender."

Simon (Logan Lerman), the teen-aged highest-ranked world player, has the best the world can offer him. He spends most of his time in a massive high-technology bedroom where he can simply lie down and interact with any of the interface screens that constitute his walls. Pop-ups of young teen women keep appearing, asking him for dates, or in the case of two British girls, reveal their breasts to him to garner his attention. Young teen girls are once again shown as sexualized and using their sexuality and ideal bodies to attract the attention of men. Dozens of heterosexual pornography sites play on the walls, along with music, advertisements and much more. It is a dazzling world of high consumerism, elite technical skills, and heterosexuality. In fact, as Simon flips through various interfaces, he repeats to himself, "Gay. Gay. Gay. Retardedly gay." His homophobic choice of words also serves to negatively frame people with mental disabilities. The glaring absence of queer men (or queer characters at all) in addition to people with disabilities, permits no challenge or contest to Simon's prejudicial language choices.

Surrogates take the next step away from traditional virtual reality interfacing, technologies, and virtual environments, though still in a manner reminiscent of *Gamer*. In the narrative universe of *Surrogates*, humans no longer directly interact with the physical world, staying at home at all times. Set in 2039, society and technology has developed to the point where people buy surrogates, robots that are usually based loosely on the actual appearance of their owner/operator. People can buy surrogates and upgrade their looks and skills based on their financial and economic status. While the physical bodies at home may not conform to the ideals of beauty, be aging, have disabilities, or exist in marginalized positions, these are not present in their surrogates. As with *Gamer*, a self-aware person now controls the actions of a physical avatar, though the avatar in this case is a robot and not a human being.

Tom Greer (Bruce Willis) is a detective assigned to a strange case where a female and male surrogate couple are found destroyed in a back alley where they had been engaged in a (hetero)sexual encounter. When the police investigate, it is found out that their owners/operators are also dead. To date in the film universe, injuries to surrogates have had no impact upon their operators who feel no direct pain, and surrogates came into existence precisely to protect the physical bodies of people from the dangers of the physical world. Not surprisingly, heterosexuality is still maintained as the assumed social norm in this "paradise," though the actual sex of the operator may not match the sex of their surrogate, presumably. Images of same sex experiences or relationships are absent once again, in a world of heterosexual lovers and couples.

Here again, the "father" of technology is presented as a highly intelligent white man (James Cromwell) with advanced technological skills and abilities. Interestingly, he has several young male avatars that he has been secretly using to keep his real world identity undiscovered – and when Greer meets Canter for the first time in person, it is revealed that the inventor is in wheelchair and elderly, something he has been able to hide as a result of surrogate use. Surrogates allow for perfect functioning able-bodies to replace problematized "imperfect" bodies from being seen. In fact, other people use their surrogates to present an idealized version of themselves to other surrogates they interact with. Greer's wife Maggie (Rosamund Pike), still grieving over their loss of a child, refuses to be seen by Greer unless through her surrogate, which she uses in public as well as at home. Greer begs to be allowed to see his wife physically, but she refuses to interact with anyone in person. Her paid labor is as a surrogate salon beauty worker, providing upgrades to female surrogate clients who want better and more perfect beauty.

Common to "Caprica," *Gamer* and *Surrogates* is that technologically-mediated interactions between people with virtual and/or physical worlds are depicted as being *chosen*. Teenagers and adults constantly pop in and out of V-club or New Cap City in "Caprica"; people can choose to be players or avatars in *Gamer*; and the surrogates of *Surrogates* have become so ingrained in society that people have developed phobias and cannot cope in the real world without mediation via their technological bodies. *Surrogates* is the most critically contemplative film to address this framing of increasing addiction and technological reliance, and in an unexpected conclusion, shows Greer choosing the intentional global destruction of all surrogates to force people to once again participate in every day life as human beings.

Avatar still reinforces the same social norms that benefit specific members of society, namely heterosexual able-bodied white men, the twist here being that operators use an avatar that has been technologically manufactured and grown from the combination of a specific person's DNA with the genetic code of the indigenous Na'vi population on the planet Pandora. While inside the interface unit, humans are mentally linked to their hybrid avatars and can control them, experiencing the physical world through their avatar, much like humans operators controlling their robotic surrogates who interact with the real world. These avatars allow humans to breathe the air that is poisonous to humans, and aids the Avatar Project team in trying to develop relations with the Na'vi whose planet contains the rare mineral unobtainium that can be used for energy desperately needed back on Earth.

For a rare change, the lead character and narrating voice is not an able-bodied person. However, Jake Sully (Sam Worthington) is shown hating his own body for no longer performing as he wishes and under his control. He makes a deal with the military at the start of the film, willing to become their spy within the Avatar Program and share his knowledge of the Na'vi with them in exchange for the restorative surgery he cannot afford. This framing of the people with disabilities as negative or evil is common within mass media stereotyping.[8] A consistent thread throughout the film is the strong intense desire Jake has to live within his avatar, leaving behind his paraplegic body in favor of his able-bodied avatar. In his first experience within his avatar, his pleasure in being able to stand on his bare feet, walk, then take off in a full run is evident in his beaming smile and his refusal to learn slowly and carefully how to interact with his avatar. His need to be able-bodied surpasses the required protocols for training, and in the end, he is able to achieve full control over his avatar within the first session. Jake now spends as much time as possible in his avatar, reluctantly having to come back to his own physical body to sleep and eat. By the conclusion of the film, he is able to literally leave his dying human body behind, to live forever in the Na'vi-human hybrid avatar that allows him bodily perfection and ability.

While white masculinist militarist Earthling culture is shown as a direct threat to the lives of the N'avi, it is the slowly reborn Jake who is their ultimate savior.

Concluding Thoughts

While many of these virtual reality films were largely dismissed at the time of their release because of the fictitious fantastic elements attached to virtual reality as a new technology, they serve as excellent illustrations of how virtual reality is being socially and culturally constructed. The creators of *The Lawnmower Man* were conscious that as a cultural product, this narrative would bring virtual reality to the mass public: "This film will be the first time many people are exposed to the concept, and it is show in a dramatic and very evocative form."[9]

The Lawnmower Man, Strange Days, Virtuosity, The Matrix trilogy and other virtual reality cinematic and televised narratives recreate the ideological configuration of virtual reality as a product that is an expression of masculinity in a package easily digested by the mass public. Beliefs in heterosexuality and masculinity serve as the sexual norm assigned to virtual reality as a new cultural artifact, supporting the premise that it is a desirable, necessary and very sexy commodity. White culture continues to be presented as the dominant group who are the creators, developers and users of these virtual realities. Upper-class white men specifically are positioned as the technological innovators and entrepreneurs. In addition to women, teenagers and those with disabilities are negatively represented via stereotyping. And long before a person encounters virtual reality in the physical world (if they ever do have the opportunity), they have consumed these strong and dominating cultural messages via popular film and television. No challenging or alternative perspectives have ever been presented for the mass audience. The technologies of virtual reality and the nature of the avatar may have changed from the first to the third wave, but their messages reinforcing social inequality and structural access to social power remain the same.

Virtual reality technologies and visual narratives about VR have fallen out of the public landscape to be replaced by new stories surrounding contemporary technologies, most predominant being the rise and impact of the Internet and Web 2.0 social media with the success of films such as *Catfish* (2010) or *The Social Network* (2010). However, at a more profound level, the very nature of film-making in this digital, technological twenty-first century has become a virtual-reality experience for those behind the camera as well as for the members of the audience.

Hugo (2011) serves as an excellent illustration of this, where director Martin Scorsese uses contemporary 3D technologies and computer-generated special effects to (re)create Paris in the 1930s, a cinematic feat that would have been impossible without the advances in 3D filmmaking and special effects technologies arising in the digital era. In this loving homage to Georges Méliès (played in the film by Ben Kingsley), Scorsese is able to offer modern viewers an experience similar to that of the people who saw Méliès's short films for the first time when they debuted in Paris. The film's mysterious automaton is the literal mechanical man who brings the films of Méliès to life, his cinematic avatar. Like the children in the film, viewers watch with delight and awe as the flat page and 2D norms of cinema become fully realized in 3D, giving a depth and realism to a fictionalized and historical narrative universe. The drama and intensity of the passenger train crashing through the station (ending as a beautiful reproduction of the October 22, 1895 wreck of the Granville-Paris Express at the Gare Montparnasse) becomes a shared parallel experience for characters within the film and the viewers outside it. Virtual reality may no longer be utilized as a narrative plot device, but the process behind making films and creating a visual narrative universe that is realistic, credible, and believable to the audience has made filmmaking and the experience of films the new manifestation of virtual reality.

Notes

[1] K. Pimental, and K. Teixeira, K. *Virtual Reality: Through the Looking Glass.* (New York: Windcrest Books, 1993), 41.

[2] Like the Holodeck from the "Star Trek" universe, ideal virtual reality would be so close to the mannerisms and characteristic so the real world that the two would be indistinguishable for the participant.

[3] From the online Jargon File v4.4.7 https://www.retrologic.com/jargon/A/avatar.html

[4] H. Rheingold. *Virtual Reality*. (New York: Touchstone, 1991), 346

[5] Bright, *Sexual Reality*, 65.

[6] Murray Pomerance. "Neither Here Nor There: *eXistenZ* as 'Elevator Film,'" *Quarterly Review of Film & Video* 20: 2 (1993), 2.

[7] Susan R. Stern. "Self-aborbed, Dangerous, and Disengaged: What Popular Films Tell Us about Teenagers," *Mass Communication & Society* 8:1 (February 2005), 29.

[8] Jack A. Nelson. Broken Images: Portrayals of Those with Disabilities in American Media. In Jack. A Nelson, ed., *The Disabled, The Media and the Information Age.* (Westport CT: Greenwood Press, 1994), 6-7.

[9] R. U. Serious, "Virtual Reality goes to Hollywood," *Mondo 2000* 6 (1992), 106.

Race for the Screen

*A*fter years of anti-racist struggle, biological theories of race have been discredited by most scientists and scholars and the more blatant stereotypical depictions of the so-called races are for the most part rejected in polite discourse. Yet race still frames much of media product and racism still permeates many of our social institutions, from education to the military, the judicial system, and employment; there is no doubt that the idea of race has profound implications for the lives of millions of people. The continuation of systemic racism is necessarily legitimated by the ideology of racism itself, and that ideology takes many forms.

Susan White examines contemporary comedic coming-of-age films and uncovers some interesting messages that are common to many of them. She exposes the ideas of "white supremacy," fear of women, homophobia, and homoeroticism that are embedded in the narrative of such films and makes the reader see them in a whole new light. Peter Clandfield, in his analysis of the popular TV series "Heroes," claims that the series challenges the idea that "whiteness is normative"—an idea that is present in much of television today. "Heroes," according to Clandfield, has surprising themes of anti-racism, anti-globalization, and planetary humanism. Cynthia Fuchs's article on Juvenile is a cogent critique of popular rap music as a response to racist assumptions about African Americans, centering on the Hot Boys' resistance to the implicit assumptions about race and intelligence. Finally, Susan Searls Giroux and Henry Giroux have a fresh, provocative and interesting analysis of Paul Haggis's *Crash* and its depiction of race relations in the U.S. today. Their interpretation is a crucial and very critical addition to the debate about the effects of film on our perceptions and understanding of racism.

Chapter 12

"I felt like, 'This guy's really hurting me.' And it hurt."

Funny Men in Pain from *Zoolander* to *Anchorman*

Susan White

Even as some white Euro-American men, reflecting upon the incursions into their traditional privilege over the past several decades, have described themselves as the latest "endangered species," American culture is in the midst of a celebration of the essential white man.[1] In recent films, the celebration takes on the conflicting characteristics of a wake, a narrative of redemption, a coming-of-age story—and many permutations thereof. Never has American cinema seen so many comic renditions of the social contradictions of masculinity, films that lovingly detail compromises and negotiations made by (almost always white) men to achieve sexual and social maturity without entirely sacrificing erotic and other freedoms. These films act as apologia for and indictment of contemporary masculinity, throwing certain kinds of white male scapegoats onto the bonfire built in recent decades by the Women's and Civil Rights movements, while recuperating and reinstating most of the behaviors still associated with white men in power. That power persists, most fundamentally, in the ways that "others" are still "othered": women and minorities remain alarming even if they can be incorporated into the rituals of white masculinity. Comedy is only one of many cultural sites where the competing versions of masculinity play a perpetual game of chicken. But because much can be said under the carnivalesque banner of the comic form that would be unacceptable in "serious" literary or film genres, comedy, especially farcical comedy, with its absurd dialogue, slapstick maneuvers, and over-the-top depictions of sexuality, occupies a privileged place in any form of social negotiation. Contemporary film comedies tell us that white dudes are still *hurting* and refocus attention on just where it hurts.

Comedic pain is one of the oldest shticks in the book. The role pain plays in classical Hollywood comedy is complex and evolving. Charlie Chaplin's soul-wrenching loneliness, Buster Keaton's kinetic dilemmas, Stan Laurel's mock weeping, Oliver Hardy's palpable disgust, the brutality and compliance that trademarked The Three Stooges (Curly Howard, Moe Howard, Larry Fine), Jerry Lewis's voluble angst, all comprise gestalts instantly recognizable even to the twenty-first-century twenty-year-old who has never seen these comics' films.[2] The ease with which these situations are absorbed by current audiences is not hard to understand: contemporary "guy cinema" rehearses and recycles the dance of domination and subordination, discomfort with the male body, obsessive phobias regarding the female body, and the loyalty to working-class values in conflict with upward mobility that also characterized male-oriented (that is, most) comedy of the past century. Further, pain and suffering being malleable comic devices, characters and spectators occupy many different positions in the sado-masochistic proceedings. We enjoy the suffering of the protagonist as he attempts to gain entry into the adult world or as, adult already, he suffers through his miserable life and then gleefully regresses so that, like the ordinary viewer, he can risk being slapped down. Our enjoyment is both active and passive in that we identify with both hero and antagonist in varying degrees at different moments of the films. We feel the comic underdog's pain and cheer on the suffering nerd, who is usually willing to inflict suffering on his antagonist if he gets the opportunity. There is no need for comic nerds to hold the moral high ground of the victim if sweet revenge, shared with the spectator, is to be had. In many contemporary comedies, male suffering, following a grand tradition, is excessive and baroque, its very excess leading to a more intense pleasure in the purgative power of pain. Who or what is being punished or redeemed through this excess?

Because achieving maturity is almost by definition regarded with ambivalence by comic males, the coming-of-age theme is common and blatant in most of their films. Coming of age is generally defined as consummating a sexual relationship with a woman and leaving behind, or at least tempering, relationships with the buddies who support the protagonist during his sexual apprenticeship. The homoeroticism binding male comic duos and ensemble casts is now more aggressive and more explicitly verbalized than at any time in film history, although homosociality has been the rule rather than the exception in the history of film comedy. Writing about the startling chemistry that characterized the Jerry Lewis–Dean Martin comic partnership during the 1950s, Frank Krutnik notes that Lewis's partnership with Martin "went beyond simply refusing the claims of adulthood and responsibility. They celebrated instead an idealized alternative to postwar domestication by enacting a utopian vision of male friendship."[3] The break-up of the Lewis-Martin act in 1956 has often been represented by Lewis himself as the end of a love story.[4] But most of the recent coming-of-age comedies, like most romantic comedies, don't depict the sad aftermath of the boyfriends' breakup, unless one counts, for example, the surreal weddings at the end of *Napoleon Dynamite* (2004) or *The 40-Year-Old Virgin* (2005) as utopian visions of a male buddy paradise with tamed females. Or unless one looks to the many sequels spawned by earlier films like *Revenge of the Nerds* (1984).

Ben Stiller's *Zoolander* (2001) is a brilliant cult film that challenges the mold of male buddy films by modeling the relationship of the male protagonists on the violently antagonistic rapport between men and women in screwball comedy.[5] (There is also a woman [Matilda, played by Christine Taylor] who contributes her own antagonism to the eventual ménage à trois.) Derrick Zoolander (Ben Stiller) and Hansel (Owen Wilson) push the homosocial envelope of the buddy film by playing its male duo as fashion models rather than as the slackers and pimply faced masturbators we see in the traditional nerd movie. The great sufferer of the film is Zoolander, who moves with startling rapidity—considering his Jethro Bodine-like stupidity—through the failure of a career, the devastation of his metrosexual bonding with his fellow male models, cruel rejection by his Appalachian coal-miner father (Jon Voight), and a flimsy brainwashing plot rehashing John Frankenheimer's *The Manchurian Candidate* (1962). The film has the audacity to open with a send-up of a fashionable *cause célèbre* of the late twentieth century, child labor in sweatshops. Will Ferrell, already a suffering-white-male comedy icon, plays Mugatu, villainous head of an organization that prizes child labor in sweatshops: this entity is ripped from *You Only Live Twice* (1967) via "The Bullwinkle Show" (1961–1964) and drives the plot with one finger on the wheel. Early in the film, the self-described "ridiculously good looking" Derrick loses crucial skirmishes with Hansel (Male Model of the Year) and then endures an unforgettable fashion duel, the "walk-off"; and, after the tragically beautiful death of his fashion buddies in a joyous gasoline fight (this contradictory gay-loving gay-bashing experience has to be seen to be believed), goes home to prove himself to Dad. Approval in the old man's eyes is not so easily won, however. Down in the coal mine with the Zoolander men, Derrick is willing to sweat, voguing in a cerulean blue suit, sucking in his cheeks in his signature moue, actually using blackface to amuse his fellow miners, and suffering his father's blunt rejection in the bar after work ("You're more dead to me than your dead mother!"). Having failed to "find his identity" in the toiling class, Derrick is pulled back into the fashion world by the nefarious Mugatu working in league with agent Maury Ballstein (Jerry Stiller) to work as the face and body of the superbly politically incorrect fashion campaign known as "Derelicte." Derelicte takes its fashion cues from the homeless, crack whores, and other familiar members of the urban lumpenproletariat. Redemption arrives as Derrick joins forces with Matilda and ultimately finds refuge in Hansel's New Age paradise as they foil an assassination plot in which Derrick was to have been the brainwashed stooge. Even for surviving this script itself, poor Zoolander deserves somebody's sympathy.

Perhaps because of Stiller's gay- or certainly bi-sexually coded performance as Derrick, *Zoolander* met with a cool reception at the box office, where audiences may have been expecting the more standard (and more conventionally hetero) Stiller fare (such as *Meet the Parents* [2000]). A film whose core emotional moments are *undisguisedly* set between men; and whose efforts to defend against its audience's potential homophobia in fact parody homophobia itself, may have been too much for the young males targeted as the primary audience. The film's emotional heart lies in the scene where Derrick and Hansel confess the hurt that each experienced at the hand of the other (as Hansel so eloquently puts it, "I felt like, 'This guy's really hurting me.' And it hurt.") But *Zoolander*, whose box office was also hampered by its release date two weeks after the September 11 attacks—which did not leave Americans in a comic mood—has been resurrected as a cult film with a very strong showing in the DVD rental market and on cable. A parody of white male pain, and *decadent* white male pain, at that—pain experienced by screen males who are the very antithesis of conventional gritty American manhood—found its audience only after America began to recover from shock at its own vulnerability in the world.

William Paul has claimed that in the 1980s, "animal comedies" (such as *Animal House* [1978] and *Porky's* [1982]) pushed out the romantic comedy as the most popular comic genre. "Animal comedies" are characterized by broad physical gags in the service of "kids aggressively pursuing the dictates of their newly felt hormonal urgings."[6] (Suffering-white-male comedies have, sometimes incoherently, sometimes incompletely incorporated the characteristics of animal comedies: in *Wedding Crashers* [2005], the first half *fêtes* the two protagonists' appetite for the wedding-as-bacchanalia, although the second half veers back toward romantic comedy, remaking *The Graduate* [1967] or even a rewriting *It Happened One Night's* [1934] seminal plot involving the abduction of a bride by a hapless hero.) The need for men to tame the animal within in order to achieve heteronormativity overshadows the pursuit of the female, something that has always risked becoming an unimportant detail in stories about men. "The sense of a contest (known as the *agon* in the Greek plays) is especially important for Animal Comedy, which usually pits groups of people against each other. In fact, a good number of the films made the contest metaphor literal by a sporting event that serves to bring an otherwise loosely structured narrative to some sense of resolution."[7] Because "contests" have long been a socially permissible way for men to share physical closeness (involving even sweat and contact) these plot devices can serve paradoxically to alleviate character and audience discomfort in the highly charged homosocial environments of the competition. Like war films, those structured around competitions give men license to express their affection to one another both verbally and physically. Thus, many recent comic films use the contest as a way of bringing men closer. In films including *Dodgeball: A True Underdog Story* (2004), villainous white men like Ben Stiller's aerobicized monster White Goodman are defeated at the hands of men configured as underdogs like Peter La Fleur (Vince Vaughn), the white male head of another crew. May the most pathetic white man win! Almost all the films mentioned in this essay use the device of the *agon* to bring men together, provide catharsis for male villainy, and resurrect the (very slightly altered) male hierarchy in sweaty triumph.[8]

Male bonding calls on tradition, as is implied by the title of a film viewed by many as an important touchstone in recent male-oriented comedy, *Old School* (2003). *Old School* depicts the reluctant withdrawal of its protagonist, Mitch (Luke Wilson), from the stifling sanctum of a committed relationship with a woman back into the camaraderie of his fraternity house. Inhabitants of the house range from college-aged to elderly, and the social structure of the fraternity seems based on the patriarchal mysticism of *Fight Club* (1999), in which a charismatic leader forms a secret society of males willing to suffer extreme pain in order to belong to an elite, anti-establishment, regressively macho cult. As in each and every one of the contemporary comedies under review, membership in *Old School's* male society requires discursive manipulation—if not outright manhandling—of the penis and testicles. One of the film's first hazing rituals, testing the pledges' commitment to the fraternity, involves their allowing weights to be tied by cord to their genitals and then thrown

---

off the edge of a building. If the rope is the wrong length, the genitals will be forcibly—perhaps even catastrophically—yanked. While most of the pledges are right to have confidence in their leaders, one, an enormously fat black kid, Weensie (Jerod Mixon), meets with an accident and is pulled off the roof by his private parts. The other young men look on and groan in sympathy. Fat, black, and nerdly, this kid belongs to several protected classes in the outcast frat film (featuring fraternities that are marginal to the institution of higher learning and whose members are traditional social outcasts). Pain provides Weensie's rite of passage, his entrée to the solid front of the Frat Pack.[9] While *Zoolander* parodies the white tendency to identify with African American suffering (with not one but two outrageous blackface moments), *Old School*, like *The Blues Brothers* (1980) (if not *The Jazz Singer* [1927]) before it, continues the tradition of white cooptation of black pain. Of course, *Old School* also offers a tip of the hat to the foundational frat-boy gross-out movie, *Animal House* (1978), which glorifies—perhaps immortalizes—the gonzo hedonism of John Belushi's character, Bluto.

Stanley Cavell has described a subgenre that he terms the "comedy of remarriage," comprising films that depict the screwball comedy couple after a few years of marriage leaves them full of doubt about the viability of their union.[10] Contemporary comedy is rife with a parallel genre: what one might call the comedy of male regression. *Old School*, in which Mitch and his age peers leave the domestic sphere to re-inhabit their youth in the company of virgin boys, is certainly one such comedy of male regression. (Mostly) white men suffer in these films from a concatenation of malaises: the inability to coexist with a more "mature," domesticated, or sexually unfaithful woman; a vague longing for male companionship; a desire to recapture the youthful gift of binge drinking without serious damage, and so forth. Will Ferrell's "Frank the Tank" (an *Animal House*-worthy character re-treaded) celebrates his newfound freedom from women and sobriety by streaking (How retro!) through their small college town, only to be picked up by the wife he wants to evade and to have his breeze-shrunken male member mocked by her companions. The ritual of defeating a patriarchal male authority figure is given a twist in that the patriarch in question, Dean Pritchard (Jeremy Piven), is the age peer and former foe of Mitch, Frank, and a third Musketeer, Bernard (1996's *Swingers* alumnus Vince Vaughn, here a smooth operator who has retained his connection to immature male pastimes by building a stereo store empire).

Few individuals have dominated the early twenty-first century male comedy film as has writer-director-producer Judd Apatow, with *Anchorman: the Legend of Ron Burgundy* (2004), *The 40 Year Old Virgin*, *Superbad* (2007), *Forgetting Sarah Marshall* (2008), and many more projects behind him. Apatow has contributed to several of the white-man-in-pain subgenres, focusing with equal success on the high school geek film (*Superbad*), the "superannuated male" comedy (*Anchorman*, *Talladega Nights*, and more) and the awkward man-boy comes of age film in the tradition of Jerry Lewis or Danny Kaye.[11] *The 40 Year Old Virgin* is a hybrid, incorporating elements of "regression" films like *Old School* and the slacker comedy featuring a dead-end workplace inhabited by Gen-Xers. The slacker workplace was brought into the limelight by the independent feature *Clerks* (1994), and reincarnated on the small screen with "Reaper" (2007), in which the protagonists "work" at what is clearly meant to be a Home Depot. The immensely successful *40 Year Old Virgin* features Steve Carell, like Will Ferrell a "Saturday Night Live" (1975) alumnus and also well received in the television mockumentary, "The Office" (2005). In *Virgin*, Andy Stitzer (Carell), a consummate buttoned-down white guy, works in a low-level job at an electronics store closely resembling a Best Buy store. Although he has ritualized his bachelor existence and lives within a comfort zone of sorts, Andy is shown to suffer with resignation the painful erections, loneliness, and humiliation that (apparently) go with being a modern 40-year-old virgin. Of course the narrative purpose of the film is to get Andy laid—most especially when his work cronies warm to him and figure out his dire predicament. So the male bond is forged as a temporary measure—one that will launch the protagonist into the frightening and alluring world of, as it is often styled in the films under discussion—pussy. If films like *American Pie* (1999) and its sequels objectify women's genitals—indeed merely to say they do is sorely to understate the case—Apatow's films go even further, not only participating in the venerable tradition of objectifying the female genitals and women as their bearers but taking the linguistic expression of male fascination and repulsion by women's privates to new heights. While *Virgin*'s lead player comes across as the prototypical white guy—rigid, somewhat humorless, sartorially clueless, and so forth—the magisterial verbal assault on "pussy" is explicitly characterized as arising from the Jewish sensibility of one of Andy's cheerleading friends, Cal (Seth Rogen), and is supported and buffered by the strongly committed heterosexuality of the African American sidekick.

Seth Rogen is one of the actors who incarnates the Jewish identity at the core of many of Apatow's projects, which bring to popular consciousness the Jewish roots of vaudeville and of film comedy. Just a few of the individuals central to that history and relevant to this essay are the Marx Brothers, the Three Stooges, Jerry Lewis, Jerry Seinfeld, Jerry and Ben Stiller, and Adam Sandler. Jerry Stiller keeps up running gags based on his Jewishness in *Zoolander*, while Apatow fully exploits the sense that Jews have only recently become "white" in US culture in many of his films.[12] Ben Stiller's minstrel displays in *Zoolander* recall the complex history of identification between Jews and Blacks in the history of film and comedy as evidenced, most notably, in *The Jazz Singer*. Apatow takes a page from Phillip Roth and Woody Allen in his explorations of Jewish men's bravado and insecurity in sexual matters. *Knocked Up* (2007) another Apatow-Rogen project, is the *Bildungsroman* of a twenty-three-year-old Jewish slacker/stoner, Ben Stone (Rogen), who goes from irresponsibility to menschdom when he gets the very blonde Alison (Katherine Heigl) pregnant and decides with great difficulty to do right by her. Once again, masculine pain in the face of commitment, of humiliation and rejection, of outgrowing one's slacker buddies is foregrounded at the expense of sustained female perspective on the matter. Although she is gainfully, even glamorously, employed and quite beautiful, Alison seems to have few friends and we are not made aware of the extent of her sufferings from the unwanted pregnancy. In Apatow's films, women remain ciphers, their genitals strange and scary, their motivations based on mysterious hormonal surges. Several scenes—I found all of them funny—stand out as exemplars of this powerful othering of the female body. A telling moment in *Knocked Up* shows Alison in the act of giving birth, with Ben at her side. Although he has gained maturity, even reading the baby books he bought to impress her, his friends remain reassuringly phobic about the results of the sexual activity for which they vociferously long throughout the film (their start-up business is a web site where consumers can pay to learn the location of female nude scenes played by their favorite actresses in mainstream films). Just as Alison is in the crowning phase, where the baby's head is visible through the slit of her vagina, Jay (Jay Baruchel) accidentally enters the room and nearly faints with horror, later advising the other men in the waiting room to enter the birth room only at the risk of never achieving an erection again. In *Superbad*, a sexually loaded high school graduation film in the tradition of *Porky's*, *Risky Business* (1983), and even *Napoleon Dynamite*, young Seth (Jonah Hill) is dirty dancing with an inebriated young woman only to find that he has gotten *menstrual blood* on his pants leg. This is cause for horror and alarm for all the men at the party (not least the girl's boyfriend, who also wears menstrual blood on his leg). It's no wonder that young men take refuge in the love of their buddies when the female body proves so abject. Apatow makes a plug for Jewish culture when he depicts the protagonist of *Knocked Up* as being in the final analysis yet one more in a line of men willing to take on family responsibilities. Does he in this way legitimate the apparent marginalization of the white male by calling on the real marginality of Jews?

In a very different vein, *Anchorman: The Legend of Ron Burgundy* (produced by Apatow) is one of a series of Will Ferrell vehicles that work to redeem versions of white masculinity that have become objects of ridicule. The outrageous suffering on the part of their protagonists is usually played for broad comic effect. In *Anchorman*, for example, Ferrell's Ron Burgundy must endure the equivalent of the travails of King Lear in order to come back to home and hearth and employment. The dominant white male has never fared well in comedy, fulfilling as he often does the role of antagonist and obstacle to the struggling hero's achievement of his dreams. The male protagonist's ambivalence about taking on the mantle of dominance is a familiar theme that can be traced throughout the history of literature. Some recent comedies take steps to break down and remodel the dominant male, bringing him back into the fold, re-empowered but benign. The age-old Oedipal story of fraternal bonding in the face of a rogue patriarch still provides an underlying structure for comedy (for example, the obnoxious dean in *Old School*; the Kennedyesque politician father of the bride played by the ever-weird Christopher Walken in *Wedding Crashers*; and, with a twist, the "godfather" figure played by Robert DeNiro in the *Analyze This* series [1999, 2002]). Young males in contemporary films continue to bond together with the goal of gaining access to women—wresting them away from patriarchal control—but the comedy genre's familiar homosocial undercurrent is stronger than ever. We have also seen that as the baby boomer generation enters retirement age, one of the agendas of male-focused comedies is to allow middle-aged men to regress, to find once more the bliss of homosocial environments and to avoid committed relationships with the women they wooed and won. 1970s anchorman Ron Burgundy remains arrested in immature, "swinging" masculinity, bonded with his equally obnoxious newsroom pals. Insofar as he is depicted as decidedly immature or retarded, Ron resembles the unripe forty-year-old virgin—but Ron is about to meet the liberated female who will force him to undergo a painful metamorphosis. He takes the fall for the bad hair and shag carpets of the 1970s (much as the displaced Austin Powers (Mike Myers) absorbs the blows of outmoded masculinity in the film series of that name [1997, 1999, 2002]).[13] Christina Applegate plays *Anchorman*'s rather sour girl-reporter Veronica Corningstone, whose ambitions are a direct threat to the masculine domination of the newsroom. As Veronica's star rises, Ron's planet sets. Even his dog gets drop kicked. In this way the fallen white man becomes the oppressed white dude and can use the tools of the plucky underdog to achieve eventual nirvana—a pattern repeated in any number of comic-nostalgia films of the new century.

And why now? What leads to, and supports, the presentation of Derek Zoolander, Andy Sitzer, Ron Burgundy, and all their hopelessly confused, desperately homophobic (or desperately homoerotic), politically asleep, irresponsible, woman-fearing, regressive—yet apparently still hilarious—friends onscreen? The world of the dominant American male—he who tamed the frontier, but who could also, through inversion have become the antitype that was

Chaplin, or Keaton, or Lewis—is gone. China has become more powerful. The muscle-man incursions attempted by George W. Bush have abjectly, and publicly, failed. The economy is in disarray. The globe is warming. The infrastructure is eroded. In the face of this, white males are no longer able to reassure themselves that sneakily dominant boorishness will work to make them cool, dignified, or saved. As these new wounded white screen heroes grope against one another in the increasingly panic-filled dark, enduring relationships (of any kind) seem hopeless for them, clumsiness and self-consciousness reign, self-involvement is everywhere. And in the audience, laughter is our final frontier.

Notes

[1] For an analysis of the perception that "reverse discrimination" hampers white men's economic and social success, see Fred Pincus, *Reverse Discrimination: Dismantling the Myth* (Boulder, CO: Lynne Rienner Publishers, 2003).

[2] I speak from my experience screening silent and early sound comedy to college-age students over the past three decades.

[3] Frank Krutnik, "Sex and Slapstick: The Martin and Lewis Phenomenon," in Murray Pomerance, ed., *Enfant Terrible! Jerry Lewis in American Film* (New York: New York University Press, 2002), 114.

[4] See Jerry Lewis and James Kaplan, *Dean and Me: (A Love Story)* (New York: Broadway, 2006).

[5] *Zoolander* was based on two short films directed by Russell Bates for the VH1 Fashion Awards in 1996 and 1997.

[6] William Paul, *Laughing Screaming: Modern Hollywood Horror & Comedy* (New York: Columbia University Press, 1994), 86.

[7] Paul, *Laughing*, 87.

[8] My favorite of these contests is the news team rumble in *Anchorman*, pitting pipe-smoking Tim Robbins at the helm of the local public television franchise against the dastardly Ben Stiller and his Telemundo gang, and so on.

[9] Many of the actors featured in *Old School*, as well as actors and writers affiliated with them, came to be known in the press as the "Frat Pack."

[10] Stanley Cavell, *Pursuits of Happiness: The Hollywood Comedy of Remarriage* (Cambridge, MA: Harvard University Press, 2006).

[11] On the figure of the man-boy in contemporary film, see Murray Pomerance, "The Man-Boys of Steven Spielberg," in Murray Pomerance and Frances Gateward, eds., *Where the Boys Are: Cinemas of Masculinity and Youth* (Detroit: Wayne State University Press, 2005), 133–154.

[12] Ben Stiller's minstrel displays in *Zoolander* recall the complex history of identification between Jews and Blacks in the history of film and comedy as evidenced, most notably, in *The Jazz Singer*. For more on the topic of the history of Jews as "white" Americans, see

Karen Brodkin, *How Jews Became White Folks and What That Says About Race in America* (New Brunswick, N.J.: Rutgers University Press, 1999).

[13] One of the many delights of *Napoleon Dynamite* is its vaguely 1970s aesthetic (although the film does not seem to be a period piece), made fully manifest in Napoleon's clothes, dance style, home décor, and so forth. Napoleon's *refusal* to recognize himself as a nerd, his utter commitment to his unhip style, are partly responsible for the film's elegiac tone.

Chapter 13

"Get your mind right"

Juvenile Renewed

Cynthia Fuchs

Yeah, I'm focusin' on learnin' from all
   your mistakes now.
Was a face in the crowd, I'm a baller with
   grace now.
(Juvenile, "Around the Way")

The ghettocentric imagination has created
the energy and opportunity for black youth
to gain greater access to popular communications media resources like film, television, and music, but does it promote an
alternative worldview?
(S. Craig Watkins[1])

Juvenile has learned from many mistakes, his own
included. Back in the olden days—1999—when he and
the Hot Boys were just thrilled to be signed, they made
a video for the "Bling Bling." Gesturing happily, the rappers here show and tell the many ways to signify success
in hiphop: spending lots of "cheddar"; driving Benzes
and Jaguars; wearing massive diamonds, elaborate ink

(tattoos), and gold or platinum teeth, as well as their signature wife-beater t-shirts. As each of the four crew members—B Dwayne "Lil Wayne" Carter, Christopher "BG" Dorsey, Tab "Turk" Virgil, Terius "Juvenile" Gray—took his turn spitting lyrics, the others cavort and gesture around him in wide-angled grandeur, displaying their big jewelry and 'hood signs, "representing" their youthful potency and brash self-confidence. As Juvenile phrased it then, "The Cash Money motto is to drank 'til you throw up."

Vivid and provocative, "Bling Bling" commemorates the Hot Boys' initial explosion onto the hip-hop scene, a savvy, self-assured, and self-conscious crew, understanding the relationship between ends and means. The Hot Boys knew—and repeatedly demonstrated that they knew—how they functioned in an economy of cultural codes. Such knowledge is by now common in the business of celebrity, as the trafficking of art/artists are topics of everyday conversation and analysis. The excesses in "Bling Bling" exhibited simultaneously their material assets, a proper respect for their production company at the time, New Orleans' own Cash Money Records, and, not incidentally, their awareness of themselves as cultural signs. Repeatedly made emphatic in the group's performances, the symbols they throw simultaneously challenge and reinforce conventional notions of what it means to be young, black, and male, what it means to be famous, rich, and popular, and most important, what it means to be hot.

That was then. Now, as *Scratch* magazine announces, "Mannie Fresh & Juvenile brought the sound and fury to Cash Money Records. But with personal and professional tragedy behind them, the ragin' Cajuns are ready to rip open their own house of hits."[2] Juve was the first to leave the label, as he was also the first to have his name on CMR multi-platinum albums, *400 Degreez* (1998) and *Tha G-Code* (1999). Before Juve, the Williams brothers—Brian ("Baby") and Ronald ("Suga Slim")—signed Mannie, formerly of the New Orleans DJ crew, New York Incorporated. Early on, Mannie convinced the Williams to shift over from gangsta rap to bounce, the New Orleans sound for which Juvenile became a most famous proponent.

The label made its owners extremely wealthy, especially when they signed a distribution deal with Universal. But the artists were feeling left out. Eventually, Juvenile says now, "Muthafucka ain't paying me my money so I quit . . . It's not about what we've done together. It's beyond feelings—it's a job!"[3] According to Juve, the break-up of the Hot Boys was in process before he left, and indeed, shortly afterwards, BG signed with the independent label Koch and Turk left as well (as of March 2006, Turk is imprisoned for the attempted murder of a deputy during a drug raid in Memphis). Juvenile's first two albums, as well as a third he completed to fulfill contractual obligations with CMR, *Juve the Great* (2000), represent an acute comprehension of the ways class organizes social and political life in the United States. With exaggerated descriptions of wealth and clout, he asserts his own newly achieved super-celebrity status, while satirizing its crazy emblems and measures, the reputations and exploits that designate "success" in the hip-hop music business. In "Flossin' Season," he raps,

> Let that little girl come over here and give a millionaire a hug.
> MacGyver ain't liver than a Big Tymer,
> Big dick, a million dollars, and a Pathfinder,
> Mr. Betty Crocker, cakemaker, casino-breaker.

Here, money makes all stars equal, from the famously white guy TV hero MacGyver (Richard Dean Anderson) to a masculinized Betty Crocker, to Juve's at-the-time Cash Money labelmates, the Big Tymers (Mannie Fresh and Baby Williams). Lyrics like these expose the U.S. system of equality by class mobility as a joke: Juve will *never* be the same as MacGyver or "Mr." Crocker. On *Tha G-Code*, Juvenile refines the attack on exclusionary class structures, wielding emblems of his own newfound wealth (most often cars, cash, and women) to draw attention to the inequities of the system. In the video for "I Got That Fire," Juvenile's image appears as a dead president's, on a burning bill, while he declares,

> You need a nigga that stay sharp, always got money,
> Pockets stay full of them big-face hundreds.
> A nigga with tattoos all over his arm,
> A nigga with a gold grill, diamonds in his charm.

"Girl," he concludes in the chorus, "Holla at a nigga if you want that Oscar Meyer." As this clever bit of rhyming suggests, sex and money are of a piece in Juvenile's universe.

Recently, Juvenile—still inclined to praise booty and property—has also come to another kind of insight, following the devastation of Katrina. Moved temporarily to Atlanta (as has Mannie Fresh, who left Cash Money in August of 2005, just before Katrina), Juvenile laments the loss of his own home and the struggles still facing his Magnolia Projects neighbors. Juvenile is finding new ways to "give back" to the community that made him. In 2000, Cash Money bought the projects, and rather than becoming landlords, the company turned the property over to the people who live there, in an effort to encourage self-determination. *Vibe*'s Sacha Jenkins describes a moment when, in Magnolia, one fan spots Juvenile's diamond-encrusted pendant and wishes aloud that she had one like that. The rapper turns to the girl and says, "I works for mine."[4]

This year, after Katrina, the situation is different, of course, and Juvenile is speaking out on the aftermath, in particular, the failures of state and federal support systems. Asked whether he believes artists should speak on such matters, he replies,

> Definitely, artists should talk about it. Artists should mention if they should struggle with what they're going through. They don't realize the effect that it had on people. So, I'm not going to point the finger at them. What they should do . . . they owe it to themselves to learn. You know what I'm saying? And really find out what's going [on] out there in the world. They owe it to themselves to learn, especially if they got kids, because they got to pass on their knowledge.[5]

This shift in Juvenile's self-presentation—from a young man glad to get his to a young man determined to understand the differences he can make—is visible as well in his 2006 CD, *Reality Check*, his first for the label Atlantic, and on top of the billboard chart in March. His new self-promotional strategy takes into account the relationship between celebrity and fan, as it is at once emotional, financial, and political.

That's not to say Juve doesn't still see himself as the best in his business, and make a point of telling you all about it. For some audiences, such braggadocio is troubling, a form of overwrought posturing that barely masks insecurities and leads to acting out. The major problem with the genre, at least that part of it associated with young black males of a certain class ("underclass") and affect (anger), is precisely what he and the Hot Boys exploited and made explicit in their original incarnation. Performing as vulgar, brutal, degenerate, they affected a look that said they were uncivilized and unintelligent.

It was ever a performance, of course. For Juvenile, appearing outrageous and confrontational demonstrates not his ignorance and disaffection from the dominant culture, but a shrewd self-marketing as products of that culture's systemic oppressions and abuses. Like

Master P's No Limit before them or 50 Cent's G-Unit after, the Hot Boys made the system adapt to their Southern style, and *became* the mainstream. Their mainstream, like any other, assimilated everything—including intelligence—as style and commodity. And so, their act was simultaneously intelligent and not. Understanding that definitions of intelligence are necessarily informed by cultural contexts, I use the term here to mean not only a gauge of education or even street smarts, or an ability to make art or money, but also, importantly, as a self-consciousness concerning such ability and the socio-political system that defines and evaluates it. Juvenile's self-awareness is not so difficult to assess, though his language and conduct hardly conform to prevailing notions of "intelligence." He won't behave in a way that polite society considers "proper" or assume a fashionable pose. He puts on "unawareness" and in doing so reveals the extent to which intelligence depends on its opposite for definition.

As a provocateur, Juvenile compares to the complex workings of what S. Craig Watkins calls the "ghettocentric imagination." That is, he reframes the "postindustrial ghetto as a site of entrapment and state repression [to] reverse the dominant claims on blackness that criminalize ghetto communities," at the same time that they "reinscribe dominant ideas about the [underclass's] behavioral pathologies that ultimately cause and reproduce social and economic dislocation."[6] Further, Juvenile—conceptually, if not self-consciously—make calculated use of the idea of the underclass, which Adolph Reed analyzes in *Stirrings in the Jug*, as "myth and symbol."[7] Reed shows that the idea/term has a long and highly politicized history, under both so-called (neo)liberal and (neo)conservative regimes. He notes especially, as a ground for the manifold abuses of the underclass, Senator Patrick Moynihan's notorious 1966 report, *The Negro Family: The Case for National Action*, which contended that because young black males in the early 1960s were largely growing up in single-parent, matriarchal environments, they would be helped by (indeed, they "needed") military discipline. This argument conveniently paved the political and moral way for "Project 100,000," which set about drafting 100,000 black men for service in Vietnam in 1967. Reed maintains that since that particular sequence of events (which has been roundly condemned), various reactionary academics, journalists, and pundits have increasingly identified the underclass as identical with a set of "deviant, dysfunctional" behaviors, following The Moynihan Report's specious and overdetermined logic. In other words, the underclass has become both code and rationale for urban poverty, such that an impoverished subject is found to be poor because he is pathological, and pathological because he is poor.[8]

Such logic works to validate a class system that is in part defined by bigotry, racism, and sexism. The act of demonizing those who fail to achieve a minimum class status, constituting them as stupid, lazy, or lacking some essential aptitude or drive, preserves the system that has rewarded those with pre-existing advantages—who are then perpetually enabled to (re)define the measures of success. So, intelligence and ignorance become *the* codes for moral standards. If you lack social position and money, you must therefore lack intelligence, morality, and good judgment. Juvenile's performances underline the ways that racism and classism are interwoven, by drawing attention to his own conventionally "underclass" behavior and appearance, now reframed as "upper class" by virtue of their assets and access. He have obviously absorbed some less than progressive aspects of this system he both resists and embraces, an achievement perhaps most clearly demonstrated in his prodigious objectification of women (see, for instance, a recent single, "Rodeo," produced for *Reality Check* by Dre and Cool; here he describes a strip club: "It's not the right spot to let your daughters visit,/There's some freaks up in here and it's all explicit").

But his challenge to the system that assigns social value to wealth and conventional beauty is also clear. He wears a diamond-encrusted grill, making for a garish, conspicuously consuming mouth, representing a very "functional" ethics, such as hard work, ambition, loyalty, and media- and business-savvy; in other words, the teeth represent intelligence. In particular, they embody the primary paradox of celebrity, which reveres outrageousness, in that their success stems from their ability to offend and also to extend the mainstream. Some reviewers reject outright their "country" displays. The *New York Times'* Jon Pareles describes a concert at the Nassau Coliseum in language that not so subtly chastises the Boys' immoderation: "Cash Money's segment [the other performers were the Ruff Ryders, also mostly defunct now] fused male bonding and corporate loyalty in a show of conspicuous consumption."[9] And *Rolling Stone's* Rob Sheffield, in a generally positive review of Juvenile's *Tha G Code*, comments that the artist's style "is even cruder than Master P's, if that's possible. Forget Cristal and caviar—as the intro to this new album proclaims, "Nigga, I *still* eat Popeye's Chicken!"[10] Sacha Jenkins calls Juvenile the "money-makin' Mouth from the Dirty South."[11] Jenkins's article focuses on Juvenile's rise-up-from-the-bottom personal history, recording his various temporary career choices—as supervisor in an asbestos-removal job, regional banger, and talented MC who paid serious dues (MC contests, open mikes, hustling) for years at local clubs. The article reports that Juvenile in particular is a "workaholic," while also showcasing the extravagant manifestations of wealth.[12]

Juvenile's displays of consumption become simultaneous resistance *and* conformity, depicting the most menacing stereotypes of young black masculinity in hyperbolic, enthusiastic, and, I think, culturally insightful ways, deploying and refracting the clichés as a kind of identity-making process. For example, in "U Understand," the chorus describes the ballers' ritual violence in stylized terms that underline their threat to (and construction by) dominant culture, but also exaggerate and mediate them, by matching violent images to a playful Magnolia bounce beat:

> Shhhh, be quiet.
> Tonight is the night that we ride.
> Thirty camouflage hummers with niggaz inside,
> With choppers, doin surgery on bodies like they doctors.

This is not to say that the video's violence is insignificant; rather, the verbal wit and hyperbole (the familiar idea of the neighborhood as a war zone, the killers as surgeons) and lively cadences demonstrate its banality and outrageousness, its similarity to any big-money action movie.

In an essay on the state of black masculinity in popular culture, Michele Wallace observes that white dominated media create the impression that there are "only two kinds of black people: the successful ones who do nothing but promote themselves and the underclass ones who spend all their time robbing, stealing, doing drugs, and killing."[13] She argues that, contrary to this impression, black culture—like white or any other culture—comprises multiple modes of *expression*. Taken a step further, this impression might be revealed to allow for only *one* kind of black people, for in each case Wallace describes the figure is understood as selfish and ignoble; here, blackness *is* underclassness, and the black celebrity, in particular the young black male celebrity, can't win for losing. Quite brilliantly, Juvenile acts out the extremes of both these seeming opposite poses. They act their ostensible social deviance at the same time that they flaunt their material success, and the *New York Times* doesn't know quite what to say about them, how to categorize them. The idea that criminality and financial success might be related—two sides of a single culturally normalizing coin—is apparently unthinkable.

Such a complex combination is visible in most of their videos and live shows, including the clips for Juvenile's "Ha" (1998) and "U Understand" (1999). These videos incorporate verbal and visual images to chronicle and fictionalize the transformation and solidification of the artist's public disposition. "Ha," Juvenile's smartly conceived breakout video, opens unconventionally, with a title declaring the specific location, "Magnolia Projects." Throughout the video, the shots of residents going about their diurnal business are punctuated by titles marking the time of day, as if the video is a document, a day in the life of the projects. His lyrics seem surprisingly conventional, contesting the superficial value of flashy rides and sexual promiscuity as these presage social and personal irresponsibility:

> That's you with that bad ass Benz, ha.
> That's you that can't keep an old lady 'cause you keep fucking her friends, ha.
> You gotta go to court, ha.
> You got served a subpoena for child support, ha.
> That was that nerve, ha.
> You ain't even much get a chance to say a word, ha.

The images accompanying these vocals pay respect to a very unflashy existence, folks hanging out on their porches, kicking it with their neighbors, tinkering with their cars in driveways, looking with suspicion on the local police officers, who appear, ironically and tellingly, with their faces blurred out, resembling the criminals on the TV series *Cops* (1989). The video's attention to such local detail, alongside Cash Money producer Mannie Fresh's infectious beats and Juvenile's clever and descriptive rhymes, makes the neighborhood come alive onscreen, combining documentary and spectacular effects. In other words, the video's visuals and the lyrics do not exactly correspond, suggesting that the "message" might not be exactly what it appears to be: if the lyrics are chastising artifice, the visuals portray realness. Rather than criticizing the wannabe player, the video interrogates the social conditions—poverty and distrust of authority—that produce such a negative-seeming affect. The video demands that its viewers read attentively, noting discrepancies and nuances.

The clip for "U Understand" is similarly layered, presenting a more pointed assault on institutions. Here the Boys rob a bank, with the help of a girl to distract the guard. The several shots of the extravagant exterior and interior denote the riches the Hot Boys are plundering. Significantly, the visuals depart radically from the lyrics, which describe a night out for a crew of gangbangers looking for trouble in the 'hood. Here, the enemy is not another gang, as in the song's narrative, but a clearly representative institutional structure. The opening verse establishes that the warfare is internal to the neighborhood, black-on-black:

> I'll ride everyday of the week (ya understand).
> Ya get ya issue when ya playin' with me (ya understand).
> I'll crawl at the spot that ya sleep (ya understand).
> Get with my niggas from the block and we creep (ya understand).

But here's the twist: in the video's visual track, the Hot Boys battle with no one person or street gang, but are instead getting theirs, symbolically and in real life.

Juve continues to embrace a hybrid hip-hop superstardom, appreciating loyal fans from back home at the same time that he shows off every dramatic emblem of their great good fortune, their magical journey out of the projects. And so, they continue to play ignorance and represent intelligence—to act like mindless thugs while in fact setting themselves up "stunnin'ly" to penetrate the system at its most vulnerable. As Robin D. G. Kelley argues, rapper hardness can mean variously and simultaneously working as comedy, social illustration, and self-imagining. Explicit and exaggerated boasts concerning violence are routine, and the point is to display verbal dexterity and clever imagery, much as Hollywood movies do.[14] The vaunted "social realism" of hardcore rap is, for its perpetrators and careful listeners, most often less literal than political, a rejoinder to mainstream journalism which has for so long refused to report on street experience and has in this way denied the existence of street intelligence—the means to survival and success—and proclaimed instead, by default, a kind of hegemonic mind.

Juvenile extends this performance by using seeming ignorance as a form of reporting and illustrating. On one level, seeming ignorant means you don't have to be publicly responsible. Juvenile told me in an interview that he doesn't make "the decisions [on] the business part of it. I don't worry about that. I just try to be the best rapper in the world and make sure that my own shit is straight." But on another level, ignorance can be wily, a form of self-identification that assimilates disparagement and prejudice and turns them back around (like movie stars from the 1930s "shucking and jiving" to get over, or like Ice T proclaiming himself a "nigga" back in the early 1990s). When I asked Juvenile in 2000 why he didn't look so dour as other hardcore MCs, he said, "They knuckleheads. Some rappers wanna be hard. I know I'm a man, I know I'm hard, I ain't got nothing to prove. I don't have to be out there with all that bullshit, you feel me? I come from the projects, ain't no secret. I been through it. I been out there. But I ain't gonna keep on acting like I'm the baddest motherfucker on the earth."[15] Juvenile's refusal to "act" is itself a choreographed performance, commanding respect and systematically refuting detractors.

While his style with Mannie Fresh might be called "formulaic," in its use of signature drum machines and a particular bounce beat, on the new CD, Juvenile works with other producers. While formula can be wildly successful in terms of sales, it can also be limiting for the artistic "development" that is essential to musicians' careers in the long run. Mannie Fresh's self-repetition from song to song and album to album—a series of variations on a theme—is increasingly refined and shaded, producing hits and also cementing his reputation as an artist in his own right, a creative force is to be reckoned with. Though Mannie worked in-house only for many years, when he left CMR, like Juvenile, he reported he felt underappreciated at the label.

Juve performs a studied ignorance that recollects his project background and lack of formal education: he's a proud self-made man. Lil' Wayne, now 23 and one of the only Hot Boys who remains with CMR, frankly reports his past. At 14, he says, "My grades was low," and he was depressed, smoking a lot of weed and just hanging around the house; "the final straw came," reports *The Source*'s Kris Ex, "when Wayne accidentally shot himself in the chest with his mom's .44 glock handgun."[16] Lil Wayne's casually contrite description of the violence that shapes not only street experience but also domestic life in the projects (his *mother's* gun) demonstrates why he was once the ideal Hot Boy, and continues to claim the concept, as in his single, "Fireman," in which video he appears amid projects and grounds burning.

After the breakout success of the "Ha" video, which rotated all over MTV and BET, Juve's second single, "Back That Ass Up," was even more popular. On *Total Request Live*,

"Back That Ass Up" (transformed into "Back That Thang Up" for radio and MTV play) rotated alongside the Backstreet Boys' "Larger Than Life" and Mandy Moore's "Candy," both conspicuously saccharine videos, the first a lively paean to the Backstreet Boys' fans, the second showcasing Moore's then baby doll beauty.

The juxtaposition revealed the ways that pop culture works, the ways it absorbs and adjusts to perceived threats to its ascendancy. Juvenile wasn't so much assimilated by popular culture as he became it, an example of its perpetual mutation, its capacity to accommodate and, corrupt or co-opt original art. Consider, for instance, his appearance with the Hot Boys on the Quincy Jones-produced talk show *Jenny Jones*. When the Hot Boys performed Lil' Wayne's "Tha Block is Hot," Jones introduced them by asking her studio audience to "make some noise for Lil' Wayne," behaving as if she was experienced in such matters. The audience complies, cheering while a few young women rush the tiny studio stage. This moment—Jones's self-positioning as "down" with her famously "hip" guests—exemplifies what we might call maximum crossover: the nice white lady host was applauding the Hot Boys' ruckus on daytime TV. The censors bleeped the curse words but no one was troubled by the fierce narrative of "Tha Block is Hot." Perhaps this is because violence is common on shows like *Jenny Jones* (which features stories of vengeance and victimization), or perhaps no one watching the show translates the group's "street" slang. Lil' Wayne tells his own dire story:

> Straight off the black gold, nuts in my hand, trustin' no man.
> Got my glock cocked, runnin' this thing, ya understand.
> We be steamin', blazin', nines, pumps, and k's, and
> Holly Grove 17th, tha hood where I was raised.

Though the *Jenny Jones* audience likely knew something about hardship and privation, Lil' Wayne's biography—his easy familiarity with a variety of assault weapons, his frankly nightmarish childhood—must have seemed at least a little strange. But in performance, such vicissitude becomes safe and even sympathetic. The talk show audience can understand Lil' Wayne as a fellow victim, admirably resolved to overcome his humble, arduous beginnings.

A more telling illumination of crossover misunderstanding and approbation might be the moment when Celine Dion was a studio guest on *TRL* in early 1999. During the show, then-host Carson Daly invited his guest to comment on the videos that have been voted by viewers into the program's countdown. At the end of the video for "Back That Ass Up," Dion showed her approval. The video shows a series of young black women backing their *derrières* up into the wide-angle lens, which magnifies the ample "booties" that Juvenile is encouraging them to shake. "Girl," he raps,

> You looks good, won't you back that azz up.
> You'se a fine motherfucker, won't you back that azz up.
> You got a stupid ass yeah, make me laugh, yeah,
> Make a nigga wanna grab that, autograph that.
> I'm sweatin in the drawers, yeah, hard and long yeah.
> Wanna walk it like a dog, yeah, break you off, yeah.

At first Dion just smiled when Daly asks how she liked the video. Then she gestured awkwardly with her arms and fingers, making grim faces as she pretended to throw (gang) signs. Finally, she backed her famously skinny ass up to the studio camera, while Daly initially looked aghast, then laughed in manifest disbelief.

Dion struggled to act like she knew what the video meant to its creators and fans, and in doing so, she occupied two very different positions: that of the men soliciting women's self-display ("Wanna walk it like a dog, yeah"), and that of the women eagerly exhibiting their assets. Both positions were far removed from Dion's own celebrated, squeaky-clean image. Yet her uncomfortable performance is also instructive, illustrating succinctly the perils of cultural appropriation. Dion's imitation is a joke that, by clumsy counter-example, reveals the potential costs of "crossing over" without intelligence. Juvenile and the Hot Boys crossed over by creating controversy, specifically by evoking the stereotype of the sexually "aggressive" black male. The Hot Boys' raucous verbal and visual performances—particularly their expressions of sexual desire and possession in "Back That Ass Up" and "I Need a Hot Girl"— descended from early black comedians' work (Richard Pryor) and hypersexualized black male actors (Jim Brown, Melvin Van Peebles) as well as 2 Live Crew's incendiary work way back in the early 1990s. But there was something else going on, aside from such a familiar rebellion against gender and sexed propriety. This something else had to do with an intelligent self-situating in relation to class. The Hot Boys' class politics were less accusatory than self-assertive, as they seemed literally to incarnate "success" and class mobility within a cultural system designed to deny it to them; their politics is not intimidating, but rather, seductive and "fun."

However, this fun—however smart or subversive its execution can be—also had limits. Some of these are clear in an episode of MTV's weekly news magazine, *1515*, that showcases the Ruff Ryders/Cash Money Tour's date in Philadelphia in late 1999. Sensationalizing its news, the half-hour program—after showing performances by and interviews with Ruff Ryders DMX, Eve, and Drag-on—climaxed with a mini-story on the Hot Boys' performance of "Back That Ass Up." Juve introduced the segment—which MTV titled "Back That Fan Up"—stating, "We enjoy ourselves while we out there, we make sure everybody gets their money's worth." The concert footage then showed a female audience member who ascended the stage and backs her naked ass up to the Hot Boys: the handheld video image showed her blurred-out butt and the crew performing around her. Leading up to this shot, and after it, *1515* included interviews with very different observers—several audience members, BG, and finally Eve, the only woman MC on the tour. BG observed that many women offered such displays, then grinned, adding that in Philadelphia, "They had one up there that gave us a shout-out to the world!" Several brief interviews with young black women fans at the Philadelphia show followed, evincing their disgust at the woman who got on stage. One girl said, "We were singin' along until that nasty girl got up on the stage and started showin' her stuff: now that's triflin'!"; and another declared, "That was actually a disgrace!"

The last interview in this segment, clearly arranged as a "final word" by MTV, set up reporter John Norris in front of a unisex bathroom, where kids were lined up to get into stalls. He was talking to Eve, goading her about that she was the only woman on the tour, before he asked, "What did you think of that?" And Eve, ever-cool, showed that intelligence is relative, contextual, and provocative. Rather than condone the show as simple "fun" or condemn the individual woman for her "indecent" actions, as the previous interviewees have done, Eve took another tack. She pointed out problems with the Hot Boys' self-aggrandizing sexual entreaties as part of a larger cultural context. While she allowed that they conducted themselves well enough around her on the tour, Eve didn't hide her disapproval: "It's all in fun, but at the same time, they are a little ignorant towards women, which I don't respect. I think they can be a little bit nicer."

Eve's canny perspective takes into account a number of others, including those of her tour mates and her (male and female) fans, and significantly articulates her own nuanced feminism. While she demands mutual respect between the sexes, she also understands—in ways that Jenny Jones and Celine Dion may not—the complex tensions that occur between two oppressed classes, in this case black men and women. In writing about 2 Live Crew's obscenity trial (the rap group was acquitted of charges brought against them by Broward County, Florida officials in 1990), Kimberle Crenshaw enumerates what she calls an "intersectional critique" of the ways that sexism and racism shape black women's experiences.[17] Crenshaw uses this approach as a way to "frame the following inquiry: How does the fact that women of color are simultaneously situated within at least two groups that are subjected to broad societal subordination bear upon problems traditionally viewed as monocausal— that is, gender discrimination or race discrimination."[18] Eve's remarks illustrate her consciousness of such framing, and underline the ways that Jenny Jones and Celine Dion (not to mention the Hot Boys and John Norris) show no such consciousness. At the same time that Jones, for example, didn't need to recognize the violence or reality conveyed by Lil' Wayne's lyrics (they are part of her show's "entertainment"), his fans comprehend and appreciate them as art *and* reportage: he described his experience (and often, theirs), using language and imagery that conforms to stereotypes while simultaneously challenging them. Similarly, for "Back That Ass Up," the Hot Boys' female fans can differentiate themselves from the "nasty" girl; they appreciate the show (for its pleasures and resistances to racism and classism) but can distance themselves from the "ignorance" that Eve saw in it.

How different Juvenile appears today. Following his painful split with CMR and the hurricane that destroyed the home he was building (still no insurance payments for that, though he's clearly not as hard up as most people in the city), Juve has been through even more hardship. He tells *Zone*'s Maurice G. Garland that he's still "gangsta," and has no plans to "get on that politician shit." But at the same time, the hurricane changed *Reality Check*, nearly completed on that fateful day in August 2005. "By it hitting," he says about Katrina, "it made the album more truthful so I went and recorded some new songs. I got my reality check from seeing my [four] kids and my family have to move somewhere else."[19]

Some version of this "truthfulness" is visible in the first two videos released to promote *Reality Check*. For the first, "Rodeo," Juvenile revisits and revises his well-known appreciation for wide-bottomed women. But here the beautiful objects are introduced first by their names ("Dark & Lovely," "Obsession," "Innocent," "Cha-Cha") listed on a sign-in sheet, and then as they pass before Marc Klasfeld's camera. They move in somber slow motion; the beat still bounces, the song is observant and reflective rather than lustful: a woman says good-bye to her young daughter, they walk inside a strip club, where a worker polishes the stage poles while the women prepare backstage, one juggling a baby on her lap as she applies her makeup. For most of the video, Juvenile appears alone and in artful shadow, not ogling or rowdy, but descriptive: the girls put on a show, men pay for their fantasies ("See how I'm holdin' the steering wheel, controllin' the ride./And y'all comin' out of park because I got it in drive"), and the video's viewers are implicated in the exchange, or at least made aware of the women's labor, the structuring of the desire. Dancers strap on their bikinis and thongs, some women argue backstage, another studies her biology textbook, and men with observable bling wave champagne bottles from an observation room, looking down on the stage, oblivious to the lives that extend beyond it. When the show's over, the women leave as they came in, dressed in jeans and looking weary. The video reveals a shift in understanding, an awareness of the process of ambition and need. Unlike, say, the delirious "Back That Ass Up," "Rodeo" acknowledges the ways that desire is culturally constructed, not inherent and certainly not simple.

For "Get Ya Hustle On/What's Happenin'," Juvenile, director Ben Mor, and a camera crew shot in the wreckage of New Orleans, in such a way that the mobile frame recalls at times the images in "Ha." But here the devastation is more apocalyptic, the effects of the storm still grim. The video opens with an epigraph: "This is a tribute to those who died in the wrath of Hurricane Katrina. The storm may have passed but for thousands, the struggle is just beginning." The camera, using stock that leaves faded blue hues, shows an angel statue, collapsed houses, and a videotape amid the ruins, *Armageddon*. As Juve raps, "Talk to 'em: your mayor ain't your friend, he's the enemy./Just to get your vote, a saint is what he pretend to be./Fuck him! Ah—listen to me, I got the remedy," the camera cuts to a trio of boys rummaging through debris. They come on three paper masks—Mayor Nagin, Vice President Cheney, and President Bush—with the note "Help is coming" written on the other side. The kids (whom Juvenile says "weren't no actors") put on the masks and walk through the streets, carrying sticks and dragging a sack of collected clutter, poking at garbage and pieces of buildings. Cars appear upturned. The kids pass spectral figures—bewildered citizens, abandoned, holding signs that read, "Still here" and "2005 or 2006."

Just so, Juvenile is still here, representing a population made suddenly, if briefly, visible by the storm. Renewed in his purpose and evolved in his self-identity, he has also adjusted his performance. While he hasn't altered his Nolia swagger and slang, as these reconfirm his sense of place and history, Juvenile repeatedly names himself as a husband and father, as well as mentor and producer for other artists on his Atlantic imprint, UTP (Uptown Project Playas). Having survived the projects, Cash Money, and Katrina, Juvenile is now looking grown up.

Notes

1 S. Craig Watkins, *Representing: Hip-hop Culture and the Production of Black Cinema* (Chicago: Chicago University Press, 1998), 230.

2 Charlie Braxton, "When I'm Gone," *Scratch* (Mar/Apr 2006), 69.

3 Braxton, 72.

4 Sacha Jenkins, "Soldier of Fortune," *Vibe* (May 2000), 99.

5 Brolin Winning, "Interview with Juvenile," MP3.com (3 March 2006). http://www.mp3.com/stories/3510.html

6 Watkins, 230.

7 Adolph Reed Jr., *Stirrings in the Jug: Black Politics in the Post-Segregationist Era* (Minneapolis: University of Minnesota Press, 2000), 179–196.

8 Reed, 184.

9 Jon Pareles, "Gangsta Rap's Choices in Life, Death and Love," *New York Times* (29 February 2000), B5.

10 Rob Sheffield, "Review: *Only God Can Judge Me* and *Tha G Code*," *Rolling Stone* (20 January 2000), 59.

[11] Jenkins, 97.

[12] Jenkins, 100. The magazine spread contains a sidebar on Cash Money's jeweler Sol Virani (who also made the first diamond-and-platinum No Limit tank pendant), with an emphasis on numbers: he made a set of $6000 gold teeth for Wayne, a $20,000 pendant for Juvenile, and a set of $16,000 diamond-and-platinum teeth for Baby Williams.

[13] Michele Wallace, "Masculinity in Black Popular Culture: Could it be that Political Correctness is the Problem?" *Constructing Masculinity*, ed. Maurice Berger, Brian Wallis, Simon Watson (London: Routledge, 1995), 302.

[14] Robin D.G. Kelley, "Kickin reality, kickin ballistics: gangsta rap and postindustrial los angeles," *Droppin Science: Critical Essays on Rap and Hip-hop Culture*, ed. William Eric Perkins (Philadelphia: Temple University Press, 1996), 121.

[15] Cynthia Fuchs, "Happy Rapper: Interview with Juvenile," *Popmatters.com.* February 2000. www.popmatters.com/music/interviews/juvenile.shtml

[16] Kris Ex, "Heat," *The Source* (October 1999), 196.

[17] Kimberle Williams Crenshaw, "Beyond Racism and Misogyny: Black Feminism and 2 Live Crew," *Words That Wound: Critical Race Theory, Assaultive Speech, and the First Amendment,* by Mari J. Matsuda, Charles Lawrence III, Richard Delgado, and Kimberle Williams Crenshaw (Boulder CO: Westview Press, 1993), 113.

[18] Crenshaw, 114.

[19] Maurice G. Garland, "After the Storm: Juvenile is Back, Stronger Than Ever," *Zone* (April 2006), 62.

Chapter 14

"We're all quite small, really"

Races, Classes, Globalisms in "Heroes"

Peter Clandfield

Just over halfway through the premiere episode of "Heroes" (first broadcast 25 September 2006), Peter Petrelli (Milo Ventimiglia), an earnest young New York nurse beginning to recognize his unusual abilities, catches a cab driven by Mohinder Suresh (Sendhil Ramamurthy), a young geneticist from Madras, India, who has come to New York in the wake of his father, murdered while researching the mutations behind powers such as Peter's. Peter, at the moment, is fascinated by the solar eclipse that is in progress. The eclipse mysteriously intensifies the hero-powers around which the series revolves, but of more definite interest are Mohinder's remarks on the phenomenon's social and cultural implications: "A global event: makes one appreciate just how small our planet really is, but then we're all quite small, really, aren't we?" These words evoke two crucial—

and contradictory—ideas that will resonate through the twenty-three episodes of "Volume One" of the series.

On the one hand, Mohinder's reference to the smallness of our planet is among the first of many ways in which "Heroes," in exploring links and alliances among its diverse characters, asserts the interconnection of all members of the human race. In their immediate context, Mohinder's words hint at his irritation at having to drive a cab to subsist as a foreigner in New York. But as the sequence continues, he and Peter establish a tentative mutual regard, emphasized by shots of their eye contact in the rear-view mirror. Peter proves the most important of the many "heroes" we meet in this show, able to learn, absorb, and thus mimic the powers of any other specially-abled person he encounters. Yet Mohinder is the chief investigator of such powers; he is also, in voiceovers that frame key episodes of the show, the most explicit commentator on the questions these powers raise. Although his role is complex and contradictory in its implications, Mohinder is the focal character for the series. His role as a figure both non-white and non-American is only one of the more prominent of numerous features through which "Heroes" offers some resistance to presumptions that whiteness is normative.[1]

On the other hand, Mohinder's reflections on the eclipse also set up the ambiguous role played in "Heroes" by forms of determinism other than white-centred casting or storylines. Key to these is the idea that most individual human beings, regardless of background, are too "small" to do anything but what their genes dictate. Peter's and Mohinder's initial rapport is based on common interest in "special" people, and as their conversation continues Mohinder talks about natural selection as a form of "destiny" favoring individuals whose "genetic code[s] . . . will take their species to the next evolutionary rung." An important object of pursuit in the series is the list of such individuals that Mohinder's father has compiled: people whose genetic profiles mark them as possessors of various "special" physical or psychic abilities. Accordingly, among the promotional catchphrases for the first season was "Are you on the list?" (a question no doubt intended to provoke many potential viewers into hoping or believing they are). It is true that the characters who are most adamantly deterministic in outlook are also the main villains of Volume One: Sylar (Zachary Quinto), the elder Suresh's "patient zero," a psychopathic anti-Peter who must murder other heroes and eat their brains to absorb their powers; and Linderman (Malcolm McDowell), a mysterious Las Vegas crime boss and avid eugenicist who plots a nuclear explosion in New York City to provide a clean slate for a redesigned "world order." However, while both villains are, apparently, destroyed as Linderman's plan is thwarted by cooperation among the more virtuous characters in the final episodes of the Volume, the series does not banish the deterministic idea that only heroes, and perhaps those dedicated adepts such as Mohinder who are able to understand and assist them, are "big" enough to make a difference to the future of humankind—a future which may bring globalized and commercialized racial and class divisions based on genotypic rather than phenotypic differences.[2]

Generic Inheritances

The adventurous but ambiguous exploration in "Heroes" of questions of "race" has roots in science fiction and fantasy. Comic books, inspiration for both the superhuman characters and the graphic style of the series, have often featured heroes serving progressive social causes: historian Bradford W. Wright notes that the original Superman stories "affirmed . . . an inclusive national culture" and "cast their superhero as a 'champion of the oppressed.'" Yet, as Wright points out, it was paradoxical that these stories' common people, though depicted as inherently more virtuous than the rich and powerful, required assistance from "the righteous violence" of the superhero.[3] "Heroes" similarly espouses principles of human equality, yet routinely suggests that this equality must be created and protected by a select few beings.

Additional complications arise concerning the use of science fiction and fantasy to address specifically racialized forms of inequality. As Gregory E. Rutledge points out, discourses of white supremacy can themselves be seen as "a protracted science fiction, or insidious fantasy."[4] Further, theorists such as Paul Gilroy argue that "race" itself—or the idea that visible, phenotypic differences between people or populations correlate meaningfully with underlying biological differences—is an obsolete fiction, at best dangerously archaic and at worst insidiously complicit with forms of fascism.[5] Gilroy discusses the capacities of fantasy and science fiction to explore possibilities for a human future beyond such thinking. He notes, for instance, that "American television's first interracial kiss was between William Shatner and Nichelle Nichols" on the original "Star Trek" (1966–1969). The Kirk-Uhura kiss was depicted as non-voluntary and alien-induced, but while Daniel Bernardi argues that it was thus "coded as undesirable and perverse," Gilroy, citing Nichols's comments on positive fan mail, suggests that it was decoded by many viewers in ways that "focused the widely shared sense of race consciousness as earthbound and anachronistic."[6] Bernardi's book *"Star Trek" and History: Race-ing Toward a White Future* (1998) addresses ways in which fantasy and science fiction, in looking to a future beyond racism, can gloss over its intractable present effects; Gilroy himself cautions that "deconstructing 'races' is not the same thing as doing away with racisms."[7] "Heroes" registers this distinction by combining attention to ways in which phenotypic "race" still does matter with persistent suggestions that divisions constructed in its name can and should be overcome. Although it does not neatly resolve all the issues of phenotypic race that it raises, the series evokes less a white future than a mixed present, and it succeeds notably in making whiteness (or Euro-American-ness) itself visible as one part of this mix, and not necessarily the dominant one.

A Heroic Mix

The racial mix of "Heroes" is integral from the first episode onward. We begin with images of Peter on the verge of flying, as Mohinder voices large philosophical questions. Peter awakes in the Manhattan penthouse of the wealthy African American man, Charles Deveaux (Richard Roundtree), whom he is nursing through a terminal illness. Peter's nap has ended on the arrival of Deveaux's daughter, Simone (Tawny Cypress), who praises Peter's work and tells him that he is "like a son" to her father. Boldly going where "Star Trek" went before, Peter replies, "That would make us like brother and sister . . . might be a little awkward if I ever wanted to ask you out." Simone mentions that she is attached, but she is visibly interested in him, and the fact that awkwardness arises from intimation of familial similarity rather than phenotypic difference positions interracial romance as distinctly other than the controversial topic it has been for much of American history, indeed an ordinary fact.[8] Further, Simone's light skin and eyes suggest that she is herself mixed. She and Peter disengage from their flirtation, but it will lead to a relationship—by no means the only interracial one in the first season. The action cuts to Mohinder, lecturing in India three days previously, just before learning of his father's death. Gazing at a world map, he tells his class, "We have colonized the four corners of our tiny planet, but we are not the pinnacle of so-called evolution. That honour belongs to the lowly cockroach, capable of living for months without food . . . . If God has indeed created himself in his own image, then I submit to you that God is a cockroach." I will return to the way Mohinder's idealized remarks elide the relatively recent history wherein some of "us" have colonized others; notable for now is that through shots of the Madras students' restive reactions to Mohinder's ponderous wit, the sequence constructs them as ordinary and emphasizes what they may share with ordinary peers in other corners of the world.

The episode shifts back to the United States, but continues to broaden the mix of characters. Las Vegas single mother Niki Sanders (Ali Larter) works as an internet stripper in a failing effort to repay money borrowed—from Linderman—in order to place her ten-year-old son Micah (Noah Gray-Cabey) in a private school she hopes will develop his prodigious abilities. While Niki is white and blonde, Micah, like Simone, has features indicating mixed white-black parentage. His presence both reiterates the normality of racial hybridity and sets up curiosity about his family history and about the origin of his powers, which manifest as an intuitive control of computers and other machines. The next character introduced, Texas high-school cheerleader Claire Bennet (Hayden Panettiere), is another blonde. Yet, her phenotypic similarity with Niki sets off their differences in social circumstance: Claire is comfortably upper-middle-class, and her main concern in this episode is coming to terms with her apparent physical indestructibility: she experiments with injuring herself and her body "miraculously" heals within moments. Niki, in contrast, must deal both with Linderman's pursuing (and notably malevolent) goons and with a condescending school official, who rejects her pleas for financial concessions to keep Micah enrolled, saying, "I just don't know if this school is the right *fit* for him." The word "fit" is loaded and coded, yet sufficiently non-specific to target both Niki's class and Micah's race. This sequence exposes not only the inequities of access to education in the United States but also the euphemistic ways in which underlying issues may be evaded in a masking bureaucracy. The official's bland disdain triggers the first—very brief—appearance of Niki's rather problematic hero-powers: she has a violent alter ego, "Jessica," who takes over and threatens the man, before peaceable Niki regains control.

Two additional key heroes join the mix in the premiere episode. New York artist Isaac Mendez (Santiago Cabrera) has visionary powers that inspire him to produce, in a kind of blind trance, alarming paintings of the near future, including one of a man exploding in New York. Simone is Isaac's girlfriend and art dealer, but his heroin use, apparently necessary for his visions, estranges them. Meanwhile, Hiro Nakamura (Masi Oka) is a goofy and charming Japanese office-worker with powers of time/space travel. Hiro's initial role is to provide comic relief, in the company of his powerless but loyal sidekick, Ando Masahashi (James Kyson Lee), but the nerdiness of his enthusiasm, along with its associations with stereotypes of Japanese-ness (his obsession with technology; his fascination with American popular culture), is tempered as the season progresses and he is drawn into the heroic effort to prevent disaster. An interracial romance of his own contributes to Hiro's maturation: in episode 8, "Seven Minutes to Midnight," he meets Texas waitress Charlie Andrews (Jayma Mays), whose remarkable memory powers have helped her to learn conversational Japanese in a flash. However, their bonding is cut short when Charlie is murdered by the lurking Sylar. Hiro time-travels back six months in a bid to save her; they become close, but Charlie reveals that she is dying (of a cerebral blood clot). Just as they declare mutual love and prepare to kiss, Hiro's powers fail and he is transported back to Japan, and the present. He materializes among co-workers exercising on his company's rooftop lawn, and the figure he presents as a dazed stranger in his own country hints that he has become Americanized and that the international mix of heroes could be more like a melting pot. Hiro's Japanese heritage reasserts itself, however, as he rededicates himself to his mission, which he sees, under the influence of Isaac's paintings, and later that of his father (George Takei, one of the stars of "Star Trek"), as that of a Samurai warrior.[9]

Other interracial romances in Volume One are also thwarted. Isaac's visions reveal the developing relationship between Simone and Peter, and the triangle has disastrous results in episode 16, "Unexpected," when an enraged Isaac shoots at Peter—who has acquired the power of invisibility—but kills Simone instead. Isaac himself is later killed by Sylar, though not before foreseeing the psychopath's own death by Hiro's sword. Isaac's death-sequence depicts him as nobly willing to meet a sacrificial fate as redemption for a wasted life. Of the heroes introduced at the start of the series, Isaac is the one most defined by his powers and their usefulness to the narrative, rather than by ordinary concerns of his own: there is little attention to his family or his Hispanic heritage, a heritage which can thus be seen as the kind of token gesture toward diversity that the series has taken pains to avoid in its treatment of other non-white characters.[10] Yet, whatever the blind spots in the depiction of Isaac and Hiro, racial difference itself is never the problem with their romantic relationships.

The two central white families in Volume One have significant issues of their own. Peter's brother, politician Nathan Petrelli (Adrian Pasdar), can fly like Superman but is more interested in winning a seat in Congress and has accepted Linderman's financial help for his campaign. What is more, Peter and Nathan's mother, Angela Petrelli (Cristine Rose), turns out to be in league with Linderman and privy to his plot to devastate New York and install Nathan as the leader who will subsequently restore order. Claire's Bennet's family suffers different but equally notable complications. Her seemingly sinister father Noah (Jack Coleman) works for a secretive Company that is tracking heroes and the Sureshes as well. Claire is adopted, and after much intrigue she learns that her "real" father is Nathan Petrelli. Angela Petrelli appeals to biological kinship to try to persuade Claire not to intervene in the climactic events, even though these events will result in Peter's death. However, Claire, having bonded with Peter when he saves her from Sylar (in episode 9, "Homecoming"), rightly puts her trust in him and in her adoptive father, who has by now broken with the Company—which turns out, not altogether surprisingly, to be controlled by Linderman—over the question of her future. The plot line of Volume One, then, decisively suggests that at least for white characters elective family loyalties can be more reliable than biological ones.

Yet it is also true that the defeat of Linderman's agenda requires the collective effort of Volume One's key biological, and interracial, family: Niki, Micah, and Micah's father, D. L. Hawkins (Leonard Roberts).

Attacking Determinism

In prison for murder as the narrative of Volume One begins, D.L. does not appear until the end of the fifth episode, but he is constructed in his absence as a stereotypical object of white fear: a volatile, lawless black man. But this profile is deployed in order to be undercut.[11] Once he arrives at Niki and Micah's home, having escaped using his powers of "phasing" through matter, D.L. is depicted as rational, reasonable, and committed to his wife and son. As Niki struggles both with her increasingly aggressive alter ego (who committed the crime for which D.L. was jailed) and with Linderman's attempts to enlist Jessica's homicidal tendencies in his criminal enterprises, D.L. becomes Micah's lead parent. His troubled past does cause him difficulty in the role, and in episode 13, unemployed and short of money, he appeals to Micah for understanding: "I've never felt much . . . like a man in my life. My papa never taught me. But I wanna be a good dad to you—gonna need your help." The ten-year-old Micah promptly produces a pile of cash, which his powers have allowed him to obtain from bank machines. In itself, the sequence could be seen as retrograde: D.L., the adult black man, requires his son's ethically unorthodox (and presumably obviously illegal) help.[12] Yet, the sequence fits into the larger narrative's ongoing challenge to deterministic social views, as D.L. overcomes his problems and goes on to bravely confront Linderman.

Oddly like D.L. in the early episodes, but on a larger scale, Linderman is an absent presence. Mentioned frequently as the force behind various plot events, he does not appear in person until the 18th episode. His prolonged invisibility signals his sinister efficiency, and can also be read as evoking the historical ability of powerful white people to maintain their advantages while presenting the effects of their machinations as the inevitable results of natural processes. His white hair and beard, blue eyes, and British accent emphasize Linderman's phenotypic whiteness, and details such as his vaguely Germanic name and his apparent vegetarianism link him suggestively to all-too-well-known white-supremacists, as does his plan to remake the world. (Linderman's own power of healing is both ironic and a possible explanation for his belief in dramatic biological forces over prosaic social ones.) Linderman's ultimate interest in Niki and D.L.—whose relationship he claims to have orchestrated—concerns Micah, whose abilities he plans to use on voting machines to ensure Nathan's election. Niki refuses to cooperate, but Linderman calls in his disciple Candice Wilmer (Missy Peregrym), who can morph into anyone she chooses and who impersonates Niki to get Micah to New York. In a key sequence in the penultimate episode, Niki/Jessica and D.L. phase into Linderman's headquarters and confront him. He boasts of having "craft[ed their] opportunities," and D.L. denounces him: "You think being rich makes you better than us?" Linderman's contemptuous response sums up his views: "Well, social Darwinism did play its part—I believe destiny to be intrinsic!" After trying and failing to turn Jessica against D.L., Linderman shoots at her, but D.L. takes the bullet. As Linderman prepares to fire again, D.L. rallies and phases a fatal fist into the back of his head. The sequence repeats at the beginning of the final episode, and the assault on Linderman's brain stem tempts the claim that this is Volume One's key conceptual moment, the decisive attack on determinist thinking. Yet the fact that the assault is delivered by D.L., the series character most obviously opposed to Linderman in terms of class and race, seems in itself almost too schematic—a binary reversal of old racial hierarchies. Moreover, Linderman's conspiracy goes on without him in the final episode, led by Angela Petrelli. The attack on determinism, however, does not rest only on the physical defeat of Linderman.

Linderman implies that breeding super-heroes is part of his larger plans for remaking the world, and that Micah figures importantly in these plans. Micah's visible mixed-ness can be read as a metaphor for his potential as a child of two heroes; his powers, though, remain relatively modest in their manifestations, perhaps because he is a juvenile, and his main role in Volume One is intellectual. In New York in episode 22, having sensed that Candice is not his mother and provoked her to show herself, Micah probes her ability to pass as anyone she chooses. Candice reveals that her regular appearance, as a slender white brunette, is itself a guise, and when she takes Micah to fulfil Linderman's election-rigging plan, she morphs into a middle-aged African American woman, "Ms. Baker" (Kimleigh Smith), and explains bringing Micah into the polling booth by saying he is her son, whom she wants to teach about democracy. The trick prompts Micah to speculate on Candice's powers: "You must bend light or something." Amused, "Ms. Baker" replies, "How do you know this isn't the real me?" Still laughing as they enter the booth, she morphs back into the white Candice—apparently only another disguise. The "Ms. Baker" guise itself, if it is a guise, seems tactically unnecessary on Candice's part, since Micah is mixed—as the sequence reminds us—and should thus pass readily as the biological (or adoptive) child of the white Candice just as much as the child of "Ms. Baker." Linderman, who has planned this strategy, clearly believes Micah will be less noticeable with a black woman. The sequence serves, in any case, to teach us about the racial implications of Candice's character: as someone who can look however she chooses, she is, effectively, genotypically raceless, and her choice, typically, of "normal"—white—phenotype both illustrates and invites critique of the normative status of whiteness, implicitly acknowledging that it still carries concrete privileges.

Micah's further intellectual contribution to Volume One is his response to Candice's claims that Linderman will "heal the world." Coolly (and like countless other exceptionally wise television children), he remarks, "I didn't know it was sick." In the final episode, this anti-catastrophic view is taken up by Charles Deveaux, who dies in episode 7 but remains a presence both in Peter's dreams and in sequences sketching the backstory of the heroes and the Company. During the final episode, Peter, pursuing Sylar, who he assumes will be the source of the nuclear explosion, passes out while struggling to control his own nuclear capabilities. He finds himself in a lucid dream at Deveaux's rooftop garden, revisiting his first day as the sick man's caregiver and witnessing a crucial conversation between his mother and Deveaux about Linderman's plan. Deveaux states to Angela, "I don't believe this tragedy is inevitable," and argues that the abilities he has detected in Peter, and above all his optimism, represent better hope for the future. Then, after Angela has left, Deveaux addresses the present-day Peter, whose dream he is, apparently, orchestrating and inhabiting: "You needed to hear the truth, before you could save the world . . . In the end, all that really matters is love." Deveaux's revelation as a senior-generation hero may invoke a fairly common positive Black character type: the sagacious, patient, even God-like older figure.[13] The revelation works, though, to bring the final episode unexpectedly full-circle with the opening one, and Deveaux's role as the crucial counsellor for Peter reiterates that familiality is made, not born. Then, again, the end of the episode hedges its bets in this respect, since it is Peter who goes nuclear (while Sylar is dispatched by Hiro), and Nathan, motivated by brotherly love after all, who intervenes and flies Peter off to explode at a safe distance in the stratosphere (and out of view), leaving their fates uncertain. Still, what saves the world—or at least New York—in the end is selfless cooperation among the various key characters, heroes and non-heroes alike.

The Two Mohinders and "Planetary Humanism" vs. Globalism

After the disaster is averted, Mohinder delivers a final voiceover, emphasizing humanism over heroism: "So much struggle for meaning, for purpose! And in the end, we find it only in each other: our shared experience of the fantastic—and the mundane." Mohinder himself has shared significantly in the plot events of Volume One. His investigation of his father's death leads him to be tricked temporarily into facilitating Sylar's attacks on other heroes, but he realizes what is happening and makes determined efforts to stop the psychopath. In the process, he encounters the Company and Bennet's unctuously ruthless boss, Thompson (Eric Roberts), who co-opts his help (episode 21) in fixing the Company's so-called "tracking system," a young white girl, Molly Walker (Adair Tishler), who can discern the exact location of anyone at any time. Mohinder denounces Thompson as an "untrustworthy *goonda*." Though the English adjective translates its general sense, the Hindi noun, meaning *rascal* or *thug*, asserts Mohinder's independence of Thompson and his associates. He also uses his heritage in treating the disorder that is interfering with Molly's powers. His own sister, Shanti, who died soon before he was born, had the same genetic anomaly as Molly, the same abilities and the same ailment; Mohinder discovers that he himself possesses the antibodies Molly needs. Their connection serves both to explain the origins of Mohinder's father's research and to reiterate the biological unity of humankind. The final episode of Volume One finds Mohinder helping to protect both Molly and the injured D.L. The fact that Mohinder himself apparently has no hero-powers makes his intelligence and courage all the more notable, and in turn makes him more appealing as a viewer surrogate. He is a relatively ordinary man investigating new frontiers of science and human possibility.

Mohinder, however, is like several of the heroes, most obviously Niki/Jessica, in that he has two distinct identities. Mohinder the visible character is fallible, though principled and sincere; but Mohinder the narrator implicitly claims a power of his own: omniscience. While his pomposity as a lecturer in the opening episode invites in us a skeptical view of his claims about what "we" are or have done, his voiceovers often have much the same grandiose, universalizing quality. Nor do all of his pronouncements sound quite as deterministic as the one he delivers at the end of episode 7 concerning the difficulties heroes may face with "ordinary" humans, who "cannot fathom how much you [heroes] stand to lose in failure—that you are the instrument of a flawless design, and all of life may hang in the balance. The hero learns quickly who can comprehend and who merely stands in your way." However, the fact that the voiceovers originate—as far as we know—beyond the diegetic time and space of the series implies a determining design on the part of series creators. Also notable in this context are the qualities of Mohinder's voice itself, whose inflections evoke those of British Received Pronunciation.[14] This voice may not be anomalous coming from an educated Indian, but it makes possible an association between the character and a post-racial discourse that naturalizes the effects of British colonialism and other historical white-supremacist regimes and implies that individuals, and their genes, are now solely in charge of their destinies.

As science policy scholar Jenny Reardon points out, assertions of human racial unity have often had underlying agendas other than the disinterested pursuit of truth and justice.[15] Paul Gilroy diagnoses the rise of "a corporate multiculturalism in which some degree of visible difference from an implicit white norm may be highly prized as a sign of timeliness, vitality, inclusivity, and global reach." Gilroy implies a parallel between the rise of commercialized celebrations of individual physical superiority and the eclipse of phenotype-based discriminations by genotype-based ones.[16] Viewing "Heroes" in this light suggests that hero-powers in general, and their attribution to an ethnic and phenotypic array of characters, may be governed or outweighed by a kind of bio-commercial determinism involving what Gilroy calls "the pre-packaged, body-obsessed, and body-transcending cultures of teen consumers everywhere."[17] "Are you on the list?" The series hails young viewers as an upgraded generation.

Reardon's and Gilroy's observations also illuminate political implications of the way the heroes' mission to save New York is equated with saving the world. The crime narrowly prevented at the end of Volume One has similarities with the events of 9/11; the character mix of "Heroes," then, might be read as response to an American call for global assistance, or as an attempt to sell the series globally by marketing images of a racially integrated America.[18] The Volume One finale might also resonate with Gilroy's suggestion that popular texts about the exploits of multi-racial groups of superheroes imply "the radical powerlessness produced by a chronic inability to reduce the salience of racial divisions" in ordinary life.[19] Yet, Gilroy goes on to argue that the popularity of such hero stories (which reflect the same paradox that Wright notes in Superman) also indicates "widespread hunger for a world . . . undivided by the petty differences we retain and inflate by calling them racial." He argues for what he calls "planetary humanism" as a democratic alternative to corporatized globalism.[20] It seems futile to expect a commercial television series as complicated as "Heroes" to offer a comprehensively progressive or even a coherent overview of contemporary issues of race. There would be a disabling kind of determinism, though, in the assumption that such a series has nothing to offer.

While its cheerleader is saved, its New York is protected from devastation, and its world is redeemed, one must wonder whether "Heroes" as an ongoing series, and the continually developing decodings of it by a loyal audience, will manage to preserve a progressive take on planetary nuances of "race," to save progressive thought from eclipse by grand globalisms. Therein lies the real suspense.

Notes

[1] Darnell M. Hunt, citing data on representations of race in US primetime television in 2001–2002, concludes, "In this discursive space, white characters lead and non-white characters follow." Hunt, "Black Content, White Control" in Hunt, ed., *Channelling Blackness: Studies on Television and Race in America* (New York: Oxford University Press, 2005), 299. See also e.g. Daniel Bernardi, ed., *The Persistence of Whiteness: Race and Contemporary Hollywood Cinema* (New York: Routledge, 2008).

2 The ambivalence about determinism seems mirrored in the Introduction to the first book about "Heroes," which points to ethical dangers in seeing heroism as "a genetic imperative of the few," yet remarks that "we might all agree that we could use one or more [heroes] to get the world back on track." See Lynnette Porter, David Lavery, and Hillary Robson, *Saving the World: A Guide to "Heroes"* (Toronto: ECW Press, 2007), 6, 10.

3 Bradford W. Wright, *Comic Book Nation: The Transformation of Youth Culture in America* (Baltimore: Johns Hopkins University Press, 2003), 11, 13.

4 Gregory E. Rutledge, "Futurist Fiction & Fantasy: The *Racial* Establishment," *Callaloo* 24: 1 (2001), 237.

5 Gilroy points out that "raciology" cannot answer such basic questions as how many distinct races there are. See Paul Gilroy, *Against Race: Imagining Political Culture Beyond the Color Line* (Cambridge, MA: Harvard University Press, 2000), 37, 47. This seems a good place to be explicit about "racial" terminology in this essay: for convenience I use the standard terms "white" for someone phenotypically European, "black" for someone phenotypically African, and "mixed" for someone whose appearance suggests combined white-black heritage; for others, I use terms based on ethnicity (Indian, Japanese) or language and culture (Hispanic).

6 The "Star Trek" episode was "Plato's Stepchildren," shown on 22 November 1968. See Gilroy, *Against Race*, 344; Daniel Leonard Bernardi, *"Star Trek" and History: Race-ing Toward a White Future* (New Brunswick, NJ: Rutgers University Press, 1998), 39. Nichelle Nichols herself appears in the strike-shortened second season of "Heroes," as Micah's New Orleans grandmother.

7 Gilroy, *Against Race*, 251.

8 Even Leon E. Wynter, a business-oriented black commentator who suggests that commercialized forms of racial mixing are doing more than political activism can to relegate racism to the past, acknowledges that it was only in the 1990s that mixed romances began to reach mainstream television and movies. Leon E. Wynter, *American Skin: Pop Culture, Big Business, and the End of White America* (New York: Crown Publishers, 2002), 147–148.

9 Hiro's father brings ambiguities of his own, since the role is played by George Takei, who remains probably best-known as Sulu on "Star Trek," and whose presence, like Hiro's own allusions to the classic series, functions to mitigate his son's foreign-ness.

10 On the history of relative invisibility for Hispanics/Latinos on U.S. television, see e.g. Hunt, 285–286.

11 "Heroes" features a second mysterious black man in "the Haitian" (Jimmy Jean-Louis), an initially silent figure who works for the Company, which employs his mind-control powers in its project of tracking individuals with "abilities" and managing knowledge of the phenomenon. Like D.L., the Haitian is other than the brute he initially resembles; his loyalties and ultimate aims, however, remain ambiguous throughout Volume One.

12 Presumably, D.L. himself could have obtained cash using his own powers of "phasing," but his doing so might have compromised his depiction as someone determined to do the right thing. The fact that it is young Micah who, in effect, steals money allows the story

itself to do a kind of "phasing," passing through a narrative obstacle while leaving its ethical substance untouched.

[13] Such characters are frequently played by Morgan Freeman, most obviously in *Bruce Almighty* (2003) and *Evan Almighty* (2007).

[14] By birth and upbringing, Sendhil Ramamurthy is neither Indian nor British, but American, and the very fact of his generally convincing and consistent rendering of Mohinder's voice suggests that the character could just as easily have had a different accent.

[15] Jenny Reardon, "Decoding Race and Human Difference in a Genomic Age," *differences* 15: 3 (2004), 45.

[16] Gilroy, *Against Race*, 21.

[17] Gilroy, *Against Race*, 196. Such bio-commercial determinism is evoked in the commentary to the DVD edition of episode 16, which introduces Hana Gittelman (Stana Katic), who uses her mind to communicate with computers, but whose more striking quality, to the commentators—who temporarily sound like the teen cartoon duo Beavis and Butthead—is that she is "hot." They go on laughingly to note that "it is somewhat odd that all of the genetically mutated people who are, you know, starting to change the earth are hot." This same episode does introduce a middle-aged female hero, Montana mechanic Dale Smither (Rusty Schwimmer), who has ultra-acute hearing, but she has only a few minutes of screen time before being killed by Sylar.

[18] On the "9/11-ish" aspects of the Volume One finale, see Porter et. al., 82–83.

[19] Gilroy, *Against Race*, 355.

[20] Gilroy, *Against Race*, 356. Gilroy elaborates on his distinction between the "global" and the "planetary" in his book *Postcolonial Melancholia:* "The planetary . . . specifies a smaller scale than the global, which transmits all the triumphalism and complacency of ever-expanding imperial universals" (New York: Columbia University Press, 2005), xv.

Chapter 15

On Seeing and Not Seeing Race

Crash and the Politics of Bad Faith

Susan Searls Giroux and Henry A. Giroux

> "*Crash* is not 'about' race. It's about strangers, others. About how we love to divide ourselves. . . . And that's so much who we are, as human beings. We will always manufacture differences."
> —Paul Haggis

Public reaction to the summer 2005 blockbuster *Crash* is a study in paradox. Well before it received the Oscar for Best Picture of the Year, Paul Haggis's directorial debut generated a great deal of discussion and no small amount of controversy in the mass media. In step with the marketing of the film as "a provocative, unflinching look at the complexities of racial conflict in America," critics in general lined up to praise Haggis's dramaturgical economy, technical acumen and political courage. David Denby of the *New Yorker* suggested that *Crash* "makes previous movie treatments of prejudice seem like easy and self-congratulatory liberalizing"[1] and

Ella Taylor of the *Los Angeles Times* hailed it as "one of the best Hollywood movies about race."[2] Very few reviewers took aim at the film's tendency to universalize and naturalize racist presumption. Richard Kim, blogging for *The Nation*, insisted that "easy and self-congratulatory liberalizing is the epitome of the film." "Compassionate conservatism" was the preferred political descriptor Kim invoked to summarize the moral of *Crash*: "Don't worry, everyone's a little bit racist." Whereas many reviewers like Roger Ebert of the *Chicago Sun Times* extolled Haggis's intricately woven plot and multi-dimensional characters, others read the "humanizing" and ultimately forgiving treatment of racists as deeply reactionary. "Haggis writes with such directness and such a good ear for everyday speech," Ebert urges, "that the characters seem real and plausible after only a few words. His cast is uniformly strong; the actors sidestep clichés and make their characters particular."[3] In contrast, Ty Burr writing for the *Boston Globe*, insisted the film's "characters come straight from the assembly line of screen writing archetypes, and too often they act in ways that archetypes, rather than human beings, do." Far from sidestepping clichés, Burr argues, *Crash* "underscores that while Haggis thinks he's exploding racial clichés he's really just rearranging the ones we already live with."[4] Similarly, A. O. Scott of the *New York Times* was unsparing in his assessment of the film's flawed characterization: "Mr. Haggis is eager to show the complexities of his many characters, which means that each one will show exactly two sides. . . . No one is innocent. There's good and bad in everyone."[5]

In the end, for all its pyrotechnics, *Crash* gives off more heat than light. It renders racism visible, only to banish it once again to invisibility by erasing its deeply structural and institutional dimensions. Theorizing racism as a function of private discrimination—a matter of individual attitude or psychology—denies its role as a systemic political force with often dire material consequences. For these reasons, Robert Jensen and Robert Wosnitzer refer to the film as "white supremacist" by virtue of the fact that it "minimizes the reality of white supremacy. Its faux humanism and simplistic message of tolerance directs attention away from a white-supremacist system and undermines white accountability for the maintenance of that system."[6] Resisting the film's reduction of racism to the public face of private despair, A. O. Scott concludes: "A frustrating movie: full of heart and devoid of life; crudely manipulative when it tries hardest to be subtle; and profoundly complacent in spite of its intentions to unsettle and disturb."[7] Gritty realism or sentimental manipulative melodrama; believable characters or utterly stock; thematically committed to unmasking racism or reabsorbing it in pious nostrums about the tragically flawed propensity of all humans to fear and distrust "the other"—the heated debates over *Crash* show little sign of abatement. Indeed, on that most combustible of public issues—race—some critics even went so far as to publicly challenge colleagues who penned unfavorable reviews of the film, reducing hermeneutic integrity to a political litmus test in which disparagement of the film translated into an unqualified endorsement of racist expression and exclusion.

The public conversation about *Crash* in all its vivid contradiction, we assert, reveals widespread confusion over the meaning and political significance of race in an allegedly colorblind society. That the same film can be read as a searing indictment of America's deep-seated racism and also as its very denial, in the form of grand and forgiving assessments of the all-too-human tendency toward misunderstanding and fear, reflects the kind of schizophrenia that marks the politics of race in the post-civil rights era. That such a film can win an Oscar in a time marked by rabid racial backlash only underscores this tension. With the formal dismantling of institutional, legal segregation most Americans believe that racism is an unfortunate—by now bygone—episode in American history, a past that has been more than adequately redressed and is now best forgotten—even as informal, market-based reseg-regation proliferates in the private sector. If inequality persists today between blacks and whites, so mainstream opinion goes, it is a function not of structural disadvantage (i.e. dilapidated, dysfunctional schools; rampant unemployment or underemployment; unequal access to loans and mortgages; police harassment and profiling or mass incarceration, etc.), but rather of poor character. The blunted insights and tiresome clichés about race that inform much of the critical reception of *Crash* belie a mood of serious engagement with the persistence of racial injustice and are more reflective of what James Baldwin once called America in a liberal convulsion. The excision of civil rights and social justice from the main-stream national political agenda in favor of a privatized language of personal responsibil-ity and individual over group rights over the last three decades has resulted in a lobotomized public consciousness—a collective inability or unwillingness to think critically about our own racial history or to theorize common political interests.

    Crash narrates the interconnected lives of some fifteen characters—black, white, Latina, Asian—within a thirty-six-hour time frame on a cold Christmas day in post-riot, post-9/11 Los Angeles. The film begins with a paradox that captures the dominant mood about the pol-itics and representations of race in America. Rear-ended on their way to a murder scene, Detective Graham Waters (Don Cheadle) and his partner and girlfriend Ria (Jennifer Espos-ito) respond to the accident in ways that say something not merely about the literal colli-sion of metal and glass parts on foggy Mulholland Drive in car-obsessed Los Angeles but also about what happens when strangers are forced to rub against and engage each other across the divisive fault lines of race, class, ethnicity, and fear. For Waters, the collision gives rise to a doleful rumination about the loss of contact, if not of humanity, in a city where people appear isolated in their cars, homes, neighborhoods, workplaces, and daily lives. Desperate for a sense of community, if not for feeling itself, melancholic police detective Waters pon-ders, "It is the sense of touch . . . In any real city, you walk, you know? You brush past people, people bump into you. In LA, nobody touches you. We're always behind this metal and glass. I think we miss that touch so much that we crash into each other, just so we can feel something." Ria is less philosophical about the collision and jumps out of the car to confront the Asian woman who hit them. Any pretense to tolerance and human decency soon dis-appears, as the crash becomes a literal excuse for both women to hurl racial epithets at one another.

    A scene that begins with a rumination about the loss of community and meaningful contact ends in an exchange of racist slurs inaugurating the polarities and paradoxes that are central to the structural, ideological, and political organization of the remainder of the film. Humanity does not disappear from *Crash* after the opening scene. That scene simply provides a crucial theoretical lens both to make the pervasiveness of race visible on the American landscape and to complicate the ways in which we understand its presence and effects. Like *Amores perros* (2000), *21 Grams* (2003), *Magnolia* (1999), and *Short Cuts* (1993), among other films, *Crash* then maps a series of interlocking stories with random characters linked by the gravity of racism and the diverse ways in which they inhabit, mediate, repro-duce, and modify its toxic values, practices, and effects. Episodic encounters reveal not just a wellspring of seething resentment and universal prejudice, but also a vision of humanity marked by internal contradictions as characters exhibit values and behaviors at odds with the vile racism that more often than not offers them an outlet for their pent-up fear and hatred. Put on full display, racism is complicated by and pitted against the possibility of a diverse polity inhabiting a shared set of values and public space, a possibility that increasingly appears as a utopian fantasy as the film comes to a conclusion.

The unexpected confrontation, the nerve rending shocks, the random conflicts often require us to take notice of others, sometimes forcing us to recognize what is often not so hidden beneath the psychic and material relations that envelop our lives. But not always. Crashing into each other in a unregulated Hobbesian world where fear replaces any vestige of solidarity can also force us to retreat further into a privatized world far removed from the space of either civic life and common good. Haggis plays on this double trope as a structuring principle that appears to make people uneasy yet also, in a more profound and troubling sense, more comfortable, especially if they are white. When racist acts are exposed in a progressive context, it is assumed that they will be revealing, furthering our understanding of the history, conditions, and agents that produce such acts. Equally important is the need to undue the stereotyping that gives meaning and legitimacy to racist practices. Haggis moves beyond the opening scene of his film to explore in detailed fashion the power of racial stereotyping and how it complicates the lives of the perpetrators and the victims, but he does very little to explore the historical, political, and economic conditions that produce racist practices and exclusions and how they work outside of the visibility of serendipitous interpersonal collisions in ways that might reveal the continuous, structural dimensions of everyday racism. *Crash* seems to put racism on full display, mimicking the logic of color-blindness currently embraced by both conservatives and liberals, but Haggis runs the risk of reabsorbing racist practices into the liberal logic of "flawed humanity" in an attempt to complicate the individual characters who bear the burden of the forceful prejudices that govern their lives. Put differently, as *Crash* unfolds it is caught in another paradox in which everyday politics becomes more racialized and more exclusionary just as the ensuing discourse and representations of racism become increasingly privatized, a theme we will explore more fully at the conclusion of this chapter.

The intersection of racism and what we call its "humanization" comes into full view in a number of scenes that, rather than simply building on each other, weave a diverse tapestry of actions held together by the intersection of race, violence, and fear that merge and disappear into metaphysical notions of innocence and guilt. Characters enact a number of ideological assumptions about racist stereotypes and how they are often taken up by whites. Unsurprisingly, Haggis begins the task of making racism visible—while implicating its victims and perpetrators—by structuring one of the most important scenes in the film around a car-jacking. Haggis and his wife actually experienced a car-jacking in LA, an experience that provided the backdrop for writing the script.

Circling back to the afternoon before the initial crash on Mulholland Drive, two young black men in their twenties emerge from a classy restaurant in an upscale white neighborhood. Anthony (Chris "Ludacris" Bridges) complains to Peter (Larenz Tate) about the daily stereotyping and humiliations visited upon poor people of color from both blacks and whites. He launches into the beginning of what will be an ongoing treatise on anti-black racism in America, ranging from the bad service he received in the restaurant by a black waitress to corporate hip-hop as a way of perpetuating black-on-black violence. Given a city wracked by two major racial uprisings and infamous for the racist violence of its police force, Anthony's assessment of internalized white supremacist beliefs would appear on target. His tirade is interrupted when he spots a wealthy white woman react in fear upon seeing him with his friend. Anthony is outraged: "Man, look around you, man! You couldn't find a whiter, safer, or better-lit part of the city right now, but yet this white woman sees two black guys who look like UCLA students strolling down the sidewalk, and her reaction is blind fear? I mean, look at us, dog!Are we dressed like gang-bangers? Huh? No. Do we look threatening? No. Fact: If anybody should be scared around here, it's us. We're the only two black faces surrounded by a sea of over-caffeinated white people patrolled by the trigger-happy LAPD. So you tell me, why aren't *we* scared?" Anthony responds with irony to this classic Fanonian moment of being "caught in the gaze," making it clear that if anyone should be afraid of racial violence it should be he and Anthony, not white people, and especially not rich whites. Rather than allow his audience to ponder this insight, Haggis performs a cheap reversal. Peter responds to Anthony's rhetorical question in wry tones, "Because we got guns." In a startling turn of events, the two young men then force the wealthy couple out of their black Lincoln Navigator, and speed away from the crime scene. An encounter that at first seems to underscore the indignity and injustice of the racist gaze is dramatically cancelled out when the white woman's fear proves legitimate. The stereotype of the dangerous black man is suddenly made all too real, an empirically justified fact. In an effort to underscore the basic contradictions that mark us all as human, Haggis undercuts whatever insight the film offers about the contemporary racist imagination, which often equates the culture of blackness with the culture of criminality.

Haggis continues to reproduce this stereotype about the criminality of black culture in the following scene. Waters and his partner now find themselves at the scene of another crime: a white undercover detective named Conklin (Martin Norseman) has shot and killed a black man driving in a Mercedes. Unfortunately for Conklin, the black man turns out to be a police officer in the Hollywood division. Conklin claims he shot in self-defense, but this does not ring true to Waters who quickly discovers that this is the third black man that Conklin has killed. Haggis toys with a liberal sensibility that would understand the scene as another tragic example of the violence of racial profiling, and Conklin as a pernicious profiler. But he soon explodes this liberal presumption as the detectives discover that the black cop is dirty, having cut himself into the LA drug trade. In a series of intertwined scenes, black people appear either complicitous with racist practices or as individuals whose sorry plight has less to do with racial subjection than with their own lack of character or sense of personal responsibility. And the stereotypes cut across gender and class lines.

For all of the pious defense of Haggis's rigorous anti-racism among film critics, it is curious to note that none reflect on the utterly offensive portrayal of black women in the film, of whom we are introduced to three. The most damaging portrayal is of Waters's mother (Beverly Todd), who is represented as cruel and dysfunctional, a crack addict whose lack of discrimination and judgment results in her doting on her wayward son, Peter, who is a carjacker, to the exclusion of the more responsible and hard-working Waters, the only functional member of the family. Waters's mother is a grown up version of the infamous welfare queen, made famous in the presidential campaign of Ronald Reagan and in countless stereotypes launched by conservative and liberal ideologues to legitimate dismantling the welfare state. Similarly, the portrayal of an African American women named Shaniqua (Loretta Devine) as the heartless insurance supervisor who works for the LA public health service is equally vicious. In an instance of alleged "reverse racism," she denies a man with a severe prostate problem a visit to a specialist because his son is a white, racist cop. And if Shaniqua's racism is not clear enough in this scene, we meet her again at the end of the film when she is rear-ended at a traffic light. Emerging from her car, she angrily shouts at the Asian driver who hit her car, "Don't talk to me unless you speak American." Shaniqua stands in as the bad affirmative action hire willing to punish poor whites because of her own racial hostility. Why bother with a critique of the welfare state or the crumbling and discriminatory practices of an ineffectual welfare system when heartless, hapless, and cruel black women like Shaniqua can be conjured up from the deepest fears of the white racist unconscious? The third portrayal is of a wealthy, light-skinned Christine (Thandie Newton), first encountered when she performs oral sex on husband Cameron (Terrence Howard) while he drives home from an awards dinner. After being pulled over by a white, racist cop to whom she mouths off, and being subjected to a humiliating body search, Christine steps into the stereotype of the overly sexed and out-of-control black woman with a big mouth who has no idea as to how to negotiate racial boundaries. As humiliating as is the violence she experiences from the racist, sadistic cop, Christine appears irresponsible, and unsympathetic, if not quite deserving of the racist violence she has to endure. Even Waters, who provides a sense of complexity and integrity that hold together the different tangents of the story, is eventually portrayed as corruptible and willing to corroborate in a lie about the shooting of a black cop; he will end up framing an innocent white cop in order to keep his brother out of jail, get a promotion, and provide political advantage with the black community for the LA District Attorney (Brendan Fraser). What is disturbing about all of these scenes is that they suggests not only that black people can be racist and complicitous with their own experience of racism, but that a belief in certain anti-black racist sterereotypes is rational, and therefore not racist.

But Haggis tempers his own confusion about the constitutive elements of racism, who perpetuates it and under what conditions by powerfully organizing *Crash* around the central motif that everyone indulges in some form of prejudice, but this cannot reductively constitute all that humans are. As Haggis explains in an interview for *LA Weekly*: "We are each such bundles of contradictions . . . You can conduct your life with decency most of your days, only to be amazed by what will come out of your mouth in the wrong situation. Are you a racist? No—but you sure were in that situation! . . . Our contradictions define us." In other words, some racists can be decent, caring human beings and some decent caring human beings can also be racists. In this equal opportunity racism scenario, racism assumes the public face of a deeper rage, fear, and frustration that appears universally shared and enacted by all of LA's urban residents. This free-floating rage and fear, in Haggis's world view, is what lends itself to reinforcing racist stereotypes. Thus racism is reduced to individual prejudice, a kind of psychological mechanism for negotiating interpersonal conflict and situational difficulties made manifest in emotional outbursts and irrational fears. Without denying its psychological dimensions, what such a definition of racism cannot account for is precisely racism's collusion with rationality, the very "logical" use to which racism has historically been put to legitimate the consolidation of economic and political power in favor of white interests. Absent any engagement with a four-hundred year history of racist oppression and exclusion in the interests of white supremacy, it becomes easy to identify all forms of race consciousness as inappropriate and extreme, and further, to render them equally so.

Perhaps more importantly, once questions of history and power are excised from public consciousness, racial inequality can be "transformed from its historical manifestations and effects perpetuated for the most part by whites against those who are not white into 'reverse discrimination' against whites who now suffer allegedly from preferential treatment."[8] We offer two elaborated examples, perhaps the two most remarked upon scenes in *Crash*—one sequence involving two LAPD cops, the utterly venomous, racist veteran, Ryan (Matt Dillon) and his sympathetically drawn rookie partner, Hanson (Ryan Phillipe), who pull over an upper-middle-class black couple; and the other portraying a domestic dispute between the utterly opportunistic District Attorney, Rick Chabot and his spoiled, overtly racist wife Jean (Sandra Bullock).

The first sequence involves Ryan on the phone with the aforementioned HMO representative, Shaniqua—a conversation that ends on a very sour note. This prelude is important because it is intended to provide a context for the even more obscene event about to unfold. When Ryan returns to the squad car, he and his partner witness a black SUV glide by, and they decide to follow. It is not the car involved in the earlier car-jacking, but Ryan spies something amiss. He pulls over an African American couple, a Hollywood producer and his wife, on the way home from an awards banquet. The wife, Christine (Thandie Newton), has had too much to drink and has treated her husband to fellatio on the ride home to their Brentwood residence—and it is on this account that Ryan has stopped them. At first the couple is amused, but things turn more serious when Ryan asks the husband, Cameron (Terrance Howard), to step out of the vehicle to see if he too has been drinking. Christine takes offence and proceeds to verbally lambaste the officer as, unbidden, she too steps out of the SUV. Ryan calls the rookie for backup and insists the two put their hands against the vehicle to be patted down, a request that further infuriates Christine whose assault has turned utterly profane and inflammatory, against the protests of her husband who demands that she stop talking. But it is too late, she has crossed the line, and Ryan feels like the couple needs to be taught a lesson. He proceeds to sexually molest Christine in the guise of police procedure while demanding from her husband, who helplessly looks on, an apology for their illicit behavior on the road. The producer and his wife return to their vehicle silenced, humiliated, and broken.

While the scene renders Ryan entirely unsympathetic and hateful, our judgment is presumably to be tempered by taking account of the context in which the abuse has unfolded. It also sets us up for Ryan's utter redemption only a few scenes later when he happens upon a car wreck and saves Christine from a blaze that is about to consume her SUV. In keeping with Haggis's understanding of how racist outbursts occur—racism is repeatedly represented in a series of isolated incidents, rather than as a systemic and institutional phenomenon that informs every aspect of daily life—Ryan has been stressed. From his perspective, he has endured the assaults of two black women one after the other: he is the white victim of an allegedly incompetent affirmative action hire, as he later reveals, and of "reverse racism," since Christine called him "cracker," among other names, in a litany of personal assaults. Apparently, Ryan has regained some equilibrium when, in a rather incredible coincidence, he saves Christine's life, in spite of her aggressive efforts to resist his initial attempt. Having staged a profound disidentification between the audience and Ryan, Haggis has now repositioned us to admire the officer's bravery and selflessness. Curiously, critics have read this scene as indicative of Ryan's contriteness, even moral growth, his coming to terms with the consequences of his earlier actions and his efforts to transcend a racist attitude. But is this really what we witness? Does remorse drive his "heroic actions" in saving Christine, or is he simply doing his job, which is to serve and protect the public interest—a commitment he utterly violated scenes ago? Is there anything truly productive or uplifting in the pendulum swing of his character from racial victim to racial savior (with rapid downward momentum generating a brief sadistic lapse quickly forgotten if not forgiven in the upward arc of his transcendence), or are these precisely the subject positions open to whites who refuse to engage self-reflectively and self-critically on deeply historical and power-infused social relations?

We are similarly set up for a "surprise" reversal (though by the end of the film the gesture has become well nigh predictable) in the sequence involving the car-jacking. As we've already argued, Haggis has flipped the script on two young African American men, who initially transcend the "thug" stereotype and appear educated, even critically conscious of such racist positioning, only to morph back into mainstream America's worst fears, a pair of gun-toting nightmares now materialized in the flesh. Not only does the scene insert a kind of empirical validity to the presumption of black criminality, it manages to pathologize radical thought in the translation, a double demonization entirely in keeping with the conservativism of the colorblind commitments of the post-civil rights era that contradicts Haggis's apparent efforts to explode such presumption. But Haggis's intentions become more curious still. Shortly, we find the victimized DA and his wife at home. The district attorney consults his staff, preoccupied with how to spin the situation so as not to lose either the "law and order vote" or that of the black community—a tongue-in-cheek moment satirizing the pretence to governmental colorblindness while the language of race is invoked in private policy decisions to strategize favorable outcomes. His wife, meanwhile, whines in the kitchen as she watches a young Latino male, who she quickly surmises is a threatening gangbanger, change the locks. As with Ryan, the stresses of the evening have gotten the better of her and she explodes in an emotional fit before her husband. The scene unfolds as follows:

> JEAN: I would like the locks changed again in the morning, and you know what? You might mention that we'd appreciate it if next time, they didn't send a gang member.
> RICK: A gang member?
> JEAN: Yes, yes.
> RICK: What, you mean that kid in there?
> JEAN: Yes, the guy in there with the shaved head, the pants around his ass . . .
> RICK: Oh, come on.
> JEAN: . . . the prison tattoo.
> RICK: Those are not prison tattoos.
> JEAN: Oh, really? And he's not going to go sell our key to one of his gang-banger friends the moment he is out our door?
> RICK: Look, we've had a really tough night. I think it would be best if you just went upstairs now . . .
> JEAN: And what? Wait for them to break in? I just had a gun pointed in my face!
> RICK: You lower your voice!
> JEAN: And it was my fault because I knew it was going to happen! But if a white person sees two black men walking towards her and she turns and walks in the other direction, she is a racist, right. Well I got scared and I didn't say anything and ten seconds later I had a gun in my face. And now I'm telling you that your amigo in there is going to sell our key to one of his homies and this time it would be really fucking great if you acted like you actually gave a shit!

The exchange is of particular interest for a number of reasons. Like Ryan, Jean for the moment appears barred from the human race—but only for the moment. Like Ryan, she assumes the posture of being victimized by the social dictates and policy measures associated with anti-racism. For her, discrimination dissolves into discretion: if avoidance of certain groups is enacted through rational application of generalizations backed by statistical evidence about the dangers associated with those populations, this isn't racist.[9] Jean's fear at the very sight of two young black men proved justified—before they did anything, they were guilty of blackness; they "were" a crime. Now she is angry at being thought of as a racist, and as such exhibits what Jean Paul Sartre called "bad faith."[10] Jean throws herself into an emotional fit in order to take on an identity that enables her to evade herself. She presents herself manifestly as what she is (i.e. a racist) in order ironically to evade what she is. We have spent some time unpacking these scenes because, we argue, they reveal in synecdochal form the broader politics of the film. In similar ways, *Crash* ironically evades the question of racism in all its socio-historical force and political consequence while at the same time seeming to face it. It simultaneously insists that we take account of our own prejudices and their hateful, material consequences and unburdens us of the task at the same time by rendering such dispositions as timeless, universal attributes of a flawed humanity. Complicating further the gesture toward responsibility is the relatively unthinking way in which characters engage in racist verbal assault or physical violence and the frequently unthinking way in which they act humanely toward others. By rendering such actions as reflexive, emotive, or generally pre-reflective, *Crash* calls upon us to become consciously reflective and responsible for how we negotiate a post-9/11 urban context rife with fearsome strangers. And at the very same time it undermines that possibility.

The apparent answer to the problem of white victimization is tolerance—and for their later expressions of tolerance, both Jean (by the simple gesture of affirming her Latina maid) and Officer Ryan are cinematically redeemed. The effort to humanize stark racists has earned Haggis critical accolades and fierce bromides from critics. Critics like David Denby were quick to seize upon the importance of this alleged insight: "'Crash' is the first movie I know of to acknowledge not only that the intolerant are also human but, further, that something like white fear of black street crime . . . *isn't always irrational.* . . . In Haggis's Los Angeles, the tangle of mistrust, misunderstanding, and foul temper envelops everyone; no one is entirely innocent or entirely guilty" (italics ours). In such a context, the question of responsibility for the violence that racism inevitably produces becomes free-floating. It is a logic sadly reminiscent of the "banality of evil" that Hannah Arendt discovered operating during the Nuremberg trials; everyone, she recalled, looked for "Eichmann the monster," only to find a man very much like themselves. That such attempts at "humanization" should now equate with redemption is a tragic denial of that history. A wilful forgetting of such banality cannot elude the question of responsibility. It is apparently the very precondition for the non-cruel to do cruel things.[11]

Haggis's model of prejudice as a universal flaw has very little to say about racism as a site of power operating within the larger structural conditions that produce it. *Crash* repudiates any attempt to engage racism "as an expression of racially predicated or manifested social and political relations of domination, subordination, and privilege . . . [that] operates by positioning subjects old and new to exclusionary or demeaning purposes. Race is about the representation of difference. Sites of difference are also sites of power, a power in terms and by means of which the dominated come to see and experience themselves as "Other," as alien and strange."[12] Collapsing the concept of racism as a power-laden mode of exclusion into the register of inflamed individual prejudices, *Crash*'s delineation of racial conflict not only privatizes race, it also drowns out those discourses that reveal how it is mobilized "around material resources regarding education, employment conditions, and political power."[13] Within this equal-opportunity view of racism, the primary "insight" of the film trades in the worst banalities: there is good and bad in everyone, and, as Stephen Hunter puts it "in this movie, nobody's truly innocent and the other side of the argument is that nobody's truly guilty."[14] Forcefully arguing against this position, David Edelstein, a film critic for *Slate*, observes

> In the end, *Crash* says, when you push a vicious racist, you get a caring human, but when you push a caring human you get a vicious racist . . . All the coincidences—there are more, involving Persian and Chinese families—make for one economical narrative: Haggis wants to distill all the resentment and hypocrisy among races into a fierce parable. But the old-fashioned carpentry (evocative of '30s socially conscious melodrama) makes this portrait of How We Live Now seem preposterous at every turn. A universe in which we're all racist puppets is finally just as simpleminded and predictable as one in which we're all smiling multicolored zombies in a rainbow coalition.[15]

But this "fierce parable" about a democratically shared racism is more than simpleminded, it is also marked by a series of absences that make it complicit with the very colorblind racism it wants to expose. When the conditions that produce racist exclusions—paid for in the hard currency of human suffering—are rendered invisible, as they are in *Crash*, politics and social responsibility dissolve either into privatized guilt (one feels bad and helpless) or disdain (victims become responsible for their own plight). In a universe in which we are all racist pawns, it becomes difficult to talk about the conditions that actually produce enduring racist representations, injustices, and violence, the effects of which are experienced in vastly different and iniquitous ways by distinct groups. The universalizing gesture implicit in Haggis's theory of racism cannot address the dramatic impact of racism on individuals and families marginalized by class and color, particularly the incarceration of extraordinary numbers of young black and brown male prisoners and the growth of the prison-industrial complex; a spiraling health crisis that excludes large numbers of minorities from health insurance or adequate medical care; crumbling city infrastructures; segregated housing; soaring unemployment among youth of color; exorbitant school drop-out rates among black and Latino youth coupled with the realities of failing schools more generally; and deepening inequalities of incomes and wealth between blacks and whites.[16] Nor can it grasp that the enduring inequality that centuries of racist state policy has produced is still, as Supreme Court Justice Ruth Bader Ginsburg observes, "evident in our workplaces, markets and neighborhoods."[17] It is also evident in child poverty rates for "blacks and Hispanics, an unconscionable thirty percent and twenty-eight percent, respectively."[18]

David Shipler argues powerfully that race and class are the two most powerful determinants shaping in an allegedly post-racist, post civil rights society. After interviewing hundreds of people over a five-year period, Shipler wrote in *A Country of Strangers* that he bore witness to a racism that "is a bit subtler in expression, more cleverly coded in public, but essentially unchanged as one of the 'deep abiding currents' in everyday life, in both the simplest and the most complex interactions of whites and blacks."[19] Pushing against the grain of civil rights reform and racial justice are reactionary and moderate positions ranging from the extremism of right-wing skin-heads and Jesse Helms-like conservatives to the moderate "color-blind" positions of liberals such as Randall Kennedy, to tepid forms of multiculturalism that serve to vacuously celebrate diversity while undermining and containing any critical discourse of difference.[20] But beneath its changing veneers and expressions, racism is fundamentally about the relationship between politics and power—a historical past and a living present where racist exclusions appear "calculated, brutally rational, and profitable."[21] It is precisely this analysis of politics, power, and history that *Crash* leaves largely unacknowledged (with the single exception of a cheap dismissal by the Assistant District Attorney Flanagan [William Fichtner]) and unexamined.

At the same time, we recognize that part of the popularity of *Crash* is due to its neo-realistic efforts to make the new post-9/11 racial realities visible in American society, especially in light of a pervasive ideology of race transcendence that refuses to acknowledge the profound influence that race continues to have on how most people experience their everyday lives and their relationship with the rest of the world. *Crash* brings to the audience's attention how racial identities are played out under the pressures of class, violence, and displacement. *Crash* also provides a theoretical service by pluralizing racism, making it clear that the notion of racism not only affects black people. It is also refreshing to recognize that the LA that *Crash* portrays (in contrast to, say, the LA of *Short Cuts*) is not entirely white, and that the public sphere is a diverse one that reflects a cosmopolitan American audience. Mostly, *Crash* explodes the assumption that racism is a thing of the past in America, but does so without any particular antagonism, such as white supremacy. Instead, Haggis implies that racism may be a public toxin, but we are all touched by it because we are all flawed. But drawing attention to race is not enough, especially when racism is depicted in utterly depoliticized terms, sliding into an expression of individualized rage far removed from hierarchies and structures of power. But in spite of its cinematic strengths and edgy emotive force, *Crash* seduces its audiences, with the comfort of existence beyond the realm of either responsibility or judgment. Race opens up a space in which acts are rendered as good or bad, but not as the outgrowth of a moral failure in the face of a pervasive system of racism bounded by relations of power and structures of inequality that encourages such failures. This is not a film about how racism undermines the social fabric of democracy, it is a film about how racism gets expressed by a disparate group of often angry, alienated, and confused individuals.

* * *

Racism in America has an enduring, centuries-old history that has generated a set of economic conditions, structural problems, and exclusions that cannot be reduced to forms of individual prejudice spread out evenly among a racially and ethnically mixed polity. While the expression of racism and its burden cannot be reduced to specific groups, it is politically and ethically irresponsible to overlook how some groups bear the burden of racism much more than others. Racism in the United States is mostly suffered by poor people of color, especially black and brown populations. How does one talk about racism in strictly individual or multi-colored terms in a system when the poverty rate for blacks is 28.3 percent, more than double what it is for whites (11.2 percent)? What role do biographical solutions (i.e. individual commitments to tolerance) play in dealing with systemic problems such as the ongoing discrimination against African American and Latino youth in the workplace and schools? How does one theorize the concept of individual responsibility, character, or equal-opportunity intolerance within a social order in which the national jobless rate is about six percent, but unemployment rates for young men of color in places such as south central Los Angeles have topped fifty percent? How does one ignore the fact that while it is widely recognized that a high school diploma is essential to getting a job, more than "half of all black men still do not finish high school."[22] A spate of recent studies suggests that the plight of black men in America at the dawn of the twenty-first century is far worse than had been previously understood. As reported recently in the *New York Times*:

> The share of young black men without jobs has climbed relentlessly, with only a slight pause during the economic peak of the late 1990's. In 2000, 65 percent of black make high school dropouts in their 20's were jobless–that is, unable to find work, not seeking it or incarcerated. By 2004, the share had grown to 72 percent, compared with 34 percent of white and 19 percent of Hispanic dropouts. Even when high school graduates were included, half of black men in their 20's were jobless in 2004, up from 46 percent in 2000. Incarceration rates climbed in the 1990's and reached historic highs in the past few years. In 1995, 16 percent of black men in their 20's who did not attend college were in jail or prison; by 2004, 21 percent were incarcerated. By their mid-30's, 6 in 10 black men who had dropped out of school had spent time in prison. In the inner cities, more than half of all black men do not finish high school.[23]

It gets worse. Of the two million people behind bars, seventy percent of the inmates are people of color with fifty percent being African Americans, while seventeen percent are Latinos.[24] Law professor David Cole points out in his book *No Equal Justice* that while "76 percent of illicit drug users were white, 14 percent black, and 8 percent Hispanic—figures which roughly match each group's share of the general population," African Americans constitute "35 percent of all drug arrests, 55 percent of all drug convictions, and 74 percent of all sentences for drug offences."[25] A Justice Department Report points out that on any given day in this country "more than a third of the young African-American men aged 18-34 in some of our major cities are either in prison or under some form of criminal justice supervision."[26] The same department reported in April of 2000 that "black youth are forty-eight times more likely than whites to be sentenced to juvenile prison for drug offenses."[27] Within such a context, the possibilities for treating a generation of young people of color with respect, dignity, and support vanishes and with it the hope of overcoming a racial abyss that makes a mockery out of justice and a travesty of democracy.

In addition, it is crucial to point out that *Crash* not only ignores the diverse array of conditions that produce racist violence and exclusions or the ways in which black and brown people have to disproportionately bear its effects, it also ignores the growing violence and militarization of urban public space that are part of a "war on crime" largely waged against black and brown youth by what David Theo Goldberg has called "the racial state."[28] Haggis has no sense of how the historical burdens of racism work through the "technologies employed by the [modern racial state] to fashion, modify, and reify the terms of racial expression, as well as racist exclusions and subjugation."[29] As Goldberg points out, as the state is stripped of its welfare functions and it negates any commitment to the social contract, its priorities shift from social investment to racial containment, and its militarizing functions begin to function more visibly as a state apparatus through its control over the modes of rule and representation that it employs. What emerges is a racial state that now relies on

> physical force, violence, coercion, manipulation, deceit, cajoling, incentives, law(s), taxes, penalties, surveillance, military force, repressive apparatuses, ideological

mechanisms and media—in short, all the means at a state's disposal—ultimately to the ends of racial rule. Which is to say, to the ends of reproducing the racial order and so representing for the most part the interests of the racial ruling class.[30]

Unfortunately, the film's commitment to privatized understandings of racism denies the state's implication in racial violence and social disintegration, or its refusal to assume any responsibility for preventing it. One consequence is that *Crash* leaves intact the myth that collective problems can only be addressed as tales of individual plight that reduce structural inequality to individual pathologies—fear, alienation, selfishness, laziness, or violent predisposition. But the visibility of racism is not simply an outcome of people randomly crashing into each other. The harsh and relentless consequences of racism are not merely present when individuals collide. Racism structures everyday life and for most people is suffered often in silence, outside of the sparks of unintended crashes.[31] Only white people have the privilege of becoming aware of racism as a result of serendipitous encounters with the other.

What Haggis utterly fails to recognize is that the fight against racism will not be successfully waged simply through the inane recognition that we are all racists, a position echoed by the actress Sandra Bullock in her comment, "If you leave this film and don't see a piece of yourself, you're a liar, an absolute liar. It may not be your time to see it yet if you don't see a piece of yourself and acknowledge it."[32] Overcoming racism is about more than acknowledging it in real life (however inadequately), it is primarily about theoretically informed, concrete struggles that must be both understood and engaged within the contexts in which racism really takes place. As the historian Robin D. G. Kelley insightfully argues:

> [Any viable attack on racism cannot ignore] how segregation strips communities of resources and reproduces inequality. The decline of decent-paying jobs and city services, erosion of public space, deterioration of housing stock and property values, and stark inequalities in education and health care are manifestations of investment strategies under de facto segregation . . . [Those opposed to racism must address] dismantling racism, bringing oppressed populations into power and moving beyond a black/white binary that renders invisible the struggles of Latino, Asian-Americans, Native Americans and other survivors of racist exclusion and exploitation.[33]

Crash is less a metaphor for the extremes to which we travel to feel something, to make contact, to transgress a sense of steel-and-glass isolation that marks life in the postmodern city. Rather, it is more aptly a metaphor for the violence that frequently marks having to negotiate difference in a world increasingly hostile to its presence, and not only its presence but the responsibility for the other that marks each encounter and the resentment that responsibility engenders. *Crash* is a metaphor for the powerful ambivalences with which strangers are met and rendered intelligible, predictable (thus manageable), and containable through the discourse of race. In a post-9/11 era, the stranger as racialized other is quickly refashioned as enemy.

Films such as *Crash* become important as part of a broader public pedagogy of difference because they play a powerful role in mobilizing racial ideologies, investments, and identifications. They produce and reflect important considerations of how race and racism function as structuring principles in shaping and organizing diverse sets of relations in a wide variety of social spheres in an allegedly color-blind era. To say this differently, *Crash* provides the pedagogical conditions through which race is made visible and through which "difference is represented and otherness produced."[34] At the same time, we have argued, it makes crucial dimensions of racism invisible. If we are to read films such as *Crash* as social and political allegories articulating deeply rooted fears, desires, and visions, they have to be understood, once again, within a broader network of social spheres and institutional formations rather than as isolated texts about individual encounters. *Crash* treats racism as the distorted symptom of a deeper personal antagonism and in doing this cancels out how racial practices flow from socio-historical and political causes that have consequences for democratic public life, as well as for private individuals. The pedagogical and political character of such films resides in the ways in which they align with broader social, sexual, economic, class, and institutional configurations, understood as part of a larger battle over values, beliefs, and social relations and their possible manifestation in either expanding or closing down democracy. The popularity of a film as deeply contradictory and often reactionary as *Crash* must be understood in the context of the growing backlash against people of color, immigration policy, the ongoing assault on the welfare state, the undermining of civil liberties, and the concerted attempts on the part of the US government and others to undermine civil rights. *Crash* misrecognizes the politics of racism and refashions it as a new age bromide, a matter of prejudices that simply need to be recognized and transcended, an outgrowth of rage waiting to be overcome through conquering our own anxieties and our fears of the other. We need to do much more in fighting racism. We should therefore be very attentive not to fight ancillary battles: viewing racism as merely an individual pathology with terrible consequences. As Slavoj Zizek observes, "The focus should be on what effectively goes on in our culture, on what kind of society is emerging here as the result of the 'war of all against all.' The ultimate result of this war will be a change in our political order."[35] *Crash* is not about viewing the crisis of racism as part of the crisis of democracy, however; it is about understanding racism as the crisis of the alienated and isolated self in a pathological urban environment. Consequently, it offers no solutions for addressing the most important challenge confronting an inclusive democracy—addressing, critically engaging, and eliminating the conditions that not only produce the deep structures of racism but also destroy the historically constructed world of democratic politics. The struggle against racism is not a struggle to be waged through guilt or retreat into racially homogenous enclaves, it is a struggle for the best that democracy can offer. It is a struggle that should be waged in the media as part of a politics of cultural representation; it is a struggle that needs to be waged against the neoliberal and racializing state and its effects in distributing power, resources, social provisions, social benefits, and the basic conditions of engaged citizenship. It is also a struggle to be waged in neighborhoods, everyday relations, schools, and all of those places where people meet, talk, interact, sometimes colliding but mostly trying to build a new sense of political community, a future polity where bigotry rather than difference becomes the enemy of democracy.

Notes

1 David Denby, "Angry People—Crash," *The New Yorker.com* (April 25, 2005). Online: http://www.newyorker.com/critics/cinema/articles/050502crci_cinema.

2 Ella Taylor, "Space Race," *The Los Angeles Times* (May 6, 2005), p. 36.

3 Roger Ebert, "Crash—When racial worlds collide", rogerebert.com, May 5, 2005. Available online at: http://rogerebert.suntimes.com/apps/pbcs.dll/article?AID=/20050505/REVIEWS/50502001/1023

4 Ty Burr, "Well-acted 'Crash' is a course in stock characters," *Boston Globe* (November 11, 2005), 1.

5 A. O. Scott, "Bigotry as the Outer Side of Inner Angst," *The New York Times* (May 6, 2005), Available online at: http://nytimes.com

6 Robert Jensen and Robert Wosnitzer, "'Crash' and the Self-Indulgence of White America," *Dissident Voice* (March 21, 2006). Online: http://www.dissidentvoice.org/Mar06/Jensen-Wosnitzer21.htm

7 A. O. Scott, "Bigotry."

8 David Theo Goldberg, *The Racial State* (Malden, MA: Basil Blackwell, 2002), 230.

9 Goldberg, *Racial State*, 228.

10 For an elaborated discussion of this concept as an analytic tool for understanding racism, see Lewis Gordon, *Bad Faith and Antiblack Racism* (New Jersey: Humanities Press, 1995).

11 This theme is taken up brilliantly in Zygmunt Bauman, *Life in Fragments* (Malden: Blackwell Publishing, 1995).

12 David Goldberg and John Solomos, "General Introduction," in David Goldberg and John Solomos, eds. *A Companion to Ethnic and Racial Studies* (Malden, MA: Blackwell, 2002), 4.

13 David Theo Goldberg, "Introduction," *Multiculturalism: A Critical Reader* (Cambridge, MA: Blackwell, 1994), 13.

14 Stephen Hunter, "'Crash': The Collision Of Human Contradictions," *Washington Post* (May 6, 2005), C01.

15 David Edelstein, "Crash and Fizzle," *Slate* (May 5, 2005). Online: http://www.slate.com/id/2118119/

16 For a compilation of figures suggesting the ongoing presence of racism in American society, see Ronald Walters, "The Criticality of Racism," *Black Scholar* 26: 1 (Winter 1996), 2–8; Children's Defense Fund, *The State of Children in America's Union: A 2002 Action Guide to Leave No Child Behind* (Washington, D.C.: Children's Defense Fund Publication, 2002), xvii.

17 Ginsburg cited in Editorial, "Race On Screen and Off," *The Nation* (December 29, 1997), 6.

18 Jeff Madrick, "Economic Scene," *The New York Times* (Thursday, June 13, 2002), C2.

[19] Shipler summarized in Jack H. Geiger, "The Real World of Race," *The Nation* (December 1, 1998), 27. See also, David Shipler, "Reflections on Race," *Tikkun* 13: 1 (1998), 59, 78; David Shipler, *A Country of Strangers: Blacks and Whites in America* (New York: Vintage, 1998).

[20] For a devastating critique of Randall Kennedy's move to the right, see Derrick Bell, "The Strange Career of Randall Kennedy," *New Politics* 7: 1 (Summer 1998), 55–69.

[21] David Theo Goldberg, *Racist Culture* (Cambridge, MA.: Basil Blackwell, 1993), 105.

[22] Erik Eckholm, "Plight Deepens for Black Men, Studies Warn," *New York Times* (March 20, 2006), 18.

[23] Erik Eckholm, "Plight Deepens," 18.

[24] Cited in David Barsamian, "Interview with Angela Davis," *The Progressive* (February 2001), 35.

[25] David Cole, *No Equal Justice: Race and Class in the American Criminal Justice System* (New York: The New Press, 1999), 144.

[26] Steven R. Donziger, *The Real War on Crime: The Report of the National Criminal Justice Commission* (New York: Harper Perennial, 1996), 101.

[27] Cited in Eyal Press, "The Color Test," *Lingua Franca* (October 2000), 55.

[28] David Theo Goldberg, *Racial State*, 4.

[29] David Theo Goldberg, *Racial State*, 4.

[30] David Theo Goldberg, *Racial State*, 112.

[31] Philomena Essed, *Understanding Everyday Racism* (Newbury Park, Sage, 1991).

[32] Cited in Joanne Laurier, "The Essential Things go Unexplained," *World Socialist Web Site* (May 28, 2005). Available online at: *http://wsws.org/articles/2005/may2005/crsh-m28.shtml*

[33] Cited in Lawrence Grossberg, "The Victory of Culture, Part I," University of North Carolina at Chapel Hill, unpublished manuscript, February 1998, 27.

[34] David Theo Goldberg and John Solomos, "Introduction," 3.

[35] Slavoj Zizek, "Today, Iraq. Tomorrow . . . Democracy?," *In These Times* (March 18, 2003), 3.

Section 4

Screened Ideologies

*T*his section primarily considers ideological forces that infuse and support pop cultural media presentations. These forces are numerous and varied and they are all interconnected: they range from body image, fascism, subversion of countercultural themes by the advertising industry, anti-immigrant sentiment, sports as propaganda, popular film and its support of the status quo and, most notably, to the ideological forces that support war.

Fiona Whittington-Walsh begins this section with a challenging analysis of the current popularity of "Makeover" shows. She relates these shows to the violent aesthetic of fascism and convincingly connects gender issues to this new genre. Stephen Muzzatti explores corporate interests and their effect on popular culture in his article. He analyses the trend of using popular music in advertising and the subsequent struggles for meaning that occur. He claims that corporate advertising has merged with counterhegemonic popular music to make advertising a new cultural form that is even more significant than the products it touts. Kirby Farrell's fascinating take on the film *Men in Black* considers that film's themes in relationship to anxieties about immigration and the increase in xenophobia in the United States. He shows how fear of the other or "alien" is a prime anti-immigrant motivator (Unfortunately, too late for this edition is an analysis of the new *Men in Black 3*, which has just been released). Dan Streible's revised article looks at the films of Dutch director Paul Verhoeven and in particular the film *Starship Troopers*. His analysis nicely interconnects with the other articles in this section. He too examines ideologies which might lead to war and social pathology and questions whether Verhoeven's anti-fascist statements are consistent with the fascist aesthetic found in *Starship Troopers*.

Linda Robertson's article considers the Gulf Wars of the two George Bushes in light of the role of airborne heroism. She investigates the differences in Hollywood's depictions of airborne pilots in films from *Wings* to *Top Gun,* showing both how heroism has changed and how films directly support the effort of the state to get people on its side during wartime. William Hoynes's article on the news reporting of war is a careful and systematic dissection of the role of the journalist and television in news, and how the news itself becomes part of the state's effort to propagandize the war effort. He focuses on "embedded" news personnel in Iraq in 2003 and 2004. Both of these authors deftly uncover the reasons why it seems so relatively easy to move a country to war. Part of the answer, they say, lies in the presentation of warfare in modern culture and the role that the mass media play in that presentation. War is most often disguised as patriotism, as the fight between good and evil, and as heroism. The reality is, of course, that war is created by social institutions and those that control them. Rarely is war decided upon by those who are sent to fight.

Christopher Sharrett's critical analysis of the films *No Country for Old Men* and *There Will Be Blood* is both provocative and refreshing. These films have been awarded with both critical and public acclaim, but Sharrett challenges that acclaim and offers a different perspective on the meaning of the narrative of each. His approach is one that will be sure to provide much food for thought and discussion. Graeme Metcalf's study of the connection between professional sports and the propagation of American values around the world offers a provocative way of linking global branding, globalization, and the NBA.

Chapter 16

Beautiful Ever After

"Extreme Makeover" and the Magical, Mythical Spectacle of Rebirth

Fiona Whittington-Walsh

*I*n February 1991, just prior to the end of the first Gulf war with President George H. W. Bush leading the crusade, the "Miss USA Beauty Pageant" appeared on the ABC network and was seen across the world including the troops stationed in the Persian Gulf. Filmed in Wichita, Kansas, the auditorium was transformed into a militaristic dream sequence complete with the stage designed to resemble the deck of an aircraft carrier. The blatant fusion of aesthetics and militaristic adulation climaxed during the eveningwear part of the contest. Standing erect on center stage the uniformed US Marine Corps created a tunnel of honor out of shimmering raised swords. Off to the side, raised on platforms, the US Naval Choir serenaded with patriotic renditions of "At least I'm free/I won't forget the men who died to give that to me/'cause there ain't no doubt I love this land/God bless the USA."[1] As each contestant moved through the razor-sharp tunnel a member of the Kansas National Guard escorted her across the stage. On display were multiple versions of militarist fashions sown onto elegant gowns, representing symbols of an aestheticized militaristic strength. Some were even garnished with fringes befitting five-star generals, hanging off grossly over-padded shoulders. One of the last contestants to emerge was wearing an understated but none the less elegant white, form-fitting, silky gown, whose long train was subtly attached to the ends of equally fitted long, regal sleeves. The tunnel of honor was transformed into a symbolic birth tunnel, complete with the pulsing bodily rhythms of labor represented by the melodic tempo of the choir. As this contestant exited the "birth canal," she paused and slowly raised her arms (and subsequently the fitted sleeves attached to the long white train) to reveal that she had been transformed into the dove of peace.

This aesthetically evocative image of militaristic power through rebirth is not restricted to the Miss USA pageant of 1991 nor is it just found within hegemonic images of the first Gulf War. Fascist images of spectacular transformation and resurrection through bodily displays of "beauty" increase dramatically prior to the outset of war and are again celebrated in a heightened fever pitch afterwards. These images are grounded on the distortion of history into mythical progress, which is central to a fascist political vision. Further, central to hegemonic images of American industrial capitalism is the representation and consumption of bodies as commodities-on-display.

Phantasmagoric images in rebirth spectacles designed for the social control of politics and culture create a mass of depoliticized individuals while simultaneously fulfilling a political mandate. These fascist tactics have increased dramatically during the post-9/11 crusade against "terrorism," which has resulted in an increase in racialized, homogenized notions of bodily beauty, attacking all forms of bodily difference by creating mythical beauty ideals through technological progress and through consumption that regulates women's bodies as symbolic sites for freedom, liberation, and the new American identity.

While myth distorts history, "progress" gives the illusion that through technological advancement we have mastered nature and created an "ethical state." We have become trapped in a "system of mirrors"[2] that distorts and reduces history to a primordial occurrence, one that leaves us prisoners of fate, believing in the inability to change the course of events. The inability to recognize the past as being intrinsically linked with the present threatens the disappearance of history itself, resulting in fascist politics.[3]

It is within this perverted history that our bodies become reduced to aestheticized political puppets of capitalist consumerism. Through both everyday practices (such as dress, makeup, diet, and exercise) to more intensive practices (including skin bleaching and cosmetic surgery) women fuel the economy through the consumption of appearance products that promise to transform them into paradigms of unattainable idealized beauty (which is believed to reside primarily in white bodies). Failure to possess this aesthetically pleasing appearance leads to being seen as "ugly" and to being reduced to the status of marginalized "other." Distorted by the hegemonic push for perfection and the attainment of the mythical ideal of beauty, our bodies have become homogenized, symbolic images for the state. Fascist images of bodily rebirth become symbols for the natural progress of modernity into the perfect "democratic" state. One can recall the spectacle produced by Hitler (who perverted the Greek celebration of bodily form even more than the Greeks had) in the 1936 Berlin Olympics, where "the fittest in human bodies, rather than the latest in industrial machines, were put on display, performing for mass audiences"[4] and represented on film by Leni Riefenstahl.

Hitler was not the first to introduce the body as the centerpiece for the capitalist spectacle. P. T. Barnum, the famed circus and freak show master of ceremonies, is credited for bringing the World's Exposition to America. In 1853 in New York, Barnum dazzled patrons with the display of "General Tom Thumb" (a "perfect man in miniature,"[5] who, just months before, had performed for, and thoroughly amused, Queen Victoria and other crown heads of Europe. This very successful adventure opened the doors for the first official American 'World's Fair', which was held in Philadelphia in 1876. Ten million people, one-fifth of the population of the United States at the time, attended. On American shores the commodities on display dramatically changed. Not just given the opportunity to marvel at technological progress, patrons were able to see the reflection of their own biological progress and superiority by casting their colonial gaze upon racialized bodies that were represented as freaks and/or human anomalies. Outside the fairgrounds was a non-official version of the exposition including the display of many of the great freak show stars, including a wide array of exotic and "un-civilized creatures" such as "The Wild Men of Borneo," "The Wild Australian Children," "The Man-Eating Feejees," and "The Bearded Lady."

Key to these displays is the concept of disavowal, where a tabooed desire is both *indulged* and at the same time *denied* through a displaced form of representation. One of the most famous female "freaks" was Saartje (Sara) Bartmann (a.k.a. the "Hottentot Venus") who was exhibited as a wild animal, brought on stage chained and in a cage. It wasn't the fact that she stood only four feet six inches in height that was of interest to the colonial gaze. Rather, it was her notable buttocks (her "booty"), a definitive feature of the Hottentot group and, more importantly, the gigantism of her labia—her "primitive" "Hottentot Apron." By starring at her buttocks the spectator is simultaneously indulged and denied the true object of yearning—her genitals. As Sander Gilman notes, Sara became the embodiment of "difference" and "otherness"—she was naturalized and reduced to only her body, and subsequently her sexuality, which became concrete examples of the differences between the "races" and the superiority of the white "race."[6] This process of representation was intensified under American capitalism and cultural production and allowed for the commodities-on-display to change into bodies-as-commodities-on-display.

The celebrity cult is a critical tool for the hegemonic manipulation of the body in western, capitalist society. Roland Barthes invokes the cult-like fascination for celebrities as a phenomenon belonging to modern mythology, which confuses nature and history, in his description of the face of Greta Garbo:

> Garbo still belongs to that moment in cinema when capturing the human face still plunged audiences into the deepest ecstasy, when one literally lost oneself in a human image as one would in a philtre, when the face represented a kind of absolute state of the flesh, which could be neither reached nor renounced. A few years earlier the face of Valentino was causing suicides; that of Garbo still partakes of the same rule of Courtly Love, where the flesh gives rise to mystical feelings of perdition.[7]

Cosmetic surgeons note that when people want to experience physical transformations, celebrity features are requested the most. The Beverly Hills Institute for Aesthetic and Reconstructive Surgery states that for 2010 the celebrity body parts most requested for female clients are:

Body: Fergie Ferguson
Eyes: Penelope Cruz

Cheek bones: January Jones
Nose: Nicole Kidman
Skin: Carey Mulligan
Lips: Angelina Jolie[8]

What is of interest with this list of names is the homogeneous nature of the iconic images we are striving to emulate. All of these bodies are white, thus solidifying the myth that ideal beauty resides in white bodies only. The Nicole Kidman nose has been a feature for several years.

As with all forms of popular culture and fads, celebrity icon status can disappear as quickly as it came. Despite the fact that facial proportions of "ideal" beauty have remained the same for hundreds of years (dating back to ancient Greek society and the ideal beauty of Gods and Goddesses chiseled in stone for all to see and emulate) the cult "life"-span remains short for female celebrities. Growing old, apparently the biggest social taboo for any female, means the death of a career, causing some celebrities to visit plastic surgeons and request that they be transformed into themselves. However, despite the fact that their careers are forcefully and prematurely ended, their images, like the face of Garbo ("the most pho-togenic face in movie history"[9]), remain icons and are mythologized as perpetually young and beautiful.[10]

The ABC weekly television show "Extreme Makeover" is about the fetishization of desires by creating the illusion that dreams and wishes are granted through consumption and the rebirth of the body, signaling the dawn of a new era of technological advancement. The show premiered in the fall of 2002, as President George W. Bush attempted to gain public and senate approval for the Iraq War. Marx suggested that all great historical moments occur twice: the first time as tragedy, the second time as farce. But rather than being merely farci-cal, this rebirth of a leader (the son replacing the father) has brought a new intensive war in which rather than confining its battle to distant lands Americanism has turned its atten-tion once again to the body as a hegemonic tool for, and site of, domination and control.

"Extreme Makeover" represents the futuristic myth of historical progress, which is cen-tral to fascist ideology. The ability to recreate through technology the beauty that is mythol-ogized as residing naturally in an organic, homogeneous body is an illusion resulting in a totalizing system of control and manipulation. This weekly program revolves around the technological transformation of despondent outsiders into delirious citizens. Of the ninety-six transformations that have taken place since the show premiered, only eight "patients" (seven women/one man[11]) have been non-white. According to the fascist ideology of the beauty myth, ideal beauty resides primarily in white bodies; it is impossible to create beauty out of a body that is not white. Just as in the representation of Saartje Bartmann, these bod-ies serve the purpose of maintaining not only the ideology behind the beauty myth but also the ideology behind a fascist aesthetic. They are further objectified in the fact that they are naturalized and reduced to only their significant body parts, which is read as an absolute example of the differences between the races.

DeShante (Season 2, Episode 9) and Jeff (Season 3, Episode 19) were born with cleft lip and palate and require reconstructive surgery. DeShante's story is one of rebirth through *reconstruction* rather than rebirth through the dialectic of destruction and creation—although the surgeons spend a lot of time discussing cutting and removing flesh from her lips in order to remove excess fat that has created "grossly large lips." Similarly to DeShante's,

Kine's transformation (Season 1, Episode 1) involves "upper and lower lip reduction." Manu (Season 2, Episode 18) is described as a "family woman who's served her country with honor" yet feels she does not look "feminine." Among her numerous procedures is "laser hair removal." Abundance of body hair is symbolic of sexual prowess and subsequently animalistic appearance; Regina (Season 2, Episode 15) is applauded as being the first Brazilian "butt lift" on "Extreme Makeover." The procedure is described as the "rage for those who want to sculpt their figure like pop stars Beyoncé and Jennifer Lopez," and I would further argue is similar to the representation of Saartje Bartmann due to the emphasis on the buttocks; Kim (Season 2, Episode 13) is described as "never [going] to the dentist" which subsequently has always made her "afraid to kiss and smile." She is also described as a having "the rarity of a third nipple, the removal of which is seen as risky"; Angela (Season 2, Episode 12) wants her "lips and nose reduced, but fears that her African-American identity may be altered." "Extreme Makeover" makes sure that Angela's transformation is at the hands of Dr. Anthony Griffin,[12] "one of the foremost authorities on plastic surgery for African Americans and ethnic skin types"; while Lachele's (Season 3, Episode 17) appearance is described as preventing "those around her from taking her seriously."

All of these "patients" were chosen for the show not because they could be transformed into the beauty ideal (according to the ideology, they couldn't) but rather because they could be showcased for their "otherness"—their "unique" and "anomalous" position as racialized bodies whose representation is both feared and desired by the colonial gaze and necessary for the fascist ideology of bodily beauty.

It is within the story of a patient named Liz (Season 2, Episode 8), however, that the show is able to demonstrate the fascist rebirth spectacle as a symbolic site for the "new" homogeneous American identity. Liz's "bio" reads as significantly different than those of the above-mentioned patients, as she is not represented as an anomalous "racialized" body. In contrast, she becomes a signifier of social success and mobility and thus, ultimately, through her transformation, the definitive American citizen:

> Liz, a 51-year-old resident of Houston, Texas, hobnobs with her city's high society scene. However, she feels that her chinless face has held her back. But a routine procedure turns into an emotional roller coaster ride for Liz, as what was suppose to be a short few weeks of recovery stretches into three months of distress. No holds barred, "Extreme Makeover" unflinchingly documents Liz's tough recovery and her conflict over her decision to go through with the operations. Will her story have a happy ending? Liz had a face and neck lift, cheek implants, upper and lower eyelid lift, chin augmentation, liposuction of abdomen and thighs, upper lip augmentation, photo facial, V-Beam laser treatment for rosacia, porcelain veneers, upper dentures, zoom whitening and Lasik eye surgery.

As with all "reality" television shows, participants for "Extreme Makeover" are "chosen" based on home video and taped interviews, where they plead for happiness by being granted extreme makeovers. Liz's segment on the show is the most interesting for the analysis of fascist rebirth spectacles, and starts with her taped interview where she discusses what it is like to be reduced to self-hatred due to her negative body image and in particular her "chinless" appearance. As all myth elides history and social reality, there is no discussion in "Extreme Makeover" of the extremely negative social consequences for Liz's being seen as "unattractive" and not being seen as actively engaged in beauty production consumption.

No sooner are we introduced to Liz than the program's propagandist hegemony starts seeping through the tantalizing visual images. We find out that she was born in Glasgow, Scotland, but as an adult immigrated to Houston, Texas where, we are told, "dreams can come true." Liz admits to having three life-long dreams: (1) to live in America and become an American citizen; (2) to have a big family (since moving to Houston she has become an honorary member of a large family with six adult sisters); and (3) to be beautiful. She even confesses a "secret desire" of being called a "bimbo—because bimbos are good looking." The narrator quickly adds that she believes to be granted *that* wish (as if most other wishes are attainable) would "require a miracle."

After we witness her audition tape and interview, the camera's eye gazes on Liz sitting in a country colonial inn having dinner with friends, celebrating the Fourth of July. As the narrator confides to us that Liz is unaware of the fact that she has been chosen for "Extreme Makeover," the camera cuts to the outside of the inn, which is draped in celebratory American historic flags. Obstructing the right side of the screen is a larger-than-life modern American flag, which dwarfs everything else in the picture including the inn and all the people. Four teenage girls (representing the youth and fecund vitality of the nation) run across the lawn in slow motion waving and spinning sparklers and flags. As the camera moves inside to reveal the festive dinner, a waitress walks up to the table with a tray of decadent desserts, all designed to make our mouths salivate with desire. Centered on the tray is a large piece of chocolate fudge cake, a further reminder of how the show is focused on self-indulgence and an exciting element for the audience, a reward for watching, wishing, and ultimately consuming. It is the waitress who announces that the *special* dessert for the evening is that Liz has been chosen for an extreme makeover.

Stunned, Liz starts to weep as her honorary sisters shower her with hugs, kisses, and screams. Liz, just a few weeks after becoming an American citizen, has been rewarded with the third of her life-long dreams: she is to go to Hollywood (another place, the narrator reminds us, where "dreams *can* come true") to undergo her transformation and become "beautiful."

One of the shocking aspects of Liz's story as narrated on the show (other than the blatant propagandist display) is the amount of surgery performed on her when her only "complaint" was her chin. As with all participants, Liz is at the mercy of a "dream team" of cosmetic surgeons whose only desire is to transform her utterly, to participate in the God-like dialectic of destruction and creation—while happening, of course, to generate an economy. Here, by my own estimates, and approximated in U.S. funds (2004), is the cost of Liz's surgical procedures, not including the cost of keeping her at a deluxe Los Angeles hotel for 3 months as well as furnishing her with a new wardrobe, hair, and make-up:

Face and neck lift:[13]	$6,000–$15,000
Cheek implants:[14]	$1,845
Chin augmentation:[15]	$1,512
Liposuction:[16]	$2,223
Upper lip augmentation:[17]	$1,199
V-Beam laser:[18]	$2,243
Porcelain Veneers:[19]	$900–$2,500 per tooth

| Zoom Whitening:[20] | $500–$1,000 |
| Lasik Eye Surgery:[21] | $1,965 per eye |

As in all fascist spectacles, class oppression is eliminated here as "beauty" is created and laid on, there being no discussion at all of the financing required for any of these elaborate procedures. What supplants that discussion is a heightened sense of, and a concentrated cheer for, the illusion of nationalism.

Moments before Liz's operation we see the "renowned" surgeon drawing his treasure map of beauty in black ink all over her body, then a tender moment when they hold hands while the narrator reminds us of their "unwritten contract" that there are no guarantees.[22] As with all fascist spectacles, this operation is made of myth and magic. We do not see any blood or the cutting of flesh, just a shimmering, sterile, private operating room full of all the latest advancements in medical technology—a new phantasmagoric spectacle.

The myth of reborn beauty is timeless—both outside history and beyond the clock. The passage of time becomes the focal point, with a large clock advancing at a quickened pace. The movement of time is symbolic of how the spectacle of rebirth through cosmetic surgery is actually defying time (the clock hands are moving faster than in "real" time), and demonstrates the mastery over nature that has long been sought after. Benjamin argued that the temporal pace of modernity was projected in progress as an "endless repetition of the 'new' as the 'always-the-same.'"[23] Eternal life through the stoppage of time is central to the illusion of the beauty myth.

After Liz's painful recovery (we see her bruised and swollen face peeping through bandages similar to those worn in *The Invisible Man* [1933] or *The Mummy* [1999]), all of Liz's friends and family gather and eagerly wait to witness Liz's "Reveal." This is the climax to the one-hour show, where the transformation becomes complete and we find out if wishes have in fact been granted. "Reveals" are always shown at night, and Liz's is no exception. We follow along with Liz in the over-sized limo as it moves along luminous city streets. Blinded by the bright lights we are denied a view of Liz's new face, glimpsing only her legs and feet. Surprise is crucial to the success of this spectacle—for Liz, for her family, and for us. The camera cuts between Liz's advancing limo and the large crowd waiting her arrival. All express excitement at the thought of seeing the "new" Liz and happiness for her being "granted the wish" of beauty. Finally the limo pulls up outside a mansion decorated, again, with an American flag hanging on the right side of the screen. We watch Liz's feet and legs exit and walk towards a large banquet room where her family and friends wait for a "grand entrance."

Liz emerges from behind a large black screen to an explosion of applause, screams, and tears. In fact, the applause of approval actually starts before Liz steps out from behind the screen, for the reward and approval is not in the finished product of her body but in the process of her rebirth, in consumption itself, a specialized and now sanctified space where Liz will be rewarded by friends, family, and the greater society. As she makes her way through the room, receiving hugs and kisses from her adoring crowd, we hear her saying, "When I looked at myself tonight, I didn't believe it was me." Her mother confirms her transformation by saying, in a notable Scottish brogue, "She really [did look] beautiful. I mean [extremely lengthy pause] . . . what a difference!" We will never see how her transformation affects Liz in her everyday life.[24] The only thing worth seeing and showing is the rebirth. The emphasis on myth over history, on illusion over reality further demonstrates the power of the beauty ideal as a hegemonic tool of oppression and social control.

The French Revolutionary Convention declared in 1792 that a new calendar would be created signaling that 1792 would be recorded as the first year of a new world era. This notion of creating a new era is fundamental to images of fascist rebirth. While Mussolini mythologized the March on Rome as the start of Italy's new fascist calendar, 9/11 represents the beginning of the new epoch for Americanism: the "aestheticization of politics" is accomplished through the illusion that by creating a racialized, homogeneous, beauty ideal we are participating and winning the fight against terrorism.[25]

Larger-than-life illusion-based images that loom at us from billboards, giant movie and television screens, and magazines covers have infiltrated all aspects of our private and public lives, distracting us from the fact that progress and technology have not changed the oppressive condition of our lives. This new phantasmagoric display of bodies-as-commodities to be transformed through consumption is designed for the same purpose. As Sander Gilman concludes, "[The] political unhappiness of class and poverty, which led to the storming of the Bastille, came to be experienced as unhappiness found within our bodies."[26] The process of extreme makeover distracts us from reality and prohibits revolutionary, social change. The body becomes the symbol of the resurrection of the glorious, timeless past and of the development of a new era of American greatness.

Despite the risks and the outrage from some cosmetic surgeons, "Extreme Makeover" continued producing fascist rebirth spectacles for a mystified audience and in July 2007, the American Society of Plastic Surgeons reported that a recent study claimed that four out of five plastic surgery patients were "directly influenced" by reality television shows including "Extreme Makeover." In advertising Season 4, the "Extreme Makeover" web site boasts "more emotion, tears and joy as life long dreams and fairy tale fantasies come true." The "Extreme Makeover" web site exclaims:

> Some of the incredible makeovers you will see include two sisters, who have struggled all their lives with cleft palettes and undergone nearly 40 surgeries, now turning to their last hope to be normal—the "Extreme Makeover" team; a colorful bull rider who's had his teeth knocked out and wants to be transformed into an urban cowboy; a goth punk rocker woman who has spent her life hiding behind her appearance getting the program's first "make-under," as the extreme team tones down her shocking style; and in another first, the show will make over an entire family (children will be styled with hair, makeup and wardrobe without surgery). New procedures never before seen on the show will be performed, such as a reverse vasectomy for a man who wishes to have another child with his wife and a hair transplant for a balding young woman. Plus hear the perspectives of these medical challenges as told by the doctors, and see more updates on some of last season's most popular makeover participants.

However, the fourth season never lived up to its magical promises. In early Fall 2006, after moving "Extreme Makeover" from the coveted Thursday night prime-time slot to Friday at 8 p.m., ABC shelved the show after just one episode. Finally, in March 2007, it was announced that due to low ratings the show was cancelled altogether. But there was more to the cancellation than what ABC was willing to admit. One of the candidates chosen for Season Four successfully sued the owners of "Extreme Makeover," the Walt Disney Company et al., for wrongful death. The plaintiff, Deleese Williams, was originally chosen for the fourth season but was suddenly cut from the show the night before her scheduled surgery.

The only reason the show offered her was that one of the many procedures she was to undergo, a dental surgery, would require a longer than usual recovery period. I contend that the longer recovery period and perhaps the realization that her transformation could be problematic would in fact hamper the promise of giving her "a truly Cinderella-like experience by changing [her] looks completely in an effort to transform [her] life and destiny, and to make [her] dreams come true."[27]

After being suddenly cut from the show, Deleese returned to her home in Texas and a family in ruins. According to the lawsuit, during preliminary filming, "Extreme Makeover" coerced family members into saying horrible things about Deleese's appearance in order to make her transformation story more compelling. Exposed on camera were instances of "severe ridicule she had endured at the hands of her sisters and other family members."[28] Her sister, Karalee McGee, committed suicide four months after Deleese's degrading return from Los Angeles. The family claims that she had been "shamed and humiliated in front of the cameras, and did not forgive herself for the way she treated Deleese and the fact that Deleese now knew all of it."[29] The lawsuit, filed September 21, 2005, accused the Walt Disney Company et al of the following actions: (1) Breach of Contract; (2) Breach of Covenant of Good Faith and Fair Dealing; (3) Intentional Infliction of Emotional Distress; (4) Negligence in Duty to Avoid Harm to Plaintiffs; (5) Unfair, Unlawful, and/or Fraudulent Business Practices; and (6) Wrongful Death. The lawsuit was settled for an undisclosed amount after over a year of legal battles.

While there is no documentation or public statement citing the lawsuit as the reason for the cancellation of "Extreme Makeover," I contend that the show was terminated because the *extreme* tactics used in order to elicit "compelling" stories of fairytale transformations and rebirth were finally *revealed* to the public, thus dispelling the myth and magic that surrounded the show's success.

Beyond "Extreme Makeover" there have been numerous shows on television with rebirth-through-consumption themes. Some of the television shows focusing on rebirth through bodily transformation include: "Dr. 90210," "Fakeovers," "What Not To Wear," "I Want a Famous Face," "Queer Eye for a Straight Guy," "Nip and Tuck," "Skin Deep," "The Swan," and Britain's short-lived "Cosmetic Surgery *Live*." Not just restricted to bodily transformation, there are numerous shows dedicated to rebirth through transforming your house, your garden, your car, etc. Some of these include: ABC's "Extreme Makeover: Home Edition," "Arresting Design," "Broken House Chronicles," "Changing Rooms," "Decorating Challenge," "Ground Force," "Ground Rules," "Designer Guys," "Dream Car," "Gardening Gamble," "Home to Go," "House and Home," "House Invaders," "In a Fix," "Monster Garage," "My Classic Car," "Trading/Family," "Trading Home Free," "Trading Spaces," and "While You Were Out."

Despite the cancellation of *Extreme Makeover,* ABC continues to represent the phantasmagoric spectacle of rebirth. Most recently, in March 2010, ABC broadcast the "82nd Academy Awards," which celebrated the year's achievements in film. With an average audience of 41.3 million viewers, the show is referred to as "the Super Bowl for Women," with women accounting for 60% of the total.[30] The broadcast lasted three hours and thirty-seven minutes, thirty-nine of which were commercials which earned ABC a staggering $68.0 million.[31]

As formerly discussed, celebrities are considered to be the blueprint of bodily perfection and the "82nd Academy Awards" broadcast showcased all the glitter and glam that the Hollywood beauty dream is made of. However, despite the presence of such desirous body parts as Nicole Kidman's nose and Penelope Cruz's eyes, the spectacle of rebirth was not found just within the ceremony. The spectacle and pre-show red carpet coverage included a multitude of advertisements for cosmetic surgery procedures ranging from Botox to full-body contouring including breast augmentation and liposuction.

The predominantly female audience of the "82nd Academy Awards" was well situated to be able both to absorb the compelling rebirth spectacle and to participate in associated consumption. According to The Nielsen Company's 2008 guide to the Academy Awards, the majority of the female viewers are at least thirty-five years of age, college educated, and have an average income of $75,000.[32] This demographic mirrors the average consumer of cosmetic surgery. According to the recent statistics reported by The American Society of Plastic Surgery (2008), women between the ages of thirty and fifty-four represent approximately 56% of the total consumers of cosmetic surgical procedures while the largest web portal for consumers of cosmetic surgery, *Make Me Heal,* contends that women aged thirty to fifty-five account for 60% of their consumer base and have an average income of $75,000.[33]

"Extreme Makeover," "The Academy Awards" broadcast, and the other transformative programing all have the same goals of giving us the opportunity to regard ourselves as radically insufficient and producing the illusion of happiness by offering us rebirth and transformation through consumption. The irony is, of course, that the ideal beauty does not exist. We are fed nothing but illusions of a beauty myth in order to trap us in a hegemonic patriarchal system of social control.

As I conclude, I am struck with an image from Charlie Chaplin's satire of the McCarthy witch-hunt era, *A King in New York* (1957). The film is the story of a dethroned monarch who was King of a small European country that was overthrown by a peasant revolt. The King finds sanctity in New York where he is "looked after" by the petty bourgeois socialites. His "celebrity" status (mirroring American love of monarchy despite their own history) is channeled into media product endorsements. However, American capitalist celebrity status would not be complete without the illusion of eternal youth and beauty, so the King agrees to undergo cosmetic surgery to enhance his marketable image. This attempt to change the autocrat's image through cosmetic surgery symbolically represents the King's transformation and ultimate rebirth from autocrat to representative of the new democratic "freedom" found within America. As myth is incompatible with history, the illusion of beauty through rebirth and surgery is incompatible with life. Soon after his recovery period is over, the King ventures out in public, in a kind of "Royal Reveal." He goes to a comedy club where he suddenly bursts into laughter. His face lift falls, destroying all that the surgeons and the mythmakers of reborn glamour sought together to create.

Notes

[1] Janet Fraser, "The Best Barbie of Them All" (*Green Left Weekly,* 1991). Online at http://www.breenleft.org.au/back/1991/34/34p10aiw.htm.

[2] Walter Benjamin, *Thesis on the Philosophy of History.* In Hannah Arendt, ed., *Illuminations: Essays and Reflections* (New York: Schocken Books, 1968), 253–264.

[3] Benjamin, *Ibid.*

[4] Susan Buck-Morss, *The Dialectics of Seeing: Walter Benjamin and the Arcades Project* (Cambridge, MA: MIT Press, 1999), 325.

[5] Robert Bogdan, *Freak Shows: Presenting Human Oddities for Amusement and Profit* (Chicago: The University of Chicago Press, 1988).

[6] Sander Gilman, *Black Bodies, White Bodies: Toward an Iconography of Female Sexuality in Late Nineteenth-Century Art, Medicine, and Literature.* In Henry Louis Gates, Jr., ed., *"Race," Writing, and Difference* (Chicago: University of Chicago Press, 1985), 223–261.

[7] Roland Barthes, *Mythologies* (New York: Hill and Wang, 2000), 56.

[8] *And The HHL Goes to . . . Famed Plastic Surgeons Reveal "Hollywood's Hottest Looks".* The Beverly Hills Institute of Aesthetic & Reconstructive Surgery (2010), http://hollywood shottestlooks.blogspot.com/2010/01/2010-hollywoods-hottest-looks.html. Retrieved March 23, 2010.

[9] Tom Prideaux, *Life Goes to the Movies* (New York: Pocket Books, 1977), 11.

[10] See as well E. Ann Kaplan, "Wicked Old Ladies from Europe: Jeanne Moreau and Marlene Dietrich on the Screen and Live." In Murray Pomerance, ed., *BAD: Infamy, Darkness, Evil, and Slime on Screen* (Albany: State University of New York Press, 2004), 239–253.

[11] For the purpose of this paper I will only be examining the transformations of the women on the show.

[12] According to the extensive ABC: "Extreme Makeover" website (http://abc.go.com/ prime time/extrememakeover/index.html), Dr. Griffin is responsible for only 17% of the transformations for the second and third seasons. No data is available for the first season. He is the only surgeon who performs the Brazilian "Butt Lift." The fact that Dr. Anthony Griffin is an African American whose work centers on "retaining [patients'] ethnic identity" is interesting to reflect on but beyond the scope of this paper at this time.

[13] Consumer Guide to Plastic Surgery: http://www.yourplasticsurgeryguide.com/ face-lift/cost.htm

[14] Average surgeon/physician fees. American Society for Plastic Surgeons, 2004 Statistics

[15] *Ibid.*

[16] *Ibid.*

[17] *Ibid.*

[18] *Ibid.*

[19] http://www.porcelain-veneers-directory.com/

[20] Atlanta Dental Group. http://www.atlantadentist.com/zoom_whitening_cost.html

[21] All About Vision (2005 statistics). http://www.allaboutvision.com/

[22] The potential danger of plastic surgery has become apparent with recent documented deaths. In early April 2004, Michele Charest, co-founder of CINAR animation, expired during a reconstructive technique in Montreal, and most recently, in November 2005, Stella Obasanjo, Nigeria's First Lady, died after undergoing plastic surgery in Spain.

[23] Buck-Morss, *Dialectics*, 56.

[24] However, during a later episode, "Extreme Makeover" briefly revisits Liz in Texas, stating that the problems she encountered during her recovery period documented on the show had to be corrected. She underwent a second batch of surgeries including revised cheek and chin implants as well as another face-lift. The narrative insinuates again that the corrections were needed because of Liz's age, not because of problems associated with such invasive surgical procedures and the fact that these procedures have a short "shelf life": as our living bodies organically transform, the surgical transformations do not, hence the requirement for continual "upgrading."

[25] A further example of this: recent news stories are reporting that since the "end" of the war in Iraq, cosmetic surgical procedures are "all the rage" in Baghdad with one surgeon performing on average twenty procedures a week. See Rebecca Santana, "Nose Jobs, Tummy Tucks: After Years of War, Iraqis Join the Cosmetic Surgery Craze," *The Canadian Press* March 21, 2010. http://www.google.com/hostednews/canadianpress/article/ALeqM5iP2u_HCSmpgrxYAmX9YieQQmFi1A. Retrieved March 31, 2010.

[26] Sander Gilman, *Making the Body Beautiful: A Cultural History of Aesthetic Surgeon* (Princeton: Princeton University Press, 1999), 19.

[27] "Extreme Makeover" web site.

[28] DELEESE WILLIAMS, individually and as guardian and representative of minors KARALEE McGEE and SEAN McGEE; and as personal representative on behalf of the ESTATE OF KELLIE McGEE, plaintiffs vs. AMERICAN BROADCASTING COMPANIES, INC.; NEW SCREEN ENTERTAINMENT, INC.; NEW SCREEN CONCEPTS, INC.; GREENGRASS PRODUCTIONS, INC.; LIGHTHEARTED ENTERTAINMENT, INC.; THE WALT DISNEY COMPANY; HOWARD SCHULTZ; and DOES 1-50, defendants. Superior Court of the State of California, County of Los Angeles, Central District. September 21, 2005.

[29] *Ibid.*

[30] "Kantar Media Reports Academy Awards Spending Reached $711 Million Over the Past 10 Years," Kantar Media News, February 16, 2010. http://www.kantarmediana.com/news/02162010.html. Retrieved March 23, 2010.

[31] *Ibid.*

[32] *The Nielsen Company's 2008 Guide to the Academy Awards,* New York: The Nielsen Company, February 21, 2008.

[33] *The 2009 Report of the 2008 Statistics National Clearinghouse of Plastic Surgery Statistics,* American Society for Plastic Surgery National Clearinghouse and *Advertising Opportunities.* Make Me Heal. http://www.makemeheal.com/mmh/advertising/index.vm.

Chapter 17

They Sing the Body Ecstatic

Television Commercials and Captured Music

Stephen L. Muzzatti

> [Humanity's] self-alienation has reached such a degree that it can experience its own destruction as an aesthetic pleasure of the first order.[1]

Introduction

Over the course of the last quarter century the overlap among various forms of popular culture and mass media has expanded steadily, especially with regard to music. The use of popular music in Hollywood films and the subsequent emergence of the "movie soundtrack," infomercials, celebrity infotainment "news," music videos, TV programs (and later entire networks) devoted to airing them, television ads scripted to look like serial dramas, Hollywood films based on videogames (and vice versa), product placement in movies, TV shows and music videos, and television programs built around the re-airing of TV commercials all speak to this widespread and growing trend. Traditional divisions among news, entertainment, and advertising are breaking down and the boundaries are becoming increasingly fluid. Much of this confluence is market driven. Executives from a host of cultural industries have recognized the profitability of crossover merchandising and are devising ever more creative, some would argue insidious, ways to engage such projects. One of the more recent forays in crossover spaces is what some are calling "advertainment"—the conflation of the advertisement and entertainment. Unlike the infomercials that first appeared in the late 1980s, approximating a talk show or TV news-magazine format to shill kitchen wares, cleaning products, and exercise equipment, this most recent foray draws heavily upon the use of popular music styles, artifacts, and actors in combination with lifestyle marketing to sell everything from cars and alcohol to holiday packages and retirement funds.

History of Advertising

While it is certainly true that ads have been around for many years, advertising as we understand it is a relatively recent phenomenon. It can be argued that a placard with a picture of a shoe on it hanging outside a cobbler's shop in the eighteenth century was an early form of advertising. The fundamental difference between that and contemporary forms of advertising (such as what we are exposed to through television) is that the former was direct and purely informational while the latter are symbolic, crammed with images designed to exploit cultural metaphors and metonyms.[2] A second difference, one of tantamount importance, is that early advertisements made no pretense. They were unambiguously designed to sell a particular product or service. Indeed, contemporary ads are so imbued with cultural mythologies that the sales pitch is furtively hidden behind a multilayered veil of artifice, multiple *entendres* and postmodern lifestyle scripts.

Like many other shifts in forms of cultural production, the transmogrification of the ad from its early, simple, and direct form to its current incarnation was a complex process tied to other, broader structural changes in society—changes which occurred primarily in the twentieth century. In the time between the eighteenth century and the early twentieth century, advertisements, at least in content, changed only modestly. While they became more elaborate and sophisticated, they still focused almost exclusively on extolling "the facts" about products. The artist's rendering of a shoe evolved into a photograph with accompanying text which detailed, for example, the materials used, the workmanship contributed, the product's cost and availability—but little else. Beginning in the early 1920s advertisements began to undergo a shift which heralded their current incarnation. This shift was tied to broader economic forces, particularly advances in mass industrialization which made the production of consumer goods easier and more efficient than at any other time in history. Tied to this was Fordism and growing alienation in the workplace. In short, the expedited production process coincided, indeed was contingent upon, an increasingly disempowered workforce in factories. Faster production meant more work, greater specialization and compartmentalization, and, not surprisingly, more disenfranchisement and dissent within the workplace. In short, as much as it was driven by the need to create new markets for products the birth of modern advertising as we know it was driven by the desire to neutralize the potentially incendiary mix of discontented workers at home and militant labor movements abroad.[3]

Pleasure and Fear: Ideology and Advertising

Ads began to promote an ideology of consumerism both as a means to create a market for the products being produced and as a way to control those most closely tied with the production process.[4] Advocating a consumerist lifestyle as the gateway to social integration quelled class conflict by diverting people's attention away from the productive process (which was alienating, not to mention increasingly monotonous) and toward one filled with promises of pleasure. Transforming people from producers of wealth into consumers, advertising forged a market where none existed before while simultaneously ensuring the continued subservience of wage laborers (who would be desperate for the opportunity to buy). Widespread consumer practices, particularly those couched in the rubric of leisure and release from drudgery, quickly became a pain killer for working class folks.[5] And beyond serving as a safe and malleable outlet for class tension, consumerism provided a veneer of coherence in the face of rapidly imploding cultural traditions.

The promised pleasure through consumption, while highly effective and very much in keeping with the aesthetics of fetishized leisure that were prominent in the early part of the twentieth century, could not sustain itself alone. To rehabituate consumerism in response to waning consumer behavior around World War II, ads became more serpentine and began to play upon fears of personal ineptitude and related social insecurities, primarily, though by no means exclusively, those of women. Women were on one level obvious and vulnerable targets of such strategies because of the highly gendered division of labor and because they were responsible for a good deal of consumption work. Working class and immigrant women in particular were frequently the targets of ad campaigns designed to undermine their sense of "domestic competence" by questioning their commitment to a clean home, well-fed children and a contented husband. Product X or Y was presented to them as not only a time-saving convenience but in fact the only means by which to ensure that a given domestic chore was accomplished satisfactorily. Furthermore, ads did not only make the case for the product of a particular manufacturer. Embedded within them was the implicit assumption that irrespective of brand, the product was a necessity.

Television and the Birth of the Commercial

The general shift in advertising strategy coincided with the emergence of another cultural production, television programs. The growth of television as a medium during the post-World War II boom provided a new outlet of previously unheralded power for advertisers. This new visual medium was extremely expensive to produce, and almost from the outset relied upon outside funding sources to underwrite it. In the early days of television, much of the outside money came in the form of "sponsorship." Companies would pay to sponsor a program and in exchange have the program named after them. At the beginning of a program an announcer would proclaim, "Texaco Star Theater" or "The Desilu Playhouse brought to you by Westinghouse," with some musical fanfare and perhaps a tagline or slogan. The "spot commercial," an advertisement that interrupted the program as opposed to one that appeared only at the beginning (or end), first appeared when Hazel Bishop, a small cosmetics company, wanted to advertise on TV but could not afford to sponsor an entire program. The compromise struck between the company and NBC resulted in a 30-second message from a twenty-six-year-old Merv Griffin being inserted into the middle of "The Kate Smith Evening Hour" (1951), spawning the ubiquitous commercial spot we know today.[6]

As the spot commercial became an increasingly normalized and substantial part of TV cultures, ads became an ever more vital place of cultural and economic brokerage. Lifestyle advertising, specifically the presentation of characters that advertisers thought the audience aspired to be or already were quickly became the staple. Television provided advertisers with considerable opportunities to dynamically link the everyday/night worlds of the audience with consumption practices. As Fiske and Hartley theorize, "Television does not represent the manifest actuality of our society, but rather reflects symbolically, the structure of values and relationships beneath the surface."[7] Living thirty-second lives, the upper middle-class characters in commercials are not only acutely other-directed, but lead their gratified existences and resolve their problems (fleeting as they may be, at least until the next commercial break!) through the unreflexive acquisition and use of consumer products.

Auditory Assaults and Popular Songs

As marketplace competition increased and the testimonials of hegemony's organizing agents (meddling neighbors, doctors, professional chefs, mechanics, dry cleaners and other scripted authorities) became increasingly commonplace in television commercials, advertisers searched for ways to augment their product push. To do so, advertisers harkened back to the generations past and began to incorporate music into their TV commercials. Employing strategies from vaudeville, where music was used to candy-coat a spoken sales pitch, and from the early days of radio, where audiences first heard the "Have you tried Wheaties?" jingle,[8] advertisers began to contract with studio musicians to create musical scores to accompany their ads.

The use of jingles or "ditties" remained the industry standard until the early 1970s and continues its presence in a modified form even today, with musical bits from Coca Cola's syrupy "I'd Like to Teach the World to Sing," to Pepsi's misogynistic "Music to Watch Girls By." Production costs were high, ranging from $15,000 to $30,000 for just the musical score, but companies clearly felt that the jingle was a vital component in promoting the pleasures of consumption and enlisting audience participation. Music has a direct route to our subconscious, and while we are always aware of what we hear we process the visual and spoken messages more consciously and critically than we do music.[9] The music worked to create mood and sustain the energy level. Never seen, but also never shut out, it served as the soundtrack for consumption.

As competition for consumers' dollars continued to intensify and the marketplace became glutted with parity products (i.e., commodities differing only slightly from one another—such as Pepsi and Coke—produced by competing companies) advertisers relied ever more on imagery and suggestive symbolism to maximize the audience's emotional investment and solidify product allegiances. By the early 1970s, realizing that the jingle was devalued currency, advertisers opted for a heretofore untested strategy—the use of *existing songs* in TV commercials. Cannibalizing music archives, they began to incorporate songs from the 1940s and 1950s into commercials for products undreamed of at that time. In perhaps the most overt display of a class-lifestyle-product nexus to date, advertisers traded upon the emotionally laden cultural currency of artists such as Nat King Cole and Benny Goodman to induce middle-aged, middle-class audiences to forget that they were watching commercials and believe they had been returned to the days of their youth—a time of great promise—with subtle, yet omnipresent, promises of a good life that could be attained through the embrace of consumerism. So, too, was there hope that by trading on clichéd cultural codings younger audiences from all classes might recapture something their anxious generation had never experienced.

Well into the 1970s, rock, the popular music of the day, was still virtually absent from TV commercials. While some advertisers had massive production budgets and employed full orchestras to approximate some of the softer rock for commercials—plagiarizing a Four Tops recording for Kraft "Velveeta" Cheese—the hard-rock stylings of the dominant youth genre, like Black Sabbath and Led Zeppelin, were unequivocally shunned as too fast, too loud, too brash, and generally too countercultural. However, by the early 1980s several significant cultural and structural shifts set the stage for the emergence of rock music in television commercials. First, by the late 1970s control over popular music production was becoming consolidated in the hands of a few major recording companies. This led not only to the erosion of rock's counterhegemonic messages but to the co-optation of artists into an entertainment "business" that was part of the existing corporate structure.[10] Just such a conscription of artists by the corporate machine is central to the ideology of consumerism—the neutralization of counterhegemonic cultural artifacts, practices, and discourses.[11] A good example is the marketing of the band KISS through comic books, action figures, and a made-for-TV movie. Today, their lasciviousness and openly defiant NYC-party-hard attitude is all but forgotten as the hedonistic "Shout It Out Loud" accompanies a twentysomething devouring a Mars Bar as he strolls down a darkened urban street. Such a consolidation of ownership in the music industry facilitates access to the art and lends a greater chance that music can be appropriated by corporate agents pedaling unreflexive hyperconsumerism. Secondly, by the late 1970s and early 1980s the copyrights on many of rock's early songs were expiring, leaving them vulnerable to any corporate pillager. Advances in music recording technology made it as easy for independently employed musicians to record a rock song as a jingle. Additionally, the demographics of the advertising industry were changing. Ad executives were getting younger and were more sympathetic to, if not outright advocates for, the use of rock music in advertising. Finally, the launch of MTV in 1981 with its young demographic and its focus on music and consumption provided an outlet for rock-based television commercials—ads that wouldn't or couldn't work elsewhere.

The use of rock and, later, other popular youth music genres such as electro, emo, hiphop and power pop exploded in the late 1980s and early 1990s. Among some of the most notable early examples from this time period were the use of the Beatles' "Revolution" by Nike, the Clash's "Should I Stay or Should I Go?" by Levi's, and Michael Jackson's ill-fated Pepsi spot. Throughout the decade of the 1990s the use of popular musical genres in television advertising became an industry staple. During this time, better educated than any generation in history, Gen X and Y came of age. Facing a world where work was increasingly deskilled and jobs in the bottom-tier service sectors and the criminal justice-industrial complex seemed to be all that was available, young people were frenetically assailed by consumerist messages. The consolidation of ownership in the cultural industries has, as Mark Crispin Miller contends, "shrunk the media cosmos and created a national entertainment state"[12]; resulting in few non-corporate, non-consumerist messages. By the middle of the decade, even the promise of an alternative epistemology resulting from the militant fusion of speed metal and rap had been supplanted by hiphop's bling and promises of hyperwealth. Today, in a world where Clear Channel and SIRIUS have emerged as the overwhelmingly dominant players in radio, and the "Big Five" of AOL Time Warner, BMG, EMI, Sony, and Vivendi-Universal (along with their television and film studio holdings) control more than 95% of all music sold in the US, commercials don't so much mimic as absorb youth music culture. Just as music videos (themselves, barely disguised advertisements for cds) are the cultural offspring of televised music performances, television commercials featuring popular music tracks (and in some instances, the artists as well) were born of a confluence of oligopolistic ownership patterns, the practice of vicarious pleasure, and symbolic representations of social worth. Disheartening as these developments are, they are perhaps not surprising. As the success of MTV, MuchMusic, and their numerous ancillaries should have taught us, music and television commercials go together; both are devoted to bodily pleasure, spectatorship, and channeled consumer participation. This is perhaps no better illustrated than in the recent series of Mitsubishi commercial cocktails (2002-2006) in which intimations of both approved and underground musico-chemical pleasures delightfully swirl. Messages of sanctioned and illicit consumption here blend with the dance beats of Dirty Vegas, Telepopmusik, The Wise Guys, and Deltron 3030 as groups of young clubgoers enthusiastically navigate the night's urban landscape in their Lancers, Eclipse Spiders, and Galants.

For External Use Only

The market conditions and the newly ephemeral cultural milieu since the turn of the twenty-first century have fundamentally changed popular music and the way the public, particularly young people, relate to it. Popular music has been transformed from a form of art made primarily by, and certainly for, young people into a potentially lucrative rights package for export to diverse and disjunctive sites. Mirroring the alienation and degradation of Fordism is a contemporary situation in which most artists do not own their licensing masters—the high-quality tapes from which recordings of various kinds can be made. These original sound recordings, fruits of some of the most difficult and emotionally draining human labor imaginable, are often owned by publishing companies, such as ABCKO and the Henry Fox Agency, who, even in the face of vehement objections by the artists, indiscriminately sell to the highest bidder. By appropriating the oppositional voices and fugitive knowledges of passionate cultural critics and social justice agents, such corporate concerns as automobile manufacturers, distilleries, fast food restaurants, and discount department stores divorce the art from its social and cultural context, mute the cultural critique, and brand it in service of hyperconsumerism. Literally decades worth of some of the most subversive and counterhegemonic music from genres as diverse as country and punk through triphop, soul, and hardcore have been reduced to the status of musical accompaniment for images of fetishized leisure and consumption.[13] Raised in a time of unheralded personal avarice and lionized corporate greed, middle-class 1980s kids now find themselves ensconced in the comfortable domesticity of suburban enclaves, gated communities, and gentrified downtowns. For them, commercials deliver Blondie's "One Way or Another" (Swiffer Duster), Madness's "Our House" (Maxwell House Coffee), and The Go Gos' "Head Over Heels"(Pantene Shampoo), while their teen and preteen children consume messages that normalize the vicious bond of commerce, imperialism, and entertainment in United States Navy "Accelerate Your Life" recruiting ads featuring Godsmack's "Awake" and New York Stock Exchange commercials accompanied by Fatboy Slim's "Right Here, Right Now."

Saying and Not Saying "No"

While many artists have had their art appropriated in the service of consumer capitalism, a few have successfully resisted such efforts. Successful resistance is often attributable to an artist's relative power within the industry, yet some is clearly due to little more than artists' resolute refusal to compromise their politics and their art. Icons like Paul Simon, Bruce Springsteen, and Neil Young have consistently refused to sell their music for use in television ads. Other singers, like the relatively unknown Pat MacDonald of Timbuk 3, refused repeated offers: over an eleven-year period MacDonald turned down Clairol's request for one song, "Hairstyles and Attitudes," and McDonald's and Ray Ban's requests for another, "The Future's So Bright I Gotta Wear Shades": together these companies had offered over $1.1 million. Many in the industry point to a $14 million deal between Microsoft and the Rolling Stones for rights to use "Start Me Up" in the Windows95 campaign as a watershed moment in the acquisition of big stars. Since then, many top-name artists have willingly consented to having their music used in television campaigns. Sting, for example, not only sold "Desert Rose" to Jaguar, but also appeared in an ad driving the car, and Paul McCartney, who just a few years ago cursed Nike, saying "The song was about revolution, not bloody tennis shoes," recently appeared in a commercial for Fidelity Investments, along with his song "Band on the Run." Similarly, after years of carefully guarding his masters Jimi Hendrix's family sold "Are you Experienced?" to Excite! for over $7 million. And after years of resistance, Led Zeppelin finally acquiesced to offers for their music, resulting in Cadillac's "Break Through" commercial of 2003 featuring the anthemic "Rock and Roll." The crashing cymbals and grinding guitar supplement singer Robert Plant's sexual angst while the sleek, silver Cadillac slips across a marble surface. At this writing, the collaboration between General Motors and Led Zeppelin energetically continues. However, all is not lost, as the case of another General Motors vehicle recently illustrated. Over the course of the last year a wide array of artists ranging from multi-platinum sellers like The Talking Heads and The Smashing Pumpkins to rambunctious indie acts like The Thermals, Trans Am, and the Soledad Brothers, and the long disbanded LiLiPUT (who made virtually no money during its five-year career) all refused repeated offers for use of their songs in commercials for the military-turned-superluxury Hummer.

The successful absorption of everything from relatively unknown artists (Badly Drawn Boy, Redlife, Ringside) through the most iconoclastic indie bands (White Stripes, Franz Ferdinand, The Buzzcocks) to the larger-than-life megastars (AC/DC, Madonna, The Who) has done much to dissolve the boundaries between popular music and advertising. Since 2000, we've witnessed very active and open cooperation among corporate clients, the ad industry, and diverse musicians, increasingly initiated by the artists themselves. After several critically acclaimed but commercially mediocre releases, for example, Moby's breakthrough album *Play* had all eighteen tracks commercially licensed—the first time in history such a broad licensing has occurred—and all eighteen have been used, including "Porcelain," which was used for a Bailey's Irish Cream ad and "Find my Baby," which was featured in an American Express commercial even before the cd hit stores. So, too, Bodyrockers' track "I Like the Way" was broken out a month before the release of the cd, not on commercial radio or other traditional venues (such as MTV's "Total Request Live," or MuchMusic's "Much on Demand"), but rather in a Diet Coke commercial. Once available in stores, the cd bore a sticker that read, "As seen on the Diet Coke commercial."

Ben Neill's release *Automotive* provided another interesting first: all ten songs on the cd were expanded versions of tracks he recorded for use in Volkswagen ads.[14] Volkswagen also sponsored Neill's supporting tour, which featured visuals from their "Driver's Wanted" campaign during the concerts.[15] Other recent players in the commercial-concert tour crossover include Jay-Z, who was featured in Sprite's Liquid Mix Tour, and Jewel and Lenny Kravitz, whose respective Spirit and Freedom tours were sponsored by Tommy Hilfiger and perhaps would have been more appropriately dubbed the "Spirit of Consumerism" and "Freedom to Shop" tours.

Conclusion

Walter Benjamin's observation, printed at the beginning of this chapter, should resonate disturbingly with all critical consumers of popular culture. While Benjamin's intention was to warn readers of his day of German Fascism's efforts to aestheticize the political as a means of advancing its imperial designs, his sentiment should not be lost to those of us who strive to better understand the contemporary workings of the cultural industries in North America. Advertising, at least its modern incarnation from the 1920s onward, is at the first level of approximation a form of class warfare. It was an exercise in social engineering undertaken by cultural managers at the behest of early twentieth-century captains of industry. Advertising's goal was the control of the dangerous classes by ensnaring them in a seamless web of wage slavery, fetishized leisure, insecurity, visceral pleasure, consumption, and vaporous ameliorative distractions. Today, the confluences of art and leisure, public display and spectatorship, and insecurity and pleasure that constitute the modern television commercial enlist audiences, particularly young ones, as willing participants in the process of their own domination.

Conventional wisdom in the study of advertising has long claimed the ads are made in order to sell products—that products would in fact not make much money on their own, without the friendly assistance of advertising to boost them. But it's not the products which are at the center of the contemporary global economy, it's the ads themselves. Slick and emotional, profound and poetic, rhythmic and insistent, the advertisement, as a cultural, political, social, and economic statement of "truth," has become our most important commercial product.

Notes

[1] Walter Benjamin, *Illuminations* (New York: Harcourt, Brace and World, Inc., 1968), 242.

[2] John Fiske and John Hartley, *Reading Television* (London: Routledge, 1989).

[3] See Stuart Ewen, "The Public Mind and the Pictures in Our Heads: A Riff," in this volume.—Eds.

[4] Stuart Ewen, *Captains of Consciousness: Advertising and the Social Roots of Consumer Culture* (Toronto: McGraw-Hill Book Co., 1977).

[5] Ewen, *Captains.*

[6] Ellis Cashmore, ... *And there was Television* (London: Routledge, 1994).

[7] Fiske and Hartley, *Reading.*

[8] See David Huron, "Music in Advertising: An Analytic Paradigm," *The Musical Quarterly* Vol. 73, No. 4 (1989), 560 and Steve Karmen, *Through the Jingle Jungle: The Art and Business of Making Music for Commercials* (New York: Billboard Books, 1989).

[9] Robb Wright, "Score vs. Song: Art Commerce and the H Factor in Film and Television Music" in Ian Inglis, ed., *Popular Music and Film* (New York: Wallflower Press, 2003), 8–21.

[10] Steve Chapple and Rebee Garofalo, *Rock'n'Roll is Here to Pay* (Chicago: Nelson-Hall, Inc., 1977).

[11] Ewen, *Captains.*

[12] Quoted in David Sanjek, "Popular Music and the Synergy of Corporate Culture" in Thomas Swiss et al, eds., *Mapping the Beat: Popular Music and Contemporary Theory* (Malden, MA: Blackwell Publishers, 1998), 171–186. See also Mark Crispin Miller, "Saddam and Osama in the Entertainment State," in this volume.

[13] See www.songtitle.info and www.commercialbreaksandbeats.co.uk/comp.asp.

[14] In a similar vein, the tremendous popularity of compilation cds like *As Seen on TV: Songs from Commercials* (2001) and the *Fired Up!* series (2003, 2005, and 2006) bespeak the conflation of advertising and popular music.

[15] Allyce Bess, "The New Hit Single Might Hide a Jingle: Is it an Ad or Art?" *The Christian Science Monitor* December 9 (2003), 11.

Chapter 18

Aliens Amok

Men in Black Policing Subjectivity Onscreen

Kirby Farrell

Barry Sonnenfeld's comedy *Men in Black* (1997) imagines "about 1500" space aliens living in human guise on earth, mostly in New York City, policed by a shadowy organization known euphemistically as Men in Black. The agency resembles a corporate version of the CIA, FBI, Immigration and Naturalization Service (INS), and the National Security Agency (NSA). According to the veteran agent Kay (Tommy Lee Jones), the aliens are "intergalactic refugees" from persecution and violence, "most of them decent enough, just trying to make a living." The agency is in transition, with two white male agents recruiting replacements so they can retire. They choose a young black New York City policeman (Will Smith) who combines street smarts with the physical superiority stereotypically associated with black athletic celebrities. By the film's end, a plucky, attractive pathologist named Laurel (Linda Fiorentino) has earned the second agent's position.

The movie's villain is an alien called "The Bug" (Vincent D'Onofrio)—"a giant cockroach with unlimited strength, a massive inferiority complex, and a real short temper." The Bug has come to earth to assassinate a refugee prince of the Arquillian Empire, who lives in New York City disguised as a jeweler named Rosenberg (Mike Nussbaum). After a crash landing in upstate New York, The Bug devours a local redneck named Edgar and puts on his skin. Making his way to Manhattan, the alien-redneck murders the elderly jeweler in order to steal a galaxy belonging to the Arquillians that Rosenberg has hidden inside one of his jewels. In reaction, an Arquillian space ship threatens to annihilate the earth if the Men in Black fail to retrieve the lost galaxy.

The film parodies Cold War melodramas such as *The Hunt for Red October* (1990) and *Crimson Tide* (1995) in which heroic agents thwart an apocalyptic nuclear holocaust. With their high-tech arsenal, the Men in Black spoof the already self-parodic James Bond fantasies of Cold War superheroes. On another level, more significant in the post-Soviet era, the plot symbolically turns an American redneck into an alien terrorist who would destroy a global (intergalactic) balance of power mediated by a gentle, urbane Jewish businessman.

In this way *Men in Black* is topically engaged with some crucial fantasies of 1990s America. Although the film is slyly sophisticated about the story it tells, it unwittingly sheds light on anxieties about immigration and economic injustice that look back to the Gilded Age, even as it embodies topical concerns about globalization, an evolving corporate police state, and the effects of technological revolution on subjectivity.

The film uses the extra-terrestrials to satirize conflicted American attitudes toward immigration, as evident in such xenophobic measures as California's Proposition 187, which in 1994 denied health, welfare, and educational benefits to illegal aliens and their children.[1] In the opening scene, Border Patrol agents intercept a van smuggling Mexicans into Texas, unaware that one of the illegals is actually a criminal space alien. When two Men in Black intervene, pretending to work for a special bureau within INS, they quickly detect the impostor and, when he turns menacing, they destroy him. Afterward they calm the astounded, naive Border Patrol agents by "shooting" them with a gun-like "neuralizer" whose blinding flash destroys recent memory and awes the audience. The gun induces amnesia or dissociation, keeping the aliens' existence secret and sanitizing a reality supposedly too disturbing to be public knowledge.

Men in Black jokes about official and everyday use of dissociation to tame reality. Ironically the only inkling of truth about the aliens' presence on earth appears in preposterous tabloids like *The National Enquirer*. The Men in Black not only suppress dangerous aliens, they also use repression to protect ignorant earthlings from terrifying awareness of their cosmic vulnerability. The repression operates on two levels: to manage hostility between newcomers and native humans, and to control the basic existential terror of cosmic alienation and death that the immigrants from space represent to earthlings. With its special guns, including the memory neuralizer, the mysterious police agency keeps the groups and spheres of awareness dissociated.

From time immemorial migration has meant competition for resources and sometimes genocidal displacement. In the Old Testament, for example, God commands Israel to exterminate the Canaanites by killing the men, enslaving the women and children, and seizing their lands and goods.[2] In United States history the Statue of Liberty idealizes tolerance based on a common pursuit of liberty and justice. Ideally, immigrants to America are not competitors but fellow refugees from oppression, disposed to share the fruits of the land. But in practice, newcomers have always been a source of cheap labor and therefore vulnerable to exploitation from above even as they implicitly threaten the nation's working poor. When competition intensifies and assimilation falters, newcomers may be, or seem to be, parasites or predators: the stereotypical Mexican family with too many children, for example, or the ruthless, demonized criminals touted in the media, such as Mariel boatlift Cubans, Latino drug dealers and youth gangs, and Sicilian or Russian "mafia."

Psychologically the newcomers represent dangerous infantile orality: too many mouths to feed and in turn a threat of cannibalistic hunger and survival rage. In "One Awful Night," a pulp crime story of 1919, detectives descend into "the famous Chinese tunnels" under San Francisco's Chinatown to kill "Chinese crooks gobbling up the girls by the wholesale and shipping them to the Chinese foreign markets."[3] The story appeared during a period of immigrant-bashing after World War I, a time of civil unrest, Red scares, and labor strife. Its maidens are icons of fertility and food "gobbled up" by "slant-eyed," "yellow-skinned devils" associated with rats, snakes, and other vermin. Like the Men in Black, the detectives work for a paramilitary "agency"—presumably Pinkerton—that operates on the edge of the law.

Men in Black winks at this store of pulp imagery. It crystallizes the threat of ravenous immigrants in the cockroach-like assassin called The Bug, who reveals a horrific shark-like maw in the climactic showdown with the agents. The Bug relishes war because "that means more food for my family, all seventy-eight million of them. That's a lot of mouths to feed." Discovering an infestation of bugs in a barn earlier in the film, a human pest-control exterminator (Ken Thorley) could be speaking of immigrants when he quips, "Well, well. Moving in like we own the place." The aliens can usurp someone's skin the way immigrants may take over someone's job and social position. Ultimately, according to this symbolic logic, immigrants compete for nothing less than autonomy and identity itself. The Bug devours the redneck Edgar and appropriates his skin, acting out the immigrants' threat to bring social death to marginal members of society.

This nightmare has revealing antecedents in the tensions aroused by the great surge of immigration from 1890 to 1910. At the turn of the century, as Gail Bederman has shown, imperialistic ideology was sharply ambivalent.[4] It held that the drive to expand economic life and civilize primitive peoples would improve the world. Yet civilization's comforts and ethos of masterful self-restraint also threatened to sap manliness, and when combined with anxiety about the raw energy of colonized people, imperialism could raise alarm, and deep anger, about degeneration and vulnerable effeminacy at home. Projecting aggression onto colonial people, guiltily uneasy about their long-suppressed rage toward their masters, western nations worried about being overrun by savages. In his memoir of 1912 Rider Haggard reports waking dreams about being enslaved by barbarian invaders.[5] "As president, [Teddy Roosevelt] believed his duty was to usher the manly American nation ever closer to the racial preeminence and perfect civilization he had predicted for it."[6] The fearful underside of this compensatory chauvinism came out in Roosevelt's warnings against the specter of "race suicide."

Coined in 1901 by Edward A. Ross, the term "race suicide" was associated with "immigration and women's advancement, as well as the falling birthrate."[7] Teddy Roosevelt maintained, for example, that "civilized but inferior Japanese men were willing to settle for a lower standard of living, and would force down wages, ruining American men's ability to provide for their families. Allowing Japanese men to immigrate . . . would thus be, as TR put it, 'race suicide.'"[8] With the closing of the frontiers, distances shrank, competition over colonies increased, and surplus populations now had no room to expand—in Hitler's charged language, no *Lebensraum*. These conditions contributed to the arms races and genocidal warfare of the twentieth century, a history evoked by the ultimatum that drives the plot of *Men in Black* when the Arquillians demand that "their" stolen galaxy be returned or the earth will be annihilated. H. G. Wells anticipated this pressurized atmosphere in *The War of the Worlds* (1898), in which Martians invade Britain with devastating rays that evoke the contemporary industrial arms race and terror of a battlefield Armageddon, but also the anxiety about genocidal colonization that Conrad summed up in Kurtz's dying cry, "Exterminate all the brutes!"[9] Global "others" threaten psychic as well as bodily usurpation, as in western worries about being overrun by the "yellow peril" of faceless Asian hordes.

Men in Black's aliens neatly condense these ambivalent historical attitudes. Their insect-like and squid-like body parts suggest a closeness to nature which can make them both derisively primitive and frighteningly powerful. The aliens arouse human distrust, yet their behavior is virtually indistinguishable from human behavior, and the film satirizes the humans' visceral xenophobia. Much of the aliens' menace lies in their ambiguity. On earth the agency monitors them in a parody of late-twentieth century industrial surveillance technology. But how many aliens finally exist out in the cosmos? If they can adapt so readily to earth and mutate at will, can they be trusted to keep to any reliable form, or are they beyond any sort of psychic or bodily integrity? In this respect they suggest the relativism that has shocked people since modernism began to discover evolution and the range of cultures across the globe.

In this century's fantasies, then, immigration may presage the fall of empires and personal annihilation. Although most of the aliens in *Men in Black* seem benign, the seasoned agent Kay explains that the agency maintains strict secrecy because people would panic if they realized that aliens lived among them, already invisibly—if harmlessly—displacing them. The film maintains a deftly ambivalent attitude toward the newcomers. For one thing, the aliens seem to represent an elite that travels like intergalactic business executives and cooperates with the immigration agency on earth. They resemble the moneyed elites of post-Cold War capitalism, the new breed of global entrepreneurs and financiers who buy citizenship in countries like the United States or Canada when economic home bases such as Hong Kong become untenable. At the same time they can be despotic, as in the Arquillians' peremptory threat to destroy the earth when their disguised emissary Rosenberg is assassinated by The Bug. When the outraged Arquillians send an ultimatum to earth, most of the aliens on earth manage to flee back into space without consulting their official minders, as if they are actually more autonomous than officialdom has admitted. In their superhuman mobility and capacity for bodily transformation, these elite beings more nearly fulfill immortality wishes than their human counterparts.

The Men in Black operate on the margin of conventional awareness. Unlike ordinary people, they confront the cosmic insignificance of humankind, but they also share some of the superhuman capacities of the aliens, thanks to their surveillance technology and high-tech guns. Like St. George opposing the dragon in chivalric romance, the agents belong to an autonomous, professional warrior class and in effect the agents trade the comforts of quotidian life for the warrior-hero's conviction of immortality. "You will sever human contact," Jay is told. But in compensation, "You're no longer part of the system. You're above the system. Over it. Beyond it."

Yet there is an underlying death-anxiety that reveals itself only when age and fatigue impair the heroic dream. In the opening scene, for instance, Kay and his older partner Dee (Richard Hamilton) detect an escaped criminal space alien among some Mexicans being smuggled across the Texas border. Stripped of his disguise the monster turns on them. Dee fumbles his gun and it takes Kay's quick reflexes to blast the monster. Afterward, Dee apologizes: "I'm sorry, Kay. The spirit's willing, but the rest of me . . ." In the context of fin-de-siècle anxiety about manliness, Dee's failure dramatizes the strain of modernism, the debilitating control and vigilance demanded by the preservation of civilization. As Dee's failure to fire his gun illustrates, the role of guardian is exhausting. Dee's middle-aged fatigue signifies encroaching senescence and death-anxiety. Suddenly he is fascinated by the beauty he sees in the stars, reminders of the ultimate framework of life and presumably nature's compensation for old age and death. The scene is comic and rueful, because the human terror of death is displaced onto the criminal monster, who is the grotesque embodiment of predatory greed for life. The stars signify mortal transience to humans, whereas aliens actively travel among the stars as if, like vampires, they can endlessly elude death.

By contrast, the relatively youthful Kay is still absorbed in the warrior-police role. The film draws much of its ironic energy from his style as an agent. His coolness—the sunglasses, business suit, and nonchalance—seems to signify absolute composure. Yet in the larger symbolic context, these qualities are a comic mask for a hypervigilance, numbness, and diminished subjectivity akin to combat trauma. Kay had to abandon his wife to join the agency. He is poised but anaesthetic. By zapping his partner with the memory neuralizer, Kay releases the weary agent from his combat trauma, implicitly equating retirement with a therapy based on repression or dissociation. To protect his own memory from the neuralizer's flash, Kay dons sunglasses, which wittily associate the healer's role with coolness, invisibility, and manipulation.

The symptoms of combat trauma can be divided into depressive and aggressive reactions. Retiring into amnesia and exhaustion, Dee moves toward a depressive position, whereas active agents seem to be continually swept into the berserk state. Confronted by overwhelming terror, a berserker is apt to plunge recklessly into battle, shedding all armor ("baresark" = "without armor" in Old Norse), in a state of beast-like or superhuman rage. No one can be certain why combat trauma immobilizes one soldier and launches another into a murderous rampage. Self-protectively, we assume that a freeze response in the face of death is more logical than a "senseless" rampage. But "when a soldier is trapped, surrounded, or overrun and facing certain death, the berserk state has apparent survival value, because he apparently has nothing to lose and everything to gain from reckless frenzy."[10]

The climactic shootout is a robust convention of twentieth century industrial entertainment. Its epitome is the video game based on the paranoid extermination of dehumanized enemies. But Western, gangster, and war movies also commonly use a fusillade of bullets to represent a convulsion of rage that purges terror and hostility. The fantasy of cathartic fury is as tenacious as it is ancient.[11] It appears in the sacrificial murder of scapegoats, in exorcism of malevolent spirits, and in beliefs about the efficacy of violent purgatives and emetics in Renaissance medicine. These fantasies imagine restoring equilibrium by "fighting off" threat, using violence to expel violence. They conjure up violence by polarizing conflict, concentrating will, selecting a target, and risking all in an act of supreme exertion and release. There is a self-intoxicating or hysterical quality to rage that contributes to fantasies of transcendent or apocalyptic scope. These dynamics play out in millennial imagery and the eschatological fantasy implied in burning witches and heretics in symbolic hellfire to purge demonic forces. In *Frankenstein* (1931) and in vampire films such as *Innocent Blood* (1992) and *Near Dark* (1987), predatory greed for life can be stopped only by annihilation of the demonic criminals in a climactic inferno. In the industrial age that incendiary fury is epitomized in the fire-bombing of Dresden and the nuclear fireball that incinerated Hiroshima, images of rage which drove World War Two to a psychological climax so intense that its aftereffects haunted imaginations through the end of the Cold War.

Seen through this lens, the cinematic "hail" of bullets or "firefight" points to ancient fantasies of demonic exorcism as well as to the psychology of berserk rage. The association of guns with berserking is rooted in deep metaphors. Like gunpowder, rage "blows up," "explodes," or "erupts." Gunpowder's volatility suggests psychic impulsivity, as in a "hair trigger" personality with "a short fuse." The detonation of a cartridge, like the berserk state, is an all-or-nothing phenomenon. "Going" amok, a soldier goes beyond conventional controls, "out" of his mind. Trapped between the enemy and the military command at their backs, facing death on all sides, soldiers may experience a sense of abandonment and cultural betrayal that triggers desperate recklessness.[12] In workplace rampages, a sense of cultural betrayal and social death may goad a "terminated" worker to a suicidal shootout in the conviction that there is no place to go and no way back into his everyday life. As satirized in Oliver Stone's *Natural Born Killers* (1994), say, sensational news coverage of criminal or workplace rampages may fulfill fantasies of transcendence in berserking. Like gambling, gunplay gives the abandonment of inhibitions a magical quality grounded in fantasies about natural instinct, luck, or moralized fate. Films like the *Rambo* series (1985–1988) dramatize survival magic in firestorms of bullets and other munitions in which enemies tend to vanish bloodlessly and the hero emerges unscathed.

Like other tools, guns compensate for the physical limitations of the body. The mind readily imagines transcendence of time and space; it is the body that is deficient. Guns are mechanical, prosthetic enhancements of the body, even as they represent an evolutionary acquisition of improved armor, teeth, claws, and a superhuman phallus. Guns are indestructible fists or teeth, and by extension they are related not only to other projectile weapons such as spears and guided missiles but also to vehicles as different as the ancient war chariot, the tank, the domestic car, the airplane, and the intergalactic battle cruiser.[13] When the human body itself becomes a vehicle and potential weapon for an "alien," then the body too can be a kind of gun. With its robot-like limp and grotesque strength, the redneck's body is charged with explosive force and serves The Bug as a cybernetic weapon. What's more, the gun may serve its master by doing seemingly harmless work, as in surgery with laser "guns" or house construction with pneumatic nail "guns." This is the ambivalence behind robot and cyborg fantasies as different as Ira Levin's *The Stepford Wives* (1975) and James Cameron's film *The Terminator* (1984). In a paranoid universe, radical existential motives such as survival anxiety and striving for heroic power tend to bind self and gun so closely that they fuse.

Like magical practices, firearms have equivocal cognitive effects. They may create a conviction of superhuman power and control, but they can also evoke terrifying irrationality and disrupt culture's conventional immortality guarantees. The media, for example, use imagery of armed children, as in the Jonesboro Arkansas schoolyard killings, or teenagers' drive-by shootings, to signify "senseless" violence that, like berserking, is supposed to exceed or defy all rational social controls. In the hero's hand the gun symbolizes godlike control, yet like Faustian magic, it also threatens to dissolve inhibitions and "possess" the soul, as in so-called impulse killings.

The student gunmen in the Littleton Colorado high school massacre (April 1999), for example, stockpiled small arms and bombs, and planned a do-or-die assault against their "enemies" meant to culminate in the suicidal crash of a hijacked plane into New York City. In the high school library, they interrogated cornered students and impulsively killed some. Eric Harris and Dylan Klebold "laughed triumphantly as they meted out fate," said *Newsweek*. "'They were, like, orgasmic,' says 19-year-old Nicholas Schumann, who heard the worst of it" (May 3, 1999). The news magazine mixed military or sports victory with suggestions of psychopathic coldness ("laughed triumphantly") and godlike, tyrannical authority ("meted out fate"). The student witness interpreted the killers' excitement as sexual frenzy ("orgasmic"). The gunmen, the journalists, and the witness bring together familiar fantasies associated with guns.

Men in Black dramatizes these magical associations in its treatment of guns and the berserk state. Using the memory-zapping gun, an agent transcends ordinary "repressed" life, comprehending it but also initiated into cosmic mysteries beyond it. As in fantasies of "blowing away" a target, the agents' high-tech weapons dissolve alien bodies into harmless, lurid goo. In the final showdown at the World's Fair site in Flushing Meadow, Kay acts out the stages of berserking. When The Bug disarms him by swallowing his assault rifle, Kay taunts the monster into attacking him, then plunges headlong into its fearsome maw to retrieve and fire his weapon, exploding the creature from within. As if reborn, Kay emerges like a newborn infant, thoroughly smeared with the gooey essence of the creature. In the imagery of berserking, conventional categories magically dissolve: killing and sacrifice produce life; the macho enemy becomes perversely maternal; and reincorporation into this devouring parent-figure generates uncanny autonomy. What's more, the rebirth also marks Kay's decision to retire, surrender his memory, and finally accept mortality.

Like the aliens, the idea of berserking assumes many disguises in the film. Despite the agents' professional cool, the agency epitomizes the berserk state. Its agents transcend conventional legal and institutional restraints. Their cryptic letter names neatly evoke their dissociation, as their high-tech car does in rocketing about New York City at speeds too great for personal control, freed from traffic laws. Racing upside down on the roof of the Lincoln Tunnel, "over the heads" of everyone else, the agents' car demonstrates the magical potency of ultimate heedless daring. When Jay accidentally touches a supercharged ball in the agency's terminal, the sphere goes amok. When it ricochets wildly throughout the building, its furious trajectory magically defies the usual laws of physics.

Lest berserking be associated solely with men and men's violence, the film also implicates women in its magic. Although the rookie Jay, for example, covets the hefty assault rifle his mentor Kay requisitions in the final crisis (a "Series IV De-atomizer"), he is issued a little "ladies'" pistol called a "cricket." The screenplay, however, makes the derringer-like pistol capable of a tremendous punch whose recoil invariably knocks Jay over backward. The pistol mocks gender stereotypes and flatters women in the audience by implying that "ladies" pack a concentrated wallop that a man may lack the strength to control. An analogous inversion appears when Jay is dispatched to help an alien mother give birth in the back seat of a car. In the throes of labor the mother reverts to her underlying alien form, and her tentacles pick up and violently whirl the helpless agent about. Childbirth is akin to going amok. The woman's body that gives life is also capable of overwhelming violence. In a flattering gesture toward blacks, the screenplay insists that despite this shock, Jay has soul. Although his partner Kay is impassive, Jay can still feel, cooing over the newborn alien.

Magical berserking is of course ideologically charged. Since The Bug's berserking is depicted as atrocious, and the agency rescues humanity, we are kept from recognizing that at bottom the agency is a corporate police state with a lawless program of surveillance and enforcement. The film's ideological implications are evident in the bodies of the aliens. The disguised alien Rosenberg is a gentle, avuncular shopkeeper who is rescuing part of his "homeland"—the disputed galaxy—from the rapacious Bug. He is "Daddy" to his pet cat Orion. During the autopsy after his assassination, Rosenberg's face swings open on hinges to reveal an infantile ET-like creature inside the head who is operating the body like a machine. Innocents, the film argues, use cybernetics and illusion to compensate for their inherent vulnerability.

By contrast, the alien assassin assumes the form of a hostile if bumbling redneck, a type regularly vilified in Hollywood films. He is uncouth and abusive to his wife (Siobhan Fallon). But as the climax of the film argues, inside this skin or form of a man is a more primitive evil, the cockroach-like Bug. The monster is as intrinsically evil as Rosenberg is "really" a childlike, elderly incarnation of ET. The film's symbolic logic makes Rosenberg the admirable old man that retiring agents like Dee and Kay would become, while projecting onto the redneck monster all their darker motives as agents. After all, in his survival rage and lust for the Arquillians' galaxy, The Bug acts out a lawless greed for life that is only too human. By destroying the monster, the agents tame death-anxiety and greed for life in themselves. In emerging from the grave-like crater, animating a grotesque male body, the rampaging assassin resembles the Frankenstein monster. As in Mary Shelley's novel, the ungainly body parts evoke proletarian incoherence, in this instance not the revolutionary mob of Nineteenth-Century Europe,[14] but the marginalized white men associated today with neo-Nazi and militia terrorism. One such figure is Buford O'Neal Furrow, who was apparently acting out fantasies associated with Christian identity and white supremacist groups in the northwest when he assaulted a Jewish day care center in Los Angeles on August 10, 1999. In effect, The Bug is a caricatured redneck gone amok, and the intergalactic war threatened by the stolen galaxy actually euphemizes a more disturbing prospect of class violence suppressed by agents of the corporate state recruited from the anxious middle class.

As Teddy Roosevelt's concerns show, at the beginning of the Twentieth Century middle- and lower-class men felt their traditional status endangered, under pressure from industrialism, urbanization, immigration, and nascent feminism. *Men in Black* projects an ambivalent solution to this continuing distress. It envisions a radical gap between an invisible elite and ordinary people. It imagines a corporate state whose unseen executives manage the affairs of an even more dissociated alien elite, editing reality for everyone else. Select, gun-toting recruits from the lower ranks serve the corporate state and preserve the "galaxies" of an alien elite from brutish enemies. A liberated woman such as Laurel or a young black cop like James can "be somebody" by becoming a Praetorian security force. Teaming up against enemies, the rookie agents create a romantic bond and a potential family, humanizing the corporate state even as they free weary middle-aged managers such as Dee and Kay to enjoy the fruits of their labors. But the heroic rookies are still finally servants. Their first assignment, for instance, is to scare up luxury sports tickets for a visiting alien diplomat.

Those at the bottom of society are epitomized by the redneck monster Edgar and in turn associated with immigrant stereotypes of a century ago. As scapegoats, greedy and aggressive, they draw off guilt the corporate insiders might otherwise feel. The monstrous redneck

Edgar is abusive to "his" wife, behaving like the immigrant in Alice Guy Blache's didactic, pseudo-documentary film of 1912 called *Making of an American Citizen*.[15] In the film an immigrant husband named Ivan mistreats his wife as he did in the old world, until his new American neighbors reeducate him through chivalrous exhortation and, as a last resort, a prison term. In *Men in Black,* that despised, uncouth barbarian once again invades America's genteel shores. After debriefing Edgar's wife, preparing to zap her memory, the young black agent Jay wants to give the woman a new feisty identity to remember instead of the usual banal formula. He tells her that she "kicked out" her boorish husband and should now "hire a decorator" and get a new wardrobe. But this is Hollywood feminism, deflecting attention to personal style when the deeper problem is the woman's poverty and the ownership of "galaxies" by an armed and inaccessible global elite.

But there is also another way that immigration lore serves the film's fantasies about the present. If The Bug represents white trash subculture, his opposite is his victim, the jeweler "Gentle Rosenberg." The grandfatherly Rosenberg is an expression of a privileged business class that in the 1990s feels older and vulnerable to ruthless rivals, afraid of losing its wealth and real estate—the prized galaxy. The jeweler belongs to an "alien" Arquillian royal family, but he can also be seen as a representation of the new corporate elite, disguising its acquisitiveness and *arriviste* insecurity. Rosenberg possesses a "galaxy" that suggests the immense wealth—the business "empire"—controlled by this financial elite, just as the redneck monster embodies the rage of the underclass in an era that has been compared to the Gilded Age. This is an "alien" elite insofar as it has cut itself off from the poor. The galaxy-in-a-bauble is in fact an invaluable "sub-atomic energy source," even as the mild jeweler puts a harmless face on military-industrial aggression.

In an era of identity politics, the manipulation of ethnicity and class markers makes for especially good box office. Like the film's black and female superheroes and its de-monized redneck, Rosenberg is part of an ideological formula. Hollywood commonly idealizes "Jewishness," as, for example, Steven Spielberg has done in *Schindler's List* (1993) and Barbra Streisand does in *The Prince of Tides* (1991).[16] But in the post-Reagan world Jews are more likely to be suburban, affluent, and politically conservative than the insecure urban immigrants once well-known for liberal, working class loyalties. Rosenberg's "Jewishness" expresses Hollywood ambivalence about these conflicted changes. The film makes him a figure of commanding, vindictive power and yet also a childlike victim, in a fantasy that combines self-aggrandizement and self-effacement. Rosenberg's "Jewishness" is an honorific, sentimental marker that celebrates ethnic pride yet also leaves out the real struggles of past Jewish immigrants chronicled by Henry Roth and others.

These fantasies are also a projection of Hollywood's own situation. In their reliance on disguise and their ability to get inside ordinary humans, the aliens resemble the "galaxies" of movie "stars" who also thrive by impersonating others. And like the Arquillians, financial elites around the world and in Hollywood struggle over galaxies—"entertainment empires" such as Disney. In fact, when the agents finally discover the contested galaxy, it shimmers inside Rosenberg's bauble like an image on a television screen. But Hollywood equivocally identifies with ordinary folks as well. In making the lowly New York cop James (Jay) and the young pathologist Laurel heroic initiates to the real story of the 1990s, *Men in Black* flatters minorities and women.

Guns and the transforming magic of berserking support this equivocal stance. The selected agents can be happy serving their human and alien overlords because the agency allows them an illusion of professional autonomy signified by their high-tech guns and sur-veillance devices. Tacitly the guns make the Men in Black not servants but free agents, not only morally superior to the elite they rescue, but also capable of policing and if necessary even killing them. Just this rebellious potential makes it necessary to have demonized ene-mies like The Bug to deflect anger away from the social world. Guns and berserking keep the agents in a state of hypervigilance that separates them from awkward questions about sta-tus and social justice, while the memory-zapping neuralizer can instantly switch them into amnesiac bliss.

In their doomsday ultimatum, the Arquillians dramatize the old American wish for both exterminatory supremacy (as in the genocidal "taming" of the American frontier or General LeMay's exhortation to bomb Vietnam "back to the stone age") and innocence wor-thy of "the new Jerusalem." In euphemizing the Arquillians the film unwittingly reveals its fears that even in the prosperous, post Cold War 1990s, far removed from mid-century hor-rors, the drive for status is grounded in dog-eat-dog survival rage.

These fantasies call into question the nature of subjectivity. The idea of aliens drama-tizes anxiety that the core of self is foreign and manipulative. It personifies the Freudian unconscious, making it to some extent controllable through surveillance and guns. As in some fashionable psychological therapies, the film wishes for a frenzied, purgative abreac-tion through berserking. In plunging down The Bug's throat in the climactic confrontation, Kay dispels the threats of the primitive unconscious. He magically undoes the terror of can-nibalism associated with the man-eating insect, hungry immigrants, and aliens who can devour humans' innards and wear their skins. In plunging into the belly of the beast, shed-ding all inhibitions, going out of his conventional self, the berserker puts himself in the grip of a deeper will analogous to the alien inside a human. The berserker, that is, implicitly par-ticipates in the aliens' cosmic reality.

And yet this pseudo-religious transcendence is eerily equivocal. An autopsy discovers inside Rosenberg's head a diminutive alien being something like the philosopher's "ghost in the machine." What agency moves the ghost? The question has long haunted modern cul-tures. Industrial technology produces tremendous power by anatomizing things, reducing them to manipulable components. It can overcome death by replacing body parts in organ transplants. The factory can reproduce useful things in infinite abundance and even clone living beings. Yet these same processes also arouse fears that we are nothing more than bio-mechanical gizmos, even in mental life—that reality is always virtual and intelligence ulti-mately artificial. They invite us to look for a ground of being that can never be seen, if it's there at all. Though industrial democracies deny it by appeals to national identity, patriot-ism, and community, societies are also assemblages of competing individuals, subgroups, and classes, each manipulated by powerful external forces, from the time clock to headline news, themselves manipulated by even more remote agencies. *Men in Black* closes with a vision of galaxies being knocked about like croquet balls in an absurd game played by agents as capri-cious as the ancient gods.

Like disproportions in wealth and freedom as the century closes, the disproportions of scale in this absurd cosmology resist practical thinking. With an executive elite ever more removed and invisible, ordinary people understandably appreciate fantasies about aliens stealthily taking control of their minds. To some extent this is in fact what media monop-oly does by determining the vocabulary and arguments available to the dominant culture. But there is another problem of scale no less disturbing. At least some of the aliens are refugees from life-or-death territorial disputes, perhaps a small elite escaping from over-populated home planets.

This scenario resonates with Richard L. Rubenstein's thesis that the "demographic explosion that began in Europe during the eighteenth century" initiated "the modern, worldwide phenomenon of mass surplus population" and an "age of triage."[17] Rubenstein contends that technological, economic, and demographic pressures have been making whole groups of people expendable, resulting in mass migrations and genocidal horrors. His examples range from the enclosures that eliminated entire villages in seventeenth-century England, to the Holocaust. In the late twentieth century anxiety about triage has intensified—or resurfaced—with increasing globalization, and the economic quakes and new waves of immigration brought about by the collapse of Cold War empires. As the frontiers have closed off outlets for emigration and the great powers have lost their for-mer empires, imperialistic rhetoric has claimed space as the last frontier. Intergalactic fan-tasies such as *Star Trek* (1965 and onward) routinely envision the future in terms of expanding empires and dangerous competition over colonies. Closer to home, and symp-tomatic of the 1980s and '90s, Michael Moore's film *Roger and Me* (1989) documents General Motors' triage of its workforce, which desolated Flint, Michigan and scattered its "surplus" population to the winds in rental trucks. As in the Social Darwinist nightmare of the Gilded Age, the haunting question remains: Is there nothing but insane competi-tion at the core of experience?

Men in Black implicitly worries this question. When the fleeing alien couple gives birth to a baby in the back seat of a car, the scene evokes—even spoofs—documentaries about refugee flight and social collapse. The refugees face a twofold threat, from political may-hem and from inexorable nature. In her birth throes the alien wife is helplessly violent. Ulti-mately both threats are manifestations of survival drives. Similarly, an alien elite and paramilitary agents are joined by their shared survival dread. This is one implication of the association of the loss of identity in berserking with the sense of an alien will "taking over" personality. *Men in Black* imagines urbane wit, technology, and daring precariously keep-ing order on an imperilled planet. But behind this cool demeanor, like an alien inside a humdrum human body, is a darker fantasy that the stress of globalization, immigration, and the emergence of a corporate police state are pressuring human populations toward the berserk state, psychically disembedded, open to hair-trigger rage over life-threatening shortages: of vital energy, autonomy, and even subjectivity itself.

Notes

[1] In *New Strangers in Paradise* (Lexington: University Press of Kentucky, 1999) Gilbert H. Muller eloquently sums up his survey of "the immigrant experience and contemporary American experience" using a rhetoric that invokes globalism, tectonic shocks, and his-toric conflict. His metaphors unwittingly resonate with the cosmic immigration scheme in *Men in Black*, as when he refers to "The galaxy of immigrant women and men who populate today's fiction [and] signify the 'ex-centricity' of the nation" and to "a new nation emerging from global catastrophe, diasporic wandering, racial and ethnic resur-gence, and vast cultural change." (236)

2 "As he announces his plans for the ethnic cleansing of Canaan," says Jack Miles, "the Lord does not, to repeat, seem angry with the Canaanites, but the effect is genocidal all the same, and there is no escaping it." See Jack Miles, *God: a Biography* (New York, 1995, rpt. 1996), 117.

3 *True Confessions: Sixty Years of Suffering and Sorrow*, ed. Florence Moriarty (New York, 1979), 2–5. For a more detailed reading, see my *Post-Traumatic Culture: Injury and Interpretation in the Nineties* (Baltimore and London: Johns Hopkins University Press, 1998), 169–70.

4 Gail Bederman, *Manliness and Civilization* (Chicago: Univ. of Chicago Press, 1995).

5 H. Rider Haggard, *The Days of My Life* (London, 1926), II, 169–72.

6 Bederman, 196.

7 Bederman, 200–01.

8 Bederman, 199. For Roosevelt's attitude toward "race suicide," see 199–206.

9 Joseph Conrad, *Heart of Darkness*, ed. Robert Kimbrough (New York, 1963), 51.

10 Jonathan Shay, *Achilles in Vietnam: Combat Trauma and the Undoing of Character* (New York, 1994), 79.

11 Daniel Goleman calls it "the ventilation fallacy." See *Emotional Intelligence* (New York: Bantam, 1995), 64. See also *Handbook of Mental Control*, ed. Daniel Wegner and James Pennebaker (Englewood Cliffs: Prentice-Hall, 1993).

12 See Shay, *Achilles*, ch. 1, "Betrayal of 'What's Right.'"

13 Cf. the World War Two B-17 bomber dubbed "the flying fortress."

14 See "The Politics of Monstrosity" in Chris Baldick's *In Frankenstein's Shadow* (Oxford: Clarendon Press, 1987), esp. pp. 14–21.

15 See *The Movies Begin*, Vol. 5 (VCR cassette), from Film Preservation Associates, 1994.

16 See my further discussion of these two films in *Post-Traumatic Culture*.

17 Richard L. Rubenstein, *The Age of Triage* (Boston: Beacon Press, 1983), 1.

Chapter 19

The Wonderful, Horrible Films of Paul Verhoeven

Dan Streible

Can a contemporary Hollywood movie traffic in both Nazi iconography and fascistic philosophy and still pass as harmless entertainment, noted only for its great special effects and its use of more rounds of ammunition than any film in history? And is the presence of "men with guns" a required signifier for a film either to encourage a fascist point of view or to be symptomatic of a culture listing to the right?

Such questions were raised in 1997 with the well-hyped release of Paul Verhoeven's $100 million adaptation of Robert A. Heinlein's 1959 "classic" science fiction novel, *Starship Troopers*.[1] All of the films Verhoeven has directed since his arrival in Hollywood have generated controversy. His work has alarmed cultural guardians with its extraordinary levels of gruesome violence (*Robocop* [1987], *Total Recall* [1990]) and graphic sexual exhibition (*Basic Instinct* [1992], *Showgirls* [1995]). Comparatively, however, *Starship Troopers* received only a modicum of critical chastisement. This despite the fact that—in addition to the gory, flesh-ripping gunplay—the film offers up what its producers called a "fascist utopia."[2] Its top-gun, teenage warrior-heroes are showcased in a glossy display, steeped in Nazi aesthetics. They embrace a rousing militarism that deems democracy a failure and a martial State a success. Our young S. S. Troopers casually but willfully endorse the ideals of the Federation that teaches them "violence is the supreme authority." In short, under Verhoeven's helm, the position affirmed by all of the principal characters fails to differentiate itself sufficiently from, say, the ideology espoused by a certain well-known mustachioed orator captured on film in Nuremberg in September of 1934. A major studio release that doesn't just allude to, but looks, talks, and walks like Leni Riefenstahl's *Triumph of the Will* (1935)?

The release of *Starship Troopers* prompts a renegotiation of the critical debate around the issue of incipient fascism in contemporary Hollywood cinema. The film also represents a distressing shift in the ability of Paul Verhoeven to intervene from within the system as a potent postmodernist making blockbusters that knowingly ridicule the violent, action extravaganza mentality. Rather than critiquing such projects, *Starship Troopers* falls into a political incoherence that potentially enables viewers to entertain the idea of a fascistic military state as a viable future. While the machine gun and other instruments of firepower are fetishized in the imagery of this high-tech movie, men with guns do not necessarily rule the day. The "Morita"[3] rifles the troopers wield against hostile alien insects allow them to display a degree of bravado and power on the battlefield, but their guns do not win the war. In a cinematic age in which Texas-sized meteorites bombard the earth, guns ultimately become a symbol of impotence rather than power. However, in *Starship Troopers* this decline of the gun's dominion does not indicate a failing of the future warrior State. Rather, the film suggests that power lingers on even when weaponry fails, deriving from the lens of a camera rather than the barrel of a gun. The power of fascist force comes less from its military superiority than from its ability to captivate minds with its commanding, monumental imagery, its corporative ability to create group-think.

Given the troubling political implications of *Starship Troopers*, I'd like to examine how such a film came to be, how it was positioned for reception and how it was received. My conclusions are based on an examination of movie trade journals, promotional materials, journalistic reviews, and on-line discussions—both critical and fan-based. As secondary resources, I consider *Starship Troopers* in the light of what critical film studies have previously suggested about cinema and fascism. The key text remains Susan Sontag's 1974 essay "Fascinating Fascism," which sought to define the aesthetic markers that abetted fascist, or at least Nazi, art as evident in the work of Leni Riefenstahl.[4]

Also important is the way in which Verhoeven figures into the symptomatic readings of key films from Reagan-era Hollywood, particularly readings by critics such as Robin Wood, Michael Ryan, Douglas Kellner, David Denby, Susan Jeffords, Stephen Prince, and others. They have noted how both patently conservative films (*Red Dawn* [1984], *Rambo* [1985], *Conan the Barbarian* [1981], *Predator* [1987]) and mainstream fantasies (the *Star Wars* [1977–1983], *Rocky* [1976–1985], and Indiana Jones [1981–1989] series) revealed tendencies that had disturbing parallels with fascist culture. "Vengeful patriotism, worship of the male torso," "military spectacle" and weapons of overkill were making US commercial cinema into a showcase for what J. Hoberman called in 1985 "The Fascist Guns in the West."[5] In the decade following, Hollywood continued in a similar vein, with big-budget spectacles ranging from Bruce Willis action pictures to jingoistic sci-fi shootouts like *Independence Day* (1996). Yet cries of fascism diminished in critical circles. This was also a period when Verhoeven directed his acclaimed *Robocop* and the dense, complex *Total Recall*—two conspicuous blockbusters that retained big guns and special effects while seeming to subvert the political inflections of the genre.

Given this context, the contradictions of *Starship Troopers* require explanation. How did a Hollywood film with such in-your-face fascist imagery appear at a time when, judging from prevailing trends in critical discourse, quasi-fascist tendencies in popular cinema had diminished? And does not the film undo Verhoeven's previous reputation as a thoughtful if audacious social commentator?

Inside the Cabinet of Dr. Verhoeven

We must begin by reading *Starship Troopers* as part of the "wonderful, horrible" films of Paul Verhoeven. I appropriate the title of Ray Müller's insightful documentary film about Leni Riefenstahl, *The Wonderful, Horrible Life of Leni Riefenstahl [Die Macht der Bilder: Leni Riefenstahl]* (1993), because as an enigma Verhoeven seems parallel to her: a auteur full of self-contradiction whose work invites polarizing analyses, an artist who avows provocative artistic creation while disavowing political intention or social responsibility. In the 1990s, Verhoeven became a bête noire, a director whose horrible excesses pushed the limits of MPAA-approved violence and sex. Yet his films remained wonderful enough—in box-office terms and in stylistic distinctiveness—to keep him on the major studios' A-list. In the 1980s, he was also lauded by analysts of pop culture politics. Retaining the edge of his Dutch films, Verhoeven was credited with critiquing the retrograde aspects of the Hollywood action blockbuster by making ultraviolent, effects-laden fantasies that ridiculed the conservative, militaristic ethos of Rambo and his cohort. If Sylvester Stallone could blow away his enemy with force of arms, Verhoeven would paint a world in which everyone was subject to gunfire. Like the Dutch masters of old, he put the anatomies of corpses on display. But his bodies were ripped by disorderly bullets, not scientifically vivisected by surgeons.

Stephen Prince's perceptive book *Visions of Empire* epitomizes the critical valorization of Verhoeven. Prince discusses the director's work as part of a "dystopia cycle" that countered the conservative trend in '80s Hollywood. Arguing that dystopic films confront issues of political exploitation, corporate control, and resistance to police-state coercion, he says such ideas "receive their most intelligent and deliberate working out" in Verhoeven's *Robocop* and *Total Recall,* the cycle's "two most outstanding exemplars." Prince calls the former a "grim indictment of Reagan policies" that is nothing less than "a thinking person's action film whose politics are left of center." Like other admirers of the movie, he interprets its satirical humor as granting viewers "the Brechtian distance necessary to see ties between their world and the film's future." While *Total Recall* is a more compromised critique, it remains a "cautionary fable" that becomes "one of the subtlest but most critical imaginative transformations of the political referents of the Reagan period." Arnold Schwarzenegger's proletarian hero of the future is a rebellious freedom fighter who overthrows a villainous corporate state (headed, as in *Robocop,* by a perfectly evil boss [Ronny Cox]). In Prince's estimation, "one feels that Verhoeven would have gone much farther" in his political critique if not for the constraints of commercial production.[6]

Verhoeven's earliest cinematic credentials seem solidly anti-fascist. After learning filmmaking in the Dutch military (like Heinlein, he was a Navy man), he made *Mussert* (1968), a documentary about the head of the Netherlands Fascist Party during World War II.

Soldier of Orange (1979), which led Steven Spielberg to invite Verhoeven to Hollywood, is his historical drama about Dutch resistance fighters who take on Nazi collaborators. Far from lionizing fascistic ideals of order, monumentalism, virile posing, and perfect bodies,

Verhoeven's Dutch films undermine such values. His down-and-dirty seventies films are more at home with the work of the "degenerate" artists condemned by the Nazis; irreverent, messy and vulgar, they also demonstrate sympathy for the outsider. The bohemian sculptor in *Turkish Delight* (1971), the gay writer in *The 4th Man* (1979), and the disenchanted motorcycle riders of *Spetters* (1980) are a far cry from the cardboard super-soldiers of *Starship Troopers*.[7]

Yet his futuristic war extravaganza was consistent with a turn Verhoeven took when he came to Hollywood. The Americanized Verhoeven has taken up guns with a vengeance, and he has consistently used these high-caliber weapons to inflict grisly destruction upon the human body. The violence of what at first seems to be formulaic action escalates into deliberately unsettling presentations of blood, splatter, and viscera. Since *Robocop*, his films, marked by their excessive splashy spectacle and intense action, each contain set pieces calculated to outrage middle-class sensibilities. Many turn disturbingly comical in tone. In *Robocop*, we see police officer Murphy (Peter Weller) tortured by drug dealers who make a game of shooting off his hands and arms. After he is resurrected as a cyborg, his first turn in crime-fighting is to use his laser-accurate pistol to shoot a would-be rapist in the genitals. In *Total Recall*, the rebel hero fights off a series of machine-gun assaults, memorably using a human corpse as a bullet-absorbing shield. *Basic Instinct*'s infamous opening features an explicit sex scene that culminates with an ice-pick murder at orgasm; its astonishing finale features Detective Mike Curran (Michael Douglas) shooting his psychiatrist girlfriend Doctor Beth Garner (Jeanne Tripplehorn) at point-blank range. In *Starship Troopers*, a young enlistee, Djana'D (Tami-Adrian George) accidentally shoots off the head of her comrade Breckinridge (Eric Bruskotter) during a training exercise; Lt. Rasczak (Michael Ironside) uses a Morita on one of his own wounded soldiers, Sgt. Gillespie (Curnal Achilles Aulisio) proclaiming, "I expect anyone here to do the same for me"; and throughout, Johnny Rico (Casper Van Dien) uses his Tactical Nuclear Launcher (available at this writing in children's toy stores) to blast the really big tanker bugs into lime green slime.

Starship Troopers's deliberate flirtation with fascism and its monstrous carnage of combat, therefore, might be understood as just another wrinkle in the Verhoeven career; ironic deployment of dizzying violence, cold characters, outrageous political philosophy, and allusion to *Triumph of the Will*—all merely for the sake of provocation. However, this excursion into the postmodern politics of irony differs from its predecessors. Its irony is so "blank" that it can invite readings as a text that seems neo-Nazi itself.

Fascistical Light and Magic

In the broadest sense, this special-effects fantasy is merely a part of the post-*Star Wars* "cinema of oppressive spectacle" of which so many critics (liberal, conservative, humanist) have complained. David Mamet, for example, spells it out in a lesson on screenwriting:

> We, as the audience, are much better off with a sign that says "A BLASTED HEATH" than with all the brilliant cinematography in the world. To say "brilliant cinematography" is to say, "He made the trains run on time."
>
> Witness the rather fascistic trend in cinema in the last decade.
>
> Q. How'd you like the movie?
>
> A. Fantastic cinematography.

Yeah, but so what? Hitler had fantastic cinematography. The question we have ceased to ask is "What is the brilliant . . . cinematography in aid of?"[8]

As cultural historian Russell Berman argues in his analysis of fascist form, *Triumph of the Will* exemplifies the "fascist privileging of sight and visual representation" because fascism "transforms the world into a visual object . . . the spectacular landscape of industry and war."[9] Thomas Elsaesser points out in his assessment of Nazi-era commercial cinema, however, that this matter can be over-stressed. To take this Frankfurt School view is "to propose that all popular cinema is potentially fascistic, if by this we mean illusionist . . . using affect and emotion to overpower reason."[10] Clearly, both *Triumph* and *Troopers* stand to abet fascist politics with their visual objectification of masses, their overwhelming cinematography. But to lump them together with *Brazil* (1985), *Metropolis* (1926), *2001: A Space Odyssey* (1968), *Contact* (1997), or *Apocalypse Now* (1979) is to lose their more particular political meanings.

A discernment of fascist tendencies in recent cinema also occurs in Robin Wood's reading of Hollywood from Vietnam to Reagan. Wood identifies "Fear of Fascism" as part of a Spielberg-Lucas "syndrome": the potential for America to become a totalitarian state, for the individualist American hero to become indistinguishable from the fascist one, of the weak-minded to be taken over by a Vader-ian Force. Although George Lucas's well-known reference to *Triumph of the Will* is more discrete than Verhoeven's Wood suggests that its presence in *Star Wars* is more than just a joke. The thrill of the Jedi military victory and the spectacle of triumphant troops assembled at the movie's conclusion resonate with authoritarian overtones. He also reminds us that, historically, fascist cultures did not feed on overtly political propaganda films but on light entertainment that reinforced certain conceptions of the body, national identity, family etc. Rocky Balboa and Indiana Jones are not protagonists in fascist films, but would be at home in a fascist popular culture.[11]

Starship Troopers puts fascist ideas on the table more explicitly than the Spielberg-Lucas films. Indiana Jones still knows a Nazi when he sees one. And he opposes them unambiguously. On a manifest level, however, these films don't encourage an understanding of a Nazi enemy—however cartoonish—as anything other than Other. Verhoeven's futuristic fantasy treads on this dangerous ground by reversing this, inviting us to identify with the fascist protagonist.

To be more historically precise, we can define fascism as a political and social system marked by authoritarian rule, military force, intense nationalism, expansionist conquest, demand for racial purity, the rhetoric of "new order," supremacy of the State, and obedience to a charismatic leader (the one element absent from *ST*). It values martial discipline, sacrifice, surrender of individual will to social order, glory in combat and death, youthfulness, and a cult of the body without eroticism. None of these alone is unique to fascist philosophy and I am not suggesting that Verhoeven is advocating them. But in bringing Heinlein's novel to the screen, he creates a cinematic space where they are allowed to play amid a riot of Nazi mise-en-scène.

Johnny Gets His Gun

Starship Troopers combines Heinlein's sci-fi war story with an Aaron Spelling-styled teen love triangle. Four friends are graduating from a high school in a futuristic Buenos Aires that looks suspiciously like a Los Angeles suburb. All enlist in Federal Service: our dumb-jock hero, Johnny Rico, does it for his brainy-beautiful girlfriend Carmen Ibañez (Denise Richards), who goes to Flight Academy. Nerdy best friend Carl Jenkins (Neil Patrick Harris) goes into military intelligence, while smart-jock Dizzy Flores (Dina Meyer) gives up her career as a pro football quarterback to follow her beloved Johnny into the Mobile Infantry. Johnny is about to quite boot amp when the Giant Bugs drop a meteor on Buenos Aires, killing millions. Johnny's platoon of gung-ho roughnecks are led into battle by their high school civics teacher, Mr. Rasczak. The battle for planet Klendathu is a fiasco, as the troopers with their World War II-style machine guns prove to be no match for the deadly giant arachnids. A second battle ends in victory, thanks to Rico and Diz's sharpshooting and our hero's cowboy tactics with mini-nukes. The comrades-in-arms celebrate by having sex, Johnny finally giving in when the eugenically-minded Moral Philosopher Lt. Rasczak instructs him to procreate.

Finally comes an apparent suicide mission to Planet P, home of the giant Brain Bug. In a scene reminiscent of John Wayne's *The Alamo* (1960), we watch from inside the barricaded fort as millions of bugs swarm over the fortress walls. Diz and Rasczak die gruesome but heroic deaths, impaled by insect claws, before Carmen's fleet arrives to save Johnny. During a second attack, Carmen is captured and about to have her skull sucked dry by the Brain Bug when Lt. Rico saves the day. We end irresolutely, as Colonel Carl appears—dressed in full Goebbels regalia. He mindmelds with the captured Brain Bug and, with a cruel smile, reports "It's afraid!" Thousands of uniformed troopers, looking ever so much like an army of ants, mindlessly cheer the fear in their enemy ("Fascist art glories surrender, it exalts mindlessness," Sontag observes[12]).

As the absurdity of the plot reveals, Verhoeven's film is highly ironic and often satirical (Heinlein's high-minded patriotism having vanished), but what is this irony in aid of? In whose army do these soldiers march (an army whose sergeants insist "Your weapon is more important than you are!")? While Verhoeven's adaptation undermines Heinlein's right-wing homily, it fails on three fronts. *Starship Troopers* wallows too deeply in Nazi iconography, enjoying its "fascinating fascism"; it presents a narrative in which a fascist future works, with no suggestion of resistance or alternative; and, most egregiously, it targets an audience of teens and children, offering them the possibility of making a positive identification with the film's young fascist heroes.

Asked about the Nazi aesthetics, screenwriter Ed Neumeier said simply, "The Germans made the best-looking stuff. Art directors love it." Verhoeven added, "I just wanted to play with these [Nazi images] in an artistic way." The film's opening, a recruitment ad, "is taken from *Triumph of the Will* . . . When the soldiers look at the camera and say, 'I'm doing my part!' that's fro Riefenstahl. We copied it. It's wink-wink Riefenstahl."

Neumeier's script begins and ends with the mocking description, "Proud YOUNG PEOPLE in uniform, the bloom of human evolution." In casting Verhoeven tries to have things both ways, playing with fascist aesthetics to subvert them, but managing to privilege a racial type. This is most apparent in the lead role. Heinlein's Juan "Johnnie" Rico was a Tagalog-speaking Filipino-cum-Federation (read: American)-citizen-soldier. The movie Johnny and his Spanish-surnamed girlfriends are supposed to be Argentinian (because this is where Perón harbored old Nazis?). But the actors in these roles are quite white. The soldiers in Rico's platoon reference the WWII combat film's generic melting pot, updated for a multicultural future. But even the characters bearing Jewish, Polish, Japanese, and African American names have the same fair, too-pretty, idealized faces.

Even Verhoeven's nod to a gender-neutral military fails to undercut the fascist ideal. These full-blooded men and women shower together without sexual attraction, conjuring up the fascist cult of the body as an instrument of combat rather than eros. As in Riefenstahl's film, showering together demonstrates Spartan camaraderie—although Verhoeven and cinematographer Jost Vacano shoot their shower scene in a way that allows viewers a sexy thrill. In the other notable scene of bodily display, Johnny's hairless torso is flogged in the public square, taking the scars that mark him as a true warrior. Again, Sontag's litany of fascist motifs is borne out: the "choreographed display of bodies," "physical perfection of beauty," "virile posing," the "endurance of pain," the "exhibition of physical skill and courage."[13]

Wink-Wink Riefenstahl

As *Starship Troopers* overindulges its Nazi imagery, it does so in a narrative universe where a fascistic mentality operates without disruption. The rules are laid out for us in Mr. Rasczak's valedictory lecture on History and Moral Philosophy. As others have observed, this scene in which a teacher inspires wartime enlistment takes the anti-war *All Quiet on the Western Front* (1930) and stands it on its head.[14] The one-armed veteran explains to his class why military forces had to impose this new world order after too much democracy led to chaos. Things "work" because only those who had done State service are enfranchised. Veteran soldier-citizens are licensed to reproduce. Mere "civilians" lack "civic virtue" and cannot vote. Force is the supreme authority. The rabidly anti-intellectual, anti-bourgeois side of fascist philosophy is projected onto the only civilian characters in the film, Johnny's rich parents (Lenore Kasdorf and Christopher Curry). They discourage their son from becoming cannon fodder and insist he go to Harvard. Their soft liberalism earns them a spot on the Bug Meteor's fatality list—weak naïfs, like the people of Hiroshima, says Rasczak.

Accepting his teaching unproblematically, all sign up for military service. Comradeship replaces family. Youth are socialized into these values via the greatest of inculcation devices: football. As star athletes, Diz and Johnny become the leaders in battle. But when Johnny and friends adopt this fascistic ideal, at what point does the viewer decide to go along for the ride? Verhoeven does try to subvert the Federation's ideology by replicating the satirical framing device used in his earlier films. Just as *Robocop* intercuts scenes of mock new bulletins (showing a Reagan-figure accidentally zapped by his own Star Wars weapons), *Troopers* features a running propaganda broadcast. This "FedNet" is viewed in an interactive Web-TV format. An "Official Voice" presents vignettes about how and why to fight the insect menace and invites viewers to watch further with the refrain, "Would you like to know more . . . ?"

Does this lend sufficient critical distance? Perhaps for adult viewers, the excess, absurdity, irony, and satire make it clear this is no endorsement of a fascist future. But the conventionally character-driven plot remains in place with some expectation that viewers will identify with the hero's strivings. Unless one is willing to root for the horrific, scabrous bugs, the film offers no points of entry other than the wonderful, horrible protagonist. Verhoeven is consistently anti-humanist, but his film is confused about what it wants to articulate about fascism.

In the promotional book, *The Making of Starship Troopers,* Verhoeven speaks directly about this subject. At times, he hints at sympathy with Heinlein's philosophy, calling it "benign fascism." When pushed to defend himself, he avers his film is "subversive," decidedly not fascist. But in between, he is as contradictory as his film. He will say only that a Pat Buchanan-like cryptofascism in the US in the 1990s is "interesting," rather than alarming or wrong-headed. When the FedNet's official voice repeatedly asks "Would you like to know more?" Verhoeven maintains his film is asking its audience to consider the nature of such a world.

> [I'm] not saying that *ST*'s society is wrong because of that resemblance [to the Third Reich].... These references say, 'Here it is. This futuristic society works on this level well—and it fights the giant insects very well. Look and decide. The judgment is yours."[15]

Guns "Я" Us

What audience, then, does *Starship Troopers* address and recruit? If it were only Heinlein readers (including all U.S. Marines, who are required to read *ST*[16]), there might be less reason for concern. Most of the author's fans rejected the movie as a disservice to the book. Verhoeven's coldness and bad taste also turned off many film reviewers. Those who were ready to give him the benefit of the doubt sometimes addressed the f-word head on, particularly *The Washington Post,* in a series of sharp critiques. But more typical were puff pieces on the film's brilliant cinematography and cheerleading reviews, such as one the *Detroit Free Press* headlined with "*Starship Troopers* Sucks Out Our Brains—and It Feels Great."[17] However, we must deal with the fact that idealized Brechtian spectators and historically knowledgeable postmodernists were not the film's main patrons. The *Troopers* audience (both actual and constructed) was largely "juvenile," to use the somewhat dated industry term.

If critical perspective and sophistication are required to read subversive irony, then what interpretive position is left for those too inexperienced to be discerning? Verhoeven's film was heavily promoted to teen and pre-teen audiences, with television ads on kids' cable, interactive cyberspace games, an official comic book adaptation, trading cards, a CD-ROM, a soundtrack album, and Toys "Я" Us action figures and weapons ("for ages 4 and up"), not to mention the Disney imprimatur. The film's "Restricted" rating was problematic enough (as a *New York Post* stunt proved, showing 12-year-olds able to buy tickets).[18] But even if the gore and sex were absent, what sense might children make out of watching, desiring or identifying with Johnny Rico? Again using a sampling of online teen chats from 1997–98 as an indicator, I found that many reacted to eye candy as they might with other films: "This film rocks"; "Johnny is awesome"; "Diz is one hot babe" ("Fantastic cinematography!"). With *Trooper* characters as representatives of a fascist utopia, what will these same viewers think when confronted with other fascistic principles? Hitler addressed his youth; Heinlein wrote his book as juvenile literature. Is Verhoeven juvenile enough for ten-somethings? And what of the children of the late nineties, now grown into college-age adults? Is not this starship fantasy—with its shiny patriots exterminating an alien enemy—the type of entertainment in which the fascist soul would take pleasure? As with Hitler loving Fritz Lang's *Metropolis* for all the wrong reasons, the artist's subversive intentions cease to matter if the film lends aid and comfort to the enemy.

Nobody Alludes to Riefenstahl

"Nobody making films today alludes to Riefenstahl."
Susan Sontag[19]

When Verhoeven, frustrated by criticism, yelled at the press in 1997, "I am not a fascist! I'm a Democrat!"[20] he was right. *Starship Troopers* is not a fascist film. In a different era, Verhoeven's penchant for messy images and irreverence would have placed his work in the category of "degenerate art." Nonetheless, a film sprung from a democratic spirit shouldn't be so difficult to separate from a fascist one. Verhoeven need not become a propagandist in the malevolent manner of Goebbels or even in the transparently didactic and proselytizing manner of Heinlein to speak clearly. His filmic portrait of human societies as ugly, harsh, and depraved might have been redeemed by just a scrap of hope, by reference to an alternative. For all their depravity, *Robocop* and *Total Recall* at least center on protagonists searching for their human identity, fighting against corrupt corporate states. But with no Ronny Cox villain to deride, the Big Bug picture lacks a target. Incoherence, not irony, is the postmodern trait that best demarcates this film. With *Starship Troopers,* this incoherence becomes nihilistic, leaving the unfortunate residue of fascist-inspired images to resonate in ways that still matter.

If there is a way to read this war story in a less distressing way, it stems from the film's own construction of impotence. Despite all the gun-toting and the firing of 300,000-plus rounds of ammunition, the disciplined, devoted, clean, lean warriors of the Mobile Infantry remain no match for the intimidating space insects. An assault rifle might have been a macho problem-solver for John Rambo, but Johnny Rico proves inferior to the arachnids below him and the mind-managers above him. As we learn in the final scene, the only hope the Federation has for beating the bugs is a new breakthrough in telepathic mind reading. Carl, Johnny's Goebbels-inspired friend, has become the officer in charge of psychic research. He has (possibly) remotely controlled the foot soldier's thoughts with "psi-orders" during the final rescue mission. Able to siphon intelligence from the captured Brain Bug, the Federation's military can now out-think its enemy. Of course, mind control—mass trance through propaganda and ritual—is also a fascist weapon par excellence.

In this sense, the film's visual display shares the calculated effect of Nazi spectacles of order. Perhaps the most chilling image comes in the final scene, where thousands of young troopers jubilantly cheer the conquered enemy's fear. The pageant of bodies massed in uniform, framed in a long shot, renders a sensation not unlike that effectuated by Riefenstahl's *Triumph of the Will.* The reverberant, throaty roar with which they erupt adds to the effect, echoing "Sieg Heils" heard in the Nuremberg stadium.

Verhoeven's films certainly problematize the politics of issues like gun violence, militarism, and corporate corruption, but we might wish that this imagemaker's vision were clearer and more articulate—especially when playing with fascism. Rather than resorting to a nihilistic response to the political present, one might recall the clarity of singer Woody Guthrie. "This machine kills fascists," he scrawled across his guitar. Paul Verhoeven and Hollywood in general don't have to make the cinematic equivalent of "This Land Is Your Land" to signal what position they take on the possibilities of a fascist utopia. But neither do they need to produce films as ideologically muddled as *Starship Troopers.*

In 2002, the DVD *Starship Troopers: Special Edition* appeared in the midst of the geopolitical sea changes triggered by the terrorist attacks of September 11, 2001. "A New Kind of Enemy, a New Kind of War"—the tagline printed on the discs could scarcely have been a more obvious topical reference to the new "global war on terror." The DVD included an audio commentary done jointly by the director and screenwriter. Verhoeven begins by reacting to critics who labeled his film as sympathetic to fascism. No, he states without subtlety, things fascist are "bad, bad, bad!" "I can tell you that the movie" is saying, "war makes fascists of us all." Yet he also engages in playful dialog with Neumeier, who repeatedly retreats from a clear condemnation of fascist ideas, even saying he wanted to write "what was essentially a fascist action-adventure film." While Verhoeven offers that *Starship Troopers* should indeed function as a commentary on "American politics" and "the conflict in Iraq," again the coyness of his words muddles any attempt to interpret his work clearly. Is he critiquing "Islamofascism" and supporting a military response to al-Qaeda and the Taliban? Or is he warning against the dissentless, superpatriotic militarization of America in the Bush era? It's not clear.

Perhaps, as Mamet, Berman, and a host of cultural critics have contended, there is something almost inherently fascistic and controlling in this machine of cinema that "transforms the world into a visual object." Not all pictures and narratives are endowed with the same political meanings and historical referents, however. Contemporary filmmakers like Verhoeven, aware of a contested cinematic past, would do well to consider more carefully which side they arm for the future.

Postscript

Ten years after the release of the film, astute satirist Stephen Colbert said in his chart-topping *I Am America (And So Can You!)*:

> I say, if Hollywood absolutely must make a message movie, make one like *Starship Troopers*. It was the perfect political allegory—because I didn't get it. People tell me it was about something, but all I know is that good-guy army-guy shot bad-guy monster-bugs with lasers in space. Four stars."[21]

Indeed *Starship Troopers* was about something, but that something eluded many viewers (and still does) because of its lack of political coherence or clarity.

Hollywood and Paul Verhoeven diverged. Blockbuster special-effects movies and war stories continued, not infrequently, to bear some of the visual and thematic traits of fascist cinema. Two sequels in the *ST* franchise appeared, but as inconsequential, low-budget direct-to-video releases, *Starship Troopers 2: Hero of the Federation* (2004) and *Starship Troopers 3: Marauder* (2008). More tellingly, Sylvester Stallone returned with *Rambo* (2008). Clint Eastwood, once tagged by critic Pauline Kael as unleashing the "fascist potential"[22] of the action genre with *Dirty Harry* (1971), in 2006 produced and directed two feature films, *Flags of Our Fathers* and *Letters from Iwo Jima,* depicting the WWII battle from the perspectives of American and Japanese military men. Hollywood's historical dramas about the Second World War nominally tell the story of the Allies' defeat of fascism, but the war film genre itself often continues to celebrate the militaristic over the democratic.

Like Eastwood, in 2006 Paul Verhoeven also completed a WWII drama. With *Black Book,* a Dutch production, Verhoeven returned to his homeland to film his recreation of battles between the Dutch Resistance and the Nazi military. Based on actual incidents, *Black Book* unveils a complicated story of compromised men and women on both sides of the fight. A German officer abets the escape of Jewish resistance organizers in Holland. Dutch resisters betray one another, aiding the German side. The "good war" mentality of American popular culture—of Ken Burns's *The War* (2009), Steven Spielberg's *Saving Private Ryan* (1998), the HBO mini-series *Band of Brothers* (2001) and *The Pacific* (2010), and many productions—is nowhere to be found in Verhoeven's Netherlands of 1944. While he does not villainize these Nazis, neither does he fall into the incoherence of *Starship Troopers*. Nor does Verhoeven's *Black Book* flirt with the fascist aesthetics and philosophy of his futuristic fantasy.

More than ten years on, the 1997 blockbuster has become a cult film, one that still provokes contradictory responses. In 2010, critic Scott Tobias described it as "the most subversive major studio film in recent (or distant) memory." Noting the continuing political resonances of *ST*'s faux fascism and American politics, he concluded, "I suspect its future is bright: the lines between the world of *Starship Troopers* and Sarah Palin's Twitter feed gets thinner every day."[23]

Notes

[1] This essay relies in part upon the author's interview and classroom discussion with Paul Verhoeven, University of Wisconsin-Oshkosh, November 3, 1995.

[2] Michael Wilmington, "Bug Wars," *Chicago Tribune* (November 7, 1997), A7.

[3] According to screenwriter Ed Neumeier, the fictional Morita (a "futuristic-looking assault shotgun") was jokingly named after "a then-current Sony executive." Paul M. Sammon, *The Making of Starship Troopers* (New York: Boulevard Books, 1997), 73.

[4] Susan Sontag, "Fascinating Fascism," in *Under the Sign of Saturn* (New York: Vintage, 1980), 73–105. See also James Hay, *Popular Film Culture in Fascist Italy* (Bloomington: Indiana University Press, 1987), Marcia Landy, *Fascism in Film: The Italian Commercial Cinema, 1931–1943* (Princeton NJ: Princeton University Press, 1986), Thomas Elsaesser, "Hollywood Berlin," *Sight and Sound* (January 1998), 14–17.

[5] J. Hoberman, "The Fascist Guns in the West," *American Film* (March 1986), 42–44. Hoberman cites David Denby's 1985 critique in *New York* magazine as specifically using the fascist label for *Rambo: First Blood, Part II, Red Dawn* and other films of that season. See Robin Wood, *Hollywood from Vietnam to Reagan* (New York: Columbia University Press, 1986); Michael Ryan and Douglas Kellner, *Camera Politica: The Politics and Ideology of Contemporary Hollywood Film* (Bloomington: Indiana University Press, 1988); Susan Jeffords, *The Remasculization of America: Gender and the Vietnam War* (Bloomington: Indiana University Press, 1989); Stephen Prince, *Visions of Empire: Political Imagery in Contemporary American Film* (New York: Praeger, 1992).

[6] Prince, *Visions*, 171–84.

[7] A guide to the director's work at mid-career is Rob van Scheers, *Paul Verhoeven* (London: Faber and Faber, 1997).

[8] David Mamet, *Writing in Restaurants* (New York: Vintage, 1986), 16.

⁹ Russell A. Berman, "Written Across Their Faces: Leni Riefenstahl, Ernst Jünger, and Fascist Modernism," in *Modern Culture and Critical Theory: Art, Politics, and the Legacy of the Frankfurt School* (Madison: University of Wisconsin Press, 1988), 99.

¹⁰ Elsaesser, "Berlin," 14.

¹¹ Robin Wood, "Papering the Cracks: Fantasy and Ideology in the Reagan Era," in John Belton, ed., *Movies and Mass Culture* (New Brunswick NJ: Rutgers University Press, 1996), 211–13.

¹² Sontag, "Fascism," 91.

¹³ Sontag, "Fascism," 86.

¹⁴ Stephen Hunter's stinging critique of the movie points this out. His review was by far the most trenchant immediate analysis of the film's fascist core. "Goosestepping at the Movies," *Washington Post* (November 11, 1997), D1.

¹⁵ Sammon, *Making,* 138–39.

¹⁶ Kent Mitchell, "Movies Corps Values: 'Trooper' on Reading List," *Atlanta Constitution* (November 7, 1997), 22.

¹⁷ Hunter, "Goosestepping," D1; Stephen Hunter, "Ooze and Aahs: Why Disgusting, Slimy Movies are Hard not to Watch," *Washington Post* (December 9, 1997), D1; Rita Kempley, "Starship Troopers," *Washington Post* (November 7, 1997), D1; Terry Lawson, "Starship Troopers Sucks Out Our Brains—and It Feels Great," *Detroit Free Press* (November 7, 1997).

¹⁸ "Despite 'R' Rating, Kids Sneak into Troopers," Reuters/Variety wire report from America Online, November 1997. Sony executives, apparently trying to justify disappointing sales, sent a letter to exhibitors (citing the *New York Post* story) advising them to check for moviegoers under seventeen who were supposedly sneaking into *Starship Troopers* after buying tickets to other films.

¹⁹ Sontag, "Fascism," 95.

²⁰ Benjamin Svetkey, "The Reich Stuff: Nazi references and Fascist Images Creep Among the Bugs in Starship Troopers," *Entertainment Weekly* (November 21, 1997), 9.

²¹ Stephen Colbert, "Hollywood," in *I Am America (and So Can You!)* (New York: Hachette Audio, 2007).

²² Pauline Kael, "Review of *Dirty Harry*," *The New Yorker,* January 15, 1972.

²³ Scott Tobias, "The New Cult Canon: *Starship Troopers*," The A.V. Club, June 10, 2010. Online at www.avclub.com/articles/starship-troopers.41966.

Chapter 20

Air Wars Live from (Baghdad)[2]

Linda Robertson

No doubt remains in the minds of serious students of the War against Iraq that the American public was deceived into supporting an opportunistic war of aggression. Equally obvious, but far less widely discussed, is that the representation of the conduct of the war was also an egregious betrayal of the public trust. This is particularly the case with regard to the air war: its purpose, extent, and cost to civilians were both distorted and suppressed. Americans were invited to watch the war begin and—they were promised—end in one major aerial attack: the televised "Shock and Awe" bombing of Baghdad. The use of strategic bombing against a major city was supposed to destroy the buildings that constituted the command and control capabilities of Saddam Hussein's government. The bombing was supposed literally to stun Saddam Hussein's supporters into immediate surrender. As for civilians, well, the explanation went, while some might be killed or injured, the United States could not be held morally culpable: our bombs were "smart" and aimed only at government targets. Civilians were not targeted, their deaths were accidental—regrettable collateral damage. "How many civilians were killed or injured?" one might well ask. The official tautology was that the United States military did not count civilian casualties, because civilians were not targeted. When the "Shock and Awe" attack failed to produce the promised immediate capitulation, the use of air power in Iraq simply disappeared from news reports. It was just the ground war—"boots on the ground"—as reported by embedded reporters from Kuwait to Baghdad.

The presentation of the air-to-ground assault on Iraq ought to have tested the credulity of even a notoriously credulous public such as Americans have sadly shown themselves to be with regard to the coverage of our military actions since the 1970s. During the period of the invasion and the early years of the occupation of Iraq, the skepticism about the veracity of official reports, which arose as the Vietnam War waned, seems to have entirely dissipated, replaced with an American ethos ranging from self-censorship, jingoism, and denial, to indifference and political apathy. The Iraq invasion was a war of aggression using air-to-ground assault on major population centers. To achieve this did not require highly coercive measures to suppress dissent on the home front. This bodes ill, because it makes the United States not only the most powerful nation on earth, but the most dangerous as well. Cold analysis yields absolute clarity about the need to understand how the credulity of the American public was so easily manipulated.

One obvious cause was the orchestrated effort by the Bush Administration to galvanize public opinion in support of the war. Support in the United States for attacking Iraq had grown during the weeks leading up to the ultimatum and attack. In a CBS poll released on March 6, 45% of the respondents agreed that the threat from Iraq "required immediate action;" 51% agreed that Hussein was not a direct threat to the United States, or that it was possible to contain that threat short of going to war. In the week prior to the war, a CBS poll indicated support had risen to 69%. A Gallup poll taken soon after the beginning of the war indicated that 62% of Americans supported the war.

The Program on International Policy Attitudes (PIPA) in conjunction with the polling firm, Knowledge Networks (KN), surveyed public opinion on the subject of war with Iraq seven times between January and September, 2003. Their findings revealed that "a substantial portion of the public had a number of misperceptions that were demonstrably false, or were at odds with the dominant view of the intelligence community." Polls showed that one in five Americans incorrectly believed that Saddam Hussein had been involved in the September 11, 2001 attacks on the United States (February, 2003); a majority believed that Saddam was in league with al Qaeda (February, 2003); that weapons of mass destruction had actually been found in Iraq (May, July, August-September, 2003); and that the majority of Americans thought the rest of the world supported American military action against Saddam (May, July, August-September, 2003).

The KN study revealed, in fact, that 80% of Americans rely upon television for their news. Viewers of Fox network news had the highest percentage of viewers with the most misperceptions (45%), while NPR/PBS had the lowest (11%). The other media outlets (CBS 36%, CNN 31%, ABC 30%, print media 25%) fared better than Fox viewers. The Gallup poll showed that the greater the viewing time, the lower the relative knowledge about the war, and the higher the relative support. The poll also showed that the more knowledgeable an individual was about the Middle East and factors relevant to the war, the less support he or she was likely to give to it.[1]

These misperceptions were the result of a sophisticated propaganda campaign aimed at the American public. Colonel Sam Gardiner (USAF, retired) summarized his 2003 study of the efforts to influence American public opinion:

The United States (and UK) conducted a strategic influence campaign that:

- distorted perceptions of the situation both before and during the conflict.

- caused misdirection of portions of the military operation.

- was irresponsible in parts.

- might have been illegal in some ways.

- cost big bucks.

- will be even more serious in the future.[2]

The January, 2008 report by the Center for Public Integrity similarly found that the Administraton waged a "carefully orchestrated campaign of misiniformation about the threat posed by Saddam Hussein's Iraq." The report traces a dramatic increase in the rate of false statements beginning in August, 2002, when the Administration sought the approval of Congress for a war resolution. The number of such statements totals 935 (see table 1).[3]

The reports by Gardiner, the Center for Public Integrity, and numerous other studies of the misrepresentation of the war concentrate on the considerable propaganda campaign shaped by the Bush Administration and abetted by the mainstream news media in the United States. But they do not explain why the American public—the audience—proved so highly receptive to the manipulation of information and images. This is true to an even greater extent with regard to the public's gullibility in accepting the sanitized

Table 1

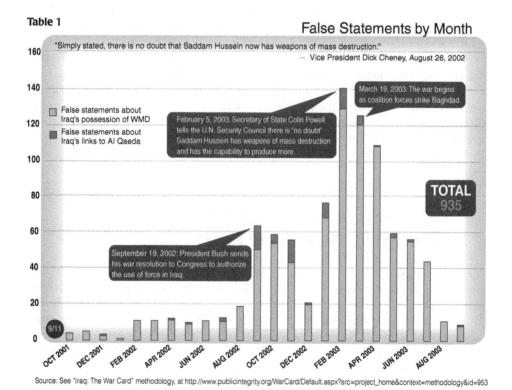

Source: See "Iraq: The War Card" methodology, at http://www.publicintegrity.org/WarCard/Default.aspx?src=project_home&context=methodology&id=953

presentation of the war itself, particularly the air war. After all, a war is tangible and has immediate material effects. Information about weapons of mass destruction or conspiratorial alliances with Al Qaeda is intangible, and requires trust in the sources of information. But it should take little imagination to conceive the effect of war waged in heavily populated urban areas.

We cannot really estimate the consequences of information control for the formation of public opinion about the Persian Gulf air wars by attending solely to the project of ferreting out what was censored, or by condemning the influence of television technology as a visual medium. Let us confine our attention to the question of why Americans seem to lack that basic moral imagination; why, that is, they seemed willing to accept that aerial bombardment is damaging only to government buildings and the psyches of those who work in them. There is no One Answer to the question; there are answers. We must inquire into the signifying practices which traditionally have been used, developed, and recombined to create the public's conception of "air wars" and of "combat pilots."

A useful approach is to consider two contributing factors:

First, how the United States military selected the images and information about not only the Iraq air war, but also the one just previous to it, the first Persian Gulf War, conducted by President Bush *père*. Both wars were conducted in the same place against the same enemy, and it would be naïve to suppose that the son did not learn from the father about how to control public perceptions of air wars. This selectivity of images and information provides a clearer context when examined in light of the cultural significance of air combat, including how pilots now understand their historical legacy.

Secondly, how Hollywood films have shaped popular conceptions of air wars. These films have been influenced in an important way by the air force: an air war film cannot be made without the cooperation of the United States Air Force (USAF) for the obvious reason that they possess all the planes. The USAF has exerted considerable influence over scripts and the visual presentation of air combat since prior to World War II.

Since our interest is in considering what cultural signifiers may have made the American public receptive to the sanitized presentation of the Iraq air war, our effort will be to compare how the military manipulated the images of the real air war—determining what was seen and what was not—with how the understanding and indeed appreciation of American air combat has been shaped by air combat films, most of which were directly influenced by the USAF.

The First Persian Gulf Air War: The Military and the Press

The suppressed information about the first Persian Gulf air war indicates what the military assumed would be unacceptable, both in the United States and around the world, while what we saw on television screens is a rather clear indication of the opposite. The televised coverage left the impression that the majority of the bombs dropped in the war zone were "smart bombs" targeted at inanimate objects—such as buildings, hangars, or runways—and that they rarely missed. However, "smart weapons" accounted for only about 8% of the total tonnage dropped, an amount which exceeded that used in all of World War II.[4] The majority were "dumb" (unguided) iron bombs ranging from 500 to 1000 pounds of explosives, or containing incendiary chemicals, land mines, or the like. The surrender of the majority of the Iraqi army was credited to the psychological and physical effects of protracted saturation bombing of men trapped in bunkers, much of it attributable to B-52s. Yet, the military imposed absolute censorship on images of B-52s, their crews, or information about their missions. There were no aerial pictures of the havoc the planes wrought on the ground below, no visual reference to them at all except brief file clips when military experts for the major networks or CNN mentioned they were being used in the air war.[5]

Americans were left with the dramatic impression that the air war was conducted and won primarily by resolute fighters flying alone or in small groups of two or three; but modern air wars are conducted by large flying armadas, a "strike package" stretching in some cases for forty miles and comprised of highly specialized planes, each having a specific function. War conducted from the air is as complex as ground maneuvering.[6]

Why was it not only permissible but highly desirable to broadcast into American homes pictures of a modern city defending itself against night aerial bombardment by American planes, but not permissible to show high-level saturation bombing over the theatre of war? Why were pictures repeatedly shown of single planes taking off or landing, but none of large, multiple-squadron armadas?

The B-52 carries the nuclear arsenal of the United States and was used for saturation bombing of Vietnam and Cambodia. So potent and negative are the images of the B-52s that there were protests in India at the news that B-52s would use bases there to refuel. Saudi Arabia and Egypt refused to allow the use of air bases for B-52s. Even granting that the United States military might not want to draw attention to the use of B-52s, why portray the air war as conducted primarily by individual planes? Why is that image more pertinent not simply for controlling public opinion, but for sustaining a sense of public "euphoria" instead of depicting the complex interdependence of an air armada?

Mechanized Warfare and the Soldier as a Symbol of National Character

Part of the answer resides in the traditional connection between the combat pilot and an idealized national character. The propaganda campaign developed by Great Britain during World War I stressed that British and Commonwealth soldiers showed individuality and initiative, while their Prussian counterparts could only follow orders blindly. This testimony to the superiority of the liberal nations in character formation was picked up by the United States and repeated in World War II and in the build-up to the Persian Gulf War.

Note, for instance, the centrality of "character" in a "prolegomenon" to a peace note written by Woodrow Wilson in November, 1916 as a response to the mechanized, stalemated slaughter along the Western Front that destroyed the capacity to regard warfare as a proof of manhood:

> Deprived of glory, war loses all its charm. . . . The mechanical slaughter of today has not the same fascination as the zest of intimate combat of former days; and trench warfare and poisonous gases are elements which detract alike from the excitement and the tolerance of modern conflict. With maneuver almost a thing of the past, any given point can admittedly be carried by the sacrifice of enough men

and ammunition. Where is any longer the glory commensurate with the sacrifice of the millions of men required in modern warfare to carry and defend Verdun?[7]

But the image of the air warrior offered a tonic to this disappointed imagination of how war should be fought. To him were transferred the values of individual initiative which, at the beginning of the war, had been ascribed to the ground soldier.

World War I saw the advent of every kind of air combat that later developed, including strategic bombing. But it was the combat pilot, and particularly the "lone wolf" who was played up for the public and who remains the central icon of that war in the public imagination. He was portrayed as an exemplar of hyper-individualism, the member of an exclusive fraternity of "aces," each one dependent entirely upon his own innate skill and will to combat. The iconographic conventions associated with the lone wolf established him as an independent hero, not as the team member of a wing or squadron. Hilda Beatrice Hewlett, writing of her visit to the front in Our Flying Men, echoed the propaganda message: "In flying, more than in any science of war, the man is alone, and on his skill and nerve depends the result."[8] In the popular imagination, war for the lone wolf was personal—he was known to his enemy either by name or by the distinctive designs painted on his plane.

Yet even as American college men were being recruited into the air service, when the United States entered the war, by images of "aces" on "lone wolf" patrols, emerging combat tactics made the role of the "lone wolf" and self-assigned missions increasingly obsolete, because they were contrary to the aim of coordinated air support for military objectives on the ground. At the end of the war, the military addressed the problem created by the publicity they themselves had fostered. In the "lessons learned" reports, the recommendation was that ways be found to temper the image of the combat pilot.[9] It was no longer useful to portray him as either a chivalric knight on a personal quest or as an entrepeneurial loner interested primarily in accruing personal glory.

The relationship of man and machine, and hence, man and weapon, also changed as the technology of the airplane developed. The most important attribute of the World War I combat pilot was his cybernetic relationship to the plane he flew and its weaponry. With the advent of synchronized, forward-firing machine guns, the combat pilot—uniquely among the soldiers of World War I—used mechanized weaponry as an extension of his skill and courage.

The weaponry of the ground war enforced a sense that one was either serving the machine as a "cog in the wheel," or, if on the receiving end of its thrust, merely a paralyzed victim of it. The advent of long-range artillery meant that men loaded shells into large barrels, stood back while they were fired, and began again. The targets were so far away that often they could not be seen by those aiming weapons at them. The same was the case with submarine torpedoes. Crews in the early tanks could see little besides the poor individual who was assigned to stand on the ground in front of them and guide them with flags. The most lethal weaponry, in addition to the long-range artillery, was gas, which required none of the martial skills either to use or to avoid. The weaponry of the ground war in World War I was at a far remove from either the skilled, highly trained maneuver of cavalry forces, or the eye-to-eye combat that was part of the romanticism associated with warfare as a test of personal strength. This reality explains much of the psychological appeal of the combat pilot. On the ground, the machine mastered the man; in the air, the man and the machine merged.

The traditional role of the warrior was nevertheless maintained, because combat pilots saw their opponents; the engagement was personalized. But by the advent of the war in Vietnam, air combat had become as highly mechanized as ground weaponry. The cockpit radar picked out enemy aircraft well before the pilot could see it; guidance systems locked on the target, so that with the squeeze of a finger a missile could be launched at the invisible opponent. Air-to-air combat and maneuvers were assumed to have been rendered obsolete by advanced technology, until the unanticipated losses in the skies over Vietnam led the air force to revive air-to-air combat training—and with it the glamorized iconography of the combat pilot—as depicted in *Top Gun* (1986).

Air Wars on Film

The values the combat pilot has been used to represent in Hollywood films have undergone a moral devolution when it comes to his accepting responsibility for causing death, either to the enemy or to those under the same command. The change can be traced from *Wings*, the 1927 silent film about a World War I "knight of the air" who is tempered by a moral code of guilt and restraint, through to the *Top Gun* stick jockey indifferent to a faceless "enemy" and concerned primarily with personal performance. It is a journey from a version—albeit diluted—of the tragic self-consciousness of Achilles to a Nintendo game that proves the "prowess" of the kid who puts the slugs in the slot. "Accepting responsibility" changes from meaning that the pilot confronts his guilt as a warrior to meaning that he learns to follow orders, tempering his sizable, competitive ego just enough to meet the needs of his command unit while showing a callous indifference to destroying the enemy in a ball of fire.

Films about air combat made prior to World War II were predicated on the pre-World War I desire to conceptualize warfare, properly fought, as enhancing rather than diminishing the humanity of the man. Seeing one's enemy called forth pity and fear, or shame and guilt; having to rely upon skill, maneuver, and courage tested the refinements of civilization on primitive instinct. Ultimately, war required accepting personal responsibility for the death of others.

Two films by John Monk Saunders, who had flown with the United States air service over the Western Front, invited a traditional catharsis by demonstrating not only the thrill of flight and combat but also the consequences of it; not only the loss of life but the moral costs to those who survived. *Wings* won the first academy award; *Dawn Patrol* was essentially an anti-war film made in two versions, one in 1930 (for which Saunders won the Academy Award for best screenplay) and the second in 1938. In both films, the preferred narrative is that the enemy is just like us, only he wears a different uniform. This point is made in a disturbing way in *Wings*, where the hero Jack Powell (Charles Rogers) shoots down his best friend David Armstrong (Richard Arlen). David is flying a German plane which he stole after he was shot down behind enemy lines. As Jack fires at him with a machine gun, David screams helplessly, "Don't you know me?" and is of course unable to return fire because he does not want to kill Jack. Jack relentlessly pursues him in a private vendetta to kill Germans because he thinks they have killed David.

Dawn Patrol is another "buddy" movie about flyers in World War I, this time men serving in the Royal Flying Corps. Scotty (David Niven) is brought down and presumed to be dead. The German pilot who shot him down is captured and brought to the rustic officer's club, where he meets Courtney, Scotty's best friend (Errol Flynn). Courtney greets him courteously, and they spend the evening together drinking and singing. Scotty shows up bedraggled, a bump on his head, and carrying six bottles of champagne. He is delighted to meet the German who shot him down, and invites him out for a night on the town; unfortunately, the German officer cannot go because he is a prisoner of war.

In *Wings* and *Dawn Patrol*, the enemy is the war itself, which divides men from men who would otherwise be friends; in *Dawn Patrol*, the enemy is also a murderously stupid command that insists upon sending untrained pilots in inferior planes on offensive patrols. In *Wings*, Jack is absolved of his guilt by David's mother, who says she has tried to hate him, but cannot, because ultimately the cause of her son's death was the war. While this may seem too glib, the point is that the film requires Jack to face the question of his moral responsibility for his role in killing "the enemy"—symbolically displaced—during war, and to seek absolution for it. Similarly, in *Dawn Patrol*, the recognition of the enemy's humanity makes the war all the more senseless—which is the point of the film. *Dawn Patrol* is an early example of what came to be called the "pressure of command film," of which *Twelve O'Clock High* (1949) is a good example from World War II. *Dawn Patrol* depicts the successive mental breakdowns of the commanders who are ordered day after day to send young, unskilled, poorly trained pilots into the air to their certain deaths. It is an oddly pacifist film, in the sense that it argues against the senselessness of war while demonstrating that men did not shirk their duty, even while they recognized the pointless waste of life caused by a murderously misguided command whose orders they were bound to obey.

World War II: "Fried Jap Goin' Down!"

In *Air Force* (1942), the enemy is the treacherous and cowardly "Japs" who are never humanized as the German pilots were in the earlier films about World War I; and the internal threat is the motive to "be a hero," acting on one's own rather than being part of a larger team. *Air Force* was made by Warner Bros., a $2 million "A" feature directed by Howard Hawks and produced by Hal Wallis. Leading men included Gig Young, Arthur Kennedy, Harry Carey, and John Garfield. The studio enjoyed the full co-operation of the commanding general of the US Army Air Force, H. H. "Hap" Arnold, who had also served as a commanding officer in Washington during World War I, overseeing the birth of the air force. He was a personal friend of Jack Warner. *Air Force* reflects a number of propaganda messages important to the air force at the time. Some were congruent with the messages typically advocated by the domestic Office of War Information; however, it is a testimony to the influence of the air force that the essentially racist anti-Japanese content of the film remains a central feature despite the energetic opposition of the O.W.I.[10]

Air Force tells the story of the crew of a B-17 named "Mary Ann," a Flying Fortress that takes off on a routine flight from San Francisco to Hickam Field, the airbase at Pearl Harbor (Honolulu), on the evening of December 6, 1941. Diverted to Maui by the attack on Pearl Harbor, the fliers are shot at on the ground by what are called "fifth column" snipers, or Japanese living in Honolulu. They fly over Hickam Field, circling it briefly before landing, so that the base is seen from the air, burning. After refueling, they are ordered to the Philippines. Shortly after they land, the base at Manila is attacked, and the "Mary Ann" takes off to confront the enemy. One of the "Mary Ann's" gunners hits a Japanese plane and shouts exultantly, "Fried Jap goin' down!"—the first of several shots in the film of Japanese pilots burning to death. The plane returns to base damaged by the attack of enemy aircraft. The entire crew works together to repair the plane and take off just before the Japanese overrun the island. En route to Australia, they spot the Japanese fleet, call in reinforcements, and successfully sink it, a sequence that splices in actual battle footage. The film closes on a base in Australia with a briefing sometime in the future when everyone's dream comes true: they are sent to bomb Tokyo.

Air Force breaks with the representation of air combat offered in the earlier films in two important ways. One is that it repeatedly invites the viewer to respond with glee at seeing the death of Japanese flyers. The second is that it openly displays World War II in the air as not being about individual heroics or the finesse of air-to-air combat. The aim is to bomb the enemy into submission. The bomber is not an extension of the fighter's skill; it is a warehouse loaded with deadly weapons carrying the war to the enemy.

Top Gun

The same message is conveyed in *Top Gun*. The time is the Cold War, when there is an enemy but no shooting war—more's the pity, the film seems to say—until the very end, an explosive battle between US Navy and enemy planes. The opening sequence is an encounter with an unnamed enemy, flying what are supposed to be MiGs. Lt. Pete Mitchell (Tom Cruise), tellingly nicknamed "Maverick," stunt-flies his plane so that his canopy is inverted over the canopy of the "enemy." In *Wings* and *Dawn Patrol*, flyers throw military salutes to those they shoot down out of respect for the man. In *Top Gun*, Maverick flips his counterpart "the bird" and takes his picture with a flash camera. Maverick has "counted coup" without firing a shot; he has "shown off" and humiliated the enemy, although to no particular purpose beyond proving that he has the skill to do it. In the final battle scene, where Maverick blows three planes apart with missiles, enemy pilots are not discernable in the cockpits; nor is the opposing nation even named.

Some faint echo of former glory is restored to air-to-air combat because of the marriage of man and machine and the encounter with hostile enemy aircraft requiring skill and courage to survive; but it is a thin veneer painted over what is essentially vainglory. Facing the enemy does not have a tempering influence, invoking the humanizing sentiments of pity, shame, and guilt. The lesson of learning responsibility is worked out through the death of Maverick's radio and weapons operator Lt. Nick "Goose" Bradshaw (Anthony Edwards), who rides behind him in the F-14 Tomcat.[11] Overly eager in a competitive maneuver, Maverick loses control of his plane because of backwash from another plane. Goose is killed during the attempted ejection when his head hits the canopy. Maverick learns from the sobering event to control his impulses and to stay in formation rather than be a maverick flier. In *Top Gun*, being responsible is reduced to the simple requirement to follow orders; the death of a comrade entails no moral encounter for the pilot because it resulted from equipment failure.

First Persian Gulf Air War: The Movie

Given the number of movies about air combat that have been made since the end of World War I, it is not an exaggeration to say that The United States Air Force has been in the business of making movies for the better part of the century. The use of the broadcast press during the Persian Gulf War provides another example of the military "producing" a movie using commercial venues to promote its own message. With the real war in the Persian Gulf, the challenge was how to portray as both interesting and admirable the use of overwhelming force to bomb an undefended enemy into submission in a lopsided war. To the extent that the representation was successful, as it evidently was, the result can be seen as arising from a number of factors in addition to the suppression of information. For one thing, it was easy for the viewer to be involved, particularly young male viewers. Because the complex interdependency of "strike packages" was not explained, and the key role of the high-altitude bombing by B-52s was suppressed, media representations gratified childhood fantasies of lone-wolf heroism and adventure in air combat. The "fighter plane" as a weapon has morphed into a bomber, but conveys the romantic iconography of personalized combat, perhaps a hint of the former glory of the "knights of the air," and most certainly the contemporary narcissistic glamour of being a "Top Gun."

The air war was represented as being about individuals taking off into the darkened sky or flying into the sun, prevailing over an opponent who could not fight well because he was the product of an autocratic regime. It was a '90s kind of war, where individuals performed feats for which they were especially trained, using technology that reflected the intellectual and economic superiority of the West. The warrior and his plane symbolized laissez-faire liberalism giving rise to a highly coordinated and successful undertaking. During World War II, the efforts by the Office of War Information to promote films that represented the war effort as socially balanced—an infantry unit, for example, would have to have included a minority soldier, an urban and immigrant youth from the Bronx, a boy from the midwest, and usually somebody with a college degree—are well documented.[12] Because this emphasis smacked of "New Deal" collectivism, conservative members of Congress reacted against the O.W.I. The representation of the Persian Gulf War, on the other hand, emphasized a predatory, elite Individualism. Images that reinforced the romance of the "lone wolf" were reiterated. Americans were repeatedly shown stunningly beautiful depictions of the F-17 "Stealth" bomber taking off into the fading light of the evening sky; or a lone Intruder launched with breathtaking force from the decks of a US carrier. Handsome young pilots were interviewed to reveal how they "felt," rather than to explain to the public complicated tactics requiring cooperative interdependence.

The referent for the televised coverage was not the real war, but celluloid air wars, what Walter Lippmann would call the images of wars "in our head."[13] As with Hollywood movies about modern air combat, the air war over the Persian Gulf did not invite a cathartic response in the traditional sense. The effort was to discharge the fear of a ground war—and the unwelcome resonance with Vietnam—by offering the air war instead. There was no invitation to guilt or shame—particularly on the ticklish matter of bombing cities—because the images were highly sanitized, the strikes "surgical." There was a profound unwillingness to invoke the moral imagination of the public, to suggest that the war would require of the average citizen anything even approaching sacrifice, never mind a sense of oneself as a responsible, historical agent for the nation's use of massive destruction. The war re-enacted on a different stage what Woodrow Wilson lamented about the advent of mechanized warfare: the Persian Gulf War had no glory to it, and hence no proof of manhood in the oldest military sense, which is why the luster so quickly faded from the Commander in Chief, and the public's "amnesia" set in so soon. The war was presented as a Saturday-matinee "summer-guy flick," such as the blockbuster *Independence Day* (1996), timed to open on July 4. This film broke all opening day records and was about single-pilot combat planes saving earth from very large, squishy aliens. Both the Persian Gulf War and *ID4* seem aimed at the same audience and were equally forgettable.

The effort to construct the Persian Gulf War with the aesthetics and moral depth of *Top Gun* indicates how much the public's responses to the face of war can influence the conduct of it. When Americans saw the "face of the enemy," they were not indifferent to it; they became sympathetic to the tattered and exhausted Iraqi soldiers who surrendered in vast numbers, having been pulverized for days from the air. There was a public outcry when pictures were shown of the wreckage and burned bodies of the unarmed Iraqi soldiers who had tried to flee Kuwait and who were attacked by British and American planes flying over Mutla Ridge. The public response to these pictures is held in some quarters to have influenced the decision by President Bush to end the war, as some military strategists put it, "one day too soon"; a euphemistic phrase suggesting that Iraqi ground forces, and especially the Republican Guard, should have been annihilated; but Bush allowed political considerations to override military pragmatism.

The representation of the air war also masked the traditions of air combat itself. What was widely reported in Great Britain but not in the United States was that both British and American flyers indicated to their commanders that they did not wish to receive further orders to engage in the kind of annihilating attack they had accomplished over Mutla Ridge. All flyers are volunteers, officers, and highly trained. While the refusal of orders would constitute grounds for a court martial, the indication that they did not wish to receive further orders certainly carried considerable weight. It is worth speculating why this resistance was not covered in the American press.

There was a hue and cry in Great Britain against the government for seeming to try and pin on the pilots the lack of political will to carry the war to the annihilation of the enemy. That interesting question aside, the reluctance of pilots to engage in the bombing and strafing of a routed army points toward the nobler legacy of air combat, a legacy which, despite the effort to dilute it in Hollywood tales of hot-shot pilots, still carries a sense of moral restraint imposed upon fliers who—part of an elite military service conceived as engaged in civilized violence rather than impersonal mechanized warfare—actually see the enemy they must encounter, and so in some way actually know him as they gun him down.

Second Persian Gulf Air War

The war against Iraq was, candidly speaking, a war of aggression, and in the euphemistic language of President Bush a "pre-emptive strike." The current logic of war was given an American-style lustre by the apparent return to the earliest attributes associated with the combat pilot: a courageous recklessness, a hypermasculine individualism. At least that is the case made in the highly favorable marks given the Secretary of Defense by the noted military historian Sir John Keegan. Keegan's laudatory profile of Donald Rumsfeld in *Vanity Fair* just prior to the invasion of Iraq touts Rumsfeld's World War II experience as a Navy pilot, one of those who "generally took risks Air Force pilots did not." This praise is for the *Top Gun* pilot, for the Maverick. The visionary Rumsfeld understands the necessity of fighting "the terrorist" because the terrorist "does not bargain, does not negotiate, and his mental processes are devoted entirely to calculating how he can successfully inflict violence on those he hates." How the necessity to "fight" the "terrorist" on these terms will allow the United States to avoid adopting the same practices as the presumptive enemy—and make it necessary to do so indefinitely—is not carefully explained by Keegan. One hint about the nature of America's wars to come is Keegan's suggestion that Secretary Rumsfeld is impatient with the legal basis given to human rights in warfare: "Although Rumsfeld has been reticent on the issue, it seems that this legalism [associated with the hindering 'Rules of Engagement' established for ground forces in the Balkans] and [the related] risk aversion were not at all to his taste." The new vision of American warfare, Keegan concludes, means that "In the battle against al-Qaeda—and the campaign against Saddam—Donald Rumsfeld seems the right man at the right time for the messy, thankless job."[14]

This ruthless mentality is praised in the name of the glory that was and is the Navy fighter pilot's, an appropriation which is the ultimate devolution of the image of the "knight in the sky": that is, the restrained warrior who fought only on equal terms and who was understood to defend civilization through his use of civilized violence. Stripped of that moral shine, regardless of how tarnished it may have been even from the beginning, the use of air power against essentially defenseless ground soldiers and civilians—so long as the "collateral damage" does not exceed a threshold the public can stomach—becomes a hollow glory. Keegan's admiring profile of Rumsfeld sadly presaged the realities of Persian Gulf War II. Keegan seemed to predict that America's wars would cross the threshold of restraint, would become blatant conquest, with the use of violence legitimized by the pragmatic belief that once America "wins," the rest of the world will love us.

Second Persian Gulf Air War: Now You See It, Now You Don't

The war against Saddam Hussein began as scheduled with the "shock and awe" bombing of Baghdad on the night of March 21-22, 2003. Vice-President Dick Cheney had made the by-now conventional assertion that America's wars are fought in the name of defending civilization. Speaking to the Conservative Political Action Conference in Arlington Virginia on January 30, 2003, he declared, "We are defending both ourselves and the safety and survival of civilization itself." He called for aggression against Saddam Hussein as part of the war against terror: "Confronting the threat posed by Iraq is not a distraction from the war on terror, it is absolutely crucial to winning the war on terror. (Applause.)"[15]

The "shock and awe" bombing of Baghdad was thus a signifier for a civilized bombing campaign conducted in defense of civilization. "Shock and Awe" refers to strategic bombing; that is, bombing of Iraq's cities or industrial areas to destroy the political and economic capacities to wage war. There were three aims articulated: "decapitation" of the regime; or, failing that, incapacitating the regime by destroying the infrastructure and so demoralizing the leadership that it capitulated; and thirdly, impressing the Iraqi people with the desirability of turning against their rulers. These are traditional aims of strategic bombing, and were used to legitimize the bombing of German cities during World War II and dropping the Atomic bombs on Hiroshima and Nagasaki. "Shock and Awe" bombing was distinguished from these earlier examples by assurances that the use of precision weaponry would reduce the risk of civilian casualties. USAF Colonel Mace Carpenter, chief strategist for the Combined Air Operations Center explained "We wanted to make it clear to the Iraqi people that we were attacking regime targets. We wanted them to see that we were clearly targetting those people who had been repressing them."[16]

The world watched the explosions and heard the sounds but did not see the effects of the seventy-two hour bombing campaign. Hundreds of strike aircraft were deployed. A total of 600 cruise missiles hit the city and bombs were dropped from 1500 sorties by strike aircraft. The entire world was supposed to be gobsmacked into a paralyzed awe at the might of the aroused America, which, like an avenging angel, destroyed only the Evildoers and spared the innocent. The staged event was spectacular, but it did not bring the regime to an end. The buildings targeted for "shock and awe"—ministries and party headquarters—had been abandoned prior to the attack.

The "Shock and Awe" Doctrine in its fullest iteration could not have been explained in such rational terms redolent of benign intent. Nor could it have been made palatable to those members of the American public with sufficient historical grasp on the air war of World War II. Naomi Klein, in *The Shock Doctrine*, explains: "In open defiance of the laws of war barring collective punishment, Shock and Awe is a military doctrine that prides itself on not merely targeting the enemy's military forces but, as its authors stress, the 'society writ large'—mass fear is a key part of the strategy." Those who devised the Shock and Awe Doctrine envisioned it as aimed "directly at the public will of the adversary to resist."[17]

The historical name given to this kind of bombing is "morale bombing." It means bombing in order to so demoralize the population as to cause them to overthrow their government. It was widely condemned during World War I when the Germans bombed urban targets in England and France; and again, when Germany engaged in the same kind of bombing during World War II. The British strategic bombing force was condemned for engaging in morale bombing of German cities, since the British had been on the receiving end of such attacks. The United States Air Force maintained throughout the war, and even after the bombings of Hiroshima and Nagasaki, that it only targeted strategic, military targets and did not engage in morale bombing.

Not only did Shock and Awe not cause the immediate collapse of the Baghdad regime, the ground war did not go as planned. The script called for crowds cheering the passing tanks and tossing flowers as if Iraq were France or Holland when the Yanks liberated them. Instead, ground forces faced heavier than anticipated resistance.

While the impression given to those watching on television was that the war was won by the ground troops, the reality was quite different. According to Captain Mike Harwood, Commander of an RAF Harrier detachment, the Republican Guard, Special Republican Guard, and Regular Army were destroyed from the sky: "Their combat effectiveness was reduced to almost zero. . . . We and the Americans were sending almost 1000 aircraft a day into Iraq for three weeks. It was a hell of an effort."[18]

Yet the air campaign basically did not appear in media reports. How was the disappearance of the air campaign managed, and why? And why was there so little inquiry into the absence of information about the air campaign? *A Washington Post* report on April 26, 2003, explained that there were several reasons why an air campaign—"that dropped 29,000 bombs and missiles on thousands of targets in Iraq—played out largely behind this scenes." For one thing, that staunch ally of the United States, Saudi Arabia, refused to allow reporters onto the bases from which coalition forces launched their attacks. But Air Marshall Sir Timothy Garden, a visiting professor at King's College and a frequent commentator on the air war, makes it clear enough that Central Command did not want the public to pay attention to the air war: "If CENTCOM could have placed those reports in the wider strategic picture, we would have had much better informed coverage—and of air power in particular. But the CENTCOM media centre was a disaster. It was scared of providing comment before Washington had taken the glory. Nor was our own MOD (Ministry of Defense) any better."[19]

After the "shock and awe" bombing, the air war turned to tactical bombing to provide close air support of ground forces by attacking enemy troops and equipment.[20] Approximately 50% of the sorties flown after the second week of the war were tactical; a total of 82% of the 15,592 targets struck by Coalition air power were aimed at Iraqi forces. This was the true "shock and awe" campaign. The rapid military success of Operation Iraqi Freedom can be put down to the effective tactical use of air power, particularly close air support. The damage to buildings and the high casualty rates among civilians that resulted were essentially unreported in the United States. Thus did the air war disappear from the television screens, newspapers, and news magazines.

Strategic Bombing and the American Imagination

Why is it acceptable to show strategic bombing to Americans? How did American public sentiment change from abhorring the idea of bombing cities during World War I to accepting and approving of strategic bombing and watching it eagerly on television, now?

From the outset, the American strategic bombing capability has been presented to the American public as necessary to prevent the strategic bombing of American cities. Indeed, the bombing of cities has traditionally been imagined so as to cast Americans in the role of victims. Among the earliest reactions to the news of the dropping of the atomic bombs on Hiroshima and Nagasaki in the elite press was that the advent of the atomic bomb rendered Americans the potential victims, and American cities the potential targets—this at a time when the United States was the only nation to possess the atomic bomb, and then as now, the only nation ever to use it.[21] The fear of a nuclear attack, which was stoked throughout the Cold War to legitimize the enormous American nuclear weapon stockpile, was irresponsibly reinvoked by National Security Advisor Condoleezza Rice in a September 8, 2002 interview with Wolf Blitzer on CNN. Blitzer asked her about Saddam Hussein's nuclear capability. She replied, "The problem here is that there will always be some uncertainty about how quickly he can acquire nuclear weapons. But we don't want the smoking gun to be a mushroom cloud." Hers was unabashed fearmongering linking the attacks of September 11, 2001, the Cold War mentality, and Saddam Hussein.

What about the effects of bombing the enemy during World War II? How has that been represented? The 1943 Hollywood propaganda film *Behind the Rising Sun* represents the same idealism about the positive effects of bombing a city as was expressed by Colonel Mace Carpenter in his explanation of the intention to use "shock and awe" bombing to signal to Iraqis that they no longer had to support their oppressive leaders. The film includes a highly diluted version of what it was like to be on the receiving end of the bombing of Tokyo. The point in this film is to demonstrate that the destructiveness of bombing cities is necessary in order to free Japan to become a civilized nation. American civilians are prisoners of the Japanese, whose atrocities against American women and Chinese women and children are depicted throughout the film. When the bombs start to fall, the prisoners are elated even though they are on the ground because the bombs mean the end of Japanese militaristic regime and the chance to rebuild Japan as a better nation. During the bombing, they are freed by a friend and escape back to the United States. The Japanese publisher who plays a key pro-militarist role in the film commits *sepuku* because of the shame he feels at the corruption of his country by the regime to which he gave such blind loyalty.

Films of this type are cultural indices. They refer to a broader contest for public opinion. No single film is, in and of itself, strictly propaganda; to be called propaganda it properly must be part of a larger strategy of public manipulation. And one cannot speak of a homogeneity of public opinion. Many Americans condemned morale bombing and the use of Atomic weapons, just as many Americans refused to accept the justifications for going to war in Iraq. But our effort has been to consider what cultural factors might account for the American public's receptivity to sanitized versions of aerial bombardment of large urban populations. Reflecting upon how the justifications were marshaled for World War I and for World War II—the war which brought America to its current position as the dominant military power in the world—helps further our understanding of the historical sources of America's willingness to watch morale bombing on their televisions as if it were an example of America's constrained use of power for civilizing purposes.

As for the factors that made the public unaware of the post-Shock and Awe bombings: the public did not notice the absence of the coverage of the air war for four reasons. First, the American vision of a bombing campaign—the air war as imagined—was essentially that air power is used for strategic strikes against military targets and is conducted within the limits of civilized warfare using precision weapons. If civilians are killed, it is also within acceptable moral limits because we did not mean to kill them, and it is sometimes necessary to destroy in order to save. Second, this war belonged visually to the ground forces who were presented as fighting a conventional war, not one aimed against civilians, and who were the objects of sympathy because they were covered by embedded reporters. The thrilling accounts of the knights of the sky were originally conceived by the military as a way to distract the public from the slaughter on the ground in World War I, and the sharp distinction between air and ground warfare has been maintained since; i.e., if the focus is on the ground war, the focus will be off the air war. A third and most important factor is that there were no disillusioning accounts from mainstream American media sources to contradict the idealized imagining of the air campaign. These three factors relate to how air wars are presented. But the fourth element has more to do with the public's complicity in accepting these idealized and sanitized representations. Surely, underlying the public's apparent gullibility was the desire not to be required to know the effects of bombing on innocent men, women, and children, as well as the infrastructure, culturally important sites, and the civil society.

Press Coverage of the Air Campaign

This raises the question of the role of the press. Tom Engelhardt, who has been highly critical of the failure of the mainstream press to cover the Iraq air war, argues that there should have been embedded reporters in the air force.[22] Attaching reporters to the air force would have provided Americans a clearer picture of the targets and the rationale for the targeting, but that alone would not necessarily have disabused them of the idealized image of air war. Indeed, to the extent that the camera would have dwelt on the awe-inspiring beauty, design, and advanced technology of the B-1 and the B-2, having reporters and camera crews assigned to the bases might have romanticized the air campaign, as was the case with the coverage of the air campaign in the Persian Gulf War.

What about the American reporters on the ground? Were they not obligated to bear witness to the damage caused by bombing? Editorial policy for the major American news outlets sanitized the pictures of casualties presented to the general public, but some offered more graphic images online. Many reporters and editors for US agencies acknowledged that they chose not to show graphic images that would "shock or revolt" their audiences. In fairness, some of this amounts to reasonable self-restraint rather than aiding and abetting propaganda. The decision, for instance, not to show the beheading of hostages seems entirely reasonable. But, the rationale in news agencies for withholding or suppressing information about civilian casualties was apparently driven not by a humanitarian concern for the dignity of the wounded, but by fear either of losing market share, or of being accused of being biased against the war. American journalists are aware that the military successfully promulgated the belief that the press lost the war in Vietnam by stirring up public sentiment against it.

Conclusion

The use of tactical bombardment for close air support in an urban war is at the furthest remove from the idealized imagery of the combat pilot rising to single-handed combat. The devolution of the imaginary air war from 1914 to 2004 is palpable to those aware of the history of both air wars and their representation. But it is not part of the mainstream reportage of the war. One reason for this is the general absence of historical knowledge among the American public. But another is that those engaged in the war do not wish the American public to be challenged in a moral sense by warfare for fear of both the political and military consequences if the public turns strongly against the war.

The need to sustain the mythic reality of warfare[23] in the hearts and minds of those on the home front accounts for all of the manipulation of information and images of the war, a manipulation devoted to: arousing fear of a "mushroom cloud" from an enemy who in reality was without either the weapons or the means of delivery (this a lingering effect of the Cold War mentality); acceptance of strategic bombing as moral and indeed humane (because of the sanitized representation of bombing in World War II); and ultimately the disappearance of the air war in reporting (a failure on the part of the press). It was necessary that we should imagine American air wars are essentially strategic, civilized, and restrained because of advanced technology. And it was necessary that we should fail to notice in the American representational repertoire reports of close air support against irregulars hidden in urban alleys and buildings. This form of warfare maximizes damage to property and puts civilians, not military target, at risk. With this most recent iteration of American air power, the American public has been doubly shielded from having to confront the realities of war, and has been complicit in accepting such a vision.

Notes

1 Steve Kull et al., *Misperceptions, the Media, and the Iraq War.* Program on International Policy Attitudes and Center for International and Security Studies at the University of Maryland (October 2, 2003). http://64.233.179.104/search?q=cache:y3mBJCObArYJ: www.pipa.org/OnlineReports/Iraq/Media_10_02_03_Report.pdf+Program+on+Inter national+Policy+Attitudes+Media+and+Iraq+report&hl=en&gl=us&ct=clnk&cd=2

2 Sam Gardiner, *Truth from These Podia: Summary of a Study of Strategic Influence, Perception Management, Strategic Information Warfare and Strategic Psychological Operation in Gulf II* (October 8, 2003). http://www.gwu.edu/~nsarchiv/NSAEBB/NSAEBB 177/Info%20Operations%20Roadmap%20Truth%20from%20These%20Podia.pdf.

3 Charles Lewis and Mark Reading Smith, "False Pretenses," Center for Public Integrity (January 2008). http://www.publicintegrity.org/WarCard/.

4 James F. Dunnigan and Austin Bay, *From Shield to Storm: High Tech Weapons, Military Strategy, and Coalition Warfare in the Persian Gulf* (New York: William Morrow and Company, 1992), 165.

5 *U.S. News and World Report* [staff], 275; "B-52s accounted for not quite 2 percent of all sorties, but dropped nearly 30 percent of all bomb tonnage." Dunnigan and Bay, 155; on effects on Iraqi ground troops in Persian Gulf War, 206; 288; General Norman Schwarzkopf with Peter Petre, *It Doesn't Take A Hero* (New York: Bantam Books, 1992), 430; on missions of B-52s: 60 B-52 sorties were flown from Europe, dropping 1000 tons of bombs. Dunnigan and Bay, 166.

6 *U.S. News and World Report* [staff], 241.

7 Quoted in John Milton Cooper, T*he Warrior and the Priest: Woodrow Wilson and Theodore Roosevelt* (Cambridge, Mass: Belknap Press of Harvard University Press, 1983), 310; See Woodrow Wilson, "prolegomenon" to peace note [circa November, 1916], in *The Papers of Woodrow Wilson,* ed. Arthur Link (Princeton, NJ: Princeton University Press, 1966, and following) vol. XL, 70–71.

8 Hilda Beatrice Hewlett, *Our Fighting Men* (Kettering, GB: T. Beaty Hart, n.d.), 6.

9 Maurer Maurer, ed. Col. Edgar S. Gorell, *The Final Report and a Tactical History, Vol I of The U.S. Air Service in World War I. 1921, 1948* (Washington, D.C.: United States Government Printing Office. 1978), 104–105.

10 See Clayton R. Koppes and Gregory D. Black, *Hollywood Goes to War: How Politics, Profits, and Propaganda Shaped World War II Movies* (Berkeley, CA: University of California Press, 1990), 78–80.

[11] Tom cruised from pretending to fly Tomcats to the moniker TomKat for his real union with Katie Holmes. The out-of-control stick jockey still seemed to be concerned mostly with personal performance and his gigantic ego when he boasted that he would eat the placenta of his baby, Suri, after she was born.

[12] Koppes and Black, 136–138; Thomas Doherty, *Projections of War: Hollywood, American Culture, and World War II* (New York: Columbia University Press, 1994), 5 *et infra*.

[13] Walter Lippmann, *Public Opinion* (1922; New York, NY: Free Press, MacMillan, 1965), 9.

[14] John Keegan, "The Radical at the Pentagon," *Vanity Fair* (February 2003), 127–129; 188.

[15] Vice President Dick Cheney. "Address to Conservative Political Action Conference" Arlington, Virginia (January 30, 2003). http://www.whitehouse.gov/news/releases/2003/01/20030130-16.html

[16] Tim Ripley, *Iraq Air War* (Pen and Sword Aviation, 2004), 61.

[17] Naomi Klein, *The Shock Doctrine: The Rise of Disaster Capitalism* (New York: Metropolitan Books, 2007), 332.

[18] Air Marshal Sir Timothy Garden, "A Commentator's View of Air Power's Role in Iraq 2003." Annual Air Power Conference (28 January 2004) http://www.tgarden.demon.co.uk/writings/articles/2004/040128airp.html.

[19] *Ibid.*

[20] Ripley, 100.

[21] Paul Boyer, *By the Bomb's Early Light: American Thought and Culture and the Dawn of the Atomic Age* (1985; University of North Carolina Press,1994), 3–27.

[22] Tom Engelhardt, "The Missing Air War in Iraq," *TomDispatch.com* (December 13, 2005). http://www.tomdispatch.com/post/42286/dahr_jamail_on_the_missing_air_war_in_iraq.

[23] Chris Hedges, *War is a Force that Gives Us Meaning* (New York: Anchor Books, 1993), 21.

Chapter 21

Embedded

The News of War and the War Over News

William Hoynes

US Senator Hiram Johnson's 1917 remark, "The first casualty when war comes is truth," has long been cliché. But the underlying insight in this quotable quip reminds us that the news media are a site of intense political contest during times of war. As the 2003 War in Iraq illustrates, the narratives and images that circulate in the news media are hard to separate from the war effort itself, as military planners see American news as one of the central battlegrounds where public attitudes toward war are molded. In this context, war reporting is both more and less than a "record" of what happened on the battlefield. War news reflects the dynamic relationship between media and military and the broader professional and cultural landscape within which journalists work. To understand war news, then, we need to begin by recognizing the political contest that places journalism so squarely at the center of the process of defining the meaning and significance of war.

While we often hear about "the media," it is important to remember that media are neither singular nor univocal. Major media pay a great deal of attention to each other, and elite papers such as the *New York Times* and *Washington Post* often define the news agenda for other news outlets, but there is a range of reporting even among the "mainstream media"—broadcast and cable networks, major daily newspapers, and national newsmagazines. In addition, alternative media, both domestic and international, are available, perhaps more than ever in the early 21st century, although their reach remains rather limited. When we identify basic tendencies in news coverage, we need not argue that all media, all the time—"The Media"—are the same.

At the same time, there is an often-striking similarity across news outlets, especially on television news. During the war in Iraq, cable news channels—CNN, Fox News, and MSNBC—despite rather small audiences, have played a central role in framing the national debate about the war. With their round-the-clock, 24/7 coverage and their apparently endless appetite for war commentary, the cable news channels played an extraordinarily important role in defining the parameters of news discourse for the North American public.

Looking Backward: World War I and News-as-Propaganda

Control of information has long been part of broader military strategy, and governments have long recognized the value of news for building and maintaining public support for war. One of the more illuminating, but largely forgotten, examples of this was the mobilization of US journalists during World War I to join the war effort, not with guns but with their typewriters. In April 1917, US President Woodrow Wilson signed Executive Order # 2594, which established the US Committee on Public Information (CPI). The CPI membership included the Secretary of State and the Secretary of War and was headed by a civilian, the well-known progressive journalist George Creel. The CPI's role was to wage a large-scale publicity campaign aimed at building public support for US involvement in World War I. The campaign was explicitly aimed at mobilizing public opinion and was waged across the range of available media at the time, involving, as Creel put it, "the printed word, the spoken word, motion pictures, the telegraph, the wireless, posters, sign boards, and every possible media."[1]

The work of the CPI represented a key moment in the development of the public relations industry in the United States, by providing a model of how to organize a multi-media campaign to mold public attitudes. The CPI strategy identified a broad and complex media environment as the arena for shaping public beliefs, in large measure by saturating that environment with messages supporting the war.

But the story of the CPI also raises some important and enduring questions about the relationship between government and media in times of war. George Creel understood that his job at the CPI was to build "national unity"—he used exactly this language—to most effectively support the war. (This is eerily familiar. In the wake of the terrorist attack on the World Trade Center on September 11, 2001, politicians and journalists also stressed the importance of national unity—with "United We Stand" slogans appearing on bumper stickers, window signs, and inside newspapers and magazines.) National unity was defined as a requirement during a time of national emergency to defeat a common enemy. In the context of World War I, many reporters saw it as their patriotic duty to use their journalistic skills and training to actively build this sense of national unity.

Enduring Questions: The War in Iraq

The story of the CPI during World War I may seem like a quaint reminder of the way things used to be before journalism emerged as a profession, with a guiding norm, "objectivity," that would insulate the news from such propagandistic purposes.[2] But the War in Iraq demonstrates that we continue to face a set of enduring questions about media and war, including:

- How should news cover war?

- How should military planners handle journalists?

- Where does dissent fit at a time when national unity is emphasized?

- Is it possible for news to cover war without glorifying war?

The post-September 11 era in the United States has been a time of great political conformity. The news media have played a central role in defining the boundaries of reasonable opinion, emphasizing national resolve and unity, legitimizing a discourse that likens dissent to a soft form of treason, and spreading fear, including routine references to the color-coded "terror alert" level on the cable news channels. It is this broader cultural context that we need to keep in mind as we analyze news coverage of the war.

While the dilemmas for journalists covering the War in Iraq are similar to those faced by reporters during previous wars, news coverage of the War in Iraq had several distinctive features. What's different about news of the War in Iraq is related both to the development of new media technologies and to new norms emerging in the news business.

Media critics have referred to Vietnam as the "living room war"[3] to emphasize the ways that American citizens saw daily war images on their television sets for the first time during Vietnam. But the War in Iraq pushed this to a new level. The War in Iraq, more than any previous war, was reported in real time, "live," by reporters on the ground with US and British troops. The sheer speed of the transmission of news reports, with journalists filing stories full of choppy images via video phone as they rode through the desert, helped to change the pace of how citizens in the United States experienced the war.

In addition, televised coverage of the War in Iraq was not limited to the evening or late-night newscasts. In this era of 24-hour cable news, war news followed the saturation coverage approach that has become the norm for cable news. Taking cues from coverage of O.J. Simpson and Monica Lewinsky, the cable networks devoted virtually all day and night to coverage of, and commentary about, the war. In this fast-paced context, prior constraints imposed by the news cycle—in which news was gathered and produced on a specific deadline for the evening news or morning newspaper—no longer hold. With cable news channels competing to fill up 24 hours of news each day, the news cycle literally never ends.[4] However, news organizations do not have the resources to gather enough news to fill this enormous news hole. As a result, cable news channels rely on vast amounts of commentary, with pundits looking for something new to say when they have no new information to report. This is one of the reasons why war coverage is often so full of speculation; especially during the early days of the Iraq war, unconfirmed reports about weapons of mass destruction and the whereabouts of Saddam Hussein were a regular part of cable news fare.

The role of journalists on the ground was also distinctive during the Iraq war and contrasts sharply with journalistic activity during the 1991 Gulf War. While reporters were kept at a distance from the battlefield during the Gulf War, given very little access to military units, and forced to do their reporting almost exclusively from US military bases in Saudi Arabia or on military organized "press pool" junkets, hundreds of US reporters were "embedded" with troops during the war in Iraq. While embedded, these reporters traveled, and were protected by, specific military units and reported the war largely from the perspective of the troops with whom they traveled. Critics have argued that the embedded-reporter program was a brilliant strategic move by the Pentagon, since it pre-empted adversarial reporting that results from denying access to the battlefield and, at the same time, gave journalists, who rode on tanks with soldiers from Kuwait to Baghdad, an active role in the war effort.[5]

Reporting War for a US Audience

One of the most striking features of news coverage of the War in Iraq was its clear *national* perspective. This was most clear in the use of pronouns by reporters and commentators, who frequently employed an "us versus them" framework, emphasizing that US news media were part of the American team. Especially in the early days of the war, many journalists were quite explicit about foregrounding their national identity, using the language of "we" in discussing the goals and strategies of the US military and "they" when referring to Saddam Hussein and the Iraqi regime.

The news media also adopted military language in their coverage. Cable shows were full of journalists talking about "softening up," "mopping up," or "taking out"—all euphemisms for various forms of military action—and reporters frequently used the language of "the enemy." Such an approach, one that talks the military talk and implies a tough attitude, may give viewers a sense that they are getting an insider's view of the war. But it is a powerful, albeit subtle, form of framing the news to systematically highlight some aspects of the war while neglecting others.

For example, one of the consequences of the "us vs. them" approach is an almost exclusive focus on the deaths of US soldiers, with comparatively little coverage of Iraqi military or civilian casualties. Certainly, the death of US service men and women is significant news for US news media. But the nationalistic coverage was remarkably disproportionate in its definition of whose deaths were newsworthy. Even when military casualty rates were as high as 300 to 1 in the early weeks of the war, the deaths of "enemy" soldiers never took center stage in the US press. The nationalistic tone of the coverage emphasized the tragedy of American deaths, but failed to emphasize the equally profound tragedy of Iraqi's killed by American troops.

As the conflict dragged on and the number of US deaths rose to more than 700 by April 2004, US news media focused significant attention on American casualties. ABC's "Nightline" dedicated its entire April 30, 2004 program to reading the names and showing photographs of all of the American soldiers who had died during the War in Iraq. When the politically conservative owners of Sinclair Broadcasting refused to air this edition of "Nightline," calling it biased reporting for over-emphasizing the costs of the war, a public controversy erupted over the reporting of US military deaths.

Controversy also swirled around the US Defense Department's policy that bans news photographs of military coffins with the remains of military personnel returning from war zones, a ban first imposed during the 1991 Gulf War. The Pentagon ban was no doubt aimed at sanitizing war coverage, with the military trying to keep images of the human costs of war at a distance from the US public. The ban was upheld as legal after a post-Gulf War law suit,[6] and the policy was universally respected but rarely discussed until the *Seattle Times* published a photo of flag-draped coffins on its front page on April 18, 2004. After the *Seattle Times* front-page photograph and the posting on the website thememoryhole.org of more than 200 photographs of coffins of war dead (obtained from the US Air Force through a Freedom of Information Act request), the Pentagon reaffirmed the ban in the face of public criticism—and fired the photographer of the *Times* photo, a woman from the Seattle area who had worked for a military contractor in Kuwait.

Even as debate raged about the appropriate tone and content of news reports of American casualties, reports of Iraqi casualties remained marginal in the US news media. Given the scale of the death and destruction in Iraq—from US bombs during the first phase of the war and in continuing battles across Iraq during the occupation—the limited focus on Iraqi casualties is a stunning reminder of the national loyalty of the US media and stands in sharp contrast to the images broadcast daily on television news programming in Europe and the Arab world. When the prestigious British medical journal, *The Lancet*, published an October 2004 study concluding that the number of Iraqi deaths from the US-led invasion was probably around 100,000, the US news media largely ignored the study. In contrast, the British press gave the study's findings much more attention, with some newspapers running front page stories about the estimates of Iraqi deaths.[7]

The Militarization of Television

Throughout the Iraq war and the subsequent occupation, military leaders played a leading role in the dramatic news coverage. Daily briefings from US Central Command were a regular feature on the cable channels and most information about the war came from the US military or reporters embedded with US forces.

But television news did much more than report official statements of military leaders. The military presence on US television was even more pronounced, as a virtual army of former military officers took on prominent roles on national and local television news. Retired military officers seemed omnipresent on television news, interpreting troop movements, battle plans, and military strategy. These ex-military officers were hired as consultants, not journalists, but they regularly appeared on camera, helping to give newscasts a militarized tone. MSNBC went so far as to hire a former general to staff its "war room," backing him up with colorful maps that tracked the US military's march to Baghdad.

News coverage included more than just former generals as lively personalities who gave viewers an insider's view of war and military strategy. Television news also focused sustained attention on the weapons of war. During the first Gulf War in 1991, television news had a video game quality to it, with pictures of the precision targeting and delivery of weapons.[8] During the War in Iraq, television news once again defined weaponry as a newsworthy topic, reporting on everything from what specific weapons look like and the training required for their use to their power and accuracy. News coverage regularly included images and simulations of military equipment, and reporters treated viewers to detailed reports about the use of Bradley fighting vehicles, Abrams tanks, and Apache helicopters, among other military resources.

The focus on weapons and, more generally, the technological apparatus of war, produced war coverage with an entertainment-like quality. Combining aspects of the feature film—where high-tech special effects often produce a kind of "shock and awe," the Pentagon's official name for the air strikes in Baghdad—with the qualities of the video game—where players fire weapons and destroy targets in high-resolution animated environments—the news adopted a familiar aesthetic that made the programming fit comfortably with standard television fare.

War as Sport

Reporting on sporting events, especially football, often employs war metaphors, including "battles" on the field and "generals" in the huddle. During the war in Iraq, however, this relationship was reversed. War coverage adopted the conventions of sports coverage, depicting the war as a big, albeit high-stakes, game.

Indeed, television news in the days leading up to the bombing of Baghdad in March 2003 resembled the extended pre-game show for the Super Bowl. All of the cable news stations had serious-sounding theme music that led into and out of each segment, along with computer-generated graphics and images of the key players in the conflict (especially President Bush and Saddam Hussein) that gave the event, the impending war, a program identity. The news channels each gave their war coverage a catchy title, with "Showdown with Saddam" and "March to War" prominently displayed on the screen. (When the war began, some of the news channels adopted the Pentagon's official title, "Operation Iraqi Freedom," for their news coverage of the war.)

The commentators for the war resembled the regular sports commentators: former players (retired military officers) served as the experts, breaking down the "game plan" and giving regular assessments of the game's "score." Reporters outside the Pentagon, State Department, and White House played the role of sideline reporter, providing updates on the views of the coaches and players (political and military leaders and soldiers), interpreting the day's events, and forecasting what would happen next. Fox News went so far as to run a "Head to Head: US vs. Iraq" feature, providing comparative information on the military strength of the two nations in a way that invoked the match-up reporting that regularly appears prior to major sporting events.

This kind of coverage does more than simply make war seem palatable by domesticating war through the familiar language of sports. The reframing of war as a game, to be analyzed in strategic terms that emphasize winners and losers of that game, serves to simplify and narrow our understanding of the complex issues and events that surrounded the build up to war, the active combat phase, and the aftermath.

War as Human Interest Story

Perhaps the most substantive coverage of the War in Iraq focused on the American soldiers fighting the war. News coverage of the War in Iraq made the soldiers in the field the heroes of the television coverage, often noting quite explicitly that the young men and women fighting the war should be recognized for their skill and courage. There were good reasons for paying careful attention to the people who were fighting—and killing and dying during the war—especially since war news has historically neglected soldiers in the field, instead focusing on political and military decision makers.

This war coverage was unique—and was widely touted as such—because of the heavy emphasis on the lives and experiences of US soldiers. The embedded reporter program gave journalists daily access to soldiers. In sharing daily experience with these soldiers, the "embeds" were privy to, and often provided viewers and readers with a glimpse of, the hopes and fears of US military men and women as they prepared for and engaged in combat.

However, the emphasis on the experience of US soldiers was often wrapped in a celebratory package. News coverage often seemed to be equal parts reporting and cheerleading for "our side." As pledges to "support our troops" became a political requirement in the United States, with even critics of the war working hard to make sure that they communicated their support for the troops, news media played a vital role in emphasizing the support-our-troops message. Coverage was often zoomed so narrowly, telling stories of soldiers who the embedded reporters came to know and admire, that the reporting often lacked any broader context.

In addition, news outlets also emphasized their own reporters' experiences as part of the human interest drama of the war. During the most active military phase of the war, in March and April 2003, news coverage often exhibited a self-congratulatory tone, as journalists patted each other on the back for their good work under difficult circumstances. Certainly, many reporters faced hardship during their time embedded with troops, and several US reporters died tragically during the War in Iraq. But the focus on embedded reporters as courageous adventurers obscured the goals and tactics of the news management strategy that motivated the Pentagon's embedded reporter program and, at the same time, effectively marginalized the reporters trying to cover the war from outside the official framework.

News as a Weapon of War

The practice of embedding journalists with American troops was part of a broader Pentagon plan aimed at building and maintaining public support within the United States for the Iraq War. But US military efforts to shape the content of news media have been even more extensive within post-invasion Iraq. Even as the State Department and US Agency for International Development spend money to support the development of a western-style, independent press in Iraq, the fledgling news media in Iraq have been the centerpiece of the Pentagon's information campaign focused on influencing Iraqi public opinion.

Even before the US bombing of Baghdad started in March 2003, the US military has tried to exert control over the Iraqi news media, beginning with the Commander Solo aircraft that flew over Baghdad several hours a day, broadcasting pro-American newscasts over Iraqi radio and television. In the months after the US-led invasion of Iraq, US officials publicly touted the importance of press freedom in Iraq, but the Coalition Provisional Authority, which administered the US occupation of Iraq until June 2004, placed controls on the content of Iraqi media and closed down several independent Iraqi-run newspapers including Moqtada al-Sadr's weekly *al-Hawza*, citing its inflammatory stories about the US occupation.

With US troops facing a growing insurgency throughout 2005, the Pentagon intensified its information campaign, using media as a weapon in the battle for Iraqi public opinion. The US military's Information Operations Task Force in Baghdad has led a multi-pronged campaign focused primarily on Iraqi media. According to the *Los Angeles Times*, the task force "has purchased an Iraqi newspaper and taken control of a radio station, and was using them to channel pro-American messages to the Iraqi public. Neither is identified as a military mouthpiece."[9] In addition, the *L.A. Times* report revealed that the US military, working with a private contractor, covertly paid Iraqi newspapers to publish stories that promoted US interests and paid regular stipends to Iraqi journalists to write pro-US news stories.

Efforts to control media in Iraq and the covert program aimed at disseminating pro-US stories through the Iraqi press are two sides of the same coin, and are indicative of the continuing role of censorship and propaganda in wartime. In this continuing war over news, independent journalism is a very dangerous profession, and more than sixty journalists were killed on duty in Iraq between 2003 and the end of 2005, making Iraq the deadliest site for reporters in more than twenty years.[10]

Explaining News Coverage

It is hard to underestimate the effectiveness of military public relations staff in shaping the news of war in Iraq in 2003. Indeed, the Pentagon's embedded reporter program was an essential part of the military's well-organized plan to prevail both on the ground and in how the war was represented, in the war over news. But journalists were not simply passive recipients of military spin. Several key factors, some broadly cultural and others relating to the profession of journalism, help to explain why news coverage looked and felt the way it did.

First, the broader ideological climate in the United States in the post-September 11 era emphasized a narrow version of patriotism. In this climate, news outlets and individual journalists did not want to be perceived as undermining the war effort with critical reporting. Secondly, news outlets responded to what they thought would be popular with the US audience, seeking to provide news coverage that would please and certainly not offend the public. When the "Donahue" show was cancelled on MSNBC, for example, programming executives indicated that "Donahue" was out of touch with the marketplace, noting that "Donahue" was "a difficult public face for NBC in a time of war."[11] In short, a cheerleading, support-the-troops tone was defined as responding to audience demand in an industry that is, after all, dependent upon selling audiences to advertisers.

Core professional norms of journalism were also at work here. War reporters, both in the United States and abroad, seeking efficient and legitimate sources of information, relied almost exclusively upon a limited set of sources, largely from in and around the US military, and war coverage reflected this narrow lens. In addition, the event-orientation of the news media focused the attention of reporters on the public statements of officials (who have the cultural power to define happenings such as press conferences as "events") and developments on the ground in Iraq. In this reportorial framework, there was little room for critical perspectives on the war's aims or justification. Even when hundreds of thousands demonstrated against the war in February 2003, news covered the spectacle but paid little attention to the substance of the opposition to the war. The embedded reporter program, as we have seen, was remarkably effective at focusing attention on the professionalism, commitment, and humanity of US soldiers and building solidarity between reporters and the military.

Finally, the widespread support for the war among political elites made it unlikely that news would include critical perspectives in its coverage. Since the norms of objectivity direct journalists to the two political parties to maintain balance in their coverage, the support for the war by the leadership of the Democratic Party virtually guaranteed that news would include little criticism of the war. Only during the campaign for the Democratic Party's presidential nomination in the winter of 2004 did leading Democrats begin to speak critically about President Bush's policies in Iraq, and these criticisms opened up some space within the major news media for a broader discussion of the war.

Conclusion

The idea that citizens should not speak out against war once a war has begun is peculiar. It suggests that people should fall in line, and that those who don't are not sufficiently patriotic. The US news media helped to nourish this belief, in large measure by their narrow coverage of the War in Iraq. But times of conflict are precisely the times when we need wide-ranging discussion, not the stifling of debate. During the war in Iraq, the major centers of American journalism largely failed to provide citizens with the wide-ranging debate and discussion that democratic societies need and, in failing, provided a nationalistic and entertainment-oriented lens on the war that gave us a view of the struggles of American soldiers but did little to help citizens understand the complex meaning and consequences of the war in Iraq.

Notes

[1] Quoted in Stuart Ewen, *PR! A Social History of Spin* (New York: Basic Books, 1996), 112.

[2] For a valuable discussion of the development of objectivity in American journalism, see Michael Schudson, *Discovering the News* (New York: Basic Books, 1978).

[3] See Michael J. Arlen, *Living Room War* (New York: Viking Press, 1969). The best scholarly account of news coverage of the Vietnam War is Daniel Hallin, *The "Uncensored War"* (New York: Oxford University Press, 1986).

[4] See Bill Kovach and Tom Rosenstiel, *Warp Speed* (New York: Century Foundation Press, 1999).

[5] For further discussion of embedded journalists in Iraq, see Lance Bennett, "The Perfect Storm? American Media in Iraq" *OpenDemocracy*, August 28, 2003; and Amy Goodman and David Goodman, *The Exception to the Rulers* (New York: Hyperion, 2004).

[6] See John R. MacArthur, *Second Front: Censorship and Propaganda in the Gulf War* (Berkeley: University of California, Press, 1993).

[7] See Lila Guterman, "Dead Iraqis: Why an Estimate was Ignored," *Columbia Journalism Review* (March/April 2005), 11.

[8] See William Hoynes, "War as Video Game," in Cynthia Peters, ed., *Collateral Damage* (Boston: South End Press, 1992).

[9] Mark Mazzetti and Borzou Daragahi. "US Military Covertly Pays to Run Stories in Iraqi Press," *Los Angeles Times* (November 30, 2005), A1.

[10] *Attacks on the Press in 2005: A World Survey by the Committee to Protect Journalists*, 2006. Online at: http://www.cpj.org/attacks05/pages05/aop05index.html.

[11] Quoted in Rick Ellis, "The Surrender of MSNBC," CommonDreams.org, February 26, 2003.

Chapter 22

A Spanish Summer Spreads Around the World

Hoop Dreams and Globalization

Graeme Metcalf

*I*n the January 25, 2010 edition of *Sports Illustrated,* Kevin Collison, a player for the NBA's Oklahoma City Thunder in speaking about teammate and young burgeoning superstar Kevin Durant states, "It's kind of refreshing, someone with that much talent and ability, a guy who's been on the cover of magazines since he was 18, but all he wants to do is play basketball and hang out. He's not trying to rule the world or become a global marketing icon—he just wants to play ball." While this seemingly innocuous comment may be lost on some, to others it is understood as a not so discreet insult directed at LeBron James, arguably the most popular player in the NBA since Michael Jordan, the star who in many respects saved the league and is primarily responsible for its international influence and global footprint. Much like McDonald's and Starbucks have endured and negotiated questions surrounding their relationship to America's dominant ideology and mainstream culture, professional sports leagues based in the U.S. have increasingly been examined as propagating

American values through the stars the league employs and celebrates. A young fan of Lebron James in Taipei, Krakow, or Istanbul may unwittingly become complicit with a political position or "way of life" through endorsing and consuming him.

James is at the center of the global production of a sport text (an NBA game), and provokes the consequences of local (outside the U.S.) consumption of that text. The ever-expanding reach of global broadcasting signifies the potential for people, places, and identities to be conveyed through sports broadcasting, allowing the televised sport text to be repurposed as a cultural text. Although Mark Falcous and Joseph Maguire assert that texts "do not possess the capacity to dictate what audiences think, they do hold the potential to construct agendas, frame issues within certain parameters, and impose and reinforce hierarchies, while simultaneously cutting off alternative interpretations."[1]

Within the emergence of globalized sports broadcasting possibilities, the NBA has surfaced as a prominent force, capitalizing on globalization's process by which the people of the world are unified through a similar interest often in aid of the substantiation of Western hegemony. For example, media mogul Rupert Murdoch's move into televised sport in 1995 provided evidence to support the claim that the relationship between globalization and media had rendered national geographical boundaries in sport all but irrelevant.[2] Murdoch's move provoked discussion examining the globalization of sport, and in particular, the many benefits the league stood to reap including merchandise sales, sponsorship, fan idolatry, and news dissemination.[3] Interestingly, this argumentation on Murdoch is similar in tone, if not content, to Jack Banks's examination of MTV's move towards an international audience. For Banks, overwhelmingly the international outposts of MTV reflect American music and stars. He argues the programing system is two-fold. First, the programing lends itself to the interests of transnational major-label record companies specializing in Western acts within the genres of pop, rock, and hip hop.[4] Banks further argues that the relationship between record companies and MTV—with an international reach—allows the two to jointly ensure the direction and popularity of "endorsed" artists or bands globally.[5]

Of particular relevance to the success of stars—whether music, sport, or Hollywood—is fan idolatry, and while MTV is able to heavily program Western artists, these stars must also resonate with international viewers in order to suture MTV into the viewing practices of an international audience. The relationship between fandom, consumption, and major cultural institutions such as music, as well as less dominant institutions such as comic books or science fiction, has long been examined. However, while studies have been conducted examining the *internationalization*—rather than globalization—of sport and national identity, there remains a dearth of research examining the relationship between fandom, consumption, and sport, and the potentiality for problematic global consequences.

Contrary to this lack is Cornel Sandvoss's informed look at fandom and English football in his text, *A Game of Two Halves: Football, Television and Globalization*. In referencing Pierre Bourdieu's seminal text, *Distinction* (1984), Sandvoss draws a connection between fandom and taste, employing Bourdieu's framework of consumption as a structuring principle articulating one's social position and identity; in effect introducing the correlation between one's consumption habits and their attendant social and cultural capital as a result.[6] In explaining fandom, Sandvoss notes that to be a fan is to engage in a series of acts of often media-based consumption;[7] fans became consumers of the source of their idolatry. The connection between social and cultural capital and the ideology of consumption is explained through the relationship between the consumption of popular culture and globalization and cultural imperialism. The consuming of an ideologically specific sport text such as the NBA is able to both confirm the seductive nature of popular culture and provide an opening through which dominant culture is able to enact its imperialist designs through the mechanisms provided by globalization. Moreover, a link is drawn between sport fandom and the positioning of international spectators to willingly or unwillingly reproduce "American values" through the consumption of NBA superstars.

It is here, in relation to the NBA, that the buying and selling of ideology succeeds through the seductive nature of celebrity and consumerist desire. The mediated sport text has been long understood as having a primary role in the production and reproduction of dominant social ideals. In this global incarnation of the same process we are able to recognize the intersection at which U.S. dominant culture comes to be produced and reproduced through a carefully constructed and definitively ideological sport text.

The Jordan Era and Dream Team

Beginning with David Stern taking over as league commissioner in 1984, the NBA has used television and commerce to grow the game as a globally consumed product fueled by television and marketing.[8] Stern made basketball into a global, cultural, entertainment-based "spectacularization"[9] beginning with the league's selling of, and reveling in, the rivalry between the Boston Celtics' Larry Bird and the Los Angeles Lakers' Ervin "Magic" Johnson. The decade before Stern took over saw the league stagnant, plagued with various drug and alcohol scandals while predominantly ignored on television, and with little in the way of national markets. Since the time of his takeover, franchises have increased in value from $15 million to $300 million, gross revenue from licensed products has increased from $10 million to $3 billion, and league revenue is up from $118 million to $3 billion.[10] The marked increases in franchise value and product revenue were the result of the benefits of the "Jordan Era" beginning in 1984, shortly after Stern's takeover. The arrival of Michael Jordan provided not only a new star but a star that Nike recognized as being potentially marketable on a global scale, a significant revelation in the NBA's desire to communicate with the rest of the world through the context of basketball and also, importantly, through the adoration of its stars or icons. Nike used Jordan as a means to spread basketball to previously undiscovered global markets.[11] At a time when global connectivity was exploding and the world seemed to be looking for a hero, Jordan became bigger than the sport,[12] proving to be the star able to grow the league outside the U.S. through expansion—teams were awarded to Vancouver and Toronto beginning play during the 1995–6 season—as well as through international appeal, as Jordan became perhaps the biggest, most widely known sport star since soccer's Pele. Couching Jordan's impact on "the bottom line" or profit, it becomes overwhelmingly clear just how literally valuable the man was, and continues to be. For example, in 1998 *Fortune Magazine* calculated Jordan's impact on the economy—aka "The Jordan Effect"—to be roughly ten billion dollars. Unsurprisingly, the primary beneficiaries of Jordan's popularity were the NBA and Nike. According to *Fortune,* Jordan's impact on the league totaled 3.1 billion in revenue generated through attendance, television deals, and merchandise sales. Equally staggering is Jordan's overall impact on Nike, estimated at 5 billion dollars through his Air Jordan sneakers and his Jordan-related Nike merchandise (timewarner.com).

Here Comes the Dream Team: Look Out, World!

As vital as Jordan's presence proved in providing the NBA with the necessary inroads to expand into the global marketplace, it was the 1992 Summer Olympics in Barcelona that offered the NBA a world stage for its biggest stars. Prior to 1992, the Olympics were an amateur affair. However, the preceding 1988 Olympic basketball tournament saw that status come into question after the U.S. lost to the Soviet Union in the gold medal game. This loss was as much political as it was sporting, as the twentieth century had seen sport become increasingly international while also pointedly political in tone. Various 1980s Olympic boycotts took on a political role, ostensibly "politicizing" an event colloquially understood as promoting global relationships, the spirit of fair competition, and general goodwill. Moreover, boycotts were largely facilitated through television, jointly acting as both propaganda and commercialism. In 1984, for example, the transmitting of ideology came through visual nationalism and culturally specific revelry while persistent advertising contributed to the subsequent financial gains of the many American companies clamoring for those lucrative advertising opportunities.

The key event which led to the NBA participation was most certainly the loss to the Soviet Union, but the build-up to the inclusion of professionals playing in the Olympics may have begun as early as 1972 when the United States lost to the Soviet Union in the Olympic gold medal men's basketball game. Before 1972, the U.S. had won the previous seven Olympic gold medals and the end of U.S. domination in basketball came to mean two things: first, basketball was now being played and understood on a more global scale, becoming more popular; and secondly, the United States was now in the position of needing to regain their dominance. While the 1972 loss can be explained away as an aberration— one team "just having their day"—more telling is the U.S. loss in 1988, as it came at a time when the game was rapidly gaining popularity.

The inclusion in the 1992 Olympics of the NBA's biggest stars and most iconic players, known as the Dream Team, provided global exposure to a sport that had already begun to take off in global popularity. Led by Jordan, Magic Johnson, and Larry Bird, the Dream Team won all its games by an average of forty-four points, on their way to gold in Barcelona, and as a result of the team's commanding the interest and fandom of a global audience it is understandable that sport has been referred to as the "new Hollywood." Of particular pertinence here is the relationship that developed between the Olympics and advertising in regards to the inclusion of professional stars, many of whom arrived with a number of sponsorship deals already in place. According to Lawrence Wenner, the Dream Team's presence saw the sponsorship and advertising of the Olympics become "dirty," or parasitic.[13] For Wenner, "dirt" refers to "the cultural borrowing that allows one cultural entity to adopt the logic of another."[14] This is consequential in that Hartley argues the mainstream ideas, or dominant ideologies, expressed in televised sport simultaneously reproduce celebrations of heroism, equality, and commitment[15] creating a fluid system in which American nationalism and patriotism are reproduced in the consumption of these larger-than-life stars. The consumption of the Dream Team compels a cultural borrowing in which a viewer seduced by the spectacle may unwittingly adopt the logic—the beliefs—central to American capitalism. In effect demonstrative of Rowe's processes of *culturalization* and *mediatization*, the cultural borrowing of the meaning of the Dream Team is simultaneous with the infiltration of American capitalist culture, turning the consumption of a basketball game, including its stars and its spectacle, into a meaningful experience laden with specialized symbols that despite arriving on the television screens of a diverse international audience work to produce a response reproducing a homogeneous ideology within the meaning of the sport text, or game. Sport is able to act interchangeably with advertising and consumption, at once connecting audiences to its text while collapsing traditional boundaries of space and time, the local, national, and international audience all consuming the same text and in much the same way. This is especially important in realizing that the NBA is now seen on television in at least 212 countries across 128 networks and forty-two languages and reaching an audience of 750 million people (www.nba.com).

Globalization has resulted in drastic increases in NBA revenue as international customers now comprise nearly fifty percent of merchandise sales. Further, the Internet has helped spread the popularity of the NBA brand: half of NBA.com traffic is from outside the U.S. and the league's TV deals include over 100 countries. Significant global markets targeted by the NBA include Asia and Africa where official NBA offices have opened. Key to the league's reach is the conducting of basketball clinics under the title of "NBA Cares," an operation that has so far taken place in Africa and Asia. According to Commissioner Stern, the league is actively eyeing other potential markets as well. As Stern explains, 2010 "will also see us opening offices in India and in the Middle East, because the ultimate compliment to our players is that the world is really embracing our game and the way it's played."[16]

Globalization and the NBA

Scott Howard-Cooper of NBA.com has recently (March 2010) revisited those Barcelona Olympics on the eve of the Dream Team's 2010 induction into the Basketball Hall of Fame. He concludes that the inclusion of the best basketball players in the world in the 1992 Olympics prompted the rest of the world to play catch-up—to increase funding to basketball programs both grassroots and professional in order to develop the type of players they had just witnessed so easily defeating their national teams, and comically so in some cases. While the drastic imbalance between the U.S. and the rest of the world has closed with Yugoslavia winning the gold medal at the 2002 World Championships and Spain duplicating the accomplishment in 2006, what has gone mostly unexamined are the political or economic ramifications of that summer in Spain almost twenty years ago.

Central to the NBA's global expansion is a symbiotic relationship between the league's business model and the continual arrival of players from outside the United States. Foreign players are a key component of successful global expansion. This is a marked break from a tradition in which foreign athletes played bit parts. Central to the NBA landscape now are Steve Nash (Canada), Yao Ming (China), Dirk Nowiztki (Germany), and Tony Parker (France). Moreover, according to NBA.com there are eighty-three foreign players from thirty-six countries, and nine out of ten NBA teams have at least one international player led by the Milwaukee Bucks with seven. The global initiative of the league's business model is certainly reflected by the number of foreign players on NBA rosters. Foreign players represent eighty of the 430 roster positions on NBA teams.[17] Perhaps the most demonstrative statistic reveals that on the sixteen teams who qualified for the 2007 playoffs, sixty foreign players hailed from twenty-eight countries while nine international players ultimately played in the finals.[18] The NBA has played exhibition games in a number of Asian cities, including Beijing and Taipei, as well as informal "pick-up games" in Athens, Madrid, Rome, Istanbul, and London. The NBA plans to hold its first regular season game outside North America during the 2011/12 season, in London. Proponents of globalization argue the understood merits of a world collapsed onto a screensaver in Canada, India, or Israel; however, opponents argue that the overwhelming, ubiquitous global presence of U.S.-owned films, television programs, brands, and fast food franchises is one of the negative results of a smaller, quicker world.[19] Missing from the above list is the NBA, despite the league's now obvious status as a burgeoning global industry whose reach is seemingly without restriction.

There is clearly no denying how significant the sport has become from a global financial, consumerist, and cultural standpoint. And to this effect, in his essay "Globalization of Basketball: Examining the Globalization of Basketball Financially and Culturally" Jay Wachtel reflects David Andrews's claims that basketball is a "legitimate cultural industry" that has replaced manufacturing as a global product.[20] It is tough to argue this notion when one considers the league's staggering financial success, as well as the number of households in which the league is now to be found. The popularity of the league's stars has created a condition allowing scholars to critically harness the game's popularity, examining, among other issues, the global social, political, and economic impact of the NBA. This examination may best use the league's television reach as a starting point, a reach extending in over forty-two different languages to 212 countries around the world.[21] The importance of these numbers is reiterated nicely by sociologist Anthony Giddens, who in describing globalization as "the intensification of world-wide relations which link distant localities in such a way that local happenings are shaped by events occurring many miles away"[22] allows a reframing of any argument that might suggest the NBA's reach is simply business. Giddens reads the league's reach as reflecting the transmission of ideology and the "American Dream." As Giddens describes it, globalization permits the bringing together of distant places, where people and communities draw on the same content and encounter the same signs and symbols, each loaded with specific ideological content. And given that a signal effect of globalization is the elimination of cultural distinctions—or difference—a by-product of a globalized American corporation may be the reproduction of the ideology of that corporation.

Globalization and Basketball Imperialism

If globalization means the dilution of a literal space into a global or mediated one in which we all draw from the same culture industry, reading the same best sellers, watching the same blockbusters, drinking coffee from identical paper cups adorned with the same logo, the growth of the NBA and its relationship to the culture industry may mean we all watch the same superstar basketball players dunk and block the same kinds of shots. The sociologist Zygmunt Bauman has conceived of a model that enables an understanding of one of the more discreet or naturalized strategies that the NBA has employed in branding itself as desirable on a global level. For Bauman, globalization has created a hierarchy of those able to travel to outside destinations—tourists—that those who remain fixed to their homeland—

vagabonds.[23] When the process of globalization redefines physical distance so that it is no longer an obstacle to experience, the NBA experience can take place anywhere, a state of affairs reminiscent of Roland Barthes's *Mythologies* (1957). Barthes reveals how dominant culture's materials are used to exert influence and ultimately power over others. Seen in Barthesian light, the NBA has become a myth that plays to universal desire.

At this point we are able to synthesize the relationship between the NBA, popular culture, and globalization and cultural imperialism. Falcous and Maguire examine the NBA's presence in Great Britain, for example, through the broadcasting of "NBA 99," a half-hour magazine-format television program.[24] The program includes highlights, a "star" player feature, a plays-of-the-week segment, and a "destination USA" segment in which the home city of a team would be profiled.[25] Encoded with visual and textual messages lending credibility to the league, "NBA 99" is understood as a cultural text in which the league is constructed as "world class."[26] Accordingly, the "Americanness" of the NBA is "reinforced by highlighting the social and cultural contexts of teams, and conveying dominant readings of the US" to viewers.[27]

It is to be hoped that understanding global cultural economy and popular culture will inform cultural practice in a way as to enable people to construct their own strategies of resistance against the hegemonic practices that continue to infect both global and local popular cultures and societies. The NBA has certainly proved successful in capitalizing on the opportunities for global success that globalization has provided. As boundaries continue to blur and connectivity continues to develop there is no way of knowing where the NBA will arrive next. Given the consistent spreading of the game, however, and more importantly, perhaps, given the vast expansion of the league, the brand, and the stars themselves, it is conceivable to believe that the National Basketball Association could soon be reshaped, renamed, and mythologized in wholly new ways. Meanwhile, although they have been asked to comment on the potentially problematic effects of their league or brand on a global scale, NBA mega-stars like Michael Jordan, Kobe Bryant, and LeBron James have been reluctant to participate in any serious discussion.

Notes

[1] Mark Falcous and Joseph Maguire, "Imaging 'America': the NBA and Local–Global Mediascapes," *International Review for the Sociology of Sport* 41 (2006), 63.

[2] Brian Stoddart, "Convergence: Sport on the Information Superhighway," in David Rowe, ed., *Critical Readings: Sport, Culture and the Media* (Berkshire: Open University Press, 2004), 328.

[3] Ibid.

[4] Jack Banks, "MTV and the Globalization of Popular Culture," *International Communication Gazette* 59: 1 (1997), 53.

[5] Banks, "MTV," 54.

[6] Cornel Sandvoss, *A Game of Two Halves: Football, Television and Globalisation* (London: Routledge, 2003), 19–20.

[7] Sandvoss, 17.

[8] David L. Andrews, "Disneyization, Debord, and the Integrated NBA Spectacle," *Social Semiotics* 16: 1 (April 2006), 91.

[9] Andrews, "Disneyization," 97.

[10] Andrews, "Disneyization," 91.

[11] David L. Andrews, Ben Carrington, Steven J. Jackson, and Zbigniew Mazur, "Jordan-scapes: A Preliminary Analysis of the Global Popular," *Sociology of Sport Journal* 13 (1996), 432.

[12] Ibid.

[13] Lawrence A. Wenner, "One Part Alcohol, One Part Sport, One Part Dirt, Stir Gently: Beer Commercials and Television Sports," in L.R. Vande Berg and Lawrence A. Wenner, eds., *Television Criticisms: Approaches and Applications* (New York: Longman, 1991), 12.

[14] Lawrence A. Wenner, "The Dream Team, Communicative Dirt, and Marketing Synergy: USA Basketball and Cross Merchandising in Television Commercials," in L.R. Vande Berg and Lawrence A. Wenner, eds., *Television Criticisms: Approaches and Applications* (New York: Longman, 1991), 72.

[15] John Hartley, cited in Wenner, "Dream Team," 72.

[16] *Toronto Star* editorial (22 February 2010), 3.

[17] "Local Heroes," *Economist* 388: 8591 (2 August, 2008), Special Report 11.

[18] Chuck Johnson, "Game Grabbing Globe, Ilgauskas Says," *USA Today* (11 June 2007), 6c.

[19] Susie O'Brien and Imre Szeman, *Popular Culture: A User's Guide* 2 ed. (Toronto: Nelson, 2009), 322.

[20] Andrews, "Disneyization," 91.

[21] Falcous and Maguire, "Imaging," 61.

[22] Anthony Giddens, *Runaway World: How Globalization is Reshaping Our Lives* (New York: Routledge, 2000). 64.

[23] O'Brien and Szeman, 339.

[24] Falcous and Maguire, 41.

[25] Ibid.

[26] Falcous and Maguire, 40.

[27] Falcous and Maguire, 73.

Chapter 23

American Sundown

No Country for Old Men, There Will Be Blood, and the Question of the Twilight Western

Christopher Sharrett

Joel and Ethan Coen's *No Country for Old Men* and Paul Thomas Anderson's *There Will Be Blood* dominated the 2008 Academy Award season, two grim films that contemplate the assumptions and consequences of the American civilizing process. The films might be viewed as contributions to the "twilight western," the subgenre that includes such distinguished but undervalued films as David Jacobson's *Down in the Valley* (2005), Tommy Lee Jones's *The Three Burials of Melquiades Estrada* (2005), Ang Lee's *Brokeback Mountain* (2005), and, if one looks at its thematic conventions rather than its iconography, Paul Haggis's Iraq-era film *In the Valley of Elah* (2007), all of which relocate concepts of the western in a contemporary setting to meditate on the disintegration of American life. The twilight western isn't new: David Miller's *Lonely are the Brave* (1962), Martin Ritt's *Hud* (1963), Peter Bogdanovich's *The Last Picture Show* (1971), and Sam Peckinpah's *Bring Me the Head of Alfredo Garcia* (1974) were postwar, late Hollywood manifestations of the sense that the white civilizing process had long since collapsed; society is presented as dilapidated or encroaching, its latter-day heroes lost or deranged. These films are to be distinguished from the revisionist westerns of Sam Peckinpah, Sergio Leone, Robert Altman, and others, which are concerned chiefly with commenting on the western as a genre, that is, the representation of the Wild West frontier experience as it occurred in the late nineteenth century, or in the case of films like *The Wild Bunch* (1969) the early twentieth century, with its violent male characters fighting a last stand against an oncoming technological epoch even more awful than the bloody nineteenth-century expansionist moment.

No Country for Old Men would seem to join the project of looking at a post-Vietnam/Watergate America (the time period of the narrative) begun by much of the more intelligent 1960s-70s cinema, but with the added critical perspective of an artwork created during the horror of the Iraq moment, although the seriousness of the film's critical project needs interrogation. *There Will Be Blood* seems to resemble the revisionist western since it is a period piece (the Southwest from the end of the 1890s to 1927), or simply a gritty return to the western itself, accompanied on screens at the same time by James Mangold's remake of *3:10 to Yuma* or Andrew Dominik's *The Assassination of Jesse James by the Coward Robert Ford* (both 2007). *There Will Be Blood* might be close in sensibility to the latter films primarily through a kindred strained seriousness, but Anderson's film shares more in common with the Coens' at the level of ambition, and like the Coens' film, Anderson's needs to be examined for its realized achievement. Like *No Country for Old Men*, *There Will Be Blood* takes on questions about foundational assumptions of the United States; despite the differing time-frames of their narratives, both Anderson and the Coens share the idea that America was "always already" condemned by the nature of its assumptions. From my perspective now, the value of this interrogation is in question.

No Country for Old Men offers an image of a desiccated America brilliantly rendered by Roger Deakins's photography, showing a bleached-out frontier overtaken by strip malls and wretched motels, with an older image of family, homestead, and community in tatters. But the Coens' frequently sarcastic gestures tend to divert whatever criticism their work intends, and the fatalism and dread it constantly reemphasizes is divorced, as in all of their films, from any meaning outside of the perversely personal, a sensibility that undermines the epic pretenses of this supremely ambitious film.

Many reviewers have noted the supposedly felicitous conjunction of the talents of the Coen brothers and their source material, the very hard-boiled novel by Cormac McCarthy, a contemporary writer already so revered he has been compared to Melville. The film adapts McCarthy's novel very faithfully, down to the peanut wrapper discarded at one point by the psychopathic Anton Chigurh (Javier Bardem), although several scenes and some philosophical ruminations by Sheriff Ed Tom Bell (Tommy Lee Jones), the story's moral center, have been wisely removed. But despite, or perhaps because of, the faithfulness of transcription, the film gives us a sensibility very different, it seems to me, than that of the novel.

Much of McCarthy's overall literary project, especially his most celebrated novel, *Blood Meridian*, has been centered on the hellish aspect of the American civilizing project from a perspective that is simultaneously violent, hallucinatory, allusionistic, and bombastic, for all the terseness of style. His mannered prose (he drops certain punctuation marks on the assumption, it appears, that they encumber the voices he wants to convey) and ambition hearken to the high modernism of James Joyce and Gertrude Stein. The concern of the novel *No Country for Old Men* is nothing less than humanity at the precipice, confronting The

Void made evident with God's departure. When reading McCarthy, I can't help but think of Georg Lukacs's remarks, in *The Meaning of Contemporary Realism*, on the limits of the ideology of modernism. Lukacs comments on the "religious atheism" that encumbers much modern fiction, as authors tremble with the realization that there is no ultimate Truth, wallowing in the alienation of the God-forsaken world that capitalist society—and they—have created, with no thought to an alternative society, or the processes that have brought us to where we are.

Although all of McCarthy's preoccupations are materially present at some level in the Coen brothers' adaptation, the movie seems essentially a comedy, drawing on the cynicism that informs most of the previous Coen films, especially *Fargo* (1996), their most successful film prior to this release, a comparison to which might illuminate *No Country for Old Men*.

Among the most disturbing aspects of the Coens' films is the sense that they have contempt for their characters, or at least find them peculiar, certainly in regard to the "little people" whose oddball lives fill out their landscapes. *Fargo* was preoccupied less with the terrible crimes of ordinary people than with the quirky habits of "funny looking" characters (an expression used in the film, identified with *Fargo* itself). In *No Country for Old Men*, there is the Barney Fife-style deputy (Zach Hopkins) who turns his back on the very sinister suspect he has just arrested, allowing the villain his punch-line deadly assault just as the dumber-than-a-post fool assures his boss on the telephone that things are well in hand. Even at this early point of the film we know that this woebegone lawman has, somehow, arrested the Noonday Devil himself—we have been keyed to this by the downbeat introductory voiceover by Sheriff Bell against vistas that render the Southwest as an empty, ineffable wasteland: Bell talks about the great frontier lawmen of the past and the moral clarity of the world they policed, the awfulness of the current world, and his anxiety over the real prospect that he may "meet something I don't understand" (given the gruesome nature of crime in the late twentieth century). The woes of this world are somehow of cosmic, apocalyptic proportions—beyond human repair, and thus a reason for despair—an idea emphasized with numbing regularity. Drug deals and local perversity are way out of control it seems, but while Vietnam is (somewhat) in the background of this narrative, America's other ills (like racism, wage slavery, and the triumph of corporate capitalism) have no bearing on the approaching four horsemen. McCarthy's apocalypticism survives fairly intact, but with the Coens' tongue-in-cheek flourishes that suggest a disconnect between two forms of cynicism, one that broods self-indulgently over the unfixable state of the world and one that aloofly sees the problem as a subject of snide derision.

But the threats of this world go past most of the stupid people who live in it, like the obese manager of the trailer park where Llewelyn Moss (Josh Brolin) lives, a person unaware that she is confronting Satan when Anton Chigurh asks her a few simple questions. One could say she is principled ("We don't give out no information!") or adamantly thick, which seems a real possibility given the way the Coens frame the scene. Then there is the motel owner who rents rooms to Moss ("You tell me the option") or the uncommonly unflappable owner of the Western clothing store who outfits the bathrobe-clad Moss ("No sir, it's unusual!"). The border guard who lets Moss back in the U.S. quizzes him with an exaggerated drawl about his service in "Nam," and after he gets the right answers he lets Moss through. Such an encounter is marginally plausible, but the issue is the degree to which all this tomfoolery produces a cartoon of the existential dread the film first offers us. When Llewelyn's wife Carla Jean (Kelly MacDonald) complains to him about his bullying, she gripes, "I'm used to a lot of things—I work at Wal-Mart;" the remark is funny and anachronistic (the film takes place before the triumph of the big-box stores), but is among the lines that tend toward the deflation of characters and our sympathy for them. While the film is different in tone from *Fargo*, its attitude toward humanity underscores a view of the Coens as nihilists, the landscape merely shifting from the frozen, brain-dead northern Midwest of the earlier film to the arid Southwest, and the focus remaining a critique of American society from an essentially conservative perspective, given the sweeping dismissal of all these nitwits good and bad. The studied compositions of the film, especially the reaction shots of silly-ass yokels, give *No Country for Old Men* an affected aspect, making hollow the ominous notes from McCarthy's novel it repeatedly tries to hit.

The film's story pivots on one of the hoariest plot devices of modern fiction, the drug deal gone wrong, a favored concept of beginning student filmmakers. It may still have resonance as an emblem of avarice and savagery, and of the cruelty basic to American history (Bell's deputy calls the initial murder scene "the OK Corral"), but why it should be regarded as a crime of awful portent is undeveloped except as a grisly image (of flyblown bodies rotting on the sunblazed panhandle) within an increasingly grim *mise-en-scène*. And portent undergirds every moment of the film, beginning with the relentless march of the unstoppable devil Anton Chigurh, armed with his powerful, arcane weaponry. Chigurh crosses the implacable figure of Death in Ingmar Bergman's *The Seventh Seal* (1957) with any number of omniscient, all-powerful serial killers who litter recent cinema—Anthony Hopkins's risible, scenery-chewing Hannibal Lecter is a degraded but obviously influential example. Or he might be Fate, that ultimate threat to hyperreligious modern America, with his assurance that God has indeed left the premises (Chigurh virtually defines himself as a harbinger of Destiny). Or he might be as banal as Two-Face, the villain from the Batman comics who also uses a flipped coin (go through the history of crime fiction to find this gimmick) to decide what horror will next befall his victims. Bardem's character is well-modulated, but he stands out the way good monsters usually do.

The film's constant emanations of Armageddon feel taken with a grain of salt (since people aren't to be taken seriously). Sheriff Bell tells his numbskull deputy about a news story detailing the torture and murder of an elderly couple for their social security checks, then notes that the unthinking neighbors complained only after one of the hoodlums walked in the yard clad only in a dog collar—for Bell this is a signifier of modern degradation, his image of "all-out war." Is Bell this naïve, the last in a line of tough Texas lawmen? Or is the film making fun of his narrow, ignorant conservatism? As always, Tommy Lee Jones has the idiom down pat, but the Coens stretch it to the breaking point, almost to the degree that Bell loses his dignity.

The notion of the film as essentially a send-up is given special credence when Bell chats over coffee with an El Paso lawman (Rodger Boyce) who is railing against the "children walking the streets of our Texas towns with green hair and bones in their noses." Bell replies "Once you quit hearin' 'sir' and 'ma'am' the rest is soon to follow." Given that the narrative takes place at the start of Reaganism, the shared tirade might be seen as a (parodied?) response to the archetypal backlash to 60s youth culture, with Anton Chigurh's mod haircut the key emblem assuring us that the world is indeed going to hell in a hand basket. For Bell, instances of moral decay are part of the "dismal tide," and "signs and wonders" foretelling the end time. But one could argue that the Coens want to leaven the seriousness of McCarthy's over-the-top vision of a nation losing its way—that is, if one believes that

McCarthy accepts, and is not merely commenting on, redneck America's conflation of punk rock with the drug trade and serial murder.

For all the apparent sarcasm, the film keeps reasserting a serious intent when it returns to McCarthy's central concerns, particularly in a final scene where Bell visits his aging uncle Ellis (Barry Corbin), who reminds him, referring to a gruesome incident in 1909 Texas, that things were always bad, and that Bell's retirement due to his belief that he has become "over-matched" by the current world is a self-consoling delusion. The exchange, in Ellis's filthy lean-to, seems to side with McCarthy's bleak rendering of American history—although it is a very wrongheaded one, uninterrogated by the Coens. The 1909 murder was carried out by diabolical "Indians" on a rampage, apparent precursors to Anton Chigurh, "foreign" elements whose monstrous behavior has no rhyme or reason—it flows merely from the pure bloodlust that is America, especially that of the Other within.

The final apocalyptic vignette is the denouement where Bell recounts to his wife (Tess Harper) a pair of dreams, both of which reference his father and patriarchal authority disappearing from the American scene. In Bell's telling, the dreams suggest that the son didn't properly follow in the father's footsteps. In the first, the father gives Bell money, which he loses. In the second, Bell sees a ghostly image of his father wrapped in a blanket, carrying a horn of fire, as if to lead his son into the inferno. Like the ghost scene from *Hamlet*, this poetic moment has potentially strong resonance that is suddenly lost as the film comes to a dead stop. The Fate that drove the hapless Llewelyn Moss to take a valise of drug money he couldn't possibly keep, for all his blind macho resourcefulness (thus starting the story rolling), is replaced once and for all by an unquestioned image of the doomsday to which we are all heading, one predicated, it seems, on betrayed paternal law. Yet, too, even this law, and the fathers it represents, are objects of the Coen brothers' relentless smirk.

There Will be Blood is adapted, as the ad copy and much pre-release publicity noted amply, from Upton Sinclair's novel *Oil!*, which was written in response to the Teapot Dome scandals of the Harding Administration but was more broadly concerned, like Sinclair's other novels, with capitalism's war on the working class. It has been noted with little critical comment that none of this is in Paul Thomas Anderson's film, and that calling this film an "adaptation" seems a form of obfuscation. The entirety of the novel's narrative of socialist challenge to the oil tycoons of the early twentieth century has been removed. What remains is the story of prospector Daniel Plainview (Daniel Day-Lewis, in a performance that overwhelms the film), and his climb from hardscrabble silver miner to deranged oil baron. His story corresponds roughly to the "Dad" narrative of Sinclair's novel, although in the book the son joins forces with Paul, a socialist organizer. In the film, Plainview's son H.W. (Dillon Freasier) has nothing to do with revolt; the film might be seen as a representation of patriarchal capitalism in microcosm, with the frontier population portrayed as vulnerable, largely mute witnesses to the patriarch's rampage. In one early scene, Plainview is shown in close-up, attempting to sell his good intentions (in order to buy up land) to a confused, cacophonous group of townspeople—the American population as mob. There is a question as to whether the director intends for us to see them from the pathological Plainview's perspective or from his own, a significant question.

The high seriousness of *No Country for Old Men* is met many times over by that of *There Will Be Blood*, beginning with the score by Radiohead guitarist Jonny Greenwood, an admirer of avant-garde composer Krzysztof Penderecki, whose apocalyptic compositions include "Threnody for the Victims of Hiroshima." Penderecki enjoyed a particular moment in the Vietnam aftermath, his pieces used by Stanley Kubrick (in *The Shining* [1980]), and his influence everywhere in industrial/electronic musical experimentation. The film opens with a still image of a hilly, parched Southwest expanse, a shrill chord by Greenwood on the soundtrack. Although the film is supremely allusionistic (George Stevens, Orson Welles, Michael Cimino, Sergio Leone, Robert Altman are here in abundance, as is Kubrick in the film's mannered denouement), it divests itself of even the slightest romanticism that the humanism of revisionists like Leone and Cimino allowed. The opening shot is decidedly *not* anything from *Giant* (1956) or even *Once Upon a Time in the West* (1968). Greenwood's shrill noise (compare this to the expansiveness of the old scores by Dimitri Tiomkin or Max Steiner, or the hyperbolic anguish of Ennio Morricone) coupled with the arid image erases all notion of the West as emblem of possibility. Yet this pronounced condemnation, with no touch of elegy, also has a good deal of preciousness. Robin Wood has noted that Anderson's films tend to announce their importance, to the degree that *Magnolia* (1999) is showcased as a masterpiece.[1] Particularly in their DVD packaging, Anderson's films since *Boogie Nights* (1997) tend to trumpet their sophistication and importance, regardless of their apparent achievement (in the case of *Punch-Drunk Love* [2002] even the ambition seems confused and confusing—all that is reasonably recognizable is something like a florid, over-designed comic rendering of *The Red Desert* [1964], suggesting that alienation is a goof). The pomposity of *There Will Be Blood* begins with its title, insistently, repeatedly written in a Gothic typescript to create not just a title but a logo. The title is derived from the blood injunctions in the Book of Exodus (depending on which translation of the Bible one has at hand), Pharoah's curse on the male first-born of Israel, which the God of Moses causes to backfire. Blood oaths against male children—and the sacrifice of children—saturate the Bible, and in this narrative may be said to have some sensible application. Yet in this theme the film plays its strongest suit. At its heart is a narrative about the manipulative power of fathers, and their use of sons to provide an extension of self and social legitimacy.

There Will Be Blood puts me in mind of the classic 1950s television western "The Rifleman" (1958–1963); the film might be thought of as the inverse of the famous series. In "The Rifleman," Lucas McCain (Chuck Connors) is a widower raising his young son Mark (Johnny Crawford) on their homestead in 1880s New Mexico. Lucas gains enormous sympathy from the people of North Fork for "raising his son right" without a woman present, as Lucas makes fairly evident both through the pain caused by his wife's death and the emotional shrine he retains for her. Lucas's story is the romance of the widower, the narrative of a sensitive man who retains "family values" while still keeping a stiff upper lip taking care of business the way a man must. Daniel Plainview's narrative is similar, except the devious Plainview is very conscious of the ways by which his (bogus) widower status plays to public sympathy (his sex life is nowhere in evidence—one can read the film as an essay on the homoerotic aspect of all pioneer narratives, or, if one chooses the puerile, adolescent option offered by reviewers, Plainview's gushing oil wells displace his penis, suggesting his angry sublimation or impotence).

Plainview answers the query of a strict-looking woman by vowing that his wife "died in childbirth, ma'am." He repeats the notion that his enterprise is "a family business," referring to his son H.W., who occasionally looks a bit shell-shocked, as his "partner." When one of Plainview's rivals tells him jokingly that his son is a useful "sweet face" to have about in order to cajole people out of their land, the charge seems unwarranted until we follow the accretion of details surrounding the false father-son relationship (Plainview gently bullies the child, and uses alcohol to anesthetize him when necessary to his plans) and the monstrous finale, wherein Plainview tells a grown and married H.W. that he is no more than a "bastard from a basket," a perverse take on the Moses legend and very true here, since Plainview adopted H.W. in a calculated move after the death of the real father, one of Plainview's original employees.

At moments, Plainview's affection for the boy seems genuine (his huddling with H.W. after the explosion of the first big well), until we see the son merely as a much-needed instrument for the father's plans, and more importantly as the archetypal projection of the father's sense of self. Those who see "mixed emotions" in Plainview's hugging of his adopted son miss a crucial point: a child receives affection in abundance so long as he (and I say "he" very deliberately: the "first born male child" has a significance in society that the female can never enjoy under patriarchal assumptions—the *Godfather* films [1972; 1974; 1990] are an effective operatic cartoon of the situation) toes the line and provides the father with the required assurances that all will go as planned in keeping patriarchal will in place. When the father's ego projection disintegrates in the final scene of *There Will Be Blood*, as H.W. now becomes Daniel's "competitor" in the oil business, the goals of patriarchy are neatly exposed. The son competes with Daniel's business interests since he has learned his lessons so well (a frightening thought to be sure), but offers no threat to Plainview's basic assumptions. The film's best scene shows Plainview to be a sociopath who says, "I have a competition in me—I want no one else to succeed." He proclaims, "I look at people and see nothing worth liking," spitting out the word "people" with a joking contempt. The absolute irredeemability of patriarchal capitalism and its linkage to an adamant, destructive self-interest are well-realized in these moments.

At the heart of the film's weakness is Plainview's relationship to the smarmy young preacher Eli Sunday (Paul Dano), who would co-opt him toward religious fervor and fealty to a fundamentalist frontier church. Plainview would seem to be pure instrumental reason at war with the intellectual snake oil peddled by Eli (in a deleted scene Plainview refers to Eli as a "lunatic"). At certain points the film suggests that the population is caught between two forms of madness, capitalism and religion. The final moment, the smashing of Eli's skull by a decrepit, fed-up Plainview, appears to suggest the final triumph of the one evil over the other, but this entirely ignores the long history of capitalism's close cooperation with religion, each scratching the other's back.[2] Also ignored is any sense of public challenge to either religion or capitalism, even in a slight, nascent form (for which, see Cimino's *Heaven's Gate* [1980]), as if Anderson doesn't want to be bothered with "all that old stuff." What we get instead is the archetypal scene of the mad old millionaire coming apart in the midst of his own wealth (even though the wealth itself—and its necessary consequences for the public—remain undisturbed). By not wanting to be "preachy," or because he wants to distill his narrative to the unremitting male ego that is the essence of capital, Anderson relies too much on a sense of capitalist expansion as a psychological matter residing simply in the will of the strong male, or the male group.

There Will Be Blood is a frequently chilling mood piece about individualism (the *sine qua non* of American narratives of success) and the unrelenting, destructive force of patriarchal will. But in refusing all suggestions of revolt (especially in H.W.'s decision to *continue* in the oil business rather than try to destroy it) Anderson's film is yet another effective portrait of the horrors of capital embodied in a perverse set of men. As with *No*

Country for Old Men, its deep immersion in aestheticism causes it to stay clear of the material dynamic of history and the resistances to it.

Notes

[1] Robin Wood, *Hollywood from Vietnam to Reagan and Beyond* (New York: Columbia University Press, 2004), xxxiii. I would say that while this tendency is evident, it is nowhere near the self-importance of the films of the truly awful, oh-so-sophisticated other Anderson, Wes, most of whose films somehow immediately arrive for the home market on the Criterion Collection label, giving them the imprimatur of significance that they don't in the least deserve.

[2] For a good overview of big oil's use of born-again religion, see Gerald Colby and Charlotte Dennett, *Thy Will Be Done: Nelson Rockefeller and Evangelism in the Age of Oil* (New York: HarperCollins, 1995).

Cultural Moments

This final section deals with some of the most current and interesting themes in popular culture today.

Angela Ndalianis takes an insightful look at the current crop of horror films and shows how the narrative has changed reflecting as she calls it "the Return of the Horror Apocalypse" and its relationship to societal collapse. Tarantino's critically acclaimed take on the Holocaust in his film *Inglourious Basterds* is dissected in Sean Springer's critical look at the implications of the film. Michael Jackson's gender identity is scrutinized in Dominic Lennard's look at the crotch shot in his performances. His conclusions are an interesting and unique take on one of pop music's most discussed stars. Julie Turnock takes a fascinating look at the history of special effects as they culminate with the hugely successful film *Avatar;* her address to the connection between politics and special effects makes for an interesting approach. And finally Thomas Doherty examines the TV series "Lost," one of the most talked about and analyzed dramatic series on television. Time travel and parallel universes are just two of the themes that make that series such an interesting phenomenon; Doherty challenges us to make sense of it.

Five brand new articles range over topics like *Harry Potter* films, the continuing fascination with vampire films and TV series like "True Blood," post 9/11 apocalyptic movies like *The Road* and *The Hunger Games*, the continuing successful teen high school series "Glee," and the "Dexter" serial killer series and films.

Matthew Leggatt takes an interesting look at Post 9/11 apocalyptic films and analyses why they are different from earlier similarly themed films. He poses some very challenging ideas as to why some Post 9/11 films (*Legion* and *Children of Men*) are often not as successful as the earlier pre 9/11 blockbuster films (*I Am Legend*). What does it mean when society no longer has a utopian ideal with which to measure the current situation? Leggatt successfully gets the reader to ponder such important questions and asks us why *The Hunger Games* as the dystopian view of the future, is so popular.

Steven Woodward gives us a penetrating glimpse of the financial success of J.K Rowling' s Harry Potter series of books and films. He speculates that essentially Rowling takes the "orphan-at-school" theme so common in culture and refreshes it with the addition of magic. He even manages to give an interesting real-life assessment of the English boarding school experience in comparison to the fantasy world of Harry Potter.

Cary Elza explores that enduring fantasy monster, the vampire. Bram Stoker's *Dracula* may have started it all so long ago, but the genre continues to change to suit the modern cultural mood of the audience. *Twilight* and "True Blood" are but two of the most recent film and television adaptations of the vampire myth. It seems that so-called evil vampires are still with us, but now they are accompanied by a more romantic version, one which yearns for love and redemption. Elza perceptively delves into everyday gender issues and provides a thoughtful social analysis of the popularity of this mythic creature.

Stephen Gaunson's article is a comprehensive look at society's interest in serial killers through the history of film. His list of serial killer films is exhaustive. He encourages us to consider the implications of our fascination with such films and series in a new and challenging way. From Fritz Lang's *M* to Hitchcock's *Psycho*, to *Silence of the Lambs* and to "Dexter," he gives us an interesting critique of this enduring genre and speculates as to why such films are so popular.

And finally James Morrison's clever and insightful look at the success of "Glee" is another new addition to the book. He calls the show "sweet with an edge" and says its success has included the hot-button issues which have rarely been dealt with so thoroughly on prime time television. The third season dilemmas that all series face are analyzed in a new and fresh fashion, as is the show's influence in many different cultural areas, like gay teen suicide, homophobia, teenage pregnancy, bullying and diversity, teen drinking, and teen texting while driving. The show has even popularized social change as in the "It Gets Better" movement.

Chapter 24

Return of the Horror Apocalypse

Angela Ndalianis

Since the emergence of Alfred Hitchcock's *Psycho* in 1960, the direction of the contemporary horror film has increasingly led to a more disturbing confrontation between the spectator and his or her worst fears about the collapse of identity, system, and order. The entry of the monster—whether Nosferatu, King Kong, Count Dracula, or Michael Myers—serves a crucial function in the horror film: by embodying society's dark side, the monstrous tests the rules, morals, and ideological structures that operate in our culture, holding these structures up for analysis, contesting their worth, and exposing the instability of the system that informs the social order. The horror film is about crossing boundaries. One side of the border constitutes order, the other chaos: the horrific manifests itself where meaning, which is established by civilization, collapses. The horror genre has been one of the longest surviving and most consistently popular genres in the cinema and, over the last decade it has made its presence felt intensively through the influx of what has come to be known as New Horror, which is the subject of this essay. Contrasting the trend toward playful, self-reflexive, and parodic horror that dominated in the 1990s and which is typified by Wes Craven's *Scream* (1996) and its sequels, the films of the first decade of the 2000s show a different agenda: in Eli Roth's *Cabin Fever* (2002), James Wan's *Saw* (2004), Roth's *Hostel* (2005), and Greg McLean's *Wolf Creek* (2005), the audience is relentlessly confronted with violence, intense gore, and, often, a social critique that refuses to hold back the punches. In these films, the horror spectator is permitted to enter a space that operates as a ritualistic violation of taboos. In the process, fears and desires are unleashed that often threaten "normal" society and its ideologies onscreen. Murder and displays of sadomasochistic violence, perverted sexual acts, incest and interbreeding, the return of the dead, cannibalism: these themes are at the core of New Horror.[1]

Whereas in the past horror narratives clearly coded the flawed characters who were marked for destruction at the hands of the monster (by exhibiting sexual promiscuity, lacking morality, being obnoxious, and so on), New Horror is unforgiving; in films like *Hostel* and *Hostel II* (2007), *Wolf Creek* (2005), *30 Days of Night* (2007) and the remakes of *Texas Chainsaw Massacre* (2003) and *The Hills Have Eyes* (2006) there is little rhyme or reason as to why the films' multiple victims become the targets of monstrous acts of bloody destruction. While the story premise, main characters, and nature of the monstrous may differ markedly in these films, one thing that does dominate across the board is the depiction of human beings (and, by extension, society) coming apart at the seams. In fact, Rob Zombie's remake of *Halloween* (2007), the horror classic originally directed by John Carpenter, provides greater detail of the events that pushed the child Michael Myers into becoming "the boogieman." Unlike Carpenter, who played on the powerful ambiguity of Michael Myers's nature—is he sociopath (and therefore the rational outcome of his social environment) or boogieman (the product of irrational forces that cannot be rationalized)?—Zombie releases Myers's identity from the realm of the unknown and supernatural, blaming his monstrous nature on the social environment that nurtured him: repeated bullying at school, the backdrop of a horrific home life, an abusive stepfather, a self-obsessed and sexually zealous older sister, and a mother who had to spend more time at the strip joint that brought home the bacon than at home providing support to her ten-year-old son. In case we miss the blame being placed on the social context (on the reality of class and poverty, as opposed to the supernatural), Zombie further drives home the trigger to Michael's violent nature by exposing his predilection for the torture of animals, a clear sign of disintegrating personality and social disintegration in general. Whereas earlier horror cinema unleashed horror to test the borders that demarcate society, order, and normality from the anti-social, chaotic, and abnormal, it always ensured that the social status quo was reinstated in the end. New Horror, on the other hand, often tests the limits of the social order to such a degree that there can be no turning back.

Zombies

Much has been made of the social and political undercurrent that runs through the new wave of horror films and many of these films have been read against the socio-political backdrop. Axelle Carolyn (2008), for example, is typical of many writers on New Horror in establishing a correlation between the rise of hardcore, apocalyptic horror with the aftermath of the events that took place on September 11, 2001. As a result, with the release of Danny Boyle's *28 Days Later* (2002), the year 2002 is seen as a turning point that ushers in a developing horror film renaissance, which aims to terrify its viewers as much as its film victims by reminding them of the grand-scale horrors that also lie "out there." For Carolyn, there are "obvious parallels between *Hostel* and real-life atrocities that the Western world was only too familiar with, from Kana (Jennifer Lim)'s burnt face recalling the blowtorch torture Saddam Hussein's troops used against Iraqi dissidents to the image of Josh (Derek Richardson) hooded, stripped to his underwear and tied to a chair directly mirroring photographs from Abu Ghraib published by the U.S. media a couple of years earlier."[2]

A high percentage of the New Horror boom is comprised of the living dead/zombie films that follow in the tradition of George Romero's Living Dead trilogy and, according to Kyle Bishop, there is a parallel between the success of this sub-genre of horror and current political events. Just as *Night of the Living Dead* (1968) was placed by critics against the backdrop of the 1968 assassinations of Martin Luther King and Robert Kennedy, student riots, racial unrest, and the involvement of the United States in the Vietnam War,[3] so too the zombie comeback—as witnessed in *28 Days Later, Dawn of the Dead* (2004), *Land of the Dead* (2005), *28 Weeks Later* (2007), *Day of the Dead* (2008), *Zombieland* (2009), and so many other films—can be placed in the current socio-political context of the September 11 events and their aftermath.[4] Bishop states, "This renaissance of the subgenre reveals a connection between zombie cinema and post-9/11 cultural consciousness."[5] In fact, some films move beyond the zombie as allegory for social issues to directly address the post-9/11 crisis. The post-apocalyptic backdrop present in the New Horror living-dead films stresses "the collapse of societal infrastructures, the indulgence of survivalist fantasies, and the fear of other surviving humans. All of these plot elements and motifs are present in pre-9/11 zombie films, but they have become more relevant to a modern, contemporary audience."[6] And in the opening title sequence of the *Dawn of the Dead* reboot, Kyle Cooper (who directed the title sequence) makes this relevance very clear as he intercuts the titles of the film with scenes of mayhem and destruction. "Real" and fictional news footage bombards the viewer with scenes of riots, abandoned buildings, police beatings, burning bodies, explosions, zombie attacks, crowds in states of mass hysteria, and micro-images of blood flowing through veins, while news readers report with utter disbelief the events that have befallen the world. To the accompaniment of Johnny Cash singing "When the Man Comes to Town," snippets of audio interrupt to tell the story of viral infections that are spreading and bringing the dead back to life—an infection that even contaminates the film's titles as the red text leaks blood and disperses the titles across the screen. Through this title sequence placed firmly within the context of real world events the zombie invasion and scenes of global apocalyptic destruction are meant to be read allegorically as concrete symbolizations of historical events; and to drive home the connection between the zombie invasion and the 9/11 events, the titles begin with one seemingly anomalous act that stands apart from the destruction dominating in this scene: thousands of Muslims are depicted bowing their heads repeatedly to the ground in mass prayer, the suggestion being that religious zeal initiates the events that follow.

In *Homecoming* (2005) Joe Dante develops this connection further still. No plot summary can do justice to what Dante delivers with his typically satirical wit and flair, but this is what Brian Lowry has to say about the film:

> It would be difficult to find a more subversive hour than this weekend's installment of "Masters of Horror"—Showtime's anthology series featuring a dozen horror luminaries. Directed by Joe Dante, "Homecoming" is a full-frontal assault on

the Bush administration, and as subtle as a punch to the jaw. Adapted by Sam Hamm from Dale Bailey's short story "Death and Suffrage"—but also vaguely reminiscent of Irwin Shaw's 1936 antiwar play "Bury the Dead"—Dante's hour darkly satirizes zombie movies, as dead soldiers arise to vote against the politicians who shipped them off to war.[7]

And in his *Village Voice* review, Dennis Lim explains that "As if in defiance of the Pentagon's policy to ban photographs of dead soldiers' coffins, Dante's film shows not just the flag-draped caskets at Dover Air Force Base but their irate occupants bursting out of them . . . as *Homecoming* suggests, there are ways in which the current administration is essentially beyond satire."[8] According to Bishop, "Horror films function as barometers of society's anxieties, and zombie movies represent the inescapable realities of unnatural death while presenting a grim view of the modern apocalypse through scenes of deserted streets, piles of corpses, and gangs of vigilantes—images that have become increasingly common and can shock and terrify a population."[9] From "the torture, rape and possible homicide of Iraqi prisoners in Abu Ghraib by American soldiers" to "accounts of cruel and inhumane methods of interrogation and treatment of prisoners at the Guantanamo Bay detention camp in Cuba, which were reported to the media by soldiers, FBI agents and non-governmental organizations," to the hurricanes Ivan, Jeanne, and Katrina, to the SARS epidemic and mad cow disease,[10] New Horror is understood as reflecting on and interpreting these events—manmade and natural—in self-consciously apocalyptic terms.

Horror Redux

Aside from the many examples of New Horror that were produced in the United States, Australasia, Europe, and Latin America, it comes as no surprise that many of the films (and some of the most successful) have been the remakes of a wave of independent, low-budget horror films that hit the screens in the 1970s. Along with the zombie virus, which began in the late 1960s with *Night of the Living Dead,* a number of these low-budget classics—*Last House on the Left* (1972), *The Texas Chainsaw Massacre* (1974), and *The Hills Have Eyes* (1977)—led the way to the New Horror aesthetic, in particular in their focus on a dark, apocalyptic horror from which there appears to be no return. Rebooting the classics, the New Horror versions revisit the horror, but this time, from within the mainstream and with bigger budgets.

Consider Alexandre Aja's *The Hills Have Eyes* (2006), which was based on the 1977 classic directed by Wes Craven. Both films place the family as institution at the center of the horror. Traveling across the desert is the Carter family, which includes Bob and Ethel Carter, who are celebrating their fiftieth wedding anniversary, the two teenagers Brenda and Bobby, their other daughter Lynn, her husband Doug and baby daughter Catherine, and the German Shepherd couple, Beauty and Beast. Soon after the film's opening, a parallel is established between the "normal" Carter family and a mysterious mutant family that appears to be living in the desert mountain caves, led by Papa Jupiter. Of course, any horror fan knows that ever since the days of *Psycho,* leaving the safety of the freeway (a structure that symbolizes the link to civilization) means trouble, and the Carters find trouble by the bucket load! Stuck in the desert (their caravan is damaged by the mutants) the Carters endure a series of attacks that rob them of Bob the father, Lynn the daughter, Ethel the mother, and Beauty the dog (all brutally murdered). After the initial attacks, the Carters take a more defensive stance against the mutants and, while Doug treks into the mountains to find his baby daughter who has been kidnapped, Brenda and Bobby stay behind and think of ways to protect themselves from further attacks. In the end Bobby, Brenda, Doug, and Beast all survive, revealing a resilience and capacity for violence that had seemed barely possible in the first part of the film. Despite the similarities, however, there are a few differences between original and remake that are worth considering.

Both films are vicious in terms of their depiction of violence, but Aja's version is far more graphic and gruesome. Consider a scene in which the mutant Lizard suckles milk from Lynn's breast before shooting her in the head and kidnapping her baby; or, another when Brenda is raped. However, there's something much harsher about Craven's version that makes these acts appear to be less about represented violence and more about "real" violence, which becomes for the spectator a more uncomfortable experience. Like many of the originals on which the New Horror remakes are based, the 1977 version of *The Hills Have Eyes* was independently produced on a low budget of approximately $250,000 and belongs to an exploitation tradition of filmmaking. The 2006 version, on the other hand, was produced for $15 million and released by Fox Searchlight Pictures.[11] *Hills* 1977 was produced by the independent Blood Relations Company, and found theatrical distribution through New Line Cinema and United Artists Films. As such it belongs to the semi-independent rather than mainstream model of production and distribution. Finding funding from independent sources, Craven then found mainstream support for distribution of his film. Commenting on the interest among film critics of the 1980s on "[exploitation horror] films, which situated themselves on the margins of the industry," David Rodowick (among others) has claimed that this is because "the low-budget horror film is often considered as presenting an ideological alternative to mainstream film practice."[12] Aside from the rawer, almost documentary style of filmmaking, which is due as much to budgetary limitations as to aesthetic choices, sitting on the margins is not what makes the *Hills* 1977 a powerful film.

While it may be that producing films within an independent or semi-independent circuit did facilitate greater freedom in the treatment of a film's subject matter and content in the 1970s and 80s (and I have grave doubts about this because it is tied up with a myth that associates independent production with freedom of expression, including freedom from ideological control), this argument can't be used in a contemporary context. Most independent production houses have now been devoured by the ever-ravenous system of conglomerates that is Hollywood. Speaking with my Marxist-Althusserian film theorist hat on, I must ask whether this means that, because they come from within a mainstream model, New Horror films can't possibly present ideological alternatives to the norm. I'd have to answer, "No"! The very core of horror is about opposition to, and flipping, the norm; some horror films do this extremely well, others are less successful at it; some disturb normality in order to reinstate it (with the pleasure of horror still residing in the disturbance), while others disturb the order in order to see it annihilated once and for all. As Rodowick concedes, being produced outside the mainstream does not automatically open up the way to the creation of a "progressive" text. Independent and mainstream films alike contain examples of regressive and progressive texts; in fact, both regressive and progressive elements are often contained within a single film.

Both versions of *The Hills Have Eyes* films are gutsy and in your face, and have no qualms about sticking it to the system. The 2006 version provides answers that explain the reason for mutations of the "monsters" in the desert and, whereas the 1977 version implies that the desert had been used for bomb testing the 2006 film makes this central. In his search for the kidnapped Catherine, Doug discovers one of the abandoned towns that had been used as a site for nuclear testing in the 1940s and 50s. It comes as no surprise that, rather than being cave dwellers, as is the mutant family in Craven's film,[13] Aja's mutants live in this town, and even have the convenience of television. Meeting Big Mama and Ruby (the young mutant who decides to help him), Doug is also granted an audience with Big Brain (yes, he has a really big head that holds his—presumably—big brain), who tells him the story of the mutants, who as inhabitants of the area were exposed to fallout from the nuclear tests. Aja explains,

> We wanted to keep its savage, realistic aspect but at the same time add a story that involved the tests that the US army conducted in the forties and fifties in the New Mexico desert—the armed forces conducted about 350 atmospheric tests, each time asking the people to leave the area, but not always making sure that they'd all gone ... That is how we wanted to explain why the region was deserted and where the mutant family comes from. It allowed us to tell a larger, more epic story elaborating on the original material.[14]

Social Horror

In his influential article, "Return of the Repressed," Robin Wood provides a basic formula for the function of the horror film: normality is threatened by the monster.[15] Normality is defined as an order that conforms to dominant social norms of heterosexuality, monogamy, the family, and social institutions such as the police, the Church, and the military, which defend them. Wood's argument depends on the Marcusian thesis that, in a society based on monogamy and the nuclear family, there will be an enormous surplus of sexual energy that must be repressed. As a result, that which is repressed must inevitably return. New Horror is, indeed, brimming over with sexual surplus, and its unleashing is played out violently, bloodily, and without forgiveness, a fact attested to by the nickname "torture porn," which often accompanies the more extreme of these films. While the sexual surplus definitely rears its ugly head in both *Hills* films, the primary repression and the rationale given for the monster that exists is directly aimed at the social. But it is in the particulars regarding the social that the two films differ.

Craven's film opens up a social critique that is far more apocalyptic in scope than what might flow from Aja's version. Both films do place blame on the government and military as institutions that were clearly responsible for the horror families that are the films' monsters. However, Aja chooses to be more specific about the back story of the mutant family: they are specifically the government and military's repressed, the result of the cover-up and failure to remove all residents from the testing ground. The mutant community comes back with a vengeance and attacks all who pass through the land with an extreme violence that, like the nuclear tests, has no respect for morality and civilized values. While this may be more of an "epic story," Craven's *Hills* goes back to the beginning of white American history.

Craven establishes a far more direct parallel between the "normal" Carters and the mutant Jupiter's family, his aim being to invite comparison between the two and to inspire the growing discovery, as the film progresses and as members of both families take out members of the opposition, that it is the "normal" family that has the greater capacity for violence (the teenagers even use their dead mother's body as bait to draw Jupiter into a trap). We also get to know more about Jupiter's clan, which is smaller than the community of mutants who live in the nuclear town in the 2006 version. The result is that in the 1977 version the attack is far more explicitly on one of the foundations of civilization: the family, whose drive to continue is represented in three generations. On the side of normality we find Bob and Ethyl, the children Lynn, Doug, Bobby, and Brenda, and the baby Katy; and the monstrous family mirrors this in old Fred, whose absent wife is ripped apart giving birth to Jupiter who, with Mama Jupiter, give birth to Mars, Pluto, and Ruby.[16] The struggle in *Hills* 1977 is the struggle for the survival of patriarchy. When Bob dies, the mantle of patriarch is taken over by Doug, and the men of the Jupiter tribe are murdered one by one. While at the end of *Hills* 2006 we are invited to cheer on the transformed cell phone salesman/hero as he wreaks havoc on the mutants (even managing to stick a mini-American flag into the throat of one of them along the way!) and escapes with his baby and the mutant helper Ruby, *Hills* 1977 leaves the spectator with little to cheer about as the camera freezes on Doug's bloody form as he pounds down on one of his dead mutant victims.

Apocalypse

Discussing the Tobe Hooper version of *The Texas Chainsaw Massacre*, Christopher Sharrett makes the observation that "Hooper's apocalyptic landscape is . . . a deserted wasteland of dissolution where the once vibrant myth [of the frontier] is desiccated."[17] In *Massacre*, we see the end product of the frontier myth in the form of the decaying mansions and families who can no longer make a living from the land because of the new concerns that drive the nation: "The long-term shifts in American culture, society and the US economy have together conspired to spawn many monsters."[18] Merging horror with the western, *Hills* also evokes the ghost of frontier history, not only in the presence of the Carters who travel west across the desert—in what is seen as an act of invasion—but in Papa Jupiter's family (for whom we develop more and more empathy as the film progresses), clearly coded through their clothing to echo the American Indian. Where the journey of Republican family and Democratic son-in-law may be read in *Hills* 2006 as an allegoric invasion of the Middle East by U.S. Forces, a connection driven home more forcefully in the sequel, in *Hills* 1977 it goes back to the beginnings of U.S. history, recalling that the nation was established through violence. When Papa Jupiter addresses his speech to the decapitated head of Big Bob (while staring directly at the camera and, by extension, the viewer), the curse he wishes upon the seed of Bob and his progeny—"I'm gonna suck the brains of your children's children!"—is a curse on Western civilization and the European "civilizers" who invaded America. What Jupiter wishes is to wipe out frontier history. Despite the apocalyptic undercurrent present in *Hills* 2006, it doesn't share the extreme apocalyptic vision that's present in its predecessor or in the New Horror living-dead films.

Conclusion

The study of genre films has often turned to myth studies and structuralist analysis in order to explain the formulaic, binary logic that is so central not only to the horror film but to all genres. Adapting the structuralist model made famous by the anthropologist Claude Lévi-Strauss[19] in understanding genre as a modern version of myth, genre theorists such as Thomas Schatz, Steve Neale, Will Wright, Mark Jancovich, and many others have explored genres as reflections of the collective unconscious (and not so *un*-conscious) of human culture. In his *Structural Anthropology* Lévi-Strauss presents the idea that, culture being a system of symbolic communication it is the role of the structuralist to find the patterns that repeat themselves in these symbolic communications that comprise culture's myths.[20] Here, and in *The Raw and the Cooked,* Lévi-Strauss explains that universal patterns are typical of myths (which explains the reproduction of similar stories across time and across cultures). An integral feature of these patterns is a binary structure whereby "mythical thought always progresses from the awareness of oppositions toward their resolution."[21] But what happens when the binaries are no longer clearly demarcated? Or when the main "patterns that repeat themselves" are about the collapse of clear-cut meaning, oppositional structure, and, therefore, resolution? The full-blown apocalyptic themes that are embraced by the earlier wave of horror and their recent remakes—in particular, as tackled in the zombie film—present a social rupture that is seen as being far too great to allow for a return to any state of "normalcy." In exploring the limits of human nature and uncovering an evil and darkness that test human nature by the films' conclusion, 1970s horror powerfully fails to imagine any source of light that could wipe this darkness out. The myths have become nightmares and civilization has collapsed.

Notes

1. Thanks to my horror buddy Alexandra Heller-Nicholas for the many lively horror chats and for her feedback on this essay.

2. Axelle Carolyn, *It Lives Again!: Horror Movies in the New Millennium* (Tolsworth, Telos Publishing, 2008), 129.

3. See, for example, Carolyn, *It Lives,* 13.

4. While it is technically not a zombie film, *I Am Legend* (2007), the film remake of Richard Matheson's 1954 novel, retains the hybrid logic of Matheson's monsters; while the creatures are a revision of the vampire tradition with a science-fiction twist, many of their traits went on to later influence the living-dead tradition. Unlike the earlier film versions—*The Last Man on Earth* (1964) and *The Omega Man* (1971)—*I Am Legend* reveals this connection to the zombie tradition through the traits of the infected (their tendency to congregate in groups, preference for human flesh, and bad skin condition). More significantly, the apocalyptic theme is also a convention associated with the social chaos instigated by zombies (symbolically, the effect of nature tampered with by science) rather than with the more personalized methods of attack generally favored by vampires.

[5] Kyle Bishop, "Dead Man Still Walking: Explaining the Zombie Renaissance," *Journal of Popular Film & Television* (37: 1, 2009), 17.

[6] Bishop, "Dead Man", 20.

[7] Brian Lowry, "Political anger finds 'Homecoming' on TV," *Daily Variety* 11/30/2005, (Vol. 289 Issue 42), 4. See Cyril Pearl, "Zombie Politics," *Video Business*, 6/19/2006, (Vol. 26 Issue 25), 16.

[8] Dennis Lim, "Dante's Inferno: A horror movie brings out the zombie vote to protest Bush's war," *Village Voice* (Tuesday, Nov 22 2005). Available at: http://www.village voice.com/2005-11-22/film/dante-s-inferno/

[9] Bishop, "Dead Man", 17.

[10] Carolyn, *It Lives*, 78.

[11] See Carolyn, *It Lives*, 11.

[12] D.N. Rodowick, "The Enemy Within: the Economy of Violence in *The Hills Have Eyes*." In *The Planks of Reason: Essays on the Horror Film*, ed. Barry K. Grant and Christopher Sharrett (Lanham, Scarecrow Press, 1984), 321.

[13] Craven's inspiration for the desert family was the infamous story of Sawney Bean, the fifteenth century murderer who set up a family based on incest and interbreeding in the caves of Bannane head in Scotland, surviving on the corpses of the living who invaded the area . . . or so the story goes.

[14] Carolyn, *It Lives*, 118.

[15] Robin Wood, "Return of the Repressed", *Film Comment* (14: 4, 1978) 27.

[16] This propagation of the nuclear family is parodied ruthlessly in both versions of *Texas Chainsaw Massacre*, where three generations are again represented, but this time in the monstrous, cannibal family: Leatherface (who also performs the role of mother), his brother, father, grandfather and the mummified grandmother of the 1974 *Texas*, and the barely alive granny of the 2003.

[17] Christopher Sharrett, "The Idea of Apocalypse in *The Texas Chainsaw Massacre*", In *The Planks of Reason: Essays on the Horror Film*, ed. Barry K. Grant and Christopher Sharrett (Lanham, Scarecrow Press, 1984), 272.

[18] Sharrett, "The Idea of Apocalypse," 98.

[19] For an account of the impact of myth studies and structuralism on genre study, see Pam Cook (ed). *The Cinema Book* (London, British Film Institute, 2007), 137–46.

[20] Claude Lévi-Strauss, *Structural Anthropology* (New York, Basic Books, 1963), 224.

[21] Claude Lévi-Strauss, *The Raw and the Cooked* (New York, Harper & Row, 1970), 10.

Chapter 25

Looking for Laughs in All the Wrong Places

Quentin Tarantino and the Holocaust

Sean Springer

Inglourious Basterds: *A Tale of Two Types of Pleasure*

Whenever a director releases a film set amidst the Holocaust, critics will rightly discuss the extent to which the film faithfully memorializes the genocide of approximately six million Jews during the Second World War. A faithful memorial emphasizes, above all, the trauma brought about by Nazi Germany's designs to torture, enslave, and ultimately murder the millions of Jews living across Europe. And yet, interestingly enough, upon the release of Quentin Tarantino's World War II alternate history *Inglourious Basterds* (2009), the filmmakers explained that *Basterds* provides something better than a faithful memorial. Apparently, it lets audiences, particularly Jewish audiences, live out a revenge fantasy, as expertly crafted by Tarantino. In an *Atlantic* essay on *Basterds,* Jeffrey Goldberg relays the filmmakers' testimonials:

> [Eli] Roth [who plays Sgt. Donny Donowitz] told me recently that *Inglourious Basterds* falls into a subgenre he calls "kosher porn."
>
> "It's almost a deep sexual satisfaction of wanting to beat Nazis to death, an orgasmic feeling," Roth said. "My character gets to beat Nazis to death. That's something I could watch all day. My parents are very strong about Holocaust education. My grandparents got out of Poland and Russia and Austria, but their relatives did not."
>
> Tarantino's producer, Lawrence Bender, says that after reading the first draft of *Inglourious Basterds,* he told Tarantino, "As your producing partner, I thank you, and as a member of the Jewish tribe, I thank you, motherfucker, because this movie is a fucking Jewish wet dream." Harvey and Bob Weinstein, the film's executive producers, also reportedly enjoyed the film's theme of Jewish revenge.
>
> Tarantino told me he has received only positive reactions from his Jewish friends. "The Jewish males that I've known since I've been writing the film and telling them about it, they've just been, 'Man, I can't fucking wait for this fucking movie!'" he told me. "And they tell their dads, and they're like, 'I want to see that movie!'"[1]

Each statement made to Goldberg implies that the film's inducement of pleasure absolves the filmmakers from any perceivable wrongdoing. For example, to the argument that *Basterds* exploits the trauma of real victims by treating the Holocaust as a mere pretext for an entertaining Hollywood blockbuster the filmmakers can retort that the film brings satisfying pleasure to Jewish moviegoers the world over. For proof, they can refer to the film's premiere in Tel Aviv where, according to the Israeli independent newspaper *Haaretz,*

> Tarantino's exuberant introduction was perfectly pitched at Israelis, many of whom can name the family members who perished in the Holocaust. The "chapters" of the movie showing Nazi-scalping, baseball bat-wielding Jews instilling fear into the hearts of the German army (and Hitler), as well as the bloodbath finale, elicited cheers and hearty rounds of applause, and the man himself won a standing ovation as the end credits rolled. . . .
>
> Like Madonna and her devotion to all things kosher, Tarantino's latest movie should ensure him a warm welcome in the Jewish state, now and for many years to come.[2]

In any event, notwithstanding a modicum of discussion in the press and the blogosphere over whether the film retroactively legitimizes Nazi war crimes by glorifying a group of American soldiers who carve swastikas into their German victims' foreheads,[3] few critics took issue with *Basterds'* representation of the Holocaust. With few exceptions, among them *The New Yorker's* David Denby who accused Tarantino of "moral callousness," American critics by and large praised Tarantino's aesthetics (the soundtrack featuring four songs composed by Ennio Morricone, the performances, the cinematography, the witty dialogue, the allusions to spaghetti westerns, etc.) while seeming either indifferent or enthusiastic toward its comic representation of an inherently traumatic historical event. "Will *Basterds* polarize audiences?" *Rolling Stone* critic Peter Travers asks. "That's a given. But for anyone professing true movie love, there's no resisting it."[4] Echoing Travers's sentiments, *The New York Observer*'s Rex Reed writes,

> Mr. Tarantino knows how to frame a scene. The color, movement and sound are as good as in *Pulp Fiction,* the dialogue is a slight improvement over *Reservoir Dogs'* and the scene where the Gestapo invade a French farmhouse to massacre a Jewish family hiding under the floor is better than anything in *Kill Bill.* World War II was more serious, complex and horrifying than all this comic embellishment, but if I sound critical, I apologize in advance. I had a helluva time watching *Inglourious Basterds.*[5]

In other words, it's not so much the revenge fantasy that wins Reed over, but rather Tarantino's "comic embellishment," an altogether different source of pleasure.

I want to distinguish between the two aforementioned types of pleasure that *Basterds* can be said to afford its viewers. While I do not take issue with anyone indulging in the retributive pleasure they might derive from watching Donowitz and Pfc. Omar Ulmer (Omar Doom) unloading their MP40 submachine guns on Hitler (Martin Wuttke) and Goebbels (Sylvester Groth), I do take issue with the specific way in which Tarantino has comically embellished an inherently traumatic historical event. By criticizing *Basterds,* I intend not to condemn the film but to call Tarantino out for his problematic use of humor, which treats the Holocaust as little more than an occasion for gaining pleasure.

The Holocaust: An Occasion to Gain Pleasure?

In *Jokes and Their Relation to the Unconscious,* Freud identifies three comedic forms: jokes, the comic, and humor, each of which gives us pleasure insofar as its occurrence persuades us to conserve psychic energy we customarily expend. The comedy in Tarantino's films falls into the third category, humor, giving us pleasure because "an emotion is avoided which we should have expected because it usually accompanies the situation."[6] In the case of films depicting the Holocaust, we expect to grieve the victims, and yet throughout *Basterds* Tarantino frames episodes that one expects to find traumatic as ironically humorous. As Freud explains in a short essay published in 1927, humor uses "traumas" as "occasions . . . to gain pleasure."[7] He elaborates: "The main thing is the intention which humour carries out, whether it is acting in relation to the self or other people. It means: 'Look! here is the world, which seems so dangerous! It is nothing but a game for children—just worth making a jest about!'"[8]

In *Basterds,* the spectator laughs because the energy usually expended in empathizing with Holocaust victims is saved once he or she realizes that the film's traumatic moments have occurred within an ironic, contrived context. The comedy always resides, then, in the sense that "This looks like the Holocaust, but it isn't the Holocaust." For example, in the opening scene, in which Col. Hans Landa (Christoph Waltz) orders his men to gun down a

Jewish family hiding under a farmhouse's floorboards, the film directs our attention not toward the tragic loss of lives but rather toward the ironic twist that leads to their (then presumably inevitable) deaths: Landa's decision to converse with the Christian homeowner in English because he suspects that the French-speaking Jewish family is secretly listening. This scene, in fact, is the only one in the film that offers a glimpse into a Jewish victim's trauma. The rest of *Inglourious Basterds* erases any trace of the Holocaust as an historical reality; instead of European Jews enduring the Nazis' brutality, German soldiers endure the brutality of Lt. Aldo Raine (Brad Pitt) and his company of mostly American Jewish soldiers known as "the Basterds." But even with German soldiers serving as victims in place of Jews, Tarantino nevertheless diverts the audience's attention away from their trauma as well. When Raine orders the execution of a German soldier who refuses to provide valuable information, Tarantino directs our attention not toward the soldier's terror but rather toward the ironic mode of execution: Donowitz, also known as "the Bear Jew," bashing his brains in with a baseball bat.

Referring to a number of recent Holocaust-related films, including *Basterds*, author Steve Lipman interprets "the continuing viability of films that deign to introduce humor into the sacrosanct subject of genocide and cruelty, a tacit sacrilege in the immediate wake of the war," as a sign of "a confidence both in the abilities of the producers and the sophistication of the public." The rise of such films, he argues,

> makes the statement that while artistic memorializing of the era guarantees that the survivors' legacy will not fade, their voices speak in a less-solemn tone. This points to the Jewish community's confidence in its ability to look at its collective trauma in a non-traumatic way. . . .[9]

While reading this statement, we might wonder why one would *want* to describe the Holocaust in a non-traumatic way, except perhaps to coolly save the psychic energy conventionally expended toward empathizing with the victims' trauma. We might also wonder whether one can adequately memorialize the Holocaust *without* speaking in a solemn tone. Regardless, we must ask whether by structuring *Basterds* so as to divert the audience's attention away from the victims' trauma Tarantino does anything to ensure that "the survivors' legacy will not fade."

Naughty Nazis

In order to memorialize the Holocaust, we must not only empathize with its victims but also understand that it resulted from an odious ideology which manifested itself in the form of Nazi Germany. Predicated on the mythical existence of an Aryan master race and a Jewish-Communist conspiracy to undermine the German state, Nazism authorized the cold-blooded extermination of tens of millions. *Basterds*, however, underplays the central role of the Third Reich in perpetrating the Holocaust, presenting the Nazis instead as the historical equivalent of naughty celebrities—a bunch of bad apples who have come to serve an important cinematic function, that of the perfect villains. Specifically, the film portrays Nazis not as mass murderers but as entertaining bad guys through whom the spectator can live vicariously. A conventionally "fun-loving" movie villain, the fictional Landa is a handsome, suave, witty polyglot who carries out his crimes with devilish glee, his arch facial expressions cutely calling up Disney's 1953 Captain Hook. "Real" Nazis receive the same treatment: Martin Wuttke's portrayal of Hitler makes the German leader out to be a frustrated crime boss, not unlike Big Boy Caprice (Al Pacino) in *Dick Tracy* (1990); whereas Sylvester Froth portrays Goebbels as a wisecracking womanizer whose goal in life is to have a svelte female next to him when he gobbles his *schlag*. One gratuitous shot, included primarily to reduce the propaganda minister to a lecher, shows Goebbels sodomizing his French translator (Julie Dreyfus).

Tarantino further elevates the Nazis to the level of humorous screen villains through the use of title cards. Goebbels is a historical character whereas the Jewish cinema owner (Mélanie Laurent) is fictional; however, Tarantino blurs the boundary between history and fiction by using the same font to identify them onscreen. Legitimizing the Nazis' status as celebrities, Tarantino uses titling to identify Hermann Göring and Martin Bormann when they enter the frame. As if the shots have been taken from a paparazzo's point of view, the titles' subtext seems to exclaim, "Oh, look—an evil Nazi!" and hence implies that the characters' significance lies more in their infamy (their caricature in *our* tranquil postwar perception) than in the specific role each played in the Holocaust. Ultimately, the Nazis come off as glamorous historical figures instead of war criminals who helped to engineer the Holocaust.

A deliberate misspelling of *The Inglorious Bastards* (*Quel maledetto treno blindato*), a 1978 Italian film with which *Inglourious Basterds* has virtually nothing in common (apart from being set during the Second World War), the film's title gestures toward Tarantino's curious attitude toward the relationship between signs and their referents. As Tarantino seems to suggest throughout his film, even though the new title is a distorted copy (a "bastardization") of the original title, the relationship between the new title and its referent is just as legitimate as the relationship between the original title and its referent, the fictional story of five American soldiers who try to escape to Switzerland after being sentenced to military prison. Tarantino's title, therefore, serves as a metaphor for his film's representation of the relationship between Nazi icons and their referents (both as configured in popular culture): in *Inglourious Basterds,* Nazi icons no longer refer to anti-Semitic ideology and its role in the Holocaust; they uncritically refer to entertaining screen villains. Exploiting the Saussurean notion that the relationship between a sign and its referent is arbitrary, Tarantino ultimately advocates humorous resignification for the sake of an enjoyable moviegoing experience.

Further protecting himself against accusations of wrongdoing, Tarantino implicitly equates his resignification of the Holocaust with artistry. This equation occurs on each of two occasions when the audience sees Raine carve a swastika into a Nazi's forehead. The first time, as he and the Bear Jew stare into the camera, the Bear Jew says, "You know, Lieutenant, you're getting pretty good at that," to which Raine replies, "You know how you get to Carnegie Hall, dontcha? Practice." The second time, Raine says, "You know something, Utivich? I think this just might be my masterpiece." These two lines leave the lasting impression that resignification—thus, the resignification of the Holocaust—can be artistic and, hence, above reproach. Indeed, the Holocaust's trivialization apparently qualifies as artistry, certainly as entertainment, because Raine and Utivich find it funny: just before the film cuts to black, they are, to quote Tarantino's screenplay, "giggling ghoulishly."[10]

The Point-of-View Shot: Trivializing Trauma

Regardless of whether Tarantino has consciously intended to hinder efforts to memorialize the Holocaust by treating it as an occasion for gaining pleasure, an application of auteur theory to his previous films reveals a consistent trivialization of trauma in them. Proponents of auteur theory hold that if a director's films exhibit a consistent structure, then by uncovering this structure we can see how it gives rise to certain meanings throughout the director's corpus. In an essay dismissive of Tarantino's films, critic Gary Groth describes their structure by noting that each of them must include:

> (a) a grisly torture scene in which a witty monologue is usually delivered by the torturer to the great discomfort of the torturee; (b) intense violence alternating with goofball humor, which more often than not derives from the characters' arcane knowledge of American junk culture; (c) an unending stream of "homages" or rip-offs of dialogue, scenes, or premises from a vast array of American and European movies; and (d) a Mexican stand-off in which everyone or nearly everyone dies.[11]

This list, which Groth compiled in 1997—after Tarantino had directed *Reservoir Dogs* (1992) and *Pulp Fiction* (1994) and written the screenplays for *True Romance* (1993) and *Natural Born Killers* (1994)—applies to *Inglourious Basterds* (although not to all four feature films Tarantino went on to write and direct after *Killers*). A recurring motif not mentioned in Groth's list, but one that still plays a critical role in the audience's reception of Tarantino's films, is a shot made from a traumatized character's exact point of view (POV). Every one of Tarantino's films includes at least one of these shots. In *Reservoir Dogs,* as Mr. Blue (Michael Madsen) shows Mr. White (Harvey Keitel) and Mr. Pink (Steve Buscemi) the contents of his car's trunk, the spectator first sees a shot of the three criminals looking eagerly into the camera. Then we cut to the anguished expression of a bound policeman, revealing that the previous shot had been from his POV. In *Pulp Fiction,* we take the POV of a little boy (Chandler Lindauer), looking up at a U.S. Army Captain (Christopher Walken) handing him a pocket watch once owned by his father, who died in a P.O.W. camp. The POV shot in *Jackie Brown* is a variant: as the film cuts from Jackie (Pam Grier) and Ray Nicolette (Michael Keaton) staring into the camera to the now-deceased Ordell Robbie (Samuel L. Jackson) staring back, the audience senses the trauma Robbie would have experienced upon realizing the woman he had been exploiting had fatally outsmarted him. *Kill Bill* (2003, 2004) includes several shots from the point-of-view of a traumatized Beatrix Kiddo (Uma Thurman): as she remembers Bill (David Carradine) about to fire a gun into her head; as she visualizes the bullet just before it rips into her; as she peeks out at two men, one of whom intends to rape her; and as she stares up at the Deadly Viper Assassination Squad after they've gunned her down. And in *Death Proof* (2007), as Pam (Rose McGowan) nears death, the film cuts to her POV, in which her sadistic killer (Kurt Russell) gazes maliciously at her.

In *The Subject of Semiotics,* Kaja Silverman describes the "classic" moviegoing experience as one in which the film "sutures" the spectator; in other words, the spectator imagines that a particular character onscreen represents his or her own subjectivity:

The classic cinematic organization depends on the subject's willingness to become absent to itself by permitting a fictional character to "stand in" for it, or by allowing a particular point of view to define what it sees. The operation of suture is successful at the moment that the viewing subject says, "Yes, that's me," or "That's what I see."[12]

Although Silverman does not mention it, I would contend that the POV shot "sutures" the spectator more than any other type of shot, given that no other shot requires the spectator to view the world as though directly through a character's eyes. In this sense, throughout his films, Tarantino provides moments in which viewers can easily indulge their desires to adopt a character's subjectivity. "[W]e want suture so badly," Silverman explains, "we'll take it at any price, even with the fullest knowledge of what it entails—passive insertions into pre-existing discursive positions . . . ; threatened losses and false recoveries; and subordination to the castrating gaze of the Other."[13]

Further, none of Tarantino's POV shots requires the spectator to experience displeasure, given that he repeatedly sets the POV shot within a strikingly ironic context which distracts the viewer from "the castrating gaze of the Other." Instead of sustaining empathy for the doomed cop in *Reservoir Dogs,* the spectator goes on to marvel at the sudden reversal of power (the criminals holding a cop prisoner); an ironic reversal of power, with Jackie now in a position of power over Ordell, has the same effect in *Jackie Brown;* the spectator's empathy for the boy in *Pulp Fiction* falls by the wayside as soon as the Army Captain ironically reveals that he'd "hid this uncomfortable hunk of metal up [his] ass for two years"; *Kill Bill's* rape scene turns into a black comedy when Beatrix rips the rapist's lips off his face; and in *Death Proof,* the killer's absurdly contrived *modus operandi*—while he sits safely in a "death proof" driver's seat, his erratic driving sends Pam flailing throughout the car's interior—diverts attention away from his victim's pain. In each instance, the net effect of situating a traumatized character's POV within an ironic context trivializes the character's trauma altogether, turning it into a source of pleasure. Tarantino's irony reminds the audience that they are merely watching a contrivance: the irony enables the viewer "to seek refuge within the film's fiction"[14] and to cease imagining themselves as victims or perpetrators of certain cultural problems (e.g. violence against women or extermination of Jews). As already discussed, *Basterds'* ironic moments counteract Holocaust memorialization, given that it excuses the audience from performing the psychic work that Holocaust memorializing requires.[15]

Keeping in mind this analysis of Tarantino's POV shots, we see that the filmmaker handles two such shots in *Basterds* in much the same trivializing way. The film ends on a shot from Landa's point of view, which Tarantino again situates within an ironic context in order to let viewers disassociate themselves from the Nazi's morally problematic subjectivity. As Raine finishes carving a swastika into the man's forehead, the film takes his perspective, which shows Raine and Utivich admiring Raine's handiwork. The irony is that after negotiating a cushy retirement on Nantucket in exchange for helping end the war, Landa must live out his life branded as a Nazi. As such, the film has again invited the spectator to imagine him or herself as a Nazi, yet a Nazi on the verge of making it in America. Once again, the irony discourages the spectator from reflecting upon Landa's wickedness and moral depravity, as the Nazi officer in charge of tracking down and murdering Jews in France ("The Jew Hunter"). We are encouraged to laugh at the poetic "justice."

We get another POV shot earlier in the film, when Raine calls for the execution of a German captive, Sgt. Werner Rachtman (Richard Sammel). From a shot of Rachtman staring stoically into the camera, the film cuts to what initially appears to be his vision but turns out to be a point-of-view shot from immediately beside his head, still sympathetic to his angle if not exactly behind his eyes. We see a darkened, arched doorway from which emerges the Bear Jew wielding a baseball bat. By dollying out and revealing that the shot is from just to Rachtman's right the camera removes us from his point of view, not as much to let us breathe a sigh of relief as to facilitate our sitting back and taking in Donovitz the Bear Jew as he slays and mutilates Rachtman. We can cheer while he screams, "Teddy fucking Williams knocks it out of the park! Fenway Park on its feet for Teddy! Fuckin' ball game! He went yard on that one!" As with the trivialization of traumatized characters in Tarantino's previous films, the German soldier's trauma in this scene turns into just another ironic contrivance once we see the Bear Jew's summative performance, in which he treats cold-blooded murder as if it were a climactic moment in a baseball game. The performance jolts the spectator away from the victim's traumatic subject position, which the film resignifies as humorously ironic.

In general, Tarantino structures the ironic POV shot like a monologue joke: in the setup, the hypothetical spectator takes a victim's point of view and prepares to expend his or her psychic energy toward painful identification with a destitute subject's position; in the punch line, and upon learning that the entire scene is an ironic contrivance, the spectator feels relief because psychic energy has been saved. The jokes of *Inglorious Basterds* thus excuse the spectator from directing any energy toward Holocaust memorials. Although the suturing process has the potential to force viewers to reflect upon the historical impact of victims' subjectivity, Tarantino lets viewers "off the hook," to use Silverman's words, by implying that the Nazis' worldview and, by implication, their horrific legacy were nothing more than one of history's humorous ironies.

Notes

[1] Jeffrey Goldberg, "Hollywood's Jewish Avenger," *The Atlantic* (September 2009), 74–77.

[2] Sara Miller, "Israelis go wild for Tarantino's Inglourious Basterds," *Haaretz* (17 September 2009). Available online at http://www.haaretz.com/hasen/spages/1115023.html

[3] See http://pajamasmedia.com/blog/inglourious-basterds-a-german-fantasy-not-a-jewish-one/ and http://www.independent.org/blog/?p=3200

[4] Peter Travers, "Die, Nazis, Die!," *Rolling Stone* (3 September 2009), 91. Available online at http://www.rollingstone.com/reviews/movie/27810109/review/29774751/inglourious_basterds.

[5] Rex Reed, "I Had a Helluva Time Watching Inglourious Basterds," *The New York Observer* (18 August 2009). Available online at http://www.observer.com/2009/movies/i-had-helluva-time-watching-inglourious-basterds

[6] Sigmund Freud, *Jokes and Their Relation to the Unconscious,* trans. and ed. James Strachey (New York: Norton, 1963 © 1905), 292.

[7] Freud, "Humour," *Standard Edition of the Works of Sigmund Freud,* trans. and ed. James Strachey (London: The Hogarth Press, 1966 © 1927), 162.

[8] Freud, "Humour," 166.

[9] Steve Lipman, "Holocaust Humor Losing Its Shtick," *The Jewish Week* (22 September 2009). Available online at http://www.thejewishweek.com/viewArticle/c344_a16807/The_Arts/Film.html

[10] Quentin Tarantino, *Inglourious Basterds: A Screenplay* (New York: Little, Brown and Company, 2009), 164.

[11] Gary Groth, "A Dream of Perfect Reception: The Movies of Quentin Tarantino," *Commodify Your Dissent: Salvos from the Baffler,* eds. Thomas Frank and Matt Weiland (New York: Norton, 1997), 185.

[12] Kaja Silverman, *The Subject of Semiotics* (New York: Oxford University Press, 1983), 205.

[13] Silverman, 212–3.

[14] Silverman, 213.

[15] For an intensive discussion of what memory of the Holocaust implies, opens to examination, and requires, see Jean-Michel Frodon, ed., *Cinema and the Shoah: An Art Confronts the Tragedy of the Twentieth Century* (Albany: State University of New York Press, 2010).

Chapter 26

"I have the stuff that you want"

Michael Jackson and the Crotch Shot

Dominic Lennard

Michael Jackson was hardly a figure accused of adherence to traditional gender roles. The star's sexual identity was the subject of extensive public and media comment, owing largely to what was perceived as the increased feminization of his image throughout his career. Jackson's high-pitched squeals and shivery, sexual shrieks and stutters, and his experiments with plastic surgery (largely coded in the media as the domain of women), had a significant hand in steering his public image away from the traditionally masculine. Many male celebrities have been under the knife prior to and since Jackson (albeit less extensively), such as Gary Cooper, Elvis Presley, Kenny Rogers, and Mickey Rourke. In each of these cases, though, the rugged, heterosexual masculinity central to the performers' image would have compromised any inclination to view them as "feminine." The appearance achieved through Jackson's procedures gave the public license to question his gender identity more directly, and led to frequent comparisons with Diana Ross.[1] In 1995, Australia's *New Idea* magazine reported news of a photograph of Jackson dressed as the diva when he was a teenager, an artifact that "[held] the singer up to more ridicule"; the article derisively concluded with the revelation that "it was not the first time he dressed like a woman."[2] Jackson's refusal to embrace traditional models of masculinity made him the favorite scapegoat of a broad cultural desire to punish gender treachery. The cross-dressing accusation reemerged numerous times prior to and following his death on June 26, 2009, and most of us are familiar with the popular joke that emphasizes Jackson's gradual transformation from "a black man to a white woman" through cosmetic surgery.

Looking back after the star's death with more sympathy, David Gates of *Newsweek* paints Jackson as "energetic, charismatic, and supremely gifted, but sexually unassertive[3]— unlike swaggeringly heterosexual black male performers from Big Joe Turner ("Shake, Rattle, and Roll") to Jay-Z ("Big Pimpin'")."[4] In fact, Jackson had openly challenged "macho" masculinity in the video clips for "Beat It" (1982) and "Bad" (1987).[5] The self-consciously "masculine" clothing often worn by Jackson in later years critiqued traditional constructions of manhood and their investment in phallic symbols of power. Clad in military regalia, badges, epaulettes, and bandolera-like sashes, the star habitually drew attention to a kind of manhood to which he refused to subscribe: there was something unmistakably parodic about the slender, feathery-voiced star wearing the macho garb of imperial patriarchy as he sang songs with titles like "Heal the World."

Through the lens of Jackson's persona, manhood could clearly not be defined by adherence to a set of macho signifiers. And following this, Jackson may be read as a figure who, in the face of tabloid mockery, exposed gender as a social construct, one who questioned the connotations of power associated with binary notions of masculine and feminine. After all, if heteronormative versions of masculinity are neither stable nor physically determined but rather ideologically constructed, so is the claim to power and superiority that men traditionally make.

However, I want to briefly explore the idea that as Jackson's image became outwardly more gender-ambiguous, his active representation of heterosexual male-dominance in fact became more pronounced. I argue that this signaling of dominance is exemplified in the crotch shot and crotch grab: choreographic and cinematographic moves that draw intense attention to the star's penis. Through consideration of these techniques in Jackson's presentation of himself in music videos and live performances, we can see that despite his apparent subversion of traditional masculinities, Jackson reaffirmed male over feminine superiority, dramatically restating the "power of the penis." In focusing on this specific aspect of Jackson's image, I do not mean to sweep aside other aspects of this unique and capricious man's public persona but rather to bring to light an evocative aspect of the Jackson image that has been overlooked in discussions of his complex relationship to gender norms.

It was around the release of "Bad" in 1988 that Michael Jackson's image became increasingly sexualized. Early solo videos such as "Billy Jean" (1982) and "Thriller" (1984) contain the signifiers of sexuality (particularly insofar as dancing itself may be accepted as a display of sexuality) but in a clearly less overt way than the videos that succeeded them. In the video for "Bad"'s title track, for instance, Jackson wore a leather outfit adorned with buckles and clips reminiscent of a bondage outfit, and caressed his own body in gestures both sleek and explosive. In the video for the more subdued "The Way You Make Me Feel" from the same album, Jackson pursues a young woman through the streets with provocative dance moves: at one point the target of his desire steps into a parked car and Jackson literally dives in after her as if a sexual act will take place. The woman escapes from the other side of the car, although it is clear from this cheekily performed maneuver that his interest in her is in fact hardly unwelcome and will be satisfied at some later point (the song's conclusion).

The most popularly recognized manifestation of this new sexualization of the Jackson image was the star's tendency to touch himself, particularly his crotch, in a way that suggested masturbation. Throughout the remainder of Jackson's career, our attention was regularly drawn to his crotch in music videos and live performances.[6]

The most sustained example of the focus on Jackson's crotch occurs in the extended video for the highly successful 1992 single "Black or White." The video "proper"—that is, the period of it in which the song itself is featured—pays plenty of attention to this area of Jackson's anatomy through both camera and choreography. It is the video's extended conclusion, however, in which these antics reach their (even alarming) zenith. As Jackson enters a nighttime street, he tilts his fedora brim over his eyes, his obscured face redirecting our attention to his body for the duration of the scene. A shot capturing his whole body reveals that the hand not securing the hat's downward tilt is clutching his crotch. He steps confidently through the blue windswept street flanked by broken down cars and recommences dancing without musical assist for a further four minutes, the camera's focus entirely on the physicality of the performance and the momentum of his body. Throughout the scene Jackson sporadically smashes a series of car windows which have been vandalized with contrived racist slogans ("KKK Rules," etc.). However, these moments clearly go no way to substantiating our preoccupation with and spectacularization of Jackson's crotch—watching it, and watching him touch it. The vandalism equates to nothing more than emptily symbolic dance moves intended to hamfistedly inject social purpose into what is, irrepressibly, a fetishistic display. The scene is gobsmackingly punctuated when Jackson squares his legs, extends one arm way out from his body, grips his crotch with the other, and thrusts repeatedly toward the lens. Sufficiently warmed up by this performance, we are treated to a close-up of Jackson's hand sliding gradually down his clothed genitals; seconds later, he zips up the fly that was—oops!—apparently open the entire time! We are thus treated to a voyeuristic shot combination that brashly assumes the viewer's fascination with Jackson's concealed—or perhaps not-so-concealed—penis.

As well as through his dancing, Jackson's crotch was emphasized through his costume choices, such as the oversized belt worn by the singer in the "Bad" video and his subsequent 1988 tour. A shimmery golden costume featuring silver strap-on leg pads ascending to the crotch region, worn during the 1996–1997 "HIStory" tour, had a similar effect of emphasizing Jackson's concealed penis. In this costume, largely padded with Velcro armguards and gloves suggesting Robocoppish body armor, the crotch region remains "exposed." The most pronounced accentuation of Jackson's crotch through his costuming was provided by the pseudo-military uniform worn during the "Dangerous" tour (1992–93), which featured gold underwear worn on top of the star's trousers (black, presumably for maximum contrast).[7] The "HIStory" tour also featured a similarly crotch-centric golden, one-piece suit worn over long black trousers. These provocative costume combinations focused maximum attention on the crotch: the point at which Jackson's legs emerged to distinguish the perimeter of his genital area. The contrast of gold with prosaic black clearly defined the limits of his crotch and our interest. Then, of course, throughout his performance, Jackson would again channel our attention to this location—lay his hands on the gold.

Our interest in his penis and the ostensibly tantalizing possibility of having it revealed to us was central to Jackson's stage persona. The striking emphasis given to this spectacle demands our consideration of its interaction with the more "feminine" aspects of Jackson's image, since it's with female performers that the crotch shot is traditionally associated. Nadine Wills focuses on the crotch shot in the Hollywood musical, a stylistic move which, she argues, "whether through women spreading their legs, through their skirts flying up to reveal their underwear, or through costumes which draw attention to the genital area,"[8] forms an iconographic mainstay of the genre. Wills discusses how the crotch shot as a move through heterosexual femininity is projected onto a woman's actual body, stamping it with a set of culturally-based ideals and assumptions. She points out that the crotch shot, among other functions, "certainly served a reductive purpose in the musical, embodying femininity as a universal female attribute to be put on display for male desire."[9]

In Jackson's case, the crotch shot/grab similarly situated the performer's sex in one totalizing location, overriding his sexually ambiguous image and constructing him, through this hidden organ, as a heterosexual object of desire. Rather than situating Jackson as a passive object of a female gaze, though, this process powerfully restated the phallocentric assumption of the mystical penis that women both "want" and "need." In the song "Dirty Diana" from "Bad," Jackson narrates a scenario in which he resists the sexual charms of a fame-seeking groupie, despite her hypnotic promise that, conversely, "[she] has the stuff that [he] want[s]." This song precisely encapsulates the relationship between Jackson and the fan put forward in his videos, except that it was Jackson, in reality, who tantalizingly withheld a sexualized body, his penis in particular—constructing the male organ as a symbol of fame, desirability, and power. For the female fan, Jackson's penis was both desired and unattainable: the key to both her attraction to him, and the division between them—that is, the power he held over her.

This display can be clearly seen in Jackson's official live DVD, filmed in Bucharest.[10] In this performance, the interaction depicted between performer and fan is blatantly sexual. Throughout the film, shots of Jackson's pelvic thrusts or crotch grabs are frequently juxtaposed with shots of screaming girls' faces, as if he were in fact pleasuring them through some astonishingly potent though invisible sexual act. The frequent use of this shot combination serves to empower Jackson's crotch, immediately demonstrating its power over his female fans. At several points throughout the concert their limply post-coital bodies are carried or stretchered from the crowd by venue security; an official attempts to slap one exhausted girl back to her senses. The overwhelming majority of fans shown are female, and the focus on them as individuals—suddenly distinguished from an indistinct mass of swaying heads—reemphasizes the star's superiority in this imagined sexual encounter by implying the lowly fan's good fortune at having been involved in it.

The orgiastic response attributed to these fans confirms Jackson's heterosexual masculinity, in spite of his effeminate image, by powerfully demonstrating his ability to master the feminine. It provides spectacular "evidence" of both Jackson's legitimacy and potency as a heterosexual male through the subordination of a feminized audience to his concealed penis.[11]

There is, however, another way to read these "encounters." Rather than representing an imaginary yet ecstatically potent sexual act, the Jackson fan display might instead indicate the intolerable *denial* of such an act: the fan frustratingly refusing real sexual contact. It is not such a stretch to argue that we could accept that Jackson, through the feminization of his appearance, might in fact have become an object of desire *for himself,* and the crotch grab symbolizes the masturbatory evidence of this. Following this we might read the excitement generated by the crotch grab as an indication of a competition: the fan's erotic inter-est in Jackson (however constructed) vying with the star's erotic interest in himself. What we are seeing is an act of teasing. Michael's withholding is thus depicted as simultaneously exciting and intolerable. The required response is for the fan to cry or tremble, reduced to an infantile state through sheer frustration.

In both interpretations male superiority and sexual power becomes incontrovertibly bio-logical, an advantage based on the female's lack of and desire for the penis. The crotch shot is used to naturalize gender difference by, as Wills puts it, "collapsing it into physical differ-ence,"[12] ensuring that the penis is dramatically located as the ultimate signifier of not only heterosexual maleness but of a male's desirability to the female and power over her.

Peter Lehman has demonstrated that cultural accounts of sexual difference and male superiority place an emphasis on the size of the penis, particularly its visibility as dramatic spectacle.[13] Any failure by the penis to live up to this drama risks ridiculing the man's sex-uality: "At the one pole," Lehman writes, "we have the powerful awesome spectacle of phal-lic masculinity, and at the other its vulnerable, pitiable, and frequently comic collapse."[14] Because the penis can never live up to the power and grandeur of the phallus, Lehman points out, the rhetoric of masculine superiority it represents, "the awe we attribute to the striking visibility of the penis" is best served "by keeping it covered up."[15] In this sense, while Jack-son's dominance was certainly linked to his (real) penis, the organ's continued concealment promised an abstract grandeur, something clearly demonstrated in the Bucharest video. Not only did the focus on Jackson's crotch remind us of the difference between men and women, it reproduced the masculinist assumption of the mystical phallus that all women want and need. Jackson's remarkable talent as a dancer was one aspect of the star's persona that was not ruthlessly questioned during his lifetime, and it is not my intention to ques-tion it here. Following this theme, though, the repeated embedding of the crotch grab—hardly a demanding maneuver—within otherwise dazzlingly (even bewilderingly) skillful routines itself aggrandized the move, and lent to it some extraordinary mystique. During the crotch grab, the invisible Jackson penis was as overwhelming as the visible Jackson dance moves that contained it.

In the video for "Remember the Time," Jackson dances in ancient Egypt for a pharaoh (Eddie Murphy) and his fussy wife (Iman). The video depicts the androgynous male as a threat to a heteronormative "macho" masculinity, the competition indicated through the visible arousal of the pharaoh's wife during Jackson's performance. Although this routine is uncharacteristically bereft of overt crotch grabs, at one point Jackson waggles a finger slowly down his torso toward his genitals, a display that provokes the queen to exhale deeply and the cranky pharaoh to order the performer's arrest for his effrontery. The queen's hypnotic fixation on Jackson's sexual body is thus used to validate Jackson's heterosexual manhood against that of the stuffy pharaoh. Murphy's appearance in this video is itself certainly a conscious rebuttal in a conversation about manhood: the comedian had mocked Jackson's masculinity in his 1983 TV special "Delirious," and as Jackson biographer J. Randy Taborelli recalls, Murphy played an "effeminate and affected" Jackson in an episode of "Saturday Night Live."[16] Toward the end of the video, the queen reclines on a bed and caresses the shaft of a royal staff as Jackson dances before her: not only is the penis here, yet again, the key to the woman's desire, but its concealment means that, as in the Bucharest video, its power and mys-tique can be fantastically inflated.

While Jackson may not have been popularly considered the most familiarly masculine performer (as Murphy's "Delirious" routine cuttingly illustrates), his concealed penis was constantly offered as a way of disambiguating his gender identity once and for all with its assertion that Jackson could be a man without "being a man" in the sense of adhering to dominant ideals of heterosexual masculinity. His version of masculinity was validated through its dominance over the feminine, specifically its imagination of a slavish desire for the concealed penis, a powerful reimagining of the mystical, all-powerful phallus. His performances implied an intensely phallocentric female gaze, and used this to affirm traditional models of masculinity defined by possession of the penis (or its representatives) and the desire for it.[17] In his biography of Jackson, Taborelli comments on the public's interest in the star's sexuality in the 1980s in light of his seemingly distant and asexual relationships with the women with whom he publicly appeared. He recalls that in 1984, Jackson's manager Frank DiLeo called a press conference to dismiss the public's various curiosities about the singer: "No celebrity," writes Taborelli, "had ever gone to such lengths to proclaim his or her heterosexuality."[18] Through the crotch grab and crotch shot, Jackson additionally refuted accusations of homosexuality by ensuring that the sexuality communicated through videos and live performances was emphatically heterosexual. However, in doing this he fell back into the very masculinist paradigms he apparently rejected.

Notes

[1] Taborelli, J. Randy, *Michael Jackson: The Magic and the Madness* (London: Pan Books, 2004), 347.

[2] May, Pamela, "Crisis Time for Jacko," *New Idea* (January 21, 1995), 9.

[3] Jackson's perceived removal from heteronormative adult sexuality was increased by his choice of residence, Neverland Ranch, a private amusement park and shrine to childhood, and the child sexual abuse alleged to have occurred there.

[4] Gates, David, "Finding Neverland," *Newsweek* (July 6–13, 2009), 57.

[5] For all music videos cited here see *Michael Jackson: Video Greatest Hits / HIStory* (SMV, 1995).

[6] Yahoo! Music felt the crotch grab significant enough to include in a list of the dance superstar's nine greatest moves (http://new.music.yahoo.com/blogs/getback/135138/michael-jacksons-greatest-dance-moves/).

[7] Also the same outfit depicted in statues of Michael Jackson positioned throughout Europe to promote *HIStory*, and rendered on the album's cover.

[8] Wills, Nadine, " '110 per cent woman': The Crotch Shot in the Hollywood Musical," *Screen* 42:2 (2001), 124.

[9] Wills, 125.

[10] *Michael Jackson: Live in Bucharest: The Dangerous Tour*. Sony/BMG. DVD. 1992.

[11] We might also note that Jackson's movements constitute more luridly suggestive versions of Elvis's iconic pelvic thrust, both relying upon and exaggerating an already familiar male-performer/female-fan dynamic.

[12] Wills, 121.

[13] Lehman, Peter, *Running Scared: Masculinity and the Representation of the Male Body* (Philadelphia, PA: Temple University Press, 1993), 109.

[14] Lehman, Peter, "Crying Over the Melodramatic Penis: Melodrama and Male Nudity in Films of the 90s," in Lehman, ed., *Masculinity: Bodies, Movies, Culture* (New York, NY: Routledge, 2001), 26.

[15] Lehman, *Running Scared,* 111.

[16] Taborelli, 328.

[17] Of course, the particular image Jackson put forward of himself as a sexual object cannot have hoped to account for, or control, his subjection to more diverse gazes, such as homosexual or bisexual ones. Rather, it constituted a self-endorsed role marketed toward a heterosexual female audience, and at the same time a role as open to subversion by male viewers as it was to rejection by female ones.

[18] Taraborrelli, 330.

Chapter 27

From Star Wars *to* Avatar

Contemporary Special Effects, Industrial Light and Magic, and the Legacy of the 1970s

Julie Turnock

We knew we'd have a lot of visual effects scenes that we could not originate on film, but I desperately wanted this film to feel analog and real, and rooted in an emotional reality.
—J.J. Abrams, director of *Star Trek* (2009)[1]

In 1977, *Star Wars* (retrospectively renamed *Star Wars: Episode IV—A New Hope*) was released to broad popular acclaim. Critics lauded its stunningly convincing and complex special effects work, as well as the film's fast-paced sense of movement within an impressively realized diegetic world.[2] It begins with a famous special effect sequence: the flyover on an empty star field, with the camera tilting down to partial view of a planet in the lower quarter of the frame. A small ship moves quickly from the top right in the frame into deep perspective, shooting brightly colored laserbeams into off-screen space, causing the screen to strobe. Then from the upper frame, an imperial cruiser looms into view, filling the overhead portion of the screen with its heft for an inordinate amount of time (about twenty-five seconds) as it moves into the deep space after the small ship. It, too, is firing laserbeams forward and furthering the strobing effect.

Moviegoers were awed by *Star Wars*'s opening sequence, as the large space ship appeared to hover over the head of the audience and converge into the middle distance. Most impressively, the entire sequence was built element by element, frame by frame, by special effects artists with no live actors or "real" locations. For the planets and ships, the *Star Wars* effects team used carefully executed matte paintings (paintings combined with live action footage, animation, or models to produce a realistic composite image) and miniature ship models (of which parts originated in off-the-shelf model kits). The star backgrounds and the laserbeams were meticulously hand-animated, frame by frame, through traveling matte composites (a composite technique used to combine two separately filmed elements when the foreground element [e.g. a person] changes shape or position from frame to frame—necessitating a new matte for each frame) and rotoscoping (tracing film images projected onto paper or cels, as a basis for lighting, ghosts, or other hand animated effects; the artwork is then rephotographed and optically combined with the original footage). The sense of pace and excitement was created most notably through the newly refined technique of motion control, which computer-mapped the motion of both the ship and the camera filming it, allowing for numberless identical repeat takes. All of these elements were finally assembled in post-production, frame by frame, with an optical printer (a device that manipulates photographic images while copying [printing] them from one film to another). The colorful and pulsating laser beams, combined with the strobing of the screen and the movement of the models into the middle distance, enliven the frame and encourage the movement of the eye into the plane of action. The aggregate effect (along with the innovative sound design) suggests a "you are there," quasi-documentary style. This thirty-second sequence quickly establishes a seamless, expansive, and credible world in which the action of the film will unfold.[3]

What may be most surprising to us today is that this sequence (along with many of the other elaborate special effects sequences in *Star Wars*) can be said to largely hold up to contemporary standards of photorealism. Although subjective, this judgment is certainly a testament to the meticulousness and creativity of the technicians of Industrial Light and Magic (ILM), Lucasfilm's still dominant special effects wing, formed in the late 1970s for *Star Wars* and its sequels *The Empire Strikes Back* (1980) and *Return of the Jedi* (1983). However, the primary reason why the effects in *Star Wars* do not look dated is that much of contemporary digital effects draw upon an aesthetic that is nearly the same as the photorealist aesthetic of this film.[4] It was ILM that invented our contemporary sense of cinematic photorealism.

From professional critics to casual cinema-goers, everyone seems to know when a movie's special effects are "good" or "amazing," or when they look "amateurish" or "fake."[5] But where do our standards of photorealism come from? What makes us judge things in movies as looking "real?" Where does it fail, and under what criteria? What may seem like a simple visual testing (does it look as it does in the world?) is in fact a complex combination of many aesthetic, historical, and technological factors. Rather than assuming that special effects belong to a transhistorical notion of photorealism, the digital special-effects aesthetics of recent blockbusters can be historically contextualized within a range of practices that demonstrate continuity with the special effects blockbusters of the 1970s. Moreover, the components and models that comprise the aesthetic of photorealism carry implications for issues of representation that reveal the filmmakers' political inclinations in the depiction of fantasy worlds.

ILM's fairly consistent aesthetic, tweaked over time as new technologies are introduced, can still be recognized in such recent (mostly ILM-produced) special-effects extravaganzas as *Star Trek* (2009), *Transformers* (2007) and its sequel *Transformers: Revenge of the Fallen* (2009), and *Terminator Salvation* (2009). The ILM model is so strong that for other films not produced by that company, namely *District 9* (2009), *Cloverfield* (2008), and *The Host* (2006), filmmakers implicitly and sometimes explicitly reference ILM examples as their model for photorealism. Further, this photoreal aesthetic began with, but extends beyond, special effects production, and goes deeper than simply influencing the look of photoreal special effects. With the permeation of digital technology into nearly all areas of filmmaking, including cinematography, editing, production design, and post-production color timing, the ILM aesthetic has seeped into nearly all areas of contemporary cinema production.

Of course, special effects have appeared in cinema throughout its history. What was different about *Star Wars* and especially its sequels was their sheer volume. They did not restrict special effects to a small, climactic showcase sequence (as was the case with "classical" 1950s science fiction like *Forbidden Planet* [1956] or *War of the Worlds* [1953]). Instead, the original *Star Wars* trilogy greatly increased the number of special-effects shots in a science fiction film, while accelerating the pace of the action within the special-effects sequences. As already described, the ILM team both innovated and looked to the past, re-engineering and enhancing traveling matte composites and rotoscoping while using a combination of traditional techniques such as matte paintings and miniatures. Finally, they refined or invented other techniques, most notably motion control. On top of the techniques developed for specific Lucasfilm productions, such as the original *Star Wars* trilogy, ILM also prioritized the repeatability of their methods, creating a reusable industrialized structure for future productions.

For ILM and Lucas, the advantage of investing so much energy and money to develop special effects techniques and a post-production timeline would be a more intense form of audience absorption in the worlds on display.[6] Special-effects artists designed techniques in the late 1970s and early 1980s in order to construct a more fully-realized, seemingly boundless and seamless world. For filmmakers like Lucas and Spielberg, the benefit of a convincingly constructed diegetic world was the way they could visually and dynamically present their version of what was popularly understood as a "New Hollywood" brand of intellectual filmmaking.[7] A perfectly achieved, seamless world would not distract the viewer (through attention to unconvincing special effects) from the ideas and worldviews presented to them. Perhaps idealistically, these filmmakers strove for a seamless visual manifestation of metaphorical lines of reasoning in order to explore science fiction's "big ideas" of the limits of humanity, the role of the individual within the group, and the dangers and potentials of technology.

In order to achieve the desired level of convincingness, 1970s ILM special-effects leaders such as Dennis Muran and Richard Edlund believed that their techniques had to conform to contemporary standards of live-action photorealism. Granted, because the term "realism" (a commonly used catch-all term by professionals and laymen alike) is far too vague and amorphous, one must concede that within cinematic representation, the more precise and apt term is "photorealism." But how can we define photorealism? The commonly held special-effects industrial formula for photorealism seems obvious: If *x* existed in our world (an alien spacecraft, a Gollum, a fairy-tale castle) and was photographed, how would it look, and how would it move? Common sense suggests that special effects objects should look the way they do when our eyes behold things in the real world. However, the real formula for photorealism is: If it existed *and if it were photographed,* how would it look? We are so used to cinematic conventions, we typically do not even notice the transformation that ordinary objects undergo when they are placed on a set in front of a camera lens, professionally lit, recorded on film or a hard drive, developed or processed, copied onto a release print, and finally projected at our local theater. In other words, the simple glass of juice in a movie that seems to look exactly like the glass of juice in front of us at breakfast has gone through a number of artificial processes, and appears at a particular point in history with certain industrial and aesthetic conventions in order for us as moviegoers to accept that it looks exactly as we expect a glass of juice to look.

Histories of special effects tend to revolve around the premise that they are always "improving" in the direction of "greater" photorealism. But notions of photorealism change and shift historically as new and different image-capture (analog or digital) techniques and technologies become standardized or expected in filmmaking practice. Therefore, if we imagine our glass of juice in a Douglas Sirk film (say, *All That Heaven Allows* [1955]), or in a Robert Altman film (say, *A Wedding* [1978]), or a Michael Mann film (say, *Miami Vice* [2006]), it will have different aesthetic contours in 1955 than in 1978 or 2006.

All that being said, what is astonishing about contemporary notions of special effects is that well into the 2000's, filmmakers and technicians use much of the same rhetoric from 1977 to describe how they achieve photorealism in special effects, this despite the huge technological changes the film industry has undergone with respect to digital technology. More likely, however, it is exactly *because* of those technological changes.

Contemporary Photorealism

In reading director and technician statements and watching DVD extras for recent films admired for their photoreal special effects, including *Transformers, Star Trek, Terminator Salvation,* and *District 9,* I see a number of imaging strategies emerge over and over again. *Star Trek* director J.J. Abrams says he "desperately wanted this film to feel analog and real." In order to create this analog effect—the unpixillated look of *not* having been created through computer digitalization—they shot on film and used hand-held (film) cameras to capture the action whenever possible. The filmmakers also enlivened the picture plane through near obsessive lens flaring (shining a bright light directly into the lens, to create a reflection that resembles a non-uniform haze or expanding bright spots), both in live action with the actors on the U.S.S. Enterprise's bridge and in wide (effects) shots of the ship in battle. *Transformers* also shot many of its action sequences with a hand-held camera. Additionally, the ILM strategy of making giant alien robots appear photoreal centered around surface texture and reflections on the shiny car bodies and moving mechanical parts. More specifically, producers wanted the robot parts not only to move and transform convincingly but to have a roughened, scratched texture that would play against the extra-shiny chrome and polished finishes of the cars.

The team on *Terminator Salvation* also emphasized the gritty surface textures of machines, using a hand-held camera and lens flares to suggest photorealism. In a related but somewhat novel variation of this theme, director McG's primary photoreal strategy for this hugely complex special-effects film involved replicating as often as possible the look of a hand-held long take. In one particular two-minute sequence, invisible editing and digital compositing create the appearance of a single, unbroken shot from a single tracking camera (a technique strongly associated with the qualities of authenticity, integrity, and the traditional aesthetic of realism, not to mention the tradition of virtuoso filmmaking), as hero John Connor (Christian Bale) climbs out from an underground bunker, surveys the landscape, runs toward and mounts a helicopter, and begins to take off. The camera stays on him as the helicopter takes a missile hit and spins out of control, then whips around to a medium shot of the helicopter in a tailspin, rockets back to Connor's side and flips over as the helicopter hits the ground and lands upside down. Connor releases his safety belt, and the camera rights itself. Connor staggers out of the helicopter, stands and observes a mushroom cloud explosion, and is attacked by a terminator. Visible cut.[8]

Careful lighting and manipulation of lighting schemes have long played a role in photoreal special effects strategies. For *District 9* director Neil Blomkamp, lighting played a particularly important role due to his much smaller budget. *District 9* has received a great deal of praise for its convincing photoreal special effects completed on a comparatively low budget (reported $30 million to *Terminator Salvation*'s $200 million). As Blomkamp (a protégé of *Lord of the Rings* director Peter Jackson) asserts:

> One way to help sell photoreal effects is if you give the visual effects artist something that is conducive to being lit in a photoreal way. Secondly you provide them an environment that will help them, [such as a hard metallic surface that doesn't absorb light] ... but bounces light, and put it inside a harsh lighting environment, like a directional single light, like sunlight. ... And you'll get a good hard shadow that will sit in that place in quite a photoreal way.[9]

Along with *Star Trek*'s and *Transformer*'s lens flares, the digital replication of light patterning serves as an important marker in recognizing a space as "credible" or "realistic."

For all but one of these films mentioned, *District 9*, ILM was the lead special-effects house for the production. Through these examples (and many others could be enumerated), we can summarize the characteristics and techniques of creating photorealism in recent special effects films: lens flares (and other textural light patterns); a hand-held camera; directional "natural" light; textured, gritty surfaces; imperfect frame corrections; rack focus (a change in depth of field during a shot); and long takes. If these characteristics recall a 1970s Robert Altman or Monte Hellman film, that is not a coincidence. ILM was incorporated in the late 1970s, and grew out of George Lucas and his collaborators' situation within the New Hollywood movement that valued that (European-inflected) historical aesthetic as a badge of realism opposed to the polished and slick professionalism of the Hollywood studio look.

The special-effect photoreal aesthetic designed to conform to Lucas's 1970s cinematography has proven surprisingly durable. Adherence to 1970s photographic aesthetics today can be understood as both continuity with the ILM past and the acknowledgement of a house style. However, it is also a reaction to the early digital-era "problem" of what computer-generated (CG) images should look like, and a continued dissatisfaction with the existing limitations of digital technology. When J. J. Abrams and his team asked, "What can we learn from *Star Wars*?," and Blomkamp enthused about 70s and 80s design geometry, they were not only evincing nostalgia for the films of their youth. Their work is also a backlash against the perceived shortcomings of CGI, especially in replicating "realistic" (that is, photographic) weight, movement, and solidity.[10]

The Animation Approach

An argument that begins with the insistence that early twenty-first century filmmakers strive to maintain the look of the 1970s photoreal aesthetic may seem somewhat counter-intuitive or even wrong in the age of the nearly fully animatable CGI blockbuster. Computer animation, not unlike traditional 2-D animation, seems to offer the unlimited possibilities and transformations that are not bound by the limitations of photochemical technologies. On one hand, it seems that CGI has realized Kubrick's much-quoted dictum: If it can be written, or thought, it can be filmed.[11] On the other hand, many critics loudly bemoan the "over-animated" look of contemporary CGI, with awkwardly moving, fuzzy-edged synthetic figures zipping about in an overcrowded mise-en-scène ruled by dodgy physics. About *300* (2006), for example, Mark Harris bemoaned:

> oatmeal-colored CGI skies that don't look skylike; CGI hills that don't appear hard to climb; CGI blood that spurts in unconvincing geysers; a dinky CGI thunderstorm that looks like a tempest in an iMac. Nothing in *300* has weight, dimension, or density; every overstylized, joysticky frame has been sprayed with a coat of I Can't Believe It's Not A Movie.[12]

How can we account for this much remarked upon aspect of CGI special effects work with regard to the attention it gives to a photographic aesthetic?

Animation techniques in special-effects work are far from new, and pre-date the popularization of digital effects by several decades. Moreover, the animated look of contemporary special effects can be placed in a dialectical historical context. The goal of 1970s special-effects production was not merely to establish a seamless sense of photorealism. Through films like *Star Wars* and its sequels, *Close Encounters of the Third Kind* (1977), and *Blade Runner* (1982), artists like Douglas Trumbull wanted special effects to achieve the level of flexibility, as well as an expressivity, that has long been associated with both traditional and experimental animation. I call this aesthetic *optical animation*. Filmmakers developed a hybrid style merging the perceived solidity and realism of the photographic "optical" aesthetic and the imaginative plasticity of animation, allowing for the building of complex diegetic worlds from multiple photographic and animated components. The *Star Wars* opening fly-over remains a striking example of this approach.

At effects houses like ILM, the filmmakers' (usually unstated) goal has been to maintain a perfect solidity/flexibility balance between the optical and animated elements of special-effects work.[13] In the late 1970s and through the 1980s, the "optical" side of the coin certainly received the bulk of research and development. Not surprisingly, however, the popularization of CGI special effects in the early 1990s prioritized an animation approach. Again, the goal remained to maintain a balance. Nevertheless, since the 1970s, we can generalize the two broad approaches towards special-effects aesthetics as putting faith in optical or animation techniques.

What is surprising about contemporary digital effects is that in theory, digital images can take on any aesthetic the filmmakers might choose. Yet filmmakers rarely choose to exercise their options. They typically go to great lengths to replicate the photochemical, ILM aesthetic that we have accepted as "correct" over the last thirty or so years. Certainly, ILM has maintained a remarkable consistency in its maintenance of an "optical" photoreal look even in the digital era. Artists there seek to digitally imitate the visible marks of optical photographic equipment, capture, processing, and finishing. (A remarkable exception to this approach can be seen in the 1999–2005 *Star Wars* prequels, in which the ILM team appears to be exploring the limits of not only digital technology but also digital aesthetics. However, since the completion of *The Revenge of the Sith*, ILM has seemed to refocus their efforts on the optical end of photoreal aesthetics, instead of the animation end.) It is worth noting that unlike pre-digital 1970s effects that made use of animation approaches and techniques (most notably multiplane effects—arranging artwork in a number of layers in front of the camera—and rotoscoping), in order to gain greater plasticity of a photographic composite mise-en-scène CGI has to do the opposite. Its mutable technological aesthetic is more closely aligned with animation than with photography, and so photorealism must be built in the computer. Effects artists do this through a number of techniques: by adding motion blur to their creatures and crafts; by studying how light is absorbed or reflected by real objects like skin or car finishes (and how light molds those shapes); and by applying laws of physics to allow for the proper sense of weight and heft. As in the case of the 2009 *Star Trek*, the contemporary mode of photoreal special effects typically uses digital animation to maintain the photochemical look by transforming an image almost entirely into a set of cues and strategies.

Nevertheless, a "soft" animation aesthetic predominates in a number of late 1990s and early 2000s special-effects benchmarks. In films such as the Wachowski Brothers' *The Matrix* (1999), Peter Jackson's *Lord of the Rings* trilogy (2001–2003) and *King Kong* (2005), Tim Burton's *Charlie and the Chocolate Factory* (2005), and Zach Snyder's *300*, filmmakers embrace the potential for stylization and plasticity in animation while keeping a close relationship to norms of photorealism. Tellingly, the ILM model of optical photorealism is so powerful, films like Jackson's and Snyder's are often criticized for their stylization.

There are two main benefits of a "faith in the animated" approach for contemporary filmmakers. They are able to build stylized fantasy worlds based on a number of photographic and non-photographic aesthetic models—thus, to borrow from, and exploit, a wide range of source "looks": comic books and graphic novels (*Sin City* [2005], *Watchmen* [2009]), 1930s (thus relatively early) color cinematography (*The Aviator* [2004], *Sky Captain and the World of Tomorrow* [2004]), historical painting styles (*Master and Commander* [2003], *The Girl with a Pearl Earring* [2003]) or even stop-motion animation (*Pirates of the Caribbean* [2003], *Lord of the Rings*), just to name a few options. Further, they are at least theoretically able to realize the 1970s *auteurist* ideal of visualizing an uncompromising totality, whether that means rebuilding 1970s San Francisco (*Zodiac* [2007]) or removing anachronistic electrical towers and other unwanted elements for a rural mise-en-scène (*There Will Be Blood* [2007]). Meanwhile, other fantasy films mark a swing back to optical photorealism: *Iron Man* (2008) and *The Dark Knight* (2008), to name two. Decisions about which route to take have implications that go beyond choice of subject matter or personal style, and touch on cinema's perceived real-world impact.

In the politically charged 1970s, filmmakers were expected to make a political choice in both their film's subject matter and its aesthetic. Filmmakers who took on science fiction subject matter in the 1970s and 1980s, like Lucas, Spielberg, John Carpenter (*Starman* [1984], *They Live* [1988]), Nicolas Roeg (*The Man Who Fell to Earth* [1976]), and John Boorman (*Zardoz* [1974]), explicitly understood filmmaking's potential for a "real world" intervention. That is, how can we use cinema to show audiences a politically charged vision of the world they actually live in? In the 1970s, filmmakers often explicitly understood the consequences of their aesthetic choices and were expected to defend them in terms of activism of one kind or another. How was social change to be achieved? Through a radical social overhaul, or a modification of the familiar? Stated more simply (albeit schematically), 1970s filmmakers designed their special effects films to address the ecological and ethical questions facing filmmakers: does the world need a total re-design and introduction of an entirely new paradigm, or do we find the good or useful in what is already there, by re-arranging or reconfiguring it? In either case, the film had to depict the "actual" world about which one framed one's political case.

Filmmakers in the 2000s, even those who initiated the special effects boom of the late 1970s such as Lucas and Spielberg, rarely acknowledge special-effects aesthetics in similarly politicized terms. Nevertheless filmmakers still respond polemically (albeit obliquely) to cinema's role in such issues of the day as corporate globalization (*Iron Man* [2008]), militarism (*Iron Man,* the *Hulk* films [2003, 2008]), political unilateralism and imperialism (The *Star Wars* prequels [1999–2005]), terror and extremism (*The Dark Knight*), discrimination (*District 9, X-Men* [2000–2006]), exploitation and resistance (the *Matrix* films, *Wolverine* [2009]), the role of personal action and responsibility (the *Spiderman* films [2002–2007]), environmentalism (*Wall-E* [2008], *Avatar* [2009]), and responsible and compassionate leadership (the *Harry Potter* series [2001–2011]), among others. Polemics can cut either critically or conservatively. For example, in an article about recent Iraq War movies, director and screenwriter Paul Haggis states, "To make a film like *Transformers* at a time of world war is a political act," by which he of course means a retrogressive political act.[14]

When the ability to generate present new worlds is the expected mode of big-budget filmmaking, the "message" borne by the technological aesthetic necessarily changes. Commentators often note the irony that so many highly technologized blockbusters nearly always feature anti-technology narratives. However, this impulse seems to be not just a simple irony of special-effects-heavy cinema. The anti-technology narratives do not only simply visualize our anxieties. Instead, these special-effects blockbusters give the audience a context for their anxieties by allowing them space for exploring the limits of what technology can and should do. The push and pull of attitudes towards technology and illusionistic visioning systems means that the narrative of special-effects cinema *requires* such tension and irony. The obsessive attention to developing new illusionistic photoreal imaging technology in the production must be allayed in the narrative by an anti-technology message.

In addition, many contemporary filmmakers recognize a certain political value in the strategies introduced to the industry by special-effects technology through its accessibility and relative inexpensiveness, but also unimagined level of control over the image. Similar to the way Stanley Kubrick was known to make twenty to thirty takes of the same shot until it was exactly as he wanted it, filmmakers now use the many levels of CGI to tweak all aspects of the mise-en-scène. In another nod to the 1970s auteur, digital technology can reinforce the place of individual creative control and the value of a single viewpoint in the vast conglomeration and synergistic world of global filmmaking. The polemics of CGI thus manifest not only in what kind of world the self-styled auteur is creating but also in her creative personality and access to control. Lauded filmmakers such as David Fincher, Paul Thomas Anderson, and Quentin Tarantino tweak the look of a film in post-production for months if they are contractually able to do so. In this way, many filmmakers find the benefit of digital technology and CGI less in the actual images it allows than in more total control over their "vision."

Conclusion

The overwhelming financial and popular success of *Avatar* late in 2009 leads us to ask whether there is any such thing as a special-effects movie anymore. Through the 1970s, "special effects" (even as industry usage changed to "special visual effects" or just "visual effects") was a meaningful term. Special effects were typically understood by the industry as material produced or generated apart or independently from the principal photography. Special effects were material generated in post-production, or in a production parallel to the principal photography that would be edited together in post-production. They were also produced for their value as an industrial attraction: the "wow" of what movies can do "now." They had an identifiable "special" status. Through the 1980s, the 1990s, and even into the 2000s, big-budget blockbuster filmmaking renewed its allure through more striking and more intense concentration of special-effects sequences. But does the sheer concentration of special-effects sequences in mainstream filmmaking make the notion of a special-effects film meaningless?

With nearly all feature-length films touched by digital manipulation on nearly every level (editing, color timing, digital removal of unwanted elements, motion capture, production design, camera image capture, projection, and so on), is the "special-effects film" a term with any currency? Nearly every mainstream feature film's budget includes a "digital intermediate" (where the edited film is scanned digitally, manipulated in post-production, and then "filmed back out" to a release print). One way to look at this problem is to tally the number of the effects shots in a given film (meaning the number of shots that required the post-production skills of specialized effects artists). For example, *2001: A Space Odyssey* in 1968 boasted 201 special-effects shots out of 602 total shots, an enormous number at the time. *Star Wars* in 1977 nearly doubled that amount, with 365, again, a previously unimaginable amount (out of 2089 total shots). To emphasize how much things have changed, *Star Trek* (2009) claimed 860. Roland Emmerich's disaster epic *2012* (2009) claimed an astonishing 1,300. And a film like *Avatar* could scarcely be considered to contain *any* shots that are not classified as "special-effects shots." *Avatar*'s official count: 2,500 effects shots.[15] Ultimately, *Avatar* could well be the benchmark film that explodes the already artificial distinction between special-effects film and cinema more generally.

A number of influential filmmakers such as James Cameron, Peter Jackson, Kathryn Bigelow, Robert Zemeckis, and Michael Mann have seemed to embrace the notion (in their own unique ways) of a digital aesthetic as one with a distinct form and with different potentialities from photographic capture. But what can we make of filmmakers like J.J. Abrams, Christopher Nolan, and McG, who insist upon shooting big-budget special-effects extravaganzas on film, and persist in, as Abrams put it, a "real, analog" look? Perhaps this phenomenon is a transitioning phase for filmmakers and filmgoers alike who cling to the increasingly nostalgic look of celluloid, or perhaps it will be the mark of a future digital aesthetic. However, it is clear that for the time being, the aesthetic developed in the 1970s by ILM still maintains its status as the apex of "photorealism." Nineteen-seventies photorealism is available for filmmakers to mine as an historical aesthetic, now as recognizable a style as German Expressionism or Film Noir.

I would like to gratefully acknowledge the assistance of Christina Petersen, Jonathan Knipp, and Nathan Holmes. This essay was completed with the support of a Mellon/ACLS Early Career Fellowship, and the backing of the Davis Humanities Institute at the University of California, Davis.

Notes

1 Joe Fordham, "A New Enterprise," *Cinefex* 118 (July 2009), 42.

2 See contemporary reviews, for example, by Vincent Canby, "Star Wars," *New York Times* (26 May 1977), 66; A. D. Murphy "Star Wars," *Daily Variety* (19 May 1977), and Roger Ebert, "Star Wars," *Chicago Sun-Times* (1 January 1977). Interestingly, the much-hyped "mythopoetic" narrative structure relying on historical cultural archetypes was largely understood as tongue-in-cheek homage to serials like *Flash Gordon,* rather than an interesting innovation.

3 See Richard Rickitt, *Special Effects: The History and Technique* (New York: Billboard Books, 2000). For a more detailed discussion of these techniques in relation to ILM in the 1970s, see Julie Turnock, *Plastic Reality: Special Effects, Art and Technology in 1970s US Filmmaking,* forthcoming from the University of California Press.

4 This despite Lucas's digital fiddling in the 1997 "special edition" theatrical and DVD release in which the computer generated additions, ironically, look more dated than in the 1977 work.

5 As an example, see the *Popular Mechanics* "Top 10 VFX Scenes of 2009" which rates "convincingness" a strong criteria for inclusion in the list. Online at http://www.popular mechanics.com/technology/industry/4340952.html?page=1.

6 For Lucas's frequent statements on the importance of credible special effects, see Sally Kline, ed., *George Lucas: Interviews* (Jackson: University of Mississippi Press, 1999). On Kubrick, see Gene Phillips, ed., *Stanley Kubrick: Interviews* (Jackson: University of Mississippi Press, 2001). On Spielberg, see Lester D Friedman and Brent Notbohm, eds., *Steven Spielberg: Interviews* (Jackson: University of Mississippi Press, 2000).

7 For discussion of the use of the term "New Hollywood" and other terminology such as American auteurs, American New Wave directors, see Elsaesser, Horwath and King, *The Last Great American Picture Show* (Amsterdam: University of Amsterdam Press, 2004).

8 Mid-century critic André Bazin is mostly closely associated with the valorization of the long take (and deep space composition) aesthetic, especially in the cinema of Welles, Renoir, and de Sica. It is also largely through Bazin's championing of the technique that

the long take is associated with virtuoso filmmaking, though often with different purposes in mind.

[9] As quoted in the *District 9* DVD extras. As Blomkamp puts it, a bad choice (that is, difficult to replicate in the computer) for recreating photorealistic lighting effects would be "a translucent jelly fish in disco lighting."

[10] Counter-examples may include the lack of respect for Earth physics in *Wolverine* (2009), or the weightlessness of creatures in the *Narnia* films (2005–2008), or the smudgy edges of the disaster sequences in *2012* (2009).

[11] Though well circulated, this quote may be apocryphal. Quoted in Jerome Agel, *The Making of Kubrick's 2001* (New York: Signet, 1970) and Halliwell's *Filmgoer's and Video Viewer's Companion*.

[12] Mark Harris, "Micro Mangling," *Entertainment Weekly* 926 (March 23, 2007).

[13] See, for example, Weta Digital's work for *Avatar*, Jody Duncan, "The Seduction of Reality," *Cinefex* 120 (January 2010), 128.

[14] Ali Jaafar, "Casualties of War," *Sight and Sound* (February 2008), 22. Many writers (including Jaafar) have criticized *300* in similar terms.

[15] For *2001* and *Star Wars* number of effects shots: Herb Lightman, "Filming *2001: a Space Odyssey*" *American Cinematographer* (June 1968), 442; John Dykstra, "Miniature and Mechanical Special Effects for STAR WARS," *American Cinematographer* (July 1977), 704. All total shot data from cinemetrics.com. For *Star Trek* (2009), Fordham (2009, *op.cit.*),118. For *2012*, Jody Duncan, "The Seduction of Reality," *Cinefex* 120 (January 2010): 128. On *Avatar*, Duncan, 146.

Chapter 28

Terra Incognita

Thomas Doherty

Perhaps in solidarity with the viewer—at sea, adrift, washed up, cast away, without moorings, entangled in the tall grass—the show is called "Lost." Has a television series ever been so convoluted, plot-twisted, character-threaded, and flashback-ridden? At once so determinately obtuse and so insistent on full-body immersion in the slipstream? "I don't know what is more disquieting," commented Sayid, the former Iraqi Republican Guardsman turned sensitive survivalist, upon sighting a typical WTF?! visitation, "the fact that the rest of the statue is missing, or that it has four toes."

Premiering on ABC on September 22, 2004, "Lost" sailed onto the cultural radar with a loud ping. At a time when HBO, Showtime, and even basic cable had seemed to suck all the cool oxygen and prize demos out of the lumbering dinosaurs of the alphabet triad, ABC's gamble on metaphysical melodrama in a serpent-infested paradise lent *cachet* and buzz to a creaky remnant of three-network hegemony. From 2004 to 2010, closing out with a syndication-friendly package of 121 episodes, the magic realism of an atoll that abided more by Einsteinian than Newtonian physics generated (perhaps) the last great outbreak of serial addiction on broadcast television.

Built around plots of Dickensian complexity and Dostoveyskian depth, with generous doses of Tristram Shandyesque convolutions laced with Oliver Stoned paranoia, "Lost" found its niche with a web-savvy, well-read, and upscale fan base. The ratings ebbed and flowed—the long hiatus between seasons and the breaks between episodes mitigated against the ritual viewing habits that bond the faithful to the video hearth, TIVO and PVR notwithstanding, and the intricate detail work befuddled viewers late to the party or too slow to keep up.[1] Yet even as the audience dwindled, "Lost" never lost its high profile on the media catwalk. In 2010, at the height of the build-up for the premiere episode of the sixth and final season, White House spokesman Robin Gibbs had to assure the American public that President Obama would not interrupt the premiere of "Lost" with a televised address on his most urgent domestic priority.

The initial spark for "Lost" was ignited not by a television writer flaunting an M.A. in Philosophy but by Lloyd Baum, head of ABC Entertainment. Baum looked over the dirt cheap megahit "Survivor" (CBS, 2000–) and figured a more painstakingly scripted show about a group of plane-crash survivors stranded on a Pacific island might revive the sagging fortunes of the network.[2] He brought together J.J. Abrams, best known for the co-ed bildungsroman "Felicity" (WB, 1998–2002) and the hipster spy show "Alias" (ABC, 2001–2006), and Damon Lindelof, a writer from the forensic noir "Crossing Jordan" (NBC, 2001–2007), to flesh out his skeletal high concept.

Abrams, a Rod Serling acolyte, and Lindelof, a comic book geek, spread a "Twilight Zone" mist over the "Survivor" blueprint: the show would be dense, trippy, non-linear, and, most importantly, serial not self-contained. Having been blessed by management in the first place, the project went from notion to pilot at warp speed. It also went in style. Filmed, scripted narrative shot on location in Oahu, Hawaii, with real actors being less cost efficient than exhibitionist wannabes being followed around by hand-held video cameras, "Lost" swallowed up a huge initial investment. By the time of airing, the $12 million dice throw was one of the most expensive and highly anticipated pilots ever produced.

Taglined in the *New York Times* as a "high-tension supernatural soap" and soon as a "breakout hit drama," "Lost" turned into the treasure island ABC had been hunting for. After the first season, Abrams left the show to administer life support to the fading "Star Trek" franchise, handing off the mythos to Lindelof, who with Carlton Cuse, a veteran film and television writer, became the bylined auteur-showrunners, stars in their own right.[3]

To attempt a plot recap and personnel flow chart for "Lost" is a sucker's bet, but as near as I can figure: Oceanic flight 815, departing Sydney, Australia on course for Los Angeles, crashes on a remote Pacific island and ejects a passenger manifest of mixed ethnic, class, and body types.[4] "The show is about an international flight that crashes somewhere in the Pacific," Abrams explained, "so the cast is going to look more like the world looks and less like *Beverly Hills 90210*."[5] Not that the unknown zip code lacks its share of lookers: a statistically unlikely sampling of buff dudes and hot babes washed up with the ordinary driftwood seated in coach.

The survivors are not alone. Two groups of not-quite-indigenous peoples have staked prior claim to the beachfront property: a tribe known as The Others, seemingly shipwrecked since the mid-nineteenth century, and a 1970s-vintage band of jump-suited inhabitants known as the Dharma Initiative, part hippie commune, part Jonestown loony bin. The three tribes—Oceanic 815, the Others, and the Dharma Initiative—criss-cross and double cross, flashback and flash sideways, and hunt and gather across what turns out to be two discrete islands honeycombed with underground tunnels and silos and pockmarked with Quonset huts, temples, shipwrecks, plane wrecks, and submarine docks.

Like Billy Pilgrim in Kurt Vonnegut's *Slaughterhouse-Five,* the islanders have a tendency to get unstuck in time. Forward narrative motion whiplashes back to the past and, in the valedictory sixth season, sashays "sideways" into a parallel universe of alternative life lines. The first two threads are more or less linear, familiar from film noirs and melodramas. Once upon a time cued by dissolves and Theremin music, the temporal disruptions on "Lost" unspool with no-fuss leaps across time zones, signaled by a simple jump cut. The real-time present thread (including time travel backwards), the flashback thread, and the sideways thread trace a Möbius strip of time rifts and intersecting storylines that exist at once in the temporally unsteady now (transmutable in time), the flashbacked then (real time, pre-takeoff of Oceanic 815), and the might-have-been (or maybe is) had Oceanic 815 landed at LAX and not on the island. Got that?

But if the island is Not What It Seems, neither are the passengers, who through interlaced back stories disgorge carousels of psychic baggage not mislaid by Oceanic Airlines. A core triad enjoys elite status and priority screen space:

- Jack (Matthew Fox): the rock-solid good boy, healer of broken bones and interpersonal squabbles. Although saddled with a serious father complex, he is the natural leader of the beached and the aimless. Jack saves the lives of four people in the first five minutes of the pilot.

- Sawyer (Josh Holloway): the co-equal alpha male, a rakish bad dude, huckster not healer, whose blond mane and sculpted torso are best glimpsed shirtless. Judging by his voracious reading of quality literature, Sawyer's Eastwoodian exterior belies a sensitive interior.

- The Exquisite Kate (even the actress's name flies on gossamer wings: Evangeline Lilly): a bad good girl or a good bad girl, but definitely a dream girl. Kate faces the dilemma of every romance novel heroine since Samuel Richardson and Jane Austen first set feminine hearts a-palpitating with tales of virtue rewarded or seduced: Mr. Reliable or Mr. Excitement? The guy you can count on or the guy who rocks your world?

If the Jack-Sawyer-Kate triangle occupies the top of the character pyramid, the support beams are sturdy and multifarious, numbering (literally) in the dozens. A systematic census of the island community would be even more confusing than the timeline, but the stand-out inhabitants include:

- John Locke (Terry O'Quinn): Alone of the castaways, the island is for him home turf. Miraculously granted mobility, he experiences a glorious resurrection from a wheelchair bound life of quiet desperation. A major player in the fields of the lord, he was born for the crucible of island survival.

- Sayid (Naveen Andrews): A man with literal skeletons in his closet, he possesses lethal warrior skills and electronic ability, as well as what is either brooding intensity or post-traumatic stress syndrome. The inclusion of a humane Iraqi character at the height of the Second Gulf War was audacious, but of all the eye-rolling plot points in the annals of "Lost," none was more unbelievable than the notion that a member of Saddam Hussein's Republican Guard would need the tutelage of the American military to instruct him in the finer points of torture.

- Jin Kwon (Daniel Dae Kim) and Sun Kwon (Yunjin Kim): An inscrutable Korean couple, each of whom initially feigns mono-lingualism and whose marital conversations are subtitled (though not for viewers in Korea). Emotion-wise, Jin and Sun find their Confucian restraint melting under the glare of American-style feelings-mongering.

- Ben Linus (Michael Emerson): Irresistibly hissible, the slithery, bug-eyed villain is a link between the homeless people-like Others and the Dharma bums, a man of infinite cupidity, sociopathic zeal, and affectless vocal patterns. Ben is responsible for the death of his father *and* his daughter.

- Hurley aka Hugo (Jorge Garcia): A laid back, surfer-dude-speaking So-Cal comic book guy and numerologist, Hurley may be the largest endomorphic protagonist in the history of television. Though the object of the occasional fat joke (Sawyer, who has a nickname for everyone, calls him Lard-o and Stay Puft), the guy you never want sitting next to you in the middle seat is the audience surrogate and fan favorite, as was acknowledged in an episode from Season 6 entitled "Everyone Loves Hurley."

Besides being a sop to global marketing, the composition of the cast of castaways reflects the rise of the new American melting pot—not the Jewish/Italian/Irish immigrants who docked at that other island (Ellis), but a first generation whose flight path to the New World terminated at LAX or JFK. Still, for every nod to the new persons of color, the show bows before the British Empire in the figures of the lovelorn, shipwrecked, button pusher Desmond Hume (Henry Ian Cusick), like his namesake a Scott; Claire (Emilie de Ravin), the pert Aussie sheila; and Charlie (Dominic Monaghan), the D-list, drug-addled Brit rocker.

The ruthless triage of serial melodrama periodically demands that certain ill-fated members of the ensemble be deep-sixed. Shannon (Maggie Grace), the spoiled California princess, and her well-meaning stepbrother-lover Boone (Ian Somerhalder), were jettisoned after the first season; Harold Perrineau (Michael Dawson), an absentee father trying to connect with his son in a tiresome C-plot, was also voted off the island with his son; and the contract of the likeable Charlie expired with his heroic death by drowning in Season 3. Yet while the betas may die, the alphas are immortal—literally raised from the dead. The rewards of syndication are too tantalizing for an artistically transgressive act of audience alienation that might depreciate the resale value of the package. Tony Soprano will not be whacked midway into season 3 of "The Sopranos," Jack Bauer will not be blown up in hour 9 of "24." In television, Q-score is destiny.

Seriality—or rather the complexity of the seriality and the tandem philosophical musings and quantum physical mind games—was "Lost"'s most distinctive contribution to long-form television storytelling. For most of the history of the medium, serial television was a misnomer. Picaresque sitcoms and self-contained melodramas of ritual stylization and emotional stasis defined prime-time programming: Lucy wailing in angst as her latest wacky scheme implodes, Joe Friday soliciting just-the-facts from a rambling eyewitness. Television characters existed in a realm with slight back story and no future: Gilligan and his fellow castaways will always be marooned on their island. TV was the medium whose flow you could dip into anywhere and still stay afloat. There was no need for a season finale because nothing much ever happened season to season.

Thankfully, by the late 1960s, the droning rhythms of serial sameness were being broken up by a fifth column of long-form subversives. Patrick McGoohan's psychedelic British import "The Prisoner" (CBS, 1968), another story with a convoluted plot about a guy on a weird island; the multi-night mini-series of the 1970s; and "Wiseguy" (1987–1990), the first regularly scheduled television program built around overarching narrative "arcs," helped make the viewer's relationship with a television show something more than a one-night stand.

The televisual arc—a long-running narrative thread connecting more or less stand-alone episodes of a regularly scheduled series—took inspiration not from its obvious cinematic forbearer, the classic Hollywood serial, but from the nineteenth-century novel, especially the episodic serialization practiced by deadline-driven writers like Charles Dickens and Wilkie Collins. No longer a picaresque telling of random adventures, a television show could be an epic journey built around the progress of its pilgrims. Like a thickly descriptive novel of manners, it spun plotlines of infinite circuitousness and probed the subterranean recesses of its *dramatis personae.* As a token of its density, "Lost" preceded the premieres of its new season with hour-long recaps of the past season, complete with a voiceover Virgil, so the slower students in the Nielsen demo could catch up. Likewise, in a "Lost" innovation, repeat telecasts included "pop-up" text explaining plot points and cross-references in "remedial 'Lost'" sessions.

The aesthetic payoffs from novelistic serial programming can be, well, novelistic. Consider one of the great bushwhacks in the gallery of television art, the false flashback that closed out Season 3. Having established a conventional flashback structure for the pre-island back stories of the main islanders, the episode entitled "Through the Looking Glass" (which really should have been a heads up) featured a frazzled Jack in deep emotional angst during a bad patch in what was assuredly his past. In the show's last moments, he stops by the outskirts of LAX for a rendezvous. A jeep pulls up next to him. Out from the driver's side steps—Kate!—who should not be in Jack's flashback—unless this is a flash *forward*—which means Jack and Kate are off the island, back in the American civilization that is Los Angeles—but how? Not simply a head-spinner, the twist also neatly derailed the binary limitations of the desert-island genre (will the marooned get off or not?) and unfurled a wider canvas of narrative possibilities.

No wonder the aura of high serious literary ambition—and the resulting chin-stroking critical esteem—enveloped "Lost" like a coastal fog. "Amid the love triangles and chases through the South Pacific island brush, viewers can expect a lesson in quantum mechanics and the multiverse hypothesis of physics," gushed the *Boston Globe.* "Yes, you can enjoy 'Lost' as a good-versus-evil adventure show. But you'll like it even more after you've schooled yourself in the theory of Schrodinger's Cat."[6] "Lost" had morphed into the television equivalent of *Finnegan's Wake,* the first television show to require footnotes.

But if acolytes craved the intellectual rewards and aesthetic buzz of a series that demanded what television had traditionally eschewed (namely, a long attention span and memory for detail), a broader slice of the demographic came down with headaches. As *New York Times* critic Mike Hall put it: "The mania for answers—the tendency to define the show as a problem to be solved rather than an entertainment to be enjoyed—can get exhausting."[7]

Not to mention silly. If "Lost" firing on all pistons was hypnotic, "Lost" stuck in the deep muddy of its metaphysical quicksand was ludicrous. Especially in the first two seasons, amid the polar bears and smoke monsters, apparitions and numerology, "Lost" seemed to have no coherent five-year plan. The dominant vibe was of a room crammed with desperate writers diving deeper and deeper into a whirlpool, frantically bailing to keep the vessel afloat, tossing marginal characters overboard and reaching out for life-preserving newbies. In 2006, a "Saturday Night Live" sketch depicted a group of "Lost" fans encountering guest host Matthew Fox in an elevator. Each of the passengers quizzes Fox on the show's controlling metaphor. "You have no idea," scoffs a skeptic. "Purgatory," blurts out the voice of smug certainty. "You're all in purgatory."

Frustrated or just antsy, many viewers gave up on the show, defecting to the linear plots and soothing resolutions of the "Law and Order" and "CSI" archipelagoes, where the DNA evidence is so tangible, at the tip of your white gloves, ziplocked, swabbed, and q-tipped. "Take this to the lab," orders the brisk ratiocinator. All will be explained, unlocked, tied up.

For the loyalists who remained, the pleasures of unraveling a labyrinthine plotline and bonding with a kindred spirit were obvious enough commitment points, but the show that played so deftly with time had a suitably timely resonance for the rest of American culture. Just as "Bonanza" (NBC, 1959–1973) bucked up the Cold War patriarchy (a nuclear family without women) and "The Mary Tyler Moore Show" (CBS, 1970–1977) rode the crest of second-wave feminism (a single woman without men), "Lost" took the measure of time and space, early twenty-first-century-style. Where better to meditate on the technology of modern communication and transportation than an isolated, primitive island?[8]

For an age of global positioning systems and spy-in-the-sky google mapping, the conceit of a lost island teeming with danger and sensuality harkens back to a bygone epoch of romantic adventurism, a time when pith-helmeted heroes in safari gear trekked into landscapes commensurate with the white man's sense of wonder. In Joseph Conrad's *Heart of Darkness* (1899), Western Civilization's original run through the jungle, the world-weary narrator Marlowe recalls opening an atlas and gazing dreamily at the blank spaces on the map of darkest Africa, a terra incognita he would fill with his imagination. Jules Verne's *Around the World in Eighty Days* (1873), Sir Arthur Conan Doyle's *The Lost World* (1912), and Edgar Rice Burroughs's *Tarzan of the Apes* (1914) were like-minded fantasy projections. All shared a prophetic sense that in a shrinking world a return to rugged primitivism was the adventure story of the future. The impulse was to light out for the territory, away from the metropolis and the machines.

No organ of popular culture better tapped into the fear factors and pleasure centers of the white man's primitivism than the Hollywood travelogues and adventure films of the 1930s. "Lost" owes a special debt to two cinematic prototypes for mysterious islands, which between them dug up creepy science in a tropical location and a smokin' monster with sentience: Dr. Moreau's House of Pain in *The Island of Lost Souls* (1932) and Skull Island in *King Kong* (1933). Moreau's man-beasts and the gargantuan Kong may have been evolutionarily dubious, but the notion of an uncharted island, shrouded in fog, off the shipping lanes, still beyond the longitudinal lines of mapping, was not totally off the charts of narrative probability.

Indiana Jones, Lara Croft, and *The Mummy* franchises are contemporary expressions of the same desire for adventure and archeology in uncharted territories. So too is the outdoorsy *oeuvre* of Jon Krakauer, whose best-selling true adventure books—*Into the Wild* (1996) and *Into Thin Air* (1997)—chronicle the lengths to which modern man must go to get back to nature. In *Into Thin Air,* even at the top of Mt. Everest, a doomed climber beyond the reach of rescue is still connected by satellite phone to his wife in New Zealand.

The communication links are ties that bind—but not always as comforting arms, sometimes as suffocating tentacles. "Lost" satisfies a palpable longing for an earthly space beyond the reach of digital gadgets, Wi-Fi hot zones, or cell phone ring tones. Hence, the Dharma Initiative exists in a low tech, pre-chip, office space: their clunky computers date from the 1970s and the 16mm projector that unspools orientation films is a visual aid from a Cold War classroom on the red menace.

Unlike 1933, these days it is well nigh impossible to get lost, to slip off the grid. The real fantasy island is an uncharted speck of land. You always know where you are—and they can always find you. "But they'll find us!" bleats Charlie, in an early episode from Season 1. "They have satellites in space that can take pictures of your license plate." Charlie is not shocked that he is lost; he is shocked that they can't find him.

The air space around "Lost" is also abuzz with the technology and rituals of modern travel. Focusing on how to escape the island detracts attention from how the passengers got there in the first place. An ordinary miracle, the transcontinental jet—a mundane mode of transportation latent with unholy terror—is the most practical way to jump between time zones.

Hollywood discovered the melodramatic machinations of an ensemble trapped in a shaky fuselage as soon as passenger plane travel became an affordable transportation option for middle-class moviegoers in postwar America. In *The High and the Mighty* (1954) and *The Crowded Sky* (1960), on through the mid-1970s' *Airport* disaster movies and 1980s' sky-jacking thrillers, the roll call of passenger types in the cabin was as schematic as the ethnicities in a WWII platoon: pregnant woman, criminal, faithful older couple. At least Abrams and Lindelof overlooked the spunky nun and the girl on dialysis.

Whatever the safety statistics say, passenger planes are vessels that bespeak disaster, an intimation of mortality for even the most jaded business traveler, never more so than in the wake of 9/11. Of course, the soothing rituals of air travel conspire to conceal such unpleasant thoughts. Airport ticket lines, security procedures, duty free shops, and customs clearance reassure the nervous traveler with the routine of bureaucratic procedure. The interior of a Boeing 747 itself is a comfort zone decorated like a living room, complete with cushions, magazines, and television. The illusion is persuasive until what the pilot calls "a little chop" nosedives into a white knuckle, sphincter-tightening rollercoaster ride in one direction. The oxygen masks drop down, baggage ricochets around the cabin, and the back of the plane rips off. Death will not be quite instantaneous.

The disintegration of Oceanic 815 in "Lost" borrows from *Alive* (1993)—"unquestionably the most chilling portrayal of a plane crash in movie history," said Leonard Maltin—and the crash site carnage took a page from *Fearless* (1993), which opened with the aftermath of the crash, not the on-board moments before impact. Abrams and Lindelof also introduced the "Lost" world with Jack's quiet awakening on the ground, followed by the sounds and images of wreckage strewn on the beach and passengers in varying states of shock. The crash—or rather the gut-wrenching moments prior to impact—can thus be experienced again and again through the perspective of each character: Jack reassuring a fellow passenger, Kate handcuffed to a federal marshal, Charlie snorting heroin in the lavatory.

Back on solid ground, the reversion to human propulsion is a relief. With the exception of an occasional VW mini-bus, the islanders are earthbound pedestrians, trekking with torches, talking around open-air campfires, and sleeping outdoors, blithely immune to sunburn, malnutrition, insects, malaria, and bad hygiene. Shot on location on transcendently gorgeous Oahu, "Lost" boasts a natural vista of unparalleled beauty. Indeed, the visual pleasure of the show—gaping not just at the beautiful bodies but the sheer splendor of the landscape—is crucial to its primal attraction. Throughout the latter half of the twentieth century, the small screen was a low-definition medium good for close-ups but little else, but when television officially graduated from blurry analog to crystal-clear digital, the bigger screens, higher resolution, and greater horizontal space of the new hardware put the subaltern medium within pixels range of theatrical cinema. Against the dreary sameness of sunny LA and rainswept British Columbia, a sunlit tropical landscape shimmering in azure ocean blues and shades of vegetative browns and greens was a HD vision of paradise in 50-inch flatscreen.

If the terrain (natural and media) of "Lost" is a digital free zone, excepting CGI smoke monsters and green-screen backdrops, the wraparound viewing experience partakes of the full range of computer-based outreach. The show is a case study for the varieties of modern spectatorship and synergy: TIVO'd, streamed on the web, watched in marathon "binge viewings" of the DVD box sets, chatted, twittered, blogged, vlogged, and podcast.

By common consent, "Lost" fans exhibit a level of cultish fixation that creeps out Trekkies. Diagramming the plotlines, peeling back the onion skin of the back story, and tracking down arcane references, a coterie of obsessive-compulsive camp followers, website nerds, and fanboys exploits the full range of Internet-age participatory culture "in numbers unlike any other television show," according to the *New York Times,* catering to "a fan base with a seemingly bottomless appetite for postmortem chat."[9] Websites such as www.thefuselage.com and www.4815162342.com crackle with the enthusiasm of true believers bent on missionary work. The celebrity hounding website TMZ "live blogs" the show. On "The Transmission," a weekly podcast at hawaiup.com/lost, a mild-mannered husband and wife critique each episode with an attention to detail that is at once touching and spooky.

The showrunners for "Lost"—not too far away from nerd-dom themselves—are willful aiders and abettors. Damon Lindelof and Carlton Cuse ("Team Darlton" in web lingo) regularly sit down and talk with *Entertainment Weekly*'s "Totally 'Lost'" team of Dan Snierson and Jeff Jensen, rapping about the mythos and doling out tidbits. In connecting all the dangling threads into a whole clothe, the showrunners are rightly mindful of an audience with zen-like powers of concentration. "Because we're inviting the fans to look at it with such a degree of specificity, the margin for error is razor thin," says Lindelof. Burbles Jenson, "Is there a relationship between Island reality and sideways reality? Will they run parallel for the remainder of the season? Will they fuse together? Might one fade away?"

The toxically high geek quotient has invited ripe satire. Of the myriad YouTube mock ups and *SNL* jibes, a faux news clip from the Onion News Network entitled "Final Season of 'Lost' Promises to Make Fans More Annoying than Ever" may be the definitive send up, mainly because Lindelof and Cuse themselves blather mumbo-jumbo that sounds not all that dissimilar from their discourse on *EW*'s "Totally 'Lost'" link. "All I'll say about the eye at the end of Season 5 is that the person's identity really can't be revealed unless you apply the Valenzetti Equation and that only works if you change one number—and fans should basically ask their friends who don't watch the show what they think that means," deadpans Lindelof.[10]

Given that level of emotional investment, the end of "Lost" was not a consummation devoutly to be wished by the hard core. Alas, the announcement that the sixth season would be the last and that the finale episode would air on May 23, 2010 was a countdown to anni-hilation that not even Desmond Hume could forestall. Though "Lost" support groups were caught between denial and curiosity, critics mainly welcomed the gutsy gambit.[11] "Indeed, the smartest thing ABC ever did (after considerable cajoling, and a little threatening, by pro-ducers Damon Lindelof and Carlton Cuse) was to set an end date, offering hope of defini-tive answers before the show's fringe audience throws its hands up in exasperation," argued Brian Lowry in *Variety*.[12]

Yet the risks of closure for a television series are both financial and artistic. A wrap-up that renders the previous episodes emotionally superfluous turns the wares into used goods. Television executives well remember how the syndication prospects for *The Fugitive* (1963–1967) were ruined by the finale, which resolved Richard Kimble's fugitive status when he killed the one-armed man. At the same time, a dud of a send-off can wipe out years of good will and audience investment, the best example being the despised blackout that brought *The Sopranos* (HBO, 1999–2007) to a fizzle.

Part of a "'Lost' Weekend" heralding "the television event of the decade," the two-and-a-half-hour endgame for "Lost"—boldly titled "The End"—concluded neither with the cus-tomary bang nor cop-out whimper but a long, wistful sigh interrupted by some well-earned sniffles. Lassoing six seasons' worth of characters and knitting up three time-and-space zones worth of plot strands needed more than slick editing. Lindelof and Cuse opted for an elegiac tone poem with symphonic tides and hymnal melodies.

Island time was real time, "sideways" time was dream-time, or transcendent realm time, or maybe time in heaven, a privileged mystical space collectively imagined by the castaways. Linked in life, the (no longer) survivors are united in a church for the funeral of Jack's father, the lost passenger from Oceanic 815. The stained glass windows bear the emblems of many religions, but Roman Catholic iconography infuses the set design and the promise of redemp-tion and resurrection is inscribed in the very name of the father. "Christian Shephard?" asks Kate. "Seriously?" By way of exposition for all of us, the father delivers the word to the son who has been sacrificed back on earth. "This is the place you all made together so you could find one another," he tells Jack of the congregation of islanders assembled in the pews. "The most important part of your life was the time that you spent with these people."

Back on the island, Jack—of course—has done the right thing, embraced his destiny as healer and savior, killed the demon who had become John Locke, saved the island, his friends, and his beloved Kate. With an almost mathematical beauty, the final shot of the last show was a mirror image of the opening shot of the first show: a close-up of Jack's eye, whose open-ing began the pilgrims' progress, the lid now closing shut, the curtain come down, the cir-cle complete.

"There will be answers!" blared the promos for the last season. Yes—but "Lost" was never really about answers—solving puzzles, figuring out equations, tying up loose ends. It was about questions—the search down dark corridors leading who knows where, the treks along jungle pathways lit by tongues of fire, the what-if scenarios, the plunge into a world that is either destiny driven or a jumble of chaos theory. In "Lost," the unsteady ground for the walkabout that is the human condition was an existential and, in the end, very private journey. A television show might point in the vague direction but, to its credit, it never pre-sumed to draw a precise map in response to Charlie's breathless query at the end of the pilot episode: "Guys, where *are* we?"

Notes

[1] Although "Lost" ratings declined over its broadcast run, from roughly 19 million viewers per episode in Season 1 to twelve million per episode in Season 6, the show remained strong with the prize 18–49 demographic and consistently scored astronomically in DVR and online viewing. The *Lost* finale averaged 13.5 million viewers, with nary an eyeball straying during the two-and-a-half hour telecast. Bill Carter, " 'Lost' Finale Lifts ABC to a Big Night," *New York Times*, May 25, 2010: C5.

[2] Being keen to surname associations, "Lost" viewers might mull the callback to L. Frank Baum, author of *The Wizard of Oz*. Being conspiratorial minded, they might also mull the experience of screenwriter Jeffrey Lieber, whose pitch to ABC of a show entitled "Nowhere" was similar enough to "Lost" to win him a Writers Guild of America arbitration as co-creator of "Lost." Although Lieber has nothing to do with the show, his name appears on the "created by" credit of every episode of "Lost" with Abrams and Lindelof.

[3] "Damon's been running *Lost* brilliantly since [2005], so my day-to-day involvement is about as much as yours," Abrams good naturedly told an online interviewer in 2008. http://www.avclub.com/articles/jj-abrams,14297/.

[4] A more meticulous mapping of the contours of "Lost" can be found in the seasonal editions of Nikki Stafford's *Finding Lost: The Unofficial Guide* (Ekw Press, 2006) and Tara Bennett and Paul Terry's *Lost Encyclopedia* (DK Publishing, 2010), which has the official imprimatur of the series. Of course, websites abound and Wikipedia entries on "Lost" may soon consume more disk space than the Civil War.

[5] Joe Rhodes, "How 'Lost" Careered into Being a Hit Show," *New York Times*, November 10, 2004: E1.

[6] " 'Lost'; Network TV Gets Brainier," *Boston Globe*, February 9, 2010.

[7] Mike Hall, " 'Lost,' Nearing End, Nods to Beginnings," *New York Times*, February 3, 2010: C1.

[8] From both a time and space continuum, "24" is the obvious companion piece to "Lost," ying to its yang: in "24," human beings are relentlessly tracked by the new technology of surveillance—monitored by video cameras, pinned and nailed by satellites, reduced to blips on a computer screen. Sitting at keyboards in cubicles, the Counter Terrorism Unit tracks fleeing suspects and careening SVUs through the streets of LA, DC, and NYC, everywhere, anytime, anywhere. "24" is about time, "Lost" is about space. "24" is the digital clock; "Lost" is the island. "Lost" may traverse the corridors of time, but "24" punches the clock. Both serial narratives were zeitgeist avatars of post-9/11 America that ended within weeks of each other, "Lost" bowing out, "24" forced out.

[9] Michael Wilson, "Finding Themselves in 'Lost,'" *New York Times*, April 4, 2010.

[10] http://www.theonion.com/video/final-season-of-"Lost"-promises-to-make-fans-more-an,14394/.

[11] In the superhero send-up *Kick-Ass*, released on April 16, 2010, the hapless teenage hero faces death with regret for all he will never live to experience: learning to drive, becoming a parent, finding out how "Lost" ends.

[12] Brian Lowry, "Lost," *Variety*, January 15, 2009.

Chapter 29

Melancholic and Hungry Games

Post-9/11 Cinema and the Culture of Apocalypse

Matthew Leggatt

*T*he question of why we choose to watch certain films can be one of the most rewarding paths to social criticism. It is a question that becomes particularly interesting when it is applied to the apocalyptic film culture, which has retained a popular appeal throughout the last decade and more. Apocalyptic films invariably depict massive-scale destruction and the end of life as we know it. Are they popular because the experience is cathartic, because it is escapist in a particular cultural frame, or because our obsession with the end of things has been spoken across the ages as something inbuilt in the human species? There is no easy way to answer such a question, but to examine the way in which these films have changed in accordance with recent history can perhaps allow an inside glimpse into their power and enduring appeal.

My personal interest in apocalyptic film originated some time ago when I came upon Fredric Jameson's statement, "It is easier to imagine the end of the world than the end of capitalism."[1] However bleak this idea is, recent history has demonstrated that even major shifts in global power relations, such as those witnessed on 9/11 and in the aftermath of the still ongoing global financial crisis, can do little to disturb the embedded social principles of capitalism. I wish to take Jameson's statement a little further and talk about the price we pay for this inability to imagine a future without capitalism, and suggest that it has further implications with regards to the virtual disappearance of utopianism in contemporary culture. Of course, there is a slight contradiction in this statement: clearly, to imagine the end of the world is, at the same time, also to imagine the end of capitalism. Given that apocalypse and utopia are two quite radically different (although admittedly not mutually exclusive) ways of looking beyond capitalism, it is fascinating to consider that one is popular today, while the other is not. And so there are two things to consider here, quite beyond our inability to get loose from what has become the capitalist imperative: not just the cost of the absence of utopia, but also the cost of our obsession with apocalypse.

The continued popularity of apocalyptic films is surely a testament to our cultural preoccupation with the end of the world, but why is it that an event such as 9/11—an event that certainly threatened global change—has seemingly offered a reinforcement of the self-same structure that provoked the strikes on the Twin Towers in the first place? Why is it that, when change threatened, many chose to stop believing in it altogether? Barack Obama's successful 2008 presidential campaign was fought on the back of the slogan, "Change we can believe in," a slogan that highlights widespread cynicism in not just the ability of politics to make a meaningful contribution to global change but also the possibility of change at all. Indeed, it is somewhat ironic that 9/11 has been so frequently pronounced as the moment when "everything changed," since most people who were not directly involved got up, brushed themselves off, and went back to work. On the day of the attacks, President George W. Bush immediately signaled to the American public that it would be business as usual: "Our financial institutions remain strong and the American economy will be open for business as well."[2] The attacks were couched not as attacks on U.S. ideology, on capitalism, or on globalization but as attacks on "freedom." This was the beginning of a careful and systematic attempt to reinforce the status quo that had been threatened by 9/11, an agenda supported not only by government policy and rhetoric but, in large part, by culture and the media, too.

For those scholars who have begun what will inevitably be a long process of analysis, evaluation, and re-evaluation of the cultural response to 9/11, claims that the attacks "changed everything" are to be found at almost every turn.[3] But this claim begs a more serious analysis. Just how did 9/11 *change everything?* While I do not wish to dispute that there has been a sweeping historical, political, and cultural impact, such a globalizing statement is intentionally confrontational. Surely the two planes striking the twin towers that day did not *change everything*, they merely fostered the perception that everything had changed.

It is true, however, that 9/11 did demand a new way of thinking and talking, not least because it seemed to trivialize the voices of scholars who had declared experience and culture bankrupt at the end of the twentieth century. This time, experience had come back to bite us, and it was a collision between the image and reality which became the focus. As Jean Baudrillard argued, "The terrorist act in New York has resuscitated both images and events."[4] Yet, with this statement in mind, it seems odd that the actual make-up of the apocalyptic image has featured so little in the theoretical literature surrounding the event.[5] While much of the published criticism to date seems to be primarily concerned with what films are being made, the important question of how films are being made remains relatively untouched.

This is where rather than being merely descriptive about the landscape of post-9/11 film analysis should place an emphasis on the aesthetic and narrative consistencies evident in post-9/11 film and culture.[6]

Apocalypse as Genre

Contemporary genre theory, chiefly associated with such critics as Steve Neale and Rick Altman, establishes that the popularity of various genres is cyclical, and therefore periods of generic proliferation repeat themselves. These cycles can frequently be traced to periodic societal concerns. The term "cycle" is an attempt to take genre studies, which has traditionally adopted a synchronic view of film history, and make it diachronic. But beyond this, it is a way of examining the evolution of genres and sub-genres which helps to account for the problems of maintaining novelty and creation in the film industry. As Altman states, "New cycles are usually produced by associating a new type of material or approach with already existing genres."[7] What we tend to see when we discover new themes, materials, locales, and aesthetics in what would otherwise fit an older mode within a pre-existing genre, is not a new genre but a new cycle.

While it could be argued that the current wave of disaster/apocalyptic films is a continuation, and decline, of an earlier cycle, which began in the late 1990s, there are reasons why this current wave should be considered a cycle in its own right. First, films that appeared in the latter half of the 2000s exhibit significant stylistic differences from those in the late 1990s. Secondly, the two film cycles appear to respond to different historical events. Films from the late 1990s have distinct millennial concerns, whereas those in the late 2000s respond to a cultural pessimism imbued by the events of 9/11. The 1990s wave of Hollywood disaster movies itself represents a recycling of the invasion movies of the 1950s—*Radar Men from the Moon* (1952); *Invaders from Mars* (1953); *Target Earth* (1954)—and the disaster movies of the 1970s—*The Andromeda Strain* (1971); *The Poseidon Adventure* (1972); *The Towering Inferno* (1974). In his book *Disaster Movies: the Cinema of Catastrophe*, Stephen Keane identifies the following reasons for the 1990s re-emergence of disaster movies:

1—The public's fascination with the impending millennium.

2—The absence of any concrete set of villains (after the end of the Cold War).

3—The advancements in special effects technologies allowing for a cinematic experience in which literally anything imaginable could be realized onscreen.

4—The ease with which these films could be watched as largely escapist entertainment.

5—The fact that they were making money. [8]

Interestingly, not even one of these reasons is particularly applicable to the current spate of post-9/11 apocalyptic films.

Although millennial fears have been replaced by fears about climate change and ecological disaster, as well as the pervasive threat of terrorism, there is now a tangible villain figure (that of the terrorist himself). While there have been advancements in technology, and these have been evident in contemporary apocalyptic cinema, there is little that can be achieved onscreen now that could not have been visualized in the late 1990s. Furthermore, films today are often *not* easy to watch and *not* family films. Instead, the majority tend to be violent and gritty films about the inevitable destruction of our way of life. Finally, and perhaps most tellingly, they are not even making that much money compared to the 1990s films: although it is true that most of the films made after 9/11 saw reasonable returns, the recently acclaimed adaptation of Cormac McCarthy's novel *The Road* (2009) grossed less than thirty million dollars at the box office, world-wide.

A brief examination of box-office receipts shows that in general post-9/11 apocalyptic films have been less successful than their late 1990s counterparts. Throughout the last decade there have been some significant successes: *I Am Legend* (2007) grossed $256 million (sixth highest grosser of that year), *War of the Worlds* (2005) $234 million (fourth highest of the year), and *The Day After Tomorrow* (2004) $186 million (seventh highest of the year).[9] But for every success there was also a flop: *Legion* (2010, with Paul Bettany and Dennis Quaid) grossed a paltry $40 million (ranked seventh-seventh for the year); *The Core* (2003, with Aaron Eckhart and Hilary Swank), $31 million (ranked ninetieth); *28 Weeks Later* (2007, a sequel to *28 Days Later* [2002]), $28 million (ranked eighty-seventh). *Sunshine* (2007, with Cillian Murphy as an astronaut sent off to reignite the failing sun) failed to make the top 100 in the same year.[10] Comparatively, 1998 had three apocalypse films in the box-office top ten: *Armageddon* in second rank, with a $36-million opening weekend and more than $350 million worldwide so far; *Deep Impact* in eighth rank, opening with $41 million and running to a similar global figure now; and *Godzilla* right behind it, opening with $44 million and accumulating almost $380 million to date. In 1997, *Dante's Peak*, *The Fifth Element*, and *Volcano* made respectable opening-week returns of $50 million between them and have, as a trio, grossed some $565 million so far. In 1996, *Independence Day* topped the box-office chart with a gross in excess of $300 million. Add in the fact that these figures are not inflation-adjusted for the earliest years and the margins appear even larger. This all begs the question: why these films and why now?

The End of Optimism: Apocalypse Film post 9/11

When we sit down to watch *Armageddon*, *Independence Day*, or *The Fifth Element*, we already know that, come the eleventh hour, humanity will save itself. Redemption is the point of these films: the world must be saved so that in films to follow it can be blown up all over again. In the current post-9/11 environment as seen onscreen it is the end of the world itself that is inevitable, so taken for granted that the cause has become almost irrelevant. In Albert and Allen Hughes's *The Book of Eli* (2010), we are merely told that "The war tore a hole in the sky." Is this a reference to nuclear explosion, to some futuristic weaponry, or to God's judgment? In John Hillcoat's *The Road*, the issue of what caused the apocalypse is sidelined by the protagonists' simple need to survive; we are left to make assumptions: perhaps it was environmental, perhaps nuclear. All we know is, "The clock stopped at 1:17. There was a long shear of bright light, then a series of low concussions." In Alfonso Cuarón's *Children of Men* (2006), humans have inexplicably become infertile. It is not that the causes of disaster in these films are insignificant or petty. There is no doubt that the audience wants to know why apocalypse has happened. But by not telling us, the films make a statement about our world today, about the inevitability of destruction and its source in a zone beyond our ability to question, comprehend, or strategize.

On the whole, Post-9/11 apocalyptic fiction represents a movement away from the escapist images of destruction seen in the late 1990s. While there are still a number of films which revel in over-the-top and brilliantly graphic set pieces of destruction—particularly Roland Emmerich's *The Day After Tomorrow* and *2012* (2009) (he is a director who certainly seems to relish the prospect of disaster)—it remains the case that most post-9/11 apocalypses are depicted in dark and thought-provoking films, bringing home the harsh realities of a world gone to hell and a planet slowly dying. The worst visions of destruction seen in such films as *Independence Day* were made concrete and witnessed on September 11th. Post-9/11 films no longer need to offer speculation about the future, but instead purvey a realization of what is occurring in the here and now, perhaps implying that although we understand our eventual plight we are powerless to prevent it. There is something sublime in this very description; the idea that we are careening towards a dramatic and spectacular end; that the finale will be glorious, vast, universal in scope. Just as the images witnessed on our television screens on September 11, 2001 were sublime in themselves, they have re-configured the audience's perception of scenes of destruction. Post-9/11 apocalyptic films have frequently traded in a different kind of sublime effect, moving away from the depiction of destruction itself and focusing instead on aftermaths, huge and unbounded expanses of devastation and waste, and the fate of the survivor.

Post-9/11 apocalypse films tend to be isolationist. In the 1990s, apocalyptic blockbusters' scripts concentrated on the problem of working in teams. Lead characters relied upon a network of partners, sidekicks, agents, assistants, and functionaries to help guide them to a solution that would save the planet. Thus, in *Independence Day* we have the macho Captain Steven Hillier (Will Smith) bringing his brawn to the aid of traditional science boffin David Levinson (Jeff Goldblum). Along the way we meet many side characters, most notably the American President (Bill Pullman) and a group of pilots who also have important roles to play in the eventual defeat of the alien invaders. In Emmerich's *Godzilla* there is a very similar set-up, the science boffin, Dr. Niko Tatopoulos (Matthew Broderick), needing the assistance of French secret service agent Philippe Roaché (Jean Réno). Once again we have the interference of an authority figure, Mayor Ebert (Michael Lerner), as well as a romantic sub-plot, the American military, and the cameo comedy performance of "Animal" (Hank Azaria). In Michael Bay's *Armageddon*, Bruce Willis's Harry Stamper escorts a drilling team into space in an attempt to prevent an asteroid from hitting the Earth, an operation that is only possible with the help and support of NASA, and which would also have failed if it were not for the exploits of a crazy Russian astronaut, Lev Andropov (Peter Stormare). Stephen Keane notices the importance of a team mentality within the film:

> Repeatedly throughout the film Stamper is referred to as a Red Adair, "the world's best deep core driller," but fundamentally his leadership principle is tempered with the value of teamwork: "I'm only the best because I work with the best."[11]

Lev's portrayal of stereotypical Russian eccentricity is somewhat indicative of these films' attitude towards notions of racial or ethnic difference. As played by a Swedish actor who moved to the U.S. in 1993, Lev's role as the comic relief brushes over nearly half a century's worth of Cold War history. The 1990s liberal sensibility, which also seems in these films to be dealt with reductively in the space of an hour-and-a-half to two hour script, is all pervasive; as Lev himself pronounces, "Components. American components, Russian components. All made in Taiwan!" The message of these films is clear: by working together, we can avert any possible disaster, from erupting volcanoes and asteroids to giant lizards and alien invaders.

When this is contrasted with contemporary post-apocalyptic films we tend to find a rather different approach in the latter. Here our characters are lone survivors. They are often hardened types: men who have learnt how to survive in the harshest of worlds, men who take no prisoners and who stop for no one. A particularly pure example can be seen in *The Road*, as much an apocalyptic drama as an action movie. A man and his son (Viggo Mortensen, Kodi Smit-McPhee) wander through a post-apocalyptic wasteland, heading south to the coast in search of warmth and food. In this place where hope does not exist and survival is everything (but also, apparently, a fruitless endeavor), the pair struggle to keep sight of their humanity. Father and son endure through extreme circumstances, constantly on the look out for groups of cannibals, their greatest fear. That this is to be the darkest of films is established early on when the father shows his son how to shoot himself in case they are captured. When the two finally reach the coast they find not salvation and respite, but as grey and dead a landscape as we have seen throughout the movie. Despite the narrative strategy of the son being adopted by a family at the end of the film, after the father has died leaving him to fend for himself, this is without doubt a film harboring a deep pessimism towards the future.

The Road is filled with isolation. While the father relies on the boy for survival—emotional, not physical—this is still a film in which they do not find a society to join. When they do meet a character who does not want to eat them, the father's survival instincts tell him they should move on as quickly as possible, and so bonding with the other is foreclosed. These principal figures are also isolated by the camera, long-shots of the pair framed against the hostile environment predominating. These shots have become a staple of post-9/11 apocalyptic cinema and can be seen frequently in other films such as *28 Days Later*, *The Book of Eli*, and *I Am Legend*. Culture, sociability, relationship, bonding—all are broken away.

I Am Legend begins with a scene in which Robert Neville (Will Smith) speeds through the streets of a totally evacuated Manhattan chasing deer. There is a playful, fantasy element to the way he drives, with the shiny red sports car reflecting light and Neville skilfully using sidewalks as shortcuts. This is his city, now. He is free to break into houses, take DVDs from the rental store, hit golf balls at cars left abandoned. His only companion is a dog whose primary function in the narrative appears to be to give Neville someone to talk to for the first half of the film. When his dog dies after being bitten by one of the infected who, a strange cross between vampire and zombie, populate the city at night, he is for the moment left utterly alone. Hardened and self-centered, the men in these films are not removed from emotion. They cling to a shred of life without which they see no reason to be. In *The Road* this talisman is the boy, in *I Am Legend* it is the dog. Neville's response is to attempt to commit suicide while taking as many of the infected with him. Fortunately he is rescued by a woman and now, with companionship (if not also sexual availability) restored, he is able to carry on and eventually complete his quest to find a cure for the devastating infection.

I Am Legend may have a hopeful ending, as Neville's cure is taken to a survivor's colony, but ultimately he has given his life to protect it. This is a familiar ending for the contemporary post-apocalyptic film: we have already seen that Mortensen's character dies at the end of *The Road*, along with the centrally important Eli (Denzel Washington) in *The Book of*

Eli and the hero figure Theo Faron (Clive Owen) in *Children of Men*. But if, as these films would suggest, the apocalypse is unstoppable, and if our heroes die for just a small glimmer of hope, what is it that is finally being offered? Why do we continue to watch them? The fantasy elements we see in the story of the lone survivor do not seem escapist in the way that 1990s cinema sought escapism through the destruction of the "indestructible" (our buildings and way of life). In the 1990s we knew that when a lead character actually died (Harry Stamper in *Armageddon*, or Arnold Schwarzenegger in *End of Days* [1999]), he died in order to save our world. What, however, are we saving now through the sacrifice of the hero in the post-apocalyptic world?

Conclusion: A Hungry and Literal End

It is always important to reflect consciousness of context in any piece of work. It can be all too easy, when focused so closely on one small area of culture, to overlook the bigger picture. While I have labelled all of these films as post-9/11, this does not mean that they are a product of 9/11 alone. These films are of course products of the decade just passed since 9/11, a decade that has seen the advent of new kinds of war and that has been plagued by financial collapse, economic and global strife, and concerns about the future sustainability of the planet and of our way of life. While 9/11 may be the defining moment in Western culture over the past decade, there is no doubting the influence of these other forms of social disaster.

Gary Ross's 2012 adaptation of Suzanne Collins's novel *The Hunger Games* is a film that draws on many of these contemporary fears and issues. In many ways an old fashioned dystopic text in the mold of Orwell's *1984*, *The Hunger Games* thrusts its audience into a world that has been vividly and clearly divided along class lines. Ross creates a film charged with a visual style that plays to the idea of social division and expresses the rich/poor dichotomy upon which the futuristic dystopia is—somehow unavoidably—founded. The economic consciousness of the film reflects only one aspect of today's concerns. The film also deals with over-indulgence, fascism, state propaganda, and the manipulation of the workforce primarily through fear and surveillance. To this extent it is a classical dystopia, extrapolating current conditions in order to examine the problems of the present in the "safe" context of sci-fi futurism. The ruler, President Snow (Donald Sutherland), is not shy about expressing the dark agenda which underlies the Hunger Games themselves, a brutal gladiatorial-style conflict in which twenty-four young men and women, selected at random, compete in a battle to the death to win honor for their districts. Snow tells Seneca Crane (Wes Bentley), the impresario who runs the Games, "Hope . . . is the only thing stronger than fear." But, too, in Snow's eyes "A lot of hope is dangerous." Certainly the higher authorities in this futuristic nation of Panem spare no opportunity for bloodshed in order to maintain the status quo that keeps the wealthy in power. Their personal visual excess, emphasized through extreme style and garish make-up, marks them out as the vestiges of a decadent society destined for decline.

What defines the post-9/11 apocalyptic film is a concern with the inevitability of destruction, and the presentation of a future in which all that we have left is faith. In *The Hunger Games* it is the catchphrase of the elite, "May the odds be ever in your favor" that is perhaps most revealing. Of course it is ironic, since in a nation like Panem, the odds are never in your favor if you are poor enough to need them to be. Just as the working class are dominated and exploited, the odds of 24/1 for you to survive the games themselves are anything but in the participants' favor. This and the other post-9/11 films discussed here are systematically characterized by a loss of belief in change. Human agency has been lost. In these bleak depictions of the future there is no room left for the utopian impulse, only the desperate need to survive in a world that has been destroyed not by one specific threat as such, but by any one of a number of end-game scenarios. These are certainly not films which celebrate the end. Rather their purpose appears to be to mourn the loss of the future. Why do we watch them? Perhaps in order to find something that lies outside the system of capital, circulating around the globe, touching every aspect of life. Maybe because Jameson's assertion, that it is easier to imagine the end of the world than the end of capitalism, is the resulting reality of a catastrophic loss of faith in change. Or maybe we watch in order to remind ourselves of the bleakness of the future, like trying to pinch oneself in order to wake-up as if from a nightmare unfolding.

Lars Von Trier's late 2011 film *Melancholia* is an example of just how far the inevitability of destruction has come in post-9/11 film. *Melancholia* is one of those rare examples of a film in which the world does actually end, and, as the filmmaker would have it, for good. Given that the main protagonist, Justine (Kirsten Dunst), is battling against depression, there is certainly nothing light-hearted about this apocalypse, a cosmic one portrayed as the collision of the Earth with another planet (mirrored in a preparatory opening scene). No science can prevent the world from ending, and it is entirely beyond the control of the characters. This is a fact made overt through Justine's brother-in-law John, played by Kiefer Sutherland – normally renowned for his almost omnipotent powers in fighting terrorist apocalypses in the popular TV show "24." John is an astronomer, a man of science, convinced that the two planets will pass harmlessly by each other. By the end of the film it has become obvious that science will not win the day and that in fact the world will end. John promptly commits suicide. Is this the logical conclusion of the kind of end-of-worldism that has been prevalent over the last decade? Fascinated as we are by ends, perhaps in our current state it would be far better off to think about beginnings and re-imaginings than what is perhaps the easiest of ways out: the end of all. While post-9/11 apocalyptic films may often have more to say about society and the future of the planet than those 1990s Hollywood spectaculars, surely their message of hopelessness leaves no room for building a better future. On some level, those crass and populist blockbusters at least sent the message that something could be done to change the world, that yes, humanity *could* save the planet.

Notes

[1] *Archaeologies of the Future*, (London: Verso, 2005), 199.

[2] articles.cnn.com/2001-09-11/us/bush.speech.text_1_attacks-deadly-terrorist-acts-despicable-acts?_s=PM:US

[3] It is rare to find a book or essay that does not begin by suggesting that 9/11 "changed everything," or at least that does not begin by dealing with this concept, perhaps in order

to dismiss it as oversimplification as Susan Faludi does in *The Terror Dream: What 9/11 Revealed about America*, (London: Atlantic Books, 2008), 2.

[4] *The Spirit of Terrorism*, (New York: Verso, 2002), 26-7.

[5] Even those film articles that seem to profess an interest in post-9/11 aesthetics, such as Mathias Nilges's "The Aesthetics of Destruction Contemporary US Cinema and TV Culture," seem to fall short of really addressing this change in the nature of the image on display talked about here by Baudrillard.

[6] Stephen Prince's book *Firestorm American Film in the Age of Terrorism*, (New York: Columbia University Press, 2009) provides a very adequate groundwork for dealing with the question "what films were produced after 9/11" but is shy when it comes to placing these cultural products within a critique.

[7] *Film/Genre*, 60.

[8] London: Wallflower Press, 2001, 79.

[9] Figures courtesy of www.boxofficemojo.com.

[10] Interestingly enough both *World Trade Center* and *United 93* also failed to live up to their billing, only managing roughly $100m between them, perhaps justifying studios' hesitancies with regards to dealing directly with 9/11.

[11] *Disaster Movies*, 93.

Chapter 30

Notes on Detecting Serial Killers

Stephen Gaunson

*T*he forgettable police drama "Cops" (1988), based on James Ellroy's 1984 novel *Blood on the Moon*, seems to be the first drama to utter the words "serial killer." "Serial murder" and "serial murderer," however, are punctuated throughout the 1966 John Brophy book, *The Meaning of Murder*. Pop culture's serial killer is drawn from the newsstands of real life, with stories often retelling and re-enacting real-life events: *The Boston Strangler* (1968), *The Deliberate Stranger* (1986), *Summer of Sam* (1999), *Zodiac* (2007), *Monster* (2007). Popular narratives commonly blur the *modus operandi* of several real serial killers to create one superpredator: Thomas Harris's *Silence of the Lambs* (1991) brainchild, Jame Gumb/Buffalo Bill, is drawn from at least six different serial killers: Ed Gein (also the inspiration for Norman Bates in Robert Bloch's 1959 novel *Psycho*), Ted Bundy, Gary M. Heidnik, Edmund Kemper, Gary Leon Ridgway and Jerry Brudos.

The serial killer of popular culture has traditionally (but not always) been a male killer of women: Charles Chaplin's Henri Verdoux (*Monsieur Verdoux*, 1947), Michael Powell's Mark Lewis (*Peeping Tom*, 1960), Don Siegel's Scorpio (*Dirty Harry*, 1971), Harold Becker's Terry (*Sea of Love*, 1989), Michael Winterbottom's Lou Ford (*The Killer Inside Me*, 2010). Alfred

Hitchcock repeatedly explored the story of an accused killer of women, who must either attempt to get away with it—*Shadow of a Doubt* (1943), *Psycho* (1960), *Frenzy* (1972)—or prove his innocence—*The Lodger* (1927), *Suspicion* (1941). The novels on which the latter two films were based, Marie Belloc Lowndes's 1913 *The Lodger* and Francis Iles's 1932 *Before the Fact*, were both stories of guilty men. While viewers of each assumed they would see a faithful adaptation, instead they found the guilty man turned out as yet another victim of the witch-hunt community. In *The Lodger*, the central figure's ultimate innocence does little to annul the audience's deeper anxieties. If he is innocent, the killer still lurks out there somewhere, but where? And will he keep killing?

Serial killing is not always an act of single lonely-heart sufferers. Sometimes men act in tandem—*Henry: Portrait of a Serial Killer* (1986), *Popcorn* (1996), *Snowtown* (2011)—but more often we find heterosexual couples choreographing the mayhem: *Natural Born Killers* (1994), *Karla* (2006), *See No Evil: The Moors Murders* (2006), *Sweeney Todd: The Demon Barber of Fleet Street* (2007), *Appropriate Adult* (2011). In such films, women often accompany their men on killing sprees in fear of abandonment and rejection, this trope raising the heteronormative bond to a status higher than life itself and highlighting the male, from women's point of view, as a treasure worth killing for and a power compelling submission. In *The Honeymoon Killers* (1969), remade as *Deep Crimson* (1996), and *Lonely Hearts* (2006), the female partner has no issue with the killer male swindling women he meets through want ads. Yet, when it comes to him seducing, and probably bedding, such rejects, she insists on being part of his "work." Her jealously and confrontation of younger better-looking versions of herself—versions more apt to seduce the male gaze—is persuasion enough for murder.

"Dexter"

A persistent question punctuated by the genre is why seemingly normal people kill, since a recurring characteristic of the serial murderer character is his or her distinctive nondistinctiveness. Confronting such a question often leads to symptomatizing the serial killer as having experienced a signal and ineradicable traumatic event in childhood. Utterly negating the role social forces might play in making serial murder possible (or making it less impossible), such a premise is fleshed out in the popular Showtime series "Dexter" (2006) adapted from Jeff Lindsey's novel series. The idea here is that as a toddler, Dexter Morgan experienced first-hand the savage butchering of his mother. (The character is played by Maxwell Huckabee as an infant; then, as the child grows up, by Dominic Janes and Devon Graye; and by Michael C. Hall in the adult version.) Left to stew in a puddle of maternal blood, he is deeply traumatized when finally rescued. The trauma leads him to acquire a bloodlust, which is developed as his adoptive police officer father, Harry (James Remar), teaches him a "code" for killing without detection. Cardinal rule: kill only killers (serial killers mostly) who have evaded police capture. Thus, morally legitimate the action through the rhetoric of civil justice in a stressed-out postcapitalist dystopia where the penal system does not function. Dexter's "day job" as a Blood Splatter Analyst for the Miami Homicide Division gives him open access to exclusive police databases, etc. His code—killing, thus punishing, "bad people" who themselves kill "good people"—elevates him to the status of noble vigilante and situates him with other vigilante serial killers in pop culture, such as John in *Snowtown* (2011), Rooster in *Righteous Kill* (2008), and Aileen Wuornos in *Monster*. A central controversy of "Dexter," indeed (as with all serial-killer vigilantes), is the heroization of its killer. In *Snowtown*, at least, the protagonist's vigilante, chest-pumping, serial-killer rhetoric is exposed as bogus; he is nothing more than a manipulative, bloodthirsty Svengali. Dexter's morally transparent vigilantism, however, is more perverse. To refrain from exploiting his killing habit is precisely his character arc: he summons his own demons in order not to create chaos but to overcome what he calls his "dark passenger." Dexter wants to be normal. ("What would Dexter do?" has been a catch-phrase branded on a plethora of Showtime paraphernalia.) "You're just like me!" serial killer Trinity (John Lithgow) snaps at him. "I know," Dexter mournfully responds, "but I don't want to be," before, ironically, driving his knife into his chest.

Pied Piper Killers

Amy Taubin demarcates the serial killer genre into three male oriented archetypes of pathology: the child murderer figure (who victimizes young girls); the Bluebeard figure whose victims are wives (that is, "good women"); and the Jack the Ripper figure who specializes in killing prostitutes (that is, "bad women"). The adult murderer of children remains the most controversial. Fritz Lang's *M* (1931) still seems like a hugely audacious film today: Beckert (Peter Lorre), a depraved pied piper type, lures and kills innocent, vulnerable, and sweet children. Finally he is tracked and surrounded by the police, but before the law can punish him he falls into the clutches of the criminal community, whose members exercise their own justice without remorse. The child murderer has been a relatively eclipsed figure of popular culture; stories concerning such figures tend to concentrate more readily on the trauma experienced by the victim's family: *Humanité* (1999), *The Pledge* (2001), *Mystic River* (2003), *Changeling* (2003). English author David Peace's *Red Riding* quartet, *Nineteen Seventy-Four* (1999), *Nineteen Seventy-Seven* (2000), *Nineteen Eighty* (2001), and *Nineteen Eighty-Three* (2002), which explored the media reaction and political cover-up of a series of murders including the Yorkshire Ripper case, was adapted into three feature-length television episodes for Britain's Channel 4 between 1999-2002.

Casting a child as the murderer of children has functioned as a trope both to underline the theme of inherent, genetically inherited "evil" and to centre the narrative on the personality and actions of the killer: *The Bad Seed* (1956), *Communion* (1976), *The Changeling* (1980), *Child's Play* (1988). Critic Roger Ebert cheekily dubbed *The Good Son* (1993) as "Henry, Portrait of a Future Serial Killer."[1] Evinced in the persona of Chucky from the *Child's Play* franchise—*Child's Play 2* (1990), *Child's Play 3* (1991), *Bride of Chucky* (1998), and *Seed of Chucky* (2004)—horror's baroque nature and suspension of plausible reality gives the child murderer narrational carte blanche to reap havoc upon the pious community's preschoolers and parents. With the weapon-wielding child killer, we can be lured into having the sense that he is equal to his victims, not towering over them with a brutalizing power. The power of the murderer appears to flow not from age and status but from personality.

Beyond the pubescent children is the teenie splatterpunk serial killer, as found in *Scream* (1996), *I Know What you Did Last Summer* (1997), *Urban Legend* (1998), or *Trick 'r Treat* (2007). The radically disfigured dream stalker Freddy Krueger (originated by Robert Englund and reincarnated by many others, including Jackie Earle Haley and Chris Greene) is the archetypal centrepiece of splatterpunk, starring in nine feature films at the time of this writing, as well as featuring in the novelization of each of these in addition to another twelve films, one television series, comic books, and video games. His only worthy rival is Jason Voorhees from the *Friday the 13th* franchise (originated by Ari Lehman and played by a number of performers since, including most recently Timothy Whitfield), the star of twelve feature films and thirteen novellas. These two slasher killers deliciously fought it out in the crossover film *Freddy Vs. Jason* (2003, with Englund and Ken Kirzinger), which of course ends with both killers remaining alive, in order that their respective franchises may be continued along with the panic-inducing terror that corpses will pile up, on and off the screen, without limit. The fear of death nearby is a marvellous tonic for consumerism. Pop culture's penchant for resuscitation and immortalization allows the serial killer to remain with us . . . lurking somewhere, anywhere . . . waiting! WAITING FOR YOU!

The serial killer narrative uniformly ends with a haunting image of the still-killing killer . . . uncaged. For many, the most chilling moment of Jonathan Demme's *The Silence of the Lambs* (1991) comes with the final shot of Hannibal-the-cannibal-Lecter (Anthony Hopkins) casually strolling down the main street of Port-au-Prince in his creamy tourist suit: Hannibal *lives*. *Henry: Portrait of a Serial Killer* chillingly concludes with Henry (Michael Rooker) leaving his suitcase at the side of a deserted road. The sudden absence of his sort-of-girlfriend, Becky—they were together the night before—and gooey stains on the suitcase's covering suggest her whereabouts; the muffled non-diegetic screaming overdubbed from an earlier scene as the camera lingers on the suitcase suggests her death even more. Henry *lives*. As much as the sequels, prequels, and other forms (Internet sites, chat rooms) allow us to keep tabs on the serial killer's manifestations, the narrative formula of the serial killer genre confers immortality. As Taubin suggests, it is "the killer's ability to rise from the dead in film after film–rather than his appearance, his physical strength or even the extreme sadism of his actions–that demonizes him. Thirty years of these films have primed audiences to bind the words 'serial' and 'killer' into the image of a superhuman monster."[2]

Bluebeard Killers

Even feature film producers who terminate series and announce their killer's time of death, refusing any further editions, seem unable to stop the zeitgeist invoked by their brainchild serial murderer. After his groundbreaking 1960 splatterpunk horror film, Alfred Hitchcock was uninterested in further exploiting Robert Bloch's novel *Psycho*. But no one could stop subsequent features from being made and released by others: *Psycho II* (1983), *Psycho III* (1986), and *Psycho IV: The Beginning* (1990), as well as the telemovie (intended as a pilot for a series) *Bates Motel* (1987)[3] and the meta-narrational *Alfred Hitchcock and the Making of Psycho*, from Stephen Rebello's critical book of the same name, in production now for a 2013 release, with Anthony Hopkins and Helen Mirren as Hitchcock and his wife and Ralph Macchio as screenwriter Joe Stefano.[4] In 1998, Gus Van Sant remade Hitchcock's original film (supposedly, but not entirely) shot-for-shot. Norman Bates has also appeared in comic and manga publications. Mostly recently he has re-emerged in the porn item *Psycho Parody* (2010) and the short film *Psycho in 60 Seconds* (2011).

Norman Bates exemplifies Taubin's Bluebeard figure (killer of good girls). There have been many films based on the French Bluebeard myth about the wife-killing nobleman, the earliest being perhaps the first serial killer film ever, George Méliès's *Barbe-Bleue* (1902). The Bluebeard killer tingles the spine of affluent and privileged middle-class cinema audiences. It is often the story of lower-class killers hunting girls from pious, wholesome families where anyone could be their next victim. The splatterpunk horror film *Scream II* (1997) opens in a movie house with an audience watching, of course, a serial-killer film, *Stab*, based on the events depicted in Wes Craven's original *Scream*. During this screening, Phil Stevens (Omar Epps) and his girlfriend Maureen Evans (Jada Pinkett), two college students, are stabbed by an anonymous person in the killer's Ghostface costume from the Craven film. Other audience members gleefully watch this spectacle, believing it to be only an elaborate publicity stunt. The Bluebeard figure is petrifying because he targets "good" (that is, affluent) people depending on potential victims' ethnicity, gender, age, and body shape. In general he seeks the good-looking young avatars held up by advertising and media fictions as worthy, essential, and successful in capitalist culture. "What do you want?!" pleads Casey (Drew Barrymore) in the original *Scream*; she is a model of swank privilege. Jame in *Silence of the Lambs*, trying to fashion a woman's suit from real skin, picks plump young women he intends to starve (at one and the same time shrinking them away from their epidermis to make it more easily removed and performing what the popular culture simultaneously adulates as a beauty makeover ceremony). Serial killer John Doe (Kevin Spacey) from David Fincher's *Se7en* (1995) also chooses his victims based on their body shape, in order to stage elaborate deaths related to each of the Christian Seven Deadly Sins: Gluttony, for example, involves an obese man force-fed until his stomach ruptures.

Hitchcock's Norman Bates, played by the androgynous and sylphlike Anthony Perkins, became pop culture's post-1960s serial-killing poster boy: lean, still youthful (Perkins had just turned twenty-eight when the film was released), and white. (Black serial killers are rare, even in blaxploitation. *Blacula's* eponymous killer [William Marshall, 1972] is one of the few examples. Blacks are quite common, however, as victims.) Prior to Norman, killers were uniformly unattractive, overweight, bald, and older: Méliès's Bluebeard, for instance, is an ogre; Bloch's 1959 conception of Norman Bates was pyknic, bald, and ugly. Nor have portly serial killers been entirely elided. Richard Attenborough's John Reginald Christie in 10 *Rillington Place* (1971) is entirely unattractive, as is Michael Badalucco's chubby "Son of Sam" in Spike Lee's *Summer of Sam* (1999), yet since the end of the Production Code and the introduction of the ratings system (between 1966 and 1968), directors have had more luxury to cast handsome and charismatic celebrities as serial killers. Thus, we have Terence Stamp, sleek, cold, and sculptural in William Wyler's *The Collector* (1965), darkly brooding Tony Curtis as Albert DeSalvo in *The Boston Strangler*, blockbuster hunk Kevin Costner headlining *Mr. Brooks* (2007), crossover pretty boy Harry Connick Jr. in *Copy Cat*, seductive Johnny Depp as Sweeney Todd, and TV star Dominic West in *Appropriate Adult* (2011). The more attractive serial killers are, the more audiences are positioned to identify with them and what they do. The serial desire to see images in film after film is wedded to the killer's serial need for victims. Like a serial killer, the film viewer fully consumes a seemingly endless array of "products."

Jack the Ripper Killers

Jack the Ripper has a pop-cultural genre to himself, and now constitutes a killer type much reproduced.[5] Before Christian Bale was catapulted to global stardom as the caped crusader Batman, he was the business-suited avenger Bateman, a yuppie Manhattan businessman-cum-serial killer in Mary Harron's adaptation of Bret Easton Ellis's disturbing satire novel

American Psycho (1991). Dechen Thurman (*This Is Not an Exit: The Fictional World of Bret Easton Ellis*, 2000) and Michael Kremko (*American Psycho 2*, 2000) also played versions of Bateman in corny spin-off filmic adaptations. Bateman also makes multiple appearances in Ellis's novels bookending *American Psycho*, *The Rules of Attraction* (1987) and *Lunar Park* (2005), as the classic Jack the Ripper killer: a slayer of bad girls (prostitutes). Ellis's sardonic detail and fetishization of his "hero" makes the first-person narration powerful and disturbing, so much so that the book was sometimes sold shrink-wrapped. Even Lester Ballard, the necrophilic serial killer of Cormac McCarthy's *Child of God* (1973), is granted first-person narration only at fleeting intervals. For the most part, the reader is protected by McCarthy's third-person prose.

American Psycho's epistolary style (the book is written as sporadic diary entries) is an important literary mode of the serial killer narrative. Other examples include *Paul's Case: The Kingston Letters* (Lynn Crosbie, 1997), *Dear Mr. Capote* (Gordon Lish, 1987), *The Executioner's Song* (Norman Mailer, 1980), *The Secret Diary of Laura Palmer* (Jennifer Lynch, 1990), and *The Diary of Jack the Ripper* (James Maybrick, 1998). Video recording is also a popular form of diarization, as we see from Michael Powell's *Peeping Tom, Henry: Portrait of a Serial Killer, Man Bites Dog* (1992), *Natural Born Killers, How to be a Serial Killer* (2008) and *Saw* (2004), the killers in all of which use video as a means of archiving themselves into history. *The Last Horror Movie* (2003) is one of the more interesting, if not successful, examples of this type. It starts as a tried-and-true splatterpunk film with the screen fuzzing, then a face (Max) explaining himself as a notorious killer and playing recorded clips of his killings. Unknowingly, the killer has recorded partly over a copy of a film entitled *The Last Horror Movie* which has migrated its way onto the shelf at the video store. *The Last Horror Movie* has been dubbed over by (literally) "The Last Horror Movie." Viewers become complicit to the killer's "confessions" and crimes. The gimmick works only with DVDs; the celluloid in theatrical release cannot be recorded over.

"Home movie footage" is seminal to the true-crime documentary to explain the crimes that did eventuate. The home footage is often investigated for its telltale signs of "peculiar" behavior. The complicit community is expected to explain themselves. Family members—especially mothers—are interviewed alongside school friends and former lovers. If the killer survives, prison interviews give him or her an opportunity to accept guilt and blame the complicit community. More shamelessly, the killer may be seen gloating over how he or she did it. In Nick Broomfield's documentary *The Selling of a Serial Killer* (1993) and its follow up *Aileen: Life and Death of a Serial Killer* (2003), Aileen Wuornos blames the Florida police for "allowing her" to keep killing. Their permissiveness let her notoriety gain currency, enabling them to profit handsomely from selling her story. ("You sabotaged my ass, society, and the cops, and the system. A raped woman got executed, and was used for books and movies and shit.") Seemingly aware of the serial killer's role in popular culture—to continue rampaging without cease—in her final statement Wuornos chillingly warned, "I'm sailing with the Rock, and I'll be back. Like Independence Day with Jesus, June 6, like the movie, big mothership and all. I'll be back."

SCUM Killers

And back she was in *Monster*. A barely recognizable Charlize Theron sympathetically played Wuornos in the role that won her an Academy Award. The film (controversially) posited that as a street prostitute, Wuornos was merely acting in self-defence when she killed lowly and sexually repressed clients who had their own pent-up murderous intentions. A female Travis Bickle vigilante type, morally cleansing the corrupt society in which she is trapped: "One day a rain will come and wash all of this *scum* off the street." Aileen and Travis both reckoned themselves to be that therapeutic "rain." Like most women-killing-men serial killer films, *Monster* is a realization of Valerie Solanas's 1967 SCUM (Society for Culling of Men) Manifesto, which opens: "'Life' in this 'society' being, at best, an utter bore and no aspect of 'society' being at all relevant to women, there remains to civic-minded, responsible, thrill-seeking females only to overthrow the government, eliminate the money system, institute complete automation and eliminate the male sex."[6] Punctuating the manifesto, Solanas lists a series of grievances including, among others, Niceness, Politeness, "Dignity," Conformity, Hate, and Violence.

Films about misandrist serial killers, such as *Black Widow* (1987) and *I Was a Teenage Serial Killer* (1993), reckon men as dim-witted, weak-minded, weak-willed, and chauvinistic. Wuornos is the perfect embodiment of Solanas's thesis, a victim of man's "shitpile" and someone willing to react against it. Lesbian also, her envy—like man's, as Solanas claims—is "pussy," not "penis." She needs or wants nothing from men. Her mission is to cull them. Lesbianism is a recurring feature of the misandrist serial killer in such films as *Arizona Heat* (1988), *Basic Instinct* (1992), *Butterfly Kiss* (1995), *Mercy* (2000), *Dr. Chopper* (2005), and *Overkill* (1992), used either to dehumanize the female by morphing her into a weirdly misanthropic sex freak or to titillate the audience with the spectacle of softcore lesbian sex.

Before the sexy and sexual SCUM there was the biddy psycho character, initiated by Joan Crawford in a series of pictures dubbed hagsploitation and/or hag horror: *What Ever Happened to Baby Jane?* (1962), *Hush . . . Hush, Sweet Charlotte* (1964), and *Straight Jacket* (1964). Shelley Winters continued it in *What's the Matter with Helen?* (1971) and the deliciously titled *Whoever Slew Aunt Roo?* (1972). John Waters's slasher-biddy satire *Serial Mom* (1994) pays homage to this hag sub-genre, with Beverly Sutphin (Kathleen Turner), a muted suburban American housewife, slaying her victims over the smallest insult; her pious, goodly, hygienic facade allows her to operate without drawing any initial suspicion. Once she is caught she is heralded a feminist heroine—as Solanas proclaimed herself—until she proves to be just a deranged killer; Solanas did likewise when she attempted to assassinate Andy Warhol.

In popular culture, serial killing can be passed from mother to child, and the Biddy Mother is often blamed for this. Henry from *Portrait of a Serial Killer* blames his "whore" Mother for dressing him as a girl, confusing his sexuality by making him "watch her doin' it. Then they'd laugh at me . . ." *Silence of the Lambs's* Jame wants to actually *be* Mother. Norman Bates is the archetypal blame-Mother killer. Dressed as her, talking as her, and becoming her, he kills anyone who threatens her babe in the woods. "You reap what you sow," or, as Mother explains to her serial killer son in *We Need to Talk About Kevin* (2011), "So the Daddy bear plants his seed in the Mommy bear and it grows into an egg." Serial killers are terrifying monsters of the community, for, like every one of us, they are the community's fruit, Mother's fruit, let loose.

Notes

[1] Roger Ebert, *I Hated, Hated, Hated This Movie* (Andrews McMeel Publishing: Missouri, 2000), 141.

[2] Amy Taubin, "Killing Men," *Sight and Sound* (May 1991), 16.

[3] A & E is currently developing a new series entitled "Bates Motel" for a 2013 airing. A prequel to Hitchcock's movie (and no connection to the abandoned pilot) it focuses on Norman's relationship with his mommy, Norma. The backstory will also reveal how Norma helped to transform her son into a serial killer.

[4] Regardless of Bloch writing also *Psycho II* (1982) and *Psycho House* (1990), these were unrelated to the other film sequels.

[5] For more on Jack in popular culture see Denis Meikle, *Jack the Ripper: The Murders and the Movies* (Surrey: Reynolds and Hearn Ltd., 2002).

[6] Valerie Solanas, SCUM *Manifesto* (London: Verso, 2004), 1.

Chapter 31

All My Vampires

Cary Elza

Since the publication of Bram Stoker's original 1897 *Dracula* (and arguably before that), the vampire has represented, among many other things, a dark, repressed side of the human psyche that can't ever be completely escaped. "Traditional" vampires—descendants of Dracula—don't let trivial matters like morality or social acceptability get in the way of a good time. Vampiric pastimes might include, but are not limited to, violence, sexual or otherwise (blood drinking is associated with the act of penetration, a symbolic rape), excessive sexuality that violates social conventions, necrophilia, and/or an obsession with death. Forged in the fires of Freudianism, the figure of the vampire as it developed over the course of the twentieth century is often interpreted as giving symbolic expression to humanity's deepest, darkest fears and desires.

But modern retellings of the vampire story are not at all like Stoker's. *Twilight's* Edward Cullen (Robert Pattinson) is *not* like Bram Stoker's original Count Dracula: he's neither Transylvanian nor foreign but American; the sun doesn't weaken him but makes him sparkle; mirrors are no problem for him; he has a loving, albeit adoptive, family, with whom he enjoys good clean fun like playing baseball; he goes to high school; and he doesn't feed on people. In short, he's a sorry excuse for a vampire—he doesn't even have fangs. What Edward and his literary ancestors have in common is a tendency to obsess over a woman.[1] For Dracula, this might not be love, but for Edward, vampiric bloodlust has been sublimated in favor of all-consuming devotion to Bella Swan (Kristen Stewart), the heroine. Like Edward, many other contemporary vampires are a far sight from Bram Stoker's seductive, murderous fiend. From Stephenie Meyer's sparkly *Twilight* vampires (2008, 2009, 2010, 2011, 2012) to the Southern gentlemen of "True Blood" (2008) and "The Vampire Diaries" (2009), recent vampires are more likely to buy you dinner than dine upon you.

In order for the traditional vampire narrative to do its ideological work—keeping the repressed repressed—the monster must be destroyed at the end. But almost as soon as the vampire made it onto the screen, the idea of seriality became part of the narrative's appeal. *Dracula's Daughter*, Universal's 1936 sequel to Tod Browning's *Dracula* (1931), picks up right where the previous film left off, with the emergence of the titular villain. The death of the vampire becomes even more reversible with the Hammer films in the 1950s and 1960s—there, all it takes to bring Christopher Lee back to life is a ring, a blood sacrifice, and some magic words. In this way, the vampire narrative's vanquishing of society's shadow side can happen over and over again. What happens, however, when the vampire doesn't move others to destroy him, because he's not such a bad guy?

The twisting of genre conventions that characterized much Hollywood fare in the late 1960s-1970s offered alternatives to the evil, animalistic vampire, and even suggested that the love of a woman might have the potential to tame the wild beast. Throughout the 1980s and 1990s, vampires became metaphors for everything from disease and drug addiction to gang violence and generational discord. But punk vampires, cowboy vampires, and other bad-boy types also shared the screen with a more Romantic incarnation—the self-loathing, poetic, sensitive vampire on a mission of redemption. This broody, heroic vampire appears on the scene like a knight in tarnished armor, saving the heroine from peril and tugging at her heartstrings. By his sad, shiny eyes the heroine can tell that he's *really* deep. As a relic of a bygone era, who has learned to operate within the boundaries of current-day social norms, he offers an antiquated, chivalrous ideal of masculinity that seems, at first glance, like an antidote to identity politics and unstable norms of morality, gender, and sexuality.

The anti-hero oozes confidence and sexuality, and makes a point of excoriating his broody friend's solipsistic self-sacrifice as a denial of who he "really is," i.e., a blood-sucking monster from the Id. While, as Karen Backstein writes, a "'bad vampire' usually throws the hero's chivalrousness into relief," the "bad vampires" seem to have more fun.[2] And more often than not, the stronger vampire's commitment to hedonism is a form of repression as well—the repression of his humanity. These two vampires form a kind of dyad. If the vampire figure traditionally represents the dark, primitive side of humanity, a shadowy double of "civilized" man, then the prevalence of vampire pairs suggests that in order to be tamed, made into suitable boyfriend material, the vampire needs his own figure of the repressed.

These new vampires aren't static. They represent changing modes of masculinity, and play out moral struggles that persist through history. Importantly, both vampires in the pairing can't ever be fully good or fully evil at the same time—they have to trade. At all times, one represents the shadow side, so he has to be at least a little evil, and one represents the human, repressed side, so he has to be at least a little good. Whether they're playing good vamp or bad vamp, though, they make present decisions based on a conception of the past that's always in flux. The structure of the vampire pair allows for the expression of both taboo and inappropriate desires related to sexuality and violence and the fascination with reactionary ideals of masculinity, in which the "assimilation" into polite society means a return to patriarchal policing of feminine sexuality. The heroine has a choice: she can stick with the knight in tarnished armor, who offers unconditional love and protection, but only on his own nefarious terms, or she can check out his fixer-upper cousin, whose carefully constructed evil mask hides a soft, squishy interior.

Or she can give both of them a try. To complicate matters further, critiques that attempt to make definitive statements about the vampire as romantic lead in a given TV series or film quickly become dated. For example, after the first few seasons of "True Blood," Southern gentleman Bill (Stephen Moyer) was hailed as a "guardian angel with fangs" in *Film Quarterly*, which didn't foresee his return to evil.[3] Buffy (Sarah Michelle Gellar) on "Buffy the Vampire Slayer" (1997) eventually breaks up with vampire-with-a-soul Angel (David Boreanaz) and takes up with snarky, unpredictably violent Spike (James Marsters). The same pattern repeats on "The Vampire Diaries," where heroine Elena's (Nina Dobrev) on-again-off-again relationship with soulful, introspective Stefan (Paul Wesley) is jeopardized by her powerful attraction to his far more morally suspect—but secretly romantic—brother Damon (Ian Somerhalder). Pitting love at first sight against a slow burn of banter-filled seduction, such love triangles point not only to competing ideals of masculinity and romance, but also to the heroine's understanding of herself as an agent in the writing of her own history.

Vampire narratives offer viewers, especially female consumers, different ways of negotiating the impact on identity and memory of both romantic and familial relationships. All of "True Blood," "The Vampire Diaries," the *Twilight* films, "Buffy the Vampire Slayer," and its sequel "Angel" (1999) are serial narratives aimed at primarily female audiences—often *young* female audiences, whose members might be intimidated by the commitments and obligations of adulthood—and as such they dip from a common well of generic traditions. Conventions of melodrama, and especially the centrality of female protagonists, speak to women's negotiation between romantic ideals and the complexity of social realities. While *Twilight* offers the comfort of absolute love, truth, and belonging—in the end Edward and Bella will live happily ever after—the TV series challenge patriarchal metanarratives of "true love," genealogy, and official history by denying viewers narrative closure, instead offering their female protagonists more complex choices, acknowledging that people change and that identities can be tried on and discarded, and that history can be rewritten.

Vampire's Girls

Importantly, these are all texts with female protagonists. As Backstein notes, they encourage "audience identification with the heroine—her strength, her extraordinary capabilities, her status as an object of desire, or a combination of all these traits."[4] Like the classic figure of the romance novel heroine, who, as Janice Radway points out, is usually distiguished from her peers by "unusual intelligence or by an extraordinarily fiery disposition" or who "exhibits special abilities in an unusual occupation," targets of the vampire affection have unique personal qualities.[5] Sookie on "True Blood" (Anna Paquin) is a telepath and a fairy-human hybrid. Buffy is a vampire slayer with superhero powers. Bella has particularly enticing blood and a natural resistance to the vampire's mind tricks. Elena is a doppelgänger whose blood has special powers. The supernatural element of each heroine's identity is often more a burden than a gift, and comes along with responsibilities. As a result, much of the narrative revolves around her asserting her own wishes and priorities while being bombarded with the demands and expectations of others.

Faced with the amorous attention of the vampire, the heroine learns to reconcile herself with the way others—the vampire especially—see her. Peter Brooks notes that the heroine's project is "the formation of an inner drive toward the assertion of selfhood in resistance to the overt and violating male plots of ambition."[6] In a certain sense, the heroine's self-image is fragmented and thrown into confusion with the arrival of the vampire hero, whose commitment to her safety and welfare often stifles her independence. The way she handles her new limitations helps to redefine her identity.

These heroines come from broken families, a detail that, as Ben Singer points out, also characterized 1910s serial melodramas using female protagonists to offer "an antitraditional conception of womanhood, one appealing to a generation of young women eager to differentiate their worldview from that of their mothers."[7] Current vampire narratives are surprisingly similar in a number of ways: spunky heroine, hunky boyfriend skilled at last-minute rescues, insatiably sadistic villain. Even a hundred years after *The Perils of Pauline* (1914), the heroine's disconnect from one or more parents speaks to a target audience of young women. Sookie's and Elena's parents are dead; Buffy has a mother (only until season six) and an absentee father who's almost never mentioned; and Bella comes to Forks, Washington to live with her father after her mother remarries. None of these young women inhabit a traditional nuclear family. Instead they seek alternate forms of community and kinship. Vampires appear in their lives as concrete, tangible ties to a stable (if sorely limiting) patriarchal past, yet offering a different and even reactionary version of family, along with the fulfillment of sexual and emotional needs.

Bloody Crushes

All four series also feature more than one suitor competing for the love of the heroine. *Twilight* pairs Bella with Edward, the sensitive Adonis who drinks only animal blood, but he is given a rival in Jacob (Taylor Lautner), the Native American werewolf. Where Edward is cold, Jacob is hot; where Edward is somewhat otherworldly and courtly, Jacob offers friendship before making his move; and where Edward is very protective—early on he demonstrates his affections when saving Bella from an out-of-control car—Jacob allows Bella more leeway, even helping her to rebuild a motorcycle. Although it might seem at first glance as though Bella has a choice between the two males, *Twilight* cuts her options by introducing the idea that mating is destined, with Jacob "imprinting on" Bella's unborn child.[8]

In contrast, "True Blood," "Vampire Diaries," and "Buffy" each allows its heroine the luxury of choosing between at least two vampires who literally fight over her. The "good vampire" appears as a crush-worthy savior, while the "bad vampire" first appears as a villain. At the beginning of "Buffy," vampire-with-a-soul Angel is Buffy's benevolent stalker, upon their first meeting not only providing her with vital information but also gifting her a silver cross, which later saves her life. They trade barbs at first, but once Buffy sees the pain in his eyes antagonism gives way to attraction. Evil Spike, in contrast, arrives in town during season two, with his crazy vampire girlfriend Drusilla (Juliet Landau) in tow, and wastes no time in finding Buffy, threatening to kill her, failing at this, and then assuaging his frustrations by terminating other vampires and assuming control. In "The Vampire Diaries," Elena has her first encounter with broody, mysterious Stefan by trading steamy looks with him across a classroom. Having saved Elena's life when she and her parents are in a car crash (the parents don't make it), Stefan then reveals his chivalrousness by returning, without reading, the journal she left at the cemetery. His darker brother Damon, however, announces his arrival by nearly killing one local teen and seducing one of Elena's friends. He continues to kill and eat people off and on throughout the series, and even once kills Elena's brother Jeremy (Steven R. McQueen) (he revives).

On "True Blood," Sookie first meets Bill, a relic of the antebellum South, at the restaurant where she works as a waitress. Again, love at first sight. They gaze at each other so intensely that the lights lower behind him and he appears to glow. Her telepathic abilities go mercifully silent when Bill is around, which adds to his appeal. After she saves him from two redneck drug dealers, he returns the favor—and reclaims his masculinity—by rescuing her from the same thugs, then healing her by forcing her to drink his blood. By contrast, domineering Viking Eric (Alexander Skarsgård) is introduced as the Sheriff of Area 5—the organization of the vampire authorities exists apart from human law—and as the owner of Fangtasia, a seedy vampire bar. When first they meet, Eric hits on Sookie, asking Bill if he's "quite attached" to her, and later in the series tricks Sookie into drinking his blood and establishing a bond with him. Like Spike and Damon, Eric manipulates and threatens those around him, kills people regularly, and at least initially disenfranchises Sookie as he bonds with her.

The morally dark Spike, Damon, and Eric appear shirtless onscreen more often than do their well-behaved counterparts. If the heroic vampire is introduced via an exchange of gazes with the heroine, the anti-hero is more likely to be the object of an accidental glance and of the camera's leisurely objectifying (and fetishizing) gaze. (During their shows' first episodes of season three, Elena walks in on Damon naked and Sookie walks in on Eric). Further linking the "bad" vampire to changing ideals of masculinity, these shows also present Spike, Damon, and Eric as having a flexible sense of sexual identity—they are often depicted flirting with men and women alike, having casual sex, and unnerving the heroine with innuendos. The vampire's association with oft-repressed sexualities is especially evident in "True Blood," which draws an overt parallel between "vampire rights" and gay rights ("God hates fangs," reads a roadside sign in the show's opening credits). And importantly, all three of these series have vocal and lively fandoms that often pair the two vampires together in fanfiction and other fan practices—even Stefan/Damon, whose status as brothers adds another subversive tickle to fans' imaginative works (see for one example salvatoreslash.livejournal.com).[9] Finally, the focus on their physical beauty—shots tend to linger more frequently on the bare torsos of the bad vampires than on the garbed torsos of the good ones—further suggests an emphasis on façade, which is vital to their character development. For these vampires, bad behavior and overt, excessive sexuality act as layers of a hard exterior persona meant to hide or sublimate some deep emotional pain underneath. As the heroine and the anti-hero become friendly, it becomes more apparent to the heroine and to viewers that his commitment to hedonism is a desperate attempt to escape the human side of his persona.

Soapy Vampires

Recent television vampire narratives owe a great deal to the form of the soap opera, which draws from melodramatic devices as well. But a key difference is the serial format's vexed relationship to the past. It not only denies the certainty of patriarchal lineage but, as Lynne Joyrich puts it, "reject[s] the notion of progress, the belief in a visible difference between past and future."[10] Vampires are the definitive soap opera figures. They have wildly complex family trees, are prone to socially unacceptable, destructive, and excessive behavior, engage in dramatic moral struggles, fall extravagantly in and out of love, deceive those around them, and most importantly, live forever—and into syndication. It's no coincidence that one of the first truly sympathetic vampires to drive viewers wild was literally from a soap opera: Barnabas Collins (Jonathan Frid), whom creator Dan Curtis introduced on "Dark Shadows" (1966) in an attempt to boost ratings. Although his role was supposed to be short-lived, audiences were so smitten with Barnabas, as indicated by fan letters and improved ratings, that Curtis gave him a bigger role. At first Barnabas appeared charismatic but cold-hearted, killing people, kidnapping a character and convincing her that she was the reincarnation of his long lost love, and so on. But as he became the center of the show, he was given a redemptive arc, to struggle against his vampiric nature, wallowing in self-hatred and misery.

A pair of vampires who antagonize each other throughout history lets cultural producers imagine a never-ending serial narrative. Mimi White writes that in soap operas, "ongoing narratives are . . . formally or structurally characterized by redundancies, reversals, and discontinuities. All narrative developments are virtually, and usually literally, reversible. Dead and disappeared characters revive and return to these fictional worlds," and furthermore, "Heroes and heroines transform into villains, while villains transmute into good guys—gradually or suddenly—and back apart." In sum, writes White, "the only narrative certainty is that things change, albeit slowly."[11] In the vampire narrative, of course, the dead literally come back to life, and like soap operas, they repeatedly return to the same tropes: the evil twin, the return from the dead, the discovery of one's past.

Unstable human and vampire lineages require characters to delve into family histories, digging up skeletons in closets and uncovering old lies. Elena's problematic parentage (her Uncle John is actually her father, and her mother is now a vampire), Buffy's absentee father and uncertain Slayer heritage (the show doesn't reveal how Slayers were created until the seventh season), and Sookie's fairy ancestry (as well as the fact that she was molested by her great-uncle) all come to light gradually, raising questions of selective memory and drawing the viewer's attention to the failure of the traditional family. This is not the case in *Twilight*, however; Bella's family might be broken, but her parents are who they say they are. Unlike Elena, Buffy, and Sookie, Bella's knowledge of her own history does not challenge the basic structure of patriarchy.

In addition to revelations about the heroine's identity, the serial narrative enables long, drawn-out character arcs that revisit the past, call the hero's virtue into question, and reveal the essential goodness of the anti-hero. In order for his human side to become visible, each of our three TV vampire antagonists undergoes a reversal that makes the heroine give him a second look. In the process, new information is revealed that forces her, along with viewers, to revisit past events through a different perspective. On "True Blood," this happens to Eric more than once: during the second season, Sookie witnesses his emotional pain as he watches his sire die, and during the fourth season he loses his memory. Although he can still bite, his vampire swagger disappears along with his memories, and he becomes so charmingly clueless that Sookie rushes to care for him like a wounded bird. This state of innocence fires up Sookie's nurturing side, making her reconsider his suitability as a romantic (and sexual) partner. Meanwhile, Bill goes missing at the end of season two, breaks up with Sookie for her "own good" in season three, and starts killing people again, eventually assassinating the queen of Louisiana and becoming king himself. Spike first demonstrates his capacity for goodness at the end of the second season when he teams up with Buffy to defeat Angel, who loses his soul after experiencing a "moment of happiness" while having sex with her. He goes on a murderous rampage and attempts to open a portal to hell. Spike becomes a possible replacement, however, only after the re-ensouled Angel decides that Buffy is better off without him and leaves for Hollywood (and his own spinoff). In season four, a secret government organization implants a chip in Spike's head that prevents him from harming humans. As with Eric's amnesia, the chip strikes at the core of his identity as a vampire, forcing Spike to alter his lifestyle and reminding him of the helplessness he felt as a nerdy Victorian poet. Though Buffy doesn't quite match Sookie's maternal instinct, she does take Spike in and offer him help, this détente laying the groundwork for a future romantic pairing which occurs in season six. The mutually destructive relationship culminates in Spike's attempted rape of Buffy, and his subsequent quest to earn his soul back, after which point a "real" relationship becomes possible. On "The Vampire Diaries," Elena regards both brothers differently when she finds out that Stefan forced Damon to become a vampire, then, while Damon retained the core of his personality, turned into a vicious, blood-addicted monster. At the end of season two, both brothers attempt to sacrifice themselves to protect Elena, but while Damon sticks around, Stefan's martyrdom requires him to return to his evil, murderous ways. Like Angel's and Bill's (and Edward's—he leaves Forks in the second *Twilight* film, allowing Bella to pursue Jacob's friendship), Stefan's absence gives the heroine the space she needs to realize that her first "true" love wasn't quite as true as she thought. In fact, his old-fashioned notions of romance, while initially appealing, could also be stifling. On these series, the cyclical patterns of relationships and reversals draw attention to the ways in which past event, values, and ideals impact the present—and they allow these young women to move forward with a better understanding of their own priorities. At the same time, ironically, they relegate past events to a state of perpetual confusion, an oblivion where meaning seems elusive.

The *Twilight* saga does not dwell as much on vampire or human history as do these television series.[12] Edward is the ideal American, willing to completely assimilate into the present and forget his past. Further, his problems are ontological, stemming from what he thinks of as his nature, not social or political. He hates the irritating fact that he wants to suck Bella's blood, but with his morals firmly in place he probably won't go on a killing spree because she stood him up. In fact, the certainty of morality at the center of the *Twilight* series, which both popular and academic analysis has also linked to Meyer's Mormonism, ties it more closely to traditional melodrama, with its Manichean conflicts, than to the more mutable moralities of the televised vampire series. There is a dark side to Edward, however. Any human boyfriend who blackmailed his girlfriend into getting married, disabled her car so she couldn't visit another guy, left her bruised after lovemaking, and tried to force her to get an abortion might qualify as an abusive partner. But because Edward is a vampire who represses his violent nature for the sake of living as a human, his more aggressive characteristics can be rationalized as stemming from his rigorous self-control. Bella's father recognizes the intensity of the relationship, and worries that Bella's high-school romance is eating up her entire life, but viewers are encouraged to shrug off Dad's concerns—after all, he doesn't know about the vampire thing. Besides, in *New Moon* (2009), Edward is so romantic that he attempts suicide when he thinks that Bella's dead, just as in *Romeo and Juliet*. Bella is *so sure* that she's making the right decision with him that she's willing to marry at the age of eighteen (saving her virginity for the wedding night, of course), carry a vampire hybrid baby to term at the cost of her own life, and leave her friends and family permanently in order to know the bliss of being a part of a vampire family. Edward whisks her away like a knight in sparkling armor, away from her humdrum existence and her broken family and into a world where fantasy becomes reality.

Telling the Vampire Story

The vampire's position in a purgatory of un-life parallels the narrative experience of the viewer, who grapples with the constant deferral of meaning-making that results from the lack of closure. The vampire can never grasp his life in its totality, because, as Walter Benjamin points out, "It is not only a man's knowledge or wisdom, but above all his real life—and this is the stuff that stories are made of—which first assumes transmissible form at the moment of his death."[13] What kind of story can be told, however, when the act of dying is never completed? Living forever necessarily entails an infinite deferral of meaning, and that means that things—even the perception of past events—can always change.

Twilight and the other vampire narratives discussed here offer two different pleasures related to the consumption of past ideals of masculinity, and of the past in general. The *Twilight* model offers a break from the past, and from the difficulties in determining truth that are often associated with postmodernism. Is Edward right for Bella? We hope so, because once she makes the decision to carry his vampire baby to term, there's no going back. In this formulation, whose commitment to black-and-white notions of good and evil harkens back to the traditional melodrama, the vampire offers a master narrative in which the heroine can lose herself, one that privileges the present—and a fairy-tale future—over the trauma of the past, and stasis over mutability. For narratives with the vampire dyad, however, the past can be rewritten over and over again seemingly without limit, and so can identity. On one hand, this might be considered a license for reckless behavior; certainly the rejection of responsibility and the denial of consequences speak to the fears of these series' young female audiences. On the other hand, the instability of historical narratives means that every time the past is revisited, something different emerges—something that affects the understanding of the present, and has an impact on the future. The development of identities and relationships is linked with a constantly changing sense of history. Unlike Edward, vampires in "True Blood," "Buffy," and "The Vampire Diaries" don't take the heroine away from herself or what she was, they make her more aware of her own agency and her own past, her own identity, her own family. Her past is drawn into her present. The heroine ends up with many more perspectives on history, from those who were there—her eyes, in short, are opened up to the world around her, for better or worse.

The immortal figure of the vampire demonstrates to the heroine and to the viewer the value of revisiting the past in order to better understand the present. As "Buffy," "The Vampire Diaries," and "True Blood" suggest, just because our understanding of the world and of ourselves will never be complete doesn't mean the pursuit of self-knowledge should be rejected for the relative comfort of belief in a given metanarrative, as *Twilight* advises. Buffy, Elena, and Sookie may never get the satisfaction of being "happy ever after," like Bella, but at least they have the chance to change their minds.

Notes

[1] This is true of female vampires as well, generally speaking. The prototype for this type of vampire is J. Sheridan Le Fanu's *Carmilla*, published in 1872, which features a female vampire who courts the "friendship" of a young girl; the novella has distinct lesbian undertones.

[2] Karen Backstein, "(Un)safe Sex: Romancing the Vampire," *Cineaste* 35: 1 (December 2009), 38.

[3] J. M. Tyree, "Warm-Blooded: *True Blood* and *Let the Right One In*," *Film Quarterly* 63: 2 (2009), 32.

[4] Backstein, 32.

[5] Janice Radway, *Reading the Romance: Women, Patriarchy, and Popular Culture* (Chapel Hill, NC: University of North Carolina Press, 1991), 123.

[6] Peter Brooks, *Reading for the Plot: Design and Intention in Narrative* (New York: Alfred A. Knopf, 1984), 39-40.

[7] Ben Singer, *Melodrama and Modernity: Early Sensational Cinema and Its Contexts* (New York: Columbia University Press, 2001), 231-2.

[8] The idea that Jacob was really in love with a yet-to-be-conceived vampire-human zygote resulted in a bit of a backlash for Meyer when the book was released; once the choice was taken away from Bella—and not because she was totally satisfied with her decision, but because the decision was made for her—some fans rebelled. See http://www.cbc.ca/news/arts/books/story/2008/08/08/meyer protest.html, http://latimesblogs.latimes.com/entertainmentnewsbuzz/2008/08/twilight-what-d.html, http://www.mtv.com/news/articles/1592457/twilight-author-reacts-breaking-dawn-complaints.jhtml, and http://www.goodreads.com/topic/show/47297-the-backlash.

[9] See also the popular CW series "Supernatural" (2005), which focuses on two brothers, one snarky and overtly sexual, the other more reserved and brooding. Without a female protagonist to provide the third point of a love triangle, the show offers viewers (many of whom belong to these other shows' fan bases as well) a romantic and often tragic vision of brotherly love.

[10] Lynne Joyrich, *Re-Viewing Reception: Television, Gender, and Postmodern Culture* (Bloomington: Indiana University Press, 1996), 57.

[11] Mimi White, "Women, Memory, and Serial Melodrama," *Screen* 35: 4 (Winter 1994), 337.

12 Meyer's vampires don't even sleep, which means, at least in terms of human physiology, that they are not capable of turning short-term memories into long-term ones.

13 Walter Benjamin, "The Storyteller," *Selected Writings, Volume 3: 1935-1938*, Howard Eiland and Michael W. Jennings, eds. (Cambridge, MA: The Belknap Press of Harvard University Press, 2002), 151.

Chapter 32

J.K.'s Potion

Harry Potter, Orphans, and the British Boarding School

Steven Woodward

*I*t is extraordinary that J. K. Rowling chose to have Harry Potter save the world by sending him to school. School, especially the British boarding school, typically features in children's books as the most repressive of institutions, and the school story, as configured by Thomas Hughes with *Tom Brown's School Days* (1857), is often about the child protagonist's dramatic and comic evasion of the horrors enshrined by that system yet crucial to its functioning. For those unfamiliar with those horrors, consider Hugo Rifkind's recent description of his own, barely credible experience:

> We were 16. My Scottish boarding school (of the sort that lots of my friends went to, but none of their children will) had this thing about sending people off to a cadet corps camp after their GCSEs [General Certificate of Secondary Education, a standardized test for British secondary-school students]. It was day three. We'd learned to abseil [rappel] and canoe. Then we were sent off to a windowless, corrugated-iron shed, where a fat, jolly ser-

geant major welcomed us to the sound of cheery bagpipe music. He sat us down at the front, and started showing us a Tom and Jerry cartoon. Then, just as we were starting to relax, he cut the power and opened up with a machine gun.[1]

As Rifkind's disorienting testimony suggests (and my own experience corroborates), the most salient aspects of a boarding school's education come not from academic study but from a sustained state of anxiety interspersed with moments of terror like this (the firing of a real machine gun—most likely loaded with blanks—in an enclosed space filled with relaxing teens), a state maintained by a network of bullies, prefects (often indistinguishable from bullies), neurotic or sadistic masters, and the masters' various agents, like Rifkind's sergeant major. (One of my own masters was both my Latin and trumpet teacher and an army captain; he eventually ran off with the married mother of one of my schoolmates. Perhaps such schools are "private" precisely because their perverse culture would never be publicly allowed.)

All children who attend boarding school are orphans of a kind, wilfully abandoned by their parents, often for months at a time. The boy boarder is expelled from the sanctuary of the maternal home and enters a site of sustained Oedipal conflict, the school acting as the agent of the father to make a man of him. Rowling's series simply renders the schoolboy's feeling as fact: Harry (in the film versions, Daniel Radcliffe) is indeed an orphan whose parents have "died" and who at the age of eleven enters the liminal world of Hogwarts, until he can finally defeat his ultimate paternal enemy, Voldemort (Ralph Fiennes), a father who refuses to yield the world to his son. It is no wonder that, within this liminal world, the allegiances of other paternal figures—Severus Snape (Alan Rickman), Remus Lupin (David Thewlis), Sirius Black (Gary Oldman)—are deeply uncertain and suspect, at least at first, while the maternal figures—Molly Weasley (Julie Walters), Minerva McGonagall (Maggie Smith), Rubeus Hagrid (Robbie Coltrane)—are reassuringly nurturing and protective. Within this schema, the headmaster Albus Dumbledore (Richard Harris until his death in 2002; subsequently Michael Gambon) holds the queerest place, demonstrating both maternal and paternal attitudes; and Bellatrix Lestrange (Helena Bonham Carter) is perhaps the most monstrous, inverting the maternal with her homicidal glee, most disturbingly when she kills the child-like Dobby.

Nevertheless, Rowling's use of the emotional and symbolic potential of the orphan at school, if an engaging aspect of her story, is not exactly original. After all, the orphan's plight has been a popular motif of literature at least since the late-sixteenth-century broadside ballad *The Babes in the Wood*, but it perhaps runs strongest in children's literature, becoming a powerful means of figuring the state of everychild. *The Adventures of Tom Sawyer, Anne of Green Gables, Charlotte's Web* all take their interest and emotive power from the vulnerable condition of their orphan protagonists and their narrative shape from the quest for selfhood on which the orphan must necessarily embark. The orphan is a paradox, possessed of the ideal freedom about which the child fantasizes as the ultimate ego ideal, but bound, sometimes unconsciously, to a quest after a love that will reflect that ideal back to him.

Harry's position at the beginning of the series is a classic case of splitting: the parents who loved him unconditionally are gone; the foster parents (Richard Griffiths, Fiona Shaw) who hate him are all too actively (and far too irritatingly) alive. And so, given the ambiguity of his situation, Harry must embark on a journey to substantiate himself, to decide his own case, to *prove himself.* That that journey should involve an immersion in a private school environment is fascinating. Within this environment, mother love is typically completely absent and the individual becomes subject to widely deployed, disciplining authorities (notably scraggly, mean-spirited caretaker Argus Filch [David Bradley]), authorities that insist on treating the individual primarily as a body that must sit without fidgeting in its seat, a body that must be hardened through daily sports, immersions in freezing pools, and nakedness. It is with this institution that Rowling sends Harry off to do battle. And Voldemort turns out to be not a force in opposition to the "civilizing" Hogwarts but its most successful creation (like Darth Vader, a logical outcome of imperialism).

Harry comes into this environment with his trademark circular spectacles intensifying his wide-eyed gaze, making him simultaneously more perspicacious and more vulnerable. And yet he does not suffer as he should, protected as he is by the celebrity that he has not yet earned (here, celebrity cannot be earned, but must be conferred) and by the cyclical reappearance of maternal figures. In fact, by the beginning of the second instalment, *Harry Potter and the Chamber of Secrets*, Harry has become entranced with Hogwarts and feels its absence physically while back at the Dursleys for summer vacation:

> He missed Hogwarts so much that it was like having a constant stomach ache. He missed the castle, with its secret passageways and ghosts, his lessons (though perhaps not Snape, the potions master), the post arriving by owl, eating banquets in the Great Hall, sleeping in his four-poster bed in the tower dormitory, visiting the gamekeeper Hagrid, in his cabin in the grounds next to the forbidden forest and, especially, Quidditch, the most popular sport in the wizarding world (six tall goalposts, four flying balls and fourteen players on broomsticks).[2]

Notice how this focalized enumeration of Hogwarts's singular experiences serves very nicely as Rowling's advertisement for the charms of her fantasy world, at just that moment, perhaps, that she was beginning to realize how her own fortunes might be turning around because of the sparkling popularity of the initial book. Empowered by just one year of study, just as Rowling had been, in a way, through publishing her first book, Harry has only to mention the word "magic" to the self-satisfied Dursleys to send them into a frenzy of terrified outrage.

As to the author's success with this creation, Harry Potter may be just another orphan story, but no previous one has ever done the business that Rowling's has. The first Harry Potter book was published in the U.K. by Bloomsbury in a run of 500 copies on June 26, 1997, but more than 70,000 copies had been sold by the end of that year. The U.S. edition, from Scholastic, appeared in August 1998, selling 190,000 copies by the end of the year. By the time the third book was published in the U.S. in September 1999, thirty million copies of the books were in print globally, in twenty-seven languages, and Rowling had received her first royalty cheque exceeding U.S.$1 million. By the fourth book, U.S. and U.K. release dates had been synchronized, the publications hyped by midnight release parties at Edinburgh Castle or London's Natural History Museum. For the U.S. release of the final book, Scholastic ordered twelve million copies and sold 8.3 million *in the first twenty-four hours.* So radically did Rowling's books distort the *New York Times* bestseller list that a separate children's list was created in July 2000. Because translations could be released only several months after the English-language releases, non-anglophone fans began to buy English copies, so that the English version of *Harry Potter and the Goblet of Fire* reached the top of France's bestseller list, and that of *Harry Potter and the Deathly Hallows* reached the top of Germany's within five days of its release. Rowling is the first author ever to become a billionaire from the proceeds of writing. By the time the last film was released, in July 2011, 400 million copies of the books had been sold globally, and the film series was already the most successful in cinema history.

Harry Potter lore is infused through cultures globally. As Brian Bethune observed in an article for *Maclean's*, "Academics have found references to every aspect of Harry's world in sources as diverse as Turkish editorials and Swedish parliamentary debates."[3] The books have more global coverage than the United Nations, having been sold in 200 publishing "territories," even though the U.N. only recognizes 192 member countries. Even real public spaces have been inscribed by Rowling's fantasy: King's Cross station now has a sign for "Platform 9 ¾" with a luggage trolley half-disappearing into one of its walls. Not surprisingly, author, publishers, film studio, and fans do not want such an extraordinarily profitable and culturally profound phenomenon to disappear. Rowling launched Pottermore.com just before the release of the final film, a website through which she is herself marketing e-books of the series, the rights for which were never bought by her publishers (having not been a point of consequence in the mid-1990s, when contracts were originally arranged) and which she has refused to sell to Amazon or Apple for their proprietary e-book platforms. Warner Bros. has taken the opportunity of the 2012 London Olympics to open its own *Studio Tour London, The Making of Harry Potter*. And the world of Harry Potter continues to inspire more fan fiction than any other source (though perhaps it will ultimately be displaced by *The Hunger Games* [2012]).

It may well seem that the success of Rowling's series is not attributable to her use of the orphan-at-school motif, however elaborately it is rendered in the seven books and eight films, but must instead stem from the addition of magic to this formula (just as Rowling added the K to her own initials, transforming herself from Joanne Rowling to the more androgynous J. K. Rowling, to avoid alienating male readers). For Hogwarts is a "School of Witchcraft and Wizardry," taking in pure-bloods, half-bloods, and mudbloods, so long as they possess some innate ability with magic. Magic represents the possibility of both transformation and power—a fictional possibility, to be sure, since no child in any school can levitate an obnoxious and power-hungry teacher figure by pointing a pencil and singing "Wingardium leviosa!"—and so perhaps all schools are ideally schools of magic, enabling their students to re-make the world for themselves according to their own desires and beliefs. Yet schools, according to such an understanding, should be the most powerful places in the human world. Notice that for Rowling teachers outside Hogwarts seem to have very little import or significance—like Slughorn in retirement—but they become extraordinarily influential on the fate of the world when they take up teaching at Hogwarts. No previous text of children's culture has made the school so much the "still center of the turning world," so that on school grounds at the end of *Harry Potter and the Deathly Hallows* nothing less than an epic battle to decide the future can take place. In fact, real schools function very differently, more like Hogwarts does under the upstart Dolores Umbridge (Imelda Staunton), who announces that she has no intention of empowering the students: "It is the view of the Ministry [of Magic] that a theoretical knowledge will be sufficient to get you through your examinations, which, after all, is what school is all about."[4] School is, for most of us, just such an inconsequential place. That is perhaps why C. S. Lewis had his child protagonists save the world of Narnia precisely by abandoning their limited roles as schoolchildren. In many ways, the Potter series is an update and inversion of Lewis's Narnia stories (published between 1950 and 1956). Lewis offered his child readers, through identification with his schoolchild protagonists, an epic role in the action of Narnia, a magical parallel world discovered by the first of these, Peter, Susan, Edmund, and Lucy Pevensie, in the back of a wardrobe. Likewise, we first meet Harry Potter living in a cupboard under the stairs at the Dursley home.

Surely a large part of the appeal of Harry Potter is that the text itself is metaphorically magical, adaptable to all kinds of personal and transcultural contexts. John Fiske theorized that television (at least network television) captivates a broad spectrum of viewers by letting them be smarter than the shows they are watching. This is accomplished through TV routinely offering what Fiske calls activated or producerly texts, combining the accessibility of closed texts with the enriched semiosis of open texts: "The producerly text . . . relies on discursive competencies that the viewer already possesses, but requires that they are used in a self-interested, productive way."[5] Gregory Bassham picks up on this particular aspect of Rowling's saga in his foreword to *The Ultimate Harry Potter and Philosophy: Hogwarts for Muggles*: "As you read these pages and personally grapple with their important issues, you will experience anew the real magic that will forever animate J. K. Rowling's immortal tales."[6] For Bassham, that "magic" is the chance to discover the deepest and most personally urgent philosophical questions within the pleasurable text:

> What is love? Is it, as Rowling says, the most powerful magic of all? Is there an afterlife? If so, what might it be like? Is death something to be feared--or "mastered," as Harry ultimately was able to do? Do people have souls? If so, how are they related to their bodies? Can souls, if they exist, be divided, as Voldemort fragmented his by means of the Horcruxes? What can shape-shifters like Animagi and boggarts teach us about personal identity and the self? Does power inevitably corrupt? Is Hogwarts a model school, or are there real shortcomings with the education students receive there? Is it true, as Albus Dumbledore says, that our choices reveal far more about us than our abilities do? What can the complex and intriguing character of Severus Snape teach us about moral conflict, character judgment, and the possibility of redemption? Would it ever be ethical to use a love potion? Is it true, as Kingsley Shacklebolt proclaims, that "[e]very human life is worth the same"? Is it true, as Dumbledore says, that something can be real even if it exists only inside a person's head?[7]

In short, Bassham seems to agree with William Wordsworth that children are indeed the "best philosophers." However, the producerly nature of the text does not necessarily have to be intellectual or philosophical. One undergraduate student, now twenty-three years old, started to read the Harry Potter books when he was the same age as Harry, literally growing up with them. He recognizes, he says, that the books are terribly written, at least the first few. But even now, he makes a point of re-reading the entire series every year. It has become a ritual for him to replay his own childhood this way, often enacted when he is at his busiest with his studies. Then, he takes any of the books out and simply reads, finding a nostalgic comfort in the experience. "Nostalgic comfort" is perhaps an exact parallel to Harry's situation in the series, since nostalgia is both painful, reminding us of what has been lost, and soothing, marking how far we have come and reassuring us that the past really existed, really strangely still exists in our memory as a structural support.[8]

But to the stories' textual magic, we must add several other kinds, including the rapid development of visual effects (VFX) both before and in the Harry Potter films, the development of the social Internet more or less simultaneously with the appearance of the series, and a marketing plan that capitalized on synergy across media.

The magic effects of Harry Potter could not have been realized filmically without the visual effects developed (at his Weta Workshop and Weta Digital in New Zealand) for Peter Jackson's generically related *Lord of the Rings*, released as three films, in December of 2001, 2002, and 2003. The eight Harry Potter films, released over a ten-year period (2001 to 2011), have themselves been a laboratory for new techniques. Thus, to the charm of the story of the foundling child, coming into his own, the movie of *Harry Potter and the Philosopher's Stone* adds the considerable interest of such effects: an avalanche of letters hurtling down the Dursleys' chimney, a magical London (scarcely more marvellous than the actual one) of Diagon Alley and the vaults of Gringotts Bank, Hogwarts itself, presented as a polished version of Mont St. Michel, magical creatures like the mountain troll, Hagrid's three-headed elephant-sized guard dog Fluffy, and the Norwegian Ridgeback dragon who scorches Hagrid's beard on first seeing his "mummy," or the Centaur, Ferenz, who saves Harry from Voldemort in the Dark Forest. Thus, the films become even more "producerly," as they would have to, considering their very considerable cost. Every film in the series has in some way to expand on such charms. And so, in the second film, we are given the flying car, the whomping willow, the howler letter, and the repotting of the mandrakes. Even Quidditch, which we had witnessed in the first film, is given some variation in the form of a rogue blodger that relentlessly pursues Harry. We might only add that the most awesome, advanced digital effects are those associated with Harry's antagonists, while the magical powers of Harry and friends are often represented through anachronistic effects, like flying in the Weasleys' car or on broomstick, or speaking in parseltongue, the language of snakes. Just as the saga becomes darker as it progresses, so do the effects become less charming or spectacular, more genuinely unsettling. VFX supervisor Mark Breakspear has noted, "I liked the development of the characters and visual effects over time. You see the same companies honing and improving the visual effects, refining them, and making them work. In [*Harry Potter and the Goblet of Fire*], the characters are old enough to be involved in darker, more mature situations, and the visual effects were far more refined and mature."[9] The Triwizard Contest of this installment provides an ideal context through which to highlight them: close encounters with Swedish Short-Snout and Hungarian Horntail dragons in a gladiatorial arena; entanglements with grindylows and merpeople at the bottom of the Black Lake: and of course the electric arcing duel of wands with a newly embodied Voldemort amidst the tombs of the Little Hangleton graveyard.

A final element of magic is the marketing of Harry Potter, which largely amounts to a conscious exploitation of the producerly qualities of the series already mentioned, those qualities that make it possible for the widest range of readers and viewers to find themselves in the saga. In *Harry Potter: The Story of a Global Business Phenomenon*, Susan Gunelius explains that "Cult brands always entail a certain level of personalization by consumers."[10] The personalization of Harry Potter was enabled by a wide variety of marketing techniques, like the three-year space between July 2000 and June 2003 when no new books were published but the first two films appeared. In "Harry Potter and Me," a documentary about Rowling first broadcast on BBC-TV in December 2001, Rowling pulled a thick folder out of the piles of her notes, a folder which she teasingly claimed contained the last chapter of the last book of the series. That folder, fans soon learned, had subsequently been locked in a safety-deposit box, but it was revealed that the last word of the chapter contained therein was "scar." At the same time, her publishers and Warner Bros. carefully guarded details of the next, more immediate installments. Nevertheless, into this space, fans began to inject their own speculations and to express their desires, in the form of websites, blogs, online commentary, and fan fiction and videos. It was in response to this response that Rowling formed her own website, thereby implicitly recognizing the importance of her fans and their desires. After that, the publishing of the books was steadily interspersed with the release of the films and the extension of the brand into other media, including Universal's reworked theme park in Orlando. The whole phenomenon, of course, has been seasoned with constant and amazed reiterations of Rowling's remarkable rags-to-riches biography—she is the richest author of all time but came from the humblest roots, writing after a bitter divorce to bolster her spirits--and rendered natural through "vertically integrated marketing," possible through Warner's parent company, AOL Time Warner, which also owns TV channels like CNN and Cartoon Network and magazines like *People* and *Fortune*: "Online promotions, television ads, interviews and magazine articles were released concurrently or in strategic succession to generate buzz and momentum around the brand, books, and movies."[11]

Now that the saga is over, Daniel Radcliffe, whose net worth was estimated in 2011 in the *Sunday Times Rich List* at U.S.$78 million, a tiny fraction of Rowling's, needs to move beyond his identification as Harry Potter if he is to find fulfilling new roles. Despite his own desire to do so, in a recent radio interview on the occasion of the release of *The Woman in Black* (James Watkins, 2012), when asked if he felt he had missed some important childhood experience by being embroiled in production of the Harry Potter films for a decade, from the age of ten, he reveals the degree to which he is Harry.[12] Taken out of a private-school environment in which all the students were essentially the same and plunged into a production environment of extraordinary diversity, he prides himself on having been on set every day and developing his primary friendships with the crew rather than his fellow stars. Radcliffe essentially claims that the production became his ideal school. Hogwarts is, of course, exactly a school of this kind, staffed by teachers who are more technical experts than philosophers, and not a genuine representation of real private schools; it is a place in which Harry chooses to ignore his celebrity and assert his merit (unlike Gilderoy Lockhart [Kenneth Branagh], who does precisely the opposite), mingling with mudbloods like Hermione Granger (Emma Watson) rather than hobnob with pure-bloods like Draco Malfoy (Tom Felton).

But perhaps the ultimate student of the saga is neither Radcliffe nor Harry, but Rowling herself, who has invented a most extraordinary new potion, connecting the producerly magic of her own orphan-at-school story to the capital reserves of publishers and film studios and the unprecedented transmedia marketing now made possible by the INTERNET. Whether that potion has been effective at transforming our beleaguered world into a more equable and productive one or has instead merely strengthened the "imperius curse" that the culture industries have over our lives and destinies remains, with or without empowering spectacles, to be seen.

Notes

[1] Hugo Rifkind, "How Not to ... Kill an Animal," *GQ* British Edition (April 2012), 50. For another, at least equally scathing, take on the British private school, see George Orwell, "Such, Such Were the Joys," in Peter Davison, ed., *Orwell's England* (London: Penguin, 2001), 362-408. Orwell could be describing the Rowling phenomenon when he writes, "It is difficult for a child to realize that a school is primarily a commercial venture" (378).

[2] J. K. Rowling, *Harry Potter and the Chamber of Secrets* (Vancouver: Raincoast, 2000), 8.

[3] Bethune, Brian. "The Afterlife of Harry Potter," *Maclean's* 124: 27 (18 July 2011), 52-4.

[4] *Harry Potter and the Order of the Phoenix* (David Yates, 2007).

[5] John Fiske, *Television Culture* (London: Routledge, 1987), 95.

[6] Gregory Bassham, *The Ultimate Harry Potter and Philosophy: Hogwarts for Muggles* (Hoboken, N.J.: John Wiley, 2010), xiii.

[7] Bassham, 2.

[8] My thanks to Matthew Doucette Pilles for describing this experience to me.

[9] Debra Kaufman, "Here Comes Oscar," *Computer Graphics World* 32: 12 (Dec 2009), 28.

[10] Susan Gunelius, *Harry Potter: The Story of a Global Business Phenomenon* (Houndmills, Basingstoke: Palgrave Macmillan, 2008), 29.

[11] Gunelius, 45.

[12] "Q," CBC Radio, 30 January 2012.

Chapter 33

"Glee" at Three

James Morrison

*I*t takes a very special TV show to defang the cattiness of James Wolcott, the rotund professional grinch of pop culture, but here he is, writing in *Vanity Fair*, on the first season of "Glee": It's "a show that restored our faith in the power of song, the beauty of dance, and the magic of 'spirit fingers' to chase our cares and woes into somebody else's backyard . . . a rocking confection that has achieved the wondrous feat of making musical theater look hip, mainstream and sexily redemptive . . ."[1] The declamatory rhetoric, the sentimental quaver in the voice—had the wielder of that poison pen, one wondered, swapped out its arsenic cartridge for one filled with aspartame? Nor was Wolcott alone, though his heart's cockles were the least likely to be warmed. Everyone loved "Glee"—at first.

By its third season (this one pirouetted to a finale in spring, 2012), nearly every show has to either renew itself or settle into the comforts of familiarity. Third seasons are especially fraught on network television, in light of the three-part structure of traditional narrative. By this logic, the first season corresponds to beginnings, the second to middles, and the third, by rights, to ends. But who wants their show to end? In serial time, third seasons are often about the deferral of endings and the distention of middles—or else they might trigger a re-set that can render the show unrecognizable to fans. A show like "Glee"—with a format defined by predictability, yet a fundamental reliance on novelty—faces special challenges in contending with the rigors of serial time. Whatever the reasons, the blogosphere has come awash with wounded plaints and cries from current and former fans and the snark of early dropouts and never-rans. The first group prays for "Glee" to reclaim its former glory while the second, on websites like Glee sucks.com, claims vindication, due to the show's alleged precipitous decline.

What "Glee" had going for it from the start was sweetness with an edge. It did not deny outright the rampant Social Darwinism of the American high school, as its blander precursor *High School Musical* (2006) essentially did, but the kids were all too twinkly, and a bit too long in the tooth, to raise any portents of real predation or carnage. The birth dates of the regulars ranged from 1982 to 1990, meaning that the youngest of them turned twenty during the show's first season in 2009-10, and though the cast works up enough of a sprightly sweat to smell like teen spirit, this heady odor subsides dependably into the more comforting aroma of post-pubescence. True, the Mean Girls on the cheerleading squad conspire to keep their wayward guys in line and romantic rivals at a distance, but you can tell they're not really out for blood—this isn't the world of *Heathers* (1988) or *Mean Girls* (2004). The jocks are feistier than their counterparts in *High School Musical*, but they're nowhere near as randy or crude or lowdown or brutal as such cadres have been known to be in life. Above all, "Glee" presents a fantasy of communal bonding across common social barriers. On the margins, it depicts what high school is "really like"—the galling everyday oppressions and petty squabbles that can seem epic, and the half-witted hostilities that take on a frightening intensity—but at its core, it shows what high school could be, if things were different.

The third season of "Glee" redoubles its commitment to this vision of community in acknowledgment that, of course, things *are* different. While the second season was airing, a rash of suicides by bullied gay and lesbian teens swept the media and prompted a national campaign to raise awareness of the risks this population faces: the "It Gets Better" project. Originating in September 2010 with a video posted on YouTube by sex advice columnist Dan Savage, the project has since archived on its own website (itgetsbetter.org) thousands of videos with messages of encouragement and support for LGBT teens, including contributions from President Barack Obama, Ellen DeGeneres, and Matthew Morrison of "Glee." Much about "Glee"'s third season reacts directly to these events. The narrative stakes are raised, with life-threatening catastrophes, unheard of in the first two seasons, becoming common. The show does not so much lose the edginess of its sweetness, as abandon it. Despite those catastrophes conflict ebbs, and the most seemingly hateful characters turn out to have hearts of gold in the end. (They just want to be loved—is that so wrong?) Bullies see the error of their ways, snobs and rotters from other schools' "Glee" clubs form mutual admiration societies, ceasing their previous efforts to take the regionals or nationals by devious means. In fact, the show has always tended in such directions—that was part of its sweetness—but by season three its emotional tenor, struggling to retain buoyancy and bounce, seems post-traumatic. Its address of queer teens as a target audience becomes ever more overt, and its dominant goal—like that of "It Gets Better"—is to reassure. "Glee" has come to a point where it repudiates hate, refuses to traffic in it, even so much as to use it as a dramatic device—and forthwith, the ranks of the "Glee"-haters swell. Maybe, in the realm of popular culture, we never really get so far beyond high school after all.

The first season of the show is notable for the cheerful leisure with which it unfolds, especially in the first half. It begins with Will Scheuster (Matthew Morrison), a frustrated

Spanish teacher and aspiring song-and-dance man, replacing the previous director of the "Glee" club at McKinley High School in Lima, Ohio. A blithe implication is that his predecessor has been dismissed for molesting his charges, this suggesting that the show will partake of the bumptious perversity of "Nip/Tuck" (2003), the previous brain-child of "Glee"'s highest profile co-creator, Ryan Murphy. But with Will energetically recruiting a lineup of unlikely choristers to revive the languishing club as the rechristened New Directions troupe, the show's essential warmth asserts itself, its cock-eyed affection for misfits taking centerstage. Each member of the ensemble is introduced by turn, her or his foibles breezily noted with an air of mild satire and just as breezily forgiven. The spirit is egalitarian; no member is given priority over any others, and in the first big production number—a rousing cover of Journey's tacky anthem of optimism, "Don't Stop Believing"—they blend seamlessly, effortlessly, as a group. By the end of the second episode, Kurt Hummel (Chris Colfer), a closeted gay boy, is embraced by the football team when his voguish dance moves prove handy for kicking field goals, and before hundreds of cheering fans the whole team sings and struts to Beyoncé's "Single Ladies" on the scrimmage line to back him up. When, fortified by this approval, Kurt tearfully comes out in the next scene, his blue-collar father (Mike O'Malley) doesn't bat an eye. "I've known since you were three," says he. "I love you just as much."

With such unconditional love in the wind, how could even such usually vitreous eyes as James Wolcott's remain tear-free? But at the same time, the show was attuned enough to its own ironic age to include a hedge against all-out sentimentality. Key to Wolcott's approval, in fact, was the show's brisk nod to the forces of evil. As Wolcott noted, the "genius coup is to give us a villain of seething hostility and cunning antagonism—a Taser in a track suit."[2] The show's resident Iago arrives in the person of the acid-tongued gym teacher Sue Sylvester (Jane Lynch), one part Eve Arden and three parts Caligula, whose loathing of the "Glee" club knows no bounds. Sue's greedy pursuit of the paltry funds allotted to extracurricular activities leads her to seek the club's downfall at all costs to keep it from sucking up the resources she covets for her own self-serving schemes, especially the glorification of the cheerleading squad. Like Satan in Milton's *Paradise Lost* (1667), she squats at the center of the "Glee" universe exuding a deliciously unwholesome energy that sheds its odious light everywhere. And because it's clear that the show thrives on her corrosive misanthropy, she's as beloved a character in the emotional landscape as any of the lovable underdogs, beautiful losers, and tenderly regarded social rejects who surround her and provide such comic grist for the mill of her understated but over-the-top scorn. Because Satan was Milton's liveliest character, William Blake quipped that Milton was of the devil's party without knowing it. "Glee" is of Sue Sylvester's party—and never doubts it for an instant.

In the first season, that is. By season three, Sue is much more Eve Arden than Caligula--and late Arden at that, the ingratiating Arden of "The Mothers-in-Law" (1967), whose brittle sourness is all the showy, defensive cloak of a gentle soul—or the batty Arden of *Grease* (1978), whose doddering wit is a mere byproduct of senility. In a late-season episode, Lynch is in her office days before the prom, literally channeling Arden from *Grease* as she makes public-address announcements from her desk. Originally, Sue infiltrated New Directions with no-talent cheerleaders, openly mocked her ill-suited assistant (Lauren Potter) for having Down's Syndrome, and sniped at everyone relentlessly, especially Will, for everything from his Supercuts-special hairstyles to his soft-in-the-sneakers humanism. By now, we know it's all an act; the hidden agenda of Sue's Machiavellian plots is not to enrich her own fiefdom or to end civilization as we know it but to spread the love, and by the hundredth glimpse of her shedding furtive tears over an inspiring performance or pumping her fist at news of the club's latest victory her big-hearted gestures of support are among the most open of secrets. She's downright motherly—a figure of pathos; in fact, a main subplot of season three involves her unexpected but welcomed pregnancy. The show gestures wanly toward acknowledging the unlikelihood of this development, and decks it out with whatever toothless, bleary-eyed humor the writers have left—the joke being that Sue claims she's been knocked up by a major star whose identity she refuses to disclose. But mostly the point is to get some milk of human kindness flowing both to and from Sue's direction. Halfway through the season, she is advised that the ultrasound shows abnormalities in the fetus, and the closeups that render her reactions to this news would be perfectly at home in any tear-jerking melodrama, from *Penny Serenade* (1941) to *Terms of Endearment* (1983).

Kurt's character arc is less dramatic than Sue's but almost as instructive about the transformations of the show over time. In the first season he's the only gay kid, and the only reason he seems less like a token queer than wheelchair-bound Artie Abrams (Kevin McHale) seems like a token paraplegic—or so many of the other characters seem tokens of various sorts—is that he's so expressive of the show's sensibility as a whole. Even so, there's some ambivalence in the treatment of the character, who alternates between being a weepy, doe-eyed sprite and a bitchy, resentful dandy. The first time we see him, in the pilot episode, he's being hoisted into a garbage dumpster by a gaggle of chortling bullies. The tone is comic, the joke being that this abuse is a daily ritual performed mechanically, to which Kurt submits with mild, disdainful exasperation. "One day you will all be working for me," he sneers as he's tossed into the trash. Although it is nowhere in evidence in Kurt's dealings with his father, when he is with others this aesthete sense of superiority in the face of material subjugation becomes a recurrent theme. Later in the first season, remarking on his real status at the bottom of the social heap, Kurt confides to his fellow club members, "The only thing that gets me by is the knowledge that we are superior to all of them."

By season three, Kurt's status as a pariah has diminished considerably. Just as, from season one onward, there seems to be a direct pipeline from Tin Pan Alley to McKinley High—with Broadway's finest, from pixieish but big-voiced chanteuse Kristin Chenoweth to stalwart Tony Awards emcee Neil Patrick Harris, popping in regularly to torch it up with New Directions—so, by season three, does Lima, Ohio appear to have become the Center of the Queer Universe. The group's Streisand wannabe, Rachel Berry (Lea Michele) proudly presents her two gay dads (Jeff Goldblum and Brian Stokes Mitchell); former members of the Celibacy Club become lesbian lovers; the football coach declares himself transgendered, out-and-proud Matt Bomer and former closet-case Ricky Martin put in high-profile guest appearances, and Kurt himself is duly equipped with the perfect boyfriend, Blaine Anderson (Darren Criss). The show's tireless aspiration to provide role models for queer youth could hardly be more laudable—though it tends, surprisingly and as a side-effect, to make Kurt *less* likeable as a character. The security of his relationship turns him complacent and brings out his irritable side. Though this tendency reflects the show's bid to keep some comedy in play, "Glee" doesn't always seem aware of Kurt's turn for the worse. When Blaine's narcissistic brother (Bomer) visits, Kurt seems to intend a compliment to his own stepbrother, Finn Hudson (Cory Monteith), but prefaces it with the casual observation that Finn is "not even my real brother"—a stinging remark that passes without notice, unregistered as the oblivious slight of a loved one that it manifestly is. Since Kurt has been obsessed with hunky but hetero Finn since the second episode, it's clear that the newfound sense of acceptance his relationship brings is what enables this thoughtless slight.

The aspiration to show Kurt coming into his own is understandable and heartening. It is meant to stand as a concrete reinforcement of the idea that, yes, *It Gets Better*. Who except the Sue Sylvester of season one wouldn't want to tell kids that? But, lodged in serial time, the show's stuck with the Kurt it has invented and the imaginative landscape it has bulldozed and planted, just as surely as it is stuck, like the rest of us, with a world it never made. And once Kurt's status as a victim of bullying has been used as fodder for jokes, how deeply satisfying can his subsequent apotheosis as a confident young man with a hot boyfriend really be? And is that really all it means for "it" to get "better"?

As if to erase the distasteful memory of those early missteps, the show introduces a subplot about bullying, with more gravity. "Glee" had already done some penance by the end of season one, stepping up its own condemnations of bullying and going so far as to have Kurt transfer to another school to escape harassment, then form an anti-bullying club on his return. But the subplot goes further than anything in the show before. In it, a homophobic football player, Dave Karofsky (Max Adler), taunts and threatens Kurt mercilessly, and though Kurt's peers rally to his defense this depiction of bullying is genuinely harrowing, conveying the victim's fear and vulnerability with an outright sense of moral indignation. More telling still is the culmination of this subplot in the third season. Kurt's acquisition of the boyfriend is presumed to guard him from harm, and the threats appear to diminish, but in fact, witnessing the spectacle of Kurt's redemptive coupling, Dave confronts his own sexuality and reveals that the torments he had formerly unleashed on Kurt were actually motivated by a repressed attraction to him. A horrified Kurt spurns Dave, whose teammates promptly denounce him and bully him in turn, in a locker-room scene that evokes the opening set-piece of Brian DePalma's *Carrie* (1976) in its screechy hothouse surrealism. Devastated, Dave goes home and hangs himself.

By any measure, this tragic outcome must be seen as a major turning point in the course of the show. "Glee"'s determination to attest to the real-world crisis of gay teen suicide is evident in the highly willed quality of the plot turn. The question remains whether the show *could* meaningfully attest to teenaged self destruction as a real problem, given the contexts it had established or inherited—and if not, what it might mean to try. As it happens, Dave survives. In the next episode, he is discovered in a hospital bed to which a repentant Kurt duly repairs, lamenting the insensitivity of his own treatment of Dave. Eyes welling—he's in doleful-sprite mode, not bitchy-queen mode—he clasps Dave's hand and professes support and friendship. It. Gets. Better.

Clearly, there are limits to what "Glee" can adequately acknowledge. At this point in the show's evolution, few who have experienced the brittle reality of American prime-time television would expect otherwise. In short order, another real-world crisis intrudes: the hazards of texting-while-driving. Quinn Fabray (Dianna Agron), a former cheerleader turned "Glee" club convert, is T-boned at the wheel by another car that rams full speed into her driver's-side door when, preoccupied by punching letters into her iPhone's key pad, she runs a light. The impact of this collision is difficult to overstate in narrative terms as well as in the obvious literal ones—it's as sudden and shocking as the car crash in *Adaptation* (2002) that it's modeled on.

In previous seasons, by the logic of TV-series storytelling, Quinn could have been seen as expendable before season three, if the specter of prime-time mortality hovered anywhere near the show. She had been a minor and unsympathetic character, thus a suitable candidate for elimination, if it should ever have come to that. In the interim, however, she was redeemed as avidly as anyone on the show, renouncing her jealousy over her former boyfriend Finn and warmly accepting his new relationship with Rachel; in fact, what she's texting at the time of the accident is her explanation for being late for Finn and Rachel's marriage. Had Quinn been brought over to the side of the angels only to be so unceremoniously dispatched? In the subsequent episode, to everyone's relief, it is revealed that she has survived the accident. So casual is this disclosure that the miraculous nature of her survival, given the extremity of what we have witnessed, barely registers, eclipsed by the wave of gratitude generated at the mere sight of her—consigned to a wheelchair, to be sure, but otherwise looking none the worse for wear.

What these events—Quinn's accident and Dave's suicide attempt—have in common is their function as reminders of the always impending possibility of disaster. Without such awareness, assurances that "It Gets Better" ring hollow indeed. Thematically, these catastrophes serve to bring forth and legitimate such assurances. That is also why catastrophes are required in their function to produce so little in the way of consequence. In both cases, the immediate aftermath is sharply elided—we cut away from the crash and the hanging, in the split second of their transpiring—and a subsequent recovery stands in place of any image of the crushing pain of impact. Dave disappears calmly from the show, while Quinn, in some agony as she undergoes physiotherapy, is suddenly awakened to the beneficial presence of a born-again Christian (Samuel Larsen) who wants to be with her. That the show acknowledges at all that such horrendous things as attempted suicide and car accidents could happen is viewed as sufficient condition for the insistence that they won't—or that they are, in the worst-case scenario, mere springboards to the greater triumphs ahead. Even these whiffs of mortality have no real place in "Glee," as is evident in the marked awkwardness with which they are processed through one of the show's staples, the spry summary of previous installments that comes at the start of each episode. Accompanied by an upbeat jingle, these recaps are provided by a high-pitched, chirpy voice played at an accelerated speed that makes it sound even more whimsical. Judging by the tone of the voice, its take on the events it recounts is arch and more than a little sarcastic. Most of what occurs on the show lends itself readily to such attitudes. If the style is modified slightly to accommodate the turns of season three, it remains disconcerting to hear this voice, in quite this manner, dispensing news of mayhem and near death.

If a popular show loses it following—or its way, by no means the same thing—this will often happen in season three. According to Sean O'Sullivan, this is because the narrative has moved beyond establishing itself, as it does in the first season, and—at least provisionally—fulfilling itself, as it may in the second. Third seasons typically vault into a different order of story time, no longer concerned with the possible—what's in the range of what could happen—or the necessary—what happens, within that range—but with the possible disguised as the necessary, the unexpected turn that responds to the news of the day, say, more than to internal dictates of story logic.[3] Potential narrative directions are multiplied yet deferred, and contingency proliferates. In season three, unanticipated events commonly violate given norms—for an interesting case see "Deadwood" (2004-06)—and exceed spectators' always fickle desires for new developments. Nostalgia for seasons past kicks in as viewers' capacities to assimilate the increasing accumulation of plot and character data are strained. And then—let the hating begin.

As we know, or should know—but "Glee" doesn't tell us—suicide is a leading cause of death among older teenagers. Queer youth have been dying in this way for decades. The question "Glee" raises in its third season is, how is it possible to acknowledge this while maintaining a feel-good ambience? And the answer is, it's not—at least not without acknowledging head-on the endemic and well organized hatred that gives rise to the crisis in the first place. Almost every partisan of the "It Gets Better" project knows that it usually does not get better, unless conditions requiring such amelioration change. So present to our social and political lives, slogans may be vehicles of such change but they are no match for realities that can be faced only in part, or perceived always as new and unfamiliar. "Glee" is too dismissive of tragedy to convince anyone that "It Gets Better." At least thirty percent of teen suicides are gay and lesbian. A third of lesbian and gay teenagers report having attempted suicide. They are two or three times more likely to succeed than other teenagers. The figures are still more extreme for minority queer adolescents. Although they are as pressing now as ever, these statistics are yesterday's news. They derive from a task force on teen suicide conducted by the U. S. Department of Health and Human Services in 1989—twenty years before the premiere of "Glee" and the start of the "It Gets Better" project.[4] The report's findings were minimized and its recommendations to stem the crisis ignored by the United States Congress, with a Democratic majority, under George H. W. Bush.

Queers have been excluded from all orders of time—past, present, and future—for so long that it's not hard to see why some do not want to be party to any of those orders, as they stand. Such refusal may very well be a prerequisite for change. As Lee Edelman writes in *No Future*, "What . . . would it signify *not* to be 'fighting for the children'? How could one take the *other* 'side' when taking any side at all necessarily constrains one to take the side *of*, by virtue of taking a side *within*, a political order that returns to the Child as the image of the future it intends?"[5] Yet it's just as easy to see why the drive to reclaim the future should be so powerful in this cultural moment. To say that children are the future—that the future is children—excludes queers all over again by tying the concept to logics of reproduction. There are and have been many queer children who may or may not choose to reproduce (gays and lesbians can and do reproduce). Affirmative culture can admit the negative only very selectively. People forget things. This makes change difficult. None of this is news.

Let's say this. If we can imagine a negative past as fully and honestly as we bring hope to our imagination of a positive future, and if we can reach an understanding of the conditions in which we exist, then we can make lives for ourselves, even here, and even now. Just do it. It gets better.

Notes

1. James Wolcott, "Of 'Glee' I Sing," *Vanity Fair* (January 2010). Online at www.vanityfair.com/culture/features/2010/01/wolcott-201001. Accessed May 2, 2012.

2. Wolcott, "Of 'Glee' I Sing."

[3] Sean O'Sullivan, "Reconnoitering the Rim: Thoughts on *Deadwood* and Third Seasons," in Pat Harrigan and Noah Wardrip-Fruin, eds., *Third Person: Authoring and Exploring Vast Narratives* (Cambridge Mass.: MIT Press, 2009), 323-32.

[4] Paul Gibson, "Gay Male and Lesbian Youth Suicide," in M. Feinleib, *Report of the Secretary's Task Force on Youth Suicide* (Washington D.C.: Department of Health and Human Services, 1989), volume 3, 110-42.

[5] Lee Edelman, *No Future: Queer Theory and the Death Drive* (Durham N.C.: Duke University Press, 2004), 3.

Contributors

Jennifer Brayton is an Associate Professor in the Department of Sociology at Ryerson University. She teaches and publishes primarily in media and popular cultural studies, including research on on-line fans and fandoms, queer identity and language, representations of disability in television, and numerous articles on the intersections gender and technology. She is currently working on an undergraduate textbook on Canadian popular culture. Jennifer is co-moderator and web manager for Canada's first electronic feminist organization, PAR-L (www.unb.ca/PAR-L), founded in 1995.

Peter Clandfield is Assistant Professor in the Department of English Studies at Nipissing University, North Bay, Ontario. He has published essays on racial aspects of popular texts in the collections *Closely Watched Brains* and *Race and Religion in the Postcolonial British Detective Story*. Among his other interests are contemporary Scottish literature, representations of urban development, and theories and practices of censorship.

Michael DeAngelis is an Associate Professor and Director of Loop Campus at DePaul University's School for New Learning, where he teaches in the areas of media and cultural studies. He is the author of *Gay Fandom and Crossover Stardom: James Dean, Mel Gibson, and Keanu Reeves*, and he has published widely in such journals as *Film History, Cultural Critique*, and *Spectator*. He is currently working on a study of art cinema distribution and exhibition practices of the 1960s and 1970s.

Thomas Doherty is a professor of American Studies at Brandeis University. His books include *Pre-Code Hollywood: Sex, Immorality and Insurrection in American Cinema, 1930-1934, Teenagers and Teenpics: The Juvenilizatiion of American Movies in the 1950's, Projections* *of War: Hollywood, American Culture, and World War II, Cold War, Cool Medium: Television, McCarthyism, and American Culture,* and *Hollywood's Censor: Joseph I. Breen and the Production Code Administration.* He is an associate editor for the film magazine *Cineaste* and film review editor for the *Journal of American History.*

Cary Elza is an instructor in the College of Communication at DePaul University, where she teaches courses on film history, media dn cultural theory, and vampires. Her dissertation examines *Alice in Wonderland* narratives in the context of technological and social change. Her publications include articles and anthology chapters on "Pokémon," "The X-Files," "Veronica Mars," Michael Moore's online presence, and "Smallville."

Stuart Ewen is Distinguished Professor of Film & Media Studies at Hunter College, and of History, Sociology and American Studies at The Graduate Center of the City University of New York. He is the author of a number of influential books, including PR! *A Social History of Spin, All Consuming Images: The Politics of Style in Contemporary Culture, Captains of Consciousness: Advertising and the Social Roots of the Consumer Culture;* and, with Elizabeth Ewen, *Channels of Desire: Mass Images and the Shaping of American Consciousness* and *Typecasting: On the Arts and Sciences of Human Inequality.*

Kirby Farrell is the author of *Post-Traumatic Culture: Injury and Interpretation in the 90s, Berserk Style in American Culture,* and *The Mysteries of Elizabeth I.* His other work includes several books on Shakespeare and several novels. He is Professor in the Department of English at the University of Massachusetts Amherst.

Cynthia Fuchs is the author of *Eminem* and Associate Professor of English, African Ameircan Studies, Film & Media Studies, and Cultural Studies at George Mason University. She is also the film, video, and tv editor for the weekly cultural studies magazine, *PopMatters* (at popmatters.com), as well as weekly film reviewer for the *Philadelphia Citypaper* (citypaper.net), *Nitrate* (Nitrateonline.com), and *Reel Images Magazine* (reelimagesmagazine.com). She has published articles on hiphop, Prince, Michael Jackson, the Spice Girls, queer punks, gender on the INternet, and race and racism in Vietnam War movies and is the editor of *Spike Lee: Interviews* and co-editor of *Between the Sheets, In the Streets: Queer, Lesbian, and Gay Documentary.*

Stephen Gaunson is a teaching and research fellow in the School of Media and Communication at RMIT University, Melbourne. His research covers history films, adaptation, and genre. His New book, *The Ned Kelly Films,* is forthcoming from Intellect.

Henry A. Giroux currently holds the Global TV Network Chair Professorhip at McMaster University. He has published numerous books and articles and his most recent books include: *Disposable Youth: Racialized Memories, and the Culture of Cruelty, Education and the Crisis of Public Values, The Mouse That Roared: Disney and the End of Innocence, Stormy Weather: Katrina and the Politics of Disposability, Youth in a Suspect Society, The University in Chains, The Terror of Neoliberalism, Against the New Authoritarianism, Take Back Higher Education* (with Susan Giroux), *America on the Edge: Henry Giroux on Politics, Culture and Education,* and *Beyond the Spectacle of Terrorism.*

Susan Searls Giroux is Assistant Professor of English and Cultural Studies at McMaster University. She is the author of *Take Back High Education* (with Henry A.l Giroux) and *The Theory Toolbox* (with Jeffrey T. Nealon) and managing editor of the *Review of Education, Pedagogy, Cultural Studies*. She has also published numerous articles on the crisis of the university/ 9/11, the history of English studies, W. E. B. Du Bois, Homi Bhabha, and Toni Morrison.

Kristen Hatch is an Assistant Professor of Film and Media Studies at the University of California, Irvine. She is completing a book on child performers on the American stage and screen through the 1930s.

William Hoynes is Professor of Sociology and Director of American Culture at Vassar College, where he teaches courses on media, culture, and social theory. He is the author or co-author of several books about the contemporary media industry, including the award-winning *Public Television for Sale: Media, the Market and the Public Sphere* and *The Business of Media: Corporate Media and the Public Interest*, as well as (with David Croteau) *Media/Society: Industries, Images and Audiences and Experience Sociology*.

Douglas Kellner is George Kneller Chair in the Philosophy of Education at UCLA and is author of many books on social theory, politics, history, and culture, including *Camera Politica: The Politics and Ideology of Contemporary Hollywood Film*, co-authored with Michael Ryan and an *Emile de Antonio Reader* co-edited with Dan Streible. Other works include *Critical Theory, Marxism, and Modernity; Jean Baudrillard: From Marxism to Postmodernism and Beyond*; works in cultural studies such as Media Culture and Media Spectacle; a trilogy of books on postmodern theory with Steve Best; and a trilogy of books on the media and the Bush administration, encompassing *Grand Theft 2000, From 9/11 to Terror War*, and *Media Spectacle and the Crisis of Democracy*. Author of *Herbert Marcuse and the Crisis of Marxism*, Kellner is editing collected papers of Herbert Marcuse, four volumes of which have appeared with Routledge. His *Guys and Guns Amok: Domestic Terrorism and School Shootings from the Oklahoma City Bombings to the Virginia Tech Massacre* won the 2008 AESA award as the best book on education. Forthcoming in 2010 is *Cinema Wars: Hollywood Film and Politics in the Bush/Cheney Era*.

Matthew Leggatt teaches at the University of Southampton, UK, in English and Film. His work centers on post-9/11 popular culture. Areas of interest also include: terrorism, the sublime, apocalyptic film, and the financial crisis. He has also published work on the 9/11 memorial site entitled, "9/11 and the Cost of Remembering" and intends to turn his thesis, from which the article featured here is adapted, into a book.

Dominic Lennard is an Honorary Research Associate in the School of English, Journalism, and European Languages at the University of Tasmania. He currently teaches in the sociology program, as well as lecturing on academic writing and research skills. His research interests include versions of masculinity in popular culture, genre film, and the representation of children on film. He is writing a book on the horror film's child villains.

Curtis Maloley is an instructor in the department of Liberal Arts and Sciences at Humber College in Toronto. He teaches courses in Sociology, Humanities, and Film Studies.

Graeme Metcalf teaches in the Department of Sociology at Ryerson University. He also teaches a course on popular culture through Ryerson's RUN (Ryerson University Now) program, an arm of the University's Continuing Education program aimed at high school youth at risk.

James Morrison's memoir, *Broken Fever: Reflections of Gay Boyhood*, was published by St. Martin's Press in 2001. Professor of Literature and Film at Claremont McKenna College, he is also the author of a novel, *The Lost Girl*, a collection of stories, *Said and Done*, a novella, *Everyday Ghosts*, and several nonfiction books on film, including *Hollywood Reborn: Movie Stars of the 1970s* and *Roman Polanski*.

Stephen L. Muzzatti is an Associate Professor of Sociology at Ryerson University, where he teaches courses in media and popular culture. He's written on such diverse topics as youth culture, the news media, moral panics, crimes of globalization, motorcycle culture, and street racing. He is an Executive Officer of the American Society of Criminology's Division on Critical Criminology, and the editor (with Vince Samarco) of *Reflections from the Wrong Side of the Tracks: Class, Identity, and the Working Class Experience*.

Angela Ndalianis is Associate Professor in Cinema Studies at Melbourne University. Her research focuses on contemporary entertainment culture, media histories and the transmedia collisions of films, computer games, television, comic books and theme parks. Her publications include *Neo-Baroque Aesthetics and Contemporary Entertainment (2004), The Contemporary Comic Book Superhero* (editor, 2009), *Science Fiction Experiences* (In press, 2010) and *Media Interfaces and the Horror Sensorium* (In press, 2010). She is currently completing the book *Spectopolis: Theme Park Cultures*, which looks at the historical and cultural influence of the theme park.

Murray Pomerance is Professor of Sociology at Ryerson University and the author of *Hitchcock's America, Michelangelo Red Antonioni Blue: Eight Reflections on Cinema, The Horse Who Drank the Sky: Film Experience Beyond Narrative and Theory, Edith Valmaine, Johnny Depp Starts Here, An Eye for Hitchcock, Savage Time*, and *Magia d'Amore*, as well as editor or co-editor of numerous anthologies including *Shining in Shadows: Movie Stars of the 2000s, A Little Solitaire: John Frankenheimer and American Film, A Family Affair: Cinema Calls Home, City That Never Sleeps: New York and the Filmic Imagination, Cinema and Modernity, American Cinema of the 1950s: Themes and Variations, From Hobbits to Hollywood: Essays on Peter Jackson's Lord of the Rings, Where the Boys Are: Cinemas of Masculinity and Youth* and *Enfant Terrible! Jerry Lewis in American Film*. He is editor of the "Techniques of the Moving Image" series at Rutgers University Press and the "Horizons of Cinema" series at SUNY Press; and co-editor of both the "Screen Decades" and "Star Decades" series at Rutgers, with Lester D. Friedman and Adrienne McLean respectively.

Tison Pugh is Associate Professor in the Department of English at the University of Central Florida. He is the author of *Queering Medieval Genres* and *Sexuality and Its Queer Dis-*

contents in Middle English Literature, as well as the co-editor of two film collections: Race, Class, and Gender in "Medieval" Cinema (with Lynn Ramey) and Queer Movie Medievalisms (with Kathleen Kelly).

Linda Robertson is founder of the Media and Society Program at Hobart and William Smith Colleges, where she teaches. The author of *The Dream of Civilizaed Warfare: World War I Flying Aces and the American Imagination* and of numerous articles on the rhetoric of ecnomics and war propaganda, she is the co-host of a weekly radio commentary program, "Plato's Cave."

John Sakeris is Professor Emeritus at the Department of Sociology at Ryerson University. He is co-editor of *Pictures of a Generation on Hold: Selected Papers, Bang Bang, Shoot Shoot! Essays on Guns and Popular Culture*, and *Closely Watched Brains*. He has written on the convergence of political economy, gender, and popular culture.

Christopher Sharrett is Professor of Communication and Film Studies at Seton Hall University. He is the author of *The Rifleman*, and editor of *Crisis Cinema: The Apocalyptic Idea in Postmodern Narrative Film* and *Mythologies of Violence in Postmodern Media*, and co-editor (with Barry Keith Grant) of *Planks of Reason: Essays on the Horror Film*. His work has appeared in *Cinema Journal, Cineaste, Film International, Senses of Cinema, Postscript, Cineaction, Kino Eye, Framework, Journal of Popular Film and Television*, and numerous anthologies.

Timothy Shary is an independent scholar and the author of *Generation Multiplex: The Image of Youth in Contemporary American Cinema*, editor of *Millennial Masculinity: Men in Contemporary American Cinema*, and co-editor of *Youth Culture in Global Cinema*. His essays and reviews have appeared in numerous journals, and he has contributed chapters and entries to such books as *The Encyclopedia of Children, Adolescents, and the Media, The Schirmer Encyclopedia of Film*, and *Rebel Without a Cause: Approaches to a Maverick Masterwork*.

Dan Streible is Associate Professor and Academic Director of Cinema Studies at New York University and organizer of the biannual Orphan Film Symposium. His publications include the books *Emile De Antonio: A Reader* (with Douglas Kellner) and *Fight Pictures: A History of Boxing and Early Cinema* as well as (with Melinda Stone) "The Small-Gauge and Amateur Film" issue of *Film History*. In 2005 he was appointed to the National Film Preservation Board by the U.S. Librarian of Congress.

Fred Turner is Associate Professor and Director of Undergraduate Studies and of the Program in Science, Technology and Society in the Department of Communication at Stanford University. He has written extensively on media and American cultural history. He is the author of *Echoes of Combat: The Vietnam War in American Memory* and *From Counterculture to Cyberculture: Stewart Brand, the Whole Earth Network, and the Rise of Digital Utopianism*.

Julie Turnock is Assistant Professor of Cinema and Media at the University of Illinois, Urbana/Champaign. Her dissertation, *Plastic Reality: Special Effects, Art and Technology in 1970s US Filmmaking*, forthcoming from Columbia University Press.

Thomas E. Wartenberg is Professor in the Philosophy Department at Mount Holyoke College, where he also teaches in the Film Studies Program. He is the author of *Unlikely Couples: Movie Romance as Social Criticism*, editor of *The Nature of Art*, and co-editor of *Philosophy and Film* (with Cynthia Freeland), *Thinking Through Cinema: Film as Philosophy* (with Murray Smith), and *The Philosophy of Film* (with Angela Curran).

Susan White is Associate Professor of Film and Literature in the Department of English at the University of Arizona in Tucson. She is the author of *The Cinema of Max Ophuls* and many essays and book chapters on gender and cinema.

Fiona Whittington-Walsh is Instructor in the department of sociology at Kwantlen Polytechnic University in Surrey, British Columbia, where she teaches in the areas of gender, culture, media, and inequality. Her research includes work examining disability and the media, beauty and physical difference/disability, beauty and cosmetic surgery, and media and cosmetic surgery.

Steven Woodward is Associate Professor at Bishop's University in Quebec, where he teaches courses on film, media, and popular culture. The editor of *After Kieslowski: The Legacy of Krzysztof Kieslowski*, he researches and publishes on film franchises like James Bond and Harry Potter, and the cringe comedy of Ricky Gervais, Larry David, and Sacha Baron Cohen.

Index